INSIDE THE VICTORIAN HOME

A Portrait of Domestic Life in Victorian England

Judith Flanders

W. W. NORTON & COMPANY

NEW YORK   LONDON

Copyright © 2003 by Judith Flanders
First published as a Norton paperback 2006

Originally published in Great Britain under the title *The Victorian House:
Domestic Life from Childbirth to Deathbed*

For information about permission to reproduce selections from this book, write to
Permissions, W. W. Norton & Company, Inc., 500 Fifth Avenue, New York, NY 10110

Manufacturing by LSC Communications, Crawfordsville
Book design by Lovedog Studio
Production manager: Julia Druskin

Library of Congress Cataloging-in-Publication Data

Flanders, Judith.
[Victorian house]
Inside the Victorian home : a portrait of domestic life in Victorian England /
by Judith Flanders.—1st American ed.
Originally published under the title: The Victorian house : domestic life from
childbirth to deathbed. London : HarperCollins, 2003.
Includes bibliographical references and index.
p. cm.
ISBN 0-393-05209-5
1. Family—England—History—19th century.
2. England—Social conditions—19th century. I. Title.
HQ615.F58   2004
306'.0942'09034—dc22
2003027693

ISBN-13: 978-0-393-32763-2 pbk.
ISBN-10: 0-393-32763-9 pbk.

W. W. Norton & Company, Inc., 500 Fifth Avenue, New York, N.Y. 10110
www.wwnorton.com

W. W. Norton & Company Ltd., 15 Carlisle Street, London W1D 3BS

7 8 9 0

For my mother, Kappy Flanders

ACKNOWLEDGMENTS

MY GRANDMOTHER, Elsie Flanders, and my great-aunt, Sylvia Morrison, endlessly supplied me with information about their childhood homes, and memories of their parents' and grandparents' houses. For these living memories of the Victorian era I am more than grateful.

I would also like to thank Cathie Arrington, Jessica Axe, Vera Brice, Julie Cass, Kate Colquhoun, David Crane, Bob Davenport, Julia Druskin, Will Eaves, Ann Edelman, Helen Ellis, Robin Gibson, Maria Guarnaschelli, Sloan Harris, Erik Johnson, Georgia Liebman, Fiona Markham, David Miller, Ravi Mirchandani, Ann Parry, Arabella Pike, Aisha Rahman, Katya Rice, Denise Shannon, Digby Smith, Rowan Routh, Fergal Tobin, Tilly Ware, and Anthony S. Wohl.

The Victoria Mailbase is an invaluable resource, both of information and of scholarly collegiality. I would especially like to thank Patrick Leary and the individual members who have discussed particular points: Gerri Brightwell, Miriam Elizabeth Burstein, Liz Calvert Smith, Eileen Curran, Martina Droth, Marguerite Finnigan, Lesley Hall, Mary Haynes Kuhlman, Terry Mayers, Beth Sutton-Ramspeck, Malcolm Shifrin, Kathryn Smith, Chris Willis, and Melanie Wilson. Lee Jackson's www.victorianlondon website has been a wonderfully useful tool.

Jim Endersby answered my questions on the science of everyday life with great patience; Anna Kythreotis not only corrected my Greek pronunciation, but gave me the joke about Parthenope Nightingale; Frank Wynne rescued my hard disk, and me, while politely pretending not to notice both my ignorance and my hysteria.

I would like to thank the following for permission to quote: Edinburgh University Press (for Keele University Press), Faber and Faber, Manchester University Press, Oxford University Press, Sutton Publishing, and Virago. I also thank the Bodleian Library, the British Library (particularly the staff of the Rare Books Reading Room), Cambridge University Library, The Society of Authors as agent for the Provost and Scholars of King's College, Cambridge, and the London Library.

CONTENTS

A QUICK GUIDE
TO BOOKS AND AUTHORS

Beeton, Mrs. Isabella (1836–65), journalist, translator, and author, she compiled *Mrs Beeton's Book of Household Management*, published in parts between 1859 and 1861 by her husband's publishing company.

Bennett, Alfred Rosling (1850–1928), one of the earliest telephone engineers, and author of such books as *Telephone Systems of Continental Europe* (1895), as well as a memoir of his childhood, *London and Londoners in the Eighteen-Fifties and Sixties* (1924). He also invented a caustic alkali and iron battery in 1881.

Bennett, Arnold (1867–1931), novelist, born in Staffordshire, son of a small-town solicitor. His novels *Anna of the Five Towns* (1902) and *The Old Wives' Tale* (1908) draw on his childhood in the Midlands. He was heavily influenced by the French realists, and in these books, and the Clayhanger series, attempted to show provincial life in almost photographic terms.

Berkeley, Maud (1859–1949), author of diaries later published as *Maud: The Diaries of Maud Berkeley*. The youngest daughter of a mathematics master at St. Peter's School, York, she lived subsequently on the Isle of Wight before her marriage in 1892, when she moved to London with her husband.

Bradley, Marion Jane, author of an unpublished diary in the British Library. She was the wife of George Granville Bradley (1821–1903), master at Rugby School, 1845–58; headmaster of Marlborough, 1858–70; master of University College, Oxford, 1870–81; dean of Westminster, 1881–1902.

Brookfield, Jane (1825–96), married William Henry Brookfield, a clergyman, in 1841, after an engagement of three years. Her husband was never particularly successful, usually serving as curate to fashionable parishes; in 1848 he became an Inspector of Schools to supplement their income, remaining in this position for seventeen years. However, as the daughter of Sir Charles Elton, she was a cousin of Tennyson's close friend Arthur Hallam. After her marriage she moved in literary circles, which brought her friendships with Carlyle, the biographer and man of letters Monckton Milnes, the traveler Alexander Kinglake, the actress Fanny Kemble, Tennyson, and, in particular, Thackeray (q.v.), friendships that caused her letters to be collected as *Mrs Brookfield and Her Circle*.

Butler, Samuel (1835–1902), son of a clergyman and grandson of a bishop; religious doubts prevented his continuing the family tradition. After five years in New Zealand, he returned to England and began a career as an artist; he showed occasionally at the Royal Academy. He published the satire *Erewhon*, based on his time in New Zealand, in 1872, which used Darwin's recent theories to depict a society where beauty is morality and illness criminal. He later wrote on science and art, as well as writing travel books. *The Way of All Flesh* (written 1873–80), his only thinly fictionalized autobiography, was published posthumously in 1903.

Carlyle, Thomas (1795–1881) and **Jane** (1801–66). Thomas, philosopher and historian, and his wife, Jane Welsh, daughter of a doctor, whose acquaintances included the Italian revolutionary Mazzini, Browning, Tennyson, and Geraldine Jewsbury (q.v.). The Carlyles moved to Cheyne Road, London, in 1834, where Carlyle wrote his *History of the French Revolution* (1837). The book made his name and lessened their financial hardships. Jane Carlyle's wit and aptitude for friendship found an outlet in a wide correspondence. *The Collected*

Letters of Thomas and Jane Welsh Carlyle number twenty-eight volumes and are yet to be completed.

Chavasse, Dr. Pye Henry (1810–79), Birmingham surgeon and author of advice books for women, including *Advice to a Mother on the Management of Her Offspring* (1839), which went through many reprintings over the next hundred years. Other books included *Advice to Wives on the Management of Themselves, during the Periods of Pregnancy, Labour and Suckling* (1843), *Counsel to a Mother* (1869), and *Aphorisms on the Mental Culture and Training of a Child* (1872).

Collins, (William) Wilkie (1824–89), novelist, son of the landscape painter William Collins, about whom he wrote his first book. His second novel, *Basil* (1852), brought him to the attention of Dickens, who asked him to contribute to *Household Words*. Collins is, however, best known for *The Woman in White* (1860), *Armadale* (1866), and *The Moonstone* (1868), novels of the "sensation" school, which encompassed mystery, crime, madness, and wildly carefully complicated plotting. Collins maintained throughout his life two common-law relationships with working-class women.

Corke, Helen (1882–1978), met D. H. Lawrence when she was teaching in Croydon. She had a relationship with her violin teacher which Lawrence reproduced in *The Trespasser* (1912). She wrote *In Our Infancy: An Autobiography, Part I: 1882–1912*, as well as memoirs of Lawrence and Jessie Chambers, Lawrence's friend and the model for Miriam in *Sons and Lovers* (1913).

Craik, Dinah Mulock (1826–87), novelist, short-story writer, poet, essayist, and children's writer. Her first novel was published in 1846, *Olive* in 1850, then in the next six years another nine novels before her most famous, *John Halifax, Gentleman* (1856). Her essays, *A Woman's Thoughts about Women*, appeared in 1858.

Cranford, see Gaskell, Mrs. Elizabeth.

Creighton, Louise (1850–1936), author of a diary later published as *Memoir of a Victorian Woman*. Her husband, Mandell Creighton, was a fellow at Merton College, Oxford, then incumbent of a parish in Northumberland, Rural Dean of Alnwick, the examining chaplain to Bishop Wilberforce, Honorary Canon of Newcastle, first Dixie

Professor of Ecclesiastical History at Cambridge, Canon of Worcester, Canon of Windsor, Bishop of Peterborough, Hulsean and Rede Lecturer at Cambridge, Romanes Lecturer at Oxford, and Bishop of London.

Cullwick, Hannah (1833–1909), servant and author of diaries later published as *The Diaries of Hannah Cullwick*. Born in Shropshire, she went into service at the age of eight. At fourteen she became sole nurserymaid to a family with eight children. She then worked as under-housemaid for a county family, from which job she was sacked after eight months, when her mistress saw her, aged seventeen, "playing as we was cleaning our kettles." She then worked for an aristocratic family, who took her with them to London. There she met the upper-middle-class Arthur Munby (q.v.), beginning a liaison that was to last both their lives. In order to be near him she began to work in middle-class households in London: for an upholsterer, a beer merchant, a widow and her daughters, as well as in lodging houses, which gave her more freedom from supervision. In 1873 she and Munby were secretly married, and she moved to his lodgings in Fig Tree Court, Inner Temple, where she lived as his servant. In 1877 she returned to Shropshire and domestic service. From 1882 Munby was a regular visitor until her death.

Daisy Chain, The, see Yonge, Charlotte M.

Diary of a Nobody, The, see Grossmith, George and Weedon.

Dickens, Charles (1812–70), with Eliot, Thackeray, and Trollope, the giant of Victorian literature. His father, a clerk in the navy pay office, was arrested for debt when Charles was twelve, and he was sent to work in a blacking warehouse. It was only for a few months, but it blighted his childhood and cast a shadow over the rest of his life, giving dramatic impetus to many of his novels. After becoming a Parliamentary reporter and a journalist, Dickens shot to fame with *The Pickwick Papers* (published in parts from 1836). *Oliver Twist* appeared in 1837, with *Nicholas Nickleby* (1838–39), *The Old Curiosity Shop* (1840–41), *Barnaby Rudge* (1841), *Martin Chuzzlewit* (1843–44), *A Christmas Carol* (1843), and *Dombey and Son* (1848) following in quick succession. In 1850 Dickens started *Household Words*, a weekly

magazine (in 1859 it became *All the Year Round*). His later novels—
David Copperfield (1849–50), *Bleak House* (1852–53), *Little Dorrit*
(1855–57), *A Tale of Two Cities* (1859), *Great Expectations* (1860–61),
and *Our Mutual Friend* (1864–65)—focused, in varying degrees, on
the state of England and on Dickens's own history, both physical and
emotional. He died with *The Mystery of Edwin Drood* (1870) left
unfinished.

Dresser, Christopher (1834–1904), designer and writer on design.
Trained as a botanist, by 1857 he was merging his two interests in a
series of articles in *Art Journal*, "Botany as Adapted to the Arts and
Art Manufactures." He later published *The Art of Decorative Design*
and *The Development of Ornamental Art* (both 1862) and *Principles
of Design* (1871–72). His design work took in carpets, silver and elec-
troplated items, wallpaper, pottery, glass, and metalwork. He was a
director of Linthorpe Pottery and imported Japanese goods into
Britain.

Eastlake, C. L. (1836–1906), architect, and secretary to the Royal
Institute of British Architects (1866–77), which led him to write *Hints
on Household Taste* (1867). The influence of this book was particularly
strong in America, where "Eastlake furniture" became popular in the
last quarter of the century. He later became keeper of the National
Gallery (1878–98).

East Lynne, see Wood, Mrs Henry.

Ellis, Sarah Stickney (d. 1872), author of many books for women:
The Wives of England, *The Women of England*, *The Mothers of England*, and *The Daughters of England*, among others. She also set up a
school for young ladies, Rawdon House, which was to promote
"moral training, the formation of character, and in some degree the
domestic duties of young ladies." In 1837 she married William Ellis,
secretary to the London Missionary Society, and with her husband
worked to promote temperance. After thirty-five years of marriage,
they died within a week of each other.

Farjeon, Eleanor (1881–1965), daughter of Benjamin Farjeon, the
author of popular melodramas. She wrote novels, poems, and plays for
children, including *Nursery-Rhymes of London Town* (1916), *Silver-*

Sand and Snow (1951), and *The Little Bookroom* (1955). In 1935 she published *A Nursery in the Nineties*, a memoir of her own childhood.

Father and Son, see Gosse, family.

Forster, Laura (1839–1924), the daughter of a country clergyman, and the author of an unpublished diary and reminiscences in King's College Library, Cambridge; aunt of the novelist E. M. Forster.

Gaskell, Mrs Elizabeth (1810–65), the daughter and wife of Unitarian ministers. Her first novel, *Mary Barton* (1848), was admired by Dickens, who invited her to contribute to *Household Words* and, later, *All the Year Round*. *Cranford* (1853) was a picture of Knutsford, in Cheshire, where she had been brought up, as was the town in *Wives and Daughters* (1866). In *Mary Barton, North and South* (1855), and *Ruth* (1853) she focused on the gap between the working classes and the middle classes. She wrote a biography of her friend Charlotte Brontë, which fixed forever the image of the hermit-like family in the wilds of Yorkshire.

Gissing, George (1857–1903), expelled from his Quaker school when caught stealing to support a prostitute. He worked and starved in America before returning in 1877 to London, marrying the prostitute the same year. His first novel, *Workers in the Dawn*, appeared in 1880. In 1883 he separated from his wife, now an alcoholic, and she died in 1888; two years later he married a working-class woman but began to move away from novels about poverty, which had been the focus of his fiction thus far, in order to explore the problems of men like himself—well-educated, middle class, but with no money and often no means of supporting themselves. *New Grub Street* (1891), which deals with this, remains his best-known work. In *The Odd Women* (1893) he turned to women in a similar position. In 1902 Gissing's wife, from whom he had parted in 1897, was certified insane; Gissing moved to France because he could not divorce her to marry his new partner.

Gosse, family: Philip Henry (1810–88), naturalist, author of *Introduction to Zoology* (1843), *Rambles on the Devonshire Coast* (1853), *The Aquarium* (1854), and *Manual of Marine Zoology* (1855–56); husband of Emily (1806–57), religious-tract writer; and father of Edmund

(1849–1928), littérateur, author of the autobiographical *Father and Son* (1907). It has recently been suggested that the Gosse parents' religious fundamentalism was not as oppressive nor their lives as dour as Gosse *fils* portrayed in this work.

Greatest Plague of Life, The, see Mayhew, Henry and Augustus.

Grossmith, George (1847–1912) **and Weedon** (1852–1919), brothers, both actors as well as comic writers. Weedon specialized in playing small unhappy men; George originated many lead roles in Gilbert and Sullivan's comic operas, 1877–79. *The Diary of a Nobody* (1892), the supposed diary of a lower-middle-class clerk, has been recognized as a comic masterpiece since its first appearance in *Punch*. (George Grossmith's son, also a George, continued the family tradition, appearing in the original production of *No, No, Nanette* (1925), and being the first to introduce cabaret into England, in 1922.)

Haweis, Mrs. Mary (d. 1898), was, like her fellow journalist Mrs. Panton, the daughter of an artist, although in her case a not particularly renowned one: Thomas Musgrave Joy. She was the author of many books on decoration, dress, and household care, such as *The Art of Dress* (1879), *The Art of Decoration* (1881), *The Art of Beauty* (1883), and *The Art of Housekeeping* (1889), as well as children's books, such as *Chaucer for Children* (1877). She also painted, and exhibited at the Royal Academy. With her husband, the Rev. Hugh Reginald Haweis (1838–1901), she pioneered Sunday openings for museums. He wrote *Music and Morals* (1871), which went through sixteen editions before the end of the century.

Hawthorne, Nathaniel (1804–64), American novelist, author of *The Scarlet Letter* (1850). Hawthorne worked in the customs house in Boston, 1839–41, and as the surveyor of the port of Salem, 1846–49. From 1853 to 1857 Hawthorne was the American consul in Liverpool. *The English Notebooks: 1853–1856* and *1856–1860* contain his diaries during his residence in England; *Our Old Home* (1863) is a series of sketches of his life at the same period.

Hughes, M. Vivian ("Molly"), daughter of a London stockbroker, wrote three autobiographical memoirs: *A London Child of the Seventies*, *A London Girl of the Eighties*, and *A London Home in the Nineties*.

James, Alice (1848–92), sister of the novelist Henry (1843–1916) and the philosopher and psychologist William (1842–1910). Born in Boston, Alice James suffered from a nervous illness that began in adolescence. After the death of her parents she became a permanent invalid, usually looked after by her friend Katharine Loring. She moved to England in 1884 and remained there until her death. Her diaries of her nervous illness and long-expected death were published in the twentieth century as *The Diary of Alice James* and *The Death and Letters of Alice James*.

Jewsbury, Geraldine (1812 90), the daughter of a cotton manufacturer, she was a novelist and a friend of Jane Carlyle, with whom she carried on an epistolary relationship from her home in Manchester, published as *A Selection from the Letters of Geraldine Jewsbury to Jane Carlyle* (1892). Her friendships extended also to the actress Helen Faucit, as well as Darwin's great supporter, T. H. Huxley, and the poet and artist D. G. Rossetti and others.

Last Chronicle of Barset, The, see Trollope, Anthony.

Levy, Amy (1861–1889), novelist and poet, educated at Newnham College, Cambridge. Her *Xantippe and Other Verses* (1881) contains a poem in the voice of Socrates' wife; her novel *Reuben Sachs* (1888) portrayed Jewish middle-class life in London, and it, together with *Miss Meredith* (1889), highlighted her feminism, which she shared with her friends, the feminist campaigners Olive Schreiner (author of *The Story of an African Farm*, 1883) and Karl Marx's daughter Eleanor Marx. Growing deafness and depression contributed to her suicide at the age of twenty-seven.

Linton, Eliza Lynn (1822–1898), journalist and novelist. The daughter of a clergyman and the granddaughter of a Bishop of Carlyle, in 1845 Eliza Lynn arrived in London as a protégée of the poet Walter Savage Landor. She initially wrote historical novels with titles like *Azeth, the Egyptian* and *Amymone, A Romance of the Days of Pericles*, but she soon turned to journalism. She married James Linton, a wood engraver and Chartist agitator, but the marriage was unhappy and in 1865 they separated. Her most famous essay, "The Girl of the Period," first published in the *Saturday Review* in 1868, vehemently attacked feminism. Her obituary in *The Times* described her "animosity towards all, or rather, some of those facets which may be conveniently called the 'New Woman'" but added that "it would perhaps be difficult to reduce Mrs Lynn Linton's views on what was and what was not desirable for her own sex to a logical and connected form."

Mackenzie, Compton (1883–1972), was born into a theatrical family. His father was Edward Compton, an actor-manager; his sister was Fay Compton, who starred in many of J. M. Barrie's plays, including *Peter Pan* (1917). Mackenzie was a wildly prolific journalist, novelist, biographer, travel writer, children's writer, and author of many volumes of memoirs, including *My Life and Times: Octave One, 1883–1891* and *Octave Two, 1891–1900*. His most famous novels include *Carnival* (1912), *Sinister Street* (1914), and—the basis for a successful film—*Whisky Galore* (1947).

Marshall, Jeannette (1855–1935), daughter of John Marshall, a surgeon and lecturer in anatomy. From the age of four to nine she lived in Kentish Town, in northwest London, but for the rest of her childhood, and until she was thirty-five, Marshall and her family lived a prosperous upper-middle-class life in Savile Row in central London. In 1890 the family moved to Chelsea. Within two years, and in the face of much opposition from her family, Jeannette married Edward Seaton, a widower and the First Medical Officer of Health for Surrey, and moved to Clapham. She kept a diary from the age of fifteen for more than two decades, parts of which were later published as *Precariously Privileged* (edited by Zuzanna Shonfield).

Mayhew, Henry (1812–87) **and Augustus** (1826–75), brothers, authors of theatrical farces and comic fiction together, including *The Greatest Plague of Life* (1847), *The Image of His Father* (1848), and *Living for Appearances* (1855); Henry Mayhew was also one of the founders of *Punch*, and its first editor. He was the originator of charitable reportage; his eighty-two essays for the *Morning Chronicle* were the foundation for the monumental *London Labour and the London Poor* (1851).

Munby, Arthur (1828-1910), poet and civil servant in the ecclesiastical commissioners' office from 1858 until his retirement in 1888. He published poetry, including *Benoni* (1852) and *Verses New and Old* (1865). He also taught Latin at the Working Men's College for a decade, and his interest in the working classes was revealed to be deeper than that when, after his death, it was discovered that he had sustained a relationship for over thirty years, and in 1873 married, Hannah Cullwick (q.v.), a maid-of-all-work. The marriage remained a secret from all but a few close friends; he told his brother only after his wife's death, and two months before his own. Munby's papers, which include Hannah Cullwick's diaries, are now at Trinity College, Cambridge, and reveal the depth of his obsession with working-class women, hinted at in his last publication, *Faithful Servants: Being Epitaphs and Obituaries Recording Their Names and Services* (1891).

Murphy, Shirley Forster, doctor and medical writer, author of *Our Homes, and How to Make Them Healthy* (1883). In the 1890s he served as the London County Council's Chief Medical Officer.

Nightingale, Florence (1820–1910), crusading nursing and hospital reformer. After much family opposition, she trained as a nurse in Germany in 1851, and became the superintendent of the Hospital for Invalid Gentlewomen in 1853. At the request of the Secretary for War, on the outbreak of war she embarked for the Crimea with a group of nurses, where she revolutionized conditions in the Scutari and Balaclava hospitals. She returned to England in 1856, and four years later the Nightingale School and Home for Nurses was set up at St. Thomas's Hospital in recognition of her work. She published *Notes on Nursing* in 1860, which went through many editions, and worked for improvements in nursing and in civic sanitation for the next forty years, despite being a chronic invalid. She wrote "Cassandra" (1852), a seemingly autobiographical fragment, which remained unpublished in her lifetime.

New Grub Street, see Gissing, George.

Odd Women, The, see Gissing, George.

Old Wives' Tale, The, see Bennett, Arnold.

Olive, see Craik, Dinah Mulock.

Our Homes, and How to Make Them Healthy, see Murphy, Shirley Forster.

Panton, Mrs. Jane Ellen (1848–1923), daughter of the artist William Powell Frith, and a journalist and pioneer of "interior decoration," who set up a "Home Decoration and Management by Correspondence" company, run by middle-class women who needed work. She was the author of many books, including *From Kitchen to Garret*, which went through eleven editions in a decade.

Patmore, Coventry (1823–96), son of the editor of the *New Monthly Magazine,* and a friend of the essayists Charles Lamb and William Hazlitt. Patmore married his first wife in 1847; she inspired his long poem in praise of married love, *The Angel in the House* (1854–63), which came to epitomize Victorian womanhood for many. Patmore was a friend of Tennyson and Ruskin, but on his second marriage, in 1864, to a Roman Catholic, he converted, and his friendships thereafter were with Catholic writers, including Gerard Manley Hopkins and Alice Meynell.

Pedley, Mrs. Frederick, author of the influential *Infant Nursing and the Management of Young Children* (1866) and *Practical Housekeeping; or, The Duties of a Home-Wife* (1867).

Potter, Beatrix (1866–1943), children's writer and illustrator, daughter of wealthy parents who moved in artistic circles; her father was a friend of John Everett Millais. She remained at home with them until she married, much against their wishes, at the age of forty-seven. Her first book, *The Tale of Peter Rabbit* (1901), was published at her own expense, and it was not until her third that she achieved any success. As a young girl she kept a diary in code which was deciphered only in the 1960s, when it was published as *The Journal of Beatrix Potter, from 1881 to 1897.*

Raverat, Gwen (1885–1957), wood engraver and illustrator, granddaughter of Charles Darwin, and author of a childhood memoir, *Period Piece: A Cambridge Childhood* (1952). She studied at the Slade School of Art, and in 1911 married Jacques Raverat, an artist and hanger-on of the Bloomsbury Circle. She was a founder of the Society of Wood Engravers.

Reuben Sachs, see Levy, Amy.

Ruskin, John (1819–1900), the son of a sherry importer, Ruskin inherited a large fortune and was able to follow his interest in art history and social reform without having to earn a living. He admired Turner, and with *Modern Painters* (1843) began to champion him publicly. This book brought him great fame, and he went on to produce several further volumes, as well as *The Seven Lamps of Architecture* (1849) and *The Stones of Venice* (1851–53). He married Euphemia (Effie) Gray in 1848; she left him for John Everett Millais in 1854, citing non-consummation as the reason. He later conceived a passion for Rose La Touche, eleven years old when he first met her. Despite his own poor history with women, his *Sesame and Lilies* (1865), on the respective roles of men and women, was deeply influential.

Ruth, see Gaskell, Mrs. Elizabeth.

Sala, George Augustus (1828–96), journalist. He contributed to *Household Words* from 1851, and at the end of the Crimean War Dickens asked him to travel out to Russia to report on the situation. He then made his name as a special correspondent covering the Civil War in America for the *Daily Telegraph* in 1863. He wrote a column called "Echoes of the Week" for the *Illustrated London News* from 1860 to 1886, and he reported for the *Sunday Times* from 1886 to 1894. He published collections of his journalism and travel writing, as well as novels.

Small House at Allington, The, see Trollope, Anthony.

Surtees, R. S. (1805–64), a solicitor, he was a founder of the *New Sporting Magazine* (1831), for which he also wrote comic sketches of Mr. Jorrocks, the hunting grocer, which were published as *Jorrocks' Jaunts* in 1838. A legacy allowed him to return to Durham, where he continued to write comic novels, including *Mr Sponge's Sporting Tour* (1853), *Ask Mama* (1858), and *Mr Facey Romford's Hounds* (published posthumously, 1865).

Taine, Hippolyte (1828–93), French philosopher and historian, focusing especially on aesthetics. Among his travel books were *Notes on England* (1872).

Taylor, Caroline Louisa (1874–1952), the first daughter and sixth child of an unsuccessful engineer in Birmingham. Her grandfather was a "manufacturing jeweller," her father the youngest of thirteen. Although he bettered himself, he was never financially successful.

Caroline studied as a pupil-teacher and taught for some years before marrying in 1903. In 1954 her son published the memoir of her childhood which she had written for her family.

Thackeray, William Makepeace (1811–63), born in Calcutta, the son of a prosperous collector in the East India Service. By the 1830s Thackeray had lost most of his inheritance, and he began to earn a living through journalism. He became a regular contributor to *Fraser's Magazine*, the *Morning Chronicle*, and other periodicals. Soon after the birth of his third child in 1840 his wife became incurably insane. Thackeray contributed to *Punch* from its earliest days. In 1847 *Vanity Fair* began to appear, published in monthly parts. His later novels include *Pendennis* (1848–50), *The History of Henry Esmond* (1852), and *The Newcomes* (1853–55).

Thomas, Sarah (1826–1906), the daughter of a Baptist minister, she and her sister lived together in Fairford, Gloucestershire, a prosperous market town. Her two brothers had emigrated to Australia, and her half brother farmed nearby. At the age of thirty-six she married a widower, Captain Thomas Milbourne, who had combined missionary work, the exploration of West Africa, and a naval career.

Trollope, Anthony (1815–82), son of a failed barrister; his mother, Frances Trollope, wrote over forty books in order to support her family. Trollope began work as a junior clerk in the Post Office in 1834; in 1841 he moved to Ireland and his career began to progress. Soon after, his first novel appeared, *The Macdermots of Ballycloran* (1847). With *The Warden*, in 1855, the first in the "Barsetshire" series, set in a cathedral town in the West Country, he found fame. He returned to England in 1859. The Palliser series of political novels began with *Can You Forgive Her?* in 1864. The author of some fifty novels, he also found the time to write travel books, biography, and an autobiography, travel to Australia, South Africa and Egypt, among other places, for the Post Office, and invent the pillar box.

Warren, Mrs. Eliza, journalist, writer of advice books for the lower middle classes.

Wichelo, Lily (1855–1945), author of unpublished journal in King's College Library, Cambridge. Mother of the novelist E. M. Forster.

Wood, Mrs. Henry (1814–87), novelist. Brought up in Worcester, she used it as background to many of her stories, but after her marriage to a banker in 1836, she lived for twenty years in France and then in London. She found great success with *East Lynne* (1861), a "sensation" novel of marital betrayal, crime, and revenge. She wrote more than three dozen novels, and her great strength was to set these lurid stories in middle-class backgrounds that her readers could immediately recognize. She owned and edited *Argosy* magazine, using it as a source for her stories about Johnny Ludlow. The famous tag line from *East Lynne*—"Dead, and never called me Mother!"—is actually from one of the many stage versions.

Yonge, Charlotte M. (1823–1901), novelist, author of the bestsellers *The Heir of Radclyffe* (1853) and *The Daisy Chain* (1856), among many others. She also wrote books for children, and edited a girls' magazine, the *Monthly Packet*, from 1851 to 1898. Heavily influenced by John Henry Keble, who was vicar near her childhood home, her work is permeated by moral and religious undertones.

CURRENCY

F ROM 1 8 8 4 THE government banks took over all issuing of bank-notes in England; previously any bank could issue notes (and in Scotland, nongovernment banks still produce their own notes today). However, most money circulated as coins, which the Royal Mint continued to produce; the smallest note was £5.

Pounds, shillings, and pence were the divisions of the currency. One shilling was made up of 12 pence; one pound of twenty shillings, that is, 240 pence. Pounds were represented by the £ symbol, shillings as "s.," and pence as "d." (from the Latin *denarius*). "One pound, one shilling, and one penny" was written "£1.1.1." "One shilling and sixpence," referred to in speech as "One and six," was written "1/6."

A guinea was a coin to the value of £1.1.0. (The coin was not circulated after 1813, although the term remained and tended to be reserved for luxury goods.) A sovereign was a 20-shilling coin, a half-sovereign a 10-shilling coin. A crown was 5 shillings, half a crown 2/6, and the remaining coins were a florin (2 shillings), sixpence, a groat (4 pence), a threepenny bit (pronounced thrup'ny), twopence (pronounced tuppence), a penny, a halfpenny (pronounced hayp'ny), a farthing (¼ of a penny) and a half a farthing (⅛ of a penny).

Relative values have altered so substantially that attempts to convert nineteenth-century prices into contemporary ones are usually futile. Food, for example, made up an extremely high proportion of a middle-class budget, whereas now it is a relatively small part; by contrast, rent was expected to be 20 percent of a middle-class London family's budget, which today makes Londoners laugh enviously. Where possible, I have indicated the costs of everyday articles, or salaries, to give some sense of the value of goods. However, if a more precise attempt to convert is wanted, the website http://www.ex.ac.uk/~RDavies/arian /current/howmuch.html is useful.

INSIDE THE VICTORIAN HOME

HOUSE AND HOME

IN 1909 H. G. WELLS—not an author usually associated with domesticity—wrote a novel about Edward Ponderevo, a purveyor of patent medicines who is the "terror of eminent historians." Ponderevo says:

> "Don't want your drum and trumpet history—no fear . . . Don't want to know who was whose mistress, and why so-and-so devastated such a province; that's bound to be all lies and upsy-down anyhow. Not my affair . . . What I want to know is, in the middle ages Did they Do Anything for Housemaid's Knee? What did they put in their hot baths after jousting, and was the Black Prince—you know the Black Prince—was he enamelled or painted, or what? I think myself, black-leaded—very likely—like pipeclay—but *did* they use blacking so early?"[1]

It is a comic view of history. Or is it? History is usually read either from the top down—kings and queens, the leaders and their followers—or from the bottom up—the common people and their lives. Political history and social history, however, both encompass the one thing we all share: that at the end of the day, after ruling empires or finishing the late shift at the factory, we all go back to our homes. Different as those homes are, how we live at home, where we live, what we do all day when we're not doing whatever it is that history is recording—these are some of the most telling things about any age, any people. Mme Merle in Henry James's *Portrait of a Lady* notes how "one's house, one's furniture, one's garments, the books one reads, the company one keeps—all these things are expressive."[2]

This is true of any age, but the Victorians brought the idea of home to the fore in a way that was new. As the Victorians saw "home" as omnipresent, it has seemed to me useful to rely on the sources that surrounded them and formed their notions of what a home should be—magazines, advertisements, manuals, and fiction. In describing people's daily lives, I look first at what theory prescribed and described in these new print sources, and then try to discover the reality in reportage, diaries, letters, and journals. Novels are used frequently, as fiction straddles the two camps in that it both set standards for "proper," or "normal," behavior in theory and also described this behavior in actuality. In using fiction as a source for how people actually behaved I have primarily relied on novels for information that the authors regarded as background material rather than as key plot devices, and have always balanced them with other, more conventional, documentary sources for corroboration.

By the mid-nineteenth century the home and what it contained were omnipresent in theory as well as in fact. Magazines in the middle of the century epitomized this centrality, their very titles boasting the growing middle class's new allegiance: *The Home Circle*, *The Home Companion*, *The Home Friend*, *Home Thoughts*, *The Home Magazine*, *Family Economist*, *Family Record*, *Family Friend*, *Family Treasure*, *Family Prize Magazine and Household Miscellany*, *Family Paper*, and *Family Mirror*.[3] They were not alone in their focus. Services were provided by "Family Drapers," "Family Butchers," even a "Family Mourning Warehouse."[4] As the Industrial Revolution appeared to have taken over every aspect of working life, so the family, and by extension the house, expanded in tandem to act as an emotional counterweight. The Victorians found it useful to separate their world into a public sphere, of work and trade, and a private sphere, of home life and domesticity. The Victorian house became defined as a refuge, a place apart from the sordid aspects of commercial life, with different morals, different rules, different guidelines to protect the soul from being consumed by commerce. Or so it seemed.

Domesticity began to acquire a new importance in the late eighteenth century, and in half a century it had made such strides that the house as shelter from outside forces was regarded as the norm. The eighteenth century had been the age of the club and the coffeehouse for those who could afford them, the gin shop and street gatherings for those who could not. Male companionship in leisure time was the norm for men. Now women at home were looked at in a different light: they became, as John Ruskin was later to describe the home, the focus of existence, the source of refuge and retreat, but also of strength and renewal.

It was not one thing alone that created this powerful urge to domesticity. It sprang from a combination of the rise of the Evangelical movement and, almost simultaneously, of Methodism and other dissenting sects; improvements in mortality figures; and the creation of the factory as a place of employment. It is for these reasons that I have chosen to focus primarily on the period 1850 to 1890—from the rise of the High Victorian era to the end of the recession that marked the 1870s and 1880s and led to the long Edwardian summer. These forty years were dynamic years, of much change. Yet it seems that this very dynamism led people to try to create a still center in their homes, where things changed as little as possible. In many areas this period can be discussed as a unity, because that is how its own participants hoped to see it: a stable period. At the same time, changes—particularly technological changes—meant that the desire for stasis was almost ludicrous in its hopelessness. The desire for stasis and the inevitability of change are, I hope, represented with equal weight here.

One of the first forces of change came with the wave of Evangelical fervor that swept the country in the early part of the century. Evangelicals hoped to find a Christian path in all their actions, including the details of daily life: a true Christian must ensure that the family operated in a milieu that could promote good relations among its members, between themselves and their servants, and between the family and the outside world. The home was a microcosm of the ideal society, with love and charity replacing the commerce and capitalism of the outside world. This dichotomy allowed men to pursue business in a suitably capitalist—perhaps ruthless—fashion, because they knew they could refresh the inner man by returning at the end of the day to an atmosphere of harmony, from which competition was banished. This idea was so useful that it was internalized by many who shared no religious beliefs with the Evangelicals, and it rapidly became a secular norm.[5]

Meanwhile, advances in technology were changing more traditional aspects of home life. With improved sanitation and hygiene, child mortality was falling. The middle classes had more disposable income, and thus anxiety about the fundamentals of life—enough food, affordable light and heat—diminished. With the increase in child survival rates came coincidentally the gradual phasing out of the apprenticeship system for middle-class professions such as doctors and lawyers, which meant that for the first time many parents could watch their children reach adulthood in their own homes. The Romantic movement's creation of the cult of innocence promoted an idealized view of childhood and produced what has sometimes been referred to as "the cult of the child": the child-centered home was developing.

That work was moving outside the home was the third essential factor in the creation of nineteenth-century domesticity. Previously, many of the working classes had found occupation in piecework, which was produced at home. With the coming of the factories, work moved to a place of regimentation and timekeeping. The middle classes too had been used to working at home: at the lower end of the scale, shopkeepers lived above their shops; slightly higher up, wholesalers lived above their warehouses. Doctors and lawyers had consulting rooms at home, as did many other professionals. Women who had helped their husbands with their work—serving in the shop, doing the accounts, keeping track of correspondence or clients—were now physically separated from their husbands' labor and became solely housekeepers. Slowly the cities became segregated: those who could afford it no longer lived near their work. An early example was the suburb of Edgbaston, on the edge of Birmingham, which had been created in the early part of the century by Lord Calthorpe to provide "genteel homes for the middle classes." These homes were for the families who owned and ran the industries on which the town thrived—the families who owned and ran them but did not want to live near them. The leases for houses in Edgbaston, known as the Belgravia of Birmingham, were clear: no retail premises were permitted, and no professional work was to be undertaken in these houses.[6] Over the century this same transformation—the separation of where people lived from where they worked—occurred across the country. In London the City became a place of work, the West End a place of residence; gradually, as the West End acquired a work character too, the suburbs became the residential areas of choice.

Charles Dickens, the great chronicler of domestic life in all its shades, was well aware of the perils of promiscuous mixing of home and work. In *Dombey and Son* (1848), Mr. Dombey, the head of a great shipping company, is unable to leave his business behind him when he returns home; his only thoughts are of Dombey and Son. By allowing his work life to contaminate his family life, he destroys the latter—and, by extension, the former. In *Great Expectations* (1860–61), the law clerk Wemmick bases his life entirely on the separation of work and home: "The office is one thing, and private life is another. When I go into the office, I leave the Castle [his house in the suburbs] behind me, and when I come into the Castle, I leave the office behind me . . . I don't wish it professionally spoken about."[7]

That the fictional Mark Rutherford, nearing the end of the century, thought no differently confirms that this attitude was not simply a jeu d'esprit of Dickens. William Hale White (1831–1913) wrote a series of supposedly autobiographical books under the name Mark Rutherford. White was a Dissenter who had trained for the ministry before he lost his faith; he then became a civil servant at the Admiralty. His alter ego, Rutherford, was also a minister who had lost his faith. About his private life Rutherford wrote that at the office "nobody knew anything about me, whether I was married or single, where I lived, or what I thought upon a single subject of any importance. I cut off my office life in this way from my home life so completely that I was two selves, and my true self was not stained by contact with my other self."[8]

That "true self" was the real man, on view only at home: Ruskin's father wrote, "Oh! how dull and dreary is the best society I fall into compared with the circle of my own Fire Side with my Love sitting opposite irradiating all around her, and my most extraordinary boy."[9] With this the good Victorian was supposed to—and often did—rest content. As the clerk Charles Pooter put it so eloquently in *The Diary of a Nobody* (1892), George and Weedon Grossmith's comic master-piece of genteel English anxiety: "After my work in the City, I like to be at home. What's the good of a home, if you are never in it?"[10] Mr. Pooter's ideal of the good life, recounted here in diary form, centered on his dream house in the suburbs.

In continental Europe the opposite was happening. The Goncourt brothers wrote in their diary in 1860: "One can see women, children, husbands and wives, whole families in the café. The home life is dying. Life is threatening to become public."[11] Europeans socialized in pub-lic—in restaurants (a French invention), in cafés (perfected by the Viennese), in the streets (Italians still perform the *passeggiata* in the evenings). But the English house became ever more inward-turning. The small wrought-iron balconies that had decorated so many Geor-gian houses vanished, seemingly overnight. Thick curtains replaced the airy eighteenth-century windows, as much to block out passers-by who might look in as to prevent the damage from sun and pollution.

For the house was not a static object in which changing values were expressed. In the eighteenth century and before, rooms had been multipurpose, and furniture had been moved and adapted to serve the different functions each room acquired in turn. (The French for "building" and "furniture" are a legacy of this: *immeuble* is a building, or, literally, "immovable," and *meuble*, furniture, is literally "mov-able.") Now, in the nineteenth century, segregation of each function of the house became as important as separation of home and work; both home and work contained an aspect of both a public and a private sphere, like a series of ever smaller Russian dolls. The house was the physical demarcation between home and work, and in turn each room was the physical demarcation of many further segregations, involving hierarchy (rooms used for visitors being of higher status than family-only rooms), function (display rating more highly than utility), and further divisions of public and private (so that rooms used for both public and private, such as the dining room, alternated in both use and importance). "Subdivision, classification, and elaboration, are certainly distinguishing characteristics of the present area of civilisation," the journalist George Augustus Sala noted in 1859.[12]

In the eighteenth century and before, servants and apprentices had slept in the same rooms as family members, who themselves were not separated in sleeping apartments by sex or age. Gradually the Victorian house divided rooms that were designed for receiving outsiders (the dining room, the drawing room, the morning room) from rooms that were for family members only (bedrooms, the study) and, further, from rooms that were for servants only (the kitchen, the scullery, servants' bedrooms). Parents no longer expected to sleep with their babies, and children no longer slept together—boys and girls needed separate rooms, at the very least, and it was preferable that younger children be separated from older ones. The desire for additional rooms meant that most rooms became, of necessity, smaller, and houses became taller, but the extra privacy made these inconveniences worthwhile. Even those forced to live in houses small enough to require multipurpose rooms felt that "nothing conduces so much to the degradation of a man and a woman in the opinion of each other" than having to perform their separate functions together in the same room, as Francis Place wrote. Place, a radical tailor, went on to detail these separate functions once he had managed to reach a financial level where he and his wife could afford to live with enough space so that they could work separately: "It was advantageous . . . in its moral effects. Attendance on the child was not as it had been always, in my presence. I was shut out from seeing the fire lighted the room washed and cleaned, and the cloathes [sic] washed and ironed, as well as the cooking."[13]

In theory, home was the private space of families. In practice—unacknowledged—houses were another aspect of public life. "Home" was created by family life, but the house itself was inextricably linked with worldly success: the size of the house, how it was furnished, where it was located, all were indicative of the family that lived privately within. His family's mode of private living was yet a further reflection of a man's public success in the world. Income was no longer derived primarily from land: the professional and merchant classes were now substantially wealthier as a group than they had ever been, and they

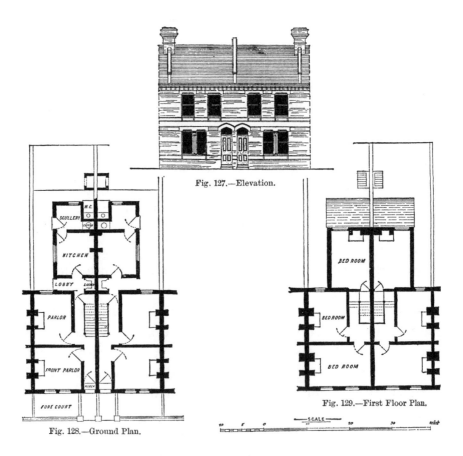

Fig. 127.—Elevation.

Fig. 128.—Ground Plan.

Fig. 129.—First Floor Plan.

Plans for terraced houses for the lower middle classes, *c.* 1870s. Note there is no bathroom, and the lavatory is still reached from the outside. The kitchen is spacious, however, with a separate larder (opposite the lobby), and a scullery with a copper. These houses rented for about £30 a year.

imitated the style of their social superiors in order to live up to their new status. Household possessions, types of furnishing, elegance of entertaining and dress, all these "home" aspects were a reflection of success at work. Therefore the public rooms, as an expression of achievement and worldly success, often took up far more of the space in the house than we today consider convenient. The money available to be spent on household goods was lavished first on those rooms that were on public display. The economist Thorstein Veblen noted the phenomenon in the United States in 1899, although it held good for Britain too: "Through this discrimination in favour of visible consumption it has come about that the domestic life of most classes is relatively shabby, as compared with the éclat of that overt portion of their life that is carried on before the eyes of observers."[14]

Dickens devoted a great deal of attention to the different types of home that were available to his characters. His biographer and friend John Forster remembered: "If it is the property of a domestic nature to be personally interested in every detail, the smallest as the greatest of the four walls within which one lives, then no man had it so essentially as Dickens, no man was so inclined naturally to derive his happiness from home concerns."[15] The novelist gave no less attention to his characters' home concerns. There was, first, the ideal, which he elaborated in his "Sketches of Young Couples":

> Before marriage and afterwards, let [couples] learn to centre all their hopes of real and lasting happiness in their own fireside; let them cherish the faith that in home . . . lies the only true source of domestic felicity; let them believe that round the household gods, contentment and tranquillity cluster in their gentlest and most graceful forms; and that many weary hunters of happiness through the noisy world, have learnt this truth too late, and found a cheerful spirit and a quiet mind only at home at last.[16]

That even Dickens became entangled in a circular notion that defined itself by referring to itself—the domestic realm was the place where one found domestic happiness—that even he could not (or found no

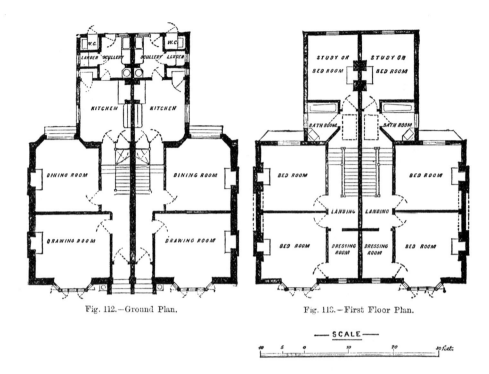

Fig. 112.—Ground Plan.   Fig. 113.—First Floor Plan.

— SCALE —

Semi-detached houses in Ealing, built for the prosperous middle classes, with five bedrooms, a dressing room, and a bathroom. As well as a larder, there is a storeroom opening off the kitchen. These houses rented for about £50 a year.

need to) explain this idea better, is surely telling. Domesticity was so much a part of the spirit of the times that simply to say "It is what it is" was adequate.

Dickens also used the language of domesticity both to create and to mock the role of women at home. In *Edwin Drood* the young heroine, Rosa, works at her sewing while her chaperone, Miss Twinkleton, reads aloud. Miss Twinkleton does not read "fairly," however:

She . . . was guilty of . . . glaring pious frauds. As an instance in point, take the glowing passage: "Ever dearest and best adored, said Edward, clasping the dear head to his breast, and drawing the silken hair through his caressing fingers . . . let us fly from the unsympathetic world and the sterile coldness of the stony-hearted, to the rich warm Paradise of Trust and Love." Miss Twinkleton's fraudulent version tamely ran thus: "Ever engaged to me with the consent of our parents on both sides, and the approbation of the silver-haired rector of the district, said Edward, respectfully raising to his lips the taper fingers so skilful in embroidery, tambour, crochet, and other truly feminine arts; let me call on thy papa . . . and propose a suburban establishment, lowly it may be, but within our means, where he will be always welcome as an evening guest, and where every arrangement shall invest economy and the constant interchange of scholastic acquirements with the attributes of the ministering angel to domestic bliss."[17]

However comic the intent in the passage above, a "ministering angel to domestic bliss" was what both Dickens and the majority of the population believed women should be. Evangelical ideas had linked the idea of womanliness to women carrying out their biological destiny— to being wives and mothers. That was their job, and to expect to have any other job was a rejection of their God-given place, despite the fact that, by the second half of the century, 25 percent of women had paying work—of necessity, in order to survive. Most of the remaining 75 percent worked at home. As will be seen, among the middle classes only the very top levels could afford the number of servants that made work for housebound women unnecessary. In spite of this uncomfortable reality, the hierarchy of authority was undisputed: God gave his authority to man, man ruled woman, and woman ruled her household—both children and servants—through the delegated authority she received from man. One of the many books on how to be better

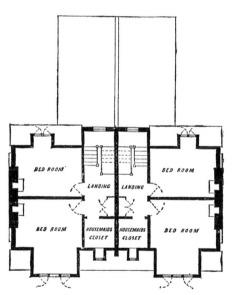

Fig. 114.--Second Floor Plan.

wives and mothers reminded women: "The most important person in the household is the head of the family—the father . . . Though he may, perhaps, spend less time at home than any other member of the family—though he has scarcely a voice in family affairs—though the whole household machinery seems to go on without the assistance of his management—still it does depend entirely on that active brain and those busy hands."[18] Sarah Stickney Ellis, an extremely popular writer for women, was even more blunt: "It is quite possible you may have more talent [than your husband], with higher attainments, and you may also have been generally more admired; but this has nothing whatever to do with your position as a woman, which is, and must be, inferior to his as a man."[19] Fifty years later George Gissing still needed to explore this view in his novel *The Odd Women* (1893). The ominously named Edmund Widdowson "regarded [women] as born to perpetual pupilage. Not that their inclinations were necessarily wanton; they were simply incapable of attaining maturity, remained throughout their life imperfect beings, at the mercy of craft, ever liable to be misled by childish misconceptions."[20]

That this was generally believed, and not simply advice-book cant, can be seen in numerous letters and diaries. Marion Jane Bradley, the wife of a master at Rugby School, wrote in her diary: "How important a work is mine. To be a cheerful, loving wife, and forbearing, fond, wise, thoughtful mother, striving ever against self-indulgence and irritability, which often sorely beset me. As a mistress, to be kind, gentle, thoughtful both for the bodies and souls of my servants. As a visitor of the poor to spare myself no trouble so as to relieve wisely and well."[21] She saw herself as an entirely reactive character: without the husband, children, servants, and poor, she would have had no role. Women were there for encouragement, to help men when they were depressed. In *New Grub Street* (1891), George Gissing's novel of literary life on the edge of poverty, the wife and husband quarrel. Amy says, "Edwin, let me tell you something. You are getting too fond of speaking in a discouraging way." He responds, "Granted that . . . I easily fall into gloomy ways of talk, what is Amy here for?"[22]

Men set the agenda, while it was up to women to carry it through.

Men are present often by their absence in the pages that follow, despite the fact that men were undoubtedly the fount from which women's possibilities grew. It was on marriage that women achieved that great necessity, a home of their own. It is clear, however, that men were barely concerned with the running of the house: "Though he may, perhaps, spend less time at home than any other member of the family— though he has scarcely a voice in family affairs—though the whole household machinery seems to go on without the assistance of his management . . ." Men were the source of funds, but it was women who judged other women, women who (to the rules of men) made the decisions that activated and continued the social circles that made up the lives of most families. Although there are several fine books on the role of men at home,[23] this will not be another of them.*

Most contemporaries accepted Ruskin's views on women and home—home was not a place but a projection of the feminine, an encircling, encouraging, comforting aura that was there to protect a husband and children from the harshness of the world. "Wherever a true wife comes," Ruskin wrote, "this home is always around her."[24] Creating a home was the role assigned to women, but it was not something over which they could exercise free will. What made a good home was carefully laid down:

> Not only must the house be neat and clean, but it must be so ordered as to suit the tastes of all . . . Not only must a constant system of activity be established, but peace must be preserved, or happiness will be destroyed. Not only must elegance be called in, to adorn and beautify the whole, but strict integrity must be maintained by the minutest calculation as to lawful means, and self, and self-gratification, must be made the yielding point in every disputed case. Not only must an appearance of outward

---

*The role of men is only one of many elements I have been unable to encompass and still have a book of a manageable length. Domestic life is protean, and any reader will, with no effort at all, be able to come up with a dozen fields of equal importance that I have not touched on. The bibliography will lead interested readers to books on many more subjects.

order and comfort be kept up, but around every domestic scene there must be a strong wall of confidence, which no internal suspicion can undermine, no external enemy break through.[25]

No small task, and the success or failure would be laid entirely at the door of Mrs. Ellis's "Women of England."

Coventry Patmore's best-selling *The Angel in the House* (1854–63) portrayed women as passive and self-abnegating, while his men were driven by a desire to achieve. Housework was ideal for women, as its unending, nonlinear nature gave it a more virtuous air than something that was focused and could be achieved and have a result. Gissing allowed Edmund Widdowson a certain naïveté in order that the novelist might express a more cynical view: "Women were very like children; it was rather a task to amuse them and to keep them out of mischief. Therefore the blessedness of household toil, in especial the blessedness of child-bearing and all that followed."[26] Women's household achievements had more to them than simple cleanliness. Arnold Bennett, in *The Old Wives' Tale*, set in the Potteries in the second half of the century, shows a drunken woman, about whom the narrator reflects in horror: "A wife and mother! The lady of a house! The centre of order! The fount of healing! The balm for worry and the refuge of distress! . . . She was the dishonour of her sex, her situation, and her years."[27] It was in failing in these roles that she is repulsive, not in the act of drunkenness itself, which Bennett has shown several times in men with condemnation but not with disgust.

Housekeeping was a source of strength for women, through which they could somehow mystically influence their husbands. In Dickens's *Bleak House* (1852–53) the Jellyby home is going to ruin because Mrs. Jellyby is more interested in her charitable works in Africa than in her own family. And it is not only the housekeeping that is affected by her absence of purpose at home; her daughter Caddy warns that "Pa will be bankrupt before long . . . There'll be nobody but Ma to thank for it . . . When all our tradesmen send into our house any stuff they like, and the servants do what they like with it, and I have no time to improve things if I knew how, and Ma don't care about anything, I should like to make out how Pa *is* to weather the storm."28 Mr. Jellyby's impending bankruptcy is to be laid entirely at the door of his wife's bad housekeeping.

It went without saying that good housekeeping improved more than just the house. Caddy Jellyby is teaching herself how to run a house: "I can make little puddings too; and I know how to buy neck of mutton, and tea, and sugar, and butter, and a good many housekeeping things. I am not clever at my needle yet . . . but perhaps I shall improve, and since I have been engaged . . . and have been doing all this, I have felt better-tempered, I hope, and more forgiving."29 She has become a better person through good housekeeping. The virtues that orderly housekeeping could bring about were almost unending. When in 1860 the child Francis Kent was murdered in a middle-class family home, the shock was not only at the brutal murder but also because "it is in this case . . . almost certain that some member of a respectable household—such as your's reader or our's [*sic*]—which goes to church with regularity, has family prayers, and whose bills are punctually settled, has murdered an unoffending child."30 Note the ingredients that make up a respectable household: church, family prayer, and prompt bill-paying.

The well-kept house directed men as well as women along the path of virtue, while the opposite led them irretrievably astray. Most of the published warnings were for the working classes, who were always considered more likely to err:

> The man who goes home from his work on a Saturday only to find his house in disorder, with every article of furniture out of its place, the floor unwashed or sloppy from uncompleted washing, his wife slovenly, his children untidy, his dinner not yet ready or spoilt in the cooking, is much more likely to go "on the spree" than the man who finds his house in order, the furniture glistening from the recent polishing, the burnished steel fire-irons looking doubly resplendent from the bright glow of the cheerful fire, his well-cooked dinner ready laid on a snowy cloth, and his wife and children tidy and cheerful.31

Working-class men who were not properly looked after by their wives retired to the pub. And if their houses were not kept to a suitable level of comfort, even sober middle-class men were expected to vanish—although more likely to their clubs than to pubs. In *East Lynne*, Mrs. Henry Wood's wonderful melodrama of love betrayed, the second Mrs. Carlyle, wife to a successful lawyer, is quite sure that if children are too much in evidence at home, "the discipline of that house soon becomes broken. The children run wild; the husband is sick of it, and seeks peace and solace elsewhere." She does not blame him but instead the housewife, who is operating "a most mistaken and pernicious system."[32] Advice books echoed Mrs. Carlyle: "Men are free to come and go as they list, they have so much liberty of action, so many out-door resources if wearied with in-doors, that it is a good policy . . . to make home attractive as well as comfortable."[33]

The attractive, tastefully appointed house was a sign of respectability. Taste was not something personal; instead it was something sanctioned by society. Taste, as agreed by society, had moral value, and therefore adherence to what was considered at any one time to be good taste was a virtue, while ignoring the taste of the period was a sign of something very wrong indeed. A tiny indication of the large importance of conformity is in the use of the word "pattern" to describe something or someone who was approved of—Esther Summerson in *Bleak House* is commended by Mr. George as "a pattern young lady."[34] Conformity, conventionality, was morality. Christopher Dresser, a designer and influential writer on decorative arts, promised that "art can lend to an apartment not only beauty, but such refinement as will cause it to have an elevating influence on those who dwell in it."[35] The house, and its decoration, was an expression of the morality that resided within. Mrs. Panton, a prolific advice-book writer, was "quite certain that when people care for their homes, they are much better in every way, mentally and morally, than those who only regard them as places to eat and sleep in."[36]

What the house contained, how it was laid out, what the occupations of its inhabitants were, what its housekeeper did all day: these

E. H. Shepard, illustrator of *Winnie the Pooh*, remembered his Victorian childhood well. Here he and his brother read in the drawing room: the fireplace with its accoutrements—coal scuttle, fire-screen—and a mantel decorated with ornaments and a clock under glass, to protect them from the coal dust and smoke, were symbols of prosperous middle-class life.

were the details from which society built up its picture of the family and the home, and it is precisely these details that I am concerned with in this book. I have shaped the book not along a floor plan but along a life span. I begin in the bedroom, with childbirth, and move on to the nursery, and children's lives. Gradually I progress to the public rooms of the house and with those rooms the adult public world, marriage and social life, before moving on, via the sickroom, to illness and death. Thus a single house contains a multiplicity of lives.

•   •   •

The nineteenth century was the century of urbanization. In 1801 only 20 percent of the population of Great Britain lived in cities. By the death of Queen Victoria, in 1901, that figure had risen to nearly 80 percent. Of those cities, the greatest was undoubtedly London. London was not just the biggest city in Britain; it was the biggest city in the world: in 1890 it had 4.2 million people, compared to 2.7 million in New York, its nearest rival, and just 2.5 million in Paris.

It was not capital cities alone that were drawing in the rural population. Until 1811, only London had a population of more than 100,000 people in Britain. By the beginning of Victoria's reign, in 1837, there were another five such cities, and by the time of her death there were forty-nine: "The Victorians, indeed, created a new civilization, 'so thoroughly of the town' that it has been said to be the first of its kind in human history."[37]

To house the numbers of newly urbanized people was a challenge without precedent, and it was met in an unprecedented way. As Continental cities (and New York) grew, apartment blocks sprang up; communal living became the norm. Apart from in Edinburgh, this was rejected in an unconscious yet unanimous way across the British Isles. Instead, a frenzy of house-building began. One-third of the houses in Britain today were built before the First World War, and most of these are Victorian. In a period of less than seventy-five years, over six million houses were built, and the majority stand and function as homes still. Despite the speed with which this massive work went on, despite the often substandard building practices, the twenty-first-century cities of Britain are covered with terraced housing built by the Victorians.* This once-unique solution to a sudden problem is now so ubiq-

---

*Terraced houses cannot readily be translated into "American" from "British." Row houses are the nearest equivalent, but unlike the American row house, the English terraced house is highly flexible socially and economically, encompassing everything from a humble worker's cottage to the grandest aristocrat's mansion. The only requirement for a "terrace" is that the row, street, or neighborhood be designed in harmony, with repetitions of the initial design appearing with each house or row of houses, and with all houses sharing party walls.

uitous that we no longer regard our terraced houses as anything except the epitome of home. Yet they were a pragmatic solution to a problem that arose from major upheavals in society.

The fact that the solution was pragmatic docs not mean that it did not also meet an almost visceral need. The French philosopher Hippolyte Taine wrote of his time in England: "It is the Englishman who wishes to be by himself in his staircase as in his room, who could not endure the promiscuous existence of our huge Parisian cages, and who, even in London, plans his house as a small castle, independent and enclosed . . . he is exacting in the matter of condition and comfort, and separates his life from that of his inferiors."[38]

Thus wrote an outsider looking in. From the inside, the Registrar General pondered the meaning of "house" and "home," as revealed by the census of 1851: "It is so much of the order of nature that a family should live in a separate house, that 'house' is often used for 'family' in many languages, and this isolation of families, in separate houses, it has been asserted, is carried to a greater extent in England than it is elsewhere." He quoted a German naturalist:

> English dwelling-houses . . . stand in close connection with that long-cherished principle of separation and retirement, lying as the very foundation of the national character . . . the Englishman still perseveres . . . a certain separation of himself from others, which constitutes the very foundation of his freedom . . . It is that that gives the Englishman that proud feeling of personal independence, which is stereotyped in the phrase, "Every man's house is his castle." This is . . . an expression which cannot be used in Germany and France, where ten or fifteen families often live together in the same large house.

The German naturalist then went on to describe how the English lived—something the English themselves tended not to think about, so natural was it to them:

> In English towns or villages, therefore, one always meets either with small detached houses merely suited to one family, or

apparently large buildings extending to the length of half a street, sometimes adorned like palaces on the exterior, but separated by partition walls internally, and thus divided into a great number of small high houses, for the most part three windows broad, within which, and on the various stories, the rooms are divided according to the wants and convenience of the family; in short, therefore, it may be properly said, that the English divide their edifices perpendicularly into houses—whereas we Germans divide them horizontally into floors. In England, every man is master of his hall, stairs, and chambers—whereas we are obliged to use the two first in common with others.

The Registrar General concluded: "The possession of an entire house is, it is true, strongly desired by every Englishman; for it throws a sharp, well-defined circle round his family and hearth—the shrine of his sorrows, joys, and meditations. This feeling, as it is natural, is universal, but it is stronger in England than it is on the Continent."[39]

Although the German he quoted indicated clearly how foreign he found the idea to be, to the Registrar General the terraced house was so normal he could not bring himself to believe in its uniqueness; the most he could admit to was that it was both "universal" and "stronger in England." However, both he and his German source agreed that "an Englishman's home is his castle." This phrase, first used in the seventeenth century by the jurist Sir Edward Coke to describe a legal and political situation, had by the Victorian era become a social description.[40]

Dickens found great comic potential in this contemporary preoccupation. In 1841, in *The Old Curiosity Shop*, he had mocked the urge for suburban retreat; twenty years later, in *Great Expectations*, his affection for the idea of sanctuary from the outside world was so strong in every phrase of his description of the clerk Wemmick's home in the suburbs, that it was clear he now also sympathized:

Wemmick's house was a little wooden cottage in the midst of plots of garden, and the top of it was cut out and painted like a battery mounted with guns . . .

I think it was the smallest house I ever saw; with the queerest gothic windows (by far the greater part of them sham), and a gothic door, almost too small to get in at.

"That's a real flagstaff, you see," said Wemmick, "and on Sundays I run up a real flag. Then look here. After I have crossed this bridge, I hoist it up—so—and cut off the communication."

The bridge was a plank, and it crossed a chasm about four feet wide and two deep. But it was very pleasant to see the pride with which he hoisted it up and made it fast; smiling as he did so, with a relish and not merely mechanically.

"At nine o'clock every night, Greenwich time,"* said Wemmick, "the gun fires. There he is you see! And when you hear him go, I think you'll say he's a Stinger."

The piece of ordnance referred to, was mounted in a separate fortress, constructed of lattice-work. It was protected from the weather by an ingenious little tarpaulin contrivance in the nature of an umbrella.[41]

Houses, then, were something that philosophers, civil servants, and novelists all thought important enough to discuss at length. They were status symbols, but the status they gave was markedly different from our own preoccupations. Today in the United Kingdom we are concerned with property ownership. The Victorians as a whole found ownership of less importance than occupancy and display. Although no firm figures exist, most historians estimate that a bare 10 percent of the population owned their own homes;[42] the rest rented, with the poorest paying weekly and the prosperous middle classes taking renewable seven-year tenancies. This allowed families to move promptly and easily as their circumstances changed: either with the increase and decrease of the size of the family, or to larger or smaller houses in better or less good neighborhoods as income fluctuated. In one area of Liverpool, it is estimated, 82 percent of the population moved within ten years, 40 percent within twelve months.[43] Mrs. Panton, the Mrs.

*For precise timekeeping, see pp. 269–71 and 402n.

Beeton of home decoration, saw this constant coming and going as sensible, although she could not quite allow herself to suggest that family incomes might ever be imperiled; she said, rather, that "neighbourhoods alter so rapidly in character and in *personelle* likewise, that I cannot blame young folk for refusing more than a three years' agreement, or at the most a seven years' lease."[44]*

The type of neighborhood one lived in was as important as the type of house. It was essential to have neighbors of equal standing, so that a social homogeneity was achieved. Thus shops and other services were confined where possible to busy main streets, and the more desirable houses were tucked in on quiet streets behind—an arrangement opposite to that of continental Europe, where the bigger, more imposing houses were to be found on the wider, more imposing streets. William Morris, after a trip to an outlying suburb, despaired, "Villas and nothing but villas save a chemist's shop and a dry public house near the station: no sign of any common people, or anything but gentlemen and servants—a beastly place to live in."[46]

The notion of home was structured in part by the importance given to privacy and retreat, and in part by the idea that conformity to social norms was an outward indication of morality. This ensured that display was vested in the choice of neighborhood, and then in interior decoration. The outside by contrast was as unrevealing as the stark façade of

---

*Jane Ellen Panton (1848–1923), a journalist and early exponent of the new concept of "interior decoration," was the daughter of the immensely successful genre painter William Powell Frith. Her obituary in *The Times* said she was a "witty and outspoken conversationalist with the courage of her opinions, and under a naturally impatient temperament there lay a fund of real kindness." This, for an obituary in the 1920s, was shatteringly outspoken, and well described the startlingly rude woman of *From Kitchen to Garret*, her most successful book (by 1897 it had been through eleven editions). In it she commented on "some friends of mine who had a [dinner] service with a whole flight of red storks on, flying over each plate, and anything more ugly and incongruous it is difficult to think of," and suggested that women should write down what they wanted for Christmas and birthdays, so that "one is sure of receiving something one requires, and not the endless rubbish that accumulates when well-meaning friends send gifts qua gifts to rid themselves of an obligation."[45]

an Arab house turned inward upon its courtyard. Most thought this a virtue: in 1815 Walter Scott had Guy Mannering say about a house auction, "It is disgusting to see the scenes of domestic society and seclusion thrown open to the gaze of the curious and the vulgar." As late as 1866–67 Anthony Trollope in *The Last Chronicle of Barset* described the same feeling. Archdeacon Grantly is disappointed when Major Grantly, his son, wants to marry a disgraced curate's daughter, but he is horrified when the major puts his possessions up for auction to finance the marriage after his father has cut off his allowance.[47] That the masses should see into a gentleman's private affairs was not to be borne.

One rung down the social scale from Dr. Grantly and his like were the endless rows of brick houses that stretched out to the horizon with deadening sameness. Conan Doyle situated his hero in Baker Street, right on the edge of the new developments, and he could not help describing the "long lines of dull brick houses [which] were only relieved by the coarse glare and tawdry brilliancy of public-houses at the corner. Then came rows of two-storied villas, each with a fronting of miniature garden, and then again interminable lines of new staring brick buildings—the monster tentacles which the giant city was throwing out into the country."[48] Picking up on the same red-brick vista, the Grossmiths situated Mr. Pooter's house in the carefully named Brickfield Terrace.

In the first half of the nineteenth century, in the inner city, houses that had earlier been the homes of the Georgian well-to-do were colonized by the new professional classes, as both homes and offices. In earlier days, living outside the city and traveling on poorly lit roads was frequently dangerous and, even when not dangerous, difficult, as night travel had to be regulated by the times of the full moon. (As late as 1861 Trollope had one of his characters say, "It turns out that we cannot get back the same night because there is no moon.")[49] Now, with the progress of gas lighting across the country, that was one problem solved. Street lighting was eulogized in the *Westminster Review* as early as 1829: "What has the new light of all the preachers done for the morality and order of London, compared to what had been effected by gas lighting!"[50] With the increase in public transport it was no longer

Gustave Doré produced a series of illustrations of London life. Here the backs
of suburban London houses are seen from a railway cutting in a typical view
of the way these brick tentacles were spreading ever-outward into the coun-
tryside. Note the rear extensions, which house sculleries, with their small
chimneys for the coppers.

just the carriage owners who could live outside the bounds of the town
and travel in to work daily. Gradually, the disadvantages of these old
houses in inner London—they had no lavatories, or the lavatories had
been installed long after the original building was planned and so were
in inconvenient places; they were dark; the kitchens were almost
unmodernizable—together with the increasing desire to separate home
from work, meant that the professionals too moved to the ever-
expanding suburbs, and traveled in to work in what had previously
been their homes. John Marshall, a surgeon living in Savile Row just
off Piccadilly in central London, in 1863 moved his family to suburban Kentish Town, on the edge of the city, after his fourth child was

born: the better air and larger house made the daily trip back and forth to his consulting rooms in their old house worthwhile.[51]

Mrs. Panton was certain that for "young people" without too much money a house "some little way out of London" was the ideal: "Rents are less; smuts and blacks* are conspicuous by their absence; a small garden, or even a tiny conservatory . . . is not an impossibility; and if [the man] have to pay for his season-ticket, that is nothing in comparison with his being able to sleep in fresh air, to have a game of tennis in summer, or a friendly evening of music, chess, or games in the winter, without expense."[53] This idyll was everything: greenery, fresh air away from city smoke, and, most important, a sense of privacy—a sense that once over your own doorstep you were in your own kingdom.

It was precisely this idyll, and the consequent rejection of city life with its allurements but also its dangers—moral as well as physical—that was the impetus for the growth of suburbia. The writer Walter Besant condemned this bourgeois development: "The men went into town every morning and returned every evening; they had dinner; they talked a little; they went to bed . . . the case of the women was worse; they lost all the London life—the shops, the animation of the streets, their old circle of friends; in its place they found all the exclusiveness and class feeling of London with none of the advantages of a country town." However, the noted urban historian Donald Olsen has argued that Besant misunderstood the aims and desires of suburbanites: "The most successful suburb was the one that possessed the highest concentration of anti-urban qualities: solitude, dullness, uniformity, social homogeneity, barely adequate public transportation, the proximity of similar neighbourhoods—remoteness, both physical and psychological, from what is mistakenly regarded as the Real World." *The Builder*, in 1856, suggested that all should live in the suburbs: "Railways and omnibuses are plentiful, and it is better,

---

*Blacks were a common nineteenth-century nuisance. They were flakes of soot, black specks that floated on the air, marking everything they touched. Ralph Waldo Emerson was told when he visited England that no one there wore white because it was impossible to keep it clean.[52]

morally and physically, for the Londoner . . . when he has done his day's work, to go to the country or the suburbs, where he escapes the noise and crowds and impure air of the town; and it is no small advantage to a man to have his family removed from the immediate neighbourhood of casinos, dancing saloons, and hells upon earth which I will not name."[54]

While the fashionable (and wealthy) still colonized parts of central London, some inner neighborhoods were becoming less desirable, and it was important for the prospective resident to take care in choosing a location. In Trollope's *The Small House at Allington,* published in 1862, a couple settled in Westbourne Grove, Bayswater:

> The house was quite new, and . . . it was acknowledged to be a quite correct locality . . . We know how vile is the sound of Baker Street, and how absolutely foul to the polite ear is the name of Fitzroy Square. The houses, however, in those purlieus are substantial, warm, and of good size. The house in Princess Royal Crescent was certainly not substantial, for in these days substantially-built houses do not pay. It could hardly have been warm, for, to speak the truth, it was even yet not finished throughout; and as for size, though the drawing room was a noble apartment, consisting of a section of the whole house, with a corner cut out for the staircase, it was very much cramped in its other parts, and was made like a cherub, in this respect, that it had no rear belonging to it. "But if you have no private fortune of your own, you cannot have everything," as the countess observed when Crosbie objected to the house because a closet under the kitchen stairs was to be assigned to him as his own dressing-room.[55]

If the family's status was on display in the choice of the house, then it followed that location and public rooms were more important than comfort and convenience, and certainly more important than the private, family spaces.

Surrounding London, the choice of suburbs was endless. Because of the railway going into the City, Camberwell and Peckham (that "Arca-

dian vale," as W. S. Gilbert called it in *Trial by Jury* in 1875) were home
to clerks—Camberwell housed one in every eight clerks in London by
the end of the century. Hammersmith, Balham, and Leyton, too, were
all lower middle class. Penge and Ealing, with no direct railway, were
middle class, Hampstead was upper middle. These were not arbitrary
designations made after the event. Contemporary guidebooks allocated St. John's Wood to authors, journalists, and publishers; Tybur-
nia (Marble Arch) and Bayswater, Haverstock Hill, Brixton and
Clapham, Kennington and Stockwell to "City men"—stockbrokers,
merchants, and commercial agents. Denmark Hill, where Ruskin had
grown up, was "the Belgravia of South London." Sydenham, High-
gate, Barnes, and Richmond were, simply, for the rich.[56]*

Arthur Munby, an upper-middle-class civil servant, in his journal in
1860 noted the class distinctions of each district as naturally as we note
street signs:

> Walked to S. Paul's Churchyard, and took an omnibus to Brent-
> ford . . . In Fleet St. and the Strand, small tradesmen strolling with
> wives and children, servant maids with their sweethearts, clerks in
> gorgeous pairs: westward, "genteel" people, gentry, "swells" &
> ladies, till the tide of fashionable strollers breaks on Hyde Park
> Corner: then, beyond Knightsbridge and all the way to Brentford,
> middleclass men & women staring idly over the blinds of their
> suburban windows, and slinking back when you look that way:
> lower class ditto ditto standing & staring at their doors, equally
> idle, but much more frank and at their ease; staring openly &
> boldly, having purchased rest and tobacco by a good week's
> work.[57]

---

*Chelsea, now a prime district for the rich, does not appear on this list—it was,
and remained until after the Second World War, an area inhabited by the lower
middle and working classes. Only with the building of the Chelsea Embankment
in 1874, which stopped the Thames from regularly flooding the area, and, in the
mid-twentieth century, with the disappearance of servants, did these houses, small
by mid-Victorian standards, become the ideal size for the newly applianced rich.

Trollope was one of the finest arbiters of what made one suburb work and another a failure, although he admired, against the trend, the lawyer who was "one of those old-fashioned people who think a spacious substantial house in Bloomsbury Square, at a rent of a hundred and twenty pounds a year, is better worth having than a narrow, lath-and-plaster, ill-built tenement at nearly double the price out westward of the parks."[58]

All of these suburbs, however remote, had one focus: the city they surrounded. However segregated, secluded, and private, every morning the suburbs emptied as the workers headed off to the city, here watched by the journalist G. A. Sala:

> Nine o'clock . . . If the morning be fine, the pavement of the Strand and Fleet Street looks quite radiant with the spruce clerks walking down to their offices governmental, financial, and commercial . . .
>
> . . . the omnibuses meet at the Bank and disgorge the clerks by hundreds; repeating this operation scores of times between nine and ten o'clock. But you are not to delude yourself, that either by wheeled vehicle or by the humbler conveyances known as "Shank's mare," and the "Marrowbone stage"—in more refined language, walking—have all those who have business in the city reached their destination. No; the Silent Highway has been their travelling route. On the . . . bosom of Father Thames, they have been borne in swift, grimy little steamboats, crowded with living freights from Chelsea, and Pimlico, and Vauxhall piers, from Hungerford, Waterloo, Temple, Blackfriars, and Southwark—to the Old Shades Pier, hard by London Bridge. Then for an instant, Thames Street Upper and Lower, is invaded by an ant-hill swarm of spruce clerks, who mingle strangely with the fish-women and the dock-porters. But the insatiable counting-house* soon swallow them up.[59]

---

*Counting houses were not simply banks, but anywhere that accounts were kept—offices, in other words. The word "office" itself was more commonly used to describe a governmental or diplomatic position—"holding office." At home, the offices were the working parts of the house: the kitchen, the scullery, the pantry, and, especially, the privy or lavatory.

The segregation and classification that came so naturally to Munby and Sala permeated every aspect of Victorian life. Suburbs were ranked to keep the classes separate; neighborhoods without shops or services kept functions—home versus work—apart. Inside the house, the need to classify and divide did not end: houses were designed to keep the function of any one group of inhabitants from impinging on any other. Home was a private space, guarded watchfully from contamination by the life of the world; but within the home too, each separate space had its own privacy, and each enclosed a smaller privacy within it. Every room, every piece of furniture, every object, in theory, had its own function, which it alone could perform; nothing else would serve, and to make do with a multipurpose substitute was not quite respectable. Privacy and segregation of function, especially as the latter defined social status, were the keynotes to the terraced house. Robert Kerr, an architect, wrote in his book *The Gentleman's House* that privacy was "our primary classification" for the ideal house; he put it ahead of a dozen other desirable characteristics such as "comfort," "convenience," and "cheerfulness."[60]

Nothing was to be allowed to escape from its own particular container. Kerr's most obvious concern was that servants and their masters should remain separate: "The Family Rooms shall be essentially private, and as much as possible the Family Thoroughfares. It becomes the foremost of all maxims, therefore, however small the establishment, that the Servants' Department shall be separated from the Main House, so that what passes on either side of the boundary shall be both invisible and inaudible on the other." Some examples of the breaching of these boundaries were servants overhearing their masters, or coal or scullery noises penetrating outside the coal-hole or scullery, or, worse, smells wafting through the house, or "when a Kitchen doorway in the Vestibule or Staircase exposes to the view of every one the dresser or the cooking range."[61] When a glimpse of inappropriate furniture through a doorway is disturbing, it seems important to examine how household life was structured, what its concerns and obligations were in daily life.

•   •   •

The standard plan of the terraced house was quickly arrived at. Such houses resembled each other closely in layout, with only the differing number of rooms—and increasing height—separating the rich from the poor. The town houses of the gentry were taller, wider, and deeper, but that was the sole distinction; the layout of the houses was eerily similar. The middle classes wanted the houses that the upper classes lived in; the poorer classes were content to live in cut-down versions of the middle-class house. The great landowners encouraged this type of housing on their estates, as something familiar to them: the town houses that were their London homes had earlier conformed to this model. As cities were rapidly generated on their land, they forced the builders into repeating the older patterns. In turn, when speculative builders bought parcels of land to make investments of their own, they copied the more prestigious estates built by the upper classes.

Architects at the time (and ever since) called the houses inconvenient and impractical, but if the demand had not been there, neither would the houses have been. These estates were built to meet a need, and if the population had shown a desire for something else, something else would have appeared.

Party walls were rigidly controlled: they were the line of demarcation between houses, and ground landlords allowed no breach of them to occur. They were also the main means of fire prevention, and for this reason it was usual to require them to extend at least 15 inches higher than the roof. But those who wrote about building practices noted that all the walls were too flimsy (a thickness of half a brick, or 4½ inches, rather than the full brick, or 9 inches, that was necessary to keep water out), that foundations were not built, and that dampcourses were not laid.[62] It is not coincidental that the word "jerry-built" was first recorded in the nineteenth century. Some bricks were so rotten that when a fire was lit smoke came out through the sides of the chimney. In her diary Beatrix Potter noted other practices that were even more unsavory:

> Builders are in the habit of digging out the gravel on which they ought to found their houses, and selling it. The holes must be filled.

The refuse of London is bad to get rid of though the greater part is put to various uses. The builders buy, not the cinders and ashes, but decaying animal and vegetable matters etc. to fill the gravel parts. It is not safe to build on at first, so is spread on the ground to rot, covered with a layer of earth . . . After a while the bad smells soak through the earth and floors and cause fevers. This delightful substance is called "dry core."[63]

The result of all this was houses that were no sooner finished than they needed repair. *The Transactions of the Sanitary Institute of Great Britain* despaired over both the lack of good building practices and the preference for display over solidity:

Here is a house, empty, which was completed and occupied two years ago. Notice how the inside is finished, to take the eye: good mantel-pieces, showy grates, and attractive papers. Now look at the floors. Not one of them is level; they are at all sorts of angles, owing to the sinking of the walls . . . Notice how the damp has risen, even to the second-floor rooms, and in all the water has come through the roof, not in one, but in many places. The bath room, &c., is conspicuous, but only to the practised eye, by reason of the scamped plumbing and forbidden fittings used. Look at the exterior . . . Observe how the roof sags, owing to the scantlings of the rafters being insufficient.[64]

Alice James, fresh from Boston, was shocked at the "dumb patience" of the English, which allowed these practices:

The generality of middle class houses . . . rock and quake when one walks across the floor, and you hear the voices of your next door neighbors . . . The Ashburnes, after a nine years' search, took a large and good house and had it thoroughly "done up," and then for weeks vainly tried to warm the drawing-room sufficiently to sit in it; then they were told by the people who had the house before them, that the room could never be used in cold weather: George was then inspired to climb up on a ladder and look at the top of the windows, which had all been examined by the British workmen, who had carefully left in the setting of them, several inches of ventilation into the open street.

The immensity of London is so overpowering that a superficial impression of solidity goes with it, and it makes one rather heartsick to learn by degrees that it is simply miles of cardboard houses.[65]*

Instead of solidity of structure, what the inhabitants were looking for, and seemed to love for its own sake, was regularity of form. The upper middle classes even built isolated terraced rows set in the middle of parkland, when on the same piece of land each householder could have had a separate house surrounded by a generous parcel of land.[66] The eighteenth century had bequeathed the "building line," the most basic regulation, which ensured that the façades of the houses were kept to a straight line, with nothing protruding—not door frames, not lintels, not even window frames. By the middle of the nineteenth century, although the concept of the terrace had been internalized, ornamental ironwork and other architectural details were breaking up the starker Georgian rows, and other regulations, mostly based on hygienic concerns, took over: in the 1850s local municipal acts laid down that all new streets had to be 36 feet wide, and at the rear each house had to have 150 square feet of open space. Other elements of control were imposed by the landlord, or the residents themselves, who equated regularity and conformity with respectability: gates were to open only in one direction, fences had to be a certain height.[67]

Sara Duncan, an American visitor toward the end of the century, got to the heart of the matter. Her cousin's house, in Half-Moon Street, a fashionable address off Piccadilly, was

very tall, and very plain, and very narrow, and quite expressionless, except that it wore a sort of dirty brown frown. Like its

---

*In retrospective fairness to the jerry-builders, it is worth noting that most of these "cardboard houses" still survive some 150 years later.

neighbours, it had a well in front of it, and steps leading down in to the well, and an iron fence round the steps, and a brass bell-handle lettered "Tradesmen." Like its neighbours, too, it wore boxes of spotty black greenery on the window-sills—in fact, it was very like its neighbours . . . Half-Moon Street, to me, looked like a family of houses—a family differing in heights and complexions and the colour of its hair, but sharing all the characteristics of a family—of an old family.[68]

These houses were indeed all of a family; and the pattern-book house was simple. It could not be more than four times as deep as it was wide, or it would be too dark. Schematically laid out, the generic house looked like this:

Top floor: servants' and children's bedrooms (usually two or three)
Half-landing: bathroom (often)
Second floor:* master bedroom, dressing room (in larger houses), second bedroom
First floor: drawing room
Ground floor: dining room, morning room
Basement: kitchen, scullery, possibly a breakfast room

Smaller houses might have only three floors: basement, ground, and first. This meant a six-room house, consisting of kitchen and scullery in the basement, two reception rooms on the ground floor, two bedrooms upstairs. All houses, of whatever size and number of rooms, were built on a vertical axis, with the stairs at the center of household life. As a woman in H. G. Wells's *Kipps* noted, "Some poor girl's got to go up and down, up and down, and be tired out, just because they

---

*Divided as we are by a common language, American readers should note that the British system gives the ground floor no number; it is just called the ground floor. The next floor up is the first, equivalent to the American second story. The British style is used throughout this book.

haven't the sense to give their steps a proper rise . . . It's 'ouses like this wears girls out. It's 'aving 'ouses built by men, I believe, makes all the work and trouble."[69]

Not everyone thought the same. Nathaniel Hawthorne, in his years in England, learned to love the regularity and system. In Leamington Spa he approved of

> a nice little circle of pretty, moderate-sized, two-storey houses, all on precisely the same plan, so that on coming out of any one door, and taking a turn, one can hardly tell which house is his own. There is a green space of grass and shrubbery in the centre of the Circus, and a little grass plot, with flowers, shrubbery, and well-kept hedges, before every house, and it is really delightful . . . so cleanly, so set out with shade-trees, so regular in its streets, so neatly paved, its houses so prettily contrived, and nicely stuccoed, that it does not look like a portion of the work-a-day world. "Genteel" is the word for it . . . The tasteful shop-fronts on the principal streets; the Bath-chairs; the public garden; the servants whom one meets . . . the ladies sweeping through the avenues; the nursery maids and children; all make up a picture of somewhat unreal finery . . . I do not know a spot where I would rather reside than in this new village of midmost Old England.[70]

These were houses for the middle classes, and they are what will be discussed in the coming pages. The houses of the working classes and the poor had their own problems, and the houses of the upper classes varied too much to be comprehended in one book. But middle-class houses—from the four- to six-room house of the lower middle class to the twelve rooms or so of the upper middle class—all conformed to a pattern. All, as Sara Duncan noted, shared a family likeness.

1

THE BEDROOM

IN THE SEGREGATION that permeated the Victorian house, the reception rooms were always considered the main rooms—they presented the public face of the family, defining it, clarifying its status. Bedrooms, to perform their function properly, were expected to separate servants from employers, adults from children, boys from girls, older children from babies. Initially, smaller houses had had only two bedrooms, one for parents and young children, one for the remaining children, with servants sleeping in the basement kitchen. To accommodate the increasing demands for separation, houses throughout the period grew ever taller.

In addition, the older fashion of the bedrooms' serving as quasi-sitting rooms was, in theory at least, disappearing. *The Architect* said that using a bedroom for a function other than sleeping was "unwholesome, immoral, and contrary to the well-understood principle that every important function of life required a separate room."[1] In actual fact, bedroom function was regulated rather less rigidly than the theory of the times advocated. Throughout the period, as well as being

rooms for sleeping, for illness, for sex,* and for childbirth, bedrooms
served more than one category of family member. Alfred Bennett, in
his memoir of growing up in the 1850s and 1860s, notes that he slept
on a small bed beside his parents' bed. So did Edmund Gosse, until his
mother developed breast cancer when he was seven; after she died, he
slept in his father's room until he was eleven. In small houses this was
to be expected. Thomas and Jane Carlyle's procession of servants slept
in the back kitchen, or scullery, from 1834 (when the Carlyles moved
into their Cheyne Row house) until 1865 (when an additional bedroom was incorporated in the attic). The house was fairly small, but
they had no children and for many years only one servant at a time.
Even in large houses with numerous servants it was not uncommon to
expect the servants to sleep where they worked. As late as 1891 Alice
James reported that a friend, house-hunting, had seen

> a largish house in Palace Gardens Terrace [in the new part of Kens-
> ington: this was not an old house] with four reception rooms and
> eight masters' bedrooms; when she asked the "lady-housekeeper"
> where the servants' rooms were, she said: "downstairs next the
> kitchen"—"How many?" "One"—at [her] exclamation of horror,
> she replied: "It is large enough for three"—maids: of course there
> was the pantry and scullery for the butler and footman.[2]

Like the Carlyles, these unknown employers probably had separate
bedrooms themselves. Even couples who shared a room often found it
desirable for the husband to have a separate dressing room for himself;
this was genteel—that is, what the upper middle and upper classes did,
even if the shifts many had to go through to carve out this extra space
often reduced the genteel to the ludicrous. (See Adolphus Crosbie's
dressing room on p. 28.) Linley and Marion Sambourne, an upper-
middle-class couple living in a fairly large house in Kensington, shared

---

*It has been suggested I am more interested in S-bends than I am in sex. For the
purposes of social history this is so, and I do not plan to discuss sex at all. There
is a great deal to say on the little we know about the Victorians' attitude toward
sex, but I am not the person to say it. (For S-bends, however, see pp. 329–31.)

a bedroom, with a separate dressing room next door for Linley.* Their two children, a boy and a girl, slept in one room on the top floor, next to the parlormaid, while the cook and the housemaid slept in the back kitchen.[3] When the children were too old for it to be considered proper for them to share a room, Linley's dressing room became his son's room, and their daughter remained in her childhood bedroom; this was all fairly standard.

Many felt strongly about maintaining segregation of function even when the occupancy was dense. Mrs. Haweis, an arbiter of fashionable interior decoration, warned in one of her books, "Gentlemen should be discouraged from using toilet towels to sop up ink and spilt water; for such accidents, a duster or two may hang on the towel-horse."[4] Ink was being used in bedrooms—the only room with a towel rail—which meant that bedrooms were used for purposes other than sleeping, which troubled her. This was clearly an ongoing situation. Aunt Stanbury, Trollope's resolutely old-fashioned spinster in *He Knew He Was Right* twenty years earlier, loathed this promiscuous mixing: "It was one of the theories of her life that different rooms should be used only for the purposes for which they were intended. She never allowed pens and ink up into the bed-rooms, and had she ever heard that any guest in her house was reading in bed, she would have made an instant personal attack upon that guest."[5]

Bedroom furniture varied widely, from elaborate bedroom and toilet suites, to cheap beds, furniture that was no longer sufficiently good to be downstairs in the formal reception rooms, and old, recut carpeting. Mrs. Panton describes the bedrooms of her youth in the 1850s and 1860s with some feeling—particularly "the carpet, a threadbare monstrosity, with great sprawling green leaves and red blotches, 'made over' . . . from a first appearance in a drawing-room, where it had spent a long and honoured existence, and where its enormous design was not quite as much out of place as it was in the upper chambers. Indeed, the

---

*Linley and Marion Sambourne's house has been preserved with the reception rooms left almost entirely as they were furnished toward the end of the nineteenth century. It now belongs to the Victorian Society and is open to the public.

bedrooms, as a whole, seemed to be furnished as regards a good many items out of the cast-off raiment of the downstairs rooms."[6] As the daughter of W. P. Frith, the enormously popular painter, Mrs. Panton had hardly grown up in a house where taste either was lacking or unaffordable. Nor was her childhood home, to use one of her favorite words, "inartistic"; this make-do-and-mend system was the norm.

By midcentury, bedrooms were beginning to be furnished to the standards of the reception rooms, where possible. This meant a good carpet, furniture (mahogany if possible) that included a central table, a wardrobe, a toilet table, chairs, a small bookcase, and a "cheffonier" or "chiffonier," a small, low cupboard with a sideboard top.* The bed, if possible, was still four-postered, with curtains. There was also a washstand, in birchwood (which, unlike darker woods, did not show water stains), with accoutrements, a pier glass, and perhaps a couch or chaise longue. In Arnold Bennett's *The Old Wives' Tale*, in which he reworked some of his childhood memories from the Potteries of the 1870s, the master bedroom of the town's chief linen-draper was splendid with "majestic mahogany . . . crimson rep† curtains edged with gold . . . [and a] white, heavily tasselled counterpane."[7]

Multifunctionality: a suggestion for a bedroom writing table with, over it, a combination bookshelf and medicine case for when the bedroom was required to double as a sickroom.

---

*Not to be confused with the American chiffonier, which is a chest of drawers.

†A wool, cotton, or silk fabric with a corded finish.

Heal's & Son, the great furniture shop on Tottenham Court Road, suggested a
bedroom furnished in Aesthetic style for the prosperous. Note that by 1896
the bed has no hangings, and gas jets illuminate the dressing mirror, although
not the bed, which still has no bedside table.

The range of furniture varied with income and taste. A mahogany
wardrobe cost anything from 8 to 80 guineas, while an inexpensive
cupboard could be made in the recess of the chimney breast, simply
using a deal board, pegs, and a curtain in front. Trays and boxes for
storing clothes were common; hangers were not in general use until the
beginning of the twentieth century (when they were referred to as
"shoulders"), so clothes either hung from pegs or were folded. Small
houses and yards of fabric in every dress meant that advice books were
constantly contriving additional storage: in hollow stools, benches,
ottomans. Even bulkier items were folded: Robert Edis, another interiors expert, recommended that halls should have cupboards "with shelves
arranged for coats."[8] "Ware"—shorthand for toilet-ware—also came
in a range of qualities. The typical washstand had towel rails on each
side, and often tiles at the back to protect against splashing water. It was

expected that there would be a basin, a ewer or jug, a soapdish, a water bottle and glass, a dish to hold a sponge, a dish to hold a toothbrush, and a dish to hold a nailbrush. A chamber pot might be of the same pattern as the ware. Mrs. Panton recommended that identical ware should be bought for most of the bedrooms, as breakages could then be replaced from stock; breakages of bedroom items, she implied, were frequent. A hip bath, a portable bath large enough for a person to sit in, might also live in the bedroom, to be filled by toilet cans—large metal cans of brass or copper, which were used to carry hot water up from the kitchen.

No room was finished without its ration of ornaments. Mrs. Haweis said that even without much money one could have a pretty room: "A little distemper in good colours, one or two really graceful chairs . . . a few thoroughly good ornaments, make a mere cell habitable."[9] Mrs. Caddy, in her book *Household Organization*, suggested that, as with the furniture and carpets, second-best would do for the bedroom— "light ornaments . . . which may be too small, or too trifling, to be placed with advantage in the drawing room."[10] Certainly the desire for small decorative objects was no less pronounced upstairs than down. Marion Sambourne's dressing table in the 1880s had on it five boxes for jewelry, a brush-and-comb set, a card case, two sachets, six needlework doilies, three ring trays, a pincushion, and a velvet "mouchoir case."[11]

Bedside tables as we know them were not current. In sickroom literature, nurses were always being advised to bring a table to the bedside to hold the medicines. Mrs. Panton, with her love of soft furnishings, suggested for the healthy "a bed pocket made out of a Japanese fan, covered with soft silk, and the pocket itself made out of plush, and nailed within easy reach," to hold a watch, a handkerchief, and so on, and then mentioned, as an innovation that required explanation, "a table at one's bedside, on which one can stand one's book or anything one may be likely to want in the night," from which, she assured her readers, "great comfort is to be had."[12]

Mrs. Panton's bed was a brass half-tester, which had fabric curtains only at the head, lined to match the furniture. This was in keeping with the style of the later part of the century. As more became known about disease transmission, home decorators were urged to keep bedroom furnishings to a minimum, although this frequently given advice was apparently often ignored. A list of objects in Marion Sambourne's room included a wardrobe, a dressing table, a cupboard to hold a chamber pot, a towel rail, a sofa, a box covered in fabric, two tables, a bookcase, a linen basket, a portmanteau, a vase, two jardinières, and ten chairs.[13] Not all agreed that bed-hangings were unhealthy; *Cassell's Household Guide* as late as 1869 thought that drafts were more of a worry than the hangings that kept them away from the sleeper.[14] In general, however, four-posters were vanishing. Even if people were not switching to simple iron or brass beds, as advised, they were at least replacing the traditional heavy drapery with beds with only vestigial curtains. The simplified lines of such beds were disturbing to some; Mrs. Panton advised that "if the bare appearance of an uncurtained bed is objected to," one could mimic the more familiar style by putting the startlingly naked bed in a curtained alcove.[15] Likewise, while carpets did not disappear entirely, they were modified so that they could be taken up and beaten regularly, or rugs were substituted, so that the floor could be scrubbed every week.

As the second half of the century progressed, hygiene became the overriding concern. Mrs. Panton, still distressed about bedroom carpets, remembered a carpet that had spent twenty years on the dining-room floor, "covered in holland in the summer,* and preserved from winter wear by the most appallingly frightful printed red and green 'felt square' I ever saw." When it was no longer considered to be in good condition, it was moved to the schoolroom, then demoted once more, to the girls' bedroom. (Note that the schoolroom, a "public" room for children, got the carpet before the children's bedroom did.) After that, it was cut into strips and put by the servants' beds, "and when I consider the dirt and dust that has become part and parcel of it, I am only thankful that our pretty cheap carpets do not last as carpets used to do, for I am sure such a possession cannot be healthy."[16]

---

*Holland was a hard-wearing linen fabric, usually left undyed. It was much used in middle- and upper-class households to cover and protect delicate fabrics and furniture.

As suggested from Heal's great furniture store for a servant's bedroom.
Instead of modern peacock-feather wallpaper (p. 41), the servants make do
with old-fashioned flowers, and plain deal furniture replaces the more elaborate versions given to their employers. Many of the middle classes slept in
rooms much like these.

Hygiene was not just a matter of ridding the house of dust. Three
things were paramount: the extermination of vermin (which encompassed bugs as well as rodents), the protection from dirt of various
kinds, and the proper regulation of light. Gas lighting was not recommended for bedrooms. If gas was used, the servants lit the bedroom
lights in the evenings while the family was still downstairs, and by
bedtime much of the oxygen in the room would have been depleted by
it; the fireplace, seldom if ever lit, added no ventilation, and in cold
weather, with closed windows, a headache was the least the sleeper
could expect to awake to. A single candle, brought upstairs on retiring,
was the approved bedroom lighting, but for the more prosperous a pair
of candlesticks on the mantel, and another on the dressing table, "with
the box of safety matches in a known position, where they can be
found in a moment," was more comfortable.[17]

Many books worry away at the location of matches, and it is understandable that before electricity it was essential to be able to find them in the dark. Mrs. Panton suggested not only that the box should be nailed over the head of the bed, but that it should first be painted with enamel paint, and a small picture be cut out and stuck on it as decoration. *Our Homes*, edited by Shirley Forster Murphy, who in the 1890s was the London County Council's Chief Medical Officer, was more modern, and it recommended a new invention, Blamaine's Luminous Paint, which could be applied to a clock face, "a bracket for matches, or a small contrivance for holding a watch." It went on, in an excess of enthusiasm, that it could also go on bell pulls, letterboxes (one assumes for streets still not lit with gas), signposts, and street signs.[18]

The lack of lighting was complicated by the fact that the bed needed to be positioned carefully to meet the conflicting demands of health and privacy. The bed should be "screen[ed], and not expose[d]" by the opening of the bedroom door, and yet at the same time it could not be placed in a draft from the window, door, or fireplace, nor should there be over-much light (which could be "trying" when the occupant was ill).[19] Given these many requirements and the limited floor plans of most terraced houses, the niceties were probably acknowledged more in the abstract than observed in practice.

Protection from dirt was still more difficult. Dust was not just the airborne particles, causing no particular damage, that we know. *Our Homes* warned:

> Household dust is, in fact, the powder of dried London mud, largely made up, of course, of finely-divided granite or wood from the pavements, but containing, in addition to these, particles of every description of decaying animal and vegetable matter. The droppings of horses and other animals, the entrails of fish, the outer leaves of cabbages, the bodies of dead cats, and the miscellaneous contents of dust-bins generally, all contribute . . . and it is to preserve a harbour for this compound that well-meaning people exclude the sun [by excessive drapery], so that they may not be guilty of spoiling their carpets.[20]

Compounded with this, coal residue was omnipresent, both as dust when coals were carried to each fireplace and then, after the fires were lit, as soot thrown out by the fire, blackening whatever it touched. The most common system of protection was to cover whatever could be covered and to wash the covers regularly. As the covers became decorative objects in themselves, however, they became less and less washable. Dressing tables, for example, were usually covered with a white "toilet cover." Mrs. Panton recommended, as more attractive, her own version, a tapestry cover "edged with a ball fringe to match." She also had "box pincushions" made out of old cigar boxes to hold gloves and other small objects: the boxes were given padded tops and then covered in plush, velveteen, or tapestry, and fringed, "so that the opening is hidden." These covers were now themselves in need of covers: tapestry could be brushed and dabbed with benzene or other dry-cleaning fluids, but it could not be easily washed; nor could velvet or plush, and especially not fringes. Yet Mrs. Panton was deeply concerned with airborne dirt: she noted that "in dusty weather particularly, and especially if we drive much," it was impossible to keep a hairbrush clean—"our brushes look black after once using." She suggested that three hairbrushes be kept in rotation: one to start the day clean, the second to be washed and set out to dry for the following day, and one spare to lend a friend should she need it.[21] If hair, covered by a hat, got so dirty on a single outing, the amount of dust and dirt that landed on clothes and furniture is almost inconceivable.

The extermination of vermin was an even more pressing problem, and, apart from the kitchen, beds were the most vulnerable places in the house. Bedding was rather more complicated than we have learned to expect. Mattresses were of organic fiber. Horsehair mattresses were the best; cow's hair ones were cheaper, although they did not wear as well; even less expensive were wool mattresses. A straw mattress, or palliasse, could be put under a hair mattress to protect it from the iron bedstead.[22] Chain-spring mattresses were available in the second half of the century, but they were expensive, and they still needed a hair mattress over them. It was recommended that a brown holland square be tied over the chains, to stop the mattress from being chewed by the springs. This upper mattress then needed to be covered with another holland case, to protect it from soot and dirt. If the bed had no springs, a feather bed—which was also expensive, hard to maintain, and a great luxury—could be added on top of the mattress. An underblanket, called a binding blanket, was recommended over the hair mattress.

After the basics (all of which needed turning and shaking every day, as otherwise the natural fiber had a tendency to mat and clump), the bedding for cold, usually fireless rooms consisted of an undersheet (tucked into the lower mattress, not the upper, again to protect from soot), a bottom sheet, a top sheet, blankets (three to four per bed in the winter), a bolster, pillows, bolster and pillow covers in holland, and bolster- and pillowcases.

With all of this bedding made of organic matter, it is hardly surprising that bedbugs were a menace. Oddly, the usually fastidious Mrs. Haweis thought that blankets needed washing only every other summer, although sheets needed washing every month—"the old-fashioned allowance"—if on a single bed; if two people were sharing a bed, it was every fortnight. Not all the sheets were changed at once: bottom sheets were taken off, as were the pillow- and bolster-cases, and the top sheet was moved down to become the bottom sheet for the next fortnight.* It was recognized that it was impossible to go to bed clean: Mrs. Haweis noted that pillowcases needed to be changed "rather oftener [than the sheets], chiefly because people (especially servants) allow their hair to become so dusty, that it soils the cases very soon."²³ (The idea that servants were especially dirty—without the congruent idea that this was because they were doing the dirtiest work—is one that will be explored in Chapter 4.)

The main cleaning of bedding came twice a year, in the spring and autumn cleanings, when it was recommended that the mattresses and pillows be taken out and aired (and, every few years, taken apart, the lumps in the ticking broken up and washed, and the feathers sifted, to get rid of the dust; for airing and its purpose, see pp. 141, 156, and

---

*This system, known as "top to bottom, bottom off," was still being used in British boarding schools in the 1980s—and possibly still is?

166–167).[24] Clearly, this kind of work could take place only with substantially more space and labor than many, if not most, middle-class households could afford. As was often the case, the advice books were describing the daily routines of upper-middle-class houses, or an ideal world that did not exist at all.* The books were aspirational in nature, creating the idea that upper-class ideals should be the norm, even to women with lower-middle-class means.

It was not, however, enough simply to clean the bedding as well as possible. Although vermin had always been present, for some reason in the eighteenth century their numbers increased,[25] possibly because of rapid urbanization. After a vigorous war against them, by the 1880s Mrs. Haweis could say that fleas were not expected in "decent bedrooms," although "at any minute one may bring a stray parent in from cab, omnibus, or train";[26] consequently vigilance had to be maintained, and the bed itself had to be examined regularly. And examine them Victorians did. Beatrix Potter wrote with an air of doom fulfilled about a Torquay hotel where she was holidaying:

> I sniffed my bedroom on arrival, and for a few hours felt a certain grim satisfaction when my forebodings were maintained, but it is possible to have too much Natural History in a bed.
> I did not undress after the first night, but I was obliged to lie on [the bed] because there were only two chairs and one of them was broken. It is very uncomfortable to sleep with Keating's [bug] powder in the hair.[27]

At home, the good housewife was supposed to check the bed and bedding every week. When Thomas and Jane Carlyle moved into their Cheyne Row house in 1834, Jane claimed that hers was the only house

---

*This continues today. Cheryl Mendelson's remarkably successful book *Home Comforts: The Art and Science of Keeping House* (2001) was quite confident not only that its readers regularly washed all the cans their food came in before opening them, and then the can opener after every use, but that before starting to cook, sensible people washed their hands in a room outside the kitchen, to avoid "cross-contamination."

"among all my acquaintances" that could boast of having no bugs. For a decade all was well. Then in 1843 bugs were found in the servant's bed in the kitchen:

> I flung some twenty pailfuls of water on the kitchen floor, in the first place to drown any that might attempt to save themselves; when we killed all that were discoverable, and flung the pieces of the bed, one after another, into a tub full of water, carried them up into the garden, and let them steep there for two days;—and then I painted all the joints [with disinfectant], had the curtains washed and laid by for the present, and hope and trust that there is not one escaped alive to tell. *Ach Gott*, what a disgusting work to have to do!—but the destroying of bugs is a thing that cannot be neglected.[28]

Ten years later, she gave up that particular war—when the servant's bed was again found to be swarming, she sold the old wooden bed and bought an iron one: "The horror of these bugs quite maddened me for many days."[29] That, she thought, was that—until a few years later when Carlyle complained about his own bed. Jane was confident initially:

> Living in a universe of bugs outside, I had entirely ceased to fear them in my own house, having kept it for so many years perfectly clean from all such abominations. But clearly the practical thing to be done was to go and examine his bed . . . So instead of getting into a controversy that had no basis, I proceeded to toss over his blankets and pillows, with a certain sense of injury! But on a sudden, I paused in my operations; I stooped to look at something the size of a pin-point; a cold shudder ran over me; as sure as I lived it was an infant bug! And, O, heaven, that bug, little as it was, must have parents—grandfathers and grandmothers, perhaps![30]

The carpenter was called to dismantle the bed. The usual system at this stage was to take the pieces of the bed, and all the bedding, into an empty room, or outside, wash the bed frame with chloride of lime and water, and sprinkle Keating's powder everywhere, then wait and repeat daily for as long as necessary. If the infestation was out of control, the bed and mattress were left in an empty room that was sealed to make it airtight, and then sulphur was burned to disinfect the bed and the surrounding area, to prevent the spread of the problem to the walls and floors.[31]*

Another anxiety was that laundry sent out to washerwomen would come back infested.[33] For the same reason, secondhand furniture was distrusted—"How can we know we are not buying infection?" asked Mrs. Panton.[34]

Even if the major infections—cholera, typhoid, diphtheria—were set to one side, the women who used these bedrooms spent, by the 1870s, approximately a dozen years of married life either pregnant or breastfeeding: they were often, in terms of health, at a disadvantage in the bedroom. Women had an average of 5.5 births (although somewhat fewer children were born alive), with 80 percent of women having their first child within a year of marriage.† Marriage and motherhood were virtually synonymous to many.[35]

Advice literature, which proliferated in all walks of life, really came into its own regarding childbirth. Motherhood, the books implied, was a skill to be acquired, not innate behavior. Nor was it to be acquired simply by watching one's own mother. Books on this subject in the early part of the century were written by clergymen, and were most concerned with the spiritual aspects of child-rearing. In the second half of the century motherhood was "professionalized," and doctors, teachers, and other experts took over. *A Few Suggestions to Mothers on the Management of Their Children*, by "A Mother" (1884), was con-

---

*Sulphur was also burned to disinfect rooms after illness (see p. 355–56). It is still used today as a bactericide—in the preservation of wine and dried fruits, for example—but its effectiveness as sulphur dioxide (as it becomes on burning) may be in doubt.[32]

†To disperse another myth regarding middle- and upper-class women, it should be noted that a small but statistically significant percentage of births in the first year of marriage—some 12 women per 1,000—had a child within seven and a half months of marriage.

fident that mothers could not act "without knowledge or instruction of any kind . . . [The belief that they could] is one of the popular delusions which each year claims a large sacrifice of young lives."[36] It was not just ignorance these books wanted to combat. For their authors, what women knew was even more suspect than what they did not know: mothers "are cautioned to distrust their own impulses and to defer to the superior wisdom of the medical experts."[37]

The first signs of pregnancy were not easy to detect. Midcentury, Dr. Pye Chavasse, author of *Advice to a Mother on the Management of Her Offspring* (a book so popular it was still in use at the turn of the century) and other similar works, gave the signs of pregnancy, in order of appearance, as "ceasing to be unwell" (that is, ceasing to menstruate); morning sickness; painful and enlarged breasts; "quickening" (which would not have been felt until the nineteenth week); and increased size. That meant that no woman could be absolutely certain she was pregnant until the fifth month. As early as the 1830s it had been known to doctors that the mucosa around the vaginal opening changed color after conception, yet this useful piece of information did not appear in a lay publication until the 1880s, and the doctor who wrote it was struck off the medical register—it was too indelicate, in its assumption that a doctor would perform a physical examination. Mrs. Panton, at the end of the 1880s, felt she could "only touch lightly on these matters [of pregnancy]," because she did not know who might read her book.[38] Kipling, from the male point of view, was very much of his time when he wrote, "We asked no social questions—we pumped no hidden shame—/ We never talked obstetrics when the Little Stranger came."[39]

It would be pleasant to be able to refute the idea that middle-class Victorians found in pregnancy something that needed to be hidden, but that really was the case. Pregnancy for them was a condition to be concealed as far as possible. Mrs. Panton called her chapter on pregnancy "In Retirement" and never used any word that could imply pregnancy. Instead, it was "a time . . . when the mistress has perforce to contemplate an enforced retirement from public life."[40] Ursula Bloom, who told her upper-middle-class mother's story, noted that "it would have been unpropitious if a gentleman had caught sight of her . . . Even Papa was supposed to be ignorant of what was going on in the house . . . He did not enquire after Mama's nausea . . . and her occasional bursts of tears."[41] The class aspect was important. *Cassell's Household Guide* warned expectant mothers:

> When a woman is about to become a mother, she ought to remember that another life of health or delicacy is dependent upon the care she takes of herself . . . We know that it is utterly impossible for the wife of a labouring man to give up work, and, what is called "take care of herself," as others can. Nor is it necessary. "The back is made for its burthen." It would be just as injurious for the labourer's wife to give up her daily work, as for the lady to take to sweeping her own carpets or cooking the dinner . . . He who placed one woman in a position where labour and exertion are parts of her existence, gives her a stronger stage of body than her more luxurious sisters. To one inured to toil from childhood, ordinary work is merely exercise, and, as such, necessary to keep up her physical powers.[42]

Seclusion and lack of exercise during pregnancy were givens for many in the upper reaches of society. At the very top of the pyramid, Queen Victoria complained to her daughter that "the two first years of my married life [were] utterly spoilt by this occupation! I could . . . not travel about or go about with dear Papa."[43] By the end of the century Maud Berkeley, from a comfortably prosperous home, painted a frieze on the new nursery walls when seven months pregnant, then spent the last month making bedding for the crib.[44]

The expectant mother also needed to prepare her own clothes. By the 1840s, the idea that corsets should be worn throughout pregnancy was beginning to disappear. While the corsets lingered, at least now women were told that they could have expandable lacings over the bosom, and steel stays should be replaced by whalebone. They were also, luckily, told that stays during labor were not a good idea, although a chemise, a flannel petticoat, and a bed gown were all expected of a woman in the later stages of labor, not to mention "a broad bandage . . . [which] must be passed loosely round the abdomen as the labor advances to its close." This bandage, "wide enough to extend from the chest to the lowest part of the stomach,"[45] seemed to convey shifting meanings: some thought it for support, some for modesty. The uncertainty points out, if nothing else, its lack of real function.

For households that could afford it (and only the more prosperous of the middle classes could), a monthly nurse was engaged. She arrived a month before the baby was due, and stayed until it was three months old, if the parents could afford her that long. Her tasks were to keep the bedroom clean, wash the baby's clothes, and wait on the mother. She also cared for the baby throughout the night, bringing it to the bedroom to be fed if it was not sleeping there, or feeding it herself if it was bottle-fed.

The nurse was also useful for morale and for practical information, as gradually through the century family members were being pushed out of the sphere of childbirth. When Dickens's first child was born, in the late 1830s, his wife's sister, aged seventeen, and his mother were both present at the birth. It was not just women who had attended births, though they predominated, nor was this behavior just for the middle classes: Prince Albert was at Queen Victoria's bedside at her first confinement in 1841;[46] Gladstone was at his wife's bedside for all six of his children's births, beginning with his first son in 1840.[47] But by the 1860s Dr. Chavasse condemned the idea of having anyone except the doctor and nurse in attendance. Not even the pregnant woman's mother was encouraged.[48] If women went back to their mother's for their first child, as many (including Marion Sambourne) did, it was likely that even then she was no longer in the room during labor.

The increasing professionalization of medicine meant that experienced midwives were being squeezed out of middle-class childbirth. Doctors liked attending childbirths—they saw it as a good way for a young practitioner to forge a bond with a newly set-up family which, with luck, would continue for the rest of the family's lifespan. For this reason they fought the possibility that midwives could become formally qualified.* Even if half to three-quarters of all births were still attended by midwives, that would mean that by the end of the century as many as three-quarters of a million women a year were being attended by a doctor—possibly the bulk of the middle classes.[49]

Another reason to have a doctor was the increasing use of chloroform. It had been administered safely as early as 1847; in 1857 it gained wide recognition when it was given to Queen Victoria during childbirth. Yet the drug was not generally accepted until the late 1870s—the delay being caused not by women, who were clamoring for it, but by doctors, who were deeply resistant.[50] It was not so much the danger—medicine had not reached a stage where practitioners expected to save every patient—as the immorality of the drug: did not Genesis 3:16 remind women everywhere that, for Eve's sin, "in sorrow thou shalt bring forth children"? Dr. Charles Meigs, two years after chloroform was first administered successfully, spoke for many in his profession: "To be insensible from whisky, gin, and brandy, and wine, and beer, and ether and chloroform, is to be what in the world is called Dead-drunk. No reasoning—no argumentation is strong enough to point out the 9th part of a hair's discrimination between them."[51] Not all felt this way, however. Both Charles Darwin and his friend the botanist Joseph Hooker were, in the old-fashioned manner, present when their wives gave birth, but—new style—their wives were given chloroform, which they administered themselves.[52]

Despite this divergence on medical treatment, both women and doctors agreed in regarding childbirth as an illness. Mrs. Panton called

---

*As a consequence, continental Europe had professionally qualified midwives decades before Britain—which did not see the need, finally, until the beginning of the twentieth century. As things stood for most of the nineteenth century, midwives had to be licensed, but this was a Bishop's License, indicating moral rather than professional qualities. To receive it the midwife had simply to be recommended by any respectable married woman, take an oath to forswear child substitution, abortion, sorcery, and overcharging (note the order), and pay a fee of 18s. 4d.

it a plight, and warned that "naturally these times are looked forward to with dread by all young wives."[53] The lower middle classes, and a substantial swath of the more prosperous, did not have the servants to permit them to lie in bed for weeks (or even days). And it was they—overburdened with heavy housework that they performed themselves, and with the care, feeding, clothing, and education of children—who would probably have benefited from time in bed. Some were forced to remain in bed, whether or not they had servants: Emily Gosse, as an older first-time mother, was unable to leave her room for six weeks.[54]

Prosperous middle-class women, on the other hand, were expected to stay in bed after the birth for at least nine days; those who got up earlier did so, it was supposed, not because they felt well enough, but out of "bravado," as *Cassell's* sternly called it, and they were considered to be acting foolishly, because "the strength and health of the mother's whole life depend upon judicious treatment at such a critical time."[55] Louise Creighton, an upper-middle-class woman married to an Oxford fellow,* accepted this fully: a close friend, who had also just had a child, came to visit, and a month after Louise Creighton had given birth to her second child, in 1874, "we spent the afternoon happily together wondering which was the most fit to get up & ring the bell when we needed anything."[56] Ursula Bloom noted that in her upper-middle-class family, after giving birth the women were kept flat on their backs and fed through a feeding cup, a china cup with a par-

---

*Mandell, or "Max," Creighton was one of those Victorian dynamos who so astonish us today. As a young fellow at Merton he became engaged to Louise von Glehn, the daughter of a prosperous German businessman living in Sydenham. At this time fellows of Oxford colleges had to be unmarried; Creighton was so valued that the rules were changed to keep him. He soon became the incumbent of a parish in Northumberland, then in quick succession the Rural Dean of Alnwick, the examining chaplain to Bishop Wilberforce, Honorary Canon of Newcastle, first Dixie Professor of Ecclesiastical History at Cambridge, Canon of Worcester, Canon of Windsor, Bishop of Peterborough, representative of the English Church at the coronation of Tsar Nicholas II, Hulsean and Rede Lecturer at Cambridge, Romanes Lecturer at Oxford, and, finally, Bishop of London—all before dropping dead at the age of fifty-seven.

tial covering and a spout, through which the recumbent patient could drink. The windows remained closed and small sandbags were laid along the edges of the frames to keep out any drafts. A lamp was left burning all night, and the monthly nurse slept on a sofa in the room. This lying-in lasted a month, and was then followed by churching (which seems to have been relatively uncommon; Bloom came from a clergy family).[57] The woman was usually faint and weak at the end of the month: without any fresh air or exercise, and with only an invalid diet, all the while breastfeeding, she could hardly be otherwise.

Serious illness always lurked. Although women had a slightly longer life expectancy than men throughout the period, all joined in regarding them as the frailer vessel. The most dangerous time was childbirth: childbed fever (or puerperal fever, now called simply septicemia) was the most common cause of death in childbirth. From 1847 to 1876, 5 women per 1,000 live births died, with puerperal fever causing between a third and a half of the deaths. There was no cure available: doctors merely prescribed opium, champagne, and brandy-and-soda, trying to ease the passing, rather than making a vain attempt to cure a mortal illness.[58]

In Vienna in 1795 Ignaz Semmelweis had radically cut the number of deaths from septic poisoning among his patients by insisting that anyone who entered his wards first scrubbed with chloride of lime. A paper on the subject, noting his results, was read before the Royal Medical and Chirurgical Society in 1848,[59] but general acceptance was extremely slow: after the Female Medical Society in 1865 warned doctors against coming from dissecting rooms straight to childbed, *The Lancet* dismissed their suggestion as "all erroneous."[60] Instead, doctors insisted that "mental emotion" and overexcitement were what caused death—women suffered in childbirth because they led "unnatural lives," and therefore they were entirely responsible for their failure to thrive.[61] Many women colluded with this attitude: Mrs. Warren's imaginary narrator was ill after the birth of her child because, according to her monthly nurse, she "shouldn't have eaten all sorts of fanciful trash, but kept [her]self to pure wholesome food, for a depraved appetite soon comes."[62] The ideas behind this comment were sound enough, but the "depravity" of the mother's thoughtlessness added the requisite moral as well as a physical dimension to women's illness.

With childbirth being regularly repeated, one can see the women's insistence on their weakness as making a certain amount of sense, even if it was not always phrased in ways that today we feel an immediate bond with. Mrs. Panton was vehement that the mother "should be the first object of every one's care until she has been for at least a fortnight over her trouble, and I trace a good deal of my own nervous irritability and ill-health to the fact that after my last baby arrived I had an enormous quantity of small worries that the presence in the house of a careful guard would have obviated." The monthly nurse, she went on, should be "a dragon of watchfulness" who keeps away "all those small bothers which men can never refrain from bringing to their wives, regardless that at such times the smallest worry becomes gigantic." It was essential that "if at no other time can we obtain consideration and thought . . . for at least three weeks after the arrival of a baby the wife should have mental as well as bodily rest, and . . . she should be absolutely shielded from all domestic cares and worries." The querulous tone was unattractive, but when she pointed out that by the time a woman had had her fifth or sixth child, her husband might have become so used to the event that he would "so depress and harass his wife by his depression that she may slip out of his fingers altogether," one does feel for the overburdened woman.[63]

There was not much escape, either. Mrs. Beeton was firm that babies should not sleep with either their nurse or their mother: "The amount of oxygen required by an infant is so large, and the quantity consumed by mid-life and age, and the proportion of carbonic acid thrown off from both, so considerable, that an infant breathing the same air cannot possibly carry on its healthy existence while deriving its vitality from so corrupted a medium." The problem was exacerbated at night, when doors and windows were closed, "and amounts to a condition of poison, when [the baby is] placed between two adults in sleep, and shut in by bed-curtains."[64] The separation of the child from its mother in its own room was, however, rarely anything but a hoped-for ideal: the space was seldom available. Without a nurse, to get any sleep at all mothers had to share their bedroom with the child they were feeding. Mrs. Beeton was not keen on this: she thought there was a risk that, while the mother was asleep, the child would continue to feed, "without control, to imbibe to distension a fluid sluggishly secreted and deficient in those vital principles which the want of mental energy, and of the sympathetic appeals of the child on the mother, so powerfully produce." The mother, on waking, was then "in a state of clammy exhaustion, with giddiness, dimness of sight, nausea, loss of appetite, and a dull aching pain through the back and between the shoulders. In fact, she wakes languid and unrefreshed . . . [a state] caused by her baby vampire."[65]

Breastfeeding, indeed, she thought "a period of privation and penance,"[66] which continued for between nine and fifteen months. Many other advice books echoed this idea of the suffering of the mother in various ways, or considered preempting the penitential period altogether, suggesting not only that bottle-feeding brought improved health to the child and mother, but that "in these days of ours few women . . . have sufficient leisure to give themselves up entirely to the infant's convenience . . . a woman has as much right to consider herself and her health, and her duties to her husband, society at large, and her own house, as to give herself up body and soul to a baby, who thrives as well on the bottle."[67]

There are no statistics for the number of women breastfeeding their children instead of bottle-feeding, or, as the latter was known, bringing them up "by hand."[68] However, with the advent of prepared foods and cheaper glass bottles, the shift to bottle-feeding began. Mrs. Beeton, by 1860, was already a little squeamish: a child protractedly nursing was "out of place"* and "unseemly."[69] (Dr. Chavasse also disapproved of postponed weaning, but his concern was that women

---

*It has been suggested that Mrs. Beeton was the first to use the expression "A place for everything, and everything in its place." Even if there are earlier instances, it was very much a feeling for the time: something out of place was something that was, both practically and morally, wrong.

who fed their child for more than a year exposed themselves to consumption.)[70] Mrs. Beeton thought bottle-feeding "more nutritious," and that the babies "will be thus less liable to infectious diseases, and more capable of resisting the virulence of any danger." Breastfed children might develop "infantine debility which might eventuate in rickets, curvature of the spine, or mesenteric [intestinal] diseases, where the addition to, or total substitution of, an artificial . . . aliment" would help.[71] This might have been true, in particular among lower-income families where the women were not able to get sufficient food themselves, although these were the ones who could least afford to buy processed baby food.

Until bottles arrived, the standard infant food was a bread-and-water pap, sweetened with sugar and fed to the baby on a spoon. The slowness and difficulty of this method made it unattractive to many mothers, partly for the time every feeding took, and also because it was difficult to ensure that the baby was receiving sufficient food. Bottles were more convenient, enabling lower-middle-class mothers with both a baby and other small children to feed the former without taking too much time out from an already arduous day. However, these bottles caused illness, although it was some time before this was generally understood. Sterilization became widespread only in the 1890s. Before rubber nipples became common later in the century, a calf's teat nipple, bought at the chemist, was tied on the bottle and "need never be removed till replaced by a new one"—roughly once a fortnight, or even several weeks "with care."[72] And mothers, particularly in the lower income groups, could not always afford appropriate food for their children. Women who carefully budgeted every penny of a small income would perhaps be at the limits of their own physical endurance without breastfeeding their children as well, but processed foods, particularly in the early days, were expensive, and what the right kinds of food were was not always obvious.

The choice for many mothers in 1860 was to make their own versions of the baby foods that were newly available prepared; Mrs. Beeton suggested "arrowroot, bread, flour, baked flour." Dr. Chavasse, in 1861, followed the same route. He suggested that mothers boil breadcrumbs

Manufactured baby food began to appear in the 1860s. By the 1870s
promotions like this one, for "Dr. Ridge's food for mothers' ducks" (p. 61)
were common. Note that it promises to cure babies' indigestion, a
worrying indication of what they were being fed.

in water for two to three hours, adding a little sugar. When the child
reached five to six months, milk could be substituted for part of the
water, with more milk added as the child got older, until the dish was
almost all milk. Otherwise he suggested taking a pound of flour, putting it in a cloth, tying it tightly, and boiling it for four to five hours.
The outer rind was then peeled off and the hard inner substance was
grated, mixed with milk, and sweetened. He also liked baked flour,
which was simply that—flour baked in the oven until it was pale
brown, then powdered with a spoon—and also baked breadcrumbs.
Both formed the basis of a gruel with water and a small amount of
sugar. He disapproved of broth, which others recommended, and he
was firm that the milk for all the above foods must come from one cow
only; otherwise it would turn "acid and sour and disorder the stomach."[73] For this the mother was to make an arrangement with a dairy
that her nominated cow would be the only one used to supply the milk

for her household. (For the likelihood that the dairy would comply, see the discussion of food adulteration, p. 281ff.)

Mrs. Warren, a few years later, suggested a German prepared food for two-month-old babies: a mixture of wheat flour, malt flour, bicarbonate of potash (to be bought at the chemist), water, and cow's milk.[74] A decade after that, an instructional guide for nursery maids (or so the title indicated, but more likely it was for their employers) recommended patent food—"Swiss milk" and "Dr. Ridge's food"—as a matter of course.[75] By the late 1890s a birth announcement inserted in *The Times* would automatically bring a flood of sample proprietary products, including patent foods, from firms keen to get the new parents' business.[76]

The new foods at least alleviated the kind of situation one doctor found himself in in 1857. He wrote: "When I see the ordinary practice of a nursery . . . I am astonished, not that such numbers *die*, but that any live! It was but a day or two ago that a lady consulted me about her infant, seven weeks old who was suffering from diarrhoea. On enquiry what had been given it I was told that . . . she had given it oatmeal. She could hardly believe that oatmeal caused the diarrhoea."[77]

While patent foods were new, other aspects of infant care continued much as before. Many books and journals addressed questions that implied that bathing young babies was dangerous. Dr. Chavasse assured mothers that, while babies should not be put in a tub, they could be sponged all over, although only their hands, necks, and faces needed soap.[78] Mrs. Pedley, the author of the influential *Infant Nursing and Management of Young Children* (1866), agreed that soap was not necessary, "except in those parts which are exposed to injurious contact."[79] One rather hopes that this is a discreet reference to their bottoms; Dr. Chavasse's babies must have been awfully smelly.

The amount of clothes the baby wore, even in summer, would have ensured that all smells lingered. Mothers were told that every infant needed a binder, which was a strip of fabric—usually flannel, sometimes calico or linen—that was swathed around the baby's stomach and was variously said to keep its bowels warm, its bowels compressed, or its spine firm.[80] Throughout the century doctors and advice writers argued against these binders, never particularly convincingly. Even Mrs. Bailin, a prominent clothing reformer, thought babies needed to wear them, although instead of linen she recommended Jaeger fabric,* which would give "just enough pressure to prevent the protrusion of the bowels."[82]

Between what babies were said to need in the way of clothes and what they actually had was a large gap. A list given by Mrs. Panton included 12 very fine lawn shirts; 6 long flannels for daytime, 4 thicker flannels for nightwear; 6 fine longcloth petticoats; 8 monthly gowns of cambric, trimmed with muslin embroidery on the bodice; 8 night-gowns; 4 head flannels;† 1 large flannel shawl, to wrap the child in to take it from room to room; 6 dozen large Russian diapers (to be used as hand towels for three or four months first to soften them up); 6 flannel pilches (triangular flannel wrappers that went over diapers); 3-4 pairs of woollen shoes; 4 good robes; and 4 binders. As well as this a nursery needed at the ready thread, scissors, cold cream, pins, safety pins,** old pieces of linen, a large mackintosh (that is, waterproof) sheet, 2 old blankets, and 3 coarse blanket-sheets.[85]

---

*Dr. Jaeger, a health reformer, toward the end of the century promoted his Sanitary Woollen Clothing, made of undyed knitted woollen fabric. Jaeger all-wool underwear became extremely popular. Mrs. Haweis commended it as "the most economical, the most comfortable, and the most cleanly, seldom as the garments require washing (once a month, says the patentee), because they throw off at once the 'noxious emanations' which soil the garments, and retain the benign exhalations." Not everyone agreed. Jeannette Marshall, the daughter of a fashionable London surgeon, rejected them outright: "The workhouse colour is a great objection in *my* eyes." Darwin's granddaughter Gwen Raverat used "Jaeger" as a synonym for "dowdy" (see pp. 306–7).[81]

†Dr. Chavasse among others thought that a head covering was always necessary, and recommended flannel caps to prevent eye inflammations, "a complaint to which new-born infants are subject."[83]

**By 1866 Mrs. Pedley was telling new mothers about "clasp-pins," which should be used for all the baby's wants. In 1889, however, the Rev. J. P. Faunthorpe still felt he needed to explain to his readers that "a special kind [of pin] is known as the safety pin, which has a wire loop to act as a sheath to protect the point."[84]

Fulminations about these overloaded infants abounded:

> A broad band is so rolled on as to compress the abdomen, and comes up so high on the chest as to interfere both directly and indirectly with free breathing; then come complex many-stringed instruments of torture, while thick folds of linen, flannel or even mackintosh, curiously involve the legs; over all comes an inexplicable length of garment that is actually doubled on to the child, so as to ensure every form of over-heating, pressure, and encumberment. After a month of this process, aided by hoods, flannels, shawls, and wraps of all kinds, a strange variation is adopted; the under bands and folds are left, but a short outer garment is provided, with curious holes cut in the stiffened edges, so as to make sure that it shall afford no protection to legs, arms, or neck.[86]

Yet most mothers were no more able to achieve this magnificence than to achieve what today we assume was standard for every nineteenth-century middle-class child: the separate nursery.

2

THE NURSERY

IN AN IDEAL nineteenth-century world, all homes would have had a suite of rooms—a night nursery and a day nursery—ready and waiting for use after the birth of the first child, together with a full complement of servants: a monthly nurse for the first three months, then a nursemaid.

The nursery itself was a fairly new concept. J. C. Loudon, in *The Suburban Garden and Villa Companion*, published in 1838, had to explain to his readers that specialized rooms for children were called nurseries.[1] Only twenty-five years later the idea had been so well assimilated that when discussing the ideal house the architect Robert Kerr simply assumed that they were necessary; it clearly never occurred to him that they had not always existed. Kerr's main concern was weighing up the virtues of convenience versus segregation. Parents needed to consider that "as against the principle of the withdrawal of the children for domestic convenience, there is the consideration that the mother will require a certain facility of access to them." The size of the house and the number of servants were for him the deciding factors: "In houses below a certain mark this readiness of access may take precedence of the motives for withdrawal, while in houses above that mark the completeness of the withdrawal will be the chief object."[2]

Outside the fantasies of upper-class living on middle-class incomes, the reality was that most houses were not big enough to make Kerr's concern one that had to be addressed. The bulk of the middle classes lived in houses with between two and four, or maybe five, bedrooms: hardly big enough for two separate rooms for the younger children, not counting two bedrooms for the older children of each sex, and definitely not big enough to worry about "facility of access."

Within these limitations, some attempt could be made to find the children their own space. Most larger houses put the children at the top of the house, in a room or rooms near the servants' bedroom. One of the main troubles with rooms at the top of the house was the need to carry supplies up and down. In *Our Homes, and How to Make Them Healthy* (1883), mothers were warned that there should be no sinks on the same floor as the nursery, since "the manifest convenience of having a sink near to rid the nursery department of soiled water has to be weighed against the tendency of all servants to misuse such convenience, and it is best to decide against such sources of mischief."[3] That is, it was better to have servants run up and down the stairs all day with food, bedding, and dirty diapers—all of which were always to be

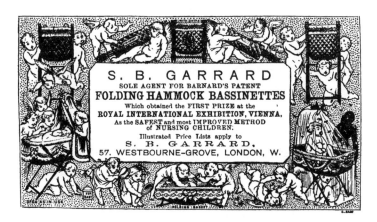

Bassinettes (also called "bercaunettes" from the French for cradle) were now lavishly decorated, as in the advertisement here, and on pages 73 and 76. Perambulators were entirely new, invented only in 1850.

removed "immediately"—rather than risk them misusing a sink, a euphemism for throwing the contents of chamber pots into them. The transmission of disease via the all-encompassing drains was a perpetual worry (see pp. 127–28), but it is likely that most houses could afford neither running water on the top floors nor the servants who might misuse the nonexistent sinks.

Health concerns were the ones given most weight—far more than convenience or affordability. One of the main reasons why it was desirable for the children to have two rooms was that they needed the "change of air" that moving from one to the other would bring, because they spent

> half of [their time]—at least for the very young—in the bed-room
> . . . The strong man after free respiration out of doors may pass
> through foul or damp air in the basement of the house with the
> inner breath of his capacious chest untouched; he may sit in a hot
> parlour without enervation, or sleep in a chilled bed-room with-
> out his vigorous circulation being seriously depressed. Not so those
> who stay at home; from these evils even the strong would suffer;
> delicate women, susceptible youth, tender children suffer most.[4]

Women and children needed fresh air and light more than men, was the conclusion, but all the suggestions that followed concerned how they should find those things inside the house.

For houses that had the space, the standard nursery was a room or two either on the main bedroom floor or higher, which was white-washed or distempered instead of painted or papered, so it could be redone every year. This too was for health reasons, to ensure that any infections did not linger. Kitchens were similarly repainted every year, but in that case it was to remove smells, and the accumulation of soot from around the kitchen range. The main ingredients of the nursery were safety oriented: bars over the windows, and a high fireguard in front of the grate, securely fastened to prevent accidents. Apart from that, the requirements were few: a central table covered in wipeable oilcloth for meals and lessons, chairs, high chairs as necessary, a toy cupboard or box, possibly a cupboard for nursery china if the children ate apart from their parents, a carpet that was small enough to lift and beat clean weekly. Mrs. Panton was very firmly against gas lighting in general, and she was particularly vehement about the danger to "small brains and eyes" posed by the "glitter and harsh glare."[5] However, many balanced this concern against the safety of a gas bracket on the wall, out of the reach of children, and the very real danger of a table-top oil lamp that could be all too easily knocked over.

The separate nursery space, in retrospect, symbolizes the distance we perceive to have been in place between parents and their children. There is no question that, however much the Victorians loved their children, they spoke of them, and thought of them, in a very different way than we do of our children today. How much was manner, how much representative of actual distance, needs to be considered. For it appears that some parents might not merely have been ignorant of children's daily routines and needs, but to a point were proud of being ignorant. Initially this might be thought of as a purely upper-class trait, fostered by having large numbers of servants, yet it occurred across the social spectrum. Molly Hughes was the child of a London stockbroker who died in a road accident in 1879, at the age of forty, leaving his family perilously near to tipping down into the lower middle class. As a young woman Molly had to go out to work as a schoolteacher. However, when she was married and able to leave paid employment, she was careful to note in her autobiography that she knew little about children and relied for information on her servant: " 'How often should we change her nightdress, Emma?' I asked. The reply was immediate and unequivocal—'Oh, a baby always looks to have a clean one twice a week.' [Emma] knew also the odd names for the odd garments that babies wore in that era—such as 'bellyband' . . . and 'barracoat.' " Molly's sister-in-law affected the same blankness when Molly was first pregnant: "She took the greatest interest, and loaded me with kindness, but in the matter of what to do about a baby she was, or pretended to be, a blank. 'When I was married,' she said, 'all I knew about a baby was that it had something out of a bottle, and I know little more now.' "[6]

Molly recognized pretend ignorance in her sister-in-law, even if she did not see the same in herself. Whether real or feigned, it indicated a gap between adults and children which was not easily breached. Caroline Taylor had a similar sort of background: she was the granddaughter of a shopkeeper in Birmingham; her father was a permanently out-of-work engineer. She described relations between her parents and their children tersely: it was one of "stiff formality."[7]

Mrs. Panton, the daughter of a successful artist, supported herself, and probably placed herself in the upper reaches of the middle classes—though it is to be questioned whether professional families would have concurred. She strove to catch the right tone in her work on domestic life. A good nurse, she said, would never allow "*her* baby to be a torment . . . She turns them out always as if they had just come out of a band-box, and one never realises a baby can be so unpleasant so long as she has the undressing of them." Later she added, "I do not believe a new baby is anything but a profound nuisance to its relations at the very first"; a new mother would require "at least a week to reconcile herself to her new fate." Children could be "distracting and untidy."[8]

Mrs. Beeton, as we saw, thought of a feeding child as a vampire. Caroline Clive, an upper-middle-class woman, thought more or less the same: she referred to her child's coming to "feed upon me," and she confessed that although she loved him now, a couple of months after his birth, "I did not care very much about him the two first days."[9] Louise Creighton said of her husband on the birth of their first child, "Max, who later was so devoted to children, had not really yet discovered that he cared about them. I am doubtful of the value of what is called the maternal instinct in rational human beings."[10]

The higher up the social scale, the more open about this distance from their children the parents were. Ursula Bloom's grandmother, at least in family legend, forgot to take her baby when leaving its grandparents' in the country. "She had never cared too much for children," said her granddaughter, perhaps unnecessarily.[11*] Those lower down the

*No one, however, can trump Augustus Hare's parents, but as an upper-class child he can only (just) be accommodated in a footnote. Hare's uncle, also an

ladder reflected the same views in smaller ways. Georgiana Burne-Jones, the wife of the then-struggling Pre-Raphaelite painter Edward Burne-Jones, referred to their first child as "the small stranger within our gates."[13] As the daughter of a Methodist minister, she knew the original Bible verse and was not just thoughtlessly parroting the standard usage whereby a baby was "a little stranger." Deuteronomy 14:21, detailing the laws concerning food, says: "Ye shall not eat of anything that dieth of itself: thou shalt give it to the stranger that is in thy gates, that he may eat it." Was the stranger within the gates a second-class citizen?

Possibly not; but the expression does reinforce the shift that has occurred over the past 150 years, from a parent-centered universe to our own child-centered one. In earlier centuries households were run by adults for adults. Children were an integral part of a functioning economic unit, whether as providers of labor in less prosperous families or as potential items of value in the business and marriage markets for the wealthier. Children were to be trained and disciplined, both to promote their own well-being and to promote the well-being of the family unit. In addition, various of the more fundamentalist versions of Christianity had said that to spare the rod was not simply to spoil the child in practical matters but to spoil his soul. Original sin, thought the Evangelicals, meant that all children were born needing to find salvation.

In less religious houses this developed into a sense of authority for authority's sake. Samuel Butler wrote of his father's childhood early in the century, as well as his own, in his semi-autobiographical novel *The Way of All Flesh*:

> If his children did anything which Mr Pontifex disliked they were clearly disobedient to their father. In this case there was obviously

---

Augustus Hare, died shortly before his godson-to-be was born; his widow, Maria, stood godmother instead, and she tentatively asked his parents if she could perhaps have the child to stay for a while. The answer to her letter was immediate: "My dear Maria, how very kind of you! Yes, certainly, the baby shall be sent as soon as it is weaned; and if anyone else would like one, would you kindly recollect that we have others." Maria Hare cared for him for the rest of her life, and he called her his mother.[12]

only one course for a sensible man to take. It consisted in check-ing the first signs of self-will while his children were too young to offer serious resistance. If their wills were "well broken" in child-hood, to use an expression then much in vogue, they would acquire habits of obedience which they would not venture to break through.[14]

As the century progressed, improved standards of living meant that many children who would earlier have gone out to work now had a childhood. Further, Rousseau's theories of child education, promoting the ideal of individual development in natural surroundings, struck a chord, and converged with the Romantic movement's eloquence on the innocence and purity of childhood. Many books agreed with the Rev. T. V. Moore in his "The Family as Government" in *The British Mothers' Journal*, when he advised parents that "the great agent in exe-cuting family law is love."[15]

Yet while physical coercion was used less as the century progressed, and persuasion more, there was little doubt about the virtues of authority and obedience. Frances Power Cobbe, a philanthropist and worker for women's rights, outlined in her *Duties of Women* what was to be expected from a child by way of obedience:

> 1st. The obedience which must be exacted from a child for its own physical, intellectual, and moral welfare.
>
> 2nd. The obedience which the parent may exact for his (the parent's) welfare or convenience.
>
> 3rd. The obedience which parent and child alike owe to the moral law, and which it is the parent's duty to teach the child to pay.[16]

Moral law was to many synonymous with religious law. It enshrined the duty of obedience owed to God. The head of the family derived his authority from God; the wife of the head derived hers from the head; and so on. Any disobedience subverted this notion of order. Therefore disobedience was, of itself, subversive, and it was the idea of rebellion that needed to be punished, not whatever the act of disobedience itself was. Laura Forster, a clergyman's daughter (and later the aunt of E. M. Forster), noted that "we were expected to be obedient without any reason being given," but she tried to give extenuating circumstances: "We shared our mother's confidence as soon as we were of a suitable age, and I think this helped to give us the conviction that we all had that nothing was forbidden us capriciously, and that some day we should know, if we did not understand at the time, why this or that was forbidden."[17]

Most parents felt that discipline could not begin too early. A mother's or nurse's refusal to feed her infant except at stated hours taught the infant the benefits of "order and punctuality."[18] Having their crying ignored taught babies self-restraint; Mrs. Warren said that if a child cried for something, on principle it should never be given— "Even a babe of three months, when I held up my finger and put on a grave look, knew that such was the language of reproof." Instead of beatings, which children earlier in the century might have routinely expected, administered by father, mother, or teachers, depending on family circumstances, children were now told of the disappointment they caused to their parents and to God. Mrs. Warren suggested that children who were disobedient should be told they were breaking the Fifth Commandment, by not honoring their fathers and mothers; Marion Jane Bradley, wife of a master at Rugby School, told her son that "God was looking at him with great sorrow and saying 'that little boy has been in a wicked passion, he cannot come up and live with me unless he is good.'"[19]

Corporal punishment, although lessened in force and frequency, vanished only slowly over the next hundred years. When Marion Jane Bradley's son Arthur (nicknamed Wa) was three, she wrote: "He was not good yesterday and surprised me by saying, 'Wa was naughty in London Town and Papa and Mama did whip Wa very hard'—I did not believe he could have remembered anything so long ago [three months before]. This whipping certainly had its effect. It was the first and last. Long and obstinate struggle who was to be the master."[20] Louise

Creighton, who said that in her own childhood she was never beaten but put in a dark cupboard that induced only boredom, punished her own children in a way that she acknowledged "may be considered brutal by some people. Cuthbert was a very mischievous boy, & used to play with fire & cut things with knives, so when he played with fire I held his finger on the bar of the grate for a minute that he might feel how fire burnt, & when he cut woodwork with his knife I gave his fingers a little cut." Despite what might today be described as savagery, she thought it important to end with "I never whipt any child."[21] What seemed harsh changed over time. A guide to the sickroom advised, almost in passing, that if a child refused medicine, "at once fasten the child's hand behind him, throw him on his back, pinch his nose to force his mouth open, and . . . pour [the liquid] down his throat with a medicine spoon." This it called acting with "firmness."[22]

It was still, however, a different world from the one in which Mr. Pontifex had ruled. Children were moving to the center of their parents' lives. This was displayed in graphic form over the century by the pattern books that furniture makers and shops produced to advertise their wares. In the early part of the nineteenth century there was no furniture made specifically for children; then in 1833 Loudon's *Encyclopaedia of Cottage, Farm and Villa Architecture* (which, despite its name, was a very metropolitan, bourgeois publication) had a short section for children's furniture, most of it miniaturized versions of adult objects. By the end of the century every shop and every catalogue had a full range of furniture designed specially for children's needs.[23]

Different families adapted to this new ethos more or less quickly and comfortably; how quickly and comfortably was based on character and on personal and social background. Many remained convinced that the marital relationship was the primary one. Louise Creighton reported that Walter Pater's sister had once said to her about the novelist Mrs. Humphry Ward and her husband that "she always preferred Mary [Ward]'s company when Humphry was present, because if he was absent Mary was always wondering where he could be; but she preferred me without Max, for when he was there I was so occupied with him & with what he was saying that I was no use to anyone else

. . . I think this was true all my life." She did not make the connection with her own mother's behavior in her childhood: when Mr. von Glehn, Louise's father, was due back from London in the evenings, "my mother always grew expectant some time before his train arrived & was very fidgety & anxious." Her husband was her focus, as it had been her mother's, and "only the fact that I nursed [my children] kept me from going about much, and this . . . did prevent me sharing many of Max's expeditions & walks which was a very real deprivation."[24]

COMPLETE LAYETTES,
£5 to £100.

THE
NEW FOLDING COT,
Untrimmed, from 15/-; Trimmed, from 29/6

TRIMMED BASSINETTES, from 17/6
TRIMMED BASKETS, from 8/6
ALL FITTINGS AND TOILET REQUISITES.

Every Requisite in BABY LINEN
can be had ready for use from Stock,
which is always large and carefully
selected, and replete with LATEST
NOVELTIES.
PARCELS CARRIAGE PAID.

W. SMALL & SON,
1 & 2, CHAMBERS STREET,
EDINBURGH.

ILLUSTRATED PRICE LIST SENT POST FREE.

Advice books, fiction, and reality converge here. Mrs. Warren's model housewife always made her children understand that when their father came home from work he was to be considered first in all things; otherwise she felt it was entirely to be expected if he became "cold and indifferent."[25] Mrs. Panton believed children should have rooms where they do not "interfer[e] unduly with the comfort of the heads of the establishment."[26] Many novels touched on the same theme. In George Gissing's *New Grub Street* the failed novelist Edwin Reardon looks back on his collapsing marriage: "Their evenings together had never been the same since the birth of the child . . . The little boy had come between him and his mother, as must always be the case in poor homes."[27] His view is that marriages prosper not because they become child-centered but because the family can afford servants to remove the children from the adult sphere.

Mrs. Henry Wood, in *East Lynne*, provided the clearest apologia for this adult-centered view. Mr. Carlyle's second wife expounds her views to her predecessor, Lady Isabel (who is for complex plot reasons currently disguised as a French governess, Mme Vine). The two women agree on this point, and as the reader has spent hundreds of pages learning to sympathize with Lady Isabel it is hard to imagine that her concurrence with Mrs. Carlyle does not imply that this was also Mrs. Henry Wood's view. It is worth quoting at length, for the insight it gives into the adult-centered worldview. Mrs. Carlyle says:

> I never was fond of being troubled with children . . . I hold an opinion, Madame Vine, that too many mothers pursue a mistaken system in the management of their family. There are some, we know, who, lost in the pleasures of the world, in frivolity, wholly neglect them: of those I do not speak; nothing can be more thoughtless, more reprehensible, but there are others who err on the opposite side. They are never happy but when with their children; they must be in the nursery; or, the children in the drawing-room. They wash them, dress them, feed them; rendering themselves slaves . . . [Such a mother] has no leisure, no spirits for any higher training: and as they grow old she loses her authority . . . The discipline of that house soon becomes broken. The children run wild; the husband is sick of it, and seeks peace and solace elsewhere . . . I consider it a most mistaken and pernicious system . . .
>
> Now, what I trust I shall never give up to another, will be the *training* of my children . . . Let the offices, properly belonging to a nurse, be performed by the nurse . . . Let her have the *trouble* of the children, their noise, their romping; in short, let the nursery be her place and the children's place. But I hope I shall never fail to gather my children round me daily, at stated periods, for higher

purposes: to instil into them Christian and moral duties; to strive to teach them how best to fulfil life's obligations. *This* is a mother's task.[28]

Or, as the novelist Mrs. Gaskell had the governess in *Ruth* say more succinctly to the children in her care, "All that your papa wants always, is that you are quiet and out of the way."[29] Mothers as well as fathers wanted quiet, but for women it was important that the morality of self-restraint be stressed.

Marion Jane Bradley kept a diary of her children's first years, from 1853 to 1860. In about 1891 she reread it and added a note to the manuscript: "I tried to make our children fill their proper subordinate places in the family—Father always to be first considered, their arrangements to be subject to his . . . Not to seem anxious about their health or to fuss over their comfort and convenience, but to make them feel it was proper for them to give up and be considered secondary. Of course, this is *quite* old fashioned."[30]

It was, truly, *quite* old-fashioned by the end of the century, for the mother, at least. Fathers remained more distant. Caroline Taylor's father "had a quick temper," she wrote, "and we children stood in fear of him. We were never allowed to express our ideas . . . My father had a knowledge of many subjects and was artistic and musical, but he never conversed on things to his children . . . Parents always assumed such dignity, and we felt so small."[31] Fifty years before, Mrs. Gaskell had reflected the prevailing views in her novels, even while her personal view, in her letters and journal, had long been moving toward precisely that child-centered universe which was the opposite of the children being "quiet and out of the way." Mrs. Gaskell was the wife of one Unitarian minister and the daughter of another, and thus there was nothing of Evangelical stringency in her attitude to her children. Although she was deeply concerned about their moral welfare, she did not see that children should suffer for it. She was very much of her time in reading numerous advice books, and she carefully considered the instructions they gave. She agreed with those that said that moral fiber was not developed by privation and denial:

I don't think we should carry out the maxim of never letting a child have anything for crying. If it is to have the object for which it is crying I would give it, directly, *giving up any little occupation or purpose of my own*, rather than try its patience unnecessarily. But if it is improper for it to obtain the object, I think it right to with-hold the object steadily, however much the little creature may cry . . . I think *it is the duty of every mother to sacrifice a good deal* rather than have her child unnecessarily irritated by anything. [My italics.][32]

This was not simply advice she was giving to others—she wrote in her journal, when her daughter Marianne was six months old, "If when you [that is, the future, grown-up Marianne] read this, you trace back any evil, or unhappy feeling to my mismanagement in your childhood forgive me, love!"[33]—and the view took concrete form within the Gaskell household. Earlier, children were to give things up to their eld-

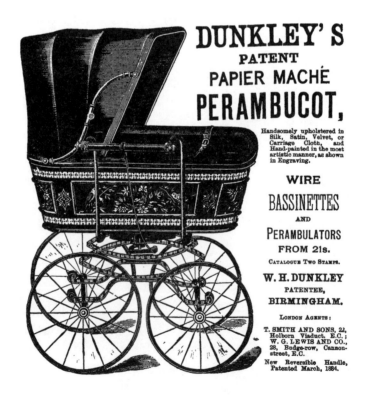

DUNKLEY'S
PATENT
PAPIER MACHÉ
PERAMBUCOT,

Handsomely upholstered in Silk, Satin, Velvet, or Carriage Cloth, and Hand-painted in the most artistic manner, as shown in Engraving.

WIRE
BASSINETTES
AND
PERAMBULATORS
FROM 21s.
CATALOGUE TWO STAMPS.

W. H. DUNKLEY
PATENTEE,
BIRMINGHAM.

LONDON AGENTS:
T. SMITH AND SONS, 22, Holborn Viaduct, E.C.; W. G. LEWIS AND CO., 28, Budge-row, Cannon-street, E.C.

New Reversible Handle, Patented March, 1884.

E. H. Shepard and his brother, by the 1880s and 1890s, were in a
very advanced type of pram, which allowed children to look about them.
Only thirty years before, small children taken out for air had to be
carried by their mothers or nursemaids.

ers; now the elders deprived themselves. Because of the cost of Marianne's schooling and the larger house they had bought, "we aren't
going to furnish the drawing room, & mean to be, and are very œco-
nomical because it seems such an addition to children's health and happiness to have plenty of room."[34]

The interest in children's happiness was new, but children's health
had always been a concern. Although mortality rates for the general
population were still high, they were dropping nonetheless: from 21.8
deaths per thousand in 1868, to 18.1 in 1888, down to 14.8 in 1908. The
young benefited soonest: children first felt the improvements as understanding of disease transmission, a drop in the real price of food, and,
most important, improved sanitation worked their way through the
population.[35] (It must be remembered that until this point the most
likely time of death was not in old age but in infancy: as late as 1899,

more than 16 percent of all children did not survive to their first birthday.)[36] A child born in the earlier part of the century would probably have watched at least one of its siblings die; a child born in the 1880s would have had fewer siblings, and would also have had less chance of seeing any one of them die.[37]

This improvement in the child-mortality rate, together with the increasingly child-centered world they inhabited, made parents ever more solicitous of the health of their children. It was difficult not to worry when a parent could expect to have to deal with the effects on a child of scalds, burns, falls, being dropped by the nursemaid,* swallowing lotions or liniment, swallowing lucifers (matches), clothes catching fire, drowning, stings, swallowing laudanum, paregoric, Godfrey's Cordial, or Dalby's Carminative (all four were opium derivatives), peas up their noses or in their ears, and swallowing glass or coins.[39]

Some fears appeared relatively trivial, but uncertain diagnostic techniques meant that many major illnesses could not be identified and separated from minor ones. Seemingly harmless childhood ailments might end in death. Mrs. Gaskell reported in her journal on Marianne's sudden attack of croup: "We heard a cough like a dog's bark . . . We gave her 24 drops of Ipec: wine, and Sam & Mr Partington both came. They said we had done quite rightly, and ordered her some calomel powders.† . . . we have reason to be most thankful that she is spared to

---

*Not, please note, the mother. The wicked or incompetent servant loomed large in the minds of the middle classes. Mrs. Warren told of a nursemaid who caused a child's death by taking the child out when she was told not to. Mrs. Beeton warned that the mother should learn to distinguish the different cries of her child, "that she may be able to guard her child from the nefarious practices of unprincipled nurses, who, while calming the mother's mind with false statements as to the character of the baby's cries, rather than lose their rest, or devote that time which would remove the cause of suffering, administer, behind the curtains, those deadly narcotics which, while stupefying Nature into sleep, insure for herself a night of many unbroken hours."[38] See a discussion on servants and their employers' fears on pp. 149–55.

†Ipecacuanha and calomel were used with ruthless regularity in Victorian households. Ipecac, as it was commonly called, was a powdered root, and functioned as an emetic, causing vomiting. Calomel, made of mercury chloride, was a purgative. Both were used routinely in attempts to "expel" various illnesses.

us . . . Poor little Eddy Deane was taken ill of croup on the same night, and died on the following Monday."[40] Poor little Eddy Deane may very well have had diphtheria; it was often confused with croup.

Even teething, that routine, ordinary, minor fret of babydom, was a major cause of anxiety. Mrs. Pedley estimated that the 16 percent of child deaths that were attributed to teething were in reality teething-related: it was not the malady but the cure that was killing children. She wrote that when their babies fretted before their new teeth began to show, worried parents decided that "milk no longer agrees with the child," so they stopped the milk and instead fed the infants on unsuitable foods. This upset the babies' digestions; they were therefore given drugs, most of which contained opium, and, not unnaturally, the babies died in convulsions—deaths put down to that dread disease, teething.[41] Her common sense, however, was drowned out by those who recommended syrup of poppies (Mrs. Warren) or purgatives (Dr. Chavasse, Mrs. Beeton, and Mrs. Warren) or surgery—lancing the gums (all of the above).

Mrs. Beeton listed the symptoms of teething, and they included, apart from the ones we would recognize today—inflamed gums and an increase of saliva—restlessness, irregular bowel movements, fever, disturbed sleep, "fretfulness, . . . rolling of the eyes, convulsive startings, labourious breathing": pretty well everything, in fact. The answer was to give purgatives and a teething ring, put the child in a hot bath, and if necessary lance the gums, "which will often snatch the child from the grasp of death . . . [Otherwise] the unrelieved irritation endanger[s] inflammation of the brain, water on the head, rickets, and other lingering affections." Indeed, Mrs. Beeton stressed that rickets and water on the brain were "frequent results of dental irritation."[42] Mrs. Beeton at least made one concession to the strength of the drugs routinely given to infants: she suggested that, before weaning, medicine could be given via the milk, the mother swallowing the appropriate dose. That was an improvement on many systems, where it was generally expected that the nurse would give the newborn infant a few drops of castor oil as soon as it was born. Mrs. Gaskell followed the general trend. Marianne "had one violent attack . . . but we put her directly into warm water, & gave her castor oil, sending at the same time for a medical man, who decided that the inflammatory state of her body was owing to her being on the point of cutting her eye-teeth."[43]

"Convulsions" were a similarly created illness: death from convulsions was common, but even at the time many attributed the deaths to the opium-based medicines used as a cure. Mrs. Beeton (whose chapter on child-rearing, it should be emphasized, was written for her by a doctor) gave a description of a convulsion: "The infant cries out with a quick, short scream, rolls up its eyes, arches its body backwards, its arms become bent and fixed, and the fingers parted; the lips and eyelids assume a dusky leaden colour, while the face remains pale, and the eyes open, glassy, or staring." This might last a few minutes only, and could surely describe almost any crying child. Yet the worried caregivers who saw a convulsion in these symptoms were advised to give the baby a hot bath and a teaspoonful of brandy and water and, an hour after the bath, administer a purgative, repeated once or twice every three hours.[44] Such "spasms" could also be treated with patent medicines such as J. Collis Browne's Cholodyne, "advertised as a cure for coughs, colds, colic, cramp, spasms, stomach ache, bowel pains, diarrhoea and sleeplessness." This contained not only opium but also chloral hydrate and cannabis.[45]

Children who had once had trouble with fits, or with their teething (and, given these symptoms, all babies did: has anyone ever had a baby who did not at some stage suffer from "disturbed sleep" or "fretfulness"?), would shortly have problems caused by the purgatives and opium that had been administered to treat them, starting off a fresh round of medication. Mrs. Pedley again tried to calm fears, pointing out that nurses often said children were subject to fits when what they meant was that they had a twitch, or blinked frequently, or moved their arms and legs after feeding (which she attributed to flatulence).[46]

Although teething seems a bizarre worry from our perspective, nineteenth-century parents had many more real anxieties than their descendants. By the time they reached the age of five, 35 out of every 45 children had had either smallpox, measles, scarlet fever, diphtheria, whooping cough, typhus, or enteric fever (or a combination), any of which could kill.[47] Lesser illnesses, such as chicken pox and mumps, were also more dangerous than today, because of the drugs given to treat them. Much of what we take for granted was simply not available, or only barely. A great deal of progress had been made by midcentury: the stethoscope, the thermometer, and the percussive technique for listening to the patient's chest had all been developed; the smallpox vaccine was routinely urged on all parents. Yet what was available and what was commonly used were not necessarily the same thing. Louise Creighton, as late as the early 1880s, was misled when her son complained only mildly of feeling ill; she therefore did nothing for some time. She finally sent for the doctor, and the child was found to have fluid on his lungs. She later said that if she had "known the use of the clinical thermometer, which was not yet considered even a desirable instrument . . . for any mother to use," she would have recognized the gravity of the illness earlier.[48]

Even something as basic as a hot-water bottle, to keep a sick child warm, was not easily obtainable. The "bottles" were generally made of stone, and corked at the top. Wriggly, fretful children had a nasty tendency to kick the corks out, sending scalding water gushing over themselves. Gutta-percha bags were available by midcentury, but they were expensive and so only for the rich.* The older method was to heat sand in a pan over the kitchen range and fill cloth bags with it, and that was more generally used.[49]

The best solution to illness was to prevent it, all agreed. All also agreed on how this was to be done: a child should lead an orderly, well-regulated daily life, simple in every element. Meals were to be plain and "wholesome"—a wonderful word embodying not only basic nutrition but also a moral element. In this moral universe food was a danger as well as a benefit: books warned against giving children specific foods, usually strong-tasting ones (especially for girls: such foods were

---

*Gutta-percha was produced from the sap of the *Isonandra gutta* tree, native to Indonesia. When vulcanized, it acted as a waterproofing, insulating material, much as we used rubber and now use plastic. It first appeared in Britain in the 1840s, becoming widely used for, among other items, hot-water bottles, golf balls, and the insulating cover for the first transatlantic telegraph cable.

thought to arouse passion, and were troublesome during puberty in particular), though vegetables and fruits could be equally hazardous. It was notable that expensive foods, or ones that tasted good enough to be consumed from desire rather than hunger, were often considered the most unwholesome. Mrs. Beeton was not alone in warning of the dangers of fresh bread. Day-old bread was infinitely to be preferred, while "hot rolls, swimming in melted butter . . . ought to be carefully shunned"[50]—especially by children, who were to have the most restricted diets. She recommended that suet pastry be made with 5 ounces of suet for every pound of flour, although a scant 4 ounces would "answer very well for children." Another of her puddings was made with eggs and brandy unless it was intended for children, when "the addition of the latter ingredients will be found quite superfluous."[51] Meat was the basis of children's diet, as it was of that of their elders, for, as Mrs. Pedley noted, "the highest form of diet is animal food. It appears that children who, at a befitting age, are judiciously fed on meat, attain a higher standard of moral and intellectual ability than those who live on a different class of food."[52]

Breakfast for children in prosperous middle-class houses was almost as spartan as it was for their lower-middle-class coevals. Gwen Raverat, a granddaughter of Charles Darwin and the daughter of a Cambridge don, throughout her childhood ate toast and butter, and porridge with salt. Twice a week the toast was "spread with a thin layer of that dangerous luxury, Jam. But, of course, not butter, too. Butter and Jam on the same bit of bread would have been an unheard-of indulgence—a disgraceful orgy." She first tasted bacon when she was ten years old and away from home on a visit.[53] Louise Creighton first tasted marmalade and jam only after her marriage, when she was in her twenties.[54] Compton Mackenzie, the novelist, had a similar prospect in his childhood:

> Nor did the diet my old nurse believed to be good for children encourage biliousness, bread and heavily watered milk alternating with porridge and heavily watered milk. Eggs were rigorously forbidden, and the top of one's father's or mother's boiled

egg in which we were indulged when we were with them exceeded in luxurious tastiness any caviar or pate de foie gras of the future. No jam was allowed except raspberry and currant, and that was spread so thinly that it seemed merely to add sweetish seeds to the bread.[55]

The bread and milk (or bread and milk and water) eaten by most lower-middle-class children was not substantially different from this upper-middle-class fare.

Mackenzie was a more rebellious child than Raverat or Creighton, and one day

> I thought of a way to exasperate Nanny by telling her that I preferred my bread without butter. I was tired of the way she always transformed butter into scrape, of the way in which, if a dab of butter was happily caught in one of the holes of a slice . . . she would excavate it with the knife and turn it into another bit of scrape. I was tired of the way she would mutter that too much butter was not good for me and, as it seemed to me, obviously enjoyed depriving me of it. If I told her that I preferred my bread without butter she would be deprived the pleasure of depriving me.[56]

No doubt his going without butter was a worry—he was removing the possibility of a lesson in the moral values implicit in food.

Morality was at the heart of home education. When Marianne Gaskell came back from her school in London, her mother was well pleased with what she had learned there: "It is delightful to see what good it had done [Marianne], sending her to school . . . She is such a "law unto herself" now, such a sense of duty, and *obeys* her sense. For instance, she invariably gave the little ones 2 hours of patient steady teaching in the holidays. If there was to be any long excursion for the day she got up earlier, that was all; & *they* did too, influenced by her example."[57] The merit of her schooling was not that she had acquired knowledge but that she had become dutiful.

Most children, boys and girls, were initially taught at home by their mothers. This might begin at a young age, although Mrs. Gaskell was concerned not to start Marianne's schooling too early—"We heard the opinion of a medical man latterly, who said that till the age of three years or thereabouts, the brain of an infant appeared constantly to be verging on inflammation, which any *little* excess of excitement might produce"—so she waited until after the child's second birthday. By her third birthday Marianne had begun to read and sew, "and makes pretty good progress . . . I am glad of something that will occupy her, for I have some difficulty in finding her occupation, and she does not set herself to any employment."[58] The expectation that a three-year-old would set herself to specific tasks and that lessons could usefully be learned so young was not uncommon. By his third birthday Marion Jane Bradley's son Wa was learning to read. Six months later his mother worried that he was very difficult to teach: one day he would read his lessons through with no problem, the next he could not. It took her six weeks to teach him to read "cab . . . which he can't remember from one day to the next." But she felt this was her fault—that she was a bad teacher because "it requires more patience than I have"—not that he was simply too young.[59]

Oddly enough, there were few instructions in how to teach small children, despite the preponderance of advice being given in all other areas of life. Mothers were supposed to know simply by virtue of being mothers. Mrs. Warren was one of the small number who did discuss this subject. Her book *How I Managed My Children on Two Hundred Pounds a Year* was precisely for mothers who could not expect to be able to afford any outside help. However, although it listed *what* subjects to teach, she never said *how* to teach most of these subjects: she assumed that all women knew.*

---

*When she did go into detail, it is hard to imagine that some of her ideas could have been considered seriously. Her children's piano lessons consisted of playing only scales and finger exercises, with the occasional "sacred piece" but no other tunes, for *seven years*. She did admit that this regime was "inexpressible weariness," but its very wearying nature promoted discipline and was therefore to be encouraged. She also taught the children drawing by letting them draw only

They did not, of course. Molly Hughes (who later became a teacher) left an account of her education at home—intended to be comic, but hair-raising in the barrenness it revealed. Midmorning her mother would "open an enormous Bible. It was invariably at the Old Testament, and I had to read aloud . . . No comments were ever made, religious or otherwise, my questions were fobbed off by references to those 'old times' or to 'bad translations,' and occasionally mother's pencil, with which she guided me to the words, would travel rapidly over several verses, and I heard a muttered 'never mind about that.' "* Then Molly would parse a verse. Her mother painted in watercolor while Molly did "a little reading, sewing, writing, or learning by heart." Geography consisted of looking at an atlas,

> but all I can recall of my little geography book is the opening sentence, "The Earth is an oblate spheroid," and the statement that there are seven, or five, oceans. I never could remember which . . . For scientific notions I had Dr. Brewer's Guide to Science, in the form of a catechism . . . It opens firmly thus: "Q. What is heat?" and the A. comes pat: "That which produces the sensation of warmth." . . . Some of the information is human and kindly. Thus we have: "Q. What should a fearful person do to be secure in a

---

straight lines, and then curved ones, for more than a year. It was lucky for these children that they were merely fictional devices, as real children would surely have ended up running amok.[60]

*Religious education, even in houses a great deal more observant than the Hugheses', was often not much more successful. Marion Jane Bradley, the wife of a clergyman, prayed every morning, first by herself, then with Wa, then with the maids (note the careful segregation). When Wa was two and a half she worried that he did not appear "capable of understanding the idea of God and Christ being the same." Later he had, she thought, understood the idea of the Resurrection; then he asked her if God would come back as a stuffed rabbit. The three-year-old appeared to understand some things better than his mother, however. On being told to thank God for his blessings, he asked why God did not give the same blessings to "poor little beggar boys." She replied, "We know that it's right because God does it."[61]

storm? A. Draw his bedstead into the middle of the room, commit himself to the care of God, and go to bed." . . . Mother's arithmetic was at the level of the White Queen's, and I believe she was never quite sound about borrowing and paying back, especially if there was a nought or two in the top row . . . Often when sums were adumbrated I felt a little headachy, and thought I could manage a little drawing and painting instead.

If the weather was good, lessons were canceled and mother and daughter went for a walk, to the West End to shop or to Hampstead to sketch. By the age of twelve Molly had never been taught how to add currency; she had never even seen the symbols for pounds, shillings, and pence.[62]

Mothers were the teachers in most houses, of their daughters for their entire school career, and their sons usually to the age of seven. Only the most prosperous could afford governesses. Our impression today is that all middle-class households had governesses for their children, but this impression is based on the aspirational nature of so much writing of the time. There were over 30,000 upper-class families by midcentury, with 25,000 governesses listed in the census of 1851. If we assume that only half of these families had young children, that leaves a mere 10,000 governesses to be spread among the families of the 250,000 professional men listed in the 1851 census. Again, assume that only half had young children. There is still only one governess for every twelve families, and that is not counting the many tens of thousands of clergy, prosperous merchants, bankers, businessmen, factory owners, all of whom would have had equal call on this precious commodity.

Even where governesses were employed, teaching was not necessarily any better. As Gwen Raverat said of her governesses: "They were all kind, good, dull women; but even interesting lessons can be made incredibly stupid, when they are taught by people who are bored to death with them, and who do not care for the art of teaching either."[63] They were among the few servants who, on the whole, did not live in the houses of their employers. (The governesses of the upper classes were an exception, not the rule.) Charles Dickens's portrait of Gradgrind, with his love of Facts, was not only a comic fiction: literature both high and low reflected this idea of education as chunks of information. Rousseau's theories of education were popular—as theorics. Theory and practice do not always overlap, however, and Charlotte M. Yonge gave a vivid picture of the boredom of rote learning in *The Daisy Chain*. There the children had a visiting French master who knew the language well and could tell Ethel, the clever child, when she had gone wrong, but he could not explain why. Ethel

> did not like to . . . have no security against future errors; while he thought her a troublesome pupil, and was put out by her questions . . . Miss Winter [the governess] . . . summoned her to an examination such as the governess was very fond of and often practised. Ethel thought it useless . . . It was of this kind:—
>
>   What is the date of the invention of paper?
>   What is the latitude and longitude of Otaheite?
>   What are the component parts of brass?
>   Whence is cochineal imported?[64]

Elizabeth Barrett Browning's *Aurora Leigh* spoke the same language as Miss Winter:

> I learnt a little algebra, a little
> Of the mathematics,—brushed with extreme flounce
> The circle of the sciences, because
> She misliked women who are frivolous.
> I learnt the royal genealogies
> Of Oviedo, the internal laws
> Of the Burmese empire,—by how many feet
> Mount Chimaborazo outsoars Teneriffe.
> What navigable river joins itself
> To Lara, and what census of the year five
> Was taken at Klagenfurt,—because she liked
> A general insight into useful facts.[65]

The Daisy Chain and *Aurora Leigh* both appeared in the mid-1850s. Many girls were still being taught the same things in the same way at the end of the century. Eleanor Farjeon, the children's writer, remembered her schoolroom days in the 1890s:

> Miss Milton taught us Spelling . . . and the Capitals of Europe, and Tables, and Dates. There was no magic in these things as she taught them . . .
>
> "What is the date of the Constitutions of Clarendon?"
>
> "Eleven-hundred-and-sixty-four."
>
> "Quite right. You know that now."
>
> "Yes, Miss Milton."
>
> But what exactly did I know, when I knew that? . . . I didn't know what "Constitutions of Clarendon" was. Was it to do with somebody's health? Who was Clarendon? Or perhaps with the way red wine was made . . . What *was* Clarendon? Miss Milton never told me, and I never asked.[66]

Eleanor Farjeon did not come from a philistine background: her father was a successful author. He could have sent her to school, as he did her brothers; that he doomed her instead to Miss Milton was not because he was unkind but because, as Louise Creighton said a quarter of a century before, "I do not think that such an idea was ever entertained."[67]

Girls and boys, once past infancy and early childhood, received gender-based conditioning. An advertisement in the back of *The Busy Hives All Around Us*, a book for children, gave a list of some "Popular Illustrated Books." Their titles were revealing. Girls got *The Star of Hope and the Staff of Duty: Tales of Women's Trials and Victories*; *Women of Worth*; and *Friendly Hands and Kindly Words: Stories Illustrative of the Law of Kindness, the Power of Perseverance, and the Advantages of Little Helps*. Boys got *Men Who Have Risen*; *Noble Tales of Kingly Men*; and *Small Beginnings: or, The Way to Get On*.[68] Even more startlingly at variance, since they were by the same author, Louisa Tuthill, were two books called *I Will Be a Lady: A Book for Girls* and *Get Money: A Book for Boys*.[69] Girls were to read of "duty," "trials," "perseverance," which would make them "Women of Worth." Boys read of ambition, achievement, success—their "nobility" would be in accomplishment, not abnegation.

Boys left home early—they were mostly at school by the age of seven if school could be afforded. Even a day school ensured that boys spent much of their time with other boys: they became socialized early. The reverse was true of girls: the more prosperous the family, the less likely girls were to leave its shelter. Instead they were encouraged to remain children as long as possible. Boys had their first emotional rupture, their first taste of the outside world, when they went to school, then a bigger rupture if they went to university, or when they started work, by which time they were considered adult. Girls who did not need to go out to work had no break to mark their passing from childhood to adolescence: they were often children until they married. Louise Creighton had barely been out for a walk alone until her marriage in her twenties—if she wanted to go anywhere she had to be accompanied by her governess; if the governess was not available she bribed her young brothers with sweets to go with her.[70] In *The Way We Live Now*, Trollope notes that "the young male bird is supposed to fly away from the paternal nest. But the daughter of a house is compelled to adhere to her father till she shall get a husband."[71]

Yet women could not be sheltered forever, though they remained hampered long into adult life by their homemade educations. Gwen Raverat's mother plagued her family with her dim grip on basic numeracy:

My mother . . . insisted on keeping accounts down to every halfpenny; but no one, least of all herself, ever understood them . . . [A]fter my father's death The Accounts became a constant menace to everyone in the family . . . It was so hopeless and so useless. It was impossible to add up one page without being dragged into the complications of all the other pages of all the other account books, which were used indiscriminately for everything. The only system was that every item had to be written down somewhere— on any scrap of paper, or any page of any account book; and then, from time to time, everything must be rounded up and added together in one enormous sum. Fortunately no odious deductions were drawn from the resulting total, as quite often the Credits had got mixed up with the Debits, and they had all been added up together.[72]

Fortunately for Mrs. Darwin, she had married into a wealthy family, and the accounts were more form than content. For the much larger number of women who needed to work, a similar lack of basic education meant blighted lives. A pamphlet called "A Choice of a Business for Girls," published in 1864, warned: "The power of making out a bill with great rapidity and perfect accuracy is also necessary, and this is the point where women usually fail. A poor half-educated girl keeps a customer waiting while she is trying to add up the bill, or perhaps does it wrong, and in either case excites reasonable displeasure. This displeasure is expressed to the master of the establishment, who dismisses the offender and engages a well-educated man in her place. He pays him double wages."[73]

John Ruskin spoke for many of the middle class when he set out his thoughts on the relative educational needs of men and women in his 1865 essay "Of Queens' Gardens." Woman's intellect, he wrote,

is not for invention or creation, but for sweet ordering, arrangement, and decision . . . Her great function is Praise . . . All such knowledge should be given her as may enable her to understand, and even to aid, the work of men: and yet it should be given, not as knowledge,—not as if it were, or could be, for her an object to know; but only to feel, and to judge . . . Speaking broadly, a man ought to know any language or science he learns, thoroughly— while a woman ought to know the same language, or science, only so far as may enable her to sympathise in her husband's pleasures, and in those of his best friends.[74]

His ideas were welcomed, and other reasons for the non-education of women were added. George Gissing, in many of his novels an ardent supporter of education for women, in others drew characters whose education encouraged them to move beyond their natural sphere, so that they committed the cardinal sin of not knowing their place, disrupting the ordered segregation of the world. In *New Grub Street*, Dora and Maud, daughters of a vet, have the grave misfortune to attend a Girls' High School, which gives them "an intellectual training wholly incompatible with the material conditions of their life."[75] Now that their intellectual station exceeds their income, they remain near-friendless, unable to meet their intellectual equals on an equal economic and social footing.

It was not only the cost of an education that prevented girls from being sent to school. Constance Maynard came from a wealthy family, and her father was happy to spend money on his daughters in other ways, but when she was sixteen he "said he didn't see why he should go on paying for an expensive school when I should do quite well at home with the three sisters above me who had been educated till they were eighteen," and who could therefore pass along any extra education she needed. When she said she wanted to go to Girton, Cambridge's newly created women's college, he "offered to get me a new pony if I would give it up."[76] (She did not, and later became the founder of Westfield College, now part of the University of London and renamed Queen Mary College.) Schools were, many thought, breeders of disease, places of dubious, if not downright poor, morals, and, as Gwen Raverat noted, just "Bad."

Even for girls who knew their place, social life imposed requirements that they could not fulfill while undergoing full-time education. Molly Hughes, aware that she was going to have to support herself, rushed with her friend to tell her parents that they had matriculated. She found that the friend's sister had brought her new baby for a visit, and "when we burst out with 'We've passed the matriculation . . . we're members of the University,' we received the response, 'Yes, dears? . . . and did it love its granny den!'" Molly's brother grudgingly admitted that, as Molly's fiancé was not earning enough for them to marry on, she might as well work for a degree, adding, "Don't work too hard."[77]

That was the key. Girls and young women must not give their

undivided attention to anything. Florence Nightingale, who certainly broke out of her family's expectations, wrote an impassioned essay on the subject in 1852, when she was thirty-two. She thought it important enough to warrant revision seven years later, on her return from the Crimea. On the advice of her friend John Stuart Mill she did not attempt to publish it. A great advocate of women's equality, he was nonetheless probably right: the anguish she felt was so nakedly apparent that she might have subsequently found it difficult to get men in power to take her health-care concerns seriously. She wrote:

> How should we learn a language if we were to give it an hour a week? A fortnight's steady application would make more way in it than a year of such patch-work. A "lady" can hardly go to "her school" two days running. She cannot leave the breakfast-table— or she must be fulfilling some little frivolous "duty," which others ought not to exact, or which might just as well be done some other time . . .
>
> If a man were to follow up his profession or occupation at odd times, how would he do it? Would he become skilful in that profession? It is acknowledged by women themselves that they are inferior in every occupation to men. Is it wonderful? *They* do *everything* at "odd times" . . .
>
> We can never pursue any object for a single two hours, for we can never command any regular leisure or solitude.[78]

All study had to give way to other members of the family. Maud Berkeley and her friends found that even practicing the piano, that ladylike occupation par excellence, was difficult to achieve: "[My father] came in while I was hard at work on my arpeggios, to say he had just started a course of reading Plato and found he was vastly distracted by my music. Very difficult, attempting to be studious when each attempt brings only reproach . . . Heard from Lillian later that Mr Barnes made a similar protest."[79]

Sarah Stickney Ellis, in *The Daughters of England*, was very firm. There was no point in educating women, because men had done everything before, and done it better. "What possible use," she asked rhetorically, "can be the learning of dead languages?" There were already translations available of all the major works, from which girls would "become more intimately acquainted with the spirit of the writer, and the customs of the time" than they ever could by attempting to read the works in the original. Likewise, a girl need not study science more than superficially. A mere acquaintanceship would render her "more companionable to men," because luckily "it should not be necessary for her to *talk much*, even on his favourite topics, in order to obtain his favour." Knowledge was important only for a girl to be able "to listen attentively"; otherwise she would "destroy the satisfaction which most men feel in conversing with really intelligent women."[80]

The Daisy Chain, Charlotte Yonge's midcentury novel, was enormously successful, and considered a very sound moral tale, helpful to young girls. Ethel, a bookish, hoydenish girl, is gradually brought to understand that the pinnacle of womanhood is in the renunciation of the use of her intelligence. At first she studies with her brother. He attends school and passes on to her the gist of his lessons, which she is permitted to indulge herself with after she has performed such essentials as mending her frocks. However, by being clever and untidy and having no aptitude for household work, she will, Miss Winter fears, grow up "odd, eccentric and blue." Soon her family decides that the time has come for her to stop studying Latin and Greek. Her brother, who has been her champion, agrees: "I assure you, Ethel, it is really time for you to stop, or you would get into a regular learned lady, and be good for nothing." So Ethel gives up all her aspirations and crowns the sacrifice (which she now thinks of as a triumph) by finding pleasure instead in stitching up her brother's Newdigate Prize submission in Balliol colors.[81]

Girls who were not prepared to give up all personal aspirations, as Ethel had so cheerfully, had other reasons to desist from serious study. Education for adolescent girls was a serious health risk, they were warned. *The Principles of Education, Drawn from Nature and Revelation*, by the educator Elizabeth Missing Sewell, was concerned with the upper classes, but she pointed out universal truths:

[A boy] has been riding, and boating, and playing cricket, and both body and mind have been roused to energy; and so, when he comes to study, he has a sense of power, which acts mentally as well as physically, and enables him to grasp difficulties, and master them. The girl, on the contrary, has been guarded from over fatigue, subject to restrictions with regard to cold and heat, and hours of study, seldom trusted away from home, allowed only a small share of responsibility;—not willingly, with any wish to thwart her inclinations—but simply because, if she is not thus guarded, if she is allowed to run the risks, which, to the boy, are a matter of indifference, she will probably develop some disease, which, if not fatal, will, at any rate, be an injury to her for life.[82]

Dr. James Burnett, in *Delicate, Backward, Puny and Stunted Children* (1895), assured his readers that a girl would, at puberty, always fall behind her brothers in academic achievement: her "disordered pelvic life" guaranteed that she "must necessarily be in ill-health more or less [ever after] . . . Not one exception to this have I ever seen."[83]*

Despite this consensus, many popular novelists deplored the lack of female education: Dickens, Thackeray, and also Charlotte Brontë and George Eliot painted vivid pictures of the resulting misery of ignorance, for both sexes. Jeannette Marshall's father, a surgeon and professor of anatomy at the Royal Academy, encouraged his daughters to attend lectures at University College. He even hoped they would sit exams. They refused to do the latter, and attended few lectures. It was not surprising. From the schoolroom onward, girls were never tested, never matched against others, never socialized in any way. Jeannette and her sister Ada managed one term before the requirements of their

---

*One exception, whom he saw fairly regularly but must have somehow overlooked, was his daughter, Ivy Compton-Burnett. It may be significant that her career as a novelist did not take off until after a major breakdown decades after his death, and one looks again at her gallery of tyrannical parents. (It should be noted that although Dr. Burnett was a homeopath, his opinions coincided in this matter with those of his more conventional medical brethren.)

social life supervened: they had made no friends with any of the other women attending the college; from Jeannette's diary, it is not clear that they even learned any of their names. For Jeannette, education was a matter of passing the time—she studied algebra in late adolescence as "a cure for boredom"—or, more important, of prestige. She had piano lessons with the well-known pianist (and founder of the English Wagner Society) Edward Dannreuther, and noted of some new acquaintances, "I went up 100 per cent in their estimation when they heard Mr. Dannreuther was my [music] master. A good card to play!"[84] Jeannette enjoyed her music and intermittently worked hard at it, although she never became one of those women condemned by the author of *Maternal Counsels to a Daughter*: "Who would wish a wife or a daughter, moving in private society, to have attained such excellence in music as involves a life's devotion to it?"[85]

Ignorance was, in many ways, a desirable state. Knowledge was burdensome and could overwhelm those unable to bear its weight. Mrs. Gaskell worried about sending the toddler Marianne to school, where "she may meet with children who may teach her the meaning of things of which at present we desire to keep her ignorant."[86] This need to protect girls from knowledge did not grow less when they became adult. Half a century after Mrs. Gaskell expressed her anxiety, Gissing depicted his characters arguing about the same subject. Monica, a woman who had been forced to marry for economic security, disagreed with her new husband on whether or not a mutual friend was "nice" for her to know. He responded:

> ". . . In your ignorance of the world"—
>
> "Which you think very proper in a woman," she interrupted caustically.
>
> "Yes, I do! That kind of knowledge is harmful to a woman."
>
> "Then, please, how is she to judge her acquaintances?"
>
> "A married woman must accept her husband's opinion, at all events about men." He plunged on into the ancient quagmire. "A man may know with impunity what is injurious if it enters a woman's mind."[87]

Knowledge of a fact could corrupt, not because of the fact itself, but because of the gender of the mind it resided in. This was not to say that girls and women were expected to know nothing. It was just that their accomplishments and abilities were important in reactive ways: as Mrs. Ellis had said earlier in the century, girls needed to know enough about science so that they could look intelligent while men talked. Equally, girls should be able to play the piano, not for the pleasure derived from music, but because it was useful. Mrs. Panton thought that girls' natural reason for learning to play the piano was "because they can be useful either to accompany songs and glees or to play dance-music";[88] love of music was irrelevant. Nearly half a century later the function of a daughter had not altered: "It is the daughter's privilege . . . to act the part of sympathiser and interested listener in the home circle. No other claim is greater."[89]

Girls were only to respond to others, not to have thoughts of their own. It took Molly Hughes some time before her place as a reactive rather than an active family member became clear to her:

> The family pooled what gossip they had got from school . . . discussing future plans and telling the latest jokes . . . I, as the youngest, seldom got a word in and was often snubbed when I did. Thus, after venturing, "I did well in French to-day," I had the chilling reminder from Charles [Molly's brother], "Self-praise is no recommendation." If I related a joke, "We've heard that before" would come as a chorus. Once when I confided to Dym [another brother] that we had begun America, he called out, "I say, boys, at Molly's school they've just discovered America."

Molly Hughes used the word "chilling" for her brother's crushing retort, but she seems not to have recognized quite how chilling the scene was. She ended, "In short, I was wisely neglected," and confided that "I tried to carry out the wishes of these my household gods by being as ordinary and as little conspicuous as I could."[90]

Felix and Henrietta Carbury, the brother and sister in Trollope's *The Way We Live Now*, showed similar characteristics, albeit heightened for fictional purposes. Felix Carbury was a wastrel who had run through his inheritance and was now battening on his mother, who could ill afford to support herself and her daughter. Henrietta, however,

> had been taught by the conduct of both father and mother that every vice might be forgiven in a man and in a son, though every virtue was expected from a woman, and especially from a daughter. The lesson had come to her so early in life that she had learned it without the feeling of any grievance . . . That all her interests in life should be made subservient to him was natural to her; and when she found that her little comforts were discontinued, and her moderate expenses were curtailed because he, having eaten up all that was his own, was now eating up also all that was her mother's, she never complained.[91]

This deference to men was not simply a hierarchical one: fathers at the top of the family pyramid, mothers next by virtue of authority vested in them by their husbands, and children at the bottom. The children were in their own little pyramid too, with boys, of whatever age, above girls. Eleanor Farjeon spelled it out:

> Whatever pains and penalties, whatever joys and pleasures, were dispensed to us by the parental powers in the Dining-room and Drawing-room . . . in the Nursery there was one Law-Giver who made the Laws: our eldest brother Harry.
>
> . . . he invented rules and codes with Spartan strictness; if they were to be enforced, he enforced them; if relaxed, only he might relax them . . .
>
> In our Nursery he exemplified Plato's "benevolent despotism" with so much benignity, entertainment, and impartiality, that we began life by accepting it without question.[92]

The last sentence implied that Farjeon grew out of her deference; Molly Hughes, when she came to write her autobiography nearly half a century after the events described, still thought her family's viewpoint was reasonable: "I suppose there was a fear on my mother's part that I should be spoilt, for I was two years younger than the youngest boy. To prevent this danger she proclaimed the rule 'Boys first.' I came last in all distribution of food at table, treats of sweets, and so on. I was expected to wait on the boys, run messages, fetch things left upstairs, and never grumble, let alone refuse." Yet even after all those years she tried to rationalize her family's behavior: "All this I thoroughly enjoyed, because I loved running about." And surely it must have been all right, because, after all, "the boys never failed to smile their thanks, call me 'good girl' . . ." She was unable to distinguish between herself and those who held power: "We were given a room to ourselves—all to ourselves," and in it "there were four shelves, and . . . each [of the four boys] had one to himself." It did not, apparently, cross her mind that she alone had not got a shelf. Furthermore, she was allowed to enter this room that was "ours" only with the permission of her brothers, and for the most part she spent her afternoons alone in her bedroom.[93] Laura Forster noted the same isolation: "The boys could and did come into the nursery when they liked, but they never played there or stayed long, whilst I had no other room open to me, except by special invitation [from them], until the evening, when we all went down to my parents."[94]

The responsibilities for a girl were more onerous too. Laura, as the oldest girl, looked after the younger children in the nursery, staying there longer than was customary because the nursemaid "said I could not be spared, and Miss Maber, who taught my three eldest brothers, avowedly cared only for boys and would not accept me in the schoolroom."[95] It was a given that girls waited on their brothers: Louise Creighton, as a younger sister, only once had the "privilege usually reserved to the elder ones of getting up early on the Monday to give the boys their breakfast before they went back to school."[96] Constance Maynard and her sister were also expected to defer to their eldest brother. (As they referred to him as the Fatted Calf, it appears that they had perhaps not accepted their subordinate role in quite the way they were expected to.)[97]

These were mostly girls from upper-middle-class families with no shortage of money. They were expected to perform services for their brothers not because there was no one else to do it but because that was what girls did. Slightly down the social scale, as Molly Hughes's experiences showed, things were no different. Helena Sickert, sister of the artist Walter Sickert, went to day school, as did her brothers. In the afternoons after homework was finished, the boys were allowed to play, while she "very often had to mend their clothes; sort their linen, and wash their brushes and combs."[98] And the lower-middle-class girl had more responsibilities yet. Hertha Ayrton was born Sarah Marks, the daughter of a clockmaker and a seamstress. Sarah/Hertha made all the clothes for her younger brothers and took care of the boys so that her mother could take in needlework to support them after the death of her husband.[99] (Ayrton became one of feminism's nineteenth-century success stories: she studied mathematics at Girton, with her tuition paid for by George Eliot. In 1899 she was the first woman member of the Institution of Electrical Engineers.) Alice Wichelo, known as Lily, was the eldest of ten children (and, later, the mother of E. M. Forster); her father was a drawing master who had died young. By 1872, when she was seventeen, Lily had traveled all the way to Tunbridge Wells on her own, with only her brother, a small child, for company. She took full responsibility for him, finding a childminder to look after him and settling him in lodgings.[100] (Compare this with the upper-middle-class Louise Creighton.)

It was not that all experiences of all girls were the same, but rather that the received ideas bred an attitude that many aspired to: to be the comfort-giver, whose primary function was to ensure the smooth running of the home, for the benefit of the man who financed it. The focal point of this was the kitchen.

THE KITCHEN

VICTORIANS LIKED THEIR rooms to be single-purpose, where we often see a multiplicity of function in our own usage. The kitchen is one of the few rooms we today would think of as single-purpose, or at most dual-purpose, cooking and eating. (Because of the multiplicity of purposes in this room, cooking and eating will appear, in Victorian fashion, in Chapter 7, The Dining Room.) The Victorian ideal held that the kitchen was for cookery only, with food storage, food preparation, and dishwashing going on in, respectively, the storeroom and larder, the scullery, and the scullery or pantry, depending on the type of dish and the level of dirt. The reality in most middle-class houses was that the kitchen performed a wide range of functions. Many of the middle classes with one servant, in four- to six-room houses, had only the kitchen for her to sleep in. (In houses of this size, it was always a "her": menservants were for the wealthy.) Larger houses still did not necessarily mean the kitchen was for cooking only: larger houses meant a larger staff, and the kitchen remained a bedroom to many. Less prosperous householders used the kitchen themselves: Snagsby, the law-stationer in *Bleak House*, used the front kitchen as the family sitting room, while "Guster," his workhouse maid-of-all-work, slept in the back kitchen, or scullery.

Bedroom, kitchen, sitting room: many uses, although usually the least regarded room of the house. The desire for separation meant that an often small space had even smaller portions cut out from it, to keep essential functions apart: a scullery, with running water, was for any food preparation that made a mess—cleaning fish, preparing vegetables—and for scouring pots and pans; a pantry was for storing china and glass, and silver if there was any, and it had a sink where these things were washed or polished; a larder was for fresh-food storage; a storeroom was for dried goods and cleaning equipment. Each separate room, in the ideal home, had a different type of sink: the scullery had a sink, or better yet two, for cleaning food and washing pots; the pantry sink was of wood lined with lead, to prevent the glass and crockery from chipping. If there was a housemaids' cupboard upstairs, for storing cleaning equipment, it too had a lead-lined wood sink, so that bedroom ware was not chipped, and a separate slop sink, where chamber pots were emptied. (It looked like a lavatory pan but was higher, and was also lead-lined.)[1] In addition, after indoor sanitation arrived, the servants often had their own lavatory downstairs—not for their convenience, but to ensure that they did not use the family lavatory upstairs.

This was, however, only the ideal. The actuality was often a dark, miserable basement, running with damp. The scullery might be a passageway off the kitchen, with the lavatory installed in it. The pantry was a china closet, the storeroom another cupboard, kept locked; the larder yet another, rather hopefully installed as far away as possible from the kitchen range, which, as it supplied the household's hot water, blasted out heat all the year round for up to eighteen hours a day. Below ground, the kitchen received little if any light from the area.* The gas burned all day, with at best a small window near the ceiling to remove the fumes. Often no windows were possible, and air bricks and

---

*Many terraced houses, especially larger ones, had raised ground floors with steps leading up to the front door from the pavement. Between the pavement and the house a sunken paved area, railed off from the street, was used to light the basement, to provide under-pavement storage, for coal in particular, and, most important, to produce a separate "back" door under the front door—the tradesman's entrance—for terraced houses without rear access.

other ventilation devices were the most that could be hoped for. In this miasma of cooking and gas, the servant unfolded her bedding to sleep after the day's work was over.

This was what Dickens had in mind for the kitchen belonging to Sampson and Sally Brass, the unscrupulous solicitor and his sister in *The Old Curiosity Shop* (1841): "a very dark miserable place, very low and very damp, the walls disfigured by a thousand rents and blotches."[2] Dickens was showing the turpitude of the household's occupants through the house itself, but Arnold Bennett's kitchen of the 1860s and 1870s, belonging to the entirely upright Baines family in *The Old Wives' Tale*, was an only marginally more salubrious version of the same thing:

> Forget-me-nots on a brown field ornamented the walls of the kitchen. Its ceiling was irregular and grimy, and a beam ran across it . . . A large range stood out from the wall between the stairs and the window. The rest of the furniture comprised a table—against the wall opposite the range—a cupboard, and two Windsor chairs. Opposite the foot of the steps was a doorway, without a door, leading to two larders, dimmer even than the kitchen, vague retreats made visible by whitewash, where bowls of milk, dishes of cold bones, and remainders of fruit-pies, reposed.[3]

There was a coal cellar, which contained the tap—the only running water—and another cellar, where coke for the range was kept, and ashes were stored awaiting collection twice or thrice a year by the dustman.*

Arthur Munby, the civil servant, had a long-term relationship with a maid-of-all-work named Hannah Cullwick. (They eventually married.) He was sexually aroused by the idea of working-class women, and spent a great deal of time talking to working women he approached on

---

*British usage persists in the notion that the people who remove our rubbish—the dustmen—are still taking away "dust"—coal dust from the kitchen range. Many garbage cans—still known as dustbins in Britain—continue to have printed on them "No hot ashes," as though every morning the range were raked out in suburban households across the land. Americans, with their "garbagemen," have managed to leave this behind.

A very leisurely-looking cook and housemaid, 1872. In this model (and unrealistic) kitchen, the cook has time to read the newspaper while the Sunday joint roasts on a jack behind the meat-screen in front of the range. There is even a small rug, which would in reality have quickly been covered in a sticky mix of steam, fat from the meat, gas residue, and soot.

the streets. (They were all "good" women—he seemed to have no interest in prostitutes.) Despite the unusual nature of his interest, the fact remains that because of it he had far more knowledge of their working conditions than many of the middle class. Even he was shocked when once he saw Hannah in the kitchen of the house in Kilburn where she was employed as maid-of-all-work to an upholsterer and his family:

She stood at a sink behind a wooden dresser backed with choppers and stained with blood and grease, upon which were piles of coppers and saucepans that she had to scour, piles of dirty dishes that she had to wash. Her frock, her cap, her face and arms were more or less wet, soiled, perspiring and her apron was a filthy piece of sacking, wet and tied round her with a cord. The den where she wrought was low, damp, ill-smelling; windowless, lighted by a flaring gas-jet; and, full in view, she had on one side a larder hung with raw meat, on the other a common urinal; besides the many ugly, dirty implements around her.[4]

It was generally recommended that kitchen floors be covered in linoleum, for easy cleaning, often laid over a cement base to foil the vermin.* Mrs. Panton suggested that "if the cook is careful . . . she should be given a rug, or good square of carpet . . . to put down when her work is done."[6] The carpet could not be permanently on the floor, for hygienic reasons. It is hard to imagine that after a long day's work in the conditions Munby described the thing Hannah Cullwick most wanted to do was unroll a carpet. Anyway, there were rarely upholstered chairs in a kitchen, as only wood survived the steam and mess of an active kitchen, so she would have had no place to sit comfortably.

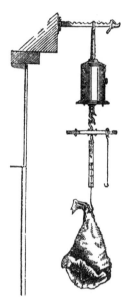

A roasting jack, which was fixed either to the top of a meat-screen (p. 103) or the mantelpiece. This is a bottle jack, with a clockwork mechanism to turn the meat in front of the fire.

The labor, steam, and dirt all centered around the kitchen range. The closed range was the first technical development in Britain to move beyond cooking over an open fire. It appeared at the beginning of the century, although it took decades before it was commonly in use. Wemmick, in his "castle" in *Great Expectations*, was still cooking with "a saucepan on the hob, and a brazen bijou over the fireplace designed for the suspension of a

*Linoleum, made of linseed oil mixed with resin and cork dust fixed onto a cotton backing, was patented in 1860. It was wipeable, and quickly became popular in heavily walked-over areas: kitchens, passages, sculleries.[5]

roasting-jack."[7]* There were many styles of range, but the main features of all of them were an oven, or ovens, and a boiler to heat water. Both were operated by means of a fire fueled by coke, which generated heat that was transmitted by flues and modified by dampers. Earlier in the century items to be baked were taken to a communal bakehouse; baking at home was for the wealthy, who had built-in brick ovens. By the 1840s *The English Housekeeper* was advising the readers on the benefits of the range: "It is a great convenience to have a constant supply of hot water, and an advantage to possess the means of baking a pie, pudding or cake."[8] The early models had boilers that had to be filled by hand, and if the water level got too low the boiler cracked; later they became self-filling, with a tap to draw the hot water off for use and a stopcock to control the inflow from the mains.

By the 1860s, the "improved" ranges that Mrs. Beeton recommended had hot plates, to keep soups simmering or other items warm, and also to heat irons (see pp. 164–66), as well as a roaster with the kind of movable shelves we now expect, which could be converted from an open to a closed oven by moving valves. These ranges cost from £5 15s. to £23 10s.[9] One of the major advantages, apart from constant hot water, was that soot no longer fell into the food that was in the oven, although it could still come down the chimney and fall into the saucepans. Soot in food remained a major problem. Most recipe books of the day constantly reiterated the need for "a very clean saucepan" and "a scrupulously clean pan"; it is difficult to remember that cooking over an open fire meant scorched, sooty pots every time. There was still no temperature control. (A legacy of this is the continuing reputation for being "difficult" of dishes that today, with modern equipment, are really very

---

*A roasting jack was a common item throughout the century, as many people thought that meat roasted in an oven tasted inferior to that cooked before an open fire. The meat was suspended in front of the fire from a bracket fixed to the mantelpiece. Bottle jacks were roasting jacks with a wind-up mechanism that turned the meat automatically to cook it evenly; otherwise even the poorest home could rig up a cord and spin the meat by hand. A dish underneath to catch the juices was essential, and a screen put around it to reflect the heat back toward the meat was useful.

The "Delight" cooking range, 1896, one of many new models. This has an
integrated chimney, instead of the range being built into the old fireplace
(p. 103). The boiler, with a tap to draw off the hot water, takes up the right
hand side, the oven the left.

straightforward—soufflés, for example.) Instead, recipes called for "a
bright fire," or "a good soaking heat," or a fire that was "not too fierce."

Closed stoves, or kitcheners, were said to use less fuel than open
ranges, but this was always qualified by "if managed well,"[10] which
probably meant they did not in practice. For those who could not
afford an oven, or where the space was not available, Dutch ovens
were frequently recommended—small brick devices that held charcoal
and were mounted on four short legs, with a trivet on top where a
saucepan could be placed. The advice books—again in flights of imagination—suggested that even jam could be made on these early versions of camp stoves, or "a light pudding or a small pie may be baked,"
adding cautiously "with care," which, again, probably indicated that it
was either difficult or impossible.[11]

Surprisingly, given the primary means of lighting in mid- to late-Victorian houses, gas cookers were rarely used: they were available from the 1880s, but were considered too expensive for the amount of cooking needed to feed a whole family. Unlike ranges, gas cookers had no boilers. As constant hot water was one of the major improvements produced by ranges, this was a serious drawback. Alternative methods of heating water had to be found, but none was as satisfactory. (See p. 325.) Some houses, where the kitchen was particularly small, used a gas stove in the summer to avoid having to light the range in hot weather, although this was not common, mostly because it cut off the hot-water supply.

Kitchen ranges and fires for heating throughout the house, together with London's foggy climate, ensured that the city was filthy, inside and out. Dr. John Simon, London's first Medical Officer, noted in Paris the "transparence of air, the comparative brightness of all colour, the visibility of distant objects, the cleanliness of faces and buildings, instead of our opaque atmosphere, deadened colours, obscured distance, smutted faces and black architecture." Approaching London from the suburbs, "one may observe the total result of this gigantic nuisance hanging over the City like a pall."[12] The gloom was not caused by climate alone. When Sherlock Holmes and Watson went to investigate a crime in a small, semi-detached house in Brixton, there was no fog, no rain, and it was midday. The Scotland Yard detective wanted to show them something: "He struck a match on his boot and held it up against the wall . . . Across the bare space there was scrawled in blood-red letters a single word."[13] Without the match, in daylight alone, they could not see the red word painted on a wall. Granted, this was for dramatic effect in fiction, yet its readers did not appear to find it remarkable.

It was coal that created this menace, a fact that was formally recognized in 1882, when the Smoke Abatement Exhibition displayed fireplaces, stoves, and other heating systems that attempted to deal with this nuisance. For decades to come, however, housekeepers simply had to accept that soot and "blacks" were part of their daily life. Latches to doors—both street and inner doors—had a small plate or curtain fitted over the keyhole to keep out dirt.[14] Plants were kept on window sills to trap the dust as it flew in; housewives nailed muslin across the windows to stop the soot, or only opened windows from the top, which diminished the amount that entered.[15] Tablecloths were laid just before a meal, as otherwise dust settled from the fire and they became dingy in a matter of hours.[16]

Fireplaces were expensive and time-consuming as well as dirty. The Carlyles, who had no children and therefore had to keep fewer rooms heated, burned a ton of coal every month, costing £1 9s. per ton.[17] In large houses, one servant could spend her entire day looking after only the fires and lights.* After all this, it is odd to note not only that fireplaces were not a particularly efficient form of heating, but that most of those who specialized in heating knew it, too. In the eighteenth century Count Rumford had developed improvements to fireplaces, which now enabled them to reflect the heat out into the room rather than having it disappear up the chimney. These were fairly common by the mid-nineteenth century, yet this was only a small improvement: most of the heat was still drawn up the flue by the drafts that allowed the fire to burn. It did not seem to matter: the idea of the fire, its importance as the focus of the home, surmounted its more obvious drawbacks. As the architect Robert Kerr noted, "For a Sitting-room, keeping in view the English climate and habits, a fireside is of all considerations practically the most important. No such apartment can pass muster with domestic critics unless there be convenient space for a wide circle of persons round the fire."[18]

Shirley Forster Murphy's book ran through the options, including German closed stoves and American steam heat. It agreed that fireplaces were the least efficient system, but rejected German stoves as dangerous, because they did not provide the ventilation that chimneys did. (It did not appear relevant that the entire German population had not yet died of asphyxiation.) It summed up: "The open fire has this advantage, that one man may warm himself at it and get as close to it as he likes, and another may keep away from its rays, and yet be in the

---

*The main reason for spring cleaning was to remove the winter dirt produced by coal, oil, gas, and candles. Spring was also when servants began to have more time, without the daily cleaning of grates and caring for fires.

society of those who profit by its heat. In a room heated by stove-pipes or warmed air this is not so."[19] This was only one of many books to say that being half burnt, half frozen was a positive feature of the English system. The architect C. J. Richardson, in his influential *Englishman's House*, acknowledged that "we are warmed on one side and chilled on the other" but considered neither burden "too great to bear." He condemned stoves, saying that they heated rather than warmed the air, which "is very different from the honest puff of smoke from an English fireplace."[20] He never explained this difference, but one feels that it was perhaps the foreignness of the stove which made it "not liked." He certainly felt no need to elaborate further.[*]

As with many aspects of the home, it may be that because the upper classes could afford large, constant fires and had enough people to look after them, those beneath them attempted the style, without the substance to maintain it, while telling themselves it was healthy. Many books reiterated that rooms that were too warm were "enervating," they sapped energy. Mrs. Caddy said that "it is not a healthy practice to heat the passages of a house," and a warm bedroom "prevents sleep."[22] A writer on eye diseases was positive that sleeping in "over-heated and unventilated rooms" was a leading cause of near-sightedness.[23] It was perhaps a miracle that anyone was near-sighted at all, if this was the case—Shirley Forster Murphy thought 50° right for a bedroom; *The Modern Householder* suggested that perhaps 60° was more comfortable for invalids but noted that "unless great care be taken, it will easily fall below this."[24] Marion and Linley Sambourne had an income putting them at the very top of the upper middle classes (often £2,000 a year), and even they tended to have only four or five fires burning regularly (probably the kitchen, drawing room, and dining room, along with either the morning room or the nursery). They never had a fire in their bedroom, and Marion's diary was full of entries such as

---

[*]Stefan Muthesius in *The English Terraced House* cites an anonymous European observer in the twentieth century on "the five priorities of a British heating appliance: 1. Safety 2. Economy 3. Ventilation 4. Looks 5. Heat." In the nineteenth century, "moral value" might replace "safety" at number one, but otherwise the order seems to me correct.[21]

"Bitt' cold, had to keep shawl on all evening" and "Lin & self break-fasted in bed . . . Lin's bath frozen."[25]

Various methods were used to keep warm. The girls in *The Old Wives' Tale* had heated bricks to put their feet on and wore knitted wraps around their shoulders.[26] Curtains across doorways were not solely to indulge the contemporary taste for drapery; they also prevented drafts.[27] Louise Creighton and her sisters warmed themselves in front of their governess's fire before going to bed: "We had flannel bags to keep our feet warm . . . & these were made as hot as possible by the fire & then rolled up tight under our arms when at the last minute we made a dash for bed."[28]

All the fireplaces had to be cleaned daily. This involved not just removing the ashes but also ensuring that the grate, the fender, and the fender irons were kept shining, by rubbing them with a dry leather. If rust appeared, then emery paper was used to rub it off, before black-lead, a pastelike substance, was applied, buffed with a blacklead brush and then polished to a shine. The kitchen range had to be cleaned even more thoroughly or the heated metal conveyed the smell of scorched fat and burning food throughout the house. To clean a range, the fender and fire irons first had to be removed. Then damp tea leaves were scattered over the fuel, to keep the dust down while the cleaning was in process. The ashes and cinders were raked out. Cinders were pieces of coal that had stopped giving off flames but still had some combustible material left in them. Thrifty housewives riddled their cinders. A tin cinder bucket with a wire sieve inside the lid was part of the housemaid's stock equipment, used to sift the rakings of all the fireplaces to separate the cinders from the unusable ash. The ash was then set aside to be collected by the dustmen, and the cinders from all the fireplaces were reused in the kitchen range. Then the flues were cleaned and the grease was scraped off the stove. The steel part was polished with bathbrick, powdered brick used as an abrasive,* and paraffin; the

---

*Before detergents, abrasives were the primary means of cleaning: rotten-stone, a powder of decomposed limestone, was used to polish steel; sand was used on pots and pans and on wooden floors.

iron parts were blackleaded and polished. In a house with one or two servants, the oven was swept and the blackleading applied only to the bars and front every day; the rest was cleaned twice a week. If there were more servants, the whole thing was done every day, including scraping out the oven and rinsing it with vinegar and water.

The kitchen range had to be large enough to cook meals for the mid-Victorian family, which might often contain a dozen people. The Marshalls had only four children, but with servants there were ten of them. Even the Sambournes, with a late-Victorian two children, were often eight at home—parents and children, Linley Sambourne's mother, who stayed for months at a time, and three servants. Lower down the scale there were fewer servants to feed, which also meant there were fewer to do the work.

The Modern Householder in 1872 gave the following list of necessities for "Cheap Kitchen Furniture":

> open range, fender, fire irons; 1 deal table; bracket of deal to be fastened to the wall, and let down when wanted; wooden chair; floor canvas; coarse canvas to lay before the fire when cooking; wooden tub for washing glass and china; large earthenware pan for washing plates; small zinc basin for washing hands; 2 washing-tubs; clothesline; clothes horse; yellow bowl for mixing dough; wooden salt-box to hang up; small coffee mill; plate rack; knife-board;* large brown earthenware pan for bread; small wooden flour kit; 3 flat irons, an Italian iron, and iron stand; old blanket for ironing on; 2 tin candlesticks, snuffers, extinguishers; 2 blacking brushes,

---

*Before stainless steel, knives were the bane of the housewife's existence. They were the only eating utensil made in two pieces—the blade, made of steel, and the handle, of silver, horn, bone, or base metals. If the knife got wet, the blade and the pin holding the blade in the handle rusted. Elaborate systems were devised to prevent this. The recommended way to wash knives was to put the dirty knives in a jug, with water and soda crystals to cover the blade only. They were whisked about briefly, then wiped dry, and the blades were polished on a board covered with emery paper, or powdered brick dust (which was sold for the purpose), to prevent rust. The handles were then wiped clean. Later, knife-cleaning machines appeared, which attempted to reproduce this procedure at the turn of a handle.

1 scrubbing brush; 1 carpet broom, 1 short-handled broom; cinder-sifter, dustpan, sieve, bucket; patent digester; tea kettle; toasting fork; bread grater; bottle jack (a screen can be made with the clothes-horse covered with sheets); set of skewers; meat chopper; block-tin butter saucepan; colander; 3 iron saucepans; 1 iron boiling pot; 1 fish kettle; 1 flour dredger; 1 frying pan; 1 hanging grid-iron; salt and pepper boxes; rolling pin and pasteboard; 12 patty pans; 1 larger tin pan; pair of scales; baking dish.[29]

While this list appears to a modern eye to be extraordinarily long, by contemporary standards it was fairly compact, even allowing for the duplication of items to ensure separation of functions—for instance, there are four different types of washing bowls for four different functions. This is repeated with the brushes and brooms. Mrs. Haweis gave "an useful [sic] little kitchen list for a very small household" which comprised 109 items, not including cutlery or dishes. Among the brushes for her little list were sets of stove brushes, boot brushes and

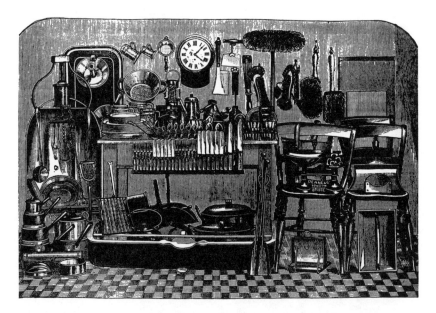

A showcard displaying goods for the well-stocked kitchen. The interior of the meat-screen with its roasting jack can be seen on the left. Note the half-dozen types of brushes on the right.

scrub brushes, a bass, or fiber, brush, a hair broom, a carpet broom, a sweep's broom, and a broom for the banisters, none of which could serve any other purpose.[30] However much space all this took up, the total cost was under £10, so it was possibly not unreasonable for many middle-class couples setting up house.

The important thing was to have the tools to keep the house clean. In the bedroom the fight against vermin was a skirmish; in the kitchen it was total war. The plagues that infested Victorian houses have been so effectively controlled for the last hundred years that for the most part we have forgotten them. For us, mice and rats are the first thought at the word "vermin"; for the Victorians it was bugs: blackbeetles, fleas, even crickets. If the struggle against them was not waged with commitment and constancy, they would "multiply till the kitchen floor at night palpitates with a living carpet, and in time the family cockroach will make raids on the upper rooms, travelling along the line of hot water pipes . . . the beetles would collect in corners of the kitchen ceiling, and hanging to one another by their claws, would form huge bunches or swarms like bees towards evening and as night closed in, swarthy individuals would drop singly on to floor, or head, or food."[31]

The only way to get rid of these creatures was to fill in all holes with cement; replace old, crumbling mortar with more cement; use carbolic acid in the scrubbing water when cleaning; and pour more carbolic through cracks in the floor every day. Mrs. Haweis did not object to rats and mice, which she thought were "nice, pretty, clever little things . . . They . . . are our friends, acting as scavengers, and are to me in no wise repugnant."[32] For those who did not agree, traps were recommended, plus a hungry cat. *Cassell's Household Guide* thought traps superior to arsenic, as the poisoned mice made a terrible smell if they died under the flooring or behind the skirting. (As an afterthought the author worried that children or animals might get at the arsenic, but that concern was very much secondary to the smell, which was thought to bring disease.)[33] *Our Homes* suggested keeping a hedgehog to eat the insects; others were scornful of this. The amount a hedgehog ate could not begin to affect the living carpet that Beatrix Potter's servants found at her grandmother's house when they visited in the summer of 1886: the first night they were there, the maids had to sit on the kitchen table, as the floor heaved with cockroaches.[34]

The war against vermin was fought for three reasons: hygiene, status, and (contingent on status) morality. Health reformers battled to convey the new information that cleanliness foiled disease. In addition, the rise of mass production gave many access to objects that only a few could have acquired earlier. Therefore the status markers moved on from the now less expensive accumulation of possessions to another, more expensive and time-consuming preoccupation: keeping clean. Respectability was signaled by many flourishes that did not make the house any cleaner but indicated that here was a decent household. George Godwin, an architect, editor of *The Builder* magazine, and promoter of sanitary housing for the poor, stressed that "the health and morals of the people are regulated by their dwellings":[35] decent houses produced decent people, not the other way around. He was not alone in this belief. Dr. Southwood Smith, in *Recreations of a Country Parson* (1861), had no doubt:

> A clean, fresh, and well-ordered house exercises over its inmates a moral, no less than a physical influence, and has a direct tendency to make the members of the family sober, peaceable, and considerate of the feelings and happiness of each other; nor is it difficult to trace a connexion between habitual feelings of this sort and the formation of habits of respect for property, for the laws in general, and even for those higher duties and obligations the observance of which no laws can enforce.[36]

Expressions that reflected this idea became commonplace. It was John Wesley, the founder of Methodism, who first said that cleanliness was next to godliness, an idea that before the nineteenth century would simply have made no sense. Good Methodists, and soon the general population, had a moral as well as physical duty to clean their houses. Thus tasks like blackleading the grates and whitening the front steps, which made the grates and the steps no cleaner than they had been before, were important in that they were time-consuming, had to be repeated daily, and therefore indicated that the householders were serious in their commitment. Front steps had to be rewhitened every morning. Whiting was made up of size, "stone blue" (a bleaching agent), whitening, and pipeclay. The stones were swept, scrubbed with water, and covered with this mixture. When it was dry they were rubbed with a flannel and brushed. In later years a hearthstone or donkey stone—a piece of weathered standstone—could be used instead of the whiting; it was rubbed over the step and did not need buffing afterward. The whiting was highly impermanent: once walked on, the steps were marked until they were whitened again the next day. But a "good" neighborhood was one where "each house you passed had its half-circle of white pavement and its white-scrubbed doorstep."³⁷ Mrs. Haweis noted that "if an old house has been lived in by respectable and careful people, it is not uncommon to find it . . . actually free from a single blackbeetle!"³⁸ Careful people who were not respectable, it was clear, would have had blackbeetles.

The link between morality and housekeeping was made time after time. Carlyle, coming from a poor farming background, thought his future mother-in-law's drawing room was the finest room he had ever seen: "clean, all of it, as spring water; solid and correct."³⁹ The same conflation of cleanliness and virtue could not have been put more clearly than by the old-fashioned newly married man in Gissing's *The Odd Women*: he thought that his wife's "care of the house was all that reason could desire. In her behaviour he had never detected the slightest impropriety. He believed her chaste as any woman living."⁴⁰ And Dickens, as usual, both adhered to and mocked the prevailing notion. In *Our Mutual Friend*, Eugene Wrayburn and Mortimer Lighthouse, two bachelors, take chambers together. Eugene insists on their having a "very complete little kitchen" where "the moral influence is the important thing . . . See! . . . miniature flour barrel, rolling-pin, spice box, shelf of brown jars, chopping-board, coffee-mill, dresser elegantly furnished with crockery, saucepans and pans, roasting jack, a charming kettle, an armoury of dish-covers. The moral influence of these objects, in forming the domestic virtues, may have an immense influence upon me . . . In fact, I have an idea that I feel the domestic virtues already forming."⁴¹

In the 1851 census, just over a quarter of a million men were of the professional ranks—doctors, barristers and solicitors, and so on. Twenty years later the number had tripled, to more than 800,000. Professionalization, a set of skills to be mastered, was not confined to the outside world; women were expected to acquire the necessary skills to be good managers, administrators, organizers in their own realm. Mrs. Beeton put it most famously in the opening sentence of *Household Management* (1861): "As with the COMMANDER OF AN ARMY, or the leader of any enterprise, so it is with the mistress of the house."[42] She was not alone. Shirley Forster Murphy's *Our Homes* twenty years later, used a similarly martial image: "If once we commence a war against dirt, we can never lay down our arms and say, 'now the enemy is conquered.' . . . Women—mistresses of households, domestic servants—are the soldiers who are deputed by society to engage in this war against dirt . . . As in a campaign each officer is told off to a particular duty, let each servant in a house, and each member of the family who can take a part understand clearly what is the duty for which she is responsible."[43] (Note how part of respectability was the ability to allocate a separate task to each person, instead of having one person perform a multiplicity of roles.)

The mistress of the house was advised to be businesslike:

> It will be found a good plan to write down the daily work of each servant in a little book that can hang in her cupboard, and the hours for doing it, as well as the days on which extra cleaning is required. The hours of rising, meals, dressing, shutting up, going to bed, and all matters relating to comfort and order, should also be inscribed in the book, with existent rules, concerning "followers," Sundays out, times for returning, the lists of silver, china, linen, pots and pans, or whatever goods are entrusted to her, the sweep's days, the dustman's days, &c., &c.[44]

Pre-printed account books were sold to simplify the requisite noting of all household expenditures. Their headings and columns for butcher, baker, rent, wages, and so on mimicked office ledgers. This was in addition to each of the tradesmen's own books: the housewife wrote her order in the book she kept for each separate supplier when he came to take her daily or weekly order. The tradesman took the book away, filled in the prices, and brought it back with her delivery later in the day. The good housewife then transferred these prices to her own ledger, and every week or month reconciled all the figures. It was, said the journal *Publisher's Weekly*, "an age of selections and collections, of abstracts and compilations, of anthologies and genealogies, indexes, catalogues, bibliographies, and local histories."[45]

These ideas were very much a part of the Zeitgeist. Linnaeus, the eighteenth-century Swedish naturalist, had been the first to propose a system for defining and classifying the animal kingdom by genera and species within an ordered hierarchy, and when his collection was brought to London to form the basis of the Linnean Society in the 1790s, it promoted and upheld the single, static classification system, which was popular by virtue of its clarity and simplicity.

The sheer amount of new information available—new inventions firing the Industrial Revolution, new flora and fauna brought back in the age of imperial expansion—fed an urge to numerate, to classify. The Register of Births, Marriages and Deaths, set up in 1837, was an approach to classifying the population at three major points in their lifespan. The census was instituted in the first attempt to number the population of the British Isles. Much of the classification followed the hierarchical patterns set down by Linnaeus. The British Museum (now the British Library) began to create its massive catalogue; the Great Exhibition of 1851 graded and classified all production into four categories ("raw materials," "machinery and mechanical inventions," "manufacture," and "sculpture and fine arts"); in 1852 Peter Roget, a physiologist, separated and categorized the entire English language into six classes ("abstract relations," "space," "matter," "intellect," "volition," and "emotion, religion and morality") in his *Thesaurus of English Words and Phrases*. (These categories gave endless trouble: the classifications at the Great Exhibition were ultimately broken down into another thirty-odd subsections, and Roget needed an additional fifty subsections for his project.)

Yet the notion that the natural world followed a relentless progressive law, that historical progress moved in a linear fashion toward a single future goal, was becoming popular in tandem with this urge to describe what was present in the here and now. *The Oxford English Dictionary*, conceived in 1857, was the first dictionary that was not a guide to current usage (or not *only* a guide to current usage), but instead a chronological ordering of the historical development of the language, a completely new approach. Darwin's *On the Origin of Species* (1859) had two themes, evolution and natural selection. Evolution was generally accepted in a very short time for such a radical thesis, perhaps because evolution could be interpreted as progress. Natural selection was at odds with historical progress; it was arbitrary, unclassifiable, and it therefore had to wait until the twentieth century for its turn. Even something as seemingly straightforward and nonscientific as how to display paintings was radically altered by this linear notion: Charles Eastlake rehung the pictures in the National Gallery to take account of school and chronology for the first time.

Women's preoccupations were not neglected in this urge to classify. Eliza Acton, in her cookbooks at the beginning of the century, was the first person to write a recipe more or less as we would recognize it today, by separating out the ingredients from the method, which no one had thought of doing before. No longer was a cook told to take "some flour" or "enough milk"; now quantities and measures were introduced. Department stores were seen as the epitome of this classificatory ideal. Whiteley's, in Westbourne Grove—one of the earliest department stores, and the biggest—was, said the *Paddington Times*, "the realisation of organisation and order."[46]

The expectation was that such organization could (and should) be replicated at home. Houlston's Industrial Library, which offered would-be servants advice on how to ready themselves for new and better jobs in service, suggested that a lady's maid keep an inventory of all her mistress's clothes, checking it every few weeks against the clothes and updating it accordingly.[47] New householders were advised to make an inventory of their entire household: furniture, furnishings, ornaments, pictures.* Then "once a year . . . the mistress should overlook every single possession she has, comparing them with a list made at the time she entered the house, which she should never let out of her own possession, and which she should alter from time to time, as things are broken or lost or bought." This must include "every glass, tumbler, cup, saucer." The maid and her employer should go through the list together, after which they should both sign and date it, so that no questions might later occur.[49]

Supervision extended to every aspect of the relationship between mistress and servant. The usual system, for a woman with one or more servants, was that in the morning the mistress would perform her household function of overseeing the running of her house. First she checked that the rooms had been cleaned properly, if there were enough servants, or cleaned the house with her servant if she had only one. Then she went to the kitchen, to look at the food left from the day (or days) before, and planned and ordered her meals accordingly. She also gave out stores from the locked storeroom. Some gave out stores once a week, but the paragon found in the advice books was to do it every day, based on the servants' requirements for that day alone.

The English Housekeeper acknowledged that few houses had storerooms that could meet the requirements of the ideal promoted in advice books, and then went on to outline them anyway: shelves for preserves and pickles, drawers for cleaning cloths, boxes for candles and soap. The price of starch varied with the price of flour, so the canny housekeeper stocked up when prices dropped. Rice could be stored for "more than three years, by spreading a well-aired linen sheet in a box, and folding it over the rice, the sheet being lifted out on the floor, once in two or three months, and the rice spread about upon the sheet for a day or two." If space was available, dried goods were to be bought only

---

*Luckily for social historians, the Sambournes did just this when they moved into their new house in 1877. Their inventory noted, among other things, that they owned sixty-six upright chairs: ten in the dining room, twelve in the drawing room, ten in the master bedroom, ten in the nursery, and another twenty-four scattered throughout the house. This did not include armchairs or easy chairs.[48]

twice or three times a year.[50] When possible, shopping was to be done seasonally, when things were cheapest: toward the end of the century coals cost about 15s. a ton in summer, £1 1s. a ton in winter. A 112-pound sack of potatoes cost about 6s. and lasted four or five people three months, which came to an outlay of about 6d. a week. If a smaller quantity was bought, or the potatoes were bought out of season, it might cost 1s. a week to feed the same number of people.[51]

Weekly stores to be handed out to the cook included "baked flour, prepared crumbs of bread, garlic, shallots, onions, black onions, burnt sugar, stock, glaze, salt, mustard, pepper, cayenne, all kinds of spice, dried herbs, vinegar, oil, string, pudding-cloths [one for every pudding ordered that week], paper for roasting, paper for fried fish, etc; fish napkins, plenty of clean towels, oatmeal, groats, flour, split peas, . . . lard, butter, eggs, etc, etc."[52] The cook also needed every week a dishing-up cloth, a dresser cloth, a tablecloth, six kitchen cloths, a dish cloth, a knife cloth, a floor cloth, a rubber (to clean the linoleum), three dusters, and a flannel.[53] Good housewives did not give these things out promiscuously; Mrs. Haweis expected her model women to inspect each old duster to ensure that it was sufficiently worn out before exchanging it for a new one.[54]

The handing out always caused problems: many servants were insulted by the implication that they were not responsible enough, or honest enough, to be allowed to take what they needed when they needed it. Gwen Raverat's mother had the same cook for thirty years, but to the end the cook "had to go through the farce of asking for every pot of jam or box of matches to be given out of the store cupboard, for she herself was never allowed to hold the key for a single instant."[55] The system mortified Hannah Cullwick. After working for more than two years for a widow and her daughter in north London, she said bitterly, "Every little thing I've to ax for & I *canna* always remember at the time what I may want to use, & so it's inconvenient—besides I think it shows so little trust & treating a servant like a child."[56] (The equation of servants with children will be discussed in the next chapter.)

Women were taught that running a house economically was a virtue in itself, regardless of income. If waste and excess were present, no matter what the household could afford, the housewife was a bad house-keeper and, consequently, a bad person: a thrifty woman was a morally upright woman. Elizabeth Grant, a Scottish woman living near Dublin, wrote in her diary: "A poor woman with a sickly baby came [to the door] . . . luckily I had some old flannel and socks of Johnny's for the little wretched thing—and mind, dear little girls, never to throw away anything . . . all old clothes I put carefully away, sure that some day some distressed person will want them. The merest rag goes into a rag bag which when full a poor woman will sell for a few pennies."[57]

By contrast, the second Mrs. Finch in Wilkie Collins's *Poor Miss Finch* was an obviously bad housekeeper, and therefore the reader knew from the outset to regard her household with a dubious eye. When the narrator first met her, "her hair was not dressed; and her lace cap was all on one side. The upper part of her was clothed in a loose jacket of blue merino; the lower part was robed in a dimity dressing gown of doubtful white. In one hand, she held a dirty dogs'-eared book, which I at once detected to be a Circulating Library novel." She was not properly dressed, not clean, *and* she read novels; the narrator was unsurprised later to find that Mrs. Finch came from a lower-class background before her marriage. She gave out the stores improperly dressed, and had no control over her household: " 'Eight pounds of soap? Where does it all go to I wonder!' groaned Mrs Finch to the accompaniment of the baby's screams. [Note that the baby is in the wrong place, emphasizing Mrs. Finch's bad housekeeping.] 'Five pounds of soda for the laundry? . . . Six pounds of candles? You must eat candles . . . who ever heard of burning six pounds of candles in a week? Ten pounds of sugar? Who gets it all? I never taste sugar from one year's end to another. Waste, nothing but waste.' "[58] Mrs. Finch, it was plain, never checked her maid's dusters before giving out new ones.

Even the charitably inclined Mrs. Grant was, by many advice books' reckoning, profligate: sheets were expected to last between five and seven years (or three to four years if there were only two sets: one on the bed, one in the wash); then, when the sheets became worn down the center, they were cut in half and sewn "sides to middle"—the sides, which tucked in and were therefore fresher, became the middle, and the old, worn center became the sides. After a few more years they were demoted to dust sheets for a further few years, to be used to cover furniture when the fireplaces were cleaned and rooms were dusted. Only then could the remnants be torn into strips for bandages, or given to the poor. To give things to the poor too soon—when they were still "good"—was as foolish as any of Mrs. Finch's behavior.

Items from the kitchen were even more urgent candidates for what we now know as recycling and was then considered simple thrift. Rubbish was divided into two parts: dust (coal dust, ashes from the fires) and refuse (everything else). From 1875 refuse was removed by the municipality as a legal obligation. Until then many suburbs had no regular collections at all, and residents had to arrange for removal as necessary, paying per collection. For this reason, as well as the moral value of thrift, housewives were encouraged to reuse everything possible.

There was, of course, less to dispose of: packaging as we know it had yet to be created, and goods came either unwrapped or wrapped in paper. Open fires allowed any overly dirtied paper (paper that had wrapped meat or fish, for example) to be disposed of immediately. Cleaner paper was kept for reuse, and really clean paper had two further uses. One was as lavatory paper (see pp. 333–34). Second, many householders used waste paper to make "spills," which were long strips of twisted paper for lighting fires or candles. In Mrs. Gaskell's novel *Cranford* (1851–53), Miss Matty, the elderly spinster, sets aside one evening a week for this. She has done her weekly accounts and her correspondence, and so uses the old bills and letters for the task. (She also makes spills out of colored paper, in decorative feather shapes, which she gives as presents.)[59]

One system of disposal that has vanished was collection by a number of street traders who regularly visited the back doors to buy various items. Paper was bought by the paper mills and by manufacturers of papier-mâché furniture and ornaments. Dealers also bought old iron, metal, wood, and lead. Mrs. Haweis, really getting into her stride, gave prices that the virtuous housewife could expect for empty biscuit boxes, jars, tins, and other household goods. "Champagne bottles *with the labels on* are worth more than without them," she advised.[60]

Old textiles and bones were bought by the rag-and-bone man, who sold his wares to paper mills and to glue, gelatin, match, toothpick, and fertilizer manufacturers. In *Bleak House*, Krook's shop carries signs that would have been familiar to all: "RAG AND BOTTLE WAREHOUSE; BONES BOUGHT; KITCHEN-STUFF BOUGHT; OLD IRON BOUGHT; WASTE PAPER BOUGHT; LADIES' AND GENTLEMEN'S WARDROBES BOUGHT."[61] By 1865 Henry Mayhew thought this type of sign very old-fashioned: rag-and-bone men now pasted up colored prints that showed characters with speech bubbles advertising their services. Mayhew describes one such print thus:

> The youthful Sammy, dressed in light-blue trousers, gamboge [bright yellow] waistcoat, and pink coat, is throwing up his arms in raptures at the "stylish appearance" of his sweetheart Matilda, who, like Sammy himself, is decked out in all the chromatic elegance of these three primary colours,* while the astonished swain is exclaiming, by means of a huge bubble which he is in the act of blowing out of his mouth, "My gracious, Matilda! how ever did you get that beautiful new dress?" To which rather impertinent query the damsel is made to bubble forth the following decided puff: "Why, Sammy by saving up all my old rags, and taking them to Mr.——, who gives the best prices likewise for bones, pewter, brass, and kitchen-stuff!"[62]

This style of advertising caught on, moving from rag-and-bone men to other working-class environments, such as fried-fish shops and stalls that produced cheaply prepared foods—stewed eels, baked potatoes— and finally soap companies (see pp. 157–58).

Kitchen waste was, of course, the main item to be disposed of regularly, and advice books were full of information on what could be got rid of, in what way. It is difficult to know how far their precepts were followed—the stress laid on the immorality of straightforward disposal

---

*Mayhew retained his middle-class anxiety about the working classes dressing too well. See pp. 150–51.

implies that probably many people threw out much more than they were expected to. Cooks who were not thrifty put all the kitchen leavings into a bucket. The content was called "wash," and the washman visited regularly to buy it; he then sold it as "hog-wash," or pig swill. Employers were warned solemnly about the evils of this system. First, it gave servants no incentive to reuse food. Some might even be encouraged to dishonesty: by telling an inexperienced housewife that she had to pay the washman to take the wash away, the cook could pocket money from both the wife and the washman.

The buckets waiting for collection also encouraged vermin, but this was hard to avoid: the local need for wash was high. Even late in the century, pigs were kept by working-class families in cities to provide a little extra income. One commentator noted that Shepherds Bush in London "might perhaps be termed *the* pigsty of the metropolis; for here every house has its piggery, and the air is sonorous with the grunting of porkers." Henry Mayhew reported that Jacob's Island, south of the Thames, near Bermondsey, had houses built out on stilts over the river: "At the back of every house that boasted a square foot or two of outlet . . . were pig-sties."[63] It was hard for the thrifty cook to see why what was waste to her should not be usefully disposed of.

Instead of simply acknowledging that some waste was inevitable, a great deal of time was spent in suggesting ways to avoid creating it. Many of these are procedures that are still accepted today, though followed by only the most conscientious of cooks: fish heads were used to make fish soup; vegetables and the water they were cooked in went to make soup or gravy, as did plate scrapings and wine; stale bread was used for breadcrumbs and for puddings. Anything that survived these operations was then fed to the dogs, cats, or chickens. Tea leaves were rinsed and scattered over carpets to aid in collecting dust when sweeping, then they were burned in the range; cold tea was used to clean windows or as a tonic for the eyes; mutton and veal fat could be clarified and used for frying.

Concern about hygiene always went hand in hand with food. Early in the century, meat mostly came from the city it was purchased in; even if the animals were driven to market there, they were butchered only on arrival, so beef, mutton, and pork were relatively fresh when bought. With the rapid expansion of the railways, by midcentury animals as far away as Scotland were slaughtered for the London markets: Aberdeen, noted one journal, was "little else than a London abattoir." More than half a million rabbits were shipped from Ostend to London alone; plovers came from Ireland, quail from Egypt. Seventy-five million eggs were imported every year from Europe.[64]

Before refrigeration, the best that could be managed at home was a cool cellar or a tiled room on a north-facing wall; neither was ideal, and even these were rarely achieved in small houses, but when meat was butchered locally, probably only the day before it was purchased, this was not too serious. As the distances grew, so did the amount of time food had to stay fresh. Likewise, milk from local dairies was preferred to milk that arrived by train, but the latter became more and more difficult to avoid as urban sprawl pushed farmland farther from the major cities.

Much advice was given to housewives on how to ensure that the food they bought was good, and on how to prolong its life in that condition. Meat needed to be examined regularly, and powdering it with ginger or pepper against flies was recommended. Charcoal kept meat fresh, and also removed the taint from already putrescent meat. Scalded milk stayed drinkable for several hours longer than fresh. To keep it for several days, grated horseradish added to the jug would help, "even in hot weather." Boiled and then packed in sawdust, eggs would keep fresh for up to three months, or they could be covered in flaxseed oil, to keep for six months. Even with these tips, menus still had to be changed with the weather. Jane Brookfield, the wife of the curate of St. James's Church, Piccadilly, noted that at her friends' house outside London, "the Salmon from Exeter and the green-pea soup and the chickens and jellies have to be eaten at an early dinner to-day . . . the hot weather not permitting any delays."[65] And, despite preventatives and precautions, Marion Sambourne's diaries are filled with entries that say "Bad fowl," "Bad mutton at lunch," "Very late dinner, duck bad, had to send out for lobster & steak."[66]

Preventative measures were laborious but could not be ignored. If butter was bought in quantity, by the tub, "the first thing to be done is to turn the whole of the butter out, and, with a clean knife, to scrape the outside; the tub should then be wiped with a clean cloth, and sprinkled all round with salt, the butter replaced, and the lid kept on to exclude the air. It is necessary to take these precautions, as sometimes a want of proper cleanliness in the dairymaid causes the outside of the butter to become rancid."[67]

Bread was known to be filthy. A Parliamentary report in 1862 had suggested that "the principal fact" about bakeries

> was their extreme dirt, and in many places the almost total covering of the entire space between the rafters with masses of cobwebs, weighed down with the flour dust that had accumulated upon them, and hanging in strips just above your head. A heavy tread or a blow upon the floor above, brought down large fragments of them, as I witnessed on more than one occasion; and as the rafters immediately over the troughs in which the dough is made are as thickly hung with them as any other part of the bakehouse, masses of these cobwebs must be frequently falling into the dough . . .
>
> Animals in considerable numbers crawled in and out of and upon the troughs where the bread was made, and upon the adjoining walls.

And then there were the smells: "The air of those small bakehouses is generally overloaded with foul gases from the drains, from the ovens, and from the fermentation of the bread, and with the emanations from [the bakers'] own bodies."[68] After this description it seems natural that a completely machine-mixed, yeastless bread was soon created: the Aerated Bread Company produced this sanitary product, and sold it in their own Aerated Bread Company tea shops. (The ABCs, as they become known, were among the first tea shops respectable ladies could patronize without a male escort; they survived well into the second half of the twentieth century.)

Even something as apparently straightforward as watercress was dangerous. Little girls sold it on the street, and door to door, but everyone knew that London cress came mostly from Camden Town, where the "beds are planted in an old brick-field, watered by the Fleet Ditch; and though the stream at this point is comparatively pure,* they owe their unusually luxuriant appearances to a certain admixture of the sewerage."[69] There was even a publication, *Water-Cresses without Sewage* (1878), which told how to grow your own, to avoid cress grown in sewage and very likely bearing typhus.[70]

For, however worrying dirt was, what it really betokened was disease. "Drains" was the shorthand used by all to indicate waterborne illness. Midcentury, when the miasma theory of disease transmission was popular, the smell from drains was thought to bring illnesses; later, with germ theory, it was the water itself. Whatever the case, drains were trouble. In a Sherlock Holmes story two houses have remained empty for some time "on account of him that owns them, who won't have the drains seed to, though the very last tenant what lived in one of them died o' typhoid fever."[71] Professionals made the same association. *The Plumber* warned: "There are a 'thousand gates to death!' Few are wider, or open more readily, than those in our own homes"— the drains.[72] After all, the linking of houses to a communal sewer was a new concept. For the first part of the century, people had continued much as they had before, with cesspools beneath their houses. And as late as 1888 Mrs. Haweis was still writing, "Between you and me, the old cesspool, *if properly emptied and deodorized,* is preferable to ill-made modern drains which connect every house with every other, and make escape from infectious maladies a clear matter of accident, whilst we are laid on by a pipe to every disease in the town."[73] The joining of each home to the next via the drains distressed her: her home was no longer her castle. This was not a rational fear, and therefore she didn't have to be consistent when she welcomed the other ubiquitous link from house to house: piped water. (For more on concerns about drains, see pp. 336–39.)

Although some great houses had had piped cold water in the seventeenth century, the middle classes began to achieve this only in the

*Comparatively. See p. 337.

nineteenth. By midcentury, most middle-class houses in cities had a connection to a water company's pipes, but it was expensive: up to 3s. a week for an intermittent supply. By the end of the century, those paying £20 a year in rent paid between 14s. 10d. and £1 10s. a year for their water; those with a £50 rent paid between £2 10s. and £4 13s. a year—nearly 10 percent of the cost of the rent.[74]

The water sometimes came into the kitchen—by midcentury, when kitcheners with boilers attached were becoming more common, water was the norm in kitchens. In smaller or less well supplied houses, there was sometimes only one tap, and then it usually was located in the scullery, where its primary use was for kitchen work and the laundry. Gradually the pipes were extended upstairs, and by the 1870s, houses with an annual rent above £35 usually had bathrooms with running hot water (heated from the kitchen range) as well as flush lavatories. This put further strain on both the sewage system and the water supply. *Our Homes* in 1883 estimated that the average person needed twenty-two gallons of water a day, divided up as follows:

Domestic usage, excluding laundry	9 gallons
W.C.s	5 gallons
Baths, one a week	5 gallons
Washing clothes	3 gallons
TOTAL	22 gallons

This, the authors went on, was for "fairly cleanly households," but the less well off, through "personal apathy and indifference," used only two to five gallons a day.[75] Their judgment ignored the many difficulties. In 1866, only 470,000 water connections existed in London (including standpipes for communal use in poor areas). The water companies rarely supplied water twenty-four hours a day, seven days a week; in the early days it was supplied for only an hour a day, three days a week, and never on Sunday, the day that the lower middle classes (not to mention the poor) might be expected to be at home. So, should the tenement dwellers be fortunate enough to have work and be out during the day, or be too sickly or too young to carry buckets of water up several flights of stairs,* or miss their turn at the standpipe at the requisite hour, or not have a receptacle for the water, well, they would have to manage with less. Or with none.

Middle-class households could, as always, make provision. Cisterns were quickly built into new houses as a matter of course, to provide water when piped supplies were unavailable. Various companies supplied water with differing efficiency: in 1874, only 10.3 percent of households in London were getting a constant supply; in 1891, only 24 percent of the houses using the Chelsea Water Company had a regular supply. Not until the companies were dissolved and the Metropolitan Water Board was created, in 1902, was a uniform standard applied across the city.[76]

As water became more easily available to the middle classes, they found it ever more necessary for health and for status. For all the middle classes, it was the work of the scullery that was the key to these activities.

---

*Those who carry bottled water back from the supermarket, our version of the standpipe, will know that it is not light work: a case of twelve 1.5-liter bottles of Evian is slightly under four gallons (that is, imperial gallons, which are about 20 percent larger than U.S. gallons; throughout this book, "gallon" refers to the imperial measure). The equivalent of five and a half cases would have had to be carried from the standpipe daily to meet *Our Homes'* average requirement. "Personal apathy"?

THE SCULLERY

MANY COMFORTABLE MIDDLE-CLASS housewives would have spent time in their kitchens. Even those who could afford servants might prefer to do the baking themselves. But no housewife who could possibly afford not to would spend time in the scullery. It was dirty, and damp, and dark. It was the repository of all the dirt of the house—where pots and pans were left for scrubbing; where, if there was no pantry (which was the case in most middle-class houses), the plates were left to be washed after each meal; where the residue of the fire-places, so carefully removed from each room, was sorted; where the laundry was done. In fact, all the jobs that could be passed over to the servants as soon as possible were performed here.

Servants and cleaning were inextricably entwined in the Victorian period. Not everyone could afford servants who were properly trained, or even full-time servants, but enough could afford at least a workhouse child, or a charwoman to come in from time to time to help with the rough work, that the standards achieved with servants became the norm, even for those who had to manage without. What could be achieved realistically was always contrasted with what *ought* to have been achieved. This was because many took having a servant as the definition of being middle class. Servants were, as consumer durables are today, a symbol of status, signaling to the world the stage that the family had reached. The wife of an assistant surgeon in 1859 said, "I must not do our household work, or carry my baby out: or I should lose caste. We must keep a servant."[1]

This idea was pervasive. A comic version was concocted by Henry Mayhew and his brother Augustus. (Before compiling his monumental *London Labour and the London Poor*, Henry Mayhew had been one of the originators of the comic magazine *Punch*.) In their novel *The Greatest Plague of Life* (1847), the daughter of a coal merchant with pretensions to gentility was about to marry, and on the eve of the wedding her mother sat her down for a mother-daughter talk:

> There was one thing that she felt it was her duty, upon my entrance into life, as it were, to warn me against—one thing, on which alone domestic happiness could be built—one thing, on which I should find my comfort depended more than any other—one thing, in fact, which might strew either my path with roses or my bed with thorns. And then she asked me what I thought this one thing was? Probably I might think she meant my husband—but no! it was something of far more consequence to me than that. Or I might think she meant fortune, or economy, or my offspring— . . . it was none of these, she told me—nor was it amiability of temper, or a proper pride in appearance, or marital constancy—no! these had but a trifling connexion with the peace and quiet of my future domestic life compared with that which she alluded to. In a word, she said, I should find the key-stone to all my future welfare rested upon those I should have about me. She referred to—servants.[2]

The census figures, however, indicate that not everyone in the middle classes could have had a servant. The number of women in service rose rapidly throughout the century: by 1851, one in three women between the ages of fifteen and twenty-four in London was a servant, and more than one in six of any age was in service.[3] Yet, between 1851 and 1871 in London, only 35 percent of the population had one servant, and 25 percent had two.[4] This left 40 percent of the population, some of whom may have had more than two servants, but the majority of whom had none, or of course were the servants themselves.

In the 1871 census there were 1.19 million servants, of whom 93,000 were cooks and 75,000 nursemaids. There were 50,000 upper-class families; this would leave only 43,000 cooks and 25,000 nursemaids for the middle classes in general—not even enough to supply the upper middle classes, the group we think of as "standard" servant-employers. It must be concluded that most families had at most one servant, and that far more women were helping their single servants do the family cooking—or doing it entirely on their own—than our perception today would allow for.[5]

Helen Corke, later to become a friend of D. H. Lawrence, wrote of her lower-middle-class childhood in Tunbridge Wells, where her father owned a shop. Her mother had no servants, and in the morning Helen, "together with my rag doll Molly, a toy rubber cat, and a picture book," was put in a swing that hung from the kitchen ceiling. There she watched her mother ironing, making pastry, setting the table.[6]

For those at the bottom of the hiring market, workhouse children were available for a few pounds a year. Ford Madox Brown, the Pre-Raphaelite painter, paid a workhouse child £5 a year, plus her food and clothing.[7] Dickens often depicted these sad little waifs: the Micawbers, in *David Copperfield*, had the Orfling—that is, the orphan—from a workhouse or charity school. Guster, in *Bleak House*, was paid 50s. (£2 10s.) a year, whereas experienced servants with references from good houses earned from £16 to £60. Children from workhouses had had no training and, having grown up in institutions, had never seen a modern house, with gas or running water or any of the various pieces of equipment they were expected to use; girls from laboring families were not in a position to know any more.

The reality of extreme poverty among the working classes was unknown to many of the comfortable middle classes; servants were probably the only representatives many of them would ever meet from

Thomas Carlyle, shown in 1859, in front of his London home, where he lived for twenty-five years. It would be another six years before the Carlyles added a servants' bedroom to the top floor: until then, their servant slept in the basement kitchen, the windows of which can be seen behind the railings.

ABOVE Older girls were quickly taught to act as surrogate mothers. In James Collinson's *Childhood* (1855), a small child sits in the schoolroom with her books at her feet while her sister supervises her lessons, mimicking the mother and child in the painting on the wall.

OPPOSITE Bedrooms varied in size and style. The governess's bedroom in Alice Squire's watercolor (*top*) is in the attic (note the sloping walls), and is only big enough to contain the necessities: a hip-bath, a washstand, a writing desk. To make room for them, the bed has had to be pushed against the fire-place. Jane Carlyle's bedroom (*bottom*), by contrast, is single-function, as the advice books recommended. Note the early Victorian lack of a bedside table.

Houses were much colder than today, and together with the high child mortality figures and the consequent worry about the health of children, many layers of clothing were considered essential. James Hayllar, a popular painter of children, showed a prosperous middle-class child in *Waiting to Go Out* (*left*). Even indoors, children were bundled up: little girls often wore two pairs of stockings, and babies were wrapped in gowns, petticoats, and flannel shawls, as well as more ornamental wrappings. In *The Introduction* by Emily Crawford (*below*), the cot is decorated in a very similar manner to the mother's dressing table, with its cover that was both ornamental and practical—washable covers were used to protect furniture from soot and coal dust.

The front kitchen at the Carlyles' house (*above*) contained only the essentials: the range, built into the fireplace, with a bottle-jack (a mechanism used to roast meat in front of the fire) and a meat-screen (to the left); gas lighting; a wooden table and chairs; and a few dishracks. At night the Carlyles' servant took out her bedding and slept in this basement room.

Hannah Cullwick, a maid-of-all-work (*left*), slept in the kitchen in some of her posts. Here, in a photograph taken by her future husband Arthur Munby, she is posed as though at work.

In Erwood's *The First Place* (1860), a young servant in her employer's drawing room is overcome with homesickness. In reality, girls were sent out to train for domestic service as young as eight: Hannah Cullwick was in her first full-time job living away from home at the age of twelve. A servant even younger than the girl Erwood depicted might have dusted this painting.

A specific time each week was set aside for certain tasks, including polishing the silver. The housemaid in this photograph is remarkably clean and tidy for such a messy job, however, and she is wearing her dress apron, which was normally put on when she was waiting on her employers. For cleaning, when not posing for photographs, she would put on a large apron of coarse fabric, without lace, and bands on her wrists to protect her cuffs.

By midcentury, wringers, machines that pressed water out of wet laundry, and mangles, which were used to give dry items a preliminary smoothing before they were ironed, had been merged into one machine. It is doubtful that any woman as elaborately dressed as the ones in this advertisement (*right*) would go near one. By the end of the century even the housemaids were well dressed, at least in advertisements (*below*), which were designed to suggest that neither laundry nor cooking was the dirty, laborious work that housewives knew it to be.

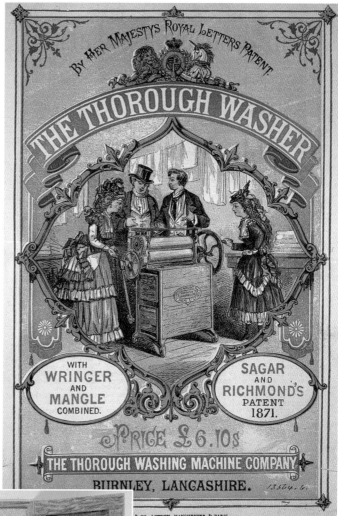

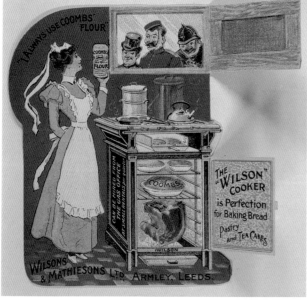

that faceless, nameless horde. Mrs. Beeton, like many others, thought that training servants was the most important responsibility a mistress had: enlightening the unenlightened, supervising their religious education, their moral welfare, and their social lives. Others, like this writer on interior decoration, were sublimely unaware of the great divide, blithely suggesting that it was important for the poor to be uplifted by "artistic" surroundings: "good art and good decoration" in the homes of their employers would repair the mindset their previous "miserable, squalid and unartistic" homes had imbued them with.[8] Friedrich Engels, in his crusading *The Condition of the Working-Class in England in 1844*, described some of these unartistic homes, in this example from Manchester: "The inhabitants live in dilapidated cottages, the windows of which are broken and patched with oilskin. The doors and the door posts are broken and rotten . . . on the average twenty people live in each of these little houses, which at the moment consist of two rooms, an attic and a cellar. One privy . . . is shared by about one hundred and twenty people."[9] It was only natural, therefore, that Guster thought her employer's lower-middle-class house was "a Temple of plenty and splendour. She believe[d] the little drawing-room upstairs, always kept, as one might say with its hair in papers and its pinafore on,* to be the most elegant apartment in Christendom."[10] Young girls from workhouses and from agricultural laborers' families often worked only for their keep in their first job, to get the training they needed in order to begin their climb up the ladder of domestic service, and also to receive the all-important character reference from their mistress, saying they were sober and industrious, and recommending them for future employment.

The turnover in servants was high, usually at the instigation of the servants. The average time spent at any one post was three years, and the households with a single servant experienced the highest turnover.

---

*That the drawing room was kept for "best" was a strong signal to Dickens's readers that the family's standing was only just in the lower middle class. Almost as clear a divide as the employment of servants, the daily use of the best room marked out the genteel from the masses.

The most mobile were the youngest servants, who, as they acquired skills, changed jobs.[11] Jane Carlyle lived at Cheyne Row for thirty-two years, and in that time she had thirty-four different servants, not including those who filled in temporarily while she looked for a new permanent servant.[12] The father and stepmother of Constance Kent (who was found guilty of murdering her brother, although suspicion always rested on her father; see pp. 17 and 25) kept three servants: a cook, a maid, and a nursemaid. A contemporary reckoned that in four years more than a hundred different women were employed in these three positions.[13] How much this was influenced by the idea of the Kents as a "bad" family cannot be known, but it is interesting that this appears to be one form the doubt took.

New servants were generally found in one of three ways: through the grapevine—via a friend, another servant, or the local tradesmen, who often acted as a clearing agency; by going to a registry office; or by advertising, or answering an advertisement. The first method was considered the best; advertisements and registry offices had the drawbacks of expense and relying on the word of strangers. All servants after their first job had to have a character reference, known colloquially as "a character," without which they could not hope to obtain work. However, the wise housekeeper, cautioned most books, did not rely on a written character alone but went to see the previous employer face to face, to ask about the prospective servant's "morals, honesty, cleanliness, capability, temper and health," in that order.[14] This enabled the prospective employer to assess the quality of the information that was being given, and also to examine the quality of the housekeeping. Women were warned that to give a false character out of kindness was not a kindness at all: the servant would still be given notice, and the whole concept of references would fall apart, leaving prospective employers with nothing to rely on.

Jane Carlyle accepted her responsibilities, and was flinty. She had had a servant, Helen, who had worked for her for nine years, then left, returned two years later, and was then sacked for drunkenness. Two years after that rupture, a woman came the other morning from *Helen*—a *decent* enough looking person *respectably* dressed . . . Her business was to ask me to give the said Helen *a character* that she might seek another place. Otherwise she (Helen) "spoke of attempting her life"— "She has been long speaking of that" I said—"Yes—and you are aware maam of her having *walked* into the Thames, after she left the last place you found her? Oh yes she got three months of Horsemonger Lane jail for *the* attempt—and if a waterman had not been looking on and *taken the first opportunity of saving her* she would have *probably* been drowned." I said it was well if she had not been in jail for anything worse . . . I recommended that she should as a more feasable speculation go into the Chelsea Work House where they would take care to keep drink from her, and *force* her to work—As for recommending her to a decent service I scouted the notion . . . Let her go into the workhouse and conduct herself decently there and then I would see what I could do for her.[15]

That was how any respectable employer was expected to behave. The only other possibility for the disgraced servant was to find one of the few places like the Industrial Female Home, in Hackney. This was to help "check" the "downward course" of servants who, "from failure in ability or good conduct," had left a position without a character. The attending servant paid 3s. 6d. a week and worked for a certificate of improvement, which would serve as a replacement character until she had once more held down a job.[16] On the other hand, if a servant had worked hard for her mistress, behaved well, and had a chance to better herself, a respectable woman would not stand in her way; indeed, she would actively help. Geraldine Jewsbury, a novelist living in Manchester and a friend of Jane Carlyle, heard of a position as lady's maid that she thought would suit her housemaid. She went and interviewed the lady herself to promote her maid's case; gave the maid a week off to go and learn the one skill she was missing; and arranged for her own milliner to teach her quilling and cap-making.[17]

Quilling was used for delicate pieces of lace. Laura Forster described the method as it was performed on a baby's cap after every washing to reshape and stiffen the lace:

> The long piece of lace to be quilled was produced, together with a bundle of straws and a board about fourteen inches by ten, the lace was put on the board and a straw placed under it and over it in close succession till the row of alternating straws was long enough to go around the baby's cap, then the lace was turned and a second and third row of straws was built on the lower one. Then came the delightful climax; the straws were tied firmly to the board, the kettle was made to boil its hardest, and the board was moved slowly backwards and forwards near the spout, till the steam had penetrated to the very lowest layer of lace. After that the board was put aside till the lace had dried and stiffened into shape, then each straw was drawn out carefully and the quilling of delicate lace was left in perfect order for that most sacred part of a baby's wardrobe, its best cap.[18]

This was a very specialized skill, and it is not surprising that Miss Jewsbury's single servant had had no call for it.

Becoming a lady's maid was a step up, beyond a doubt. Most servants' work was backbreaking, and they were rarely healthy, suffering from long-term illnesses caused by poor nutrition, confined quarters, and lack of sun and fresh air. The series of guides to service published by Houlston's Industrial Library compared the health of employers and their employees, and encouraged those who had jobs with good families to believe themselves hardy:

> It may strike you with surprise that your mistress complains so often of illness as she does. It is very possible that, comparing your own state of health with hers, you may be puzzled what to think, and at length conclude your mistress fanciful. It is certainly true that while the generality of servants go on from year's end to year's end, never interrupting their work for the sake of nursing

A fairly standard bedroom where a housewife interviews her servant: The bed
has already lost its curtains, although the half-tester remained. A table with a
writing slope and a dressing table behind, lit with candles rather than gas, plus
two easy chairs and a chaise-longue, hint at the various uses of the room.

themselves, and complaining of nothing worse than an occasional
cold, the generality of ladies declare themselves ill much more
frequently . . .

There are more reasons than one for this. In the first place, the
health of the servants is really better, on the whole, than that of their
ladies. It is better, I believe, than that of any class of people in society. They have none of the hardships of poor people, and few or
none of the cares which break down the health of the rich . . . They
have not the labour and anxiety of mind, the cares and troubles,
which break the sleep of too many of their employers . . . a lady
who has been teaching and watching over her children, or who has
been occupied in mind with her husband's affairs, may well be more
fatigued than the housemaid who has been scouring her rooms.[19]

Despite this cheery view of their lives, those in service knew the reality when they saw it. In 1864 Hannah Cullwick went to visit a lodging-

house keeper she had once worked for in Margate, to help her with "mangling the week's wash for she did all the washing with the help of her little maid from the workhouse—a fresh one from Limehouse, for the other poor wench was sent back there ill, & had died since. I felt extremely sorry for them having to work so hard & such long hours, from 5 in the morning till 12 at night, & I spoke as plain as I could to Mrs E. about it."[20] This may not have come as a surprise to Mrs E., as lodging-house keepers, much against their will, were being forced slowly to improve their servants' working conditions. In 1872 one lodging-house keeper complained "that it was now necessary . . . to allow their maids to go to bed at ten o'clock every night, and to give them an afternoon out every other Sunday, or no servant would stay."[21]

This improvement came about as more women went to work in shops and factories. A comparison of the work of a housemaid to that of a shopgirl or factory hand showed why. A housemaid worked from six every morning to ten o'clock at night. In theory she had half an hour each for breakfast, tea, and supper, and an hour for dinner, with an hour and a half for needlework in the afternoon, "which may fairly be regarded as a rest." Thus she did at least twelve hours of heavy physical labor every day, which was two hours more than a factory worker (four hours more on Saturdays), although a shopgirl often worked the same hours. Shop hours varied with locality, but suburban shops expected to open at about seven-thirty or eight in the morning, and remain open until nine or nine-thirty Monday through Thursday; on Fridays, most shops stayed open until ten-thirty or eleven, and on Saturday till midnight. The journalist G. A. Sala reported "tens of thousands" at work late: coffeehouses and chophouses stayed open to eleven, when the grocer, the cheesemonger, and the linen draper all began to close up too. By midnight only pubs, cigar shops, supper rooms, fish warehouses, and chemists were open. Most shops rarely had a full day's holiday: butchers, grocers, bakehouses, all were open on Christmas Day, and servants expected to work then too. Hannah Cullwick wrote, "I often think what a most delightful pleasure that must be, going home for Christmas, but I've never once had it."[22]

A housemaid's work, however, was of a "more severe nature," carrying coals and water, lifting weights in making beds and emptying baths: a full coal scuttle weighed between twenty-eight and thirty pounds, a bath-jug of water thirty pounds. Prams were invented in 1850; before that, babies or young children were carried by the servant on their daily walk. They must have been grateful for the change: by the 1880s an eighteen-month-old child could be expected to weigh twenty-six pounds.[23] The housemaid also had less fresh air than a factory worker. Added to this, servants rarely had Sundays off; at best there might be a reduced workload. If the family expected an elaborate Sunday dinner, then Sundays were like any other day for the servant. When a half-day was given, the servant was expected to get through the regular twelve hours' work by five o'clock before being allowed out. On Mondays, if the laundry was done at home, the servant often had to get up at three or four in the morning to start the water heating, and yet "it is well known that a housemaid's work is considered lighter than that of a cook, kitchenmaid, scullerymaid or dairymaid."[24]

Many did not stay the course. One sixteen-year-old reported to Henry Mayhew: "I am an orphan. When I was ten I was sent to service as maid-of-all-work, in a small tradesman's family. It was a hard place, and my mistress used me very cruelly, beating me often. I stood my mistress's ill-treatment for about six months. She beat me with sticks as well as with her hands. I was black and blue, and at last ran away."[25] (By the time she was sixteen, she was a prostitute—a not uncommon fate. Modern scholars have noted the high rates of illegitimate births, theft, drunkenness, prostitution, infanticide, and suicide among the servant population.[26] Although undoubtedly some, possibly many, servants did become prostitutes, one wonders how many prostitutes, thieves, and drunks merely claimed to be in service to give themselves a veneer of respectability.) Mrs. Beeton differentiated between "small tradesmen" and "respectable tradesmen," suggesting that the maid-of-all-work who was employed by the former was made to suffer because the small tradesman's wife was "just a step above her in the social scale."[27]

For families that could afford more than a maid-of-all-work, the next stage was to have either a cook and a housemaid, or a nursemaid and a cook (who then in reality performed the function of a maid-of-all-work). Gradually, noted one observer, "as her means increase every wife transfers every household duty involving labour to other hands."[28] A cook and a housemaid together divided the housework thus: the cook prepared the meals, looked after the kitchen entirely, cleaned the passages, kitchen, scullery, hall, and steps, and answered the doorbell in the morning hours, when the bell was most likely to indicate tradesmen calling for her orders; the housemaid cleaned the bedrooms and reception rooms in the morning, looked after the dining room, waited at dinner, prepared tea, answered the front door after her cleaning was done, and waited generally on the family.

Until she could afford this luxury, the housewife managed with one servant, helping as necessary but leaving the heavy work to her. The maid-of-all-work, or "general servant" (considered to be a more genteel term), had, as even Mrs. Beeton acknowledged, the most tiring, difficult job of all servants—she was "perhaps the only one of her class deserving of commiseration: her life is a solitary one, and, in some places, her work is never done. She is also subject to rougher treatment."[29]

Her daily routine began at six o'clock every morning at the latest (or five-thirty in the summer: the time was decided by weighing the cost of the candles or oil needed in the winter against the extra work the servant could manage—it had nothing to do with how the servant felt). On her way to the kitchen she drew all the blinds and curtains and opened all the shutters, except in the bedrooms where the family still slept, and the breakfast room, which she shortly would deal with. In the kitchen, the fire should have been laid night before. The range apart from the front bars was polished while the fire was drawing up. Twice a week it needed to be thoroughly cleaned throughout, including the boiler and oven. Once it was cleaned, she checked that the boiler had water, put the kettle on, and, while waiting for it to boil, cleaned the household's boots and knives.

Then the maid washed her hands and went to open the curtains in the breakfast room (sometimes a room apart from the dining room, sometimes the dining room). She took with her a sweeping cloth, to cover the ornaments and furniture. She folded up the hearth rug for shaking outside and laid a coarse cloth over the carpet so that she could put down the blacklead box, the cinder sifter, and the fire irons. Cleaning the grate, fire irons, and fender—which had to be done daily—was supposed to take twenty minutes but often took longer. The fire was then lit to warm the room before the family came downstairs for breakfast. Then she cleaned and rubbed the furniture, washed the mantelpiece and any ledges, dusted the ornaments. She strewed damp, used tea leaves, rinsed the day before, over the carpet to help collect the dust, then swept them up again.

The next area was the hall, front steps, and entrance, where the mats and rugs were shaken out. The front-hall floor was cleaned, and any brass was polished. If there was time, the steps were whitened before breakfast. All the downstairs fireplaces were emptied of their cinders, which were sifted and used to bank up the kitchen fire.

This was the last of the early-morning dirty work, and now the maid was expected to change into a clean cotton dress, apron, and cap. (This was the lower- and middle-middle-class version of the segregation of duties. The upper classes had one servant for each type of task. Some upper-middle-class families could achieve this; many more could not. In less well-to-do houses, separation of function was made clear by the different uniforms worn by the maid at different times of day as she performed different parts of her job.) She then laid the table, and cooked and brought in breakfast, when the mistress gave her her instructions for luncheon or dinner. While the family was eating, she ate her breakfast if there was time; otherwise she snatched a mouthful before going upstairs to air the bedrooms and strip the beds to air them. Many worried about bodily emanations, as they were usually called: "The water given out in respiration is loaded with animal impurities; it condenses on the inner walls of buildings, and trickles down in foetid streams, and evaporates or sinks into the walls."[30] Thus the need for beds and bedding to be aired every day. The mattresses were turned, and the servant then emptied the slops and rinsed the chamber pots with hot water and soda. The drinking-water bottles were emptied and wiped, and left ready for refilling in the evening when the beds were turned down. Three times a week in summer (less in winter for fear of damp) the floors were washed.

Washing the floor was rather more laborious than we know it today, with a mop and detergent. *The Lady's Every-Day Book* gave very clear instructions. Grease from candles was first removed by rubbing hard soap on the spot and scrubbing at it with a brush and cold water. Then a bar of soap was dissolved in two gallons of water by cutting it into pieces and heating until it melted. The dissolved soap was put in one bucket, fresh water in a second, water and vinegar in a third. A brush was dipped in the soapy water and the floor was scoured a square yard at a time, using as little water as possible. It was rubbed well with a coarse sponge to remove the soap and any dirt, and the sponge was rinsed in the clean water before being reused on the next part of the floor. A clean sponge was then dipped into the vinegar water and rubbed across the cleaned area, which was then wiped dry with coarse cloths before the servant moved on to the next area, hanging the drying cloths up to dry between patches.[31]

After the family had finished breakfast, the general servant put on a large bed-making apron, to protect the bed from her clothes, which were dirty once again, this time from the bedroom fires and slops, and from floor washing on the days she had done it. She was usually helped in making the beds by her mistress or the daughters of the house. Then she prepared whichever room was to have a thorough cleaning that day: anything that needed protecting from dust was moved out of the room, the rest was covered, and curtains and valances were pinned up out of the way. Rooms that were not going to get their weekly cleaning were quickly dusted, the washstands were cleaned, and the lamps and candlesticks were collected to take downstairs for cleaning, together with anything else that was dirty enough to need cleaning in the scullery.

Now the maid-of-all-work returned to the scullery, clearing the breakfast room on her way and sweeping the carpet again to remove any breakfast crumbs. The scullery was simply a bare room with a cement, tiled, or brick floor, a fireplace (sometimes), a counter, and a sink. If there was a copper—a separate boiler—for the laundry, it was to be found here. In the early part of the century, and in houses with only small or modest rents throughout the period, the sink frequently had the only tap for running water in the entire house. It was here that the maid-of-all-work did both the dishes and the breakfast pots and pans. If the house was large enough to have a separate pantry where the dishes and cutlery were washed, the family was most likely prosperous enough to afford two servants.

While the maid-of-all-work washed up, the mistress dusted the ornaments in the drawing room, which gave "an air of order and refinement to the room." The maid-of-all-work would then do the rest: dusting and cleaning the furniture, sweeping, cleaning the windows, mirrors, and grates, and doing any other rough work needed in the room.

Tradesmen called either daily or, preferably, on certain days each week; if there was only one servant, it was difficult for her to get through her work if the doorbell kept ringing. For this reason the postman, who made between six and twelve deliveries every day (depending on location), used an instrument that looked like a drumstick to make a double rap at the door; having recognized the knock, the servant did not have to run to open the door but could collect the letters when she had time. Sir Rowland Hill was the progenitor of the penny post, which for the first time made the sender, not the recipient, responsible for the cost. He saw this as timesaving for the carrier, not the household, but it was both. He enthused, "There would not only be no stopping to collect the postage, but probably it would soon be unnecessary even to await the opening of the door, as every house might be provided with a letter box into which the letter carrier would drop the letters, and having knocked, he would post on as fast as he could walk." He "posted" on, but was not yet known as the postman—he was still the letter carrier, and his mark of office was a quasi-military scarlet frock coat, with shiny buttons and ornamental cuffs, and a top hat with a gold-colored band. If he had a telegram, which had to be handed over personally, he duplicated his effort, giving a pair of double raps, so the servant would know to interrupt her work and open the door.[32]*

The principal cleaning for the day was done in the morning or after-noon, depending on when the main meal was served. If the family ate dinner at midday, the morning was spent getting the meal ready, and cleaning had to be postponed to the afternoon; if dinner was served in the evening (a more genteel, fashionable time), then the cleaning could be done in the morning. The dining room, breakfast room, bedrooms, kitchen, and scullery were cleaned every day as described; the other rooms each had a special day to be "turned out"—that is, cleaned and scrubbed thoroughly. Most houses operated on a system that ran more or less as follows:

Monday:	laundry
Tuesday:	servant's room,† one bedroom
Wednesday:	remaining bedrooms
Thursday:	drawing room, breakfast room, morning room
Friday:	dining room and polishing the silver
Saturday:	hall, stairs, kitchen, passageways
Sunday:	collect, sort, and soak laundry, to ready it for Monday

Having the main meal in the evening—which was not possible if there were children—made a single-handed servant's work easier. If the servant was expected to wait at table rather than simply bringing the food up, she could not be tidy at midday, having just finished cleaning the kitchen. In the evening, however, she would have had time to change into a clean uniform before the meal, and could protect it later by washing only the china and glass after dinner, leaving the scraped pots and pans stacked in the scullery until morning, when she would once more have her "dirty" dress on.

---

*The title of James M. Cain's 1934 novel, *The Postman Always Rings Twice*, reflected this many years after the actual knocking had ceased: telegrams signaled trouble. For more on postal deliveries, see pp. 260–61.

†If time was allowed for it at all. See p. 149.

Before beginning her preparations for dinner the maid put on a coarse apron. Half an hour before the meal she took it off to go upstairs and tidy the dining room: sweeping the carpet again, and possibly taking the cinders out. Then she laid the cloth and set the table. Before bringing the meal up she also needed to look into the drawing room to check the fire and close the curtains in winter or open the windows in summer. After she had brought the food up and everyone was seated at the table, she handed round the plates, then returned to the kitchen to dish up the second course. When the family left the dining room, she returned to clear the table, sweep up the crumbs once more, clean the hearth, and dust the furniture again. Then she could return to the kitchen to have her own dinner, after which she washed up, cleaned the kitchen again, and put on the kettle for tea, which earlier in the century many families had in the evening after their dinner at around five. (As dinner began to be served later in the evening, tea in turn was transferred to five o'clock.)

Then the maid was ready to wait on the family in the evening, "and employ the rest of her time in repairing or making her clothes."[33] She prepared the tea and, having changed her dress once more if she had washed up the pots and pans from dinner, carried it upstairs. She then drew the blinds throughout the house, closed the shutters, and prepared the bedrooms for the night. Then she cleared away tea and washed up, rinsing the tea leaves for use on the carpets in the morning. The final tasks were to put out all the fires and lamps, lock the front door, and turn off the gas—although these may have been tasks the master of the house liked to perform himself. In many households the silver plate was counted every night, put into a plate basket, and given to the master to keep in his room overnight, as security against burglars. The sole remaining chore before the servant could go to bed herself was to rake out the kitchen fire and lay it ready for the morning.

All this was regarded as normal, and not too much for one person. Indeed, Mrs. Beeton thought that "a bustling and active girl will always find time to do a little needlework for herself, if she lives with consistent and reasonable people. In the summer evenings she should manage to sit down for two or three hours, and for a short time in the afternoon in leisure days." Mrs. Warren agreed, adding that in her daily tasks, not too much equipment should be given to the maid-of-all-work, as any girl, no matter how much work she had to get through, "should find time to wash three cloths in a day," for constant reuse.[34] "Cre-fydd," the pseudonymous author of a housekeeping manual, conflated effort and result when she said that if every room was thoroughly turned out once a week, including washing the paintwork, beating the carpets, cleaning the windows, and brushing the walls and curtains, "the house is always clean, and with very little labour."[35]

Many housewives interiorized this concept. Mrs. Gaskell wrote to her daughter, "All our new servants do very nicely. To be sure we are a very small family, and there is proportionably very little work to be done." There were three children at home, which was not many, it is true, but her letters for the year show a house constantly filled with visitors. In one week she had "Uncle Sam" for two nights, "Annie and Ellen Green" for another two, and Selina "in a great deal." Later that year came "lectures, two dinners, one concert card party at home . . . company in the house" plus "Mr and Mrs Wedgwood, Dot and Jane . . . Annie and Ellen Green, closely packed!"—all staying for different lengths of time.[36] Hardly a sinecure for the servants. The Mayhew brothers put it more crudely in *The Greatest Plague of Life*. When the narrator's new servant arrived, she "was so quick over her work, that after I had made her scrub all the house well down, from top to bottom, and clean all the paint, and take up and beat all the carpets, and give all the furniture, and tins, and coppers, and stoves, a thorough good rubbing . . . I was hard put to it to find some odd jobs to keep her fully employed; for I had no idea of paying servants the wages I did to support them in idleness." The narrator's husband commented on how nice the new servant made everything look, which only fueled her wrath:

> Of course I told him it was like his impudence . . . how on earth he could ever be such a stupid as to fancy that the improved appearance of the house was all owing to Norah, and how much work he thought she would have done if I had not always been looking after her . . . I told him moreover I was sorry to see that

he was very ready to compliment Norah, though he never thought it worth his while to trouble his head for an instant about the labour and fatigue I had gone through, in being obliged to keep dancing all the day long at the girl's heels, as I had done."[37]

Hannah Cullwick's diaries record a routine not much different from what is outlined above, apart from the time set aside for needlework and rest, which she never got.* (She wrote her diary late at night, and it is not surprising that when she moved to Munby's chambers and had no further need to tell him of her day, she showed no inclination to continue with it.) The perpetual cleaning and recleaning was a reality, not simply advice-book fantasy. In 1860 Hannah was general servant to an upholsterer in Kilburn:

[14 July 1860] Opened the shutters & lighted the kitchen fire. Shook my sooty things in the dusthole & emptied the soot there. Swept & dusted the rooms & the hall. Laid the hearth & got breakfast up. Clean'd 2 pairs of boots. Made the beds & emptied the slops. Clean'd & wash'd the breakfast things up. Clean'd the plate; clean'd the knives & got the dinner things up. Clean'd away. Clean'd the kitchen up; unpack'd a hamper. Took two chickens to Mrs Brewer's & brought the message back. Made a tart & pick'd [i.e., plucked] & gutted two ducks & roasted them. Clean'd the steps & flags on my knees. Blackleaded the scraper in front of the house; clean'd the street flags too on my knees. Wash'd up in the scullery. Clean'd the pantry on my knees & scour'd the tables. Scrubbed the flags around the house & clean'd the window sills. Got tea at 9 for the master & Mrs Warwick in my dirt, but Ann [the nursemaid] carried it up. Clean'd the privy

*The context of Hannah Cullwick's diaries must always be borne in mind. There is no question that she did the work she described, and probably more. However, she wrote the diaries only at the request of Arthur Munby, and she was of course aware of his attraction to working women and dirt. His description of seeing her in her kitchen (pp. 103–4) leaves no doubt that the work was every bit as filthy as she described, but it must always be remembered that her insistence on it was twofold.

& passage & scullery on my knees. Wash'd the dog & clean'd the sinks down. Put the supper ready for Ann to take up, for I was too dirty & tired to go upstairs. Wash'd in a bath and to bed without feeling any the worse of yesterday [when she had gone up the chimney to sweep it].

[16 July 1860] Lighted the fire. Brush'd the grates. Clean'd the hall & steps & flags on my knees. Swept & dusted the rooms. Got breakfast up. Made the beds & emptied the slops. Clean'd & wash'd up & clean'd the plate. Clean'd the stairs & the pantry on my knees. Clean'd the knives & got dinner. Clean'd 3 pairs of boots. Clean'd away after dinner & began the preserving about ½ past 3 & kept on till 11, leaving off only to get the supper & have my tea. Left the kitchen dirty & went to bed very tired & dirty.

[31 July 1860] This is the last day of July. I have cleaned 83 pairs of boots [this month] . . . been to . . . church not at all; been out no were [*sic*] but on errands . . . I've been busy cleaning windows & glasses this month, for the flies & the dust make so much dirt. My hands are very coarse & hardish, but not more so than usual. Mrs J. [her employer] has very white hands & she often comes & lays her hand lightly on mine for me to feel how cold they are— we say it's to show the difference more than anything.[38]

This perhaps was not as bad as a later employer, who went with her family to watch the procession marking the arrival of Princess Alexandra in London for her marriage to the Prince of Wales. Hannah was left at home:

Clean'd away upstairs & wash'd the things up. Put coals on the fire. Went up & made all the beds & emptied the slops. Came down & swept the dining room all over & dusted it. Swept the hall & steps & shook the mats . . . Clean'd the windows in the hall & passage & clean'd the hall & steps on my knees, the back stairs, then I was got to the passage. I took the matting out & shook it. Swept the passage & took the things out of the hole under the stairs—Mary uses it for her dustpans & brushes. It's a dark hole & about 2 yards long & very low. I crawl'd in on my hands & knees . . . I got the handbrush & swept the walls down. The cobwebs & dust fell all over me & I had to poke my nose out o' the door to get breath, like a dog's out of a kennel. Then I swept the floor of it & got my pail & clean'd it out & put the things back in their places. I was very black as I could be, but I didn't wash till I'd clean'd the passage & 'tatoe hole out & the shelves & back cellar, & then I finish'd in the kitchen & made the fires up & wash'd my face & hands . . . The first part of the family came back at six & was ready for tea. The Mistress said she was very glad to be at home again, it'd been such a hard day for her. She said that as I carried the umbrella over her from the front gate.[39]

Munby once recorded that Hannah cried in her sleep from sheer exhaustion.[40] The only surprise is that it was just once.

When comparing Hannah's account of her days with the itemized lists in the advice books, the most noticeable difference is that hardly any of the books set aside time for the servants to clean their own rooms. Advice books that set out a cleaning schedule, with details of rooms to be cleaned weekly or fortnightly, frequently failed to allow time for the servants' rooms to be cleaned. The number of authors who then complained that servants were dirty, or did not keep their rooms nicely, is striking, including Mrs. Beeton in her hugely influential *Household Management*. Mrs. Panton, another who did not schedule in time for servants' own cleaning, warned that the mistress would have to check her servants' rooms regularly, "for notwithstanding the School Board and the amount of education given nowadays to the poorer classes, I am continually astonished at the careless disregard of the simplest rules of health and cleanliness shown by girls who ought to know a great deal better." The virtuous Mrs. Panton said she would have liked to "give each maid a really pretty room, but at present they are a little hopeless on this subject . . . No sooner is the room put nice than something happens to destroy its beauty; and I really believe servants only feel happy if their rooms are allowed in some measure to resemble the homes of their youth, and to be merely places where they lie down to sleep as heavily as they can. The simpler, therefore, a servant's room is furnished, the better." However, bedding and toiletware should be marked for each servant—"that is to say, that the property should be marked 'Cook,' 'Housemaid,' 'Parlourmaid' . . . [for] this individualises each single thing."[41]

As with cleaning, so with meals—few books allowed for servants' mealtimes in their schedules, leaving the servants to fit their meals around family meals and their own work. When the books did discuss servants' food, the main concern was not when they ate but the need to ensure that they did not eat more than their allowance. Mrs. Eliot James, in *Our Servants*, was one of the few authors to deal with the subject. She was aware that servants resented the inferior food they were usually given, and recommended that their main meal should include meat from the same joint the family was eating: "There is less reason for grumbling, if the servants know that their food is the same." Still, she did not go too far: "I do not say that any delicacies . . . in the way of game, entrees, sweets, are all to be finished up."[42] Most servants received nothing like these things. Arthur Munby was shocked when, after their marriage, Hannah Cullwick told him that she was eating the "wing of a fowl" for the first time: "What? said I—then what parts *have* you eaten? 'Only the bones . . . we never expect to get anything else—we common servants!' "[43] Ursula Bloom recorded her mother's view that the maids should not have the same food as the family, "because that would have been demoralizing for discipline, and might have given them ideas."[44]

Servants who thought they were above their station were particularly worrisome. *Punch* ran endless cartoons of servant girls in fashionable dresses, the humor of that in itself being so exquisite that rarely was an actual joke appended. The Mayhews in *The Greatest Plague of Life* told of the narrator's horror of a servant "whose godfathers and godmothers (stupid people) had christened [her] Rosetta, as if she had been a Duchess. As of course I wasn't going to have any of my menials answering to a stuck-up name like that, I gave her to understand that I should allow no such thing in *my* house, indeed, but I would take the liberty of altering pretty Rosetta into plain Susan." The worry for the narrator, only just of the middle class herself, was that she might be confused with those beneath her: Rosetta/Susan appeared on May Day, and "drat her impudence! if she hadn't on each side of her head got a bunch of long ringlets . . . hanging half down to her waist, and a blonde-lace cap, with cherry-coloured rosettes, and streamers flying about nearly a yard long; while on looking at her feet, if the conceited bit of goods hadn't got on patent leather shoes . . ." Her employer made her change her clothes, so that when she went to church, "the girl . . . was no longer dressed out as showily as if she was the mistress instead of the maid."[45]

Earlier in the century, most servants had not worn uniforms; the difference between cheap and good fabric was immediately visible, and the elaborations of fashion ensured that the working classes dressed nothing like their betters. It was only in the 1850s and 1860s, with the arrival of new manufacturing methods and cheap cotton imports from India, that uniforms had to be created so that servants could continue to be differentiated from their mistresses on sight. Even then, some of the differences between good clothes and the rest remained visible, whatever the precariously stationed might have thought. In Samuel Butler's *The Way of All Flesh*, Ernest Pontifex returns home after many years' estrangement from his parents. He has, unknown to them, inherited money, but they think him indigent. On his arrival, his father sees "at a glance that Ernest was appointed as though money were abundant with him . . . swaggering in a grey Ulster and a blue and white neck-tie," and is deeply annoyed.[46] By midcentury, many large cities had shops called Servants' Bazaars, which sold uniforms. Lewis's of Liverpool sold gift parcels for employers to give their servants at Christmas: "seven yards of double-width black merino, two yards of lining, one striped skirt, and half a dozen linen handkerchiefs"—in other words, the material for the servant to make her own uniform.[47] This fear of confusion also manifested itself in rules of behavior designed to keep employer and employed apart. Servants were not to speak until spoken to; they were to stand in their employers' presence; they were not to walk beside them on the street.[48]

Hannah Cullwick knew her place well. When her employer's adult daughter went visiting in the evening, Hannah went to fetch her home—servants could walk alone in the streets at night when a middle-class woman could not. (For more on women in the streets, see pp. 399–402.) She told "Miss Margaret" that it had been raining earlier, and "she said, 'Then I'll have my cloak & galoshes on,' & I stoop'd down & put them on for her, & the cloak. Then she give me a parcel & the umbrella to carry & we come out . . . Miss M. walks so *very* slow, it's tiring to keep behind enough."[49]

It was essential that the occupations of servants and employers were never confused. In *East Lynne*, Joyce Hallijohn, a model servant who keeps to her place, describes her sister Afy, who does not: "Her notions were fine, and her dress was fine; she was gay and giddy and very pretty, and would do nothing all day but read books . . . My father did not like it: we were only plain, working people, and she wanted to set up for a lady—the effect of bringing her up above her station."[50] Novel-reading was a serious matter. Acquaintances of Jane Carlyle were without a servant when they had to suddenly dismiss one "because 'she lied,' and 'was curious,' and 'read novels.' "[51] That Jane Carlyle put these reasons for dismissal in quotation marks at first might seem to imply that she found them unlikely. But probably not: she had a passion for quotation marks, and certainly thought dishonesty and curiosity unacceptable in a servant. Being overheard by the servants was one peril of the sort of small house she lived in, and having bells to summon servants in houses where everyone was always within calling distance was another attempt to maintain the illusion of separation and privacy.

Her friend Geraldine Jewsbury had no doubt that curiosity was a sacking matter. She wrote:

> With regard to that little servant of yours—I would not keep her if I were you; such a development of curiosity will surely be fatal to any mistress under the sun. It will not confine itself to inspecting letters, and all that, but it will show itself in listening to private conversations, and in prying into all your comings and

goings; and servants are so coarse in all their thoughts that they can understand nothing they see, but put the most abominable construction on all that passes. The best of them are uneducated in all their ideas, and those who are professedly curious and prying will not be bound by any laws of gratitude for kindness they may receive, and any respect they ought to feel. That girl will do you a mischief if she stays with you, and me, too, if she gets hold of this letter and reads.[52]

Others shared Jewsbury's overt fear of the working class. Mary Elizabeth Braddon was a successful popular novelist, and part of her success was predicated on her echoing precisely what her readers thought. In her best-seller *Aurora Floyd*, a lurid tale of bigamy and betrayal in high life, she replicated middle-class views of servants' attitudes toward their masters: "Your servants listen at your doors, and repeat your spiteful speeches in the kitchen, and watch you while they wait at table, and understand every sarcasm, every innuendo, every look . . . Nothing that is done in the parlour is lost upon these quiet, well-behaved watchers from the kitchen."[53]

Yet this fear worked both ways. Hannah Cullwick's fellow servant Clara bought a music box. "It's a nice box & sounds well," Hannah wrote in her diary, "but I'm afraid it's too loud, & will be . . . heard upstairs, & I shall always be afraid of it." Clara later decorated the kitchen for the servants' Christmas:

It was certainly very gay-looking & pretty. Colour'd paper cut & done in festoons all round the top o' the kitchen, & holly trimmings around the lower part [& on] one side o' the kitchen hung a picture of Jesus in the manger, Joseph & Mary & the wise men & the oxen there too in the stall. Then under the picture was a table spread with presents for each of us, & nuts, biscuits & oranges too, [&] in the middle was the box o' music playing & a dozen colour'd candles burning. All very pleasing & gay to the senses, but with it all I felt afraid it was *too much*—too much, for Missis to hear of & Miss Margaret to see, for Missis wouldn't

allow us 6d. worth of holly & have none themselves. I didn't like
to tell Clara but I felt that it was hardly safe.[54]

"Hardly safe"—what a terrible thing to have to say about a bit of colored paper.

The assumption that all servants were prone to dishonesty if not
kept on the path of righteousness by their employers meant that a
good housewife ought, for their sake, to keep everything locked and
under her supervision. In Anne Brontë's *The Tenant of Wildfell Hall*
(1848), in Gilbert Markham's mother's house—presented as the model
of domestic felicity, both moral and physical—the tea tray is brought
into the parlor by the maid, but it is Gilbert's sister who gets the sugar
and tea from a locked cupboard in the sideboard, where both are
kept.[55] Bad households had servants who drank and stole their masters'
possessions, either for their own consumption or to sell. The Pockets'
house in *Great Expectations* was obviously a bad one because all Mrs.
Pocket did was read, and as a result "the cook [was] lying insensibly
drunk on the kitchen floor, with a large bundle of fresh butter made up
in the cupboard ready to sell for grease!"[56] Servants who were given
their mistress's cast-off clothing would invariably "help the mistress
not to save, but to spoil her clothes, so as to hurry them into their own
pockets, and grudge her every day she wears them."[57] The clothes
ought not to be given to the servants in any case, because they were not
suitable and would give the servants ideas above their station.

Employers had a moral duty to behave in a way that would reinforce their servants' notion of their place. In *David Copperfield*, Dora
is unable to manage her household. The result, says her husband, "is
not merely . . . that we lose money and comfort, and even temper
sometimes, by not learning to be more careful; but that we incur the
serious responsibility of spoiling every one who comes into our service, or has any dealings with us . . . unless we learn to do our duty to
those whom we employ, they will never learn to do their duty to us. I
am afraid we present opportunities to people to do wrong."[58] The need
to improve servants—against their will, if necessary—showed itself in
numerous ways. Geraldine Jewsbury noted with approval that a prof-

ligate servant had been taken in hand by her employer, who "now refuses to give her any [money; presumably her wages], but has undertaken to spend it for her."[59]

The idea that all servants were dishonest was apparently ineradicable. Mrs. Warren suggested that if the mistress was not well enough to go down to the kitchen to check the contents of the larder every day, she should "have the remnants of food [from the day before] brought" to her. This was to prevent servants from dishonestly eating more than they should, which needed constant vigilance. "A maid-of-all-work should never be permitted to carve for herself," and if any food was ever missing the employer should always ask where it was, to keep such a loss from occurring again. The mistress should supervise the cutting of every loaf of bread, or the servants "will give it to beggars, who will throw it away." They could not "be left to their own guidance, but must be ruled." Soap, candles, matches should all be handed out only as needed; otherwise servants would run riot with them.[60]

The goods that servants were given for their own consumption were similarly rationed. Mrs. Haweis recommended three-quarters of a pound of soap per servant per week, for both bathing and washing the servant's smaller items of laundry.[61] That was about average. Many households still operated on the old-fashioned system of allowances— so much money was "allowed" each servant weekly for tea, for beer, for laundry. During the century the price of tea and beer dropped, and consequently allowance money gradually began to be phased out, except for the laundry allowance, which remained the norm. Toward the end of the century it was usually about 1s. a week for female servants, on the understanding that they washed their own caps, cuffs, collars, and other small items. Male servants were allowed about 1s. 6d., because they were not expected to do any of their own laundry.[62]

Laundry was an expensive business, and a major part of any household budget. If laundry was done at home, at least two people were needed. Women with only one servant were actively involved in washday; those with two either did the laundry with one servant or took over the second servant's tasks while she gave all her time to the laundry at least one day a week. A woman with one servant might co-opt a daughter, thus allowing the servant to continue with her daily routine. In houses with more spare cash, a laundress could be hired to come in by the day. If the washing was sent out the disruption and trouble were lessened, but many feared infection from the "promiscuous" mixing of their laundry with that of unknown others.* (Whiteley's Department Store opened a laundry department in 1892; it became successful only when it began to separate each household's laundry and indicated this segregation by returning the servants' laundry wrapped in paper of a different color.)[64] If laundry was sent out, the sensible householder ensured that the baskets of clean clothes were never taken upstairs, unpacking them instead in the kitchen and hanging everything before the fire for a time to be aired and checked for any bugs that might be lurking.[65] The assumption that servants were somehow hardier (as seen earlier; see pp. 136–37), so that it did not matter if the potentially infectious garments were aired in the servants' quarters, was always unspoken. Hannah Cullwick did not notice it when a friend of "Miss Margaret," who worked in a Ragged School, sent some books to be recovered: "The old ones was dirty, & poor Missis was so afrai'd they might give smallpox or something that she sent 'em down to be done in the kitchen & I help'd to do them."[66]

Having a laundress come to the house every week was safer than sending laundry out, although costly: the amount of coal used for boiling water all day was great, soap and other ingredients were not particularly cheap, and in the 1860s a laundress cost between 1s. 6d. and

---

*Dr. R. Hall Bakewell noted an instance where a woman he was treating had a child with scarlatina, or scarlet fever. She "begged me not to mention [it] . . . as otherwise it would get to the laundress's ears, and she would refuse to take the clothes. Such a request was exceedingly wrong. The danger of communicating scarlatina by means of clothes worn by a patient is very great . . . and . . . when it is known, as it most probably will be in the end, the poor laundress will lose her customers immediately." So far, so sensible. He went on, however, "It happened in this case that the lady's laundress was mine also, and I immediately gave directions to send no more things to her." Note that he did not inform the "poor laundress" but instead became one of those customers she lost, even though telling her would have removed the risk for him and solved her problem; rather, he was loyal to his prosperous patient and looked out for himself. For more on the unpleasant Dr. Bakewell, see pp. 344–46.[63]

2s. a day. By the 1870s her price had risen to between 2s. and 2s. 6d. a day, plus she expected perks—usually beer three times a day and gin and water at night. Laundry costs could reach £6–£10 a year for a family that was paying only £25 a year in rent and £70 for food.[67] These costs were so substantial in comparison to the rest of the household budget that when people stayed with friends they expected to be presented with their washing bill on departure.[68]

Until 1885, soap was sold in long bars to grocers; they cut off a portion with a wire, as cheese is cut today, and sold it by weight. Various brands had monopolies in different areas, so the type of soap available depended on the area. Soap was advertised to the kind of housewives who did their own laundry, but in the midcentury this practice was still in its infancy. The advertisement below shows perhaps why Mr. Harper Twelvetrees' Manufactory, which made penny packets of soap powder, did not become the market leader:

A FRIENDLY BIT OF CHIT-CHAT BETWEEN MRS. SCRUBWELL AND MRS. THRIFTY.

[SCRUBWELL.] Good morning, Neighbour Thrifty. How are you and your family? But how is this? I understood you had your "week's wash" today, and I expected to find you "up to the elbows" in suds; instead of which, here is a clean dry house, and the dinner-table all in apple-pie order, ready for your husband on his coming from work. Are you going to put off your wash till next week?

THRIFTY. Why neighbour, *I have done my washing!* I began at a little before 9 o'clock this morning, have washed every rag of clothes, and look, there they are on the lines in the garden, nearly dry.

SCRUBWELL. Well, I *am* surprised. But do you mean to say that you have washed all that lot of clothes this morning. *Impossible, surely!*

THRIFTY. Impossible or not, *it is quite true.*

SCRUBWELL. You amaze me, neighbour. How have you done it, and who have you had to help you?

THRIFTY. Oh, it is easy enough to get rid of the slap-dash, steam, and dribbling-slops on a washing-day, in good time. I can always make quick work of *my* washing by using "Harper Twelvetrees' Glycerine Soap-Powder," and it makes the clothes beautifully clean and white too, I assure you. I scarcely ever rub our clothes now, and you know how black my Jim's shirts get at the Foundry.

SCRUBWELL. But how do you get the clothes clean if you do not rub them well?

THRIFTY. I mean that I don't often find it necessary to rub them after I take them out of the soaking water. Of course, I always soak the white clothes over night, and soap the collars and wristbands of shirts, and rub the part most soiled; but I don't stand rubbing the clothes to pieces, and rubbing the skin off my hands at the wash-tub all the next day, as some people do.

SCRUBWELL. Well, this is really wonderful! I had no idea that washing-day could be got over with so little trouble and labour. I think I shall try this wonderful powder . . .[69]

That was addressed to a working-class market. It was only in 1885 when W. H. Lever began to sell his soap in one-pound bars, already wrapped, that a brand became generally recognizable to the middle-class customer. Lever also focused on the working classes and the lower end of the middle-class market, who did their own laundry, and for them he wrote a handbook, "Sunlight Soap and How to Use It," to promote his brand. Pears soap began advertising at the same time, aiming for middle-class customers.[70]

It was this end of the market that was most concerned with laundry. With cleanliness being next to godliness, lack thereof was a social stigma. If the money was not available, the housewife could quite simply not be as clean as she wished, which brought "a sense of degradation . . . cleanliness is a costly thing, and a troublesome thing," noted the narrator of Gissing's *New Grub Street*.[71] The morality of regular laundering was well to the fore, as a nursery rhyme of the time showed:

They that wash on Monday
Have all the week to dry.
They that wash on Tuesday
Are not so much awry.
They that wash on Wednesday
Are not so much to blame.
They that wash on Thursday
Wash for very shame.
They that wash on Friday
Wash in sorry need.
They that wash on Saturday
Are lazy sluts indeed.[72]

Monday was the only proper day to begin a wash; it became known in advertisements of the time as Blue Monday, which gives an idea of the upheaval involved, as well as nodding toward the blue dye used in the process (see p. 161). Some houses did the laundry once a fortnight to minimize the disruption, but most could not afford enough clothes to keep them a full two weeks without washing.

The first thing to be done in the weekly process was to sort the laundry on Saturday or Sunday, checking each item and entering it in a washing book, so that at the end of the process everything could be checked off again. (Households that sent some laundry out and kept the smaller things at home were advised to keep two separate washing books.) Sheets, towels, men's collars, linens, "body linen" (that is, underwear), men's shirts, nightclothes, aprons, petticoats, and diapers were separated out; then fine muslins; colored cottons and linens; woollens; delicate items like women's collars and cuffs, decorative handkerchiefs, and babies' best dresses; and finally very dirty items—kitchen cloths, household dusters, cloths used to clean out chamber pots, and so on. Each item was looked over, with each stain examined and a decision taken on how to treat it based on the type of fabric and the type of stain. Sheets and linens were covered with lukewarm water and a little soda and left overnight; greasy cloths were soaked in a solution of half a pound of unslaked lime to six quarts of water, boiled for two hours, then left to settle, strained, rinsed again in a new lime solution, and left overnight.

On Monday, if the house had only one servant, it was recommended that she get up two hours earlier than usual to light the fire, clean the washtubs and any machinery—a wringer, a mangle—that the household had, and then get through her ordinary work while her mistress made and served the breakfast. The meal would be the only hot one that day, as the range and its boiler would both be devoted entirely to heating water for the washing. Even houses that had a copper needed additional water from the range. The copper, located in the scullery, made laundry much simpler. It held about twenty gallons of water at a time, which sounds like a lot, but a single wash—consisting of washing, boiling, and rinsing—took fifty gallons. The water in the copper came to a boil more quickly than pans of water on the range, as the fire was completely enclosed, although its small, restricted chimney then had to be cleaned more frequently than the chimney of the range. (The laundress often did this with gunpowder; the process was called "skying the copper.") The copper was more economical because it saved time, and also because cinders could be used to heat it, instead of new, fresh coal. (For these reasons, it was often used to boil large puddings, especially Christmas pudding.) The enclosed fire of the copper also meant that one of the main hazards of laundry in the kitchen could be avoided. On a standard range the boiling water regularly slopped over the pan's edges onto the open fire. This filled the room with soot and ash, some of which fell back into the pan, filthying the water and the clothes in it.[73]

As soon as the water was hot, the sheets and other linens were taken out of their overnight soaking water, rinsed in hot water ladled out of the copper, and rubbed or beaten with a dolly or a possing stick. A dolly was a wooden stick with what looked like a miniature stool at one end; a possing stick resembled a lavatory plunger made of copper, and it worked by suction. Either could be used in a washtub, or in a special wooden tub with a lid with a slot which the dolly or the possing stick went through. The sheets were then wrung out, and the water was thrown away. A bar of soap—there were as yet no detergents[*]—was shaved, cut into pieces, and dissolved in boiling water to form a jelly. The jelly was rubbed through the sheets. Then the water was added to transform the whole to a soapy mass, and the sheets were agitated again. More water—as hot as could be borne by the laundress—was added, and the sheets were rubbed a third time. The water was thrown out, more was taken from the copper, and the items were put in their first rinse, then wrung out. They were then put in the copper itself, together with one teaspoon of soda to every two gallons of water, and boiled for an hour and a half, to remove the soap thoroughly. After the boiling the sheets were taken out, rinsed a third time in another tub of boiling water, and then a fourth in a final tub of cold water, which had had "blue" put in it. The soaps of the time had a tendency to turn whites yellow, and blue was a lump of dye used to counteract this. It was tied in a piece of cloth and then mixed well through the water before the items were added. If the laundress mixed carelessly, the wash came out marked with yellow and white streaks. After the blue rinse, everything was wrung out for a third and

A very tidy housemaid stirs clothes in the copper. The fuel was behind the door in the middle, and the water was drained out by the tap in the center.

final time, and hung up to dry. Thus, the first—and simplest—load of laundry took one soaking, two washes, one boiling, and four rinses: eight different processes.

[*]The first photochemical detergent, which cleaned in the hardest or coldest of waters, was produced only in 1907, in Germany; until then, boiling water had to be used. If cold water was needed for the fabric, the soap was treated as described here and then the water was allowed to cool.

Other items had other requirements. Cotton clothes, for instance, were taken out of their soaking water and put straight into hot soapy water and rubbed, stains having been first scrubbed directly with the soap jelly. Then they were wrung out, rinsed, and wrung out again before being put in the copper, which this time had soapy water in it. Depending on the strength of the fabric and the amount of dirt, they were left to boil for anything from an hour to the whole afternoon, while the laundress watched and repeatedly skimmed off the dirty froth that boiled up to the surface. Then they were rinsed in hot water, then in tepid water, then in cold water, which again contained blue.

Wringing out heavy fabrics, sodden with boiling water, was made easier by the arrival of wringing machines, which had a crank to turn rubber rollers that pressed out the moisture. In D. H. Lawrence's *The Rainbow*, Anna is given one by her father, who explains, "You screw it on to the side o' your wash-tub." This was at the very end of the century, but these devices were to be found in many middle-class houses from the 1850s. Anna, in her scullery, "turn[s] blissfully at the handle, [with] Tilly beside her, exclaiming, 'My word, that's a natty little thing! That'll save you lugging your inside out . . . It fair runs by itself.'"[74]

Most items could not be handled as described above. Many colored fabrics had impermanent dyes, woollens shrank, muslins were too delicate: all these had to be treated separately, gently, and very quickly, in waters of differing temperatures with different additives to protect them—salt for woollens, bran for colored prints and cretonnes. Where possible, woollens and silks in particular were not washed at all but were brushed, and dabbed with benzene and other cleaning fluids. Mauves and violets had their color preserved by being washed in water that had soda in it (although some violets had a nasty tendency to be damaged *only* by soda); dark green was maintained by alum or vinegar; blue by salt; brown and gray by ox-gall, bought from the butcher. Other colors were preserved by sugar of lead or oil of vitriol, from the chemist: both were poisonous (vitriol is sulphuric acid), and if too much of either was used it ate through the fabric it was intended to save. Pepper protected cambric; "three large handfuls of fresh green

A mangle, 1895. By now machines with rubber rollers did both the wringing
(to remove water) and mangling (to smooth dry items before pressing).

ivy leaves" was recommended for rinsing prints. Pinks and light greens
could be washed with impunity but lost their original coloring when
they were ironed.

Without chemical detergents, stains were a serious problem. Many
instructions were given for removing marks created by common
household accidents: grease from candles and oil from lamps could be
removed by turpentine mixed with fuller's earth and applied directly
to the stain, or by stale bread rubbed on the stain; wax from candles
was removed by a hot coal wrapped in linen or brown paper and
applied to the stain. Ink came out with lemon juice, fruit stains were
washed in hot milk.[75] Special items, or items with more than one type
of fabric in them, needed to be picked apart, to have each part washed

separately, and then to be resewn. Hannah Cullwick noted washing "my red stuff frock after I picked the body [bodice] from the skirt."[76]

Once the washing was complete, at the end of the first full day of laundry, the clothes were, ideally, hung outside—that is, if the weather permitted, and if the house was not located too near a factory whose unpleasant smells and chimney ash covered the neighborhood, and indeed if the house had a garden in the first place. If any of these conditions could not be met, then the laundry had to be dried in the kitchen, usually on a clotheshorse that could be hauled out of the way, up to the ceiling, from where the clothes dripped on everyone's head. Grace Foakes, the child of laborers, remembered that "the ceiling [of the kitchen] was not very high and most of the time the washing was dangling on our heads. The place was damp and smelly, with steam running down the windows and walls. Sometimes in bad weather the washing took two or three days to dry."[77] One of the benefits of Sir Titus Salt's model town, Saltaire, built on the edge of Bradford in the 1850s, was that it had a town laundry for the residents.[78]

Even after this herculean effort the housewife had not nearly finished her task. Items that needed starching were, once dried, dealt with separately, usually on the following day. Ordinary starch was made of potato or rice flour, diluted in water and boiled before use. It was not easy to get just the right consistency: too thick, and the starch failed to adhere to the fabric; too thin, and the materials did not stiffen. Items to be cold-starched—mainly men's shirts—were dipped in the starch solution, then rolled up until they were ironed. Hot starching was a more complicated process. Hot starch was made from a mixture of starch, melted borax, and candle wax, diluted with water and simmered to a jelly. The items treated with this glutinous mass were mainly frilled: caps, aprons, babies' clothes, petticoats, nightgowns. The frills were dipped into the starch while it was simmering, and were ironed once they had dried. Fabrics too delicate for starch were treated with isinglass, milk, or diluted glue to stiffen them.[79]

Ironing was done much as it is today, with the single difference that there was no way of keeping an iron consistently hot over the neces-

Many houses had no garden in which to dry clothes, or they were too near a factory belching soot or odors. Indoor clotheshorses were designed to dry clothes in the kitchen out of the way. The hanging clothes dripped for days, creating an atmosphere that was saturated with damp.

sary period. Mangles were used to give sheets, tablecloths, and linens a smooth finish before they were ironed.* Then flatirons were used in pairs: one sat heating on the range or a trivet by an open fire while the second one was in use, and, as the second began to lose heat, they were exchanged. Because the fire made the irons sooty, they had to be cleaned each time they were heated, with a cloth or a piece of ironing rubber. The starch stuck to the bottom too, and it had to be cleaned off with kerosene, the iron then being wiped with sandpaper or rubbed on an emery board, as knives were. Mrs. Nubbles does this in *The Old Curiosity Shop*, "coming to the fireplace for another iron . . . rubb[ing] it on a board and dust[ing] it with a duster."[80]

A cleaner type of iron was a box iron, which had a hollow core. Inside was placed a piece of iron that had been heated in the fire. This type of iron was lighter than a flatiron, however, and therefore did not press the creases out as easily, which meant it was mostly reserved for

*Technically, mangles were for items that were already dry; wringers were for wet items. But after the 1860s dual-purpose machines appeared on the market which did both wringing and mangling. As these machines were known as mangles, the belief evolved that "mangling" means only removing water from wet items.

The inconvenience of drying clothes in the kitchen meant that often they were
put away still damp. To solve this, clothes and sheets were often aired in front
of the fire before use. E. H. Shepard's nursemaid aired his nightshirt over the
gas every evening instead. (Note the fireguard in front of the fireplace,
common in rooms used by children.)

delicate items. So too were goffering irons, which looked like modern
hair-curling tongs and were used on babies' clothes, underclothes, the
trim on women's dresses, and ribbons.

After all this, and after the clothes had been checked to ensure that
no mending was necessary after the many rubbings, wringings, and
manglings they had received, everything was aired before the fire to be
certain no damp remained. Airing was rarely neglected, as many illnesses were thought to come from damp sheets and clothes. The Rev.
J. P. Faunthorpe in a book for girls said, "It is a highly criminal act to
put out for use sheets, or shirts, unaired," and Ernest Shepard, the
illustrator of *Winnie-the-Pooh*, in a memoir of his Victorian child-

hood, remembered how every night he sat in his combinations, all-in-one underwear that covered the shoulders, torso, and thighs, while his nursemaid aired his nightshirt by passing it to and fro over the gas jet.[81]

The airing was, however, the last of the week's laundry work: everything was now folded and returned to the cupboards, with luck by Friday at the latest—to begin again just two days later.

5

THE DRAWING ROOM

THE DRAWING ROOM was the center of the house, literally and spiritually. It was the status indicator, the mark of gentility, the room from where the woman governed her domain. It was not the living room of today's families—the dining room more commonly performed the functions of the modern living room or family room—but was instead a formal room for entertaining. The wife, the family, and the house were the outward indicators of a man's success in the world; it was not the ownership of the property that mattered, in an age when rental was the norm, but the appropriate style of living within the property. To fail to live up to the man of the house's success was as bad as actually failing. Mrs. Ellis, in her influential *The Wives of England*, thought it "scarcely necessary . . . to point out . . . the loss of character and influence occasioned by living below our station."[1] Thus no good housewife hoping to make her way socially could afford to neglect any part of her house; Mrs. Panton reminded her readers that even the hall would "disclose immediately to the eyes of the caller that here is the abode of people who care for their home . . . and who thus denote that they are worth cultivating, for no doubt they will turn out to be desirable friends."[2]

However, trying too hard was a black mark, an indication of inse-
curity. In Gissing's *New Grub Street*, Mrs. Yule lives in Westbourne
Park, west London, in one of the new suburbs. Although she decorates
carefully, it fools no one: "It was a small house, and rather showily
than handsomely furnished; no one after visiting it would be astonished to hear that Mrs Edmund Yule had but a small income, and that
she was often put to desperate expedients to keep up the gloss of easy
circumstances."3 To reduce the style of the reception rooms would
have reduced Mrs. Yule socially, yet she could not live up to her drawing room. For those with limited means, the only way to achieve the
necessary finish was to skimp on the parts of the house—the bedrooms
and kitchen in particular—where no guests ever went. *Building News*
noted that "bedroom accommodation is in many of [the terraces] deficient in proportion to the size of the house; everything is sacrificed to
the sitting rooms."4

Skimping was bad; so too was overdecorating in relation to one's
income. An elaborate drawing room was inappropriate for "the master of the house, who has to work so hard for his £300, or something
less, a year," warned "MBH" in *Home Truths for Home Peace*, a volume that promised to be "A Practical Inquiry into What Chiefly Mars
or Makes the Comfort of Domestic Life." After all, "when *he* comes
in tired from business, he will certainly expect to sit down *somewhere*,
and here, you would as soon think of introducing a bull into a china
shop, as of beholding a man, after a day in the city and a dusty walk
home, stretching himself at ease in such a boudoir as this." The room
was, inappropriately, "handsome enough for the richest banker's lady.
This boudoir and appointments belong to an income twenty times as
large as any which their possessors ever dream of, and to a style of living with which their *every-day* existence forms a most striking contrast."5 It was not the decoration itself that was at fault; it was the
pairing of the decoration with an income that did not match it. Not living up to one's income was bad; trying too hard was worse; the greatest sin of all was living above one's income.

So when Mrs. Ellis urged her homemakers not to "sacrifice either of
comfort or respectability for the sake of economy," she was walking a

very fine line. Extravagance was immoral; thrift was moral; the greatest good was knowing one's place and living up to it precisely. Gwen Raverat's uncle and aunt, who lived in a suburb of Southampton, were the very embodiment of this idea: "They were well off and lived in style and comfort; but it was neither for the style nor the comfort that Aunt Sara really cared. Her religion was Duty, and it was her duty to her position and her class to live like that. It was Right, for instance, for people of her kind to keep a carriage and horses. This was not a manner of speaking; she truly felt it a Duty." She was the real-life equivalent of Dickens's dustman and his wife, who inherit a fortune in *Our Mutual Friend*: Mrs. Boffin knows that "we have come into a great fortune, and we must do what's right by our fortune; we must act up to it."[6]

The cost of furnishing a house varied widely. What was possible did not always mesh with what the advice books recommended. Most families could not hope to achieve the recommendations, but nonetheless they felt they should strive for these ideals. In 1857 J. H. Walsh, in his *Manual of Domestic Economy*, thought that a house with three bedrooms and two servants, for a prosperous family, could be completely furnished for £585. A family with an income of £100 should, he thought, expect to spend £83 on the initial furnishing. As one became more prosperous, the percentage spent on furnishing went up, not down. For an income of £250, 88 percent should go to furniture; an income of £500 meant that 117 percent should be expended; and those with a £1,000 income, at the top of Walsh's scale, should pay out £1,391. (It was no wonder marriages were delayed while men waited and saved to be able to support a wife.) Twenty years later Walsh revised his figures, and it would appear that while there was a fall in the price of basic household goods, the cost of luxury items continued to rise. A man earning £150 a year (the equivalent of £100 a year in 1857) could now expect to spend a mere £64 on his house, compared to the

COMFORT FOR LADIES

The Prince of Wales' Lady's Easy Chair, Very comfortable · 32s. Superior ditto, all hair, 36s.

£83 he had had to lay out two decades before. However, a man earning £1,500 (£1,000 in 1857) would now spend £1,578—nearly £200 more than in 1857, although more than 30 percent less in real terms.[7]

This kind of outlay was not undertaken lightly. Maud Berkeley remembered preparing her first home:

> What long and weary hours have we spent, choosing furniture and decorations for the house. For the drawing-room, we chose a magnificent blue carpet decked with roses . . . Whiteleys had just the thing we desired for curtains—a bale of Chinese patterned silk. My extravagance made poor Jim blench, but I believe quality speaks for itself. We also chose linen antimacassars and table-cloths and napkins from a rich store of such delights. For chairs and tables and beds, we made our way to Christie's salesroom, and bid feverishly for set after set of dining-room chairs . . . Our meals became meetings of Council, where we debated the virtues of mahogany against teak, planned attacks on furniture ware-houses, and worried, worried, worried.[8]

And her husband was more than comfortably off.

What was bought varied with the times. At the beginning of the Victorian period, sofas, ottomans, upright chairs and easy chairs, stools, ladies' writing desks, console tables, work tables, sewing tables, occasional tables and screens, and, indispensably, a round table for the center of the room were all part of an ordinary drawing room. Coil-spring upholstery was beginning to appear, and chairs were becoming heavier and also more comfortable. Easy chairs were divided into standard and "ladies' chairs," which were smaller, had a more upright back, and had lower arms to accommodate full skirts (and, later, crinolines).[9]

The expectation was that whatever

The " Wolsey " Easy Chair.
Spring Seat, very soft and comfortable, £3 3s.
Extra size ditto, £3 17s. 6d.

was bought would stay—possibly for the rest of its owners' lives. The furniture of one of Gwen Raverat's many uncles was "really good and lasting, though often quite surprisingly ugly. Indeed, everything was so solid that most of the things we had from his house after his death, are still nearly as good as new."[10] This was the norm. In *Bleak House*, Harold Skimpole had his furniture taken away by bailiffs for nonpayment of bills. But, he said, "chairs and tables . . . were wearisome objects; they were monotonous ideas, they had no variety of expression . . . How pleasant, then, to be bound to no particular chairs and tables, but to sport like a butterfly among all the furniture on hire, and to flit from rosewood to mahogany, and from mahogany to walnut, and from this shape to that, as the humour took one!"[11] The reader had by this point learned to distrust Mr. Skimpole, and was meant to be further distrustful on learning of his desire for permanent upholstery revolution.

In the 1860s and 1870s several men began to write on home design, indicating that it was now a subject to be taken seriously. For these men, and for their anxious female followers, it was not that taste might be good or bad. It was, rather, right or wrong. Good taste came about through education, hard work, and application; it was an expression of morality. Mrs. Panton could be relied on to spell things out most bluntly: "In starting to buy the furniture . . . let us consider not what is handsome or effective or taking to the eye, but what is suitable to [the husband's] position."[12] This was no advice-book flight of fancy, although Gwen Raverat's family modified the order of preference somewhat: "When they bought an armchair they thought first of whether it would be comfortable, and next of whether it would wear well; and then, a long way afterwards, of whether they themselves happened to like the look of it."[13] Furniture was selected because it was correct, moral, worthy, not because it was comfortable or attractive.*

For this reason many design experts condemned the fashion for imi-

---

*Auction houses still sell what they refer to as "important" pieces. They may be the last place to carry on the Victorian idea that ornaments and furniture both create and reflect the status of their owners.

tation finishes, such as the frequently used "varnished paper meant to have the appearance of marble, the kind of marble imitated being supposed to indicate the financial condition of the owner."[14] If a house reflected the owners' standing, then pretending to be of a different financial standing cast the whole system of judging acquaintances into disarray. *Fraser's Magazine*, in 1850 and 1851, ran a series of articles on this worrying tendency in this "Age of Veneer," and the design writer Robert Edis was grateful that thirty years later these deceptions were being seen for what they were—"gross shams and vulgar imitations . . . [that showed] an utter disregard of moral or mental satisfaction . . . and cared little or nothing for the truth, fitness and comfort of [the home's] internal belongings." He returned to this subject again and again, stressing that "shams of all kinds are to be objected to," and summing up: "If you are content to teach a lie in your belongings, you can hardly wonder at petty deceits being practised in other ways."[15] The fact that so many people wrote on this subject, and so vehemently, suggests that their target audience was not heeding them.

Yet Mrs. Panton knew that "it is always vulgar to seem to be what one is not."[16] It was vulgar and common to have imitation objects in one's house, as Mr. Pooter did in *The Diary of a Nobody*: "I bought a pair of stags' heads made of plaster of Paris and coloured brown. They will look just the thing for our little hall, and give it style; the heads are excellent imitations."[17] A real gentleman would have known that an "excellent imitation" was a contradiction in terms. Mr. Pooter's sham, demonstrating his vainglorious aspiration and how far he fell short, would have been exquisitely comic in its time. The idea that one's possessions were a representation of one's moral worth was so all-pervasive it rarely needed elaboration. Pictures on the walls had subjects that "awaken our admiration, reverence of love," and "at times [they] prevent our going astray by their silent monitions"[18]—these were genre pictures, historical, particularly classical, scenes expressing virtue, and young girls in appropriate domestic settings. All of this underscored the basis of the designers' and decorators' advice: that "the more cultivated and refined the intellect the greater is the craving for correct and refined forms."[19] The circle was complete: a cultivated and refined mind produced a cultivated and refined room; this room then acted in its turn on the people who used it, further improving them.

The drawing room was the best room, and therefore it was the primary "teacher to the untidy or unmethodical." For it was obvious that

> fine manners are a necessity, and a certain amount of fine manners is maintained by use of a room that holds our dearest treasures, and sees little of the seamy side of life. It is on little things that our lives depend for comfort, and small habits, such as a changed dress for evening wear with a long skirt, to give the proper drawing-room air, the enforcement of the rule that slippers and cigars must never enter there, and a certain politeness maintained to each other in the best room, almost insensibly enforced by the very atmosphere of the chamber, will go a long way towards keeping up the mutual respect that a husband and wife should have for each other, and which is a surer means of happiness than anything I know.[20]

What sort of room, then, was this room that promoted domestic happiness and upheld morality?

In smaller terraced houses, the front door opened onto a passageway that in turn led to two rooms, often linked by doors that could be opened wide to join the rooms together when necessary. The back room was used regularly by the family for eating and for family leisure, women's daily activities, and household routine. The front room, or drawing room, or parlor, was kept for best, and held the most choice (and therefore most formal) furniture and ornaments. In larger houses the drawing room was usually located on the first floor—often taking up the whole floor, as it did in Linley and Marion Sambourne's Kensington house—while the two rooms on the ground floor were a morning room and a dining room. The staircase thus allowed the pageant of guests processing down, in carefully graded order of precedence, to dinner. (See pp. 286–87.)

There were as many ways of decorating drawing rooms as there were people to fill them, and the ideal decoration changed over time. A few things, however, remained desirable throughout the period: a high ceiling, a long room, a bay window. In the first half of the century a certain lightness of furniture and color was retained from the Georgian period, captured by Jane Eyre in her description of the drawing room at Thornfield, "spread with white carpets, on which seemed laid brilliant garlands of flowers . . . ceiled with snowy mouldings of white grapes and vine-leaves, beneath which glowed in rich contrast crimson couches and ottomans; while the ornaments on the pale Parian mantelpiece were of sparkling Bohemian glass, ruby red; and between the windows large mirrors repeated the general blending of snow and fire."[21] This was the drawing room of a wealthy home. By contrast, in Arnold Bennett's *Anna of the Five Towns*, set in the Potteries, the heartland of the Industrial Revolution, Anna Tellwright's father's house, which rented for a mere £30 a year, had a drawing room that

> was not a cheerful one in the morning, since the window was small and the aspect westerly. Besides the table and three horsehair chairs, the furniture consisted of an arm-chair, a bent-wood rocking chair, and a sewing-machine. A fatigued Brussels carpet covered the floor. Over the mantelpiece was an engraving of "The Light of the World," in a frame of polished brown wood. On the other walls were some family photographs in black frames. A two-light chandelier hung from the ceiling, weighted down on one side by a patent gas-saving mantle and a glass shade; over this the ceiling was deeply discoloured. On either side of the chimney-breast were cupboards about three feet high; some cardboard boxes, a work-basket, and Agnes's school books lay on the tops of these cupboards. On the window-sill was a pot of mignonette in a saucer.[22]

Still, this room had what advice writers would recognize as an honesty about it, even if they would not have approved of the mixture of mundane objects with the uplifting. By contrast, an American visitor looking for rooms in London was appalled by the mock gentility that she saw: "One of the drawing-rooms was 'draped' in a way that was quite painfully aesthetic, considering the paucity of the draperies. The flower-pots were draped, and the lamps; there were draperies round the piano-legs, and round the clock; and where there were not draperies there were bows, all of the same scanty description. The only thing that had not made an effort to clothe itself in the room was the poker, and by contrast it looked very nude."[23] This was not just a foreigner's view. H. G. Wells remembered the lower-middle-class sitting rooms of his childhood: "My most immediate impression was of the remarkable fact that something was hung about or wrapped round or draped over everything. There was bright-patterned muslin round the gas-bracket . . . [and] round the mirror over the mantel, stuff with ball-fringe along the mantel . . ."[24]

Readers of Mrs. Panton might here have recognized many of her effects, even if she was under the impression that she was writing for the upper middle classes, not lodging-house keepers or shopkeepers. She had suggested that a piano—a virtual necessity in a drawing room*—might have what she considered to be its essential ugliness covered with serge, felt, or damask, "edged with an appropriate fringe . . . which thus makes [it] an excellent shelf for odds and ends of china and bowls of flowers." The music stool in front of it might be covered with "a pretty material, nailed on, and adorned with a frill that serves a double purpose, being highly ornamental and hiding the opening of the box at the same time." Sheet music could be stored in a small cupboard, again covered with a cloth, with more ornaments "scattered" on top. If the luxury of a grand piano was possible, the drawing room's decorator could really make a statement. "A good arrangement in the bend" of the piano was a big palm in a brass pot on a stand, or even a square table, with plants and books, and a couple of chairs, "placed in a 'conversational' manner," with another stool in front of them, with yet another plant on top. "This gives a very finished look to the piano," and also made it unobtrusive, which was the best thing of all.[26] Two

---

*Even the Pooters had a piano, an upright, or "cottage," piano, bought "on the three years' system." In 1890 twice as many pianos were being made as in 1850. The Rev. H. R. Haweis, husband of Mrs. Haweis, thought a piano essential, not for its musical contribution to the household but because "the piano makes a girl sit upright and pay attention to details."[25]

years later Mrs. Panton was even more resolute in hiding the real nature of the piano: she recommended that an upright should be turned into the room, so that the player could see her audience, while the now-naked back was to be covered by hanging from a rod "a simple full curtain." A piece of Japanese embroidery could be placed on the top, and on top of that, a photograph frame in brocade, a cup for flowers, and "one or two" ornaments. A screen at one end of the piano, a tall stand with a plant in a decorative pot, and armchairs with embroidered antimacassars added the finishing touches.[27]

That people read these books and followed the advice is not in doubt. But, as with Mrs. Panton and her lodging-house-keeper follower, for the most part those who studied their precepts were not of the social stratum that the writers expected. Wilkie Collins, in his novel *Basil*—the story of an upper-class man's all-consuming passion for a worthless lower-middle-class girl—showed the sham and falsity of the woman through a description of her parents' drawing room:

> Everything was oppressively new . . . Never was a richly furnished room more thoroughly comfortless than this—the eye ached at looking round it. There was no repose anywhere . . . the books, the wax-flowers in glass cases, the chairs in flaring chintz covers, the china plates on the door, the blue and pink glass vases and cups ranged on the chimney piece, the over-ornamented chiffoniers with Tonbridge toys and long-necked smelling bottles on their upper shelves—all glared at you.[28]

This picked up one of the contradictory themes of the period: in an age devoted to the idea of progress, most people thought new equaled bad. Collins, in the same book, had the hero view the suburb that his fiancée-to-be lived in: "Its newness and desolateness of appearance revolted me."[29] *Home Is Home*, a novel published in 1851, described the ideal sitting room by furnishing it with "a book-case of no modern date."[30] And Dickens, in *Our Mutual Friend*, has a field day with the pretension of the newly arrived. The Veneerings (note their sham-surface name) were bran-new people in a bran-new house in a bran-new quarter of London. Everything about the Veneerings was spick-and-span new. All their furniture was new, all their friends were new, all their servants were new, their plate was new, their carriage was new, their harness was new, their horses were new, their pictures were new, they themselves were new, they were as newly married as was lawfully compatible with their having a bran-new baby, and, if they had set up a great-grandfather, he would have been brought home in matting from the Pantechnicon, without a scratch on him, polished to the crown of his head.

At the Veneerings' house, Alfred Lammle meets his wife-to-be, Sophronia Akershem. Both are said to be "of property": "As is well known to the wise in their generation, traffic in Shares is the one thing to have to do with in the world. Have no antecedents, no established character, no cultivation, no ideas, no manner; have Shares." Both turn out to have no more shares than they have established character, cultivation, ideas, or manner. They have fooled each other as they have fooled the world: "Veneering knew as much of me as he knew of you, or as anybody knows of him."[31]* The Veneerings and their "bran-new" house might be linked to Ruskin's comments ten years before on what he saw as the visible immorality of the kept woman's room shown in Holman Hunt's *The Awakening Conscience*. Ruskin thought that everything in the picture showed "a terrible lustre" of "fatal newness." Nothing had "the old thoughts of home upon it."[32]

At the same time, no one wanted to be thought old-fashioned.

---

*An idle thought: Did the burgeoning number of books with bigamy as their theme have something to do with the increasing mobility of population, brought about by the railways? A person could arrive from nowhere, say he was anything—including unmarried—and no one was any the wiser. In *The Way We Live Now*, Paul Montague was engaged to a woman he knew nothing about—or, as his cousin described her, "a woman whom he had met in a railway train." It appeared that the train was almost as damaging as the unknown past. More pragmatically, it may be that bigamy was merely a convenient way of allowing otherwise moral people to have immoral sex while still selling books to decent people.

Robert Edis, that arbiter of design, in his search for the new in 1882 gave a heartfelt description of the drawing room of the 1860s and 1870s:

> I can conceive nothing more terrible than to be doomed to spend one's life in a house furnished after the fashion of twenty years ago. Dull monotonous walls on which garish flock papers of the vulgarest possible design stare one blankly in the face . . . or the even worse monstrosities of imitation moiré silk, with bunches of gilt flowers tied up on gilt ribbons, and running in symmetrical lines like soldiers on parade.
>
> . . . red curtains hung on to a gigantic pole, like the mast of a ship, blossoming out at the ends into bunches of flowers, or turned finials, like enormous hyacinth bulbs in water. The curtains trailed some feet on the floor, and . . . became the receptacle for dust and dirt . . .
>
> The chairs were covered with red stuff of some kind; the table had a red cloth, printed all over with elegant designs of flowers in black, in impossible positions; the carpet was probably of some gaudy colour and pattern, covering the whole room with a sprawling pattern of gigantic flowers; the furniture of the stiffest possible kind . . . an enormous glass over the miserably ugly mantelpiece, in a still more enormous gold frame, with bits of plaster ornament, also gilt, stuck on like bats and rats . . .[33]

As a writer on the new, Edis had a vested interest in disliking the older style, but many memoirists had to navigate the difficult shoals of having once admired fashions that had since become obsolete. Louise Creighton remembered her parents' drawing room as having "a flowery paper divided into panels with gold beading and on the ceiling there was a very slight decorative painting, small bunches of flowers connected by violet ribbons running round the edge. This had been painted by Italian decorators when I was a child & very wonderful we thought it. Later, after my marriage, the room was re-papered with a blue Maurice [meaning William Morris] paper & the ceiling white washed over the flower wreaths."[34] Compton Mackenzie remembered the 1890s craze when his mother redecorated, covering the drawing-room walls "with a wiggle-waggle of flesh-coloured lincrusta mould-ing* which appeared rich and beautiful to us."[36]

Compton Mackenzie's mother also went for the new "cosy corner": in the niche created by the fireplace, two settees were built in at right angles, and had padded backs with shelves extending out of them, on which china and other objets d'art could be displayed. These were considered very stylish, and became extremely popular: there was even a song that went: "My heart's in a whirl, / As I kiss each curl / Of my cosy corner girl."[37] Mrs. Mackenzie bought hers as an integral piece, from Maple's Department Store, but they could also be created at home by the intrepid housewife. Mrs. Panton described how to do it:

> Put straight across the corner of the wall a small black table . . . covered at the top with a Turkish antimacassar; this holds a plant in the daytime and the lamp at night, and is large enough to hold all the month's magazines . . . above this a black corner bracket for china, crowned by a big pot to hold grasses or bulrushes, can be hung on the wall; and in front of the table should stand a square stool, holding a large plant and pot, heavy enough to hold its own should any one come near enough to knock it over, were it too light . . . next the fireplace, put your own particular chair, leaving room for a stool of some kind, that is broad and low, and can hold your work-basket . . . your favourite book, or your newspaper stand with the paper-knife attached;† and on the desk above and at the side of your chair hang a sabot for flowers, your favourite photographs, and any pet piece of china or ornaments you may fancy. One of mine consists of a mandarin's fan and case; the case

---

*Lincrusta was a trade name for a wallpaper made by the same method as linoleum: it had a raised pattern stamped into it, often imitating more expensive wall coverings such as wood paneling or stamped leatherwork, or even stucco.[35]

†Newspapers and periodicals as well as books were sold uncut, making small knives for slitting the pages essential. Special folding knives were sold for this pur-pose at railway bookstalls for passengers; men tended to keep a penknife handy in their vest pocket.[38]

is embroidered in silk, and gives a very pretty bit of colour, and the fan serves as a fire-screen should any one object to the cheerful blaze.[39]

Rooms could be dated from their ornaments as well as from the furniture and paint and paper. Gwen Raverat's Aunt Ellen and Uncle Frank were a little more daring than the rest of her family, and in the 1890s they adapted to the prevalent "aesthetic" style:

There was just a trace of greenery-yallery and Japanese . . . In the drawing-room hung a large engraving after a painting by Fred Walker, "The Harvest Moon," in which a rustic character with a scythe and several maidens wended their classical ways across the face of the full moon. You could almost date the marriage from that picture alone, it was so often given as a wedding present about 1883. I knew two other of the best academic houses in Cambridge where it was the chief adornment of the drawing-room. There was a small cast of the "Venus of Milo"; and all about the house there hung large photographs of the Best Pictures: the "Sistine Madonna," of course (all proper drawing-rooms had *her*; we had her ourselves, even larger, at home).[40]

Some objects were neither old nor new, just expensive. In *Our Mutual Friend* (1864–65), Podsnap's silver was "made to look as heavy as it could, and to take up as much room as possible. Everything said boastfully, 'Here you have as much of me in my ugliness as if I were only lead; but I am so many ounces of precious metal worth so much an ounce . . .' "[41] Trollope's *The Last Chronicle of Barset*, written only three years later, carries on the theme. Musselboro is at a dinner party given by his business partner. They are both social climbers, and it is displayed in their conversation. "Why doesn't What's-his-name have real silver forks?" asks Mrs. Van Siever. "What's the use?" replies Musselboro. "Everybody has these plated things now. What's the use of a lot of capital lying dead?" Mrs. Van Siever remains uncompromising, as she needs to be to maintain her position in society (although we later learn she is a moneylender): "Everybody doesn't. I don't. You know as well as I do, Musselboro, that the appearance of the thing goes for a great deal. Capital isn't lying dead as long as people know that you've got it."[42] Objects were important, and useful, for what they told about their owners.

The design writers were ambivalent. As we have seen, Mrs. Panton adored drapery, yet she was aware of the perils of rooms filled to bursting. Mrs. Haweis told of an "unfortunate acquaintance" who tried to join his dinner partner to take her in to dinner. He crossed the room,

> knocking over the chair next him, and arriving at his destination with a fringed antimacassar neatly fastened to one of his coat-buttons. He then backed into a small table, on which stood some books and photographs, and only saved this, to send another spinning; this time smashing the whole concern and depriving me of one of my pet flower-holders . . . But worse was to come: in one heroic effort to get away from the scene of the disaster he backed once more into a "whatnot" full of china.[43]

Her solution, however, was simply to ensure that the tables and all the objects on them were solidly anchored and properly weighted, not to have fewer of them.

Mrs. Panton was doubtful about some forms of ornamentation: "Large Negro lads with glass eyes and arsenic-green draperies starred with gold, are not as suitable, even in a great hall, as a bronze Hercules or a really well-modelled elephant." Mrs. Caddy, however, admired the quirky: "Souvenirs of travel, such as the quaint wooden pails seen at Antwerp or the brass frying-pan-shaped candlestick at Ghent, should be eagerly sought, as they add much to the picturesqueness and piquant liveliness which are so desirable." And while Mrs. Orrinsmith, in her *The Drawing Room, Its Decoration and Furniture*, rejected "coal-scuttles ornamented with highly-coloured views of, say, Warwick Castle . . . hearth rugs with dogs after Landseer . . . mats and footstools of foxes . . . with glaring glass eyes . . . [or] screens graced by a representation of 'Melrose Abbey by Moonlight,' with a mother-o'-

pearl moon," later in the same book she suggested that the reader/home-decorator should always be on the lookout for that special something: "a Persian tile, an Algerian flower-pot, an old Flemish cup, a piece of Nankin blue, an Icelandic spoon."[44] What was objected to was not ornamentation as such, but that the depictions of Warwick Castle or Landseer dogs were simply too local, too easy to come by.

Things that had once been stylish no longer were, and were condemned where previously they had been admired. *Exchange and Mart,* a magazine that provided a forum for people to dispose of detritus—and to collect even more items that would in turn become unwanted—saw that this fashionable transience had a market value. The first category listed in its pages when it began publishing in 1868 was "bric-a-brac." It is hard to imagine how matches were found for the various items described, yet the success of the magazine indicated that they were: "I want autographs, &c. I have a box of mathematical instruments, a blue silk chest expander, seventy autographs . . . 84 foreign stamps, 140 crests and monograms, several copied songs, books, &c.," or "Wanted, a portable desk. Offered, nine songs, some old and sacred, French dull gold buckle, prints &c."[45]

The sacred songs were probably for Sundays, when in many homes entirely different pastimes were pursued on that day. In the early 1850s, members of the Lord's Day Observance Society began to lobby for a total shutdown of all public civic life on Sunday. They did manage to get postal deliveries stopped, but only for a few months. However, their campaign against the Sunday opening of "national properties" was more successful: parks, museums, and zoos were shut, bands were stopped from performing, concerts were forbidden. This was, for the most part, a question that divided along class, as well as religious, lines. The influence of the Evangelical movement, which had expected the Sabbath to be kept as a day entirely devoted to religion, was beginning to lose its power. Many, particularly in the upper middle classes, honored Sunday more in the breach than in the observance. By the 1880s Marion Sambourne thought that although one should not play cards or gamble on Sunday, it was for her a good day to have dinner parties (ensuring that not only she, but also her servants, spent almost no time in religious duties). Indeed, her friend Mrs. Stone, wife of the artist Marcus Stone, had her "at home" day every Sunday.[46] In the same decade Mrs. Panton approved of visiting on that day, as it was "no work" for the servants—tea could be laid before they went out for their half-day. (She failed to note that they would have to wash up on their return.)[47]

Into the 1890s, Gwen Raverat's family observed the day only so far as it was incumbent on them to set a good example to the lower classes: "There were many things we might not do, not because they were wrong in themselves, but 'because of the maids.'" These forbidden activities included sewing, knitting, and cards—and if she and her siblings wanted to play tennis their racquets had to be disguised in brown-paper parcels "to avoid giving offence to the people in the street."[48] Louise Creighton's family had for years not even worried about this—her father was a shareholder of the Crystal Palace when it relocated to Sydenham, and during her childhood in the 1850s and 1860s the Creightons were therefore given access to the grounds on Sunday when the general public was barred.[49]

This sort of class-bound privilege enraged Percy Cruikshank, an engraver, and nephew of the more famous George Cruikshank, Dickens's regular illustrator. These pleasures were forbidden to the less prosperous who had worked hard all week and needed fresh air and relaxation on their one day off. The Lord's Day Society, he protested, was encroaching on their freedoms more and more. In 1854 Cruikshank produced a volume illustrating pastimes that he considered acceptable but that Sabbatarians wanted to prevent: family walks in the park, excursions on the river, fish dinners in Greenwich. As he pointed out, the society, by preventing music, dancing, fireworks, "poses plastiques," and other dubious activities at places like Cremorne Gardens recreation grounds, ensured only that the day was instead devoted to "decorous hard drinking."[50]

However, the gloomy image of the inward-turning, shuttered Victorian Sunday was a reality for a large number of people. Many families, even ones that were not particularly religious, by their behavior made Sunday a day apart. Molly Hughes, who did not come from a religious family, went to church on Sunday mornings, and then in the afternoon all amusements were forbidden and reading had to be from appropriate material only. Mrs. Gaskell, the wife of a Unitarian minister, forgot herself and mentioned a novel by Sir Walter Scott on a Sunday, "so there I am in a scrape."[51] John Ruskin, at the end of his life, remembered the limitations thus: "I never, until this time [1845, when he was in his mid-forties], had thought of travelling, climbing or sketching on the Sunday: the first infringement of this rule by climbing the isolated peak above the Gap . . . after our morning service, remains a weight on my conscience to this day. But it was thirteen years later before I made a sketch on Sunday."[52]

Edmund Gosse, whose father was an adherent of the extreme fundamentalist Plymouth Brethren sect, gave perhaps the grimmest picture of a Sunday:

> We came down to breakfast at the usual time. My Father prayed briefly before we began the meal; after it, the bell was rung, and, before the breakfast was cleared away, we had a lengthy service of exposition and prayer with the servants. If the weather was fine, we then walked about the garden doing nothing, for about half an hour. We then sat, each in a separate room, with our Bibles open and some commentary on the text beside us, and prepared our minds for the morning service. A little before 11 a.m. we sallied forth, carrying our Bibles and hymn-books, and went through the morning-service of two hours at the [meeting] Room; this was the central event of Sunday.
>
> We then came back to dinner,—curiously enough to a hot dinner, always, with a joint, vegetables and pudding, so that the cook at least must have been busily at work,—and after it my Father and my stepmother took a nap, each in a different room . . . In the middle of the afternoon, my stepmother and I proceeded up the village to Sunday School . . . We returned in time for tea, immediately after which we all marched forth, again armed as in the morning, with Bibles and hymn-books, and we went through the evening-service, at which my Father preached. The hour was now

already past my week-day bedtime, but we had another service to attend, the Believer's Prayer Meeting, which commonly occupied forty minutes more. Then we used to creep home, I often so tired that the weariness was like a physical pain.

Gosse was not allowed to open a scientific book, make a drawing, look at a specimen, despite the fact that his father was a naturalist. He could not go out into the street, "nor discuss worldly subjects at meals," nor look at his "museum" (a shelf of specimens and other educational objects). "I was hotly and tightly dressed in black, all day long, as though ready at any moment to attend a funeral with decorum," he recalled.[53]* Hippolyte Taine, visiting London, noticed a similarly funereal air generally: "Sunday in London in the rain: the shops are shut, the streets almost deserted; the aspect is that of an immense and a well-ordered cemetery."[54]

Not everyone agreed that this was what life should be one day a week. In the 1850s Laura Forster's vicar father would have preferred there to be no post on Sunday; as there was, all were allowed to read their letters. However, newspapers were looked at on the Sabbath only "in times of great anxiety," such as the Crimean War.[55] Ten years later, on the other hand, Trollope's fictional Archdeacon Grantly was "very stoutly anti-sabatarial when the question of stopping the Sunday post to Plumstead had been mooted in the village, giving those who ... were the special friends of the postman to understand that he considered them to be numskulls, and little better than idiots."[56] For those who adhered more closely to the Sabbath, there were special publications

---

*Ann Thwaite in *Glimpses of the Wonderful*, her recent biography of Gosse's father, Philip Gosse, has proved fairly conclusively that *Father and Son*, Edmund Gosse's memoir of his childhood, can no longer be read as a literal rendition of his circumstances. Yet it is important to keep it before us, if only because his portrait of his family home and his family life was believed absolutely for a century after it was published. How much of this was that *Father and Son* is a wonderfully coherent piece of writing that appears seamlessly truthful, and how much was that the picture he drew was true of so many other households, is a question that the reader will have to judge alone.

for Sunday reading for children, books that were advertised as "The Earliest Religious Teaching the Infant Mind is Capable of Receiving" or the like.[57] Ruskin, in his childhood, had made do with "the Pilgrim's Progress, Bunyan's Holy War, Quarles's Emblems, Foxe's Book of Martyrs, [and] Mrs. Sherwood's Lady of the Manor,—a very awful book to me, because of the stories in it of wicked girls who had gone to balls, dying immediately after of fever."[58]

Singing, apart from hymns, was frowned on. Toys were also segregated into the sacred and the profane. Laura Forster recalled: "I remember my brother Willie when about five being reproached for 'un-Sunday' conduct by his eight-year-old brother Eddy. We were not kept without toys and occupations on Sunday, but we were given different ones, a large Noah's Ark being specially reserved for that day. Willie's crime consisted in his making a stable of the animals, whilst Eddy held that they ought only to follow Noah in Bible fashion two by two into the Ark."[59]

With more widespread prosperity, improved manufacturing processes, and falling real costs, toys were more common in middle-class households. The difference between Sunday and weekday toys became a gaping chasm when weekday toys encompassed such items as Ernest Shepard's "soldiers in blue uniforms with spiked helmets, little horses with harnesses that would take off, and little carts filled with tiny wooden planks"; or rocking horses, or horses on wheels that could be galloped down the street. Gwen Raverat had a barrel organ with punched cards that made it play a tune when a handle was turned. (She and her brothers liked it better when the cards were inserted upside down.) The contents of the toy cupboards of Marion Sambourne's children sound closer to today's consumer-driven markets than one would have expected. Her son Roy itemized his and his sister's possessions:

> Roy has a bank of England pencil and so has Maud both of them has got a little India rubber. Roy has got a lot of pens Maud has only a few. Maud has got from twenty five to thirty five dolls and Roy has got nearly twenty boxes of soldiers with three hundred

and thirty soldiers. Maud has got a lovely theatre Roy has a fly that flys along Maud has a large dolls house Roy has a pair of horses you can drive. Maud and Roy have a nice pair of reins . . . Maud has nine or ten doll sets of chairs and tables and Roy has nine or ten boxes of bricks. Roy is fonder of soldiers little fish to swim precious stones coins and puppys that go along. Maud is fonder of dolls and little chiner tea sets.

One Christmas they received a music box and a magic lantern, with over a hundred slides of a wonderfully catholic mixture of cathedrals and comic pictures, including "a man in bed swallowing rats at a great rate."[60]

As with children's growing numbers of toys, adults' possessions had multiplied too. More and more objects began to accumulate from the 1860s, becoming a deluge of "things." A recent critic has broken these down into three categories. The functional contained such items as lamps, coal scuttles,* footstools, fire screens, fire irons, candlesticks, clocks, mirrors, workboxes and sewing boxes. The ornamental included figurines (Staffordshire figures, Parian porcelainware, Wedgwood, bronzes), graphic images (paintings, drawings, engravings, watercolors, lithographs, prints, etchings, Stevengraphs,† photographs), drapery, china, ceramics, shells, minerals, fossils, wax fruit, stuffed animals, plants, boxes, fans, and feathers. A final, "mixed" category embraced the otherwise uncategorizable: scrapbooks, commonplace books, albums, pressed flowers, magic lanterns, birdcages, fern cases, aquariums, books, trays, musical instruments, vases, cushions, wall brackets,

---

*Yet coal scuttles were not approved of by all. Mrs. Panton thought they should not be permitted: it was no trouble, she airily assured her readers, to have coals brought in whenever the fire needed more fuel. (The passive voice elides who was doing the bringing, and her assumption of the availability of labor is another bow to her supposedly upper-class audience.) Her dislike of the functional continued with fire irons. She recommended that the drawing-room fireplace should have a set of brass fire irons for display, with a black set as well for use, as the brass one could not be used without becoming "black and spoiled."[61]

†Stevengraphs, which were pieces of silk that had been woven to create an image, were developed in the 1860s. They usually had a portrait of a famous person: a politician, religious leader, or legendary figure.[62]

The cover for this midcentury sheet music shows, aside from its melodramatic elements which illustrate the lyrics, a very traditional middle-class drawing room. The furnishings, including a center table with a lamp to sew and read by, the bird in its cage, the fireplace, all go to create a picture of women secure in domestic comfort.

stereopticons, inkwells, table covers, antimacassars, doilies, and mats.[63] There were things to cover things, things to hold other things, things that were representations of yet more things. It no longer seems odd that it took a "brisk" girl three hours to clean the drawing room.

With this ever-increasing number of objects in the Victorian house, compared to the lightness and spareness of Georgian rooms, came an ever more urgent need to keep things clean. By the 1870s and 1880s it was well known that the dust trapped in a drawing room was a health risk. This letter appeared in *The Times*, from a surgeon:

> I had furnished the house in the way common to habitations of its class. There were window-curtains in [all the rooms]. There were carpets on all the floors; there were unprotected papers on the

walls; there were wardrobes and other pieces of furniture, which
had their apparent height increased by cornices, within which
were hollow spaces, seemingly made on purpose to form har-
bours for dirt. There were ponderous book-shelves, containing a
formidable amount of printed lumber, and a still more formidable
amount of dust . . . There were all sorts of fluffy things about,
which were supposed to be ornamental, fancy mats and the like,
and which blackened the fingers of any one bold enough to touch
them . . . Upon all these things the dirt of a London street poured
in without intermission. In dry weather the dust found its way
through every chink; in wet weather the feet of visitors brought
in mud, which dried into dust speedily. If the children romped for
ten minutes in a carpeted room, the dust would lie in a thick layer
upon the tables and chairs when they had finished . . . The house
. . . was a scene of perpetual malaise and ailing. Somebody always
had a "cold" or a headache, the former malady being now supposed to have little to do with temperature or with chills, but to
be produced by the poisonous influence upon the mucous mem-
brane of the respiratory passages of the septic dust which people
breathe, and which, in the majority of instances, they trample out
of their filthy carpets.[64]

The house was a dangerous place in ways we have forgotten. Painted
walls were usually primed with two coats of lead, red and white; the
top coat was then mixed into a base of white lead. This caused painters'
colic, a type of paralysis, when the wet paint was absorbed through the
skin. Wallpaper was no safer: many colors were produced by dyes
made from various poisonous materials. Green papers were particularly dangerous, often having an arsenic base, as did lilac, pinks, a variety of blues, and "French gray"; some wallpapers had concentrations
of arsenious acid that ran as high as 59 percent. In addition, vermilion
was adulterated with red lead.[65] (Prussia, Bavaria, Sweden, and France
had banned these papers long before, but in the late 1880s they were
still routinely used in Britain.) Arsenic in the wallpaper was one of the
reasons that a "change of air" often worked so well (at least in the short

term) for invalids: those who were being slowly poisoned went to the seaside, leaving their poisonous paper behind, and their health improved; but on their return to the still-poisonous room, they had a relapse.[66]

Clothing was equally impregnated with arsenic. In 1862 Charles Darwin had cut out a suggestion from *The Times* for "detecting the presence of arsenic in wreaths and dresses":

> Put a drop of strong liquid ammonia . . . upon the green leaf, or dress, or paper, and if it turns blue, copper is present; and copper is rarely, if ever present in these tissues and fabrics without arsenic being also present—the green compound being arsenite of copper . . . if every lady would carry with her, when she is shopping, a small phial of liquid ammonia, instead of the usual scent bottle, the mere touch of the wet stopper on the suspicious green would betray the arsenic poison and settle the business quickly.

This novel idea did not catch on. In the 1890s women were still being warned of the problem, and warned to look out in particular for items that were worn next to the skin—underwear, stockings, socks, and gloves.[67]

To avoid airborne infections and dirt brought in through open windows, doctors recommended that curtains, which trapped germs as well as dust, be replaced with blinds, preferably of a glazed fabric that could be wiped down, or various forms of colored-glass or ground-glass windows. Others too particularly liked such windows for the rooms children worked in: as well as guarding privacy, they prevented the children from being distracted by the world outside.[68] Less expensive imitations could be produced as a hobby by the women of the house: "Vitremanie," a sort of homemade stained-glass effect made from paper, was explained in detail in *Cassell's Household Guide*, along with a variety of other ways of transforming plain glass; *The Young Ladies' Treasure Book* recommended "Diaphanie," a method of transferring chromolithographs in transparent colors onto the windows.[69]

But curtains were, for many, not dispensable. "No house," thought

Mrs. Panton, "can possibly look pretty where white curtains are conspicuous by their absence, any more than a girl can look pretty if she has neither nice frilling or spotless collar and cuffs." She recommended white muslin curtains, with lace edging and inserts, to protect the room from the gaze of passers-by, and thicker curtains in front, with fringes, tiebacks, and pelmets with swags of material. (These thicker curtains, in rep, damask, or chintz, were replaced in the summer by lighter ones in muslin or lace if it could be afforded.)[70] As well as the two sets of curtains, many had roller or Venetian blinds. Drawing-room blinds and curtains remained drawn for most of the day, to keep the sun away from the curtains and carpets, which with their organic dyes faded easily.

The fireplace was the main culprit in the creation of dirt. Yet despite its being the source of soot and ash, fireplaces and mantelpieces were prime decorative locations. In summer the grates were filled with ornamental screens, paper or fabric, or in winter too in many houses: fires in bedrooms were often a luxury only the ill could indulge in. In Arnold Bennett's *The Old Wives' Tale* the sisters look back on their girlhood bedroom in the 1860s and 1870s, which had a "small fire-grate . . . filled with a mass of shavings of silver paper[;] now the rare illnesses which they had suffered were recalled chiefly as periods when that silver paper were crammed into a large slipper-case which hung by the mantelpiece, and a fire of coals unnaturally reigned in its place."[71] Jeannette Marshall was pleased with her family's newly decorated drawing room in 1876, noting that the fireplace no longer had the old-fashioned "long & melancholy tresses of shavings, as if an old person had been combing her head over them"; instead the grate was now "dotted with green leaves . . . P[apa] calls it *Leightonesque*."[72] The old, despised ornament sounded very like Mrs. Beeton's suggestion of 1861: "Purchase two yards and a half of crinoline muslin, and tear it into small strips . . . about an inch wide; strip this thread by thread on each side, leaving the four centre threads; this gives about six-and-thirty pieces, fringed on each side, which are tied together at one end, and fastened to the trap of the register, while the threads, unravelled, are spread gracefully about the grate."[73] The "Leightonesque" replacement appeared to be an early variant of Mrs. Panton's suggestion, made in 1888 (the Marshalls were very advanced indeed), that the ordinary fender be replaced with one

> made of virgin cork . . . and filling up the grate with great ferns and flowering plants or cut flowers [which needed to be changed frequently, since nothing survived long in the atmosphere of the chimney]. The cork fender should be filled with moss, and then jam pots sunk in it full of water; in these arrange your flowers; put a hand-basin in the grate itself, and bend large leaves of the Filix mas. fern over the edges; these completely cover the bars of the grate; then large peonies can be arranged in the basin and the whole looks like a bank of flowers.

For those slightly less enthusiastic, she did concede that a simpler version was simply to train ivy over a wire frame.[74]

It was the mantelpiece itself, however, that came in for the most concerted decorative effects. Robert Edis said that the overmantel should be the dominant feature in all drawing rooms. The most basic way to decorate a mantel was simply to set out a few ornaments: a clock in the center,* candlesticks (which would give out a brighter light by being reflected in the mirror traditionally placed over the mantel), the best ornaments, vases, and a jar of spills for the fire. However, to contain the proliferation of display objects, mantels were first enlarged by a board, covered with fabric, and then by a built-up superstructure combining shelves, cupboards, and brackets, to hold books, china, ornaments, fans, and other appurtenances of elegant living. The simplest

---

*If a separate clock could not be afforded, a watch stand, an elaborate pasteboard case in the shape of a building, could be purchased, in which a watch was inserted when its owner was at home. Clocks were essential to the smooth running of the Victorian household. See pp. 269–71 for a discussion on the importance of timekeeping. It is unlikely that a children's book in an earlier century would have begun with a rabbit with a pocket watch, much less one that worried, "Oh dear! Oh dear! I shall be too late!"[75]

way to a fashionable mantelpiece—although its simplicity must be only a relative matter—was to place a board over the mantel, cover it with a velvet cloth, add a valance to it to hang down, with a ball fringe for decoration, to match the curtains and carpet. *The Young Ladies' Treasure Book* had a more elaborate suggestion for

> an elegant and highly acceptable bridal, Christmas, or birth-day gift. White velvet . . . decorated with a wreath of orange-blossoms and leaves in oils, intermingled with fronds of that most exquisite of ferns, the "maiden-hair," is a late bridal gift. It is heavily edged with white and green silk fringe, below which falls a row of balls of white carved wood fastened to the fringe . . . For mantel-decoration above this superb hanging are two vases, four feet high, of "iridescent amber" glass-ware, over the rainbow-like surface of which trail smilax and white honey-suckle . . . The central ornament is peculiarly beautiful, being a large and unusually perfect conch shell, with a lining of pure colour, in which reclines the figure of a nymph, sleeping. Above her is a cupid, who has climbed to the top of the shell and gazes at the sleeper. The mantel-valance, the vases, the nymph and shell, all harmonize with each other most perfectly.[76]

Jeannette Marshall was only one of a large army of women who were creating various effects in the home. She herself did more than many: painting chairs and mantelpieces as well as embroidering and creating "effects." Much of what she did would be classed as fancy-work. Women who "made" their homes, who created the ideal domestic space, were supposed to spend their time looking after the men, ensuring that their material needs were filled. They were, as *Cassell's Household Guide* called them, "comfort-givers." The number of pairs of embroidered slippers, or spectacle or watch cases, or decorated tobacco jars, that any man could reasonably use was limited, so the objects that were made, both for their own homes and to be sold at church bazaars to fulfill charitable requirements, moved from the useful, to things to put useful things in, to just plain bizarre.

Alice goes through the looking glass from a typical middle-class mantelpiece, complete with velvet covering and ball-fringe, and clock and flowers under glass. The looking glass, in keeping with advice book recommendations, is taller than it is broad, always a sign of gentility.

Many items recommended by ladies' journals smacked of desperation: a guitar made from cardboard and silk scraps; a Turkish slipper made from "a couple of old visiting cards" and more silk scraps; a penwiper shaped like a hand with the motto "No Hands should be Idle" embroidered on it in beading, which rendered it incapable of wiping pens; and a wheelbarrow of card, ribbon, and gold paper.[77] Maud Berkeley participated in this creation of useless objects: "Could not think what to buy for Lilian, so have embroidered an apron which she can perhaps wear when dressing as a maid at concerts."[78] Working for financial gain was looked down on, but the skills that would have enabled these women to earn their living were prized, as long as they

A suggestion for decorating the fireplace in summer, from *Sylvia's Home Journal*, 1881. In winter the grate would replace the flower arrangement, which was unlikely to appear in any real home whatever the season: the gas fumes and lack of ventilation ensured that only the hardiest plants survived for long.

were used only to produce items that no one would buy—or perhaps even want to buy.[79] Maud Berkeley was sure that it was the making rather than the purchasing, or even the object itself, that was important: "Decided to make my Christmas presents this year, rather than to buy them." She had no doubt that "while bought baubles are more immediately attractive, our hearts warm more to the home-made offering. Never shall I forget Aunt Bertha's quince jam. I had a stomach-ache for a week after sampling it."[80]

Other suggestions for hobbies included dozens of types of needle-work (embroidery, knitting, crocheting, tatting, woolwork of all sorts, petit point and other forms of tapestry-making), beadwork, including more outré forms such as bead mosaics (where the beads were set into cement), painting on glass, modeling in gutta-percha or leather ("these arts combine usefulness and elegance"), various forms of decorating objects (painting china, decorating with paint, wool, shells, dried flowers, leaves, seeds or moss, feathers, cut paper or découpage), making molds of leaves or plants, decorative napkin-folding, making albums (of drawings, photographs, *cartes de visite*, inspirational quotes, or autographs), ornamental frames for matchboxes (truly: see right), painting on tiles, and making scrap pictures for screens.

Who engaged in these hobbies can be inferred from the fact that *Cassell's Household Guide* recommended screen-making in particular as it "fills up a good deal of spare time, entails no mental exertion, and may be done at small expense." The backing screen and frame cost "only" £1. An income of £150 a year apportioned, on average, 7s. a week for the entire family's incidentals; thus screen-making would have taken nearly three weeks' money,

The Lady's Every-Day Book (*c.*1873), and countless other magazines, suggested endless fancywork to fill in the empty hours for upper-middle-class women. This is an ornamental frame to hold matches. The border was embroidered, beaded, the "nest" to hold the matches woven, then the whole mounted on a frame.

not allowing for any other needs at all in that time. That these women had a good deal of spare time to be filled indicated that they were not helping with the housework or educating their children or their younger siblings. The time element was not unusual: making decorative albums, in which one was encouraged to paste in pictures of, say, Moses in the bulrushes and then draw a border of bulrushes around the image, was promoted enticingly as a project that would "conveniently fill up a long evening."[81] Dinah Mulock Craik, the popular novelist, wrote of women at home: "Their whole energies are devoted to the massacre of old Time. They prick him to death with crochet and embroidery needles; strum him deaf with piano and harp playing . . ."[82]

The purposelessness of the objects, and the futility of their creation, can be seen in the idea of the ceremonial pincushion. Ursula Bloom remembered:

> It was . . . of primary importance that a suitable pin-cushion should be prepared and set in the baby's basket, in readiness for its arrival. This cushion could be made of nothing but the best white satin, and small useless pins were employed to form a flowery pattern across its surface, in the middle of which was some encouraging motto, such as "Welcome, sweet Innocent," or "Bless my little one," also arranged in pins. Tassels in white chenille adorned the corner. It was an unwritten law that this cushion could never be used. It was merely a flourish of trumpets, an acclamation to the baby personally, and as such remained for ever unsullied.[83]

This was not a late-Victorian piece of extravagance. Dickens had described precisely the same thing nearly fifty years before in *Dombey and Son* (1848), when the spinster friend of Mr. Dombey's sister made a pincushion with the pins spelling out "Welcome Little Dombey."[84] And E. F. Benson, the author of the "Mapp and Lucia" novels, remembered a formidable example from his childhood in the 1870s, "a domed and elliptical oblong" of a size, shape, and scale that were "those of a blancmange for no less than eight people"[85]

Jane Carlyle, although priding herself on being a mean screen-maker, neatly encapsulated our modern views on this kind of intensive, laborious time-wasting. She wrote to her cousin on receipt of a present:

> Well! certainly! dearest Helen anything like my perplexity over that beautiful piece of work yesterday morning is not easy to conceive—*Was* it a delicate attention to my *dog*, carried out on the most foolishly extravagant principles, both as to materials and pains? . . . then if it was *not* a bag to put my blessed dog into; surely it *must be to put feet into*—but again, "what a waste" . . . The feet that went into *that* must be Venus's feet to begin with and attired in cobweb-stockings and white satin slippers!—At night came "*the solution*"—if solution it could be called! To put over a teapot!!! Mercy of Heaven! all that lovely braiding put over a teapot! *that* seems the absurdest *waste* of all! Indeed my dear, I shall do nothing of the sort—I will keep it till—I have a baby!* and as it is likely to be "*a very small one*" it shall be a little bed for *my* baby![86]

Charles Kingsley shared this contemptuous attitude toward women's hobbies in his novel *Glaucus*:

> Your daughters, perhaps, have been seized with the prevailing "Pteridomania," and are collecting and buying ferns, with Ward's cases wherein to keep them (for which you have to pay), and wrangling over unpronounceable names of species (which seem different in each new Fern-book that they buy), till the Pteridomania seems to be somewhat of a bore: and yet you cannot deny that they find enjoyment in it, and are more active, cheerful, more self-forgetful over it, than they would have been over novels and gossip, crochet and Berlin-wool. At least you will confess that the abomination of "Fancy-work" . . . has all but vanished from your drawing-room since the "Lady-ferns" and "Venus's hair"

---

*Jane Carlyle was fifty-one at the time; the Carlyles were childless.

appeared; and that you could not help yourself looking now and then at the said "Venus's hair," and agreeing that Nature's real beauties were somewhat superior to the ghastly woollen carica-tures which they had succeeded.[87]

Pteridomania, or, more simply, fern collecting, had become by the mid-1850s one of the most popular drawing-room crazes. In 1869 the journalist Shirley Hibberd published *The Fern Garden*, a popularizing work; it was to go through eight editions in ten years. Ferns were hardy and could be grown in the close, dark atmosphere of the aver-age drawing room, and if the collector was willing to go and find them herself the hobby was relatively inexpensive. In the 1830s Nathaniel Ward had noticed that a plant living in a closed glass dome had sur-vived for a year.* The glass cases were in theory tightly closed; when the sun warmed the air, the moisture in the soil evaporated, then con-densed on the glass and dripped back down to re-water the plants. (In reality, the cases leaked, water vapor escaped, and the cases had to be opened regularly to be watered again.) The cases gave protection against gas fumes and coal dust, and enabled otherwise fragile plants—not merely ferns—to survive. The simplest Wardian case was a bell glass over a pot; more elaborate were cases with entire miniature gar-dens in them, with artificial rockeries built from painted pieces of coal.

Because ferns were soberly colored, they were considered more worthwhile than frivolously colored flowers to "minds . . . schooled to simple elegance." As they never bloomed, they were equally never out of season and could be displayed year-round. Women collected and classified ferns, they cultivated and bred ferns, they made outdoor ferneries, they dried, pressed, mounted, and framed ferns. They made spatter pictures from them. (The fern was placed on the paper, colored ink was spattered over it from a toothbrush, the fern was removed, and

---

*Ward was not the inventor of the self-supporting glass case, but, as often happens with inventions, Wardian cases were named for the popularizer rather than the originator. A Wardian case survives *in situ* on the landing at Linley Sambourne House.

A combined aquarium and fern case, 1857, merged two of the most popular
hobbies, although cases this elaborate were seen mostly only in aspirational
magazines. Certainly the aquarium element here was not large enough for the
fish to survive. The positioning in a window, however, was ideal for the case
to receive maximum light in an often heavily curtained household.

the outline of spatters was preserved.) Unlike fancywork, fern collecting was educational: it taught the wonders of nature, "the beads in our
Rosary of homage to the Spirit of Beauty."[88]

For similar reasons, aquariums were fashionable at the same time.
The tanks that had become available were not only attractive enough
for the drawing room but had educational value as well: "By giving
delight to the eye as a domestic toy, and by stimulating through the
medium of recreation the spirit of scientific inquiry, [the aquarium] has
brought subjects of profoundest interest within the practical reach of

the humblest student of the ways of God in Nature."[89] More pragmatically, the popularity of both ferns and aquariums received a boost from the abolition of the glass tax in 1853.[90] Tanks operated on the equilibrium or balance theory (the understanding that the aquatic plants would produce enough oxygen for the fish to survive). As with Wardian cases, in reality the balance theory was one of those nice ideas that did not quite work in practice—the plants in a small tank could never produce enough oxygen—and instead it was mechanical pumps that made aquariums possible for the amateur for the first time.* But the *idea* of the balance theory fitted in with the times: it was evidence of God's purpose on earth, and was "a special and elevating influence."[92]

Whatever its status as an educational tool and even as evidence of God's purpose, the aquarium had to match up to the rest of the house in terms of decoration. Books vied with each other to suggest more and more intricate and elaborate designs. *Cassell's Household Guide* recommended building the rockwork up above the level of the water and having a fern garden planted on top—a sort of two-for-one idea. Henry D. Butler's *Family Aquarium* suggested facing the interior ends of the tank with cement, made jagged to look like stone, and building miniature caves in them, then draping seaweed from the top to resemble wrack-strewn cliffs. Various materials were recommended to the marine interior decorator: Portland cement, gutta-percha, or coke faced with cement.[93]

The transience of all hobbies, as well as the money that was poured into them, can be seen in the pages of *Exchange and Mart*. In the late 1860s advertisements like this one began to appear: "AQUARIUM—2ft. 7in. long, 21in. wide, and 15in. deep, enamelled ends and bottom, plate-glass front, opaque glass back, polished oak cornice. Wanted, a needle rifle. Open to offers."[94] The aquarium may have had its day, yet, as Kingsley noted, the expensive cases still had to be paid for. Women

*Philip Gosse (see pp. 185–86) was said to be the inventor of the aquarium. He was certainly the great popularizer, and he created the word "aquarium," the etymology of which is uncertain. The most obvious explanation is that "aquarium" is simply the neuter singular of aquarius, after the zodiacal water carrier, or, more fancifully, that Gosse based the word on the Latin for a watering place for cattle.[91]

practiced their hobbies in an amateur fashion at home, but there were businesses behind each one, devoted to supplying the raw ingredients, the patterns and instructions in ladies' journals, and any further equipment that was useful. The *Lady's Every-Day Book* advertised "Coloured Scraps for Screens and Scrap Books,—Flowers, Figures, Fruit, Birds and Landscape in great variety from 1s. per sheet. One dozen assorted, 10s. 6d." Another company, which made inks and dyes, focused its advertising at women. As well as mentioning the more traditional uses for its products, it pointed out that "ferns, grasses, flowers and seaweeds may be dyed most exquisite colours, Green, Crimson, Purple, Scarlet, &c."[95]

The burgeoning of fancywork, of hobbies of all sorts, came about not solely through the improving standard of living and the drop in real costs of the raw ingredients of hobby-work, although both were essential. The one factor that brought more change to domestic social life than any other was the technological advance of household lighting.

Gas lighting had been around for most of the century, but it had primarily been thought of as an aid to industrial development, for public buildings and for outdoors. A factory had been illuminated by gas as early as 1798, and by 1803 gaslight had been used in the Lyceum Theatre.[96] One of the earliest popularizers was Friedrich Albert Winsor, who gave lectures, published pamphlets, and, in 1814, founded a company with one gasometer; within eight years there were forty-seven gasometers in Britain, and two hundred miles of pipe had been laid. The adoption of gas was astonishingly rapid: by 1816 gas was common in London, and three years later many big cities had some access to it. By 1823 fifty-three cities had gas companies, and by the late 1840s, gas had reached even small towns and some villages. The speed with which gas was welcomed was a purely British phenomenon—in 1862 London alone was consuming as much gas as all of Germany. (A rough comparison shows the population of London to have been around the 3 million mark; the German Confederation in 1865 had approximately 47 million people.)[97]

Shops were among the first to take advantage of this novelty, which combined with improvements in glass manufacture to produce large plate-glass show windows that could be illuminated all evening long. A printer, Charles Manby Smith, in 1857 admired this transparent alternative world: "Broad streams of gas flash like meteors into every corner of the wealth-crammed mart—from which it may be but one invisible wall of solid crystal separates the passenger, who might easily walk through it but for the burnished metal guard which meets him breast high."[98] In other public places gas was a mixed blessing. Visiting the theater gave many people headaches, because the gas consumed so much oxygen. The temperature was also raised—in the top balcony it could reach 100°F (38°C). Many public spaces invested in a *plafond lumineux*, a transparent ceiling behind which the gas burned, lighting the area below while keeping the fumes away from the spaces illuminated. As soon as possible, many theaters turned to electric lighting, usually in the form of arc lights. The Albert Hall began to use some electric lights in 1879, and in 1881 the Savoy Theatre premiered Gilbert and Sullivan's *Patience* using 824 Swan incandescent electric lamps (the earliest prototypes of the modern lightbulb) onstage, and an additional 370 in the auditorium; it was the first time an auditorium was darkened during the performance.[99]* Other public spaces remained resolutely reliant on daylight: the British Museum, the South Kensington Museum (now the Victoria and Albert), and the National Gallery all set their closing hours seasonally, with winter dusk ensuring that the galleries had no visitors after three or four o'clock for months on end, despite the fact that the British Museum had experimented with electricity as early as 1879.[100]

Yet the very real merits of gas were not in doubt; the improvement

---

*This led to a radical change in the perception of theatrical performance, and in the nature of the audience's role in it, which shifted from participatory community to passive observer, but that subject is, sadly, even further outside the scope of this book than I normally digress. Within the range of this work, however, it is worth noting that Swan, when experimenting with different types of filament to use in his new lamps, experimented with cellulose, from which he produced reconstituted cellulose threads. His wife used the threads to make doilies and lace borders, but neither saw much future in it, and Swan sold to two of his assistants the rights to produce what shortly became known as viscose: the precursor to rayon.

it made to daily life was appreciated by all. The journalist G. A. Sala wrote enthusiastically:

> In broad long streets where the vista of lamps stretches far far away into almost endless perspective; in courts and alleys, dark by day but lighted up at night by this incorruptible tell-tale; on the bridges; in the deserted parks; on wharfs and quays; in dreary suburban roads; in the halls of public buildings; in the windows of late-hour-keeping houses and offices, there is my gas—bright, silent, and secret. Gas to teach me; gas to counsel me; gas to guide my footsteps . . . He who will bend himself to listen to, and avail himself, of the secrets of the gas, may walk through London streets proud in the consciousness of being an Inspector—in the great police force of philosophy—and of carrying a perpetual bull's-eye in his belt . . . Not a bolt or bar, not a lock or fastening, not a houseless night-wanderer, not a homeless dog, shall escape that searching ray of light which the gas shall lend him, to see and to know.[101]*

One of the inventions that most promoted the introduction of gas domestically was the Argand lamp, initially shown in Paris in 1783. Its inventor, ignored in his native land, moved to the more industrialized Britain, where the lamp's benefits were immediately appreciated and it was rapidly adopted in homes. Argand lamps burned gas at a higher temperature, which created a cleaner flame. This new flame was enclosed, for the first time, in a glass cylinder, or chimney, protecting it from drafts; and a mechanism allowed the flame to be raised or lowered, permitting the regulation of brightness, again for the first time. This brought with it the need for shades to diffuse the light and to protect the eye from the brightness—a sharp contrast with earlier systems

*Wolfgang Schivelbusch, in *Disenchanted Night*, picks up on Sala's equation of gas with safety: he suggests that Paris, where street-lighting was considered part of the supervisory function of the centralized police force, had good lighting; London, with its fragmented system of privately run gas companies, compensated with strong locks.[102]

of lighting, which had used shades to direct and focus the light. Gas could be run through pipes and tubes to fittings in the ceilings or walls, or even on tables. No longer did lights have to face only upward: gas jets could be fixed to gaseliers (a contraction of "gas chandeliers") in the ceiling, from which they slid down when in use; wall sockets had pivots near the attachment points, to direct the light to the desired object.[103]

The advantages of gas made it hard to do without, yet once it was available to all it was the demerits of gas which often seemed to pre-dominate in discussion. It was generally thought that the gasometers dotting the cities might explode at any minute. The fear of leaks was so strong that many advocated turning off the household's gas at the main every night—this despite the fact that if a gas jet was extinguished by turning off the main, and not at the jet itself, gas poured out when the main was turned back on in the morning, through the unlit jet, which no one knew had not been properly extinguished. Thus the fear of leaks ensured that a much riskier situation was created. Gas also consumed large quantities of oxygen, depleting the atmosphere of poorly ventilated rooms. New houses made provision for this—a ceil-ing ventilation grill can still be seen above the bay windows outside the dining room of Linley and Marion Sambourne's house, which was most likely installed when the house was built in the 1860s, or shortly thereafter. In older houses, many rooms were poorly ventilated, or had had their old, drafty ventilation disabled in order to improve the poor warming effects of the fire. In *The Old Wives' Tale* there were two gas jets in the parlor, but the door to the street was bordered with felt "to stop ventilation." Even experts thought it sensible that "win-dows are so placed in a room as to meet the requirements of light, and do not . . . occupy the most advantageous position for the continuous admission of air."[104]

Burning gas did not just deplete the air; it was dirty, smelly, and quickly destroyed the objects its combustion products came into con-tact with. If pictures were displayed in rooms lit with gas, their owner was advised to hang them from cords rather than wires: gas corroded the wires almost immediately.[105] Silver, furniture, and books were similarly damaged. The aspidistra reached its astonishing level of ubiquity because it was one of the few plants to survive in a gas-laden atmosphere. A warehouse in Manchester tried an experiment, exposing cotton fabrics to gas: after a few months, the dye in certain fabrics had deteriorated; after a year, the fabric itself was visibly weakened.[106] The problem was well known, and by the 1850s many shops had installed their gas jets outside the windows, so as not to damage the goods on display.[107] This did not resolve all the problems associated with gas, however. Mr. Pooter suffered representatively: "I ordered a new suit of dittos [that is, trousers] . . . by gaslight, and they seemed to be a quiet pepper-and-salt mixture with white stripes down. They came home this morning, and, to my horror, I found it was quite a flash-looking suit. There was a lot of green with bright yellow-coloured stripes."[108]*

Many tried to limit gas in their homes to places where it was hard to manage without—the hallways (where drafts from the open door easily extinguished lamps and candles); nurseries (where lamps or candles could easily be knocked off tables); kitchens (where brightness and functionality won over aesthetics); and, if absolutely necessary, bedrooms (so that a light could be struck in the dark). It was the reception rooms that relied on lamps.

At its inception, gas cost 15s. per cubic foot per hour; by 1870 the same cubic foot cost 3s. Ten years later, five cubic feet for an hour cost less than a farthing, meaning that gas—which burns at about sixteen times the strength of candles—had dropped to one-sixteenth of their cost.[109] Earlier, given the cost of gas, many people reserved its use for one or two days a year—an important dinner party or Christmas Day.[110] Later, the relative expense of candles was one of the reasons why many of the wealthy rejected the more financially accessible gas lighting. Many of the great houses had nothing but candles, at least in the rooms occupied by the family, until electricity arrived: the expense of electricity ensured its welcome by the upper classes as a status marker. That Mrs. Proudie installed gaseliers in the Bishop's palace for

---

*There remain working gas street lights outside St. James's Palace in London. The visitor can immediately see how Mr. Pooter's mistake occurred.

her first formal reception in *Barchester Towers* was an indication of her hopelessly middle-class background.[111]

Even once the prices of gas lighting had dropped, the joint-stock companies that had monopolistic rights to supply gas failed to provide a pure product. Instead they piped in inferior, adulterated gas that did not burn cleanly. The quality varied from town to town, or district to district: in Scotland the gas companies supplied the best-quality gas, which allowed homeowners to burn lamps with the illuminating power of 26 candles; in Liverpool, Manchester, and Carlisle it was 20 candles; in most parts of London it was 23 candles. Yet there were many places in London where the gas produced the equivalent of only 14 to 16 candles. To make matters worse, the supply was not constant: gas was generally piped for most of the day at low pressure, which was raised just before demand increased—at dusk, for example. When a gas jet was lit during the period of low pressure, the tap had to be almost fully open to get a moderate flame; when the pressure was increased, the light flared up to a size larger than could be supplied by the oxygen in the room. If no one was in the room to turn it down, black smoke and soot would continue to billow out until the flame was regulated.[112] "Governors," or regulators, were created to prevent this, but until they were fitted to the main inlet pipe separate ones had to be bought and attached to each light fitting.

When gas was introduced in the early part of the century, there was not much of an alternative: candles were expensive, and oil was both expensive and dangerous. Kerosene, first distilled from coal in 1846, was at midcentury the main fuel. The temperature at which kerosene vapor ignited—the flash point—was low, and in addition the construction of early oil lamps made it all too likely that the flame from the wick would come into contact with the oil in the reservoir, at which point the whole lamp would explode. Some houses used sperm-oil lamps, even though they were dangerous to move and so had to remain fixed in one room. By the 1860s better manufacturing processes had raised kerosene's flash point, and improved design had made explosions rarer, although the oil was still flammable. Colza, or rape-seed oil, became popular, as did the newly produced paraffin (commercially produced from 1856), which overcame its demerit of strong smell by its extreme cheapness. Fuel for a paraffin lamp that was bright enough to replace the light of two gas jets cost 13s. or 14s. a year, although it too was dangerous, and many insurers required higher premiums if paraffin lamps were used. (In addition, those who could afford to do so were advised to have a special room for all lamp cleaning, with as little woodwork as possible in it; for the rest, cleaning lamps on a tin tray was the most affordable substitute.)[113] The gas for just one jet cost between 19s. and 25s. for the same period. Mrs. Haweis gave the lower figure as the cost "with care," which probably meant that it was almost unachievable, except in the smallest, most frugal households. She estimated that for a year ten gas jets cost between £10 and £12; ten Duplex lamps cost a maximum of £8 18s. The equivalent price of candles was £30.[114]

Duplex lamps had double wicks, which gave up to 25-candle light with colza oil, and had, like Argand lamps, chimneys that allowed the light to be dimmed or brightened. One lamp, with colza, was considered enough to illuminate a small household, carried from room to room as needed.[115] Gas ceiling lights gave enough light for general sociability, but not for any detailed work—reading, sewing, or even card playing. For these occupations, oil or gas lamps, the latter with long flexible rubber hoses, were brought in to stand beside the participants.

Although the atmosphere of the rooms was less depleted with oil than with gas, the dirt involved with oil lamps was substantial. If oil splashed out of the reservoir that held it, the smell of heated oil filled the house; dust and dirt clogged the small airholes around the wick and had to be cleaned away everyday. The glass chimney also needed washing after every use, and the shade fairly regularly.[116] The globes or chimneys diminished the light given out if they were not kept spotless: as it was, the best-designed ground-glass globes absorbed a quarter of the lamp's light, and many absorbed up to half the available light, even before the dirt from the wick was taken into account. Duplex lamps burned at a steady light for over six hours, whereas many other lamps, through the dirt deposited on the chimney, dimmed from a 25-candle light to a 15-candle light over the same period.[117]

The amounts of light being produced artificially, while they would seem hopelessly dim to us, appeared terrifyingly bright at the time:* when the Grosvenor Gallery opened in 1877, the *Daily Telegraph* complained that the brightness of the gas "fatigued [the] optic nerve."[118] Others referred to light given out by gas as "dazzlingly white," "as bright as day," "an artificial sun." When lightbulbs were first used, in the 1890s, they were what today would be measured as approximately 25 watts; that was more or less the light being given by one gas jet.[119]

Consequently, as the century progressed, lampshades became darker and heavier, and were used together with thicker, heavier curtains and with stained-glass windows. Light had become something that needed to be tamed, domesticated. Public light was different from private light, and, as with so many aspects of daily life, promiscuous mixing of public and private was worrying. Mrs. Orrinsmith, in her 1877 treatise on the drawing room, said that light "to be beneficial . . . must be, as it were, educated to accord with indoor life."[120] Just three years earlier the *Englishwoman's Domestic Magazine* had prescribed that a dinner party "must always be given by gas light or, if you have not got gas, by lamp or candlelight. Above all, let there be plenty of light. If it be daylight outside, you must close the shutters and draw the curtains."[121] Outside light was now, in this social context, inferior to manufactured light—private light.

A part of this need to tame light, surely, was that the new lighting showed the old dirt—and much more clearly than ever before. The brighter a room, the more obvious was its dirt. Previously the mantelpiece, covered in its swags and sashes, was dirty only if it was touched; now it was dirty when it was observed.

Dirt that was visible meant housekeeping coming into the open. Despite the importance that was laid on women's great task—the creation of domestic space, with its connotations of refuge and peace—women were not supposed to speak to their husbands or family of the

---

*For the variability of our responses to light, try reading by the light of one candle, with the curtains closed to block out ambient street-lighting: what was the norm for so many centuries appears almost impossible to a modern eye, accustomed to copious electric light.

work they were doing; segregation of function was not only for activity, but even for thoughts about that activity. If women spoke of what they did all day, then it would have to be acknowledged that this private sphere was just as much a place of work as the public sphere. The artificiality of the dichotomy would be exposed. Dickens's bustling housekeepers were all young, most often unmarried, and they kept house for a guardian, a brother, or a father. Once women married, the greatest feat they could achieve was making the household machinery move in complete silence—and this machinery encompassed much of what we would today regard as the pleasures of family life. Women's greatest task was the home, but it was not proper to acknowledge it. When Jane Eyre is told that she has come into a substantial inheritance, her cousin asks her, "What aim, what purpose, what ambition in life have you now?" Jane is in no doubt:

> My first aim will be to *clean-down* . . . Moor-House from chamber to cellar; my next to rub it up with bees-wax, oil, and an indefinite number of cloths, till it glitters again; my third, to arrange every chair, table, bed, carpet, with mathematical precision; . . . lastly [the servant and I will devote ourselves] to such a beating of eggs, sorting of currants, grating of spices, compounding of Christmas cakes, chopping up of materials for mince pies . . .

Her cousin Rivers is lofty: "I trust that when the first flush of vivacity is over, you will look a little higher than domestic endearments and household joys." Jane knows that this is a mask, that for both of them such things are "the best things the world has!"[122]

She knew it, but in thinking that "the best things" were to be discussed with those who were to enjoy their fruits, she mistook her role. Mrs. Warren, however, never wavered: when her narrator's son decided on his profession, she postponed sharing this news with his father, for "you know my rule, never to worry him about home doings in the evening."[123] Mrs. Haweis believed that "the seamy side" of domesticity—that is, information about the servants who were cleaning the house—should never penetrate the male sanctuary. Like many others,

Mrs. Panton felt that the reverse also held true: "A sensible woman keeps these subjects in the background, and no more troubles her husband with the price of butter, or the cook's delinquencies, than he does his wife over the more intimate details of his office, which he keeps for his clerks and his partners generally." Certainly, if the housebound woman talked about the cook, it might have to be acknowledged that she was every bit as much an employer, a supervisor of workers, as her husband, and the myth of domesticity as a haven from work would be shattered. Mrs. Panton recommended instead talking about what was in the paper, or a book, or people one had seen—what we would regard as topics to be discussed among mere acquaintances. The pseudonymous "MBH" suggested that the man of the house should physically as well as mentally be shut away from domestic nuisances: a room was to be set aside for him, which "will provide a sanctuary from the numerous petty domestic troubles and annoyances that, as few men can comprehend or tolerate, it is much better that they should not see."[124]

Dinah Mulock Craik drew a similar picture. The selfish, foolish wife in her novel *Olive* was horrified to discover that her husband "actually expected to dine well and punctually, ever day, without being troubled beforehand with 'What he would like for dinner?' He listened once or twice, patiently too, to her histories of various small domestic grievances, and then requested politely that she would confine such details to the kitchen in future." In return, he never spoke to her about his business affairs, even (especially?) when he was on the verge of bankruptcy. Gissing's *The Odd Women* is a curious mixture. The author sympathizes with the frustrations of women entombed in a permanent round of household chores. At the same time he mocks their inability to discuss anything apart from that very domestic life he knows swaddles them:

> We went to walk about the Abbey. Now, for some two hours . . .
> whilst we were in the midst of that lovely scenery, Mrs. Orchard
> discoursed unceasingly of one subject—the difficulty she had

with her domestic servants. Ten or twelve of these handmaidens were marshalled before our imagination; their names, their ages, their antecedents, the wages they received, were carefully specified. We listened to a catalogue raisonne of the plates, cups and other utensils that they had broken. We heard of the enormities which in each case led to their dismissal . . . Now, be good enough to extend this kind of thing over a number of years.[125]

This segregation was not advice-book wishful thinking—it was reality. Letters mirrored the advice books. Mrs. Warren had specified "a comfortable fire-side, well-cooked food, no disorder, no litter of any kind; keep the home room free from disagreeable reminders . . . let no smell of washing and ironing pervade the home, no talking of Susan's short-comings, or of baby's ailments—baby should be in bed when Mr Hall returns, and then be sure that no basket of stocking-mending or household needlework be introduced to his notice."[126] Mrs. Gaskell in her daily life saw such a situation as normal: she wrote to her sister-in-law after her eldest child had had a serious infantile illness, "One can't help having 'Mother's fears'; and Wm, I dare say kindly, won't allow me ever to talk to him about anxieties, while it would be SUCH A RELIEF often."[127] It was not only the servants who should not be spoken of: even the baby's illnesses were to be hidden, as was the baby itself.

Value was placed on outward forms, not the messy, intimate details we value today. Intimacy was formalized, and turned into social rituals, with their own rules and structure. Thus women—in reality both workers and employers—portrayed themselves, and thought of themselves, as private beings whose sole public facet was the creation and promotion of social life—the creating and maintaining of the vast scaffolding of daily life, with its interspersed landmark events. The foremost of these events, both in organizational terms and as a precipitating factor for becoming a member of society, was marriage.

6

THE PARLOR

IT WAS ENTIRELY accepted by the vast majority of the population that the central event in any woman's life was marriage. Women who remained unmarried had failed to fulfill their destiny, both biologically and psychologically. It was *right* for a woman to marry; it was what she was for. In her novel *Reuben Sachs* (1888), Amy Levy wrote of a woman, with "beauty . . . intelligence . . . power of feeling," who "saw herself merely as one of a vast crowd of girls awaiting their promotion by marriage."[1] With that marriage came a home, the key to happiness; without marriage women could only hope to live on as dependents in someone else's house. Unmarried men were pitied too, and considered to be living only half a life. The perception was that for the most part they lived in lodgings where it was axiomatic that they were imposed upon by their landladies—women who did for cash what decent women gave for free. Although companionate marriage, rather than marriage for property, business, or social alliance, was accepted as the norm, the perception and reality of marriage was that it was the core of social relationships, a social rather than personal linkage. A good marriage allied families, reinforced caste, and upheld the morality of social norms. It was, for all society's insistence on private domesticity, a public act, one that was planned and executed in the public areas of the house: in the parlor, the less formal reception room, when planning the match *en famille*; in the dining room when entertaining the prospective suitor; and in the drawing room for the formalities of the ceremony.

And marriage was a necessity for women. Marriage was success, spinsterhood was failure: it was that stark. In *The Way of All Flesh*, Samuel Butler set out the possibilities running through the mind of Christina Allaby, no longer a young girl: "What else could she do? Run away? She dared not. Marry beneath her and be considered a disgrace to her family? She dared not. Remain at home and become an old maid and be laughed at? Not if she could help it."[2] The Allaby sisters, all without dowries, see Theobald Pontifex as a weak man whom they might maneuver into marriage. To decide which one is to get him, they play cards, the winner to take her chances with him. While it is unlikely that this was an actual occurrence, the fact that it was a common novelistic trope is interesting. The sisters in R. S. Surtees's *Mr Sponge's Sporting Tour* similarly play "fly loo" to settle on who gets first pick of a man. In *He Knew He Was Right*, Trollope sardonically suggests that a pair of sisters toss for the man. Marriage for love has so overwhelmed companionate marriage or financial or social alliances that the idea seems bizarre, but it was this transition point that makes these jokes possible.

Among the middle classes, the new question of "redundant" women now began to loom large. The hundred years from 1750 to 1850 were years of emigration; in addition, men had a slightly lower life expectancy. By 1851 there were 906 men for every 1,000 women; ten years later it was 879 (and in Scotland, hard-hit economically, 769) men per 1,000 women.[3]

Various solutions were put forward to resolve this problem—and problem it was, if marriage was the only satisfactory career for women. The common viewpoint was the reverse of today's: many Victorians thought that women who were independent were somehow incomplete, whereas we think the opposite—that without independence it is difficult to be a whole person. William Rathbone Greg, a mill owner turned political pamphleteer, wrote in 1862 of the women "who have

to earn their own living, instead of spending and husbanding the earnings of men; who . . . in place of completing, sweetening, and embel-
lishing the existence of others, are compelled to lead an independent
and incomplete existence of their own." Their very inability to be
appendages to men left them unfinished. His solution, for these "hundreds of thousands of women," was, oddly enough, marriage, as if
they had all been offered marriage and refused it. For those—few, he
thought, though the evidence is against him—who might have failed
even to be offered marriage, he encouraged emigration. He added
hastily that he was not referring to servants,

> all of whom are necessarily single . . . *female servants do not con-*
> *stitute any part of the problem we are endeavouring to solve.* They
> are in no sense redundant; . . . they are fully and usefully
> employed . . . they do not follow an obligatorily independent, and
> therefore for their sex an unnatural career:—on the contrary, they
> are attached to others and are connected with other existences,
> which they embellish, facilitate, and serve. In a word, they fulfil
> both essentials of a woman's being; *they are supported by, and*
> *they minister to, men.* We could not possibly do without them.
> Nature has not provided one too many.[4]

He was answered sharply (although slowly: this riposte appeared in
1870) by Mary Taylor, a feminist (and a school friend of Charlotte
Brontë), who had herself emigrated to New Zealand, where she kept a
shop; she knew whereof she spoke:

> The phrase redundant women really means starving women very
> often, and almost always women whose means have fallen so much
> below their position that they are miserably poor . . . The remedies
> he proposes amount to this—they are to marry. If the complaint is
> that they are single, the remedy is unobjectionable. With the
> poverty that makes marriage impossible he does not propose to
> deal . . . [Instead] he wishes to keep single women poor. He wants
> their life not to be so easy and attractive as that of the married.[5]

She pointed out that most men writing on the subject ended by stressing that a single life should always be made unattractive, that jobs—and therefore a living—must remain closed to women, because otherwise they would not marry: a damning indictment of marriage.

But there was not much else open to them. Cardinal Newman suggested that redundant women might enter convents, because "as matters stand, marriage is the sole shelter which a defenceless portion of the community has against the rude world;—whereas foundations for single females, under proper precautions, at once hold out protection to those who avail themselves of them . . . thus saving numbers from the temptation of throwing themselves rashly away upon unworthy objects, transgressing their sense of propriety, and embittering their future life."[6] However, this also transgressed the generally accepted notion of marriage as the one true state for women. What kind of woman would voluntarily choose to remain single? And what did that choice say about marriage? Like Mary Taylor's comments, this was something the writers did not want to consider.

However, remaining single for most men and women was not a choice: it was what happened when choice was taken away. Men without an income commensurate with their social background could not find wives. And women knew what would happen if they failed to capture a husband. They would end up like the poor relation in Arnold Bennett's *The Old Wives' Tale*: "a poor second cousin of John Baines; one of those necessitous, pitiful relatives who so often make life difficult for a great family in a small town. The existence of Aunt Maria, after being rather a 'trial' to the Bainses, had for twelve years past developed into something absolutely 'providential' for them [after John Baines was paralysed by a stroke] . . . She was a shrivelled little woman, capable of sitting twelve hours a day in a [sickroom] and thriving on the regime."[7]

Instead of living for her husband and children, a single had to make do with surrogates, whether it was "some desultory tastes to condense into regular studies . . . some faulty household quietly to remodel, some child to teach, or parent to watch over." Dinah Mulock Craik was only one of many who thought a single woman should be "the universal referee, nurse, playmate, comforter, and counsellor . . . the nucleus of cheerfulness and happiness to many another home."[8] And, as with married women performing their daily duties, she should find happiness in this. Charlotte Yonge agreed: the unmarried woman "must be ready to cease . . . to be the first with any . . . she faced the probability that they would find others to whom she would have second place . . . to be grateful for their fondness was her call; but never to count on their affection as her sole right and inalienable possession."[9]

This cannot be what any woman outside fiction desired, but it was what many had to put up with. Jeannette Marshall's mother was one of five sisters reaching adulthood in the late 1840s and early 1850s; only one failed to marry, and her blindness was considered an insuperable obstacle. In Jeannette's generation there were twenty first cousins: fifteen failed to marry as expected.[10] (A few, including Jeannette, did marry in their late thirties or forties—long after they were considered beyond the age for it.) Beatrix Potter, who did not marry until her late forties (and then only against her parents' wishes), spelled out what an upper-class girl with no prospects could expect daily. When she was nearly thirty, she wrote: "Must confess to crying after I got home, my father being as usual deplorable." She therefore occupied her time by "beginning to read Gibbon's Decline and Fall from the beginning again, after having waded to the 4th. vol. of seven, and forgotten the three first. It is a shade better than metaphysics, but not enlivening." She memorized reams of verse: she could recite *Richard III* and *Henry VI*, part II, all the way through, word for word—"not 6 lines dropped or 12 . . . wrong words," as well as most of *Richard II* and *Henry VIII*, and half of *The Merchant of Venice*.[11] Again, probably better than metaphysics, if not the same as having a real occupation, which she did ultimately find, although not until 1901, when she was in her mid-thirties.

Beatrix Potter had a completely practical attitude to marriage, one that was very much of her time. Marriage was a business transaction: a man got a housekeeper/companion, and in exchange a woman got a household and children. Her status was dependent on her husband's, and his credentials had therefore to be explored thoroughly. Over a month in 1895, she watched her family respond to one unsuitable match:

[7 September] Letter to my father from Aunt Mary announcing [her daughter] Kate's engagement to one Captain Crookshank, who has been in the Army, is now a Stockbroker "by no means rich," not a word about his religion, friends, or age. One should not judge before one hears all the case, but this sounds a silly business if nothing worse. They are to marry next month, and are going to live in a furnished house in the suburbs, where, as Kate ingeniously puts it, the pleasures of town and country life will be combined.

Aunt Mary has not a particle of sense, but I can't understand the girl not having more self-pride or ambition . . . Father is grieved and exasperated to tears . . . It was very foolish of Aunt Mary to make no fuss and stop Capt. Crookshank . . .

Not that I in the least consider position or wealth as the great objects of life . . . Too much money is an evil in most hands, but too little is a sore trial to one extravagantly brought up. Fortunately Kate's £10,000 was tied up by my grandfather in such a manner that her husband cannot meddle with it, but what is £350 a year [the income on her capital] to a girl who dresses as she does. Love in a cottage is sentimental, but the parties must be very pleasing to each other to make it tolerable.

. . . If he were in the Army even, he might rise . . . If this is what beauty leads to, I am well content to have a red nose and a shorn head [from illness], I may be lonely, but better that than an unhappy marriage.[12]

Marriage was the ultimate goal, but its very importance meant that it was better to reject a proposed connection that was not absolutely right. In addition, the custom of expecting one child (often the youngest daughter) to remain at home as a companion to the aging parents—a relic from earlier days and larger families—still seemed right to many, even though family size was dropping. Maud Berkeley was the youngest of nine children and, like Beatrix Potter's, her parents were disturbed when she decided to marry, at thirty-two. The concern was not because of the man she had chosen, who was from a good family (he was a great-nephew of Bishop Berkeley, the philosopher). But, as her father said, "who now would read to him in the evenings"?[13] The love between parents and children was supposed to be stronger than between husband and wife—"Lovers grow cold, men learn to hate their wives, / And only parents' love can last our lives."[14]

The first problem for girls hoping for marriage was the very circumscribed lives they led. Beatrix Potter, in hundreds of diary pages covering three years of her late adolescence—precisely when she might be meeting eligible young men—did not mention a single friend of her own age: the only people she wrote of in her diary in those years were family members or friends of her parents. Constance Maynard throughout her twenties had to ask her mother for permission before writing to friends. Laura Thornton noted this isolation from the outside world, and also its cause. Her mother's friend Mrs. Godfrey rarely went out, and "she expected her children to be happy and contented within their own home . . . I never remember seeing any one but the Vicar of the parish call . . . All [her daughter] Christine's friendships out of the family were treated as a grievance by her mother, who was much fonder of [her sister] Adelaide, and I remember many small indications of this in Mrs. Godfrey's comparisons of the two, which all went to shew that Ady was devoted to her family, whilst Christine cared only for strangers." Laura Forster considered her own childhood to have been supremely happy, and she was very content with her social life. Even so, it was only much later, when her mother suggested to her that she should not hesitate to talk to one of her aunts if she had trouble confiding in her mother, that Laura finally accepted that "I could be on the most confidential terms with friends outside our household without any fear of her thinking me disloyal."[15]

Once these cloistered women did meet men, it was unseemly to look for a special friendship. Monica Widdowson in *The Odd Women* remarks of some sisters, "They never *will* marry!" "Why not?" wonders her husband. "They are nice enough girls." "Yes, but . . . people see that

they want to find husbands."[16] They have breached Mrs. Ellis's fundamental rule: "The first restriction to a woman of delicacy, of course, will
be, never to entertain this sentiment towards one by whom it has not
been sought and solicited."[17] Women who flirted with men were to some
no better than prostitutes: "Female coquetry . . . is but once removed
from that position to which society gives *no character* at all." In fact, "flirtation in a woman is equivalent to libertinism in a man; it is the manifestation of the same loose principles."[18] Descriptions of courtship
make it plain that not everyone thought this way, but it is important to
note that this expression of the idea was not considered extreme.

One solution, which many still approved of, was for the parents to
arrange the marriage: a suitable man was brought into the social circle
for the girl to see if she liked him enough to marry. Or she did not even
have to like him—that could come after marriage. Charlotte Brontë
urged on her friend Ellen Nussey:

> Has he . . . common sense—a good disposition, a manageable tem-
> per? then Nell consider the matter. You feel a disgust towards him
> *now*, an utter repugnance—very likely—but be so good as to
> remember you don't know him . . . From what I know of your
> character . . . I should say you will never *love before* marriage. After
> the ceremony is over, and you have had some months to settle down,
> and to get accustomed to the creature you have taken for your worse
> half, you will probably make a most affectionate and happy wife,
> even if the individual should not prove all you could wish.[19]

A quarter of a century later, the situation remained the same: in Trollope's *The Small House at Allington*, Bell Dale is sure that her sister
Lily "will never be really fond of any man till he shall have given her
proper reason."[20] *Reuben Sachs*, nearly fifty years after Charlotte
Brontë, had a similar viewpoint:

> "I do not like Mr. Lee-Harrison."
>   "Of course not," said [her mother]. "I should be sorry to hear
> that you did. No girl likes her intended—at first."

. . . Only that afternoon Rose had said to her: "We all have to marry the men we don't care for. I shall, I know, although I have a lot of money. I am not sure that it is not best in the end."[21]

Equality of social level as well as income was essential, but the hierarchical structure devolving authority from the man remained. In Mrs. Gaskell's novel *Ruth*, the wealthy Mr. Bradshaw ticked off on a mental list why his partner might be suitable for his daughter Jemima: he was "just the right age to unite the paternal with the conjugal affection . . . [he had] a house ready furnished, at a convenient distance from her home . . . in short, what could be more suitable in every way?"[22] The other major concern, money, did not have to be considered in this case: as the business partner of Mr. Bradshaw, the prospective husband was equally matched with the family he might marry into.

Women took on the status of their husbands: women who "married down" were objects of scorn, as we have seen with Beatrix Potter's cousin. Caddy Jellyby, in *Bleak House*, knows that "Ma thinks there is something absurd in my having married a dancing-master, and she is rather afraid of its extending to her."[23] Marrying up for status was entirely acceptable to both sides. (Within limits. A man from a good background who married a servant, for example, "degraded" himself. This was why Arthur Munby and Hannah Cullwick kept their marriage secret—he could not bring himself to tell his mother.) Thackeray in *The Newcomes* was blasé about it: "Women sell themselves for what you call an establishment every day, to the applause of themselves, their parents and the world."[24] This honesty was unusual; most novels presented a more idealistic surface to a pragmatic situation. When Bella Wilfer in *Our Mutual Friend* declares that she must "marry an establishment"—that is, choose a man for his income rather than his love— she is led by the author through the narrative to discover the error of her ways, until she reaches the domestic felicity of marrying a man of her economic status (lower middle class) for love. (For this, oddly enough, she is rewarded at the end of the book with—an establishment. It is almost as though Dickens could not think what else society could reward her with, apart from money.)

That marriage was a business, for women, was often put plainly. Edmund Widdowson, in *The Odd Women* (1893), has just told his sister-in-law that he plans to marry. She had not known he was looking for a wife, and asks: "Now why didn't you come and ask me to find you a wife? Why, I know two or three girls of really good family who would have jumped, simply jumped, at a man with your money. Pretty girls, too . . . Don't you know, my dear boy, that there are heaps of ladies, real ladies, waiting to marry the first decent man who offers them five or six hundred a year? . . . I would get together a round dozen in two or three days. Girls who would make good, faithful wives, in mere gratitude to the man who saved them from—horrors."[25]

Given the necessity for financial and social equality, and the inability of the girl to become friendly with more than one man without receiving the dread designation of "flirt," the introduction was essential. Earlier, meetings were governed by small local populations, who all knew each other's circumstances, and thus were confined to social equals. By the middle of the century, the increase in the size of social groups, and the creation for the middle classes of various types of public recreation that had previously been accessible only to the wealthy— theaters, concerts, seaside holidays—made meeting by locality, of groups outside one's normal sphere, a possibility.

Jeannette Marshall's two early experiences were examples of both the old and the new ways. Her first admirer was found among her home circle: he was the nephew of a patient of Jeannette's father. They met in 1870, when she was fourteen and he in his mid-twenties, and after that he contrived "accidentally" to bump into Jeannette and her sister on their daily walks; he sent the family tickets for Drury Lane (his uncle had the ticket concession); he had sheet music specially bound for her. The Marshall parents seem to have been unequipped to deal with this situation, which they steadfastly ignored for two whole years, until the suitor's uncle approached Marshall formally. At that stage Marshall rejected him, possibly because Jeannette was too young, or perhaps because he thought the man's family was not good enough. When her rejected suitor became engaged six months later to the daughter of a jeweler, Jeannette wrote in her diary that the engagement was "a kind of Trade's Union." She may have agreed with her father, or she may simply have been saving face, even to herself.[26]

The second suitor appeared two years later, when the Marshall family was on holiday in Switzerland. Herbert Thomas, in his thirties, was staying at the same hotel. He made clear his admiration for the eighteen-year-old Jeannette, and told her "all about his birth, parentage & education"—an almost certain prelude to a proposal. Her parents handled the situation no better than they had her first entanglement. They could not feel happy about his social position: he was a freelance journalist (which was bad), although he also held a post in the offices of the Privy Council (which was good). He spent a great deal of time traveling, without any reason, and without the independent income that would have made it natural (bad again). In general, the Marshalls thought "our flirtation is becoming a trifle strong," Jeannette recorded, and they pointedly did not ask Thomas to call on their return to London. Encouraged by Jeannette, however, he called anyway; then he asked her father to dinner, "& poor Papsy was so 'took-aback' that he was incapable of refusing . . . P[apa] seemed in a mortal fright lest he shd. declare his intentions on Friday."

He did not, and the Marshalls were forced by convention to invite him back. But they could not quite bring themselves to make such a sign of approval, so Marshall invited him to dinner at his club, which met the social obligation while not appearing to be too encouraging. Jeannette complained to her diary that her father was giving Thomas no opening, but she did not know whether it was because Dr. Marshall thought she herself did not like Thomas or because her parents disapproved of him. (Apparently she did not consider speaking to her father about her feelings.) Jeannette was putting up a cool front: this was what girls were supposed to do. Unfortunately for her, however, it appeared that her father and her suitor were both taken in. Thomas began to call more infrequently, and then refused an invitation altogether. Jeannette realized that whatever may have been there was there no longer. Defiantly, she noted in her diary, "I have seen so little of him for so long that I do not like him as much as I did this time last yr., & that was not so *very* much."[27]

These two courtships may have been abortive because the Marshalls thought Jeannette too young, or possibly because they did not know the rules. At its most formal, the procedure went more or less as follows. If a man wanted to marry, his first obligation was to consider his financial position and his future prospects, to see if they justified his trying to attract a woman. If they did, he could then see if his chosen woman returned his affection—doing so with "delicacy and caution," to avoid compromising her. This, oddly, might be before they had met. He might simply have seen her in church, or perhaps met her at a ball. (In the rules of society, an introduction at a ball did not count as an introduction; the woman could with perfect politeness "fail" to recognize him afterward, cutting him dead without his having the right to be annoyed.) He might, however, be a family friend, or a friend of her brother, which made things simpler.

If he had not met her, he arranged for a mutual friend to introduce him to the family. (If he could not find a mutual friend, it was a good indication that the families could not be socially compatible and the idea should be dropped.) The introduction was a serious matter: "Those who undertake such an office incur no slight responsibility, and are, of course, expected to be scrupulously careful in performing it, and to communicate all they happen to know affecting the character and circumstances of the individual they introduce."[28] The prospective suitor must at this stage state his position and prospects, "as well as mention his family connections," and ask if he might call on the girl's family. If they agreed, the acquaintance could grow without anything definite being said, which would allow one or the other to decide against an engagement without seeming "fickle or jilting."

The two met in family circles, with at least one married family member always present. Now was the time for the girl to assess his worth. Did he speak "slightingly" of women, was his church attendance regular, did he have amusements "beyond his means, or [ones that were] . . . low and vulgar"? She should also make sure that he was

not "foppish, frivolous, slovenly, eccentric,"* and that he was sufficiently interested in business to ensure a decent income. In turn, he
needed to see that she was "attentive to her duties; respectful and affectionate to her parents; kind and forbearing to her brothers and sisters;
not easily ruffled in temper; . . . [if] her pleasures and enjoyments [are]
those which chiefly centre on the home; if her words [are] charac-
terised by benevolence, good-will, and charity." If she turned out to be
a flirt, or interested only in dress (or, alternatively, not interested
enough), or "petulant, pert, [or] inconstant," it was at this point that
he could still extricate himself with honor.

Otherwise his next step was to speak to her father and, if the father
was agreeable, to the girl herself. Until the parents' agreement was
given, nothing was really settled. Louise Creighton accepted her
suitor's proposal when she was visiting friends at Oxford, but he
could not leave his college for the next fortnight, and "until he had
seen my father he did not think we should consider ourselves engaged
or write to each other."[29] If a woman wanted to refuse her suitor's
proposal, which was "the greatest honour it is in his power to offer,"
she must be "delicate," considering his feelings. She should also examine her own conscience "to discern whether any lightness of
demeanour or tendency to flirtation" had led him on. If he wrote to
her after she had refused him, and the letter was "presumptuous and
intrusive," she should give it to her parents to answer. Whatever the
answer, it was final, and the man should attempt no further intercourse.

Parental involvement divided along gender lines: the father's role
was to check into a suitor's present finances and future prospects; the
mother's dominion was almost everything else, starting with an assess-
ment of his suitability in terms of social compatibility. If this was satisfactory, the rest followed: invitations so that the couple could meet,
opportunities for talk, appropriately modified chaperonage—in other
words, access to her daughter.

In the absence of one or both parents, the ritual was adhered to in

*For conformity as a virtue, see pp. 290–91 and 294.

A late Victorian parlor, with a central gaselier to light the table, a cottage piano
(a must in every home with pretensions to gentility), Morris-style wallpaper,
and appropriate genre and animal pictures. The room may have been used by
children to do their lessons, indicated by the globe in the corner.

modified form. In *The Daisy Chain*, Flora's mother is dead, so her
father takes on her role: "I have never heard anything of his character,
or conduct. Those would be a subject of enquiry . . . we must be
assured of his father's consent, for they may very fairly object, since,
what I can give you, is a mere nothing to them. Next, I shall find out
what character he bears . . . and watch him well myself; and, if nothing
appear seriously amiss, I will not withhold my consent."[30] In *Bleak
House*, Esther Summerson has no parent at all, so Mr. Guppy
addresses himself to her as if she fulfilled the parental as well as her
own role in the courtship:

> My present salary, Miss Summerson . . . is two pound a week.
> When I first had the happiness of looking upon you, it was one-
> fifteen, and had stood at that figure for a lengthened period. A rise
> of five has since taken place, and a further rise of five is guaranteed

Dickens's illustrator Phiz showed Mr. Guppy's proposal, 1853. Bleak House was large enough for Esther Summerson to have her own sitting room, but housekeeping was more often done from the dining room. As Mr. Guppy finishes his lunch, Esther is working at her desk, which is complete with ink-stand, paper-holders, and writing slope.

at the expiration of a term not exceeding twelve months from the present date. My mother has a little property, which takes the form of a small life annuity; upon which she lives in an independent though unassuming manner, in the Old Street Road. She is eminently calculated for a mother-in-law. She never interferes, is all for peace, and her disposition easy . . . My own abode is lodgings at Penton Place, Pentonville. It is lowly, but airy, open at the back, and considered one of the 'ealthiest outlets. Miss Summerson! In the mildest language, I adore you. Would you be so kind as to allow me (as I may say) to file a declaration—to make an offer![31]

The humor is in the confusion of boundaries: a speech that should be given to the father is instead delivered to the daughter. In this particular case the lack of segregation is played for laughs, but it is still not acceptable—and neither is Mr. Guppy, for his income is only £104 a year (which he expects to rise to £117). A clerk could marry on this; Mr. Guppy's error lies in proposing to a woman who, despite her own lack of income, is being looked after in an upper-middle-class household. She has her own maid, as well as a houseful of servants, indicating that her guardian's income is probably heading toward £1,000 a year, if not more; the potential Mrs. Guppy on £100-odd could expect to be the employer of, at best, a young maid-of-all-work in her first job. Mrs. Warren wrote for what she saw as the lower end of the market with such titles as *How I Managed My House on Two Hundred*

Card games became more popular at home with the spread of gas lighting.
In *A Game of Cards* by Nancy A. Sabine Pasley (*top*) the lamp that would have
been on the table for direct lighting is not shown. The fireplace is characteristic
of a late-century household with modern tastes: an overmantel in the Aesthetic
style, and a simple embroidered fabric covering for the mantel—no drapery, no
fringe, no swags. The Carlyles' drawing room (*bottom*) was more traditional,
especially the central table with oil lamp and the patterned wallpaper. The room
also harks back to a still earlier period in its lack of ornaments, especially
around the fireplace.

Mixie & I invariably lose our shuttlecock in the gas.

Maud Berkeley's diary illustration of 1893 shows a large gas ceiling light and a conventionally high Victorian decorated fireplace: compare the deep swags and dense layers of ornaments here with the earlier and later styles in *A Game of Cards* and in the Carlyles' drawing room on the previous page.

Augustus Egg's remarkable triptych, *Past and Present* (1858), showing the
downward path of an adulterous woman, begins in a standard midcentury
drawing room, complete with green and red decoration, central table, well-
proportioned mirror over the fireplace and suitable paintings on the walls.
But clues to disorder are everywhere in this household: the painting over her
husband's portrait on the right is of a shipwreck, over hers on the left the
expulsion from the Garden of Eden; her children play with a pack of cards, a
clear sign she is a bad mother who allows them knowledge of gambling; and,
possibly worst of all, their house of cards is built on the foundation of a
French novel—the spine is marked, firmly, "Balzac."

ABOVE James Hayllar, that painter of contented domesticity, shows *The Only Daughter* becoming engaged. The signs of a happy home are implicit not only in the tender chain of feeling displayed, but also in the piano, the pet lying in front of the fire, and the sewing machine on the floor, tangible evidence of the mother's busy industry on her family's behalf.

OPPOSITE Paintings of wedding ceremonies were very popular: this was where domestic life was seen to begin. The reality of lavish weddings was usually confined to the upper middle classes, but in paintings a mixture of classes could appear. In James Charles's *Signing the Marriage Register* the bride is elaborately dressed, with at least two bridesmaids (behind the child on the left); the group on the right, however, is less socially elevated, including a sailor and a man in rustic dress. Note the wedding favors pinned to their breasts.

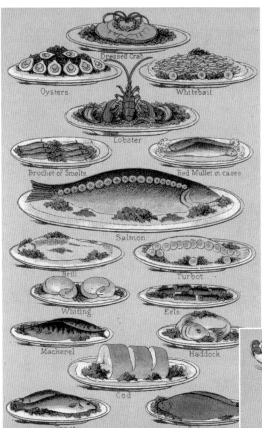

OPPOSITE In *Our Dining Room at York* (*top*), the plain room, relatively simple drapery, no gas lighting, and lack of ornamentation shows the décor in 1838, at the very start of the Victorian period. The table setting shown, however, remained constant for the next three decades at least, with the soup at one end of the table and a fish at the other, separated by corner dishes. It was the only stable element: by 1883 some dining rooms had electric light, and most contained desks, sideboards, and ornaments (*bottom*).

George Elgar Hicks's triptych, *Woman's Mission* (1863), shows three stages of womanhood: as mother, as caretaker of the elderly, and here, as wife or, as Hicks named her, "Companion to Manhood." That she is a good wife is clear: the breakfast table has been carefully set, with her husband's post neatly arranged, in front of a bright fire; he wears embroidered slippers, presumably stitched by her, and, as he flinches from the bad news contained in the black-bordered letter in his hand, she rushes to his side, half supporting, half clinging: the model wife.

Pounds a Year. Mrs. Panton suggested that her fictional couple might marry on a fairly modest income and live a "somewhat straitened and monotonous existence" until this improved. She was, however, budgeting for £300–£500 a year—an income greatly more than most of the middle classes hoped to achieve in their years of prosperity.[32]

One of the main financial considerations before marriage was that it was generally expected among the upper middle classes that a woman should move into a home that was as much like her parents' as possible. Everything was to be complete: curtains, carpets, furniture, each household object—all were to be bought before marriage, rather than saved for through the years. *Upward and Onward: A Thought Book for the Threshold of Active Life* told young men:

> . . . with care,
> Prudence and forethought, first prepare thy home.
> For 'tis not manly to allure a girl
> From peace and comfort, and sufficiency,
> To a sad cheerless hearth and stinted board.[33]

Yet for the majority of the middle classes this it was an unattainable dream: the Mr. Guppys and Mr. Pooters knew that their wives would have to save for every single item, and their houses would never be entirely finished.

Even Jeannette Marshall, from a much wealthier family, did not expect that everything would be ready before her marriage. When she became engaged to the Medical Officer of Health for Surrey, who had treated her father in his last illness, they discussed their finances. Her fiancé earned £1,000 a year, and expected to save from that £300 a year.* Jeannette had £50 a year, income from a legacy of £1,000. She told her fiancé that "that would dress me, & leave something over to

---

*Before pensions, everyone who could tried to set aside one-third of each year's income to provide for old age, or for their children after their early death. Another solution was for men without much money to insure their lives on marriage, with their wives as beneficiaries.

buy things for the house. He exclaimed & I said 'Why I have never had more than £30, & have never spent *that* on my clothes alone.' To see his face was a study; I cd. not help laughing. He said that was one thing wh. he had been worrying about, wondering if I shd. be satisfied with £75!"[34] By contrast, John Ruskin's wife brought nothing into their marriage. His father gave them £10,000 and they lived on the interest, which was probably between £300 and £400 a year.[35] Phyllis Rose, in her fascinating biographical study of the marriage, suggested that the £300 they spent furnishing their house was "exorbitant," but if the Ruskins had £350 a year, then £300 was precisely what J. H. Walsh, in his *Manual of Domestic Economy*, suggested was a sensible expenditure. (See pp. 170–71.)

Kate Thomas, the daughter of a Baptist minister, living in a country town in Gloucestershire, was less fortunate. Her sister, Sarah, noted in her diary in 1860 that a visiting minister "could speak of nothing but Kate . . . He confided . . . that he wished he had her for his wife, but after making enquiries . . . thought he would not have enough money to be of our family."[36] So Kate, unasked, remained unmarried—neither she nor her sister doubted that being unmarried was better than being married to a poor man. Not everyone felt this way. Mrs. Gaskell noted in a letter her pleasure in helping a "young couple [who] will be *very* poor" with their plans: "I like their way of bravely facing poverty in order to be together, instead of waiting till they can set off in style."[37]

Others were not prepared to tolerate such a situation. In Samuel Butler's *The Way of All Flesh*, Theobald Pontifex's father is furious when his son chooses his wife: "The ineffable folly . . . of your fancied passion for Miss Allaby fills me with the gravest apprehensions . . . [I] have no doubt that the lady herself is a well-conducted and amiable young person, who would not disgrace our family, but . . . your joint poverty is an insuperable objection to your marriage."[38] The reader was expected to despise the unlovable Mr. Pontifex, but in *East Lynne* the same situation was presented as admirable: Captain Thorn wanted to marry Barbara Hare, and "had his circumstances allowed it" he would have made an offer. They did not, however, so he suffered in silence until "he had acquired some property by inheritance, and had also been promoted a step in his profession."[39] Only at this point was he able to speak to Barbara Hare about his feelings.

Others felt even more strongly. George Gissing in his own life believed that his paltry and erratic earnings made marriage to someone of his class out of the question. (He consequently married two working-class girls, both times disastrously, although this may be because he carried his belief into practice further than most: his first wife was an alcoholic prostitute.) His sense that women required material comforts that men were content to do without played out over and over in his novels, most overtly in *New Grub Street*. Amy and Edwin Reardon live precariously in a flat near Regent's Park. He has left his clerkship to a hospital on the strength of a well-received novel. Because "the girl wasn't content to go into modest rooms [that is, a lodging house]— they must take a flat . . . He had done a fatal thing. A man in his position, if he marry at all, must take either a work-girl or an heiress."

Edwin is unable to sustain the pace of writing necessary to produce an adequate income, and his plans for remedying the situation are unacceptable to his wife: he thinks they should move to a cheaper neighborhood, where the same amount of space will cost half the amount they are paying in fashionable Regent's Park; or he could become a clerk again. To the first, she responds: "But think what it means, to give up our home and position. That is open confession of failure. It would be horrible." To the second, which would remove them to the lower middle class: "You shall not fall to that! It would be too bitter a shame." She sees his failure to provide for her as "unmanly": "You say you love me, and I try to believe it. But whilst you are saying so, you let me get nearer and nearer to miserable, hateful poverty." Finally she rejects him altogether: "You have the opportunity of making one more effort to save us from [the] degradation [of becoming a clerk and a clerk's wife, and moving out to the suburbs]. You refuse to take the trouble; you prefer to drag me down into a lower rank of life. I can't and won't consent to that. The disgrace is yours." She moves back to her mother's, which was regarded by many in society (although not by Gissing himself) as preferable to the disgrace of losing status.[40]

Nearly half a century before, the writer Ann Richelieu Lamb* had stated the same views as Gissing, every bit as harshly:

> Woman not being permitted by our present social arrangements and conventional rules, to procure a livelihood through her own exertions, *is compelled* to unite herself with some one who can provide for her; therefore in contracting matrimony she thinks principally of this necessary requisite . . . Man, on the other hand . . . seeks to find in his wife, a sort of upper servant, or female valet, who is to wait upon him, attend to his wants, instinctively anticipate his wishes, and study his comfort, and who is to live for the sole purpose of seeing him well-fed, well-lodged, and well-pleased![42]

This sounds like impassioned rhetoric, but place it beside a "comic" piece from *Punch* in 1859 and one begins to think that perhaps it was a calm statement of fact:

> The very best Sewing-Machine a man can have is a Wife. It is one that requires but a kind word to set it in motion, rarely gets out of repair, makes but little noise, is seldom the cause of dust, and, once in motion, will go on uninterruptedly for hours, without the slightest trimming, or the smallest personal supervision being necessary . . . If it does get out of order a little, from being overworked, it mends itself by being left alone for a short time, after which it returns to its sewing with greater vigour than ever.
>
> . . . the Sewing Machine may be pronounced perfect of its kind; so much so, that there is no make-shift in the world that can pos-

---

*Almost nothing is known of Ann Richelieu Lamb, apart from her one publication, *Can Women Regenerate Society?* (1844). She reappeared briefly to history once more, as an invited guest named Ann Richelieu Dryden at a meeting of the Claylands Debating Society in 1870, where the topic under discussion was "Can the claims advanced on behalf of women by Mr J. S. Mill be advantageously granted in this country?" But what she had been doing in the intervening quarter of a century has vanished.[41]

sible replace it, either for love or money. In short, no gentleman's establishment is complete without one of these Sewing Machines in the house![43]

This need to think of women as possessions was perhaps stronger now that the passage of the Divorce Act—only two years earlier, in 1857—had made it possible for a couple to divorce without an Act of Parliament. Now a women could obtain a divorce if she could prove adultery, coupled with bigamy, incest, or cruelty; a man needed to prove adultery alone. That same year a Married Women's Property Bill was defeated. This is not the place to discuss the incremental changes to the rights of women, but in summary the legal changes were as follows: 1857—Married Women's Property Bill defeated; Divorce Act passed, giving separated, divorced, and deserted women a small number of rights over their own property; 1870—a severely curtailed Married Women's Property Act passed, allowing women to retain their own earnings; 1873—separated or divorced women given access to their children aged seven to sixteen; 1878—women whose husbands had been convicted of assault given custody of children under ten; 1882—more rights granted to married women, including the right to dispose of their own property; married women given a separate legal identity, enabling them to make a will and to sue and be sued; 1886—married women entitled to maintenance, given the right to become a child's guardian on the death of their husbands; 1895—women whose husbands had been convicted of assault given custody of their children to the age of sixteen; 1925—women given equal rights over their children.[44]

But before marriage, once the financial status of the suitor was deemed acceptable and the proposal had been accepted by the woman and her family, the ceremony and its many formalities were the next hurdle. Many in the lower middle and middle classes simply had the banns read and went off to their local parish church, marrying with one or two close friends and their parents present. A new dress might be worn by the bride, although it was usually in a practical color (often black), which then took its place as her best dress for some years to come.

Grand weddings and the complicated etiquette that surrounded them were the preserve of the wealthy. No one earning under £300 a year, and not many at that level, could afford to follow all the rules laid down. That paintings of courtship, engagements, and weddings were regularly shown in this period is another clue that complex ceremonies were an upper-class preoccupation.[45] Most unusually, novels are remarkably scant in details of weddings, compared to their depictions of other ceremonies. Diaries and letters are, even more unexpectedly, not much more informative, suggesting that in middle-class life a quick trip to church was probably all that was expected. Even when more money was available, weddings were not yet given the central importance they are today. In *The Small House at Allington* (1861), the Countess de Courcy does not attend her daughter's wedding, for no particular reason, and no one thinks it odd.[46] It was only gradually that these formal rules began to be seen as the norm, whatever the underlying reality. As many changes have occurred in the years since, the elaborate prescribed structure is worth looking at.

The first matter to be dealt with was the trousseau. This was not simply clothes for the woman, which, in her new role of wife, needed to be different from her earlier girlish dress. It also included the very substantial quantity of household linen and bedding. In previous centuries the trousseau was sewn by the engaged woman herself; from the 1830s, shops (usually called the Something Linen Warehouse) produced "Marriage and Outfitting Orders" ("outfitting" was a euphemism for underwear). A sample trousseau, costing £20, included:

6 Beatrice chemises, 3 Alexandra chemises
4 Alice nightdresses, 2 Maude nightdresses
6 Paris long-cloth drawers, tucked, 3 trimmed with work [i.e., embroidery]*
2 long-cloth petticoats, tucked, 1 trimmed with work, 3 flannel
3 camisoles, trimmed with work, 3 extra good

*Note that the underclothes had the names of Queen Victoria's daughters and daughter-in-law, except for the underpants.

3 merino vests

1 printed cambric dressing-gown, 1 in coloured flannel, 1
   white hair-cord dressing jacket

12 pairs white cotton hose, 6 hem-stitched

12 cambric pocket handkerchiefs, 6 hem-stitched

1 pair French wove corsets

1 patent crinoline

6 fine towels, haberdashery (an assortment)[47]

But this was for the very wealthy only, however much the shops
wanted customers to think that everyone had a trousseau like this.
Advertisements and advice books all scaled up their descriptions of
what "everybody" needed, in the hope that at least some of their necessities would be taken as the norm. Sarah Thomas from Gloucestershire
was fairly prosperous, yet on her engagement in 1862 she thought an
appropriate trousseau was fabric for four chemises, along with giving
the local dressmaker an order for five dresses. She went to London for
her wedding dress, and to Cirencester for a silk dress, which was possibly her "going-off" dress.[48]

It was the man's responsibility to rent and furnish a house, while the
woman—as future housekeeper—supervised certain things from the
beginning. Louise Creighton's parents "gave me . . . all of my house
linen & kitchen things, my bedroom furniture & my piano"—in other
words, things for the areas of the house considered particularly
female.[49] The couple expected to receive presents from family members, usually plate, jewelry, furniture, or "items of ornament."[50] Guests
at the wedding were not expected to give presents in exchange for the
invitation: only close friends of the family joined in the gift-giving.

The many attributes we now think of as a "traditional" wedding
were in reality all fairly new: white wedding dresses had begun to be
worn by some in the middle of the eighteenth century, although many
people continued to wear colored ones. Gradually pale colors came to
the fore, until the creation of aniline dyes, combined with the legal
change that permitted afternoon weddings in 1886 (see p. 239), made
dresses of bronze, claret, amethyst, and other similarly striking colors

Sunlight soap advertised to the lower middle and working classes, which may partly explain the mixture of signals in this advertisement: the bride, in an expensive white dress and veil, is standing in the kitchen with her large bouquet resting on a chair, while an unusually large collection of servants for a house that size has gathered to admire her. Sunlight had bought the rights to a popular painting, *A Wedding Morning*, by John Henry F. Bacon, just as, earlier, Pears' soap had with Millais's even more famous image, *Bubbles*.

fashionable for a while. In the 1870s and 1880s ivory also appeared. But the supremacy of white, once it had been established for the more prosperous, was never really threatened.

Prices were as various as the dresses. Peter Robinson advertised dresses at £10 in 1874; slightly earlier, they were selling the fabric for a silk dress at £3 17s.[51] This, however, was only the beginning. A surviving bill for a wedding dress in 1850 shows that out of a total of £7 8s. 5d. for the dress, only £4 15s. 4d.—less than two-thirds of the total—was spent on the material, in this case an expensive figured silk. Whalebone, tape, cording, hooks, edging, lining, and lace cost over half as much again. A further £12 was spent on accessories—shawls, bonnet, mantle, veil, and scarf—for a final expenditure of £20.[52]

Bonnets were replaced by veils in the middle of the nineteenth century. Thackeray's *Vanity Fair* straddled this period, being set during the Napoleonic Wars but written more than thirty years later. The author had Amelia Sedley marry in "a brown silk pelisse . . . [and] a straw bonnet with a pink ribbon; over the bonnet she had a veil of white Chantilly lace."[53] In 1854, in Norfolk, the local vicar wrote in his diary: "A day of excitement in the parish in consequence of Miss Dingle's wedding and of her wearing a *veil*, supposed to be the first ever seen in Dereham."[54]* By the 1830s, orange blossom was beginning to appear. After Queen Victoria wore it at her wedding in 1840, it became more than fashionable—it was virtually required. Wax versions, however, became available for those out-of-season weddings, and for the blushing bride to put on permanent display under a glass bell in her drawing room.[55]

The only exception to this was when a widow married again. (The rules of formal mourning are elaborated on pp. 378–89.) She had no bridesmaids, no veil, no orange blossom; instead she wore a colored silk dress and bonnet. For a widow who was the mother of the bride, deep red was considered seemly in the first year of mourning (only for the wedding: black was resumed immediately after church).[56] A bride who was in mourning for a family member wore a white wedding dress (white was an acceptable color for mourning), with a white-only bouquet, a white veil with a black border, and white gloves stitched with black.[57]

Men's clothes for the event were just as carefully considered. Frock coats first began to appear in the 1850s and 1860s. The *Minister's*

---

*The Rev. Benjamin Armstrong was not a great fan of weddings. He went on: "All weddings are alike. The mind reverts to new well-fitting gloves and bouquets imported from Covent Garden—postboys with huge favours [see pp. 239–40] and smirking servant girls—a handsome breakfast with lots of champagne—wretched speeches on the part of the men and tears on the part of the women. Then come the corded boxes; the bridegroom has another glass; an old shoe is thrown into the carriage for luck and off they go. For my own part I dislike weddings and would soon attend a funeral." Apart from the last clause and the adjectives, his report is almost identical to the glowing descriptions found in etiquette manuals.

Gazette of Fashion in 1861 assured worried men of the acceptability of "Frock coat, blue, claret, or mulberry coloured . . . Waistcoat, of white quilting . . . Trousers of pale drab or lavender doeskin . . . ," though "unfortunately invisible green and even black frock coats are occasionally seen [in the congregation] at weddings but both are inconsistent with the occasion except in the case of marriage to a clergyman." Morning coats were definitely advised against. As always with fashion, what was out soon became in: by the 1870s, and through the 1880s, morning coats had once more become standard for grooms. The 1890s moved toward more sober colors, and the frock coat, on its return, was now expected to be black, worn with a dark waistcoat.[58]

Increasing formality was partly an indication of the increasing size of the wedding party, and the display that that entailed. Early in the century the family group went together to the church. Later in the century friends and distant family connections were also invited. It may be that this was related to another change, which occurred in the 1870s and 1880s: presents were now expected from all guests and were displayed the day before at the bride's parents' house.

On the morning of the wedding day, the groom sent to his future in-laws' house a bouquet for the bride, and one for each of the bridesmaids, together with presents for them: a small piece of jewelry was standard. In 1863 when one of Louise Creighton's sisters married, her brother-in-law-to-be gave her and her sisters—who were to act as bridesmaids—lockets with a photograph of the bride in them.[59] Louise and her sisters were dressed in white, to match the bride, even though for bridesmaids this was already considered old-fashioned, and by the 1870s it was the norm for them to dress in contrast to the central figure. They were also commonly adults—usually younger sisters, cousins or friends of the bride, as is the custom in America today; the current British fashion of using children was then confined to page boys, who carried the bride's train. The Mayhew brothers' comic novel of an aspirant lower-middle-class woman, *The Greatest Plague of Life*, gave their protagonist bridesmaids "who are carriage people . . . they looked truly charming, for they are dear, good, showy girls."[60]

The 1895 edition of *Mrs Beeton's Book of Household Mangement* showed
an elaborate supper laid out *à la française* (p. 271ff). By this time the style was
old-fashioned except for ceremonial meals such as a wedding breakfast,
as itemized on p. 240.

After 1886, weddings could be performed in the afternoon. Until
then, twelve o'clock was the latest a marriage service could take place;
the extension to three o'clock meant that the wedding breakfast could
be eaten at the same time as an early dinner would have been on an ordinary day, and the couple would still be able to depart on their wedding
trip in daylight.[61] This was helpful, as the day was long and the breakfast was large. The word "breakfast" was a survival from the wedding's
earlier incarnation as a morning activity; the menu was a dinner menu,
with only the name remaining as a reminder of the meal's early history.

After the ceremony, wedding favors, prepared earlier by the bridesmaids, were given to the groomsmen, the bridesmaids, and all the servants connected with the bride's family (and for the bride and groom's
carriage horse). Women's favors might be a sprig of orange blossom
with silver leaves and white ribbon; men's could be silver oak leaves

and acorns.[62] Bridesmaids and groomsmen wore them pinned at the breast; servants wore theirs on the sides of their hats.*

The breakfast was as elaborate as means would allow. The table was laid out with all the foods.† A suggested summer menu, with the correct placement of each dish, was as follows:

Forequarter of lamb

Wedding cake

Veal pie   Chicken pie

White grapes

Cold salmon   Pigeons in jelly

Cherries   Cream   Strawberries

Hams   Epergne   Tongue

Flowers

Cold ducks   Galantine de veau

Lobster salad   Blancmange   Lobster salad

Jelly

Apricots   Peaches

Pigeons in jelly   Purple grapes   Peaches

Sponge cakes

Wine jelly   Whipped cream

Chickens and tongue

Tea and coffee[63]

---

*The horse could probably do what it wanted.

†For an explanation of service *à la française*, see pp. 271–74.

After a short time at the table, the bride went to change, and soon afterward the couple departed on their wedding trip. Slippers were tied to the back of the carriage, indicating that the bride was now her husband's possession rather than her father's,[64] and in the later part of the century, rice, a symbol of fertility, was thrown—by married ladies only.[65]

The remaining obligations were entirely those of social life. The bridesmaids went to the bride's father's house the day after the wedding to arrange for the new couple's wedding cards to be sent out. These had been supplied earlier by the groom, and were folded cards with his name on the outside and the bride's—her maiden name— inside the fold. They announced to the world that the marriage had taken place. The groom had left a list of people he wanted notified; the new bride was in theory obliged to include all the acquaintances whom she normally called on, although in practice her new position was frequently used as "an opportunity of dropping such acquaintances as she may not be desirous of retaining," as one etiquette book delicately put it, and if she was marrying up, there were usually a number of former friends to be left behind. As a halfway stage, mitigating the brutality of breaking off a relationship too abruptly, cards were sent without the couple's new address on them: this notified acquaintances of the marriage, but also let them know that the couple would prefer it if the recipient did not call; those who had a card with an address understood it to mean that after the wedding trip they were expected to call. The narrator of *The Greatest Plague of Life* was careful to "request my weeping mother to take care and see that a large piece of my wedding cake was sent round to each of the better class of our friends whom we wished to have the pleasure of visiting."[66] The "wedding visit" was at the couple's new home, and was entirely formal: the bride wore her wedding dress, as she was also to do at dinner parties for the first year, and wedding cake was served, with wine to drink the couple's health in. The couple returned these visits together, the bride dressed in her going-off dress. After this, they were no longer bride and groom, but now, formally, a married couple.[67]

·   ·   ·

Being able to set up a home at marriage was the middle-class ideal, but it was not one that most people could achieve. Studies of the town of Preston at midcentury showed that at least half, possibly more, of the population lived either with their families or in lodging houses for the first few years after marriage. It was usually children, rather than marriage itself, that precipitated the couple into their own house.[68] This pattern was perfectly replicated by Dickens in his own life. On his marriage in 1836, his wife, Catherine, moved in with him to his old chambers in Furnivall's Inn, where they lived together with Dickens's brother Frederick and Catherine's sister Mary.[69]

On finally achieving that holy grail, "an establishment," the newly married woman was faced for the first time with a house to look after. The more prosperous her family, the less she had been involved with housekeeping in her unmarried state. Childhood innocence was by now treasured, and innocence was equated with lack of knowledge. Many girls came to their marriages with a lack of information not merely about married life itself but even about how a household functioned. Before her marriage Maud Berkeley hoped to be of help, but she found herself "at a loss to know what to give [her parents] for dinner in [the cook's] absence. Consulted a number of recipe books, not one of which seemed to propose anything I felt I could possibly make."[70] This lack of reliable help from books was a great burden to many women, who left their mothers knowing nothing, and found learning not as easy as they had expected. Bella Wilfer, in *Our Mutual Friend* (1864–65), on her marriage was

> under the constant necessity of referring for advice and support to a sage volume entitled The Complete British Family Housewife·* . . . [But she] was by no means an expert Briton at expressing herself with clearness in the British tongue . . . In any crisis of this nature Bella would suddenly exclaim aloud, "Oh, you ridiculous

*Dickens has highlighted the favorite words of the advice-book writers: what could be better than something that was Complete and British *and* for a Family? See p. 4 for some actual magazine titles.

old thing, what do you mean by that? You must have been drinking!" . . . There was likewise a coolness on the part of the British
Housewife, which [Bella] found highly exasperating . . . she
would casually issue the order, "Throw in a handful —" of something entirely unattainable. In these, the Housewife's most glaring moments of unreason, Bella would shut her up and knock her
on the table, apostrophizing her with the compliment, "Oh, you
are a stupid old Donkey! Where am I to get it, do you think?"[71]

By contrast, the image these books gave was one of women who, with
servants to command, did relatively little themselves. *Cassell's Household Guide* gave a great buildup to how a home could be made more
homey: "There are many little things that can be done at a small cost
. . . little things that only want a small amount of patience, goodwill,
and energy to execute, and which amply repay the trouble they give."[72]
However, when it came right down to it the only thing the author
could suggest for prosperous housewives was that they make felt borders to stop the drafts under badly fitting doors, which perhaps indicated what upper-middle-class writers really felt about women's work.
Louise Creighton's duties appeared to have been correspondingly
light. She gave "many little dinners" for six or eight people, and they
"took up a great deal of time, getting & arranging flowers & dessert."
Dessert at this period meant fresh fruit and nuts, not the sweet puddings, cakes, or other dishes that are today called dessert (see pp. 272
and 284). In Louise Creighton's household these were produced by the
cook. Sometimes, Creighton added, "most of the day" was taken up by
these tasks.[73]

Marion Sambourne, with her three servants, did a little more around
the house: she dusted the drawing room (although not regularly), and
washed the more delicate objects there herself; she helped the maid
with putting things away. A diary entry reads: "Polished two pieces of
furniture, watered plants, practised [on the piano] one hour, looked out
things for [her son], cut out cloth for armchair."[74] She never did any
cooking, although some women made pastry or baked or had a spe-
cialty for dinner parties: Louise Creighton's mother "superintended

the preparation" of her *pièce de résistance*, a Russian salad. Louise in her turn learned, she said, to cook from a German servant, but this appears to have meant only baking and making preserves, and cooking for her was "a frequent amusement for a wet afternoon," rather than part of a household routine.[75]

Much of the household work for these upper-middle-class women was more of a pastime than real work, to be taken up and dropped at will. Gwen Raverat's mother wrote that just before her marriage she had been painting—"not artistic painting, but practical painting. I thought it would be a pleasant little surprise for Mamma to come home and find the dining room entirely repainted. So I bought the paint and have been brushing it on all morning . . . Now I have given it to one of the maids to finish. It is tiresome work."[76] She fitted in well with her future family: her mother-in-law's "work" was something called peggywork, in which longs strips of knitting were produced on a frame with hooks in it. Mrs. Darwin then handed the strips over to a maid to sew together to make rugs.[77]

The Darwins were among the élite, however. Most women faced rather more than peggywork every day. Mrs. Beeton's description of daily life for a married woman mostly involved paying calls, receiving and entertaining visitors, and supervising her children and a staff, "leaving the latter portion of the morning for reading, or for some amusing recreation."[78] However, as the editor of a modern edition has astutely pointed out, while the book was written as though the mistress were delegating all her work to servants, the layout of the chapters actually better served those doing the work themselves. For a supervisor, recipes would have been most usefully grouped by dishes that appeared together at the meal; Mrs. Beeton, however, grouped them by cooking method, which for the person doing the cooking was a far more useful arrangement.[79] The fiction that her reader was upper middle class was gracefully maintained while the reality of a middle-class or even a lower-middle-class housewife doing most of the work herself was adhered to in fact.

What was suitable for a lady to do varied substantially from household to household. Mrs. Gaskell wrote cheerfully that she had been "arranging lessons and [the] children's winter things," not to mention that "there is three-quarters of a pig awaiting me in the kitchen."[80] Jane Eyre remembered staying with the Rivers family: "Happy at Moor House I was, and hard I worked; and so did [the servant]: she was charmed to see how . . . I could brush, and dust, and clean, and cook."[81] Jane Carlyle also brushed and dusted and cleaned, and more. She routinely worked with her servant, making breakfast, sweeping the parlor, blackleading the grate, making her bed.[82] When the builders spattered her new wallpaper with whitewash, it was Jane who did "such scraping and rubbing . . . which [the maid] would not touch."[83] Despite these herculean endeavors, the following year she told her cousin that her maid was going to have to leave because she had become deaf and could not hear the doorbell, leaving Jane "having to go and seek *her* to *open* it."[84] There were, after all, some things that a respectable woman simply could not do.

Yet like Jane Carlyle, the majority of women worked regularly and hard in their houses: they made the beds, cleaned the lamps, washed windows, skinned and prepared meat for cooking, and made preserves and wine, as well as cooking daily meals, dusting, sweeping, scrubbing, sewing and upholstering, doing the laundry, making curtains and clothes, and cutting and laying carpeting; many even repaired shoes and boots. All the things that it is now thought that "genteel" women of the time did not do, they did.[85] If they then discussed their work as little as the books suggested, it is not difficult to understand why men thought that their homes were so comfortable that women were pleased to remain there—and why the women were less convinced.

In Mrs. Oliphant's *Phoebe Junior*, Reginald, the older brother of Ursula, has refused a job that would have been a sinecure—he says he could not contemplate being paid for work he would not be doing. Ursula is more pragmatic: her so-called sheltered life in the home has taught her what real work is.[86] Edmund Widdowson in Gissing's *The Odd Women* is equally certain that the moral value of housework is paramount: it is the house, rather than the work, that he focuses on when he tells his new wife, "It ought to be a pleasure to you to see that the house is kept in order." Monica is unpersuaded:

> "If we were poor . . . I believe I shouldn't grumble—at least, I hope I shouldn't. I should know that I ought to do what there was no one else to do, and make the best of it. But"—
>
> "Make the best of it! . . . What an expression to use! It would not only be your duty, dear, but your privilege!"
>
> "Wait a moment, Edmund. If you were a shopman earning fifteen shillings a week, and working from early morning to late at night, should you think it not only your duty but your privilege?"
>
> He made a wrathful gesture.
>
> "What comparison is there? I should be earning a hard livelihood by slaving for other people. But a married woman who works in her own home, for her husband and children"—[87]

Widdowson, as Gissing's mouthpiece for what he saw as retrograde, if common, ideas on marriage and the relationships between men and women, had strong views on the relative positions of men and women once they married: "Never had it occurred to Widdowson that a wife remains an individual . . . Everything he said presupposed his own supremacy; he took it for granted that it was his to direct, hers to be guided. A display of energy, purpose, ambition, on Monica's part, which had no reference to domestic pursuits, would have greatly troubled him; at once he would have set himself to subdue, with all gentleness, impulses so inimical to his idea of the married state."[88] Such attitudes were not simply fictional devices. When the Carlyles married three-quarters of a century earlier, Jane suggested that her widowed mother might come to live with them. Thomas refused: he felt that his gender gave him the right to command, but feared that his mother-in-law might think that age took precedence.[89]

Who ruled the family was an issue in multigenerational households. Ruskin's parents had no doubt that parental love took precedence over wifely regard. When Ruskin and his wife, Effie, stayed with them, Effie reported to her mother: "John's cold is not away yet but it is not so bad as he had with us and I think it would go away with care if Mr. and Mrs. Ruskin would only let him alone. They are telling him twenty times a day that it is very slight and only nervous, which I think it is. At the same time they talk constantly to him about what he ought to do, and in the morning Mrs. Ruskin begins with 'don't sit near these towels John they're damp' and in the forenoon 'John you must not read these papers till they are dried.'"[90]

In houses where there was only the married couple, or the couple with their children, the assumption was that the house was to be run around the needs of the man. Jane Carlyle felt obliged to refuse an invitation to accompany friends to Astley's Amphitheatre, a variety hall, although she very much wanted to go: "Mr C has gone to make a call at a distance and left word that he will not be back to dinner till 6— which means with *him* half an hour after six—so the carriage would come to snatch me away . . . before he had done eating, and that would hurt his digestion."[91] Her desire was not expected to take precedence over his convenience. Charles Dickens, when away from home, wrote to his wife: "Keep things in their places; I can't bear to picture them otherwise."[92] She was to suit even his convenience of imagination, rather than her own practical requirements in reality.

This acquiescence was expected to filter down the generations. Laura Forster recalled her mother's insistence that whatever her father said on matters of "conduct or belief" was unquestionable: "As I grew older . . . my mother was much troubled because I could not accept . . . all the religious and political opinions of my father . . . I remember her telling me when I was seventeen or eighteen that it grieved her to feel I did not take all my father's views as she did."[93] By the end of the century, wives did not take all their husbands' views either. Amy Reardon, in *New Grub Street*, is ordered by her husband to follow him to new lodgings. "You will do what I think fit," he thunders. Her response: "Do as *you* think fit? Indeed!"[94]

But the old ideas persisted that "women were very like children; it was rather a task to amuse them and to keep them out of mischief. Therefore the blessedness of household toil."[95] Throughout the century, this view of the woman kept penned up was symbolized by the caged bird: women were confined by their husbands even while they were protected by them, just as the birds were both imprisoned and sheltered. Elizabeth Barrett Browning's *Aurora Leigh* described a woman who "had lived / A caged bird life," and the metaphor was ever-present.[96] The references to the caged bird are so many they would fill a chapter in themselves, but a random sample includes Rochester describing Jane Eyre as a "curious sort of bird [seen] through the close-set bars of a cage," David Copperfield's mother, Little Nell in *The Old Curiosity Shop*, Dorothea Brooke as seen by Casaubon in *Middlemarch*, and Isabel Carlyle in *East Lynne*. In paintings the common image of the bird in the drawing room did, of course, reproduce a popular household pet, but its frequency symbolized more.[97]

The child-woman and the woman-child were to many people the ideal of womanhood. Childhood was a time of innocence, and prosperity allowed the innocence to be prolonged—in the case of women, indefinitely. Coventry Patmore reinforced the view, with love as the tool that ensured that women regressed to infant status:

> There's nothing left of what she was;
>   Back to the babe the woman dies,
> And all the wisdom that she has
>   Is to love him for being wise.[98]

Earlier Ann Richelieu Lamb had described from the woman's side what being a perpetual child-woman meant: "She may dance, sing, and be a child as long as she pleases, write pretty stories, string rosy words in rhyme—but to help in devising or practising such schemes as may be for the real benefit of mankind, becomes in her, a matter for ridicule, a subject for merriment, impertinence not to be endured."[99]

It was this dancing, singing child-woman who flitted across the pages of fiction—usually to die beautifully, because what else could she do? She could certainly never grow up. Dora Spenlow, David Copperfield's first wife, even referred to herself as his "child-wife." Bella Wilfer, in *Our Mutual Friend*, set out to be more than "the doll in the doll's house," even though at the end of the day all that that involved was reading the newspaper to have something to discuss with her husband; she was allowed to know of his business only when he magically came into his inheritance, not when he struggled.[100]

The reality of marriage to a woman who knew nothing and was never allowed to learn (for that would mean she became adult) was seen by Dinah Mulock Craik, even if she was not one who was usually sympathetic to the ideas of the New Woman. In *Olive* (1850), Angus Rothesay married, and then "woke from the dream to find his seraph of beauty—a baby-bride, pouting like a vexed child."[101] He had loved her for her childishness, and was now dismayed and aggrieved to find she was behaving like a child.

John Ruskin, in his brief and unhappy marriage, was in a similar position. He wrote to his solicitor during the divorce proceedings that "I married [Effie] thinking her so young and affectionate that I might influence her as I chose, and make of her just such a wife as I wanted. It appeared that *she* married *me* thinking she could make of me just the *husband she* wanted. I was grieved and disappointed at finding I could not change her, and she was humiliated and irritated at finding she could not change me."[102] The only explanation he could think of was that she must be suffering from some "slight nervous affection of the brain." This was obvious: she was "always thinking that I ought to attend *her*, instead of *herself* attending me."[103] What could that signify, except madness?

It is easy to mock Ruskin, but he was not out of step with his coevals in this respect. Women were prone to madness; their reproductive functions made this so.[*] Therefore any behavior that was unconventional, uncomfortable, or unusual could be dismissed and the woman brought to heel. In fiction—most spectacularly in the sensation novels of the 1860s, where bigamy, insanity, and murder are rife—women who were deviant in refusing the roles assigned to them were

---

[*]The subject is too large to go into here, although some small part of it is discussed on p. 94. It may be sufficient for a general sense of the mood of the times to note that in 1857 *The Lancet* thought that "madness . . . is a sufficiently common result of disturbed ovarian function."[104]

consigned to madhouses: in Mary Elizabeth Braddon's *Lady Audley's Secret* the obviously sane protagonist is locked up by her family; in Wilkie Collins's *The Woman in White* the equally sane Laura Glyde is confined by her husband for refusing to sign over her inheritance.

These fictional examples are extremes, but extremes of a spectrum that had only a small area of normal female behavior and a large area of deviant female behavior. Anything that fell beyond the norm therefore approached madness. When she was twelve, Constance Kent, later to be jailed for murdering her brother, attempted to escape a very unhappy household by running away from home dressed as a boy; her father claimed publicly that she had always been unstable, as was proved by this example of lack of "feminine delicacy." It was a handy excuse for Mr. Kent, and one he was to use again when, while acting as a sub-inspector of factories, he was called up before the Board of Factory Commissioners, because rumors of his attachment to his children's nursemaid had begun to circulate, together with comments on his wife's seclusion. He found a doctor to say that his wife was insane, and had been so for nearly a decade. This was accepted without protest, despite the fact that he had had five children by her in this same period.[105] On a slightly less dramatic note, when the actor Fanny Kemble left her husband, Pierce Butler, because of his adultery, he suggested that she had "morbid tendencies" and that her "mental derangement" was in danger of becoming permanent. This was not questioned. A woman friend wrote to her: "My poor, dear Fanny, my precious, almost idolized friend, do let me persuade you that your mind is diseased."[106]

Dickens notoriously used this convenient trope when he wanted to leave his own marriage. Catherine Dickens had produced ten children in sixteen years, and had also suffered a number of miscarriages. She was permanently exhausted and left the running of her house to her sister. Dickens was not content simply to move out; everyone, via a statement he published in the *New York Tribune*, should know that Catherine suffered from "a mental disorder." What else could explain a woman who was not interested in her home? When George Eliot set up house with the married G. H. Lewes, George Combe, a phrenologist, suggested that she could scarcely be sane.

Yet, while seemingly rejecting the notion of social norms, Lewes and Eliot in reality lived in St. John's Wood in a form indistinguishable from their more conventional neighbors. They could do this because her friends moved in a social world where such an arrangement could be accepted, or were women who had no social position to begin with. For where a woman fitted into the rules and obligations of society marked her whole life.

Darwin, contemplating marriage, set out the pros and cons in facing columns, the better to clarify the situation for him. The list is so extraordinary it deserves quoting in full:

MARRY

Children—(if it Please God) —Constant companion, (& friend in old age) who will feel interested in one,— object *to be beloved* and played with. better than a dog anyhow.—Home, & someone to take care of house—Charms of music & female chit-chat.—These things good for one's health.—*but terrible loss of time*.

My God, it is intolerable to Think of spending ones whole life, like a neuter bee, working, working, & nothing after all.— No, no won't do.—Imagine living all one's day solitary in smoky dirty London House. —Only picture to yourself a nice soft wife on a sofa with good

NOT MARRY

Freedom to go where one liked—choice of Society & *little of it*. Conversation of clever men at clubs—Not forced to visit relatives, & to bend in every trifle.—to have the expense & anxiety of children —perhaps quar-relling—**Loss of time.**— cannot read in the Evenings —fatness & idleness— Anxiety & responsibility— less money for books &c— if many children forced to gain one's bread.—(But then it is very bad for ones health to work too much)

Perhaps my wife wont like London; then the sen-tence is banishment & degradation into indolent, idle fool.

fire, & books and music
perhaps—Compare this
vision with the dingy reality
of Grt. Marlbro' St.
    Marry—Mary—Marry Q.E.D.[107]

If the choice had been available to them, would women have come to
the same conclusion?

7

THE DINING ROOM

DINING ROOMS WERE to the Victorian terraced house what kitchens are to its modern occupants. For us, kitchens are often the center of our social lives, places for gathering as a family and for entertaining. They serve many functions, all of which we perform happily in public. Dining rooms by contrast are one of the few single-function rooms left in the house. Middle-class Victorians, however, had to use them for what, in larger houses, would have occupied several rooms. Many terraced houses had only two reception rooms. One was reserved for entertaining, for "best." Eating in the kitchen was what the working classes did: it was taking a private area and making it public. To avoid this the middle classes used their second reception room— usually the one at the back of the house—as both a dining room and a family sitting room.

Its decoration was of necessity less focused than that of many other rooms. It needed to serve two groups of people, at least, for many more than two activities. At midcentury, dining rooms were considered masculine spaces, even though it was women who spent the most time in them. Feminine spaces were the drawing room, the morning room, the nursery, and the bedroom—places of socialization and children, where women were acknowledged to be in charge. Masculine spaces were the study, if there was one, and the dining room (the burning importance of the dinner hour to men is discussed later, pp. 269–71).

These masculine rooms were therefore to be dark, sober, just as the feminine drawing room was to be light-colored, more fanciful. A model dining room had a "Turkey" carpet and dark paper. If the carpet had some red in it (which most did), "then you must have crimson curtains, crimson sofa, crimson everything."

A suggested model for a multifunctional sideboard in 1888. Above the shelves display china, silver, or plate, while underneath bookshelves and cupboards store items for use when the room serves as a sitting room.

Charles Eastlake, a writer on design (and later the keeper of the National Gallery), despaired of this kind of advice. He derided those who listened when they were told that these crimson wallpapers were "elegant," "genteel," and "in much request."[1] Yet this was what current fashion dictated: red flock wallpaper, in floral or arabesque patterns, with red curtains to match, draped heavily across the floor and well past the window embrasure, to stop drafts. Chairs were upholstered in red, with solid, dark wood, the sideboard was in solid, dark wood, the table was in solid, dark wood.[2] The wood was preferably mahogany, or if that was too expensive, something with a dark grain. The chimneypiece, the door handles, and the finger plates were likewise similarly dark, if possible black.[3] Dark green was generally considered a good contrasting "masculine" color, for both dining rooms and studies.

The dining room was the most public room in the house. The drawing room was where ladies congregated when calling, but the dining room was where formal displays of hospitality were made, on which the status of the family was judged. One could not, therefore, be too careful in one's choices of furnishing. The mirror that was normally placed over the mantel "by its shape or size [gave] either a common or a refined aspect to a room." If the mirror was higher than it was wide, while still extending the full width of the mantel, then it was refined; a mirror wider than it was high was common. "It is better to sacrifice something else in the room, and expend the money on a good glass," said *Cassell's Household Guide.*[4] This was standard advice-book obfuscation. A mirror wider than it was high, yet fitting the width of the mantel, meant a low-ceilinged room. The occupants were thus being reminded that they did not live in a house with good proportions.

After the mirror, the crowning aspect of the room was the sideboard. Mrs. Caddy thought that it was "the glory of the dining room" and should take up the whole of one wall, displaying a dessert service, ornaments, and table decorations. If the room was big enough, she preferred two sideboards, one the full width of the wall and one smaller.[5] This idea of display was important, although details altered as the century progressed. By the 1880s Robert Edis was suggesting that a smaller sideboard could be used if the display elements were transferred to the wall above the fireplace, which could hold a "main shelf sufficiently broad to take . . . the various ornaments, useful or otherwise, which are wanted, with perhaps a centre panel for a good portrait or subject picture, enframed in boldly carved moulding; round it, on either side, might be plain panelling, carried up to the ceiling line, with recesses for sculpture or bronzes, or tiers of shelves for those whose tastes lie in china or other bric-a-brac, the top perhaps finished with a bold curved cove, filled in with stamped leather or decorative enrichment."[6] In effect, this was the same sort of elaborate overmantel he had recommended for the drawing room (see pp. 193–94).

Colors altered rapidly. The passion for crimson was swept away when aniline dyes produced a host of new colors: now peacock blues, magenta (first known as "fuchsine"), and pinks all briefly held center stage. Others created in this first wave of enthusiasm were Tyrian purple—soon to be renamed mauve and appropriated as a mourning color—and yet others now lost to us, such as Britannia violet, as well as colors that commemorated the atmosphere of cities: Manchester yellow, Manchester brown, London dust, Dust of Ruins.[7] It was only a short time that these vibrant shades were in vogue. From the 1860s onward William Morris and the Aesthetic movement brought softer colors back into fashion. Fashion, however, seemed too frivolous a reason to undertake something so important as altering one's house, so writers on design frequently justified these alterations to colors in a manner like that of the author of *The Dining Room*. Mrs. Loftie was sure that what she proposed was "based upon scientific calculations analogous to those which obtain in the sister art of music. It is in no way connected with the caprices of fashion."[8] Nonetheless, it is noteworthy that gray, sage, and olive drab were all scientifically suitable at exactly the same moment that fashion approved of them too. The transparency of the reasoning should not mask the anxiety these changes brought. People do not bother to tell themselves that things are "scientific" if they do not seem of fundamental importance, and the dining room—the most public of the public rooms—was indeed of fundamental importance. It and the drawing room would be the first to receive fashionable updatings.

In his enormously popular comedy *Vice Versa*, the playwright F. Anstey contrasted these changes of fashion, which were given so much importance, to what people lived with year after year: the house in Westbourne Terrace, in the newly fashionable suburb of Paddington, where the play was set, was "furnished in the stern uncompromising style of the Mahogany Age . . . Here were no skilfully contrasted shades of grey or green, no dado, no distemper on the walls; the woodwork was grained and varnished after the manner of the philistines, the walls papered a dark crimson, with heavy curtains of the same colour, and the sideboard, dinner-wagon, and row of stiff chairs were all carved in the same massive and expensive style of ugliness."9

Although the fashionable led the way through Aestheticism and the Arts and Crafts movement, many dining rooms continued to be furnished in mahogany and scarlet throughout the century. These colors represented solidity and a bourgeois sense of having achieved a proper style, reflecting a proper place in the world, and this ensured that they were not to be lightly erased. As late as the 1880s Caroline Louisa Taylor's great-aunt in Leamington Spa still had in her dining room every horror that Mrs. Panton and her friends were busily rejecting. The room was "furnished in mahogany upholstered in deep red which was also the colour of the curtains. Along one wall was an escritoire . . . The top was a cupboard with fancy glass panes and in there was the plate basket, wine glasses, decanters . . . and an exquisite dessert service."10 Compton Mackenzie's mother, as the wife of an actor-manager, could afford to reject the old-fashioned standards of red and green for daring café-au-lait walls, as she lived among artists. Mrs. Panton would have claimed to approve. She warned her readers "specially against green"; she felt that it "should be avoided entirely" in the dining room. Yet even she, though wanting to be of the moment, had an automatic default mode that sent her right back to the older style. On the page following her advice to avoid green, she described her model dining room: it had a green carpet, a green tablecloth, a mantel and overmantel in green-stained wood, green-stained dining chairs and a green-stained dresser. Most people, like E. H. Shepard's aunts in the formidably upright Gordon Square in Bloomsbury, followed what

Mrs. Panton did rather than what she said. The Shepard aunts had a green dining room, "rather dark, with large bookcases; an enormous mahogany sideboard took up almost one end of the room . . . The furniture was of solid mahogany, and not very comfortable, and there was always a slight smell of dinner."[11]

Smells were always a problem. It was difficult enough to get a room warm; once it was, no one was going to open the window of an occupied room to air it. Smells went hand in hand with warmth, and only rooms that were empty for long periods could be aired properly. This was rarely the case in the dining room, which was a place where "work, reading, drawing and writing [went on all day, and] had to be hustled out of sight and out of the way . . . to 'lay the cloth' and renew the foul odours, which . . . breakfast had left behind it to poison the morning with." Smoking in the dining room after dinner was disapproved of: the house was locked up for the night soon after dinner; the room could not be aired out overnight, and the smell of tobacco lingered in the carpets and curtains to greet the family at breakfast time.[12]

Mrs. Panton warned that decorating the dining room was the most expensive part of setting up house. The amount of furniture this multipurpose room required was formidable: although the room had many functions, wherever possible each piece of furniture was to serve one purpose only. So, although there was a large table in the center of the room, it was for eating at, and most wanted to have something else, to use as a writing table.[13] This desk was often used by the husband for any household work he did—accounts, letters, and so on—and when he was out during the day it was where the woman of the house dealt with her own accounts and answered her correspondence. Louise Creighton's mother, who lived in a large house in Sydenham, still had in the dining room for this purpose her davenport, a small desk with a sloped top over a pedestal made up of drawers.[14] (It is not to be confused with the American usage, meaning sofa.) Ideally, a writing desk was no matter of a small table pushed into a corner. It needed to be large enough to hold everything that might conceivably be necessary for what was, in effect, a home office that also had a decorative, display element. Mrs. Panton listed for her ideal writing table two inkstands

The Housewife's Treasury of Domestic Information (1884) shows a model dining room, which has space for the dining table, a small tea table, and unseen
armchairs, next to the footstool at the bottom right, for use after dinner. This
imaginary room is wider than that in any real terraced house which needed to
use the dining room as a family room.

(one for red ink, one for black), "a box for string, . . . a post-card case, a letter-weigher [i.e., a scale], and a date-card and candlestick, and also a tray for sealing-wax, pens, ink-eraser . . . If possible keep a bunch of flowers on the desk . . . and . . . dictionaries, two plants, and three brass pigs taking a walk."[15]

Before the telephone, and while the telegraph was an expensive novelty, desks were even more heavily used than they are today in the home, for the post occupied a central place in daily life. Postal deliveries had changed radically in 1840, when Sir Rowland Hill pushed through his scheme of penny postage. Before this time a letter had to be paid for by its recipient, and the charge was calculated both by weight and by distance: a one-ounce letter from London to Birmingham cost 9d., to Liverpool 11d., and even to Brighton, less than fifty miles away, it cost 8d. With the penny post, letters were to be "stamped"—that is, franked at a post office at the time of posting—or, alternatively, a newfangled adhesive square could be bought ahead of time and stuck onto a newfangled envelope. The new system was feasible now that all letters weighing up to half an ounce (soon raised to four ounces) cost only 1d., no matter where in the United Kingdom they were going. Many appreciated the timesaving aspect of the envelope. Geraldine Jewsbury wrote to her friend Jane Carlyle in 1849, "I will send you a quantity of stamped adhesive envelopes, and then all the material bother of sealing &c., will be done away with." Others were less enthusiastic. In *Cranford*, one gentleman is so shocked by the wastage implicit in envelopes that whenever he receives one he turns it inside out and uses it again. But the system caught on nevertheless: in 1854 alone, 515 post offices were opened to serve the rapidly growing market, and perforated stamps had arrived, doing away with the scissors previously chained to every post office desk. The following year saw the arrival of street collections—that is, pillar boxes—in London,* and the post office frank was phased out: stamps were now compulsory.

Not everyone was impressed by a service that allowed husbands to

---

*At least in part invented by Anthony Trollope in his daytime job as civil servant in the post office.

send a note to their wives at lunchtime, to advise them of their time of arrival that evening. In a letter to *The Times* in 1851, an outraged citizen complained that a letter posted in central London at 1:30 had failed to reach its destination, a matter of a mile and a half away, until 4:00 that same afternoon. Yet most were happy. In 1840, when the system was instituted, 169 million letters were sent every year; in 1889 the system supported a staggering 1,558 million letters.[16]

As well as the desk at which to keep up this volume of correspondence, the dining room/sitting room needed a couple of armchairs for reading in, together with a bookcase; if no other space was available, a few drawers in the sideboard might double as filing space for correspondence and other papers. The women also sewed in the dining room. In more prosperous families, this meant decorative sewing or small items that were held on the lap; in the less well-off, the women used the dining table as a sewing area for making dresses and other large items. The Bradshaw women in Mrs. Gaskell's *Ruth* (1853) were wealthy, and their workboxes were permanent fixtures in the dining room; in Mrs. Gaskell's own, less well-to-do home, her daughter Meta was "working hard at the dining-room table, mending your pink gown," Mrs. Gaskell wrote to her eldest daughter, away at school.[17] Eleanor Farjeon described a family evening: "I took my book into the dining-room, and sat down on one side of the mahogany table. [Her brother] with *his* book, read opposite me. Papa, in the big leather armchair by the fire, was reading the *Globe* . . . Mama was doing wool cross-stitch on a pair of carpet-slippers for Papa's next Christmas."[18]

For the lower middle classes, the sitting room, which doubled as a dining room, often became a secondary kitchen. Even when the house was large enough to have both rooms, bits of cooking apparatus sometimes spilled over, particularly in houses with no women. Bachelors were considered likely to manage in this way, because many had lived in lodging houses where, at the mercy of their landladies—commonly portrayed as rapacious or drunken, or both—they had learned to fend for themselves in one or two rooms.

These unfortunate womenless men cooked small suppers over the fire to avoid the unpleasant and expensive food supplied from the landlady's kitchen. If they could afford it, or when they entertained, they had food sent in from coffeehouses, bakehouses, or pastry cook-shops. The cost and quality of the meal and the service provided varied. Bakehouses were the least expensive option: they simply cooked the food supplied to them already prepared in dishes;* coffeehouses, which were more costly, delivered full meals, together with cutlery, crockery, a tablecloth, and condiments, and the waiters who brought the food stayed and served it; pastry cookshops supplied "made" dishes such as pies. David Copperfield, when he moved into lodgings, invited some friends for a supper party. He decided to serve "a pair of hot roast fowls—from the pastry cook's; two little corner things,† as a raised pie and a dish of kidneys—from the pastry cook's; a tart, and . . . a shape of jelly—from the pastry cook's. This, [his landlady] said, would leave her at full liberty to concentrate her mind on the potatoes, and to serve up the cheese and celery as she could wish to see it done."[20]

What people ate, and how much, was governed entirely by income. Food was proportionately one of the most expensive items in the budget. In the 1860s and 1870s a family with an income at the lower end of the middle classes—about £140 a year—expected to spend about £30 on rent, property taxes, and water, while spending nearly £80 a year on food. The consumption for this income, per person per day, was approximately 3 ounces of meat, 2 ounces of cheese, 2 ounces of butter, 1 pound of potatoes, and ½ pound of bread. By contrast, a family with an income of between £300 and £500 a year expected to consume, per person per day, between ½ pound and 3 pounds of meat, 3 ounces of cheese, 8 ounces of butter, and over 2 pounds of potatoes, as well as the same ½ pound of bread that their poorer friends did. Tea consumption ranged from ½ pound a week for an entire family to ¼ pound per week per person.[21]

---

*Bakehouses were considered less than satisfactory for anything other than basic dishes. Because everything was baked together in a communal oven, temperature control was not possible, and pastry suffered in ovens better suited to meat. The honesty of bakehouses was a problem too; the careful customer had his bread or meat weighed when he took it in, so that sections were not cut off and sold to others.[19]

†For an explanation of corner dishes, see p. 271*n*.

Breakfast was generally a solid meal. At the end of the century a dispensing chemist and his wife, living on about £100, recorded that they had cocoa and either bread and butter with fish or eggs and bacon; their children ate bread and milk, or porridge alternating with an egg. More prosperous families had more choice, if of a similar nature: eggs, bacon, kidneys, mushrooms, grilled fish or kedgeree—an Indian-style dish made up of curried rice and smoked fish—with a cold ham or tongue on the side. Usually there was one hot dish each morning, with toast and jam. Mrs. Panton warned that hot buttered toast or hot fresh bread should never be served, as "these two items make the butter bill into a nightmare."[22] Unusually, however, she recommended that fruit should be eaten at breakfast by both adults and children. Many thought fruit, particularly fresh fruit, "unwholesome": *The Lady's Every-Day Book* warned against pears; Jane Carlyle thought any fruit gave colic to those foolish enough to consume it (which goes some way to explaining Thomas Carlyle's chronic dyspepsia); Gwen Raverat's family thought it "a pleasant treat, [but] rather dangerous."[23] Many others did not make definite statements, but the only fruit that appeared in their weekly menus was either stewed or in a tart or pudding, and then only once or twice a week. Mrs. Beeton recommended grapes as a cure for "the most obstinate cases of constipation," but she added that the pips and skin should not be eaten.[24]

Luncheon, with the men away from home, was often combined with the children's dinner, and so was a more substantial meal than if the woman of the house had eaten alone or with her friends. The table was set with a cloth, and "slips," additional narrow bands of cloth, were laid down the sides to protect it if children were present. The cloth—"of course," noted one advice-book writer—was not the same one that was used later, for dinner.[25] Luncheon cloths were among the many consumer durables that were beginning to appear for the first time, both to provide extra luxuries for people with additional income and to enforce segregation even further. With luncheon cloths, meals were demarcated by style as well as by time and menu.

A suitable luncheon for women was "the remains of cold joints, nicely garnished, a few sweets, or a little hashed meat, poultry or game," thought Mrs. Beeton.[26] If children were eating, potatoes and a pudding were added, with possibly a few vegetables, although many writers were hesitant about this. Mrs. Warren stated argumentatively, "Vegetables were not forbidden [for her children], for I consider them wholesome and easy of digestion if properly cooked," which sounds very much as though others commonly did not. Most followed the system of Dr. Chavasse, who suggested that "occasionally" a vegetable might be given.[27] (No one counted potatoes as a vegetable: they accompanied almost all children's dinners.)

The meat-plus-starch approach was standard for children and for the women who ate with them. It was also the kind of meal that servants were given once a day: plain, filling, with little or nothing elaborate, with no strong or spicy flavors. *Cre-Fydd's Family Fare* was more stringent, or, as it would have been seen, thrifty. When the dining-room dinner consisted of curried mutton, fried tripe, rice, potatoes, and baked marmalade pudding, the kitchen got "cold mutton, potatoes."[28] Sometimes what was suggested and what was actually served were at odds: Hannah Cullwick wrote in her diary of having nothing in the house, so "I went out for the children's supper & got a lobster"[29]—probably not what Mrs. Beeton had had in mind. Most children and servants, however, ate the same very basic food day after day.

Day after day in more ways than one. Leftovers were a perennial subject. The housewife was expected to examine the previous day's remains every morning, before giving orders for that day's meals. Whatever was left was to be used up as quickly and thriftily as possible. In houses with several servants, the servants were expected to finish off the less luxurious parts of the dining-room meals. Where there was only one servant, the same meals tended to arrive in the dining room time and again. (It is noticeable that the luncheon prescribed by Mrs. Beeton above was made up almost entirely of leftovers. She was not, in fact, particularly interested in anything except dinner, to which she devoted 109 pages of recipes, compared to a total of half a page for breakfast, luncheon and supper combined.)[30] Most weekly menu plans listed entirely new dinners only three days a week; the other four were made up of reheated food from previous days. *Cassell's Household*

Guide suggested that if the housewife was skilled at planning, food appeared only once, but this seems not to have been borne out in actuality. Most writers fully expected dishes to reappear. Mrs. Beeton gave numerous recipes for recooking food, usually meat—her Scotch Collops was reheated veal in a white sauce; her Indian Fowl was reheated chicken covered with a curry sauce; Monday's Pudding was made with the remains of Sunday's plum pudding—not to mention the recipes she gave for endless types of patty, potted meat, and minced meat, all of which used cooked meat as their base.[31]

The return of the same food was so regular that it was a common basis for comic stories. Beatrix Potter wrote in her diary of "some Manchester people" whose new maid "cut up a cake or some kind of sweetmeat before handing it round. She thought the old lady looked rather aghast, and the next morning received a reprimand. That cake had been offered at supper for three years and now she had cut it up."[32] The story was obviously apocryphal, yet, as with all comic stories, there had to be a basis of truth to it in order for it to be considered funny. (It is also confirmation that guests at a meal were commonly not expected to accept all the foods that were served. See p. 274.) Similarly, Mr. and Mrs. Pooter had a party where a blancmange was served; it then became one of the great running jokes of the book as it reappeared over and over.[33]

Meals with men present had more substance to them. As well as a meat dish, there was commonly expected to be soup and fish, served first—this was economical, as it took the edge off hunger with cheaper foods before the more expensive roast appeared. Then there were vegetables, puddings, and sweet dishes. Many books offered sample menus for the entire year. One, which may stand in for many others like it, suggested a week's breakfasts and dinners. (Luncheon, or the woman's meal, was ignored: the housewife presumably ate leftovers from the day before.)

SUNDAY
Breakfast: Broiled haddock, poached eggs, cold meat, honey
Dinner: Oxtail soup, boiled leg of mutton, caper sauce, mashed

turnips, carrots, potatoes; mince pies, almond pudding, Welsh rabbit

Kitchen: 1-pound beefsteak pudding, potatoes, mince pies

MONDAY

Breakfast: Broiled bacon, bloaters [cured herring], cold meat from Sunday's mutton

Dinner: "Economical soup" [made from the water Sunday's beef had been boiled in], curried mutton from Sunday, fried tripe, rice, potatoes; baked marmalade pudding, cheese, celery

Kitchen: Cold mutton from Sunday, potatoes

TUESDAY

Breakfast: Omelette, sausages on toast, sardines

Dinner: Economical soup, roast fowl, tongue, rump steak, broccoli, mashed potatoes, bread sauce and gravy; Victoria pudding, stewed cheese

Kitchen: Hashed mutton from Sunday, apple pudding

WEDNESDAY

Breakfast: Cold fowl from Tuesday's dinner, tongue from Tuesday's dinner, eggs, marmalade

Dinner: Fried cod with fried oysters, minced fowl from Tuesday, savory rice, mutton chops, potatoes, fried broccoli; brandy bread pudding, "cheesikins" [savory biscuits]

Kitchen: Irish stew with cold mutton from Sunday

THURSDAY

Breakfast: Buttered eggs, tongue from Tuesday's dinner, bloaters, marmalade

Dinner: Roast loin of mutton, lobster cutlets [i.e., patties of chopped lobster], potatoes, currant jelly; apple fritters, cheese, celery

Kitchen: Beefsteak pie from Tuesday's rump steak, potatoes

FRIDAY

Breakfast: Potted meat [made with remnants from various

meals during the week], broiled kidneys, poached eggs

Dinner: Fried sole, mutton from Wednesday's dinner stewed with pickles, veal cutlets, brussels sprouts, mashed potatoes; cheese

Kitchen: Cold pie from Thursday, leftover meat, potatoes, rice pudding

SATURDAY

Breakfast: Kippered salmon, mutton chops from Tuesday's dinner, cold sole from Friday's dinner, preserves

Dinner: "Palestine" [Jerusalem artichoke] soup, calf's head (half), bacon, broccoli, mashed potatoes; raisin pudding, cheese

Kitchen: Mutton "etc.," or general meat leftovers, potatoes, currant dumplings[34]

The two major changes that took place over the century were the times at which meals were served (and what they were called), and the manner of serving them. The timing of meals was considered of essential importance, in terms of both timekeeping itself and the social implications of when one ate each meal. Dinner had, earlier, been a meal eaten at midday; supper was served early in the evening, and tea came after, before bed. By midcentury, when most middle-class men were no longer working at home, dinner moved to the later hour of five or six, after the office workers returned home. From this hour, those who did not have to get up for work the next morning pushed dinner ever later, as a sign of leisure. The upper middle classes copied them, in order to indicate their own gentility, and the middle classes, in turn, followed their lead, in order to separate themselves from those beneath them. Improved gas and oil lighting also meant that eating after dark was no longer the expense it had been earlier, and gradually, as the century progressed, only the elderly, the stubbornly old-fashioned, or those so low on the social scale as to be unconcerned ate their dinner during the day.

Ruskin, after his marriage in 1848, entertained frequently, having guests to dinner at six o'clock; his parents disapproved of this as "unhealthy"—unhealthily late, that is. Mrs. Gaskell would most likely have won their approval: her family ate dinner between four and five (unless, like Dora Spenlow's aunts in *David Copperfield*, the elder Ruskins thought the even older fashion for dinner at three more suitable).[35] Both the Ruskins and the Gaskells expected to have tea three or four hours after their dinner. Henry and Augustus Mayhew mocked the fashionable world in their novel *Living for Appearances*, the story of an ultra-smart couple who dare do nothing that is not approved of by the beau monde:

> It was only three o'clock, p.m., and yet Mr. Wellesley Nicholls and his wife were about to dine. Such a flagrant transgression of the rules of fashionable or civilized society was the more remarkable because Mr. Wellesley Nicholls had often been heard . . . to express himself in very forcible terms on the disgusting and tradesman-like custom of early dining . . . he had been known to exclaim, "Better is a dry crust and gentility at seven, than baked mutton and vulgarity at two." His usual hour for eating was seven.

As, however, he was forced by circumstances that day to dine at three, "the parlour blinds were carefully drawn down."[36]

By the 1870s, even those less concerned than the Nichollses ate later. Hannah Cullwick's employers—a widow and her daughters—regularly ate at five, which was the same time that Mr. Pooter had his dinner on his return from the City. When his son, Lupin, invited his parents to dinner at eight, they were horrified: "I said we did not pretend to be fashionable people, and would like the dinner earlier."[37]

As dinner, for the fashionable, moved later, after-dinner tea was no longer necessary to bridge the gap until bedtime. Instead it moved earlier, to fill in the longer period between luncheon (which in families without children was a light meal) and dinner, and to greet the office worker on his return home. This change took time to be assimilated. In the 1850s the Carlyles still invited people to tea after dinner, at about seven o'clock: this was thriftier than having them for the meal itself, and made an evening entertainment.[38] As late as 1883 the advice writer Mrs. James needed to emphasize that afternoon tea was now "an institution," and she found it equally necessary to note precisely when it should be served and what kind of food was expected. For the upper middle classes it was finger food—small sandwiches or cakes.[39] Lower down the social scale, tea was more substantial: often called a meat tea or high tea, it included eggs or meat—protein of some sort—to assuage the hunger of the clerk who had not been able to afford more than a coffeehouse lunch, or of the manual laborer after hard physical activity.* The more prosperous liked this habit, even if they could not quite bring themselves to call it tea. Sarah Thomas, on a trip to Bath, went out for a "bountiful tea and supper. We had cutlets and forcemeat balls, a most handsome joint of cold beef, potatoes whole and mashed, hot plum pudding, mincepies, jam tarts, beside some others, and a beautiful salad."[40]†

The time at which meals were served was important; that they were served precisely on time was essential. It was not coincidental that the nineteenth-century obsession with time coincided with the high period of factory work and the expansion of the railway. Factory workers were called to their shifts at set times by whistles, rather than being ruled by daylight. Train schedules made every minute important; no longer did a stagecoach leave the staging post more or less at the time announced, when all the passengers were packed in. And in the

---

*This is the opposite of what many Americans refer to as high tea. The thinking behind this U.S. neologism is that if tea is genteel, then high tea must be supergenteel. Invitations for all-women gatherings, such as baby showers, often specify "high tea," and the food is very much what an English tea would be, not a high, or meat, tea.

†Sarah Thomas's fondness for salad contradicts one of our current notions of Victorian cuisine. There were many mentions of salad, and also of "salad cream"— hard-boiled eggs puréed with cream, mustard, salt, and vinegar. Mrs. Beeton also gave an olive oil–based dressing, made with three tablespoons of oil to four of vinegar, which she said was for dressing cucumbers. She added: "Generally speaking, delicate stomachs should avoid this plant, for it is cold and indigestible." With those proportions of oil and vinegar, it is hardly surprising.[41]

same period the time at which household tasks were performed became as much a part of an orderly life as the routines themselves. Mrs. Ellis warned her "Daughters of England" that "in all our pursuits . . . it is highly important to habituate ourselves to minute calculations upon the value and progress of time," for "every year, and month, and day, have their separate amount of responsibility." Time was to be "laid out" carefully, as money was.[42] To waste time was every bit as reprehensible as to waste money.

Good housekeeping meant good timekeeping. Bells or gongs marked the main events of the day: family prayers, if they were held, were announced by a bell to summon the family and servants together; meals were announced by a gong or bell, and, in prosperous families, dressing bells rang some time before dinner to mark the moment when all were expected to retire to change for the meal.[43] At Steerforth's house in *David Copperfield* a "warning bell" is rung half an hour before breakfast, so that no one is late when the breakfast bell itself rings. Mrs. Gaskell's small daughter was summoned to join her parents after their dinner by a bell: she "danc[es] with delight when she hears the bell which is a signal for her." Augustus Hare, on a visit to a friend, was told that "at whatever hour of the day or night you hear that gong sound, you will know that you are expected to appear *somewhere*."[44] In prosperous households, this was no longer absolutely necessary—even school-aged boys had pocket watches by that time—but in less prosperous circumstances, everyone would rely on one clock.

Dinner being late was a sign of disastrous housekeeping: whatever happened, whatever emergencies occurred, a good wife ensured that her husband was not kept waiting for his meal. In fiction, late dinner was a standard shorthand to indicate a wife who was lacking in either ability or love: Dora Spenlow was incapable of getting her servant to serve dinner on time; Mrs. Jellyby's family had only a "nominal" dinner hour, "for we dine at all hours." George Gissing's Edmund Widdowson stood in for all disgruntled husbands when one Sunday his wife persuaded him to pay a visit to some friends, which meant that their Sunday dinner—normally eaten at one o'clock—was postponed. On their return, he announced, "This disorder really won't do."[45]

The dinner that this prototypical husband was looking forward to at the end of the century had undergone a radical alteration in form over the previous half century, and as the old style has disappeared from modern memory, it is worth looking at that middle-class norm in some detail. Previously, dinners had been served *à la française*: much of the food was put on the table at once, and the meal was served in two or three "removes." When the diners arrived at the table, summoned by the dinner bell, the food was in place, often over dishes of hot water to keep it warm. There was a tureen of soup at one end of the table, in front of the mistress, and fish at the other end, in front of the master. (Elaborate dinner parties might have two kinds of soup and two fish dishes, in which case the soup was served first and then removed by the fish, as it was phrased.) The master and mistress served the soup and the fish with, if possible, a servant present to pass the dishes as they were filled. If there were guests, the man on the hostess's right helped her to carve the fish if there were two or dish up the soup. It was rude to ask if a guest wanted soup or fish; as one advice book noted, "He will probably take both, and it limits him to one by the question."[46] After the fish and the soup, a roast joint was put in front of the host and a fowl in front of the hostess, and again they served their family or guests. The side or corner dishes (so called because they filled the sides and corners of the table) were carried or passed round, depending on the number of servants and the level of formality.* They were dishes of single-portion meats, such as sweetbreads, cutlets, or kidneys; meat-based dishes such as patties, rissoles, and croquettes; or made dishes

---

*A side or corner dish was also known as an entrée, because it was there when the diners entered the room. This term is not to be confused with the modern word, meaning either a first-course dish (to the British and French) or the main course (to Americans). "Made" dishes were side or corner dishes that were cooked in a sauce. Being "foreign," sauces were open to some doubt as to their merit: "*Made-dishes,* as the horrible imitations of French cookery . . . are termed . . . are very unwholesome," warned *The Lady's Every-Day Book*.[47]

such as curries and stews. The main thing that defined them was that they were easy to serve and needed no carving.

The layout of a table set for dinner *à la française* was very important. A good meal encompassed not merely what was served, but in what order, and what it looked like: "No two dishes resembling each other should be near the same part of the table." If there were two soups, they were to be placed at the top and bottom of the table; if four, top, bottom, and in the middle at either side, opposite each other. The two soups should be "a white and a brown, or a mild and a high-seasoned soup," while the fish, boiled and fried, should be placed opposite each other, not together—more segregation. The meat course, likewise, was expected to have one "white" and one "brown" meat: chicken and beef, for example. If there was one principal dish it was placed at the head of the table; if two, at the head and the foot; if three, one went at the head, two at the bottom on opposite sides of the table. If there were as many as four, size helped the decision process: the largest went at the head, the next at the foot, and the other two at the sides.

Guests and family took part in the meal in a more active way than simply waiting to be served. At dinner parties the men were expected to help the women next to them to wine until the midcentury, when the servants began to take over this duty. In *The Daisy Chain*, Ethel went to a dinner that was "so grand, that no side-dish fell to her lot";[48] had it been more informal, she as a guest, or a family member, would have participated in the serving of the meal.

After the joint, the table was completely cleared and the meat was removed by the same number of dishes, this time with a sweet dish in front of the hostess and a savory one—often game—in front of the host. The side dishes were now vegetables, jellies, creams, trifles, and confectionery. At formal meals, after this the table was again cleared, and cheese, butter, salad, celery, radishes, and cucumber removed the sweet dishes. Then the table was cleared once more—and at formal dinners the cloth was taken away—and dessert arrived, dessert meaning simply fruit and nuts, with finger bowls being provided if they had not been on the table throughout the meal. After the fruit, the hostess rose and the women left the dining room. If the home was prosperous and the men had hearty appetites, then "zests" might be brought in at this point: anchovy toast, deviled dishes, or other piquant food considered too highly spiced for women.

Family dinners were less elaborate. There were normally only two removes. The first was soup and fish, removed by poultry, ham, tongue, stews, roasts, curries, or any other made dishes, with vegetables; the second was poultry and vegetables, "macaroni" (a generic reference to any kind of noodles), jellies, creams, pastry, and salad. The soup was served by the wife; after it was eaten the fish was served by the husband, and the servant passed the sauce. The servant then took clean plates from the sideboard and passed the entrées, together with vegetables, which were eaten while the joint was being carved by the master. Savory dishes and sweets were handed around on plates.[49]

The quantities that were served seem enormous to us. Mrs. Gaskell described a meal that included a sirloin of beef "at the bottom of the table, and 2 turkeys at the top."[50] A winter dinner for eight people was laid out on the table as follows:[51]

On the table as the diners enter

Hare soup

Oyster patties   Cotelettes à la Maintenon

Oyster sauce

Cod's head and shoulders

First remove

Boiled turkey

Mashed potatoes   Stewed sea-kale

Saddles of mutton

> *Second remove*
>
> Cabinet pudding
> Jaune mange*
>
> Punch jelly   Cheese fondue
>
> Brace of partridges

To see this as too much food is, however, to misunderstand the nature of the meal. No one was expected to eat everything that appeared; the variety was instead to ensure that there was something to please every appetite. A clue to this is the surprisingly short time a meal was expected to last: Lady Jeune, the author of a guide to correct behavior, said that "no dinner should consist of more than eight dishes, soup, fish, entrée, joint, game, sweet, hors-d'oeuvre, and perhaps an ice . . . and no dinner should last more than an hour and a quarter." (She added, however, that most dinner parties had sixteen dishes and lasted two hours.)[53] People were not eating eight dishes in an hour and a quarter, at a rate of nine minutes per modern "course" (or seven minutes per course at the dinner parties). Instead, they were selecting the dishes they wanted from the choice spread out in front of them.

Quantities were reduced, as was choice, by the new style of service that was beginning to appear, where each remove (soon to be renamed a course) was brought in separately. This was service *à la russe*, which had arrived in Paris in the 1830s and by the 1880s had become the norm in Britain. Mrs. Beeton, writing in 1861, did not think much of it. She included just one paragraph on the subject, and two pages of

---

*Jaune mange was a set pudding, like blancmange, but with egg yolks rather than milk giving it its color. A recipe for it instructed: "Pour a pint of boiling water on one ounce and a half of isinglass, the next day add one pint of sweet wine, the juice and peel of a large lemon, the yolks of seven eggs well beaten, sweeten to your taste with loaf sugar, mix all together. Give it one boil up stirring it frequently, strain through a fine sieve into moulds."[52]

sample meals, compared with sixteen pages of meals *à la française*, and finally dismissed it by saying that it could really be done properly only in houses with a footman. Trollope used service *à la russe* a few years later as a shorthand way of indicating a degree of pretension in society. In *The Last Chronicle of Barset* (1866–67) his down-to-earth attorney issues dinner invitations, warning "that if [his friends] wanted to be regaled à la Russe they must not come" to his house. Despite this, Mrs. Beeton did note the essential fact that was to make service *à la russe* so popular that today we do not even realize it has not always been the norm: it was cheaper.[54]

The display element of service *à la française* required large joints. Dishes remaining on the table for so long had to be completely filled to make them look attractive, even if they then contained too much food for the number of people at the table; half-filled dishes made the host look shabby and mean. The new system meant that the table was set, and dessert (fruit and nuts in display dishes) was on the table when the guests arrived, but no other food. Then, when the guests were seated, the meal was carried in dish by dish and passed by a servant in the manner we know today. Laura Forster was told by the wife of the local squire that service *à la russe* necessitated only one-third as much food as *à la française*: along with not having to fill dishes to the brim was the advantage of not having to order extra dishes to create the obligatory symmetrical table display,[55] which was provided instead by the dessert dishes and by flower arrangements (an innovation). In addition, different types of food could be kept rigorously apart: no longer were sweet dishes served with savory, nor could one diner eat fish while another had soup. Each dish now had its allocated place in an orderly system. Manufacturers liked the new way better too: as with luncheon cloths, cutlery could become specialized. Georgians ate their fish with ordinary dinner knives and forks; the Victorians extended the canteen with a special fish knife and fork—the latter not to be confused with the new oyster fork, or a salad fork, which was different again from a cake fork.

However much service *à la russe* was in keeping with the times, it took some getting used to, and trendsetters, as ever, were considered a bit odd. Tennyson's friend Arthur Hallam had a dinner party in 1849, and Mrs. Brookfield reported on his newfangled practice to her husband: "We went down to dinner, and found nothing on the table, not even soup. Harry began to redden, in embarrassment, Julia and I to giggle."[56] Accommodation had to be made to the older system for some time. Not everyone immediately reduced the amount served. In 1875 *The Lady's Every-Day Book* was still reminding its readers that they had to inform their guests of the menu, "because the great variety of dishes . . . is to give a choice to the different tastes of the company."[57] Now that guests could not see what was available, menus were necessary so that "appetite may be reserved for any dishes preferred."[58] Ladies could use menus to make an invitation to the hopeful young man sitting beside them, as Miss Demolines does as her opening gambit to John Eames in *The Last Chronicle of Barset*: "Pray look at the menu and tell me what I am to eat. Arrange for me a little dinner of my own, out of the great bill of fare provided. I always expect some gentleman to do that for me."[59]

Many people, echoing Mrs. Beeton, thought that the amount of service needed for this new system meant that one was under "the necessity of continually asking for something."[60] Edward Ricket, who in the 1870s wrote a guide to the table for gentlemen, disagreed. He described his perfect dinner: "I would have every dish served in succession, with its proper accompaniments, and between each dish there should be a short interval, to be filled up with conversation and wine." This, however, was not what normally happened at the meals he attended. Instead he saw "a small party with a dish of fish at each end of the table, and four silver covers unmeaningly starving at the sides, whilst everything pertaining to the fish comes, even with the best attendance, provokingly lagging, one thing after another, so that contentment is out of the question."[61]

Eventually a modified form of service *à la russe* was settled on for family meals, whereby the servant passed and served a number of dishes while the meat was carved by the master of the house. The banquet in Lewis Carroll's *Through the Looking-Glass*, published in 1871, is an example of what happened in this period of transition. When the mutton arrives, Alice says to the Queen, "May I give you a slice," which was the formula for the hostess when she carved for service *à la française*. The meal itself, however, is served *à la russe*, with the dishes brought out in succession.[62] Less whimsically, in 1865 Trollope in *Miss Mackenzie* described a dinner party at Tom Mackenzie's house:

> The order of the construction of the dinner was no doubt à la Russe; and why should it not have been so, as Tom Mackenzie either had or was supposed to have as much as eight hundred a year?* But I think it must be confessed that the architecture was in some degree composite. It was à la Russe, because in the centre there was a green arrangement of little boughs with artificial flowers fixed on them, and because there were figs and raisins, and little dishes with dabs of preserve on them . . . but the soups and fish were on the table, as was also the wine, though it was understood that no one was to be allowed to help himself or his neighbour.[63]

What the dishes consisted of, and how they were cooked, also altered over the period. In 1842 *The English Housekeeper* warned: "Take care not to over season, or let soup have any predominating flavour. This is a great fault, and a common one." Twenty years later Mrs. Beeton was having none of that: "Sauces should possess a decided character; and whether sharp or sweet, savoury or plain, they should carry out their names in a distinct manner."[64] English cooking has, for much of the past century, had such a bad name that it is easy to read into the cookbooks of the nineteenth century an apparent fear and dislike of food. Mrs. Panton warned her young couple on £300–£500 a year that if they wanted the kind of food that required a first-rate cook, they "must rise superior to this, for they will not be able to afford such things even if they desire them, and I do hope they do not, for I do not know a more despicable way of spending one's time or one's money

*It is interesting that Trollope thinks *à la russe* was more expensive than *à la française*. This was partly because anything new can seem so, and partly because of the need for a servant at meals. In reality, the cost of the servant was amply compensated for by the smaller amounts of food purchased.

than in squandering it over food and expensive cooks. If things are nice and are nicely sent to table, that should suffice."[65] For her, the quality of the display was of equal importance to the quality of the food, and both had merely to reach a basic level (for that is surely what her "nice" means).

Despite Mrs. Panton's desire for competence, many of the instructions for cooking the various ingredients live up to our notions of watery English food that has been boiled beyond death. Mrs. Beeton recommended "1½ to 1¾ hours to boil the macaroni." *The English Housekeeper* could not have agreed more: "It is not the general custom to cook vegetables sufficiently, which renders them indigestible." Mrs. Beeton gave large carrots up to two and a quarter hours (although young ones were ready in half an hour); a cutlet was to be stewed for two hours, "very gently." Veal, pork, and lamb needed to be "thoroughly done to the centre." One cannot even assume that her times reflect vegetables not being cut as small as we are used to: the Rev. J. P. Faunthorpe in his *Household Science* was careful to specify "thinly sliced carrots and celery" to be boiled for an hour before serving, and *The English Housekeeper* thought two hours was right for rice.[66*] Nor can lower temperatures account for these cooking times. While baking or stewing might have taken place at lower temperatures than modern cookers that give an even and regular heat, the laws of nature were not in abeyance, and boiling water cannot have been boiling at anything lower than 100°C (212°F).

In general, the breakdown of recipes supplied by Mrs. Beeton supports our notion of a starch- and meat-based kitchen: there are 160 meat dishes to only 96 vegetable dishes, and 179 puddings and pastries (both savory and sweet), with another 97 sweet dishes. Yet the particulars show a range and variety of ingredients that is much wider than today's. *Cassell's Household Guide*, in its helpful compendium of sea-

---

*For those who do not cook, the modern equivalents are (with ranges to allow for cooking method and the size and age of the ingredients): pasta, 3–12 minutes; carrots, 5–15 minutes; a cutlet, 15–40 minutes; rice, 15–20 minutes. For those who would like to begin to cook, Mrs. Beeton may be the place to start: on p. 336 she gives eighteen lines under the heading "To Make Hot Buttered Toast."

sonable foods, listed (among many other things) hare, rabbit, teal, pigeon, widgeon, lark, eel, lamprey, barbel, tench, pike, kale, cardoon, skirret, salsify, scorzonera, and sorrel.[67*] Large numbers of grains and pulses were commonly used; as well as rice, household storage cupboards also contained tapioca, sago, semolina, pearl barley, Scotch barley, arrowroot, groats, and oatmeal, together with a wide range of spices, herbs, and flavorings. One cookbook recommended, as a basic list, "vanilla, cinnamon, nutmegs, mace, allspice, cloves, whole pepper, ground pepper, black and white, cayenne, mustard, fine salt for table use, curry-powder, soy, anchovy-sauce, vinegar, Lucca [i.e., olive] oil, tarragon vinegar, Chili vinegar, Harvey-sauce, tomato-sauce, chutney, . . . mushroom and walnut ketchups, capers, all kinds of herbs in bottles, closely corked, pickles, currant jelly and other preserves, raspberry and black currant vinegar."[68] Sauces and ketchups were plentiful. Ketchups were bottled piquant sauces, the most common being anchovy, mushroom, or walnut. *The English Housekeeper* included in its list of useful sauces "Camp sauce, Gloucester, Harvey's, Oude, Reading, Tomata, Lopresti's, Universal, Essence of Shrimps, Oyster Catsup, Walnut, Mushroom, . . . Essence of Anchovy, of Lobster."[69†]

The one ketchup that was rare was tomato ketchup. In fact, tomatoes (or, as they were often called, tomatas) were themselves still rare. In 1851 a friend of Mrs. Brookfield asked her, when she went to Madeira, "Could you, if circumstances are easy, send me by any vessel fourteen or sixteen lbs. of Guava jelly . . . Mrs. Taylor tells me the Tomata jelly, or jam, is wonderful. I can't imagine it, but if so please add some."[71] It was not the idea of a jelly or chutney that she was

---

*The narrowing of taste perhaps makes it useful to identify some of these items: a lamprey is an eel-like fish with a sucker mouth; barbel is also a fish; cardoons are related to artichokes; skirret is a Chinese root that tastes like parsnip; salsify, from the sunflower family, has an edible root that tastes like skirret, a near relation; scorzonera, also called black salsify, although it is not in fact related, has a root that can be eaten and leaves that are used in salad.

†Most of these have vanished, apart from anchovy ketchup, now generally known as Worcestershire sauce, although Harvey's Sauce, another anchovy-based sauce, remains in production.[70]

uncertain of, it was the "tomata" itself, whereas guava was popular enough that she wanted sixteen pounds of it. In 1861, out of 96 vegetable recipes, Mrs. Beeton gave only three for tomatoes; only four out of her 135 sauces were tomato-based.[72]

Once-common foods that rarely appear now include calves' feet: before packaged gelatin, the bones could be used to make a very nice jelly.* Also common were bullocks' hearts ("an excellent family dish"), fried ox feet, cow heel, sheep's head, sweetbreads, pig's face ("a Breakfast or Luncheon Dish"), pig's pettitoes (feet), hare ("the ears should be nicely crisp"), and calf's head ("Put the head into boiling water . . . take it out, hold it by the ear, and with the back of a knife, scrape off the hair . . . When perfectly clean, take the eyes out, cut off the ears, and remove the brain").[74]

Other foods that have become ordinary to us were then more unusual, and only slowly did people become accustomed to them. Caroline Taylor was in Liverpool when her brother "bought a new fruit which had been brought from abroad. It was the banana and he said, 'Try this and see if you like it, [the landlady's daughters] think they taste like soap.' "[75] More and more types of food were being imported, both fresh and preserved. Canned goods were first used in bulk during the Napoleonic Wars, as a way of transporting food for the army and the navy. Before a knowledge of germ theory, and therefore without sterilization, the food inside often went bad, and the cans exploded. It was not until the 1860s that these problems were solved. In 1858 the popularity of canned items was helped by the invention of the can opener, which replaced the hammer and chisel that had been used before.† Sar-

---

*A recipe for a fairly luxurious version of this dish called for two calves' feet, six lemons, two glasses of sherry, and the whites of eight eggs: "Wash the feet well, after scalding, take out the long bone and the fat between the joints." Then the feet were boiled in two gallons of water until the liquid turned to jelly. This was strained and cooled and the sediment removed. The jelly was then reheated, the remaining ingredients were added and simmered together, and then it was sieved a final time.[73]

†The patentee of this useful gadget noted that others had described it as "part bayonet, part sickle," but he thought "a child might use it without difficulty."[76]

dines became available in cans in the 1850s, but were a luxury item: they cost nearly 3s. for a box of twenty-four. Canned meat began to arrive in bulk from Australia; beans were canned for the first time in 1880. In the 1840s "desiccated soups," or soup powder, appeared. Stocks and sauces could now be made with store-bought sauces or "gravy balls," which were used like stock cubes and cost 1s. for fifty. Egg powder was a cheap substitute for eggs when baking: a penny bought enough to make a cake.[77] (A single egg cost as little as a penny around Easter, in the laying season; at other times of the year it was much more.)

Fortunes were built by supplying processed food. Sir Henry Tate, founder of the Tate Gallery, made his money through patenting an invention in 1872 for cutting up sugar loaves, and then marketing "cube sugar." Until then sugar had been bought in large, conical loaves, which had to be chopped up—a rough, heavy job, to be done by a man if possible. The chopped pieces would then be cut into smaller pieces with sugar nippers, by the housewife or servant, until they were down to a size that was usable.[78] In the same period the Cadbury and Rowntree (both chocolate) and Huntley & Palmer (biscuit) families all thrived, although until the turn of the century most prepared food still came from small shops that made their own products on the premises. As early as 1861 Mrs. Beeton recognized that many of her readers were shopping rather than cooking: she recommended making gravies from store sauces, and curries from bought curry powder. Muffins and macaroons, she cheerfully observed, were difficult to make, and the ingredients cost more than the price of the finished product at a confectioner. However, she drew the line at pickles: "Although [they] may be purchased at shops at as low a rate as they can usually be made for at home, or perhaps even for less, yet we would advise all housewives, who have sufficient time and convenience, to prepare their own."[79] She did not say why. It was not thrift. Did homemade pickles taste better? Were you simply a better wife if you made your own in season? Or was it anxiety about adulteration?

This was not an idle fear. It was only in 1860 that a Food Adulteration Bill became law, and it was ignored almost entirely until 1872, when regulatory inspections and stiff penalties made enforcement possible.[80]

Before the Sale of Goods Act of 1885, there was no obligation in law for a seller to supply goods that were sound or that matched their description. But as early as 1851 *The Lancet* asked a doctor from London's Royal Free Hospital to look into the quality of thirty common foods on the market. Adulteration broke down into several groups. Some involved simply dilution: butter was watered down, as was milk—often by 50 percent. Bread had alum added to it for bulk: of the forty-nine bread samples analyzed, there was not one that did not have alum in it. Some breads also contained potatoes, again for bulk (not to mention carbonate of ammonia, sulphate of lime, and chalk). Oatmeal was bulked up with less expensive barley. One tea imported from China had so much bulking agent added to it that the Chinese merchants called it "lie tea"; a single sample was found to contain 45 percent sand and dirt. Cocoa and chocolate had arrowroot added to them, and they were often colored with earth. Gin had water, sugar, cayenne, cassia, and cinnamon mixed into it. Lard had potato flour, water, carbonate of soda, and caustic lime added. Coffee too was adulterated: of twenty-nine samples, twenty-eight were mixed with ground chicory, mangel-wurzel (a type of beet used for animal fodder), wheat or rye flour, sawdust, carrots, or acorns, and several also contained red oxide of lead.

The red oxide was not for bulk but fulfilled the second purpose of adulteration, which was to give the food a better appearance. Poisonous coloring agents were common: on investigation they were found in tea, preserved meats, and fish. Mrs. Beeton gave a recipe for anchovy paste, noting that in store-bought varieties, "in six cases out of ten, the only portion of these preserved delicacies, that contains anything indicative of anchovies, is the paper label pasted on the bottle or pot, on which the word itself is printed . . . All the samples of anchovy paste, analyzed by different medical men, have been found to be highly and vividly coloured with very large quantities of bole Armenian. The anchovy itself, when imported, is of a dark dead colour, and it is to make it a bright 'handsome-looking sauce' that this red earth is used."[81] Of a hundred samples of sweets, fifty-nine had chromate of lead, and seventy-four had various other poisonous colorings, some sweets containing seven coloring agents in each one.[82]

Adulterated food was so common that books on housekeeping gave methods of testing for the most common contaminants as a matter of routine. Water with muriate of lime in it could be used to test for alum in bread. If the water went cloudy, alum was present. Bread suspected of containing plaster of paris was soaked in water over heat for three to four hours. When the water was poured off, any plaster of paris remained at the bottom of the pan. Sugar could be checked for sand—"a very common cheat"—by dissolving a small amount in water and examining the sediment.[83]

Many people, however, did not want to know. In 1855, when Crosse & Blackwell changed its pickle recipe and started using a non-toxic coloring, sales slumped: the public did not want brown pickles. It was only when the company advertised the reason for the change that sales began to pick up again.[84] Even then, G. A. Sala was not happy. "Food is a gift from heaven's free bounty," he wrote; one should not "look the gift-horse in the mouth. He may have false teeth. We ought to be very much obliged, of course, to those disinterested medical gentlemen who formed themselves into a sanitary commission, and analysing our dinners under a microscope, found that one-half was poison, and the other half rubbish; but, for my part, I like anchovies to be red and pickles green."[85]

For, as we saw with Mrs. Panton, what food looked like was a serious concern. Mrs. Beeton gave a recipe for a "Miniature Round of Beef," specifying that it was a family dish, not for company. The meat was skewered into shape and cooked; then the skewer was removed "and replace[d] by a plated or silver one."[86] That is, appearances were so important that it was better to purchase an object with no function, and to let the food cool down while inserting it, than to allow the dish to lose its shape or to admit a humble kitchen utensil to the dining room. Whether the readers of her book actually followed this advice is not important; they understood that this was what was desirable, that what the table looked like was as important for family dinners as for elaborate entertainment. Mrs. Panton recommended that a plant in "an art pot"—that is, a decorative, not terracotta, pot—have a permanent place on the table.[87]

Dish of Apples

Dish of Mixed Summer Fruit

Dish of Strawberries

Suggestions for dessert displays, 1861: decorative dishes of fruit (or nuts, not shown here), which remained on the table throughout the meal. It was only when service *à la russe* became popular, and dessert was brought in at the end of the meal, that flower arrangements began to appear on the table.

After service *à la russe* became the norm, however, it was dessert that decorated the table most completely: at its simplest it was a matter of alternating short and tall dishes of fruit, sweets, and nuts down the center of the table. Candied peel soon came to be seen as essential, as did crystallized fruit, fancy biscuits, and preserves. Mrs. Beeton gave a "recipe" for a "Dish of Mixed Fruit":

> For a centre dish, a mixture of various fresh fruits has a remarkably good effect, particularly if a pine[apple] be added to the list. A high raised appearance should be given to the fruit, which is done in the following manner. Place a tumbler in the centre of the dish, and, in this tumbler, the pine, crown uppermost; round the tumbler put a thick layer of moss, and, over this, apples, pears, plums, peaches, and such fruit as is simultaneously in season. By putting a layer of moss underneath, so much fruit is not required, besides giving a better shape to the dish. Grapes should be placed on the top of the fruit, a portion of some of the bunches hanging over the sides of the dish in a négligé kind of manner, which takes off the formal look of the dish. In arranging the plums, apples, &c., let the colours contrast well.[88]

That was the entire recipe, and although it was the only one in the book where the dish's appearance was the sole thing that mattered, recipes that involved actual cooking were equally concerned with the look of the finished dish. This preoccupation with appearance needed justification, however, and Mrs. Beeton protested that the elaborate menus were necessary:

"Food that is not well relished cannot be well digested; and the appetite of the over-worked man of business, or statesman, or of any dweller in towns, whose occupations are exciting and exhausting, is jaded, and requires stimulation. Men and women who are in rude health, and who have plenty of air and exercise, eat the simplest food with relish, and consequently digest it well; but those conditions are out of the reach of many men. They must suit their mode of dining to their mode of living, if they cannot choose the latter."[89] Those who had the means were obliged—for the sake of their health—to eat more elaborately than those with less money.

The mode of dining was indeed adapted to increasing prosperity, which was what Mrs. Beeton was describing. Those on small incomes rarely socialized outside their own family groups—with the cost of food as high as it was, they could not afford to do so. Entertaining outside the family network became more usual only as one moved up the social scale, and with non-family members came formality. Informal meals for the family were one thing, but with outsiders informality was insulting: if one cared for and respected people, then one cared for and respected their status as well.

An intricate ritual of invitation and entertainment developed for those in the middle and upper middle classes who socialized outside their family circles. Invitations were issued by the hostess in both her and her husband's name, three weeks ahead of the planned event: any earlier was considered to be too much of a commitment to being in town; any later implied that the recipient was an afterthought, because a more desirable person had said no. It was unmannerly not to reply within twenty-four hours of receipt of the invitation. The Podsnaps, in *Our Mutual Friend*, issued invitations and, if they were refused, considered that it was the intention that mattered: the person had been "asked, at any rate, and got rid of."[90] Thackeray's Major Pendennis was indignant at being invited to a "second-day dinner": while service *à la française* was still current, it was not uncommon that two dinner parties were held on consecutive nights. The important guests were invited the first night; for the second night there were fewer people, and the food was the excess from the night before.[91]

By the late nineteenth century, guests were asked for dinner between 7:30 and 8:30. A quarter of an hour's grace was acceptable; arriving more than fifteen minutes after the time on the invitation was extremely discourteous. General introductions were not made at a dinner party. Instead, the host took each male guest over to the woman he was to partner at dinner and introduced them to each other; the man bowed, never offering his hand, and made small talk until dinner. He then escorted his partner for the evening down to the dining room, and sat next to her at the table. The younger, poorer, and less socially prominent the man, the less pretty, rich, or socially prominent the woman he was paired with.

Precedence—the order in which people went in to dinner, and where they were seated—was taken with extreme seriousness. There were books that listed the precise rankings of various professions— clergy lists, law lists, army and navy lists. They noted who in each field was superior to whom, and which professions took precedence over others. Women took their rank from their husbands and fathers, and therefore consideration had to be given to the position of widows who had remarried, and to that of daughters both before and after marriage. But the books did not often stoop below "Gentlemen entitled to bear arms." As Trollope's narrator lamented in *The Last Chronicle of Barset*, "Amidst the intricacies of rank how is it possible for a woman to learn and to remember everything? If Providence would only send Mrs Dobbs Broughton a Peer for every dinner-party, the thing would go more easily; but what woman will tell me, off-hand, which should go out of the room first: a C.B. [a Commander of the Order of Bath], an Admiral of the Blue, the Dean of Barchester, or the Dean of Arches [the Ecclesiastical Court]?"[92]

Even when all the guests came from the same circle, there were complications. Gwen Raverat remembered the intricate decision-making that went into the seating plan in a university town:

> The guests were seated according to the Protocol, the Heads of Houses ranking by the dates of the foundations of their colleges . . . After the Masters came the Regius Professors in the order of

their subjects, Divinity first; and then the other Professors according to the dates of the foundations of their chairs, and so on down all the steps of the hierarchy. It was better not to invite too many important people at the same time, or the complications became insoluble to hosts . . . How could they tell if Hebrew or Greek took precedence, of two professorships founded in the same year?[93]

When it was time to go down to the dining room, the host escorted the woman of the highest rank; then the couples formed a procession in order of precedence, from highest to lowest, ending with the hostess, who went in with the man of the highest rank, and was followed by any men without a partner (single men, poor men, young men). The man took his partner by whichever arm would protect her dress from the stair railings. As each couple arrived at the table, the servants and the host and hostess told them where to sit, with the most prominent male guest sitting on the right of his hostess, the most prominent woman on the right of the host. The next in rank sat on the left of their hostess and host respectively, and then in descending order of alternating men and women down to the middle of the table, where the least significant were placed. At this point only did women remove their gloves.

The table was laid with a white cloth, and it often had over that a colored runner down the center, possibly itself covered with a lace runner. If there were flowers, they were chosen to complement the runner and the china. Families who entertained formally all hoped to be able to purchase china that was kept solely for dinner parties: a "best" set and a dessert set. Mrs. Panton, rather confused, thought gilt on china was "vulgar, always suggestive of nouveaux riches," and added that "it has a way of washing off that is most trying." (Her lament that it was common to own it at all and then that it did not wear well sounds like a music-hall joke.) Her views on china were generally muddled. No china, she thought, should have a monogram on it—except the breakfast set, the best set, and the dessert set. In other words, despite her stated ban, it was only the everyday set that did not; the other three sets, if the household had them, were all monogrammed. These conflicting views may not have been much help to the rising middle classes, but they indicate to later readers how what otherwise might seem to have been a fixed set of rules was actually in a state of perpetual evolution.

If the dinner was particularly formal, two soups were offered, usually one thick, one clear. Both the soup and the fish were offered a second time, even though it was the height of bad manners to accept. When small game birds were served, a whole bird was given to each guest, although "young ladies, as a rule, do not eat any . . . delicacy of this description";[94] they were served portions of chicken or pheasant instead. Young ladies were also expected to refuse savories and cheese.

The consumption of cheese was a vexed question. The core problem was that because bread and cheese was a staple of the working classes, eating cheese might compromise one's standing. The second Mrs. Gibson, in Mrs. Gaskell's *Wives and Daughters*, loudly condemns the eating of bread and cheese by the middle classes and repeats that it is only "fit for the kitchen"—that is, for servants. Mrs. Beeton worried that "cheese, in its commonest shape, is only fit for sedentary people, as an after-dinner stimulant; and in very small quantity. Bread and cheese, as a meal, is only fit for soldiers on march or labourers in the open air, who like it because it 'holds the stomach a long time.'"[95] In other words, because cheese was both inexpensive and filling, a person of standing could not eat it in any quantity: that was what laborers were forced to do from hunger, and the middle classes did not want to be seen to be eating simply to quell their appetites.

Dinner parties involved more elaborate forms of the menus listed earlier. Marion Sambourne kept a notebook with dinner-party menus. In 1879, at a party for eight people, she served artichoke soup; fillets of salmon; leg of lamb, salad, new potatoes, stewed celery; wild duck, watercress; Aldershot pudding, plum pudding; soft roe of herring; and biscuits. In the 1890s, as the Sambournes became more prosperous, another menu, this time for a "gentlemen only" dinner for Linley Sambourne's friends, consisted of caviar; clear soup, cold salmon, pigeons, tomato salad; roast lamb, peas; haricots verts; roast chicken, salad, Russian salad; jelly, macedoine of fruit; anchovy savory, cream cheese;

ices—pineapple cream, raspberry water (that is, pineapple ice cream and raspberry sorbet); grapes, cherries, greengage plums. With this the twelve men drank twelve bottles of Ayala '80, five of Geister '74, two of sauternes, three of burgundy and fifteen of champagne.* Linley noted the next day, "Slight bilious headache which lasted all day."[97] As well he might. It was a contrast to meals of this kind that the Carlton Club had in mind when it posted a notice: "The committee, taking into consideration that the observance of a General Fast has been ordained, have directed that the Coffee room dinner shall be confined strictly to—Two soups. Fish. Plain Joints. Spring Tarts. Omelettes and Cheese."† Others entertained more simply than the Sambournes. Mr. Brookfield, a socially well-connected but modestly earning cleric, had Thackeray and the travel writer Alexander Kinglake to dinner, and he served a much less elaborate meal: "2 Haddocks, 2 road pigeons, a loin of mutton, a plum tart, Potatoes, and French beans, and cheese."[99]

When dinner was finished, the women left the room, the door being held by the man sitting nearest it. A particularly young or unimportant man might be told, "You must find it very boring—I'm sure you'd like to join the ladies," and he had no choice but to do so. The ladies retired to the drawing room, where, if necessary, they were finally introduced to each other. They then "fell into intimate, low voiced conversations about their illnesses, their children and their servants," reported Gwen Raverat.[100] The men followed shortly afterward—riotous drinking was mostly confined to the type of men-only dinners that Linley Sambourne enjoyed—and tea was brought in.

Less important guests might be invited only for this later part of the evening, and they were expected to appear between nine and ten

*It is not possible directly to compare the amount of wine drunk with modern consumption. Neither bottles nor alcohol content were standardized. It is likely, however, that the bottles contained between 375 and 630 ml, rather than the modern 750 ml. Today the alcohol content of wine is generally around 12.5 percent; in the nineteenth century it ranged from 8–9 percent, for champagne, up to 10–11 percent.[96]

†The comedy of this vanishes when one realizes that the General Fast of 24 March 1847 was to mark a calamity—the potato famine in Ireland.[98]

o'clock. There was likely to be music, and light refreshments. More elaborate refreshments were sometimes served; these might include tea and coffee, bread and butter, macaroons, plum cake, seed cake, biscuits, wafers, cream and water ices, and iced drinks—claret cup, champagne cup, sherry, soda creams, lemonade, cherryade, orangeade, or punch.[101] But these were much rarer: most entertainment relied on tea alone, or possibly tea and sandwiches. Even with this second part of the evening, guests were expected to leave between ten and eleven, rarely later.[102]

All of this was much less complicated than it appears now. The rules of society varied from social group to social group, but the idea that society ran smoothly only through adherence to an accepted set of rules was rarely challenged. Gissing despised this, but he was unusual. In *New Grub Street* he wrote scathingly of a woman who "lived only in the opinions of other people. What others would say was her ceaseless preoccupation. She had never conceived of life as something proper to the individual; independence in the directing of one's course seemed to her only possible in the case of very eccentric persons, or of such as were altogether out of society."[103] Most of the middle classes would have regarded any other viewpoint as bizarre. The Congregational minister James Baldwin Brown spoke for many when he said that all

are to set themselves under the law from the first. There are those above them whose ideas, habits, fashions, they are to observe as a primal duty . . . Nothing is more detestable, I think, than the air of self-assertion and independence in the young; the manifest expression of the feeling that it is a fine thing to be peculiar, and different in dress, manner, and habits from all the world around, which some young persons delight to wear . . . The spring of power is repression, depend upon it . . . Remember it, young people, and keep in, "don't say" [what you think], to the very utmost, before you suffer yourself to fancy that you have a better fancy to show, or a new light to offer, to those whom God has set round you in the world.[104]

Those who conformed did their duty to society, and were an example to the lower classes: "The mechanical forms of good breeding are of great consequence."[105]

These forms were of great consequence not because they kept people out, but because they allowed movement to occur. It is important to remember that Victorian society was hierarchical but porous. These social rules were intricate, but they were open to all. Money, despite a surface aristocratic scorn for "trade," was the lubricant that allowed people to slide up and down the social register. Those in trade, despised one year, had their children married into the social group above them the next; a generation later their grandchildren had effortlessly taken their places in this new world.

The rules were important, therefore, not as a barrier to restrict movement, but to indicate current status as people moved through the different levels of society. What was done, or not done, was never permanently fixed, but at any one time most people in any single group had a clear idea of what was expected of them at that level, and had books and magazines to instruct them if they were hoping to move on to the next. Who succeeded and who failed in these leaps was monitored by women, who ruled this world from the morning room.

THE MORNING ROOM

IT IS A NEAT piece of symmetry to say that men out in the world operated in the public sphere while women at home looked after the private one. In reality, homes were both the private face of public life and the public face of private life. Morning rooms, where houses were big enough to provide one, were rooms that were exclusively given over to women, but unlike the upper-class "boudoir," these were not private rooms in the strict sense, but perhaps privately public rooms. They were where women who had staff did the organizing of the household: spoke to the servants, did their correspondence, kept their accounts—all morning tasks, for the good housekeeper. In addition, it was here that many women entertained their less formal callers, their close friends, and did sewing and other household tasks.

The rooms were, of course, therefore considered female spaces, and they were decorated as a less formal version of the drawing room, with flowered chintz, the popular Indian import, often predominating in fashionable households. Curtains were important both to mask the woman of the house from prying eyes and to add feminine frills and flounces. Yet the space was not private in the sense of withdrawal. Because this was where the running of the household was done, it was part of the public persona of the house, part of the presentation a man of worth would display to the world. A prosperous man wanted to display a prosperous family: a well-kept house, filled with the artifacts that fashion suggested a man of his stature should have, together with a well-kept wife, covered in the kinds of artifacts—the fashionable clothing—that the wife of a man of his stature should equally well have, and performing the kinds of duties that the wife of a man of his stature should perform. As Carlyle noted in *Sartor Resartus*, "Man's earthly interests are hooked and buttoned together and held up by clothes."[1]

He was not alone in recognizing their central importance: all Victorians knew, even if only subliminally, that dress reflected not only what they did but who they were. The *Quarterly Review* of 1847 noted that "dress becomes a very symbolic language—a kind of personal glossary—a special body of phrenology, the study of which it would be madness to neglect . . . Every woman walks about with a placard on which her leading qualities are advertised."[2] Gwen Raverat's aunt took this seriously. To her, "dressing well was a Duty, and not a pleasure: your duty to that state of life to which it had pleased God to call you."[3]

The state of life God had called you to could fluctuate: a young medical student's wife dressed very differently from the wife of a salaried hospital surgeon, who dressed differently again from the wife of a titled society physician. Each had to do the best her rank and income permitted, and as these altered, she had to dress to reflect the change (or to attempt to hide the change, if she was moving in the wrong direction). Women were accustomed to "reading" other women's clothes; novelists used details of dress as a language of status and identity that would be immediately understood. In a society with permeable class boundaries, clothes were important: every nuance was examined and decoded.

It was not merely what was worn—how expensive it was, and whether it was ready-made or made to measure—that mattered, but also when it was worn, and how it was worn. All were essential clues. The what and the how were both complex and seemingly absolute, although in reality they evolved over the century: in retrospect so fluid, but at any one time quite precise. Being "very gaily dressed in the morning, or when walking in the streets," was "vulgar." So were gloves that were silk or cotton, rather than kid. Married women were expected to wear dressier outfits than single women. "To wear a bonnet fit for a carriage, when not in one, is the extreme of bad taste"—it was, once more, that grievous sin of mixing categories: wearing an outfit appropriate to one place in a different one. All these rules went to make up the overall rule that "a lady should never dress *above* her station; it . . . leads to all sorts of evils."[4] The small evil of mixing dress and time categories led inexorably to the great evil of confusing the boundaries of categories, by pretending to be of one class when in fact one was of another. The potential for this evil grew with the population. In small towns, one knew everyone's background and position. In *Cranford*, the ladies feel no obligation to keep up with fashion: "What does it signify how we dress here at Cranford, where everybody knows us?"[5] However, large cities meant that by taking on different clothing one could present oneself as something one was not.

Personal taste was not an issue. If one was a "pattern" woman, one aimed to fit the pattern as precisely as possible. Mrs. Brookfield wrote that she had met a woman who "was dressed oddly and had hair in long ringlets down her back, which looked singular and elf-like, and merely worn because she fancied it."[6] Singularity was not desirable, and wearing something because you fancied it was distinctly peculiar. Jeannette Marshall was every bit as conformist. She went to an "at home" given by the artist Ford Madox Brown, and was appalled by "the flood of 'artistics' in everything hideous in the way of costume." At Brown's daughter-in-law's house the company was "most singularly attired, the ladies sad & the gentlemen mad-looking"; one woman was "as usual in mouse-colour and very sloppy."[7] Yet fashion was never absolute: it was only a few years later that the Marshall women redecorated their house in this very same despised Aesthetic style, and the girls' clothing followed suit. Timing was everything. One did not want to be too far ahead of the pack—that would imply an unhealthy interest in clothes. It was, said the Rev. J. P. Faunthorpe, "the duty of girls especially to be neat and clean, tidy and nice in their dress . . . But although it is the duty of girls to be, and look, beautiful in themselves, and in their dress, they will never do so if they think too much about it."[8] This was not advice-book theory only. Many truly believed, and practiced, it. Molly Hughes's mother "wished to make me indifferent to my personal appearance, provided only that I was tidy and had no buttons missing. She snubbed me once quite severely for remarking that I thought I looked nice in my new dress: 'It's no business of yours what you look like.'"[9]

In reality it was very much her business, and every woman's business—it was just that, as with housework, they were not to talk of it. A woman who did not take care of her appearance was as disgraceful as one who cared openly about it. We saw how the second Mrs. Finch, in Wilkie Collins's *Poor Miss Finch*, was marked out as hopelessly unfit for her station, both by her disregard for dress and by her indolent habits (see p. 121). Mrs. Proudie, the Bishop's wife in Trollope's Barchester series, was condemned in the same way in *Framley Parsonage* when she failed to dress in the mornings "with her usual punctilious attention to the proprieties of high station . . . She had on a large loose cap with no other strings than those which were wanted for tying it beneath her chin"—in other words, a cap that had no decoration but was merely functional.[10]

As the century progressed, cheaper magazines, better illustrations, and paper patterns issued in magazines or sold by post spread more widely to more women what exactly was to be worn each season.* The railways dispersed the magazines farther and faster; new-style department stores made items more quickly available; sewing machines brought the possibility of these goods within regular middle-class reach. Fashion was no longer only for the rich. Its democratization meant that rules had to be laid down for those who previously had not had access to this world. "To Brunettes, or those ladies having dark

---

*The American Ebenezer Butterick developed the first paper pattern, which meant that clothes no longer had to be judged by eye and cut out in cheap fabric toiles first. By 1850 *The World of Fashion* included patterns as well as fashion plates. In 1873 the first British branch of Butterick's opened, where patterns cost from 3d. to 2s.[11]

complexions," said Mrs. Beeton, "silks of a grave hue are adapted. For Blondes, or those having fair complexions, lighter colours are preferable."[12] That there were rules which gave priority to some points of fashion over others, no one doubted. Mrs. Gaskell wrote to her daughter Marianne, who was hoping to buy a new dress in London: "If you have any gowns made in London *have them well made*; I would rather put the expense into the make than the material; *form* is always higher than *colour* &c. I don't mean that I would ever have you get a *poor* silk instead of a good one; but I had rather you had a brown Holland, or a print gown made by a *good* dress maker, than a silk made by a clumsy, inelegant badly-fitting one."[13]

What clothes cost to keep up appearances varied widely. In the mid-Victorian period it was estimated that the minimum a working-class family of five needed for clothes was 2s. 3d. a week, or £6 a year. For the prosperous middle classes Mrs. Panton thought that a man could dress well on £30 a year, a woman on £50, and a child on £10 to £15–or £120 a year for the same family of five.[14] Yet Jeannette Marshall and her sister Ada, definitely of the prosperous classes, never spent more than £30 each, and, unlike many, they had as young women vast wardrobes: up to forty new dresses every year. To produce this number on £30, they spent the time leading up to the two main social seasons, summer and winter, making clothes—more than three hours a day, every day. In addition they spent considerable time shopping for fabric, patterns, and various types of trim and decoration.[15] This was more time-consuming than it may at first appear, even for those without forty dresses a year. The choices to be made were endless. Haberdasheries sold all types of caps, cuffs, and collars, as well as decorations for them: ribbons, bows, braid, frilling, quilling. A single lace merchant advertised "Point de Bruxelles, point d'Alsace, Point de Vence, Milano, Genoa, and Greece; Medici lace, real Valencienne and imitation Ecru; real and imitation black Spanish and Chantilly laces; fichus, ties, wrappers, falls, mantillas, handkerchiefs; hand-made embroidered underlinen, trousseaux, layettes, trimmed baskets, cots, etc."[16] Well into their thirties, Jeannette and Ada often dressed alike—a custom that has now entirely disappeared except for very small children. This was not uncommon: there

A *Punch* cartoon from 1873 has one sister acting as chaperone for the second.
That they were sisters would have been immediately understood by readers
owing to their identical outfits.

were numerous cartoons of identically dressed sisters in *Punch*, and—
a more glamorous example for the Marshall girls to follow—Princess
Alexandra and her sister Dagmar were photographed in identical outfits before their marriages (to the Prince of Wales and to Alexander III
of Russia, respectively). For those without access to court dressmakers,
this style was most easily achieved by home manufacture.

Making clothes was much less expensive than buying them. The editor of her diary estimated that Jeannette Marshall saved her father £35
a year by making her own clothes.[17] An evening dress in silk brocade
could cost between £10 and £50 at a dressmaker's, while silks could be
bought from 10s. a yard; a basic cashmere costume (jacket and skirt)
cost £3 3s., whereas good-quality cashmere was 3s. 6d. a yard.[18] Women
who could afford the luxury had a daily dressmaker come to the house.*

---

*A daily dressmaker was a dressmaker who visited her clients at home; a dress-
maker, with no descriptive prefix, meant a woman with her own establishment,
ranging from a humble village dressmaker working in her front room, up to the
grandest court dressmaker employing dozens of hands.

Often the women of the house did as much preparation as possible. The dressmaker did the cutting out and the fitting, while the women of the house made the skirts, and hemmed and trimmed them. Then the dressmaker sewed the bodice, which was the most complex part of the job, while the women of the house added the trim. For plain sewing a daily dressmaker earned 2s. a day plus her food; if she was doing only the difficult parts, then she might expect up to 3s.[19] The Marshall sisters had a dressmaker only for their best evening bodices; their mother, Ellen Marshall, had her most elaborate dresses entirely made by a daily dressmaker.[20] Marion Sambourne, by contrast, in the early days of her marriage used almost exclusively dressmakers who had their own ateliers, and she spent £100 a year on her clothes. She once had a daily dressmaker come to the house, but this was a failure: the quality was just not the same. She paid £38 for one evening dress, although she also economized by doing the household mending herself.[21]

Many women expected to wear different dresses for different times of day, without the spur of society that goaded the Marshall girls and Marion Sambourne. Molly Hughes's cousin married and moved to Guernsey, where she kept to the style she had been accustomed to in the prosperous town of Guildford: "For breakfast she had a pretty flowered dressing-gown. At ten she put on a simple business-like tailor-made costume for shopping in Peterport. On returning she changed into a workaday dress and an overall for kitchen operations. The overall was removed for lunch, and then, for the afternoon, a really good dress was put on for paying calls. When we came back a little exhausted from this strain of looking well and being polite, a loose tea-gown was the thing, and this remained on until it was time to dress for dinner."[22] Seven different outfits for an ordinary day.

Further segregation of clothes followed if the wearer moved at all in society. The details were minutely graded: a trip to the opera required a décolleté gown; to the theater a less elaborate toilette was expected; the music halls required only a high evening blouse, unless one went to the Palace Theatre of Varieties, when full evening dress was worn in the stalls and boxes, although not in the balcony. Restaurants too were subdivided: the smartest restaurants required décolleté gowns, less important ones only ordinary outdoor costumes or evening dress.[23]

Most women neither could afford this nor lived the kind of life where it was necessary. Even in the upper middle classes, many thought that a wardrobe of three day dresses was sufficient, with one or two additional dresses for evening if the family was of a level of society that went out to dinner. The formidable (and wealthy) Aunt Stanbury in Trollope's *He Knew He Was Right* possessed five dresses, all of black silk—"one for church, one for evening parties, one for driving out, and one for evenings at home and one for mornings."[24] Women like this bought a new dress every year, which was saved for best while the previous year's best dress was downgraded to be worn for visiting and other ventures into the outside world. Only if the afternoon call was important did the best dress replace it. (As Aunt Stanbury lived in the Exeter cathedral close, it was natural that her best was reserved for outings to church rather than entertainment.) In the mornings, a dress from two years before was worn for work around the house. If little or no entertaining was done, the best dress also sufficed for evening wear. If the family had more disposable income, then it was likely that an evening dress was worn for parties, with a second-best evening dress kept for theaters, concerts, and dinners. In this way, a day dress had to do duty for no more than three years, although many, if not most, middle-class women expected to wear a dress for up to a decade, and replaced their best only every three to four years.

Those managing at the low end of the middle-class income could still dress, as they would have said, genteelly, for substantially less than £30, although rather more than the £6 for an entire family that working-class women budgeted for. "Espoir," a lady in reduced circumstances, assured her readers that she could produce a dignified wardrobe, and always be appropriately dressed, on £7 a year. She itemized her expenditure carefully. She bought a new dark dress every year, for 10s., and wore it daily after she had finished her household tasks, for which the dress from the year before sufficed. She wore a black silk dress in the evenings, which she expected to last for many years. Each summer she bought another dress, for 7s. The rest of her expenditure was on the details that were so important in identifying and maintaining class. As with the wedding dress on p. 236, accessories consumed the lion's share of "Espoir's" budget: less than £1 was spent on dresses, over £6 on accessories. These included two pairs of boots every year: one at 13s. for outdoor wear, and a second pair at 16s. for indoors. Colored stockings for winter and white for summer came to £1 10s. a year; six pairs of gloves—four dark and two light, at 3s. 6d. each—came to £1 1s. (Gloves were a great status indicator: as they fitted tightly and therefore split easily, they proved that the wearer did no work. They were also difficult, if not impossible, to clean, and replacing them was expensive.) She spent 5s. a year on collars and cuffs, which were colored, as these needed less frequent laundering and so were cheaper to maintain than white ones. A straw hat every year cost 18s., a new bonnet another £1. She advised her readers similarly financially constrained to buy their bonnets in the summer: that way they were new when the days were brighter, and by the time they had got shabby they were generally seen in dimmer light.[25]

Although "Espoir" said she bought "a dress" every year, this could also have meant the fabric for a dress—which, given the prices she was paying, probably was the case. In Mrs. Gaskell's novel *Ruth*, when Ruth agreed to pose as a widow to hide the illegitimacy of her child, she was asked by her benefactress (to aid the deception), "Would you object to my buying you a black gown?" She agreed, the "gown" was bought, and Ruth "stitched away incessantly" until it was ready.[26] That she was expected to make the dress was not simply because she was poor. In *The Small House at Allington* the wealthy squire gave his nieces "brown silk dresses from London—so limited in quantity that the due manufacture of two dresses out of the material had been found to be beyond the art of women."[27] Throughout the Victorian period it was also possible to buy a finished bodice, together with fabric that had already been cut out for the skirt, to be made up by the purchaser; or, alternatively, a made-up skirt and a bodice supplied as fabric and trimmings. Peter Robinson, the London department store, referred to these items as "un-made" dresses.[28] The bodices were the difficult things to buy ready-made—they were supposed to fit tightly, like gloves, and so needed individual measurements to sit properly over all their complex corsetry. Gwen Raverat's sharp eye noted that, because of this, "ladies never seemed at ease or even quite as if they were wearing their own clothes. For their dresses were always made too tight, and the bodices wrinkled laterally from the strain; and their stays showed in a sharp ledge across the middles of their backs."[29]

In 1861 a fashion plate was captioned "complete dress to be sold as one," which may have been the first fully ready-made dress to be advertised.[30] Ten years later Debenham & Freebody's *New Fashion Book*, an advertising brochure that the Cheltenham shop sent out to customers, gave the following possibilities for ladies' clothes:

- They could be made to measure in the shop.
- The shop could take the measurements for the bodice, while the skirt was bought already finished.
- The entire dress could be purchased ready-made.
- Patterns and designs could be sent to customers at no charge, together with a line drawing showing how to take measurements at home, and the measurements then returned for the dress to be made in-store, sometimes together with an old bodice to be used as a guide.[31]

Dresses that were bought ready-made were less expensive than made to measure, and gradually began to match the prices of home sewing. Marion Sambourne in the 1880s started to buy some ready-to-wear day dresses: a brown velvet dress for £2 19s. 6d., a blue serge for £4, another winter dress for £7 7s.—a vast improvement on her fashionable dressmaker Madame B, who had both charged her £38 for a single dress and made her "wait an age."[32]

Men's clothes were sold in ready-made form long before women's were, in great part because it was easier: men's clothes had less variety than women's; they were less reliant on detail and finish, less tight-fitting, and in general more uniform. Women who had disposable income made none of their husbands' clothes: Jane Carlyle had made her husband's stockings and shirts when they first married, but as soon as she could afford to buy them she stopped, and did only the mending.[33]

The expansion of the postal service promoted innovation from manufacturers.
The Bradford Manufacturing Co. encouraged sales by sending paper dress
patterns to their customers, all of which could, of course, be used to make up
dresses from their fabrics.

Still, advice books constantly reiterated, "Every woman ought to know how to make her own and her children's garments."[34] This was a moral precept rather than a practical one; it was womanly to sew for one's family, and girls began to learn when they were four or five. Sewing had great symbolic value long after sewing machines and ready-to-wear clothes had removed its practical purpose. Molly Hughes was nearly refused entrance to North London Collegiate School because she did not know how to make a buttonhole[35]—and North London Collegiate was one of the pioneers in expanding girls' educational achievements, including preparing them for university.

For parents, the appearance of their children's clothing was every bit as important as that of their own. When Laura Forster was seven, she was taken with her mother when she went calling. On the way, "I discovered a small hole in my glove . . . I asked my mother whether, as it was a right-hand glove, I should take it off before I shook hands; she agreed."[36] Her mother thought the poor condition of a seven-year-old's glove serious enough that it had to be hidden even from friends.

Children needed to look like other children of the same class: to be pattern children in pattern clothes. Mrs. Gaskell worried about her daughter Marianne, away at school: "I was a little bit sorry to hear you were wearing your *merino* in an *evening* that night when Tottie drank tea with you. Either you are getting into the dirty slovenly habit of not changing your gown in the day-time, or you are short of gowns to wear a *merino* to *tea*?"[37] Her association of disregard for social convention with dirt was revealing. She had not been told, after all, that Marianne was wearing an old, shabby, or dirty dress; she was simply wearing a dress designated for one time of day at another.

Clothes were divided up by age, by gender, by marital status, and then, over all of these, by income. Babies and small children, up to the age of three or four, were dressed alike, in what now would be called girls' clothes—petticoats and frocks. (The only survival of this today is the traditional christening gown.) As toddlers grew into young children, clothes for boys and girls became entirely distinct. There were two main types of clothing for children: outfits that were variants on adult clothes, mostly worn by girls, and outfits that embodied a fantasy world, mostly worn by boys—miniature military jackets, sailor suits, kilts, Little Lord Fauntleroy suits. Compton Mackenzie, aged six in 1889, was dressed in a velvet suit and lace collar in imitation of Frances Hodgson Burnett's small hero, who had appeared in print three years earlier. The other boys in his dancing class all wore sailor suits, and "were inclined to giggle at my black velvet, and after protesting in vain against being made to wear it I decided to make it unwearable by flinging myself down in the gutter on the way to dancing class and cutting the breeches . . . Thus not only did I avoid the dancing class, but I also avoided being photographed in that infernal get-up."[38] Many children were photographed in this kind of fantasy rig. As a child, Ursula Bloom's father wore a dress of shepherd's plaid (but made of silk, which not too many shepherds had), with plaid boots.[39]

Children were bundled under endless layers. Boys wore jackets and waistcoats buttoned to the neck, knickerbockers, stockings, hats, boots buttoned up to the ankle. C. S. Lewis remembered "choking and sweating, itching too, in thick dark stuff, throttled by an Eton collar . . . I am wearing knickerbockers that button at the knee. Every night for some forty weeks of every year and for many a year I am to see the red, smarting imprint of those buttons in my flesh when I undress."[40] Eleanor Acland, in her memoir of a Victorian childhood, described the girls' version:

> Our small persons were smothered in clothes . . . first of all, a vest. Then a chemise, a garment whose use was never apparent to us, but we were given to understand that it wouldn't be at all "nice" to go without it. It was made of calico, and reached the knees. Next "stays," a strip of wadded pique whose use was unmistakable. In addition to the five buttons that fastened our stays up the back, they had a number of other buttons at various levels and intervals round the waist. Two of these held up the elastic "spenders" of our stockings; the five buttonholes of our drawers belonged to the other three, and yet two more were buttoned into two holes in the band of our flannel petticoat. Over that came a white petticoat made with a bodice. The edges of all the white gar-

ments were decorated with rather scratchy cambric trimming. Finally there were our frocks and pinafores. I have forgotten the stockings themselves—long black stockings reaching above the knee, woollen in winter, thick cotton in summer. That was for indoors. For out of doors, except on really warm days, there were one or two more layers. A shetland-wool jersey, and coats, known . . . as pelisses . . . mufflers, or, for Sundays and other grand days, swan's-down tippets.[41]

Usually the only difference between the layers in winter and summer was that summer layers were cotton or linen and wool, and winter ones were flannel and wool. Gwen Raverat, looking back, said, "It fairly makes my heart bleed to see photograph after photograph of ourselves . . . playing in the garden in high summer, always in thick, black, woolly stockings and high boots. We wore, too, very long, full overalls with long sleeves, and of course hats or caps."[42]

It was not that children's clothes were more constricting than those of adults; for women they were less so, as boned corsets arrived only with adolescence. It was simply that adults had no expectations of clothes being comfortable: all the childhood memories of being stuffed into clothes like a sausage into its skin were retrospective, recalled in a time when clothing had given up some of its status symbolism in favor of comfort, which began to happen in a minor way in the second half of the century. Yet even then, as Mrs. Peel remembered, when women began to wear tailor-made costumes (walking skirts and blouses), which were theoretically less confining, they came with "high-boned collars which rubbed raw places on our necks, and stiff stays, and we skewered our hats through our hair with long bonnet pins, our gloves were tight and our boots buttoned." The novelist Mrs. Oliphant declared, "No one but a woman knows how her dress twists around her knees, doubles her fatigue, and arrests her locomotive power."[43]

Medical opinion was not silent on the matter. *The Lancet* reminded doctors that women patients complaining of exhaustion, or an inability to walk even short distances, were probably suffering from the loads they were carrying rather than illness or the inherent weakness of being female. By the end of the century a fashionable woman was carrying thirty-seven pounds of clothing, although the Rational Dress Society had long campaigned for women to reduce their underclothing to a maximum of seven pounds.[44]*

Two elements were at work here. The first was the permanent fear that a chill would lead to a cold, which would lead to something worse. For this reason, Eleanor Farjeon, like many children, was made to wear two pairs of stockings, one over the other: in her case, as her parents were well-to-do, cashmere stockings next to the skin, then silk ones on top.[45] (Wool and cotton was the less expensive variation.) Laura Marx, one of Karl Marx's daughters, wrote to her sister: "The weather continues to be atrocious. I caught such a cold by changing my linsey [wool] for my black silk dress that I completely lost my voice for two or three days."[46] The second reason, no less crucial, was status. Eleanor Acland, in retrospect at least, knew this: "We must not assume that the only object of the prevailing wealth of personal upholstery was to keep the body warm. It had an aesthetic moral purpose as well. I remember enquiring of a just-grown-up cousin if ladies' skirts really had to have such yards and yards of stuff in them. She answered, with a prim repressiveness, that she couldn't say that it was exactly necessary, but that 'any nice girl is very glad they do, because if they didn't—just think, people would see one's shape showing!' "[47]

She was merging the morality of maintaining one's status with propriety, or modesty, and for many they were inextricably linked. At the end of the century, "women were incredibly modest . . . even with each other," as Gwen Raverat described:

> You could see a friend in her petticoat, but nothing below that was considered decent. At school, the sight of a person in her white frilly drawers caused shrieks of outraged virtue; and I should have thought it impossible to be seen downstairs in my dressing-gown. As a consequence, decent women did not take very much trouble

---

*Today's, by contrast, weighs a few ounces. A full set of clothes—cotton trousers, wool top and cardigan, socks, underwear—weighs just over two pounds.

about their underclothes, which were apt to be rather Jaeger and patched; but they were often extremely complicated. This is what a young lady wore, with whom I shared a room one night . . .

1. Thick, long-legged, long-sleeved woollen combinations.

2. Over them, white cotton combinations, with plenty of buttons and frills.

3. Very serious, bony, grey stays, with suspenders.

4. Black woollen stockings.

5. White cotton drawers, with buttons and frills.

6. White cotton "petticoat-bodice," with embroidery, buttons and frills.

7. Rather short, white flannel, petticoat.

8. Long alpaca petticoat, with a flounce round the bottom.

9. Pink flannel blouse.

10. High, starched, white collar, fastened on with studs.

11. Navy-blue tie.

12. Blue skirt, touching the ground, and fastened tightly to the blouse with a safety-pin behind.

13. Leather belt, very tight.

14. High button boots.[48]

The condition of the underclothes was unimportant, as long as there were an appropriate number of layers to insulate the wearer from the outside world, both physically and morally. Indeed, elegant, or even just attractive, underclothing was considered slightly immoral: it betokened an excessive interest in matters that were best not thought of. Baroness Staffe, in *The Lady's Dressing-Room*, thought that colored underwear was in "somewhat doubtful taste," and that "a virtuous woman has a repugnance to excessive luxury in her underclothing."[49]*

---

*Even in France, thought by many in Britain to be a running sewer of depravity, elaborate underwear was suspect. When J.-K. Huysmans saw Manet's *Nana* (1877), he thundered: "The aristocracy of vice is recognizable today by its lingerie. Silk is the trademark of courtesans who rent out at a high price." Huysmans, the author of several novels exploring the world of sensual aestheticism, was hardly a parochial boy shocked by the ways of the big city.[50]

Raverat's friend was indicating her ladylike mentality by not caring about the quality of her underwear while having the requisite concern with quantity: less was improper.

The century had not begun that way. Dresses in the Regency period were known for their lightness: some weighed no more than a pound. This did not last. From the skin outward, the undergarments began with a chemise, which was de rigueur. It looked like a knee-length short-sleeved shirt. Over it was a corset, then a camisole, made of white cotton, shaped to the waist, the sole purpose of which was to cover the corset. In the 1850s the number of petticoats that went over these was reduced by the arrival of the crinoline, a metal or whalebone cage.

In 1856 the "cage" crinoline, a petticoat of steel, was introduced. Women appreciated it as it reduced the number of petticoats—and therefore the weight—they wore. Originally a beehive shape, by 1863 (center) it had become a pyramid, with a smaller diameter. By 1867 it had vanished, to be replaced by the crinolette (left, 1869), which created a train effect, with an open front that permitted the dress to fall straight to the ground. Through the 1870s (right, 1873) this developed slowly into the "dress improver," a cane or woollen netted fabric which the dress buttoned on to, with a horsehair pad at the small of the back to help create the fashionable "mermaid's tail," which required up to 36 yards of fabric.

Over this went an ornamental petticoat, which a looped-up skirt displayed. Finally came the skirt. Underpants, or drawers, became necessary only with the disappearance of the layers of petticoats and the arrival of crinolines, which tipped up easily. Drawers were usually flannel, and came to just below the knee. After the crinoline disappeared, in the late 1860s, a horsehair petticoat, with hoops suspended from the waist, was used to form the shape of the skirt. This gradually evolved into a "dress improver," which by the 1880s was a separate piece, a bustle attached to the bodice or the petticoat, with possibly a pad of horsehair added.

The crinoline was good for lots of jokes in *Punch*, but it was the corset that was the defining feature of women's underwear. An average corset exerted a force of twenty-one pounds on the organs, although extremely fashionable tight lacing could increase that to eighty-eight pounds.[51] Prepubescent girls wore stays, padded fabric bands that buttoned tightly but did not constrict the waist. The corsets that arrived with puberty were symbols of the changes in girls' lives. Now vigorous games played with their brothers were replaced by demure exercise; walks, or even just carriage drives, were all that many upper-middle-class girls could hope for. Housework was the exercise of the lower-middle-class woman. Fears about physical weakness brought about by the onset of menstruation ensured that many girls were put on a low-protein, bland diet; in the same way, fears of mental weakness similarly induced meant that girls' education was often curtailed at this point. And it was at just this moment that padded stays were replaced by boned corsets. It seems pat to say that the physical constrictions imposed by the corset symbolized the physical and mental constrictions imposed by society. Because it is pat does not mean it is not true, however, although it is simplistic to suggest that an all-powerful patriarchy imposed this restriction on a submissive female population: much recent work has shown how women were active in rejecting looser garments.

Writers of the time were not certain whether the corset was worn for health or for fashion; many merged the two, suggesting that it was "wholesome" to make one's dress fit better. What was certain was that it was also a moral restraint: corsets ensured that women controlled their physical appetites and reminded them to restrain their moral ones. This is not a retrospective reading. Fashion magazines constantly pointed out to their readers that "the corset is an ever-present monitor indirectly bidding its wearer to exercise self-restraint; it is evidence of a well-disciplined mind and well-regulated feelings."[52]

EXPANDS TO
ANY SIZE.
5000 IN USE WITH GREAT SUCCESS.

Expands to any figure, 20 to 30 inches waist, and 34 to 40 inches bust, and folds in 28-inch box. A triumph of success. The "Queen" says : "It expands to any size, 20 to 30 waist and 34 to 40 bust. All parts of body, waist, hips, or skirt can be altered by a child, and altered to any height." Is very strong, and folds in small box. Sent for P.O.O.   **35/-**

Home dressmaking created many subsidiary requirements for businesses. The
dressmakers' form advertised here was expandable (from a twenty- to a
thirty-inch waist) so it could be used on more than one family member. It
then folded away to meet the requirements of small houses.

Quite how tightly women were to lace themselves was a problem.
Tight lacing had first arrived in the nineteenth century for one simple
reason: technology. Until 1820, if corset strings were pulled too hard
the surrounding fabric ripped; after this date, the metal eyelets that
were used made tighter lacing possible. From the middle of the century, a further change—to corsets that did up in the front—facilitated
lacing more tightly more quickly,[53] and from then on it became a question of fashion and morals. In the early part of the Victorian age, tight
lacing was the only way to make the waist substantially smaller than
the petticoated skirt, as the waistbands of all the petticoats bulked out
the waist. When crinolines appeared, the number of petticoats
decreased and, even more important, the vast diameters of ordinary
skirts meant that waists no longer had to be so tightly compressed to

appear small. Lacing became temporarily looser. When crinolines turned into bustles, tighter lacing again became necessary to produce the required S-shape.

At the same time, tight lacing was condemned by doctors, health writers, and dress reformers. The average woman was condemned whatever she did: either she was overly concerned with fashion or she was lax and unrestrained. There was, of course, the officially sanctioned middle ground, but the extremes on both sides took up so much space that the middle seemed sometimes difficult to locate. Some women did hold out against the fashion. The Marshall girls, owing no doubt to their father's profession of surgeon and professor of anatomy, wore only unboned stays—and this quite happily, despite their love of fashionable dress. Jeannette bought regular stays and took out the bones—"only 52!" she noted of a new corset.[54]

It is difficult to say how tightly women really laced. Large quantities of writing, by both pro- and anti-lacing campaigners, seem to have been written by sexual fetishists, as a sort of soft-core porn.[55] Much of it appeared in mainstream magazines such as the *Englishwoman's Domestic Magazine*, edited by Samuel Beeton, Mrs. Beeton's husband. (It should be borne in mind that the magazine is notorious among Victorian scholars today for its columns of correspondence supposedly sent in by parents on the nature and extent of physical chastisement for girls: all, to a modern eye, clearly sexual fantasies.) What is interesting is that to contemporary readers it was not clearly bogus. A recent fashion historian, Valerie Steele, however, has noted a variation in the vocabulary of the letters. The *Englishwoman's Domestic Magazine* correspondents whom we would today guess to be fetishists used words like "suffering," "agony," "delicious," and "exquisite" to describe the effects of tight lacing, while what appears to be genuine correspondence contained words like "comfort," "ease," and "freedom."[56] Valerie Steele also looks at the actual evidence—the corsets themselves. She notes that in the Leicestershire Museums Service there is a collection of 197 corsets, only one of which has a waist measuring 18" when fastened; eleven measure 19", and the remainder are between 20" and 26"—in other words, not much below the waist sizes of many women today, who substitute exercise for corsets. She adds that we do not know why these corsets were preserved; it may have been that they were considered particularly small or pretty.[57] In other words, the 6 percent that are under 20" may be an even tinier percentage of the whole than we currently think.

While this is important, and needs more research, it is certainly the case that women were, at home and in the world, encouraged to make themselves lesser. Margaret Gladstone, the daughter of a professor of chemistry at London University, had lost her mother as a child and was brought up by four older half sisters. When she turned twelve they gave her a handwritten list entitled "Notes on Etiquette," instructions on how to comport herself as a lady. The notes included: "Take short . . . steps . . . Do not swing more than one arm at a time, & do not work that one." The notes for "behaviour at table" had seven "do nots" and only one "do": do chew each mouthful twenty times—that is, do not eat too fast. "General remarks" included: "Do not read too much. Do not eat too much butter or jam."[58] In effect: do not take up too much space, do not make yourself noticeable in any way.

Emotion in women was a negative feature. Most of Dickens's women who do not repress their emotions come to bad ends: Miss Wade and Tattycoram in *Little Dorrit*, Lady Dedlock in *Bleak House*, the second Mrs. Dombey in *Dombey and Son*—all lose their lives or, perhaps worse, their homes. Their links with decent society are severed by their passion, when domesticity can no longer contain them. In his own life, his daughter noted, Dickens had similar views. His wife "was never allowed to express an opinion—never allowed to say what she felt."[59] In *The Daisy Chain*, that paean to self-repression, a young governess, who has been rather hurt by what she perceives to be slights, learns that thinking of "one's own feelings and self is the way to be unhappy."[60] In an extreme example, Alice James, the invalid sister of Henry and William James, wrote in her journal that she had had "to peg away pretty hard between [the ages of] twelve & twenty-four, 'killing myself' . . . absorbing into the bone that the better part is to clothe oneself in neutral tints, walk by still waters & possess one's soul in silence."[61]

Of course, most women did not see self-suppression as a form of self-murder. Repression was regarded as a positive virtue, even if today it sounds like the living death that Alice James had worked toward. Mrs. Ellis, in *Daughters of England*, commended the woman whose "whole life, from the cradle to the grave is one of feeling, rather than action; whose highest duty is so often to suffer, and be still; whose deepest enjoyments are all relative; who has nothing, and is nothing, of herself; whose experience, if unparticipated, is a total blank." Girls were to spend their time in looking after the men in the house, thus becoming "too happy in the exercise of their affections to think of self," promised Mrs. Ellis in *Daughters of England*.[62] "It is essential to your making home happy," warned *Female Piety, or The Young Woman's Friend and Guide*, "that there should be much *self-denial*— a spirit of forbearance—an occasional surrender for the sake of peace . . .—willingness to forego [*sic*] what you could righteously claim as your own."[63] *The Lady's Every-Day Book* was unusually blunt in its "Advice to Wives": "Her motto must be never to irritate."[64]

Marion Jane Bradley had been well inculcated with the virtues of these views. When her daughter was about eighteen months old, she wrote: "There is something inexpressibly tender and clinging about Edith . . . I never dare speak to her in a loud or quick voice for fear of frightening and hurting her . . . such a sweet loving nature needs the food of love while it must be taught endurance." She foresaw that her daughter would "be of that sweetly loving nature that I think to be the highest kind one could desire . . . I think it so good of God both for my sake and hers to give me a child who seems only to breathe love and gentleness."[65*]

Gentleness, silence, and ignorance were almost synonymous as desirable ladylike traits. Arthur Munby offered financial help to a milliner who had fallen on hard times. She had managed to keep herself away from prostitution, the all-too-easy end for many poor seamstresses, but even so, noted Munby, "though a virtuous respectable

---

*Times changed, and women's attitudes with them. Nearly forty years later Mrs. Bradley added rather more realistically in the margin, "Edith altered much as she grew older and became quite different in *that* way."

girl, [she] has not—nor can any such girl have—that *ignorance* of vice which one desires in a lady."[66]

But it was not simply knowledge of vice that contaminated women; it was knowledge altogether, as Molly Hughes realized. She had gone to visit cousins in Cornwall, who "are rather dreading you as a 'modern girl,'" she was told. After a few days one reassured her, "They told us you were clever, but you aren't a *bit*!" This, she wrote, "gave me my cue. I must keep dark the fact that I was working for my degree, and my interest in books and pictures and politics. As heartily as I could I entered into the gossip about love affairs and 'the length to which some girls will go.' However I found it convenient to cultivate the reputation for being a bit odd. Oddity didn't matter, it was only knowledge that was to be avoided."[67] Marion Sambourne spoke too freely at a dinner party, giving her views on the merits of women novelists, which as a woman reader she might be assumed to be competent to speak of. The next day "Lin gave me a lecture on self-opinion, must try to correct this."[68] This was echoed in fiction, when the squire in *The Small House at Allington* condemned his niece as "headstrong and positive"—"positive" was a negative adjective here.[69] And, from an outsider's point of view, Sara Duncan, from America, noted tartly that "in England an unmarried person, of my age, is not expected to talk much . . . This was a little difficult for me to understand at first . . . but I have at length been brought to understand it, and lately I have spoken with becoming infrequency, and chiefly about the Zoo. I find the Zoo to be a subject which is almost certain to be received with approval."[70]

She might also have chosen Gilbert and Sullivan as her topic. In Gissing's *The Odd Women*, Everard Barfoot paid a call on an emancipated woman friend:

> "Is there anything very good in the new Gilbert and Sullivan opera?" he asked.
>
> "Many good things. You really haven't been?"
>
> "No—I'm ashamed to say."
>
> "Do go this very evening, if you can get a seat. Which part of the theatre do you prefer?" . . .

"I'm a poor man, you know. I have to be content with the cheap places." . . .

A few more such questions and answers, of laboured commonplace or strained flippancy, and Everard, after searching his companion's face, broke off with a laugh.

"There now," he said, "we have talked in the approved five o'clock way. Precisely the dialogue I heard in a drawing-room yesterday. It goes on day after day, year after year, through the whole of people's lives."[71]

Gissing quite obviously despaired, but many lived like this perfectly happily. For most women, calling on people, and being called on, was the main source of social intercourse outside familial relations. Leaving cards was how women controlled their friendships: whom they would visit, whom not, who would become a closer friend, and who would remain a polite acquaintance. The rules were elaborate, but they were understood by all.

The initial move was the introduction. This was very like introducing an eligible man, as described earlier; it too was no casual impulse. Introducing any two people socially imposed obligations on both parties; it was therefore customary, before doing so, to ask both if they wanted to meet. The introduction was also, for the person who introduced two people, "a *social endorsement*, and you become . . . responsible for the person you introduce. If he disgraced himself in any way you share, in a greater or lesser degree, in his disgrace."[72] Once a woman was introduced to a man, she had an obligation to acknowledge him socially, unless the acquaintanceship was so unwelcome that she was "compel[led] . . . to treat the other with marked coldness."[73] If he failed to take the hint she would be forced to "cut" him more obviously—to fail to recognize him in public. Florence Gaskell, aged seven, already knew how people behaved. She was left in the carriage when Mrs. Gaskell went to pay a call, and afterward said, "Mama the footman was so kind he told me all the churches we could see . . . but I thought it very odd he should speak to me as we had never been introduced."[74]

One of the ways in which girls marked their passage from childhood was by getting their own cards to leave. (It was often possible to economize: Jeannette Marshall's cards had initially belonged to her aunt, a "Miss Marshall," who had no further use for them once she had married eight years before Jeannette inherited them. Ada, as the younger sister, had to make do with "Miss A. Marshall" written on them in ink.)[75] Cards were a social passport and had an intricate etiquette all of their own. Ladies' cards were at the most 3½ inches deep. The woman's name—for example, "Mrs Linley Sambourne"—was in the center, with her address in the bottom left-hand corner. A man's cards were larger, and simply had his title and last name—"Mr Sambourne"—unless he needed to distinguish himself from an older brother or a father, in which case he was "Mr Linley Sambourne." His home address was in the bottom left-hand corner, his club on the right. If a girl had not yet achieved the dignity of her own cards, when she called with her mother the right-hand corner of the mother's card was turned down, to indicate that the daughter had been present too. Boys had no responsibilities, socially, and therefore had no cards; they made no calls until they were independent young men. A woman left three cards, one of her own and two of her husband's; hers was for the woman she was visiting, her husband's for the woman and the man.

There were two ways to call: either the caller asked at the door if the mistress of the house was at home and left a card if she was not, or she simply handed the card to the servant, saying "For Mrs. X," without attempting to visit. Calls had to be returned within a week, or ten days at the outside, to avoid giving offense. Like was usually returned with like: if a card had been left, then a card was returned; if a visit had been made, then a return visit was obligatory. If a more socially prominent woman returned a card with a visit, this was a great compliment; by contrast, if she returned a visit with a card, it was a clear indication that she wanted only a formal acquaintanceship. When social background was similar, jockeying for position took place: Mr. Pooter's son asked his mother "to call on Mrs Mutlar [his fiancée's mother], but Carrie said she thought Mrs Mutlar ought to call on her first."[76]

Women with busy social lives kept visiting books that were very like their household account books. In them they noted the name of the caller, when she had visited or left a card, and when the visit was returned, to ensure that snubs were not unintentionally given. Marion Sambourne noted her friends' "days"—when they were "at home"—in the front of her diary: Mrs. Alma-Tadema received on Monday, Mrs. Rider Haggard on Wednesdays, Mrs. George du Maurier on Thursdays. Her own day was Tuesday, and she normally had four or five callers on Tuesday afternoons. "At homes" avoided the necessity of receiving callers—or being announced by the servant as "not at home"—every day of the week. It also reduced the work for the servant on a daily basis. If callers arrived at teatime they were expected to join in, and this could mean that fresh tea and sandwiches had to be constantly ferried upstairs for a couple of hours. A typical afternoon's calling for Marion Sambourne, who was enthusiastically social, was: "Called on Mrs Kemp, Mrs Christopher, Mrs Humphreys, all out. Had tea at Mrs Holmes, stayed some time. Called & had tea at Mrs Tuer's and at Miss Hogarth's, saw Mrs Andrews and girls there, sent

Punch always enjoyed mocking women's pastimes. In "Annals of a Retired Suburb" (1882), the joys of calling were illustrated. Many women had one day a week when their friends knew they were "At Home," and waiting for callers. But those without busy social schedules might often wait in vain.

carriage home & walked back."[77] Three visits, three teas, three cards left was about average for her.

There were numerous situations in which calling was obligatory: the day after a dinner party, an evening party, or any other sort of entertainment; if there was illness in the house; after a death. It was expected that cards only would be left in a house of illness or death, but neglecting to call altogether was an oversight that could not be forgiven. Marion Sambourne noted these visits too: "After lunch called at Mrs Baines (lots of people there) Mrs Smiles (too ill to see anyone) Mrs Sington (little girl v. ill) Marion Pollock (out) Mrs Kemp (had tea there) Mrs Eykyn (out) and round park to Mrs V. Cole. Sent carriage home, tea there. Walked back, left card at Miss Winthorp's and enquired after Dr Harcourt, little better."[78] Three visits, two teas, six cards left, three of which were for people who were ill.

Calls were made between three and five in the afternoon, and were referred to as morning calls. "Morning" was originally used to refer to anything before dinner. As dinner time moved from its original place in the middle of the day, "morning" stretched to accommodate this. (Our only vestige of this practice is to refer to theatrical performances in the afternoon as matinees.) If a visit was made, the maximum length of time to stay was half an hour, and fifteen minutes was much more polite. If other visitors arrived during that quarter hour, it was incumbent on the first visitors to leave shortly thereafter. Only impersonal conversation was acceptable—light chat that had no possibility of offending anyone. Mrs. Gaskell gently mocked this inanity when the narrator of *Cranford* wondered how she was to know when her allotted fifteen minutes was up. She was told, "You must keep thinking about the time, my dear, and not allow yourself to forget it in conversation." The narrator continued: "As everybody had this rule in their minds . . . of course no absorbing subject was ever spoken about. We kept ourselves to short sentences of small talk, and were punctual to our time."[79]

To indicate the fleeting nature of the call, women left their shawls and bonnets on, and men carried their hats and sticks into the room[80]—that is, when they could be persuaded to visit at all. Social duties and obligations were the concern of women, and men rarely, and only reluctantly, participated, as Mrs. Gaskell noted: "William called the other day on Mrs Smith—no thanks to me though, as it seemed to me that he waited till I had done asking him to go before he would. Oh the obstinacy of husbands!"[81] Even returning wedding calls was a chore, although not one that could be avoided. Louise Creighton remembered that it "bored Max much . . . He considered it a good afternoon's work if we could achieve 8 [calls]."[82]

Many women felt the same way as the men. Ellen Marshall was a reluctant visitor. Her husband arranged his schedule so that on two afternoons a week she and Jeannette and Ada could have the carriage for calling. Ellen ensured that their calls were kept to the bare minimum: the obligatory condolence and illness visits, and the calls following dinner parties. The rest they avoided if possible. If, as they drove up to a house, they saw the woman they were about to call on going out, they waited at a distance until she'd left, so they would only have to leave cards.[83] Maud Berkeley was more sociable, yet even she could not work up much enthusiasm for all her obligations: "The New Year began with a duty visit to Mrs Raglan-Barnes. Admired a new sofa cushion she had worked with a motto in gold thread on moss-green sateen: 'Lie still and slumber.' Could not help but feel it was strikingly apposite to the occasion, as half the company was nearly asleep."[84]

Others accepted their duty more cheerfully. In *Our Mutual Friend*, when the Boffins unexpectedly inherited money, the wife of the "Golden Dustman" shoulders the burden: "I say [we must have] a good house in a good neighbourhood, good things about us, good living, and good society."[85] Women were expected to be the prime movers of social life; men who liked visiting, by contrast, were regarded as either comic or dubious. Florence Nightingale was angered at the way men's and women's representative responsibilities were divided up:

Suppose we were to see a number of men in the morning, sitting around a table in the drawing-room, looking at prints, doing worsted work and reading little books, how we should laugh! A member of the House of Commons was once known to do worsted work. Of another man it was said, "His only fault is that he is too good; he drives out with his mother every day in the carriage, and if he is asked anywhere he answers that he must dine with his mother." . . .

Now, why is it more ridiculous for a man than for a woman to do worsted work and drive out every day in the carriage? Why should we laugh if we were to see a parcel of men sitting round a drawing-room table in the morning, and think it all right if they were women?[86]

The answer to this was not simple, but it went to the heart of the whole question of public versus private life. Women's forays into the public world outside a domestic sphere were minimal and, particularly higher up the social scale, often grew out of their roles as nurturers and carers. Charitable work was one of the principal outlets for this public face of private virtue.

Middle-class women were active in many charitable institutions, especially in organizing bazaars, teas, fund-raising events of all kinds. Contact with the poor themselves, however, was often considered too "contaminating and degrading." In addition, too profound an interest in charitable works prevented women from performing their essential duties: "establishing a home," entertaining, and taking part in society's rituals.[87] Jeannette Marshall knew which was paramount: "Mr. Kempe preached on visiting the sick, & assured us it was our bounden duty to enrol ourselves district visitors on the spot. Now, I shd. like to know who is to find time for that!" She was also certain, as many of the middle classes were, that "(district) visiting, like charity, begins at home."[88] Or not: there was no indication in Marion Sambourne's diary that, out of an income of some £2,000 a year, she and Linley gave anything to charity, nor did she do any work sewing for bazaars or make other genteel contributions of a similar nature.[89]

Many of the middle classes were similarly against paying local taxes and rates: they felt that the working classes, who were contributing less, were receiving more than their fair share of the civic services provided. The middle classes also worried that their money was going to the "undeserving" rather than to the "deserving" poor: a constant concern, although those who were undeserving were often simply those whom the more prosperous did not know. Men waited outside the main railway stations and followed carriages home, hoping after a run of several miles to earn sixpence or a shilling by helping to carry in trunks or other baggage. Gwen Raverat's Aunt Etty "would never let [them] into the house; she had always engaged beforehand a most Respectable Person, the Square-keeper, to help the cab-driver to carry up the boxes. My father would put his head out of the cab-window, and tell the runners that they would not be needed; but they followed us all the same . . . Once one of them burst into tears, and my father, rather shamefacedly gave him a shilling after all. This was supposed to be very wrong—indiscriminate charity: helping those who begged, and not those who really needed help."[90]

The poor were instead supposed to be taught by their "betters"; the deserving poor were identifiable by being those who were willing to learn. Mrs. Beeton thought that "great advantages may result from visits paid to the poor; for there being, unfortunately, much ignorance, generally, amongst them with respect to all household knowledge, there will be opportunities for advising and instructing them, in a pleasant and unobtrusive manner, in cleanliness, industry, cookery and good management."[91] For it was simply instruction that they needed. The middle and upper classes were good at what Gwen Raverat called "telling": "Ladies . . . did not do things themselves, they told other people what to do and how to do it. My mother would have told anybody how to do anything: the cook how to skin a rabbit, or the groom how to harness a horse; though of course she had never done, or even observed, these operations herself. She would cheerfully have told an engine-driver how to drive his engine, and he would have taken it quite naturally, and have answered: 'Yes, ma'am,' 'Very good, ma'am.' "[92] Thomas Brooks's painting *Charity* (1860) showed a mother teaching her daughter how to give charitably. The rich woman and her child have come in from the sunshine; the woman carries a Bible, the child some fruit, as they step out of the light into the dark house, bringing with them moral as well as physical nourishment.[93]

Mrs. Beeton gave a recipe for a "Useful Soup for Benevolent Purposes" that the frugal housewife could make to distribute to the local poor, at a cost of 1½d. per quart: "The above recipe was used in the winter of 1858 by the Editress, who made, each week, in her copper, 8 or 9 gallons . . . for distribution . . . [It] gave . . . a dish of warm, comforting food, in place of the cold meat and piece of bread which form, with too many cottagers, their usual meal, when, with a little more knowledge of the 'cooking' art, they might have, for less expense, a warm dish every day."[94] All they needed for this improvement was a little more knowledge—and the means to make use of it, for, although the ingredients suggested by the bountiful Editress came to a mere 1½d. per quart, that was when they were bought in bulk. And if the ready cash was available to buy the ingredients, the "cottager" still required a copper, fuel to feed it for six and a half hours, a spare six and a half hours to watch over it, and the physical strength to carry ten gallons of water home.

That the more prosperous were wiser was a given, no matter what their age. The young Sarah Thomas received a note from a local townswoman asking for financial help. She did not simply send the money, but took a sovereign to her. She "held on to it" while taking the woman "round to the tradesmen to pay some bills with it."[95] The supervisory aspect was important, but to get too involved was "odd": Jeannette Marshall despised "Miss H." for leaving behind a "comfortable home for that poky place" from which she visited "the poor in the very lowest & vilest parts of London, wh. no doubt is well-meant, but rather cracked."[96]

It was better by far to give to those of the middle classes who were in danger of slipping down the ladder—perhaps to the Society for Aged and Infirm Women, which "sought money" on behalf of "those who have discharged the relative duties of wife and mother."[97] There were many similar institutions. In *Our Mutual Friend*, Dickens satirized this type of charity: "An estimable lady in the West of England has offered to present a purse containing twenty pounds to the Society for Granting Annuities to Unassuming Members of the Middle Classes, if twenty individuals will previously present purses of one hundred pounds each."[98] Dickens was mocking not the fearful newly poor but the way in which the comfortable middle classes found it so much easier to give to people who were just like themselves.

Women made forays into this world for the most part as an extension to their role as caregivers; the men actually headed up the charities, decided policy, dealt with the finances, and supervised the administration. If women wanted to operate on their own, either they were pushed into the extreme actions of Jeannette Marshall's Miss H. or they restricted themselves to handouts of disposable cash to poor people they happened across near their homes. It was generally considered preferable that, just as charity should go to the deserving—to those similar to themselves—so their nurturing should be kept for the deserving—to those inside their own homes. Their safest course was to focus their giving natures on looking after their families in health, and in illness and death.

THE BATHROOM AND
THE LAVATORY

THE SEARCH FOR health in housing quickly began to center on the newly created rooms containing baths and toilets. It was considered desirable to have two separate rooms, one with a permanent, built-in bath—the bathroom—and the other with a toilet and possibly also a bath. This second type of room was usually called a lavatory or W.C. (water closet),* as was the object the room contained.

The flush lavatory first came into widespread popular consciousness with the Great Exhibition of 1851, the bathroom following later. The middle and upper classes had previously washed in their bedrooms or dressing rooms, with water brought up from the kitchen, either hot or cold depending on the number of servants and the heating methods available. They washed using basins and ewers, and bathed in baths that ranged from tin—the least expensive—through enamel and zinc. The type depended on cost, and on how often they had to be moved: rooms with enough space for the bath to remain permanently in place could have a bath of heavier material. From the 1840s the more expen-

---

*Occasionally sinks were referred to as lavatories, as they still are in some parts of America. To avoid confusion this latter usage will be ignored.

By the end of the century, gas geysers were used to heat water in the bathrooms. They were expensive, noisy and often dangerous, but landlords liked them, as the cost was in the operation, not the installation.

sive properties began to pipe hot water upstairs, although they housed the population that had the least need for running water, as the number of servants was sufficient to ensure that hot water would be carried wherever and whenever required.

By the 1870s hot-water pipes began to appear in middle-class houses. At this time new houses renting for £50 a year often had bathrooms; those at £100 a year nearly always did. A bathroom increased the rent by as much as £10 a year—a 20 percent increase on all but the highest level of rentals.[1] Installing hot-water pipes cost about £50–£60 in the 1880s, but the increased revenue from the rent made it worthwhile for landlords to begin to install bathrooms in houses when leases fell due,[2] and soon there were bathrooms in "even tiny houses built for clerks, [which] rented at about £30 a year."[3] A decade later Mr. Pooter, who was so conspicuously proud of his dream house, did not think to boast of this now ordinary room.

Cold water only was still being supplied to the upper floors of many smaller houses at the end of the century. Geysers, or small boilers, had arrived in the 1860s, and were installed in bathrooms to heat the water just before it was used. The geyser was powered by gas, coke, or oil, although the gas geyser was the most common. Landlords liked them, as they were less expensive to install than hot-water pipes: the expense was in the running, not the installation, and this devolved naturally onto the tenants.[4] Tenants were less keen, as the geysers were expensive, noisy, and, occasionally, dangerous. (Like the kitchen range in its early stages, they exploded from time to time.)

When bathrooms were installed in small houses, and in older houses that had not originally been designed for them, the space had to be carved out of an already intensively utilized area upstairs. As the middle classes had previously bathed where they had dressed, the dressing room therefore became the logical room to be converted.

The bathroom was initially treated no differently from any other room in terms of decoration. Gwen Raverat's family bathroom was decorated in exactly the same way as all the other rooms of the house, right down to the photographs of works of art on the walls.[5] Mrs. Panton as late as 1888 gave no particular scheme of décor for this room; it was the only room in the house for which she did not give a minute description. A mere two years later she was in full flow: the walls were to be papered (the one concession to utility being that the paper should be varnished, to protect it from the water and steam); the woodwork was to be painted with enamel paint, as the harder-working rooms of the house, the kitchen and nursery, generally were. The floor was ideally tiled, but tiles were so expensive that Mrs. Panton expected most middle-class householders to have linoleum. The baths and sinks had mahogany surrounds, to make them look as much like furniture as possible.[6]

Baths and sinks in the 1880s were made of iron, tin, stoneware, or earthenware. To protect the floor, and the ceiling of the room below, the prudent housekeeper had fixed under the bath a lead sheet with turned-up edges and a waste pipe connected to the outflow pipes. With the baths came more regular bathing. In 1869, *Cassell's Household Guide* was instructing its readers that faces, armpits, feet, and "the groin and parts about" were to be washed once a day with soap; a

My first attempt to use the new invention for the hot-water was not a success.

sponge bath was also recommended every day, but soap was not suggested for this, as the sponge bath was for "invigorating" the system, not for cleanliness.[7] In 1875 *The Lady's Every-Day Book* concurred: "It is a great mistake to make this bath a regular washing one. It should only be used as a tonic." Washing was done separately, at night. Daily washing of the head was also recommended—"an excellent prevention against periodical headaches."[8] As so much bathing was therapeutic rather than hygienic, all sorts of changes could be rung on the basic bath. Gwen Raverat's family took this to what was probably an extreme. Her mother thought that if sea bathing was healthy, then the benefits could be simply reproduced in Cambridge by adding sea salt to the children's twice-weekly baths.[9]

Women and men had different approaches to bathing. Linley Sambourne and his son used the bathroom on the landing of their house in Kensington, while Marion and her daughter preferred to have warm sponge baths in their bedrooms.[10] Maud Berkeley felt the same way. In the 1890s another innovation, the shower, or shower-bath, arrived in the house. The Berkeleys' was the kind that attached to the taps: "When I attempted to take one of these new-fangled things, the hose leapt out of the bath and turned itself on me. Definitely prefer the old way of bathing in a hip bath."[11] The more elaborate, permanent types of shower were not much easier. Gwen Raverat's family bathroom "had a sort of grotto containing a shower-bath at one end; this was lined with as many different stops as the organ in King's Chapel. And it was as difficult to control as it would be for an amateur to play that organ. Piercing jets of boiling, or ice-cold, water came roaring at one from the most unexpected angles, and hit one in the tenderest spots."[12]

That the Victorians persisted with these systems until they could control the technology was probably at least in part a legacy of their struggle with indoor sanitation. Many people had seen the flush lavatories at the Great Exhibition in 1851, and many more had read about them: it was estimated that 827,000 people—14 percent of the Exhibition's visitors—had used the facilities, often experiencing such things for the first time.[13] These public lavatories were such a novelty that the *Parliamentary Papers* carried a report:

> It being a somewhat novel step to provide these conveniences for the public on a large scale, and at the same time to derive a revenue from them, the following particulars are given:
>
> The Waiting-rooms were situated near the Refreshment-courts, those in the Transept being the most frequented; the price was made higher, in order to induce the public to go to those which were not so central. No difference was made in the mode of fitting them up, or in the attendance. The amount expended in constructing and fitting up the Water-closets and Washing-places was about £1600.
>
> The Urinals for gentlemen were not charged for; 54 of the latter were provided. It would have been convenient if more accommodation had been provided in the Ladies Waiting-rooms* . . .
>
> The largest receipt from the Waiting-rooms on any one day was on the 8th October, and amounted to £32. 16. 3, on which day

---

*Some things never change.

11,171 persons made use of the Waiting-rooms. The number of visitors on that day was 109,760 . . .

No apology is needed for publishing these facts, which, throughout the whole time of the Exhibition, strongly impressed all concerned in the management with the necessity of making similar provisions for the public wherever large numbers are congregated, and with the sufferings which must be endured by all, but more especially by females, on account of the want of them.[14]

The same year as the Great Exhibition, the first "halting station," or public lavatory, was installed, in Fleet Street. The first women's lavatory was opened in the Strand in 1852. However, public conveniences for women were not widespread, and in 1879, when the local council in Paddington proposed public lavatories for women, residents objected to these "German abominations," suggesting that they would lead to loose women congregating in their district. This was probably a reaction more to the increasing presence of women in public than to any observed behavior.[15]

It was not long before "pan closets" were beginning to be installed more generally in private houses. Three pieces of technology were needed to bring the lavatory indoors. The first was the nonporous clay pipe, which appeared in the 1850s. The second was the lavatory trap or valve, and the third, closely linked, was the flushing mechanism. Lavatories have two main components: the basin or bowl and, leading from that to the waste pipe, the trap or valve. The basin simply needed to be of nonporous, easily cleanable material. With the development of glazed stoneware, this was economically viable very early. The trap or valve was more complicated. This was what allowed the disposal of waste while ensuring that smells were sufficiently blocked. A pan closet simply had three to four inches of water as a sealant in a cast-iron receptacle at the bottom of a copper pan in what was known as a D-trap. (It looked like the letter D on its side.) The pan was tipped up to dispose of waste, which emptied straight into the drains. It was unsanitary, malodorous, and found frequently throughout the century. It was not until the S-bend (or, as it was initially

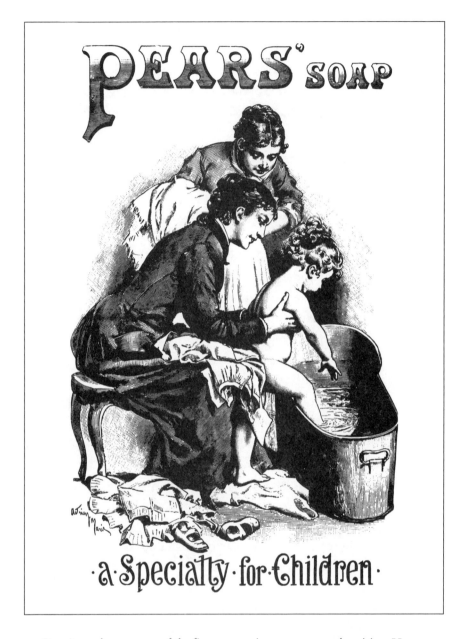

Pears' soap became one of the first companies to use mass advertising. Here a child is bathed in a hip bath, but later a more ambitious campaign included purchasing the rights to Millais's painting *Bubbles*, a portrait of his grandson Willie (later Admiral Sir William James). Did he join the navy to evade that ubiquitous ad?

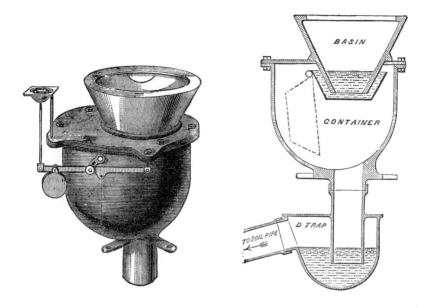

A very common pan closet, popular in the 1860s. The D-trap (bottom right) allowed odors from the drains to permeate the house. When this trap was replaced with the more sophisticated S-bend, with its double water seal, lavatories could be installed anywhere without fear of smells spreading.

called, the siphon-trap) was invented, with its double water trap, that smells could finally be abolished entirely as it carried the waste away from the bowl. This led to the wash-out, or flush-out, closet, which was extremely popular: by 1889 one company alone had sold over one hundred thousand of them.

This development coincided with improved flushing systems. In 1861 Thomas Crapper produced a lavatory with a new mechanism, which, together with his motto "A certain flush with every pull," made his lavatories the market leaders. The problem that remained was water power. Until the siphon flush, the power of the descent of the water alone was all that carried away the waste; from the 1870s new developments allowed the breakthrough valveless siphon to create a vacuum, which gave cisterns substantially more power than the force of the weight of the water alone. This was important in cities in particular: in London, for example, regulations allowed only two gallons of water to be expended per flush, which on its own was not enough to clean out the basin. With piped water and rooftop cisterns added to high-level cisterns above the lavatory, pressure was now stronger and produced improvements to hygiene.[16]

For decades, however, older systems gave endless trouble, and general instructions were routinely handed down: three to four pailfuls of water were to be poured down the pan every morning, to flush out the pipes, then the "plug"—that is, the chain—was to be held for three to four minutes to clear the (pre-vacuum) system fully. This was crucial, for "the condition of the water-closet is a more certain sign of the character of a housekeeper than is any other part of the house."[17] This might have surprised Hannah Cullwick. She worked briefly as a daily char in Eaton Square, London's most expensive neighborhood, where she cleaned "the inside room where the watercloset is. I had a very dirty job. The cobwebs was thick about the walls, & the dust & dirt too on the floors. The window was tied & I daren't try to open it, it seem'd as if it hadn't been open'd for years, & would tumble to pieces if I did."[18]

Lavatories were, after the initial phase, as heavily decorated as any other surface, with the bowls made by potteries such as Doulton, Minton, and Wedgwood. Initially the bowls were cased in by wooden surrounds and only their interiors were decorated. From about 1875 improved hygiene standards made housekeepers want to have faulty pipes and joints readily accessible. As the cabinets began to disappear, more decorative exteriors came onto the market. The possibilities of decorative art were endless. "Architectural" and geometrical styles were common, as were raised, embossed patterns, stripes of clay of different colors, or patterns of birds or fruit. A modern historian of the water closet, who noted the above, also recorded that by the end of the century there were ribbon and shell designs, "Renaissance, Empire, Gold Line, Tourain or Baronial" styles, a choice of flowers, including "Orchid . . . Carnation, Morning Glory, Chrysanthemum, Hydrangea," and designs named "Pink Lucknow, Brown York, Olive Green Chicago, Grey Plassy, Mulberry Marble, Cretonne, Mazarine Blue and Gold, Chocolate Galatz, Dacca Mulberry, Pink Teviot, Dark Blue

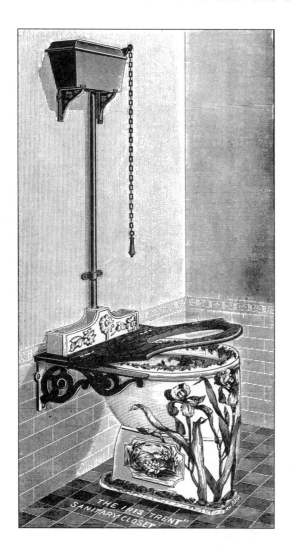

The "Iris" pedestal lavatory, 1895, was only one of many popular patterns.
Others included fruits, shells, stripes, birds—even views of Windsor Castle.

Leghorn, Décor Louis XV," not to mention Italianate garden scenes
and reproductions of Windsor Castle.[19]

While these elegant appliances were becoming more common, lavatory paper remained a homemade product, and was not commercially
produced for some time. For one thing, it was yet another way to reuse
what would otherwise be wasted; and so household paper of all kinds

was torn up into squares to serve this purpose. Diana Holman Hunt described the method in her memoir. On a visit to her grandmother, the widow of the Pre-Raphaelite artist Holman Hunt, she was told,

> "You can make yourself useful; there are many circulars, envelopes and paper bags ready . . ."
>
> "Which do you need most, spills* or lavatory paper?"
>
> "Let me see—the latter, I think . . . Here is your knife . . . You will find the stiletto, the template and string in the Indian box over there."
>
> . . . I ripped the blade through the stiff paper folded round the template. "Some of these bags from Palmer's Stores are very thick and covered with writing."
>
> "Print is all right on one side you know . . ."
>
> When I had cut a hundred sheets, I pierced their corners and threaded them with a string; I tied this in a loop to hang on a nail by the "convenience." I made a mental note of the softer pieces and put them together in the middle, between the back of a calendar from Barkers and an advertisement for night-lights.[20]

Many people continued to live without indoor sanitation—not only among the lower middle classes, but even many of the prosperous. Robert Louis Stevenson's parents lived in the best area of Edinburgh, the New Town, but in the 1860s they managed with an outdoor privy and, inside, chamber pots.[21] By contrast the Sambournes' house in Kensington, built in the 1870s, had three W.C.s. Those houses with one lavatory frequently retained an outdoor privy for the servants' use. *Our Homes* was sure that "the minor inconveniences of having at times to approach it through the rain is more than counterbalanced by the decided advantage of atmospheric connection between it and the kitchen being effectually cut off."[22] Those houses with two lavatories designated one (usually near the kitchen) for the servants, one for the family. Some books suggested that if there were two family lavatories

*See p. 122.

they should be separately demarcated for the men and the women in the family, but I have not found any instance where this was known to have been done, although people with houses large enough to have downstairs cloakrooms tended to reserve them for men—both those living in the house and visitors.[23]

The placing of the lavatory in houses with floor plans conceived before its existence was even less straightforward than the siting of the bathroom. When W.C.s first arrived, the practice was to put them in extensions against the back of the house, in a location where there was no window above it—the only way to deal with the odor. Once the smell had been conquered by the S-bend, the W.C. was commonly situated, to keep it out of the way, in areas with too little ventilation, in rooms with no outside walls: under the staircase, in dressing rooms, in a partitioned area of a bedroom. The landing on a staircase was one of the few good places ready-made in most houses, without major building work: it usually had access to an outside wall, and a lavatory there took up otherwise little-used space. But, as *Our Homes* noted, new and poorly located drainpipes often meant that "every time the contents of the basin are discharged the sound of water rushing down the pipe [was] distinctly audible" in the drawing room.[24]

The noise was an unpleasant social reminder and also, of far greater concern, a reminder of the dangers that lurked in hygienic apparatus. By the 1870s it was recognized that indoor plumbing was essential, but increased knowledge of disease transmission made the idea of taking into one's house what appeared to be the source of disease a hazardous one. With chamber pots and cesspits, one's own waste was present, but these new piping systems seemed to link each house to the next. With no generally understood concept of how disease was transmitted, the pipes were thought to be an entry point for illness. Each person's own germs were carried away in these sewage pipes, but who was to say that other people's weren't being carried in? How many deaths, asked sanitary engineer S. Stevens Hellyer, "have been caused by . . . a foul drain, a diseased water-closet trap, a bottled-up soil-pipe . . . ?"[25] Marion Sambourne repeatedly attributed her sore throats and other minor ailments to the washbasin and its attendant drain in her bathroom.[26]

In the 1830s and 1840s three waves of contagious diseases had swept across the country: from 1831 to 1833 there were two influenza epidemics, and the first-ever outbreak of cholera in Britain, which alone killed 52,000; from 1836 to 1842 there were epidemics of influenza, typhus, smallpox, and scarlet fever; from 1846 to 1849 came typhus, typhoid, and cholera again. These three waves of death had a devastating impact on a terrified population that had thought that, with the smallpox vaccination and some success against diseases like diphtheria, epidemic death might be on the wane.

Today we can understand these epidemics as the result of a lethal combination of bad weather conditions, high food prices leading to poor nutrition among much of the populace, sudden influxes of immigrants, and cities without the sewers and water supplies to cope with the sharp rise in population. The economic basis of disease can be seen most clearly in life-expectancy figures. In the Surrey countryside, life expectancy for men was 45 years; in London it was 37; in Liverpool, with its large immigrant population, 26; for working-class men generally it was 15. The official density of population for London was 42 people per acre, but this was an average, and it varied from 1 person per acre in the prosperous outer suburb of Eltham to 300 people per acre in the inner-city slum of St. Giles.[27] At the time, all that could be seen was that these diseases were bringers of mass destruction: influenza then was the killer virus of 1919, not the merely debilitating bug of today. In 1833, in the first week of an influenza epidemic London burial numbers doubled; in a single fortnight they increased by 400 percent. In the four years after a typhus outbreak in 1837, 16,000 people died of typhus every year; scarlet fever killed another 20,000 in 1840. The Irish potato famine in the following years brought a sharp rise in the number of people living in poverty in industrial cities throughout Britain. In 1848 there were 30,000 deaths from typhoid and another 13,000 from influenza, and 50,000 from cholera in 1850. It was thought that for every person who died of old age or violence, another eight died of disease.[28]

It was recognized early on that poor sanitation was at the heart of disease transmission, long before it was known why. The factor that speeded up the improvement was Asiatic cholera, which had first arrived in Britain in 1830 and spread rapidly along the waterways. In 1849, during one epidemic, 15,010 houses in the City of London were inspected. *The Times* reported that

> 2,524 had "offensive smells from bad drainage or other causes"
> 720 had "filth or rubbish in the cellar"
> 446 were "in an offensive or unhealthy state from bad or defi-
>   cient drainage"
> 1,120 had privies or W.C.s "in a very offensive state"
> 223 had "cesspools full of soil"*
> 30 had "burst or overflowed" cesspools
> 21 had "cellars used as cesspools."[29]

In other words, up to one-third of the houses examined had major hygiene problems.

As Sir John Simon pointed out in his "Report of the Medical Officer of Health to the City of London" (1848), "Part of the City might be described as having a cesspool city excavated under it."[30] These cesspools were hazardous to more than those who lived above them. Because they were expensive to clean out, they frequently overflowed, and the liquids seeped into the local watercourses and, ultimately, into the Thames itself, the main source of London's drinking water. The tributary rivers of London also doubled as sewers. Henry Mayhew listed some of his findings in them: ingredients from breweries, gasworks, and chemical and mineral manufactories; dead dogs, cats, and kittens, fats, offal from slaughterhouses; "street-pavement dirt of every variety; vegetable refuse; stable-dung; the refuse of pig-styes; night-soil; ashes; tin kettles and pans . . . broken stoneware, jars, pitchers, flower-pots, &c.; pieces of wood; rotten mortar and rubbish of different kinds . . ."[31] The fetid gas was a danger on its own: the Fleet River, long covered over, had such a buildup of gas that it exploded, with sewage pouring out with enough force to sweep away three houses.[32]

---

*"Soil" and "night-soil" were both euphemisms for excrement.

Initially, sewers had been only for rainwater; but gradually sewage was discharged into the drains and, ultimately, the rivers. In Cambridge Gwen Raverat lived by the river, and she vividly remembered the sewage that had been in it as late as the 1890s. There was a well-known story then of Queen Victoria visiting years before, and saying as she looked down over the bridge, "What are all those pieces of paper floating down the river?" and of the Master of Trinity calmly replying, "Those, ma'am, are notices that bathing is forbidden."[33] In the 1840s the builder Thomas Cubitt reported to the Select Committee on the Health of Towns that cesspools were vanishing and that "the Thames is now made a great cesspool instead of each person having one of his own."[34] By 1848 it was illegal to build houses without drains, which had to be connected to the public sewer. At first this caused increased incidences of cholera and other water-borne diseases, as the sewage was discharged directly into the rivers; Sir John Simon, a proponent of the miasma theory of disease, was concerned to get smells, which he thought bred disease, out of the house, and was less worried about what happened once the sewage reached the river.

When the unusually hot summer of 1858 caused the "Great Stink" of London, Parliament was finally "all but compelled to legislate . . . by the force of sheer stench," reported *The Times*. MPs could not sit on the river side of the Houses of Parliament at all,* and sheets dipped in chloride of lime had to be hung as disinfectant throughout the building.[36] The same year the army had issued a report: at Sebastopol, at the height of the Crimean War, mortality from both battle and disease was 12.5 per 1,000 soldiers, as against 17.9 per 1,000 in the infantry and 20.4 in the Guards quartered at home. (In towns in Britain at the same time death rates were 9.2 per 1,000, while in the country they were 7.7 per 1,000.) "In the population of one of the most unhealthy towns in the kingdom, Manchester, the mortality was then very high; but even in

---

*This is not to suggest that at other times the Thames was salubrious. Arthur Munby, returning from Boulogne the following year, wrote, "So we got back to London by seven, and the stench of the Thames gave me a sick headache, & destroyed at once all the blessings of the pure sea air."[35]

this selected spot of unhealthiness it was only 12.4 per thousand of persons of the same ages compared with the 17.5 of the soldiery [in barracks]," said the report. When the army improved the ventilation and "nuisances arising from latrines and defective sewerage" in its barracks, the death rate dropped dramatically.[37]

The evidence could not be ignored, and the first great metropolitan sewage system was begun, with huge pipes, treatment plants, and outfall sewers to carry away the city's effluent in embankments all along the Thames. The completion of the system in the 1870s made waterborne epidemics a thing of the past, while European cities continued to be ravaged. London, the largest city in the world, had therefore had the worst problems created by high-density living, and dealt with them first. Smaller cities soon followed. The last big cholera epidemic in London was in 1866. Of the 4,363 deaths in July and August, 93 percent were in the area supplied by the East London Water Company, which was still using improperly filtered water from the Thames. By contrast, France did not pass laws for a main-drainage system for another fifty years; Dresden suffered a crippling typhoid outbreak as late as 1891–92; Hamburg had cholera in the last decade of the century as well.[38]

By the 1880s it was generally understood that cholera and typhoid, even if no longer epidemic, were spread by excrement, and that contaminated groundwater was a contributing factor. Bad drains were also thought to be responsible for other diseases, such as diphtheria, ague, dyspepsia, constipation, erysipelas, "foul-air fever," and consumption—or at the least the drains were suggested as contributing factors. Thus the very rooms that had been installed to prevent disease, and which did do so much to ameliorate the health of so many, were now also seen to be responsible for the promotion of these diseases. How to treat the illnesses, which in the nineteenth century were unavoidable, was the question that faced every family.

THE SICKROOM

The London Medical Officer Shirley Forster Murphy's book, *Our Homes*, warned that "every bed-room is a possible sick-room."[1] Likewise, every woman was a possible nurse. Both the sickroom and the nurse were flexible concepts. Just as a nurse was only a nurse when necessary—in healthy times she was a wife, mother, or sister—so a sickroom appeared only in times of trouble. The rest of the time it was a bedroom. When illness appeared, the wife or mother transformed herself, and so did the bedroom, for illness was a home-based episode. Until the end of the century hospitals were where the poor went. For the middle classes, illness was something that happened at home. By extension, therefore, so did nursing.

Professional nurses were available, and many books advised on what should be looked for in a nurse for families that could afford them, although money was only a small part of the deciding factor in who looked after the patient; more hung on the availability of female relations. If a professional was to be hired, she needed to be strong enough to lift a patient, in good enough health herself to look after others, and with "a happy, cheerful, equal flow of spirits, a temper not easily ruffled, and kind and sympathetic feelings." She should be "sober, active, orderly, and clean and neat in her person" (note the order).[2] This was an ideal, however, and few expected nurses to live up to it. Before nursing reforms in midcentury, nurses were distrusted and disliked; they were expected to drink and possibly even take snuff, to be unclean and unpleasant. They were women doing a most unwomanly thing: they were nurturing and caring for others for financial gain. In *The Old Curiosity Shop*, written in 1841—the same year as the description of the ideal nurse above—Dickens portrayed those looking after Little Nell's grandfather as "strangers who made of it a greedy trade, and who, in the intervals of their attendance upon the sick man, huddled together with a ghastly good-fellowship, and ate and drank and made merry; for disease and death were their ordinary household gods . . . [Nell] was . . . alone in her unfeigned sorrow and her unpurchased sympathy."[3] It was not the care they gave the patient that Dickens doubted (although he did that too), but *why* they cared for him: mercenary motivation rendered even the best care null. The quality of Nell's care was irrelevant: her feminine emotions gave it its virtue.

As Mrs. Beeton noted, "All women are likely, at some period of their lives, to be called on to perform the duties of a sick-nurse . . . The main requirements are good temper, compassion for suffering, sympathy with sufferers, which most women worthy of the name possess, neat-handedness, quiet manners, love of order, and cleanliness."[4] Women were generally assumed to fall into one of two groups: the nurses and the nursed. The nurses tended to have their jobs imposed upon them, by circumstance and necessity. The nursed, although often truly ill, sometimes had an element of choice. In *David Copperfield*, Tommy Traddles's fiancée, Sophy, was in the first group. She found it difficult to abandon her role as the family's caregiver: 'You see, Sophy being of so much use in the family, none of them could endure the thought of her ever being married. Indeed, they had quite settled among themselves that she never was to be married, and they called her the old maid." When Sophy and Traddles told her mother of her engagement, her mother fainted, and "I couldn't approach the subject again for months." Her sister Sarah, who had "something the matter with her spine," "clenched both her hands . . . shut her eyes; turned lead-colour; became perfectly stiff; and took nothing for two days but toast and water,* administered with a teaspoon."[6]

"It has been said and written scores of times, that every woman makes a good nurse," said Florence Nightingale.[7] While she, unusually, felt that nursing had to be taught, she neglected to consider, through the strength of her own vocation, that not every woman was a nurse by inclination. Yet those who avoided this duty were condemned by other women, as well as by men. In *The Small House at Allington*, when Lily Dale gets scarlet fever, the doctor tries to persuade Bell, her sister, to avoid infection by going to stay elsewhere for the duration. Bell is resolute: "I don't ever like to hear of a woman running away from illness; but when a sister or a daughter does so, it is intolerable."[8] Beatrix Potter acted in a daughterly manner but did not enjoy the process: "Mamma was taken very ill, sick from eight on Monday morning till three next morning . . . There is supposed to be some angelic sentiment in tending the sick, but personally I should not associate angels with castor oil and emptying slops."[9]

Many other women thought less about the philosophy of nursing, but the practice was all too routine. Laura Forster's brother and sister both had consumptive illnesses: "At 12 [midnight] I gave [my sister] her pill, at three her draughts, at 4.30 I made her breakfast; she coughed again at 6, but only a little, and soon after I got up and put on her some embrocation." Laura's tone of exhaustion five months later, after her brother's death, was to be expected: "I do not fear death but the valley of the shadow is a weary place to live in."[10] Physically wearying, as well as emotionally. Soon she was called on again. Her mother died in 1869, her father in 1871, and before that she had nursed them both for over three years and "my health had been shattered by incessant nursing."[11] It was hardly surprising that fiction mirrored life and contained numerous heroines who, after nursing another woman, became a patient in turn: George Eliot, Mrs. Gaskell, Harriet Martineau and many other (women) writers saw this as a natural progression.[12]

---

*Toast and water was highly recommended for invalids. A slice of toast was put in a jug, and a quart of boiling water was poured over it. When this had cooled it was strained and ready to serve.[5]

While nursing was an exclusively female task, the sickroom was no longer an exclusively female preserve. Those values which Mrs. Beeton had listed as the most important for a nurse—compassion, sympathy, and a desire to serve—were seen as leading to a career in public service for men, but in women they were to be expressed only in a private context. This epitomized the bizarre disjunction of women's lives. As nurses, as mothers, as educators of future generations, women were able, capable, adept and proficient managers; as wives, as daughters, as sisters, women were unstable, fragile, uncertain creatures needing masculine guidance. We have seen that the professionalization of all aspects of society was well under way—in education, where mothers were responsible for their boys only until they were old enough to attend school; in charity, where women worked under men's supervision; in child-rearing, where mothers were taught by advice books to mistrust their instincts and the advice given them by their own mothers; in their households, where countless books told women how to run their homes in the newest, best way. It was no less the case with medicine. It has too readily been said that men and women occupied separate spheres—work versus home, professional life versus home life. Once the situation is examined, this can be seen to have been not remotely the case: male experts had firmly ensconced themselves in the home, commenting on and prescribing for every aspect of what was thought to be private life.

For the middle classes, the technological advances of medicine—anesthetics and surgery in general, and in relation to childbirth in particular—meant that men, doctors, now took over where previously women had ruled. Dr. Pye Chavasse in his childcare handbook had forbidden women to attend women in labor, as had been traditional for centuries. (See pp. 53–54.) The "practitioner should deliver his firm and respectful dictum in the midst of [women's] blind and exalted sentiments, which exercise the most disastrous influence on the health of the children," both during childbirth and in the infant's early life, said another advice book about mothers and their children.[13] Midwives had such poor reputations—and so few opportunities for training and none for accreditation (see p. 54)—that many middle-class mothers welcomed the arrival of doctors and their usurpation of the place of women. Doctors saw patient ignorance as an opportunity: the less the patients knew of diagnosis, treatment, and cure, the more reliant on their medical men they would have to be. This attitude was not merely subtext, nor is it a retroactive reading of the situation. Ruth, Mrs. Gaskell's eponymous heroine, hoped to become a nurse, and thought it helpful that she had learned Latin to teach her son, as it meant that "I can read the prescriptions." Her more worldly friend responded, "Which the doctors would rather you did not do."[14]

This idea that people were kept in ignorance for mercenary ends sounds harsh, but consider, as an example, Dr R. Hall Bakewell's 1857 book on the management of the sickroom—and bear in mind that this book was sold as a handbook for the home nurse. He began: "No attempt will be made in this little tract to describe the symptoms or treatment of diseases, as the writer is convinced that far more harm than good is done by works on domestic medicine . . . how unreasonable must it seem to suppose that a person quite uneducated in medicine can discover a disease, and decide on the appropriate treatment, simply from reading the short, imperfect, and generally incorrect, descriptions contained in works on domestic medicine." This, it is worth reiterating, is in a work on domestic medicine. If the home nurse wanted to treat a minor illness, Dr. Bakewell's counsel was that the best thing to do was "*do nothing at all*" (his italics) and, if things got worse, to send for a doctor.

He was not entirely without advice for those seeking help: "The first hint I would give is—always, unless in a case of sudden illness, send for a medical man *early in the day*." This was not to ensure the welfare of the patient but because "most medical men commence their rounds about ten, a.m., some at nine, and unless patients send before this time, most serious inconvenience to the surgeon and great delay to the patient is caused. [Note the order.] When your medical friend arrives, state the case to him quietly and fully, mainly describing present symptoms, and not entering into wearisome histories of what took place months ago . . . Some, like the lower class of Irish, will, if one allows them to run on, tell one everything but what one wants to know."

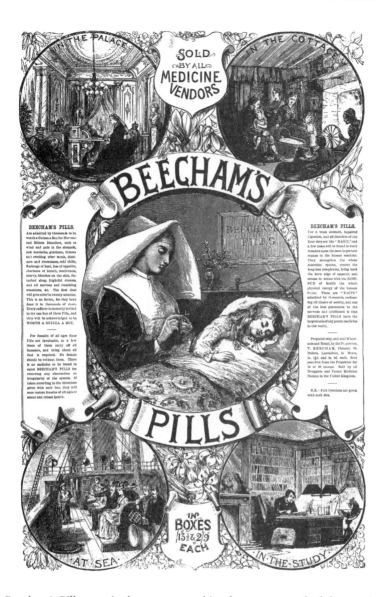

Beecham's Pills promised to cure everything from scurvy to bad dreams. In fact, they contained only aloes (a purgative), ginger, and soap. This advertisement directs itself to a wide audience, from "palace" to "cottage," as does its copy. While announcing it is "WORTH A GUINEA A BOX," the pills were, in fact, selling for 1s. 1½d. In 1909 it was estimated that the cost of the ingredients for a box of 56 pills was half a farthing.

He had stringent instructions for the home nurse: she was to "adhere strictly" to the diet "prescribed by the medical attendant . . . never making even trifling alterations without permission." When things went wrong, it was not because these instructions were wrong, or because nature was more powerful than medical knowledge, but because "it is so seldom that people will take the trouble to carry out medical instructions fully and exactly." If the patient or the family had doubts about the treatment, they had to bear in mind that "the most ignorant and unpractised surgeon will know better what to do than the cleverest of his patients . . . The question is simply this, do you think your own opinion or the surgeon's the more valuable?"

It was not that he was against second opinions, he hastened to add; it was simply that patients "commit[ted] the folly of paying a man to give . . . advice and then refusing to take the advice."[15] Bakewell was more open than most in airing his views of his patients, but not particularly unusual in holding these views. *Cassell's Household Guide* warned patients that second opinions could not be obtained without "consultation with the medical man already attending . . . and the ordinary attendant will naturally be offended if any attempt is made to seek other advice behind his back." The proper way to get a second opinion, the guide suggested, was to ask the attending doctor for the name of a colleague.[16] That this would only bring another man with similar views was overlooked. Many doctors refused even this. When Countess Lovelace, Byron's daughter, was dying agonizingly of cancer of the uterus in 1852, she attempted to consult another doctor. Her doctor wrote: "I wish to have no consultations—they will only hamper me, and I will have none of them, unless at my own proposition, feeling at a loss or in a difficulty. No one who has not watched the case as I have done can possibly judge fairly, and if I am to be bothered with strange people coming in, I decline having any further charge of you."[17]

This defensiveness was perhaps more understandable when the extreme limitations of medicine were taken into account. Most advances in health came from advances in hygiene and sanitation and from improvements in nutrition. Germ theory brought the ability to differentiate between diseases that had previously been thought of as one, and diagnoses improved: diphtheria could now be told apart from scarlet fever or croup, syphilis from gonorrhea, typhoid from typhus. The invention of the stethoscope allowed the differences between pleurisy, emphysema, bronchitis, and pneumonia to be clarified, but once the patient's illness was defined, the lack of cure was still an insuperable problem. A number of drugs were isolated or discovered in the early part of the century: morphine, quinine, atropine, codeine, and iodine.[18] Beginning in the 1820s, salicylic acid was produced from salicin, itself derived from willow bark, and was used primarily for rheumatic fever and rheumatism. Alice James wrote to her brother William in 1886, "Until lately every joint in my body was constantly pierced with rheumatic pains . . . how I should have lived without salicene I don't know."[19] The synthetic descendant of salicin and salicylic acid was first produced in the Bayer laboratories in 1897; it was named Aspirin and sold from 1899 on.*

Many avoided medical men as much as possible. A great deal of the (unspoken) reason may have been cost. In 1860 Sarah Thomas paid a consultant £3 17s. 6d. for a diagnosis of her sister's illness.[21] A decade later, *Cassell's Household Guide* gave consultants' fees as 2 guineas, plus traveling costs: 1 guinea per mile by road, or 14s. by rail, one way only. Sarah Thomas, in Gloucestershire, was being charged moderately by this reckoning. *Cassell's* suggested that half a guinea (10s. 6d.) to a guinea was standard payment for childbirth "for an artisan's wife," with rates rising to 50 guineas "in higher circles." This seems impossible: 10s. to 11s. would simply have been beyond the means of most artisans. It is more likely that *Cassell's* was replicating the standard assumptions of most advice books, and misreading the economic categories. Just as Mrs. Panton thought that the lowest middle-class income was £200–£300, which in reality situated its possessors firmly in the prosperous middle classes, it may be that *Cassell's* artisans were actually the lower and some of the middle middle classes. House calls

---

*It took two years for Bayer to bring its new drug to market because there seemed to be more promise in another discovery, a cough medicine made from the newly synthesized diacetylmorphine, which carried the brand name Heroin.[20]

cost from 2s. 6d. to 10s. 6d., usually including the medicines, with a sliding scale upward for night calls. For the most part, the doctor came to the house, and his "boy" returned later with the medicines. The "boy" was identifiable by his "natty pot-hat" (that is, top hat) and trim shell-jacket decorated with several rows of silvered buttons.[22]

It may have been for economic reasons that Helen Corke's shop-keeper parents rarely called for the doctor. Helen said that her mother "had little respect for people who 'fly to the doctor for a cold in the head,' and is quite certain that she knows how to treat whooping cough." Her father dosed the family every week with brimstone and treacle or senna tea (both laxatives), and "Mamma's faith in the small green bottles of homoeopathic pillules remains unchallenged."[23] Geraldine Jewsbury also went in for what today are called alternative remedies. She encouraged Jane Carlyle to see a Dr. Elliotson for her headaches: he "has an inspiration for knowing what ails people."[24] Elliotson was a mesmerist—a hypnotist—as well as a professor of medicine at University College London, and he had a large following, although there is no indication that Jane Carlyle saw him.

Many consulted a variety of trained and untrained, conventional and unconventional practitioners, usually for one simple reason: orthodox medicine was frequently radical, painful, and could give no relief. A not unusual story was that of Emily Gosse, the wife of the naturalist Philip Gosse and mother of Edmund Gosse.[25] Philip and Emily Gosse married in middle age: he was "nearly thirty-eight, she was past forty-two," said their son, by this circumlocution making the four-year gap in their ages appear enormous. They were members of the Plymouth Brethren sect, extreme fundamentalist Christians. Emily Gosse published over thirty Gospel tracts, and wrote proselytizing articles for various Christian publications. Their religion set them apart: the family did not celebrate Christmas, considering it a pagan holiday; Emily thought that all fiction was sinful, because it was untruthful; and, most important for this story, they both believed that illness was sent by God to chastise the sinner.

When around the beginning of 1856 Emily noticed a lump in her breast, her response was to take "the first opportunity of showing it to her friend, Miss Stacy."* Miss Stacy persuaded her to go to a doctor; he diagnosed cancer and recommended surgery, as did a second who was suggested to them by a relative who was also a doctor. The Gosses hesitated: breast cancer was a hideous disease, and the treatment not much better. A contemporary historian of medicine gives a sobering picture of the disease:

> This cancer killed, and in a particularly devastating way, almost every woman who fell victim to it. In most cases, an untreated malignant lump in the breast would slowly continue to enlarge until it burst open onto the skin surface and proceeded to eat away at the surrounding tissue. Most patients died only after years of enduring the presence of an expanding ulcer where the breast had been, painfully eroding its way through the underlying muscle of the chest wall and in time even the ribs beneath, all the while exuding the stench of foul fluid that oozed constantly from its ever-widening circumference. Few experienced physicians had ever seen a woman live as long as five years after the initial discovery of a cancerous mass. Usually, the interval between diagnosis and death was less than half that period.[27]

Surgery was almost always a failure. Eight out of ten women could expect a recurrence of their tumors within months, or a year or two at the most. It was not uncommon, therefore, to reject surgery and just wait for death. The Gosses' doctor-cousin, however, came up with another possibility: he had heard of an American, "Dr." Jesse Weldon

---

*In writing his detailed account of his wife's disease—*A Memorial of the Last Days on Earth of Emily Gosse*—from which this account draws heavily, Philip Gosse was following in a tradition not limited to Dissenters. Throughout the century many families wrote memorials of the dying as a "spiritual accounting to God." Historians find them extremely useful as, to preserve the memory of the soon-to-be-deceased, a daily record of their final days was kept, recording not only religious moments but also secular conversations and medical treatment. As the century progressed and death became increasingly an event that happened in the hospital or under professional care, these memorials began to disappear.[26]

Fell, who "professed to be in possession of a secret medicament, by the external application of which to a cancer the diseased portion gradually became dead, spontaneously separated from the healthy flesh, and sloughed away, leaving a cavity, which soon healed, and the patient was well." They went to see him, and he showed them photographs of patients and their tumors as the treatment progressed, and also tumors in jars, which he claimed had simply fallen off under this treatment. They also saw a woman having her tumor dressed; the doctor showed them how the cancerous mass had separated from the healthy breast "except for a few mucous threads, which he divided with scissors." Later the woman told them that the tumor had dropped off entirely soon after they left.

The Gosses decided that Emily would place herself under Dr. Fell's care. This was not a light decision: the cost of any medical care—traditional or alternative—was high. They were not poor: Philip Gosse's books brought in a good income, as did his very popular lectures.* At the same time, savings were not spent casually: without any pensions, a provident breadwinner would hope to lay aside 30 percent of his earnings every year, to see him through old age and to cover any family emergencies. Interestingly, their son gave a completely different picture. He wrote nearly half a century later that his parents were "proud . . . to conceal the fact of their poverty, painfully scrupulous to avoid giving inconvenience to shop-people, tradesmen or servants, their whole financial career had to be carried on with the adroitness of a campaign through a hostile country." When Emily began treatment, "every branch of expenditure was cut down, clothes, books, the little garden which was my Father's pride, all felt the pressure of new poverty. Even our food, which had always been simple, now became Spartan indeed."

Emily traveled from Islington to Dr. Fell's practice in Pimlico every other day for four months to have ointments applied to her breast.

---

*Emily Gosse's religious tracts were hugely popular: one title alone sold half a million copies.[28] However, it is likely that Emily Gosse saw the tracts as part of her missionary work, and would not take payment for them.

One of the ointments caused "a gnawing or aching in the breast, which at times was scarcely supportable," but there was no visible change in the tumor. By the fifth month there was an "intense aching and 'drawing' pain in the tumor," but still no change. The doctor therefore advised surgical removal of the tumor. By now Emily was too weak to make the thrice-weekly trip, and so she and Edmund—then no more than eight years old—moved into lodgings near the doctor. There the child became, according to his own account, "my Mother's sole and ceaseless companion; the silent witness of her suffering . . . For nearly three months I breathed the atmosphere of pain, saw no other light, heard no other sounds, thought no other thoughts than those which accompany physical suffering and weariness . . . I have now in my mind's cabinet a picture of my chair turned towards the window, partly that I might see [my] book more distinctly, partly not to see quite so distinctly that dear patient figure rocking on her sofa, or leaning, like a funeral statue, like a muse upon a monument, with her head on her arms against the mantelpiece."

Dr. Fell's surgical procedure was no more orthodox than his earlier treatment. "The whole surface of the left breast, an area of four inches in diameter, was wetted with nitric acid . . . The object of this application was to remove the skin. The smart was very trying, and continued for several hours augmenting; the effect being to blister and destroy the whole skin, exactly as if a severe burn had taken place." The next day he incised the tumor "in order that it might be penetrated by the peculiar medicament which he used for its separation. With the scalpel he drew, on the surface of the now exposed flesh, a series of parallel scratches, about half an inch apart, reaching from the top to the bottom. When these were made, a plaister of purple mucilaginous substance was spread over the whole. The next day, on renewing this plaister, the scalpel was passed again along the scratches, deepening them a very little." This was repeated every day, with the purple stuff pushed by linen rags deeper into the cuts, which were increased every day. This was the "seat of an aching, piercing pain, under which my beloved sufferer was fain to wander up and down her narrow room . . . unable from the agony to lie, sit, or stand."

After a month the incisions were an inch and a half deep, and Dr. Fell said he had reached the bottom of the tumor, and started to apply a "girdle . . . around the line where the killed tumour adjoined the living flesh . . . The object was to promote a suppuration, whereby the tumour should be gradually detached from the flesh, and sloughed off." This took two weeks more, forming a furrow filled with pus. Two days later the doctor noticed "a sort of offshoot of the tumour, in the bottom of the cavity," which, while he was not sure it was cancerous, he thought he had better remove as a precaution. So the process started over again, for another four weeks. Then he said there were two more places where he would have to remove skin, and when she asked why, he responded, "Oh, 'tis in your blood"—that is, the cancer had spread and was no longer localized.

At this point Emily decided that she could stand no more: "We had . . . been all along assured that the cancer was local . . . and therefore the announcement that it was seated in the blood, which indeed we had good reason to believe it true, took us by surprise, as contrary to the statements we had all along relied on." They decided "that our only human hope lay in an effort to invigorate the constitution, and to remove the taint from the system" with homeopathy, in which Emily had long had faith.

Emily moved back to Islington toward the end of December, and by the middle of January the cancer had become rampant: the wound was suppurating and had become infected, and her arm was unusable. She also had fever and was coughing terribly: she was permanently bedridden, and "often she was too weak to do more than pat [her son's] hand." Her homeopathic doctor was more honest than the American quack.* He "gave no hope of recovery."

It is likely that Emily simply remained in her own room, waiting for death, with Philip's cousin, who had arrived from Clifton, to nurse her, while her husband and child slept in the second bedroom. Her hus-

---

*"Quack" is not too strong a word. Fell was not a man with a genuine, if misguided, mission. He wrote to a friend in America, "I am residing in the great metropolitan babel of the world operating upon John Bull and trying to relieve him of some of his surplus gold."[29]

band's main concern was that he had no image of her to remember her by. She had had two portraits made, both in her more prosperous youth, but the second one had gone with a relative to America, and only a childhood picture remained. Two friends offered their services—a not uncommon circumstance for someone gravely ill, although more unusual at such a late stage.* One friend was to photograph her, the other would paint a watercolor miniature. Despite Emily being very obviously only days away from death, the friends' offer was welcomed, and the photographs in particular were, said her soon-to-be-widower, "characteristic and pleasing, though somewhat undefined, because of the motion arising from her laborious breathing." Another photograph was taken a mere twelve hours before her death, when her bed (with her in it, one presumes) was moved across the room, so that a better light could be obtained.

It may have been relatively easy to move the bed: the Gosses appear to have lived in a fairly austere manner. Even if they had not, instructions for the preparation of the sickroom would have encouraged a simplification. It was recommended that, at the commencement of illness, the sickroom be emptied as much as possible of all furniture and ornaments. In the second half of the century, disease theory indicated that bare, spare rooms were more conducive to patients' recovery: they could be kept clean more easily, and the attempt to eradicate what were soon to become known as germs could be carried out. Naturally, not everyone paid attention to such dictates. Alice James was photographed in her sickroom in Leamington Spa in 1889 or 1890. She sat on a chaise longue by the window, with a table beside her covered with a cloth, with books, flowers, an ornamental bowl, papers, and a lamp; lace or net curtains were covered by another pair of brocade or chintz curtains. The fireplace had a fabric overmantel, with yet more knickknacks on it.[31]

In theory, however, the sickroom was to contain nothing but the

---

*More common was the situation with Alice James. Three months after she had been told she had breast cancer her companion insisted that a photographer be brought in to take her picture.[30]

bed (with no bedcurtains or valances); a sofa or daybed, if the patient was strong enough to sit up part of the time; a washstand; a chest of drawers for towels and clean nightclothes; and two tables: one near the bed to hold drinks for the patient and the medicine for the day; a second, larger one, for items not immediately needed, together with the impedimenta of nursing: tape for bloodletting, linen for wounds, and for poultices and blisters, together with a spatula for the same, a sponge, lint, scissors, bandages, and adhesive plaster.[32]

The once common blisters and poultices are, happily, so far in the past that they need explanation today. Both were used on the principle of counter-irritation: an illness or infection was thought to be caused by an inflamed organ or area of the body, which could be countered by a manufactured inflammation nearby to "draw" the poison from the system. So stomach trouble was treated with a blister to the gut, a sore throat by a blister on the neck. Blisters were produced by pretreated blister-plaster. The area was cleaned and dried, and the plaster was held in place with strips of adhesive plaster, or a bandage. Within five or six hours the chemical on the paper caused a blister to form. If no blister-plaster was available, a blister could be raised by directing the steam from a kettle onto the area, or by touching the area with metal heated in boiling water. After the blister appeared it was punctured with scissors and the fluid was allowed to run out. Oil was put on if the place was to be allowed to heal; if not, a "perpetual blister" was created by cutting off the blistered skin with scissors and applying another blister plaster to the raw patch. "Many people faint when a blister is dressed for the first time; but such a circumstance need excite no alarm. It is a mere sympathetic effect," reassured the author of a nursing advice book. A poultice irritated the skin but did not break it as a blister did. A hot paste was created by mixing bread, meal, or the like with boiling water. A rag was placed on the area to be poulticed, and the boiling hot paste was spread over it and left on for ten to twenty minutes.[33]

Advice books warned about the kind of clutter that accumulated in sickrooms, which Trollope in *Doctor Thorne* (1858) took for granted: "There were little boxes and apothecaries' bottles, cups and saucers standing separate, and bowls, in which messes have been prepared with the hope of suiting a sick man's failing appetite. There was a small saucepan standing on a plate, a curiously shaped glass utensil left by the doctor, and sundry pieces of flannel, which had been used in rubbing the sufferer's limbs."[34] Other useful tools were a piece of oilcloth to cover the bed when washing the patient, and a rope, tied from the head to the foot of the bed, to allow the patient to move without help. Stone hot-water bottles or heated sandbags were used to keep patients warm; rooms were ideally to be kept at a temperature of 60°F (15.5°C)—or, as one advice book said depressingly, "that of summer in this climate."[35]

Despite the chill, all medical and nursing manuals encouraged ventilation in sickrooms, probably because so little was encountered in reality. The manuals advised this mainly because it was thought that "all infection is weakened by dilution with air" and that doctors could not transmit disease if they had passed through fresh air,* while the strength of the infection was "greatly increased and concentrated in the confined and impure air."[36] Even late in the century "fumigation" might consist of as little as "put[ting] the bedding in the yard for the sun to fumigate it," as was done in Caroline Louisa Taylor's house after four of her brothers had had scarlet fever and one had died from it. (She had continued to play with them throughout their illness, sitting on their beds.)[37]

Others were less cavalier. *The Modern Householder* explained in detail how to fumigate a room where infectious disease had been breeding. All the wallpaper was to be wetted with carbolic acid and stripped off the walls and burned. Then a quarter of a pound of brimstone (sulphur) was broken into small pieces and put in an iron dish over a bucket of water. The fireplace and windows were sealed by pasting paper over them, a shovelful of live coals was placed on the brimstone, and the room was quickly left, with the door being sealed for at least five or six hours. Clothes that had been in the room, together with any bedding, curtains, carpets, or hangings, were left hanging there during the process, to be disinfected at the same time. Afterward they

---

*Page 56 shows the dubiousness of this proposition.

were laundered thoroughly in the normal way, with the one addition that everything that could be was washed with carbolic acid in the water, and then boiled. The room was then lime-washed and left unoccupied with the window open for a week or two.[38] As with disinfection for vermin, it is unclear precisely how much the sulphur contributed. The carbolic acid and stripping the wallpaper off certainly helped, as did airing the room for a week. It was observed, however, that consumption in the house frequently continued even with these methods, although how much was due to lingering infection and how much to reinfection through tainted food supplies is unknown.

In novels, at any rate, this kind of thorough cleaning was taken as a matter of course by the end of the century. In *The Old Wives' Tale*, Sophia, having recovered from a fever, fumigated the entire apartment: "Pans of sulphur were mysteriously burning in each of the three front rooms, and two pairs of doors had been pasted over with paper, to prevent the fumes from escaping . . . Sophia, with brush, scissors, flour-paste, and news-sheets, was sealing the third pair of doors." She was careful to ensure that all the cracks were pasted over, including the gap between door and floor, and the keyholes.[39]

Women were more concerned than men with illness and its effects, both because women were the ones who would have to nurse the ill and because they tended to be ill more often than men. The legend of the Victorian woman has her lying on her chaise longue in a darkened room, with nothing to do all day except tell her servants to fetch things while she broods about her health. At least as many women nursed as were nursed, but it is true that many more patients were female than male. One reason for this, before the psychological elements are explored, was that women were indeed less well than men: mortality rates were higher for females than for males, starting in infancy, especially in the middle classes. This cannot for the entire middle class be laid at the door of poor nutrition, with scarce food being held in reserve for the breadwinners, although this was frequently the case for the working classes and may have affected some of the lower middle classes as well. However, girls of all income groups were regularly fed protein-poor diets, in the belief that this would ameliorate the "ill-

Prosperous middle-class women had a great deal of time on their hands. One way of using it was to produce endless "things." Often these items were made in order to sell them at charity bazaars, as shown in James Collinson's *At the Bazaar* (1857) (*left*). Another way of passing the time was to pay calls. In Frederick Walker's *Strange Faces* (*below*) a couple goes calling: it is clear that the man and the woman in the center are the visitors, as they are wearing their outdoor clothes: hats, stick, shawls. Calls were generally of 15 minutes' duration only, and removing shawls and hats indicated a worrying expectation of an over-long call.

The Carlyles maintained an old-fashioned dressing room (*left*) instead of a newfangled bathroom (*opposite, bottom*). The hip bath on the floor in Carlyle's dressing room was filled with hot water that was carried up from the basement in brass cans, and then taken back downstairs the same way. The shower in the 1851 *Punch* cartoon (*opposite, top*) shows these cans being used to fill the shower in this satire on the modern craze for new plumbing. Showers like this really existed, although the bathrooms tended to look more like bedrooms, complete with fireplaces and carpets.

More common than showers were flush lavatories: Doulton, in its advertisement for the "Improved wash-down closet" (*right*), shows only one of a range of decorations that were available.

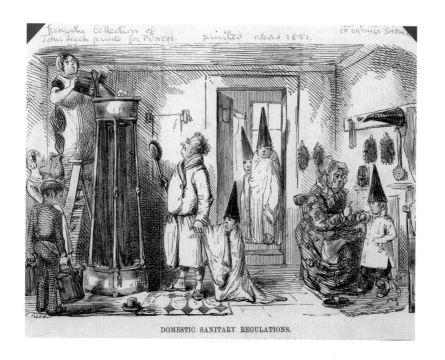

DOMESTIC SANITARY REGULATIONS.

Two sides of illness. In Alfred Rankley's *Old Schoolfellows* (1854) (*left*), the Victorian ideal of the nursing angel in the sickroom is portrayed, although the room has not been emptied of furnishings, carpets and hangings, as was recommended. In Frank Holl's *Doubtful Hope* (1875) (*below*), a harsher reality is shown: many suffering from illness could afford nothing more than a trip to the apothecary/chemist before returning to work.

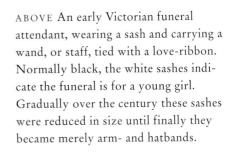

ABOVE An early Victorian funeral attendant, wearing a sash and carrying a wand, or staff, tied with a love-ribbon. Normally black, the white sashes indicate the funeral is for a young girl. Gradually over the century these sashes were reduced in size until finally they became merely arm- and hatbands.

LEFT Women bore the brunt of the mourning dress code: they were expected to spend at least two and a half years in mourning for a husband. Edward Killingworth Johnson's *Young Widow* (1877) contemplates a dress, possibly her wedding dress, which will certainly be out of fashion by the time she is permitted to return to light-colored clothes.

Omnibuses were middle-class transport par excellence: they started too late in the mornings to carry workers. Women traveled inside: initially the roof seats were reached only by ladder, and men were expected to move upstairs if the inside became too crowded. Later the ladders were replaced by stairs, but the top remained the province of men. In winter the straw covering the floor quickly became wet and muddy, and the door and windows were kept closed, creating an atmosphere that was at once drafty and stuffy.

The omnibus was hailed at any point along its route (center, front, a woman raises her umbrella to notify the driver to stop). For years there were no tickets, and conductors and drivers charged as much as they could, reporting as few passengers as they could once back at the depot: this encouraged them to pick up as many passengers as possible, sacrificing speed for profit. Hansom cabs, at the right, took only two passengers at a time, with the driver perched up above, the reins passing over the top of the cab and down in front of the passengers.

Fast food is not a modern invention: street sellers, like this baked-potato man (*left*), could be found in great numbers, with oyster sellers and stalls with sheep's trotters or stewed eels clustered around pubs, and women selling apples and oranges near theaters. Throughout the towns roamed pie-men, sherbet-sellers, muffin men, cockles-and-mussels men, watercress girls, cherry girls, and strawberry girls. In George Clausen's *Schoolgirls* (1880) (*below*) a milkmaid carries her wares in two large pails, which have smaller tin cans hanging from them to measure out the milk. On the right is another street seller, this one a flower girl.

nesses" associated with puberty. In addition, women spent more time indoors, in gas- and coal-dust-laden atmospheres. They had frequent pregnancies, although as the century progressed, the size of families was dramatically reduced, with consequent improvement in women's health. Perhaps most important, their clothes were constricting, as was their culture, ensuring that any exercise they took was at best limited.[40] The author of *The Domestic Management of the Sick-Room* saw exercise for boys and girls in stark contrast: boys too frequently suffered from a tendency toward too much exercise. By overexertion—perhaps as little as running too strenuous a race, or playing a game of cricket—it warned, boys often laid down the potential for a fatal disease. Girls, by contrast, were "too much restricted by custom [note, not their clothes] from the free employment of their limbs" and suffered from a lack of exercise.[41]

In popular imagery girls were constantly shown to be in need of protection from their own desire to do things, and from the dangers their feminine fragility brought on when, contrary to custom, they did take exercise. In *Ruth*, Elizabeth Bradshaw went for a long walk to gather strawberries in summer. She was dizzy and fainted on her return, and "it was many days before she regained any portion of her spirit and vigour." The walk had made her, for months, "listless and weary," she could not eat, and she remained bedridden until the autumn was almost over.[42] The perception was that too much exercise could not simply bring on dizziness and nausea but could unbalance a woman permanently. Women were subject to "feminine disorders." Their femaleness dominated their lives, and could not be controlled. Illnesses included puberty in general, menstruation in particular, pregnancy, childbirth, lactation, infertility, and menopause. A woman was, in terms of both her health and her psychological state, her ovaries. Dr. John Burnett wrote of a man who took his wife, who had become short-sighted in early middle age, to an oculist, only to be told that "the eye weakness was from a weakness of the womb," that she was suffering from a prolapsed womb, and that the only way to restore her vision was to perform a hysterectomy. Burnett said that on hearing this story he felt he had to write *Organ Diseases of Women*, not because of the unlikeliness of this connection, but because he knew that he could homeopathically restore enlarged wombs to their original size. This was in 1892.[43]

Puberty was a particularly dangerous time, and the "patient" needed watching in particular when "restless and excited, or melancholy and retiring; listless and indifferent to the social influence of domestic life."[44] Anything that could embrace symptoms as contrasting as restlessness and listlessness, excitation and dullness, was so all-embracing as to be meaningless—and also, of course, the perfect description of adolescence.

Women's sensitiveness and "nerves" were taken for granted, if the women were of that socioeconomic class which could give in to them, rather than that which had to cater to them. (Such catering must have been an often infuriating task. Mrs. Panton, who later in life became an invalid herself—and from her unwitting description, a very querulous one—instructed that an invalid's bed was to have a screen nearby so that the room could be cleaned without her seeing it, "and so save the invalid from the nervous strain caused by the worry of watching the movements of the servant," although even then, "the noise of the coals and the moving of the fire-irons are maddening if improperly managed." Her solution was that each lump of coal was to be wrapped separately in a piece of paper before the coals were brought in, so they could be placed noiselessly on the fire.)[45] Women with enough money and time could learn to enjoy illness. It was a way of imposing themselves on their household without breaching their role as the duty-loving, self-denying angel in the house. It was, in short, a way of finding time and space for themselves in a society that did not allow them to want either thing openly. Julia Stephen spoke more truth than she knew—or perhaps, equally, she knew exactly what she was saying—when she wrote, "The art of being ill is no easy one to learn, but is practised to perfection by many of the greatest sufferers."[46] After the early death of her first husband she had had a breakdown, and remained an invalid for a decade.

Marion Sambourne suffered from a number of unspecified illnesses that she referred to in her diary as "the old weakness." She was, from day to day, "tired," "very tired," "seedy," "weak," or "poorly." She undertook different and elaborate cures to improve her health, many of them common in the 1880s and 1890s: milk diets, Turkish baths once a week, a pint of claret a day. Frequently she stayed in bed until noon, although the latter part of an entry that began by complaining of ill health might end, "To theatre & dinner, very jolly evening." When her mother-in-law came to stay, however, as she did for several months every year, Marion became positively waspish about another's ill health: "Mrs S seedy & depressed. Mrs S not so ill as she thinks she is."[47]

Women were possessive about their illnesses, which were often pre-fixed with the pronoun "my," as in "my headaches": it was part of their public persona, and possibly gave them status. Geraldine Jews-bury had "my old nervous stupors"; Mrs. Panton recommended a chaise longue for when "one's headache is just a little too bad to bear."[48] Many positively encouraged invalidism as a state of mind. Jane Carlyle wrote to Thomas following the death of his mother: "Do you know, Dear, I dont like your always saying you are '*well*' in health. Nobody gets *really* well in that sudden way; and so you can only be feeling bodily well, either because your mind is so overfilled with sorrow, that you have not a minute to *listen to your sensations;* or, because you are in a *fever of billiousness* which passes with one for *wellness,*—till the reaction comes."[49] Even if one felt well and looked well, one was not necessarily so: illness lurked always. Thomas Car-lyle rarely needed to be told this—his attitude in the above letter was very much an exception. He was obsessed with his health, to a degree that suggests psychological rather than physiological sources. From his early twenties his letters recounted biliousness, digestive prob-lems, constipation, in a never-ending litany of general not-rightness: "sick with sleeplessness," "bilious," "My health continues very uncer-tain," "continual grinding misery of ill-health"—and then "But let me not complain."[50]

Illness was so enticing, the state of being cared for so attractive, that it was health itself that needed to be encouraged. Fiction has endless descriptions of the desirability of ill health. Lily Dale, in Trollope's *The*

Small House at Allington was in "the half-dignified, half-luxurious state which belongs to the first getting up of the invalid." Charlotte Brontë's heroines found peace in their sickbeds. Romola lay on her "delicious bed"—and on and on. Men were no less in love with illness. Oliver Twist appreciated being "tended with a kindness and solicitude that knew no bounds."[51] Back in the nonfictional world, Arthur Munby was "in bed & upstairs for a week or more, tenderly nursed & kindly tended. One may be thankful for sickness, when it comes with an 'entourage' of cosy warmth & comfort, and an atmosphere of dreamy thoughtful quiet."[52]

Perhaps the greatest invalids of all were to be found in the Darwin family. Gwen Raverat was fascinatedly appalled by her grandparents and aunts and uncles:

> In my grandparents' house it was a distinction and a mournful pleasure to be ill. This was partly because my grandfather [Charles Darwin] was always ill, and his children adored him and were inclined to imitate him; and partly because it was so delightful to be pitied and nursed by my grandmother . . . every one of [hundreds of letters] . . . contains dangerously sympathetic references to the ill health of one, or of several, of the family. Many of their ailments must have been of nervous, or partly of nervous, origin; of course there was real physical illness too, though no one now will ever know how much . . . But of one thing I am quite certain: that the attitude of the whole Darwin family to sickness was most unwholesome. At Down [House], ill health was considered normal.

Raverat's Aunt Etty was spectacular, even by Darwin standards. When she was thirteen years old the doctor had recommended, after a bout of diphtheria, that she have breakfast in bed for a time. "*She never got up to breakfast again in all her life* . . . ill health became her profession and absorbing interest . . . She was always going away to rest, in case she might be tired later on in the day, or even next day . . . She characteristically wrote to a proposed visitor: 'Don't come by the ten o'clock train, but by the 3.30, so as to give me time to put you off, if I am not well.' "[53]

Charles Darwin himself, however, was a special case, as Raverat indicated. He came from a family of doctors, and a family too that had a high degree of nervous instability. Several books have been written dedicated entirely to the subject of his illnesses, which centered on digestive troubles and skin complaints: were they nervous, or were they physiologically based? Many think that they were psychosomatic. Ralph Colp, in his 1977 book *To Be an Invalid: The Illness of Charles Darwin*, has suggested that Darwin's eczema was brought on by worry about the reception of his theory of evolution: "His feelings of anxiety and shame then caused his 'eczema attacks.' His 'eczema' cleared when he stopped talking about evolutionary topics."[54]

John Winslow, also absorbed by the subject, came up with a more ingenious theory. He suggested that Darwin suffered from chronic arsenic poisoning, after he was diagnosed with dyspepsia and began taking Fowler's solution, a proprietary drug that contained arsenic. The patient was to start with a small quantity, continuing with an increasing daily dose until the stomach problems receded, "which will seldom be the case until some of the effect of the arsenic on the stomach has been felt." If nausea set in, with tingling in the extremities and loss of appetite, this was taken as a sign that the drug was working. If more classic symptoms of arsenic poisoning occurred (conjunctivitis, catarrh, indigestion, furred tongue, cold extremities), then mercury was prescribed, even though mercury compounds often contained arsenic too.

It must be noted that Ralph Colp examined Winslow's claims for arsenic poisoning and rejected them. The coincidence of symptoms is remarkable, however. Sir James Clark, who treated Darwin for nervous dyspepsia, listed twenty-six symptoms that were to be expected in such cases. Twenty-one of them match common symptoms in cases of arsenic poisoning. Another two sometimes appear, and only three do not match arsenic-poisoning symptoms at all.[55]

It is not necessary that the theories of psychosomatic illness and arsenic poisoning are mutually exclusive. It is entirely possible that Darwin, anxious when discussing his radical theory of evolution, suffered from increased indigestion. In taking Fowler's solution to settle his stomach, he ingested the arsenic that in turn inflamed his eczema.

Darwin became ill when thinking of a theory that would destabilize his entire conception of society—and, indeed, society's whole conception of society. Invalidism in the nineteenth century appears to have been ready-made to permit highly disciplined people to relax their codes of duty and service in order to permit their putting themselves before society as a whole. Florence Nightingale was a prime example of this. She came from an upper-middle-class family, and she and her sister, Parthenope, were brought up to be polite young ladies, ornaments to their family.* Florence's wish to be of service was understood, but the means she chose was not: a young girl, or a woman, could best be of service in her father's or her husband's home, tending to the menfolk. Of that life she wrote: "Women never have a half hour in all their lives (excepting before and after anybody is up in the house) that they can call their own, without fear of offending or of hurting someone. Why do people sit up so late, or, more rarely, get up so early? Not because the day is not long enough, but because they have 'not time in the day to themselves.' " She wrote this before the Crimean War. Afterward she recognized that such a life was what she would once again be doomed to if she did not take action. It was not her single state that was the worry, because "for a married woman in society, it is even worse. A married woman was heard to wish that she could break a limb that she might have a little time to herself. Many take advantage of the fear of 'infection' to do the same."[56] For the next fifty years, with dogged determination, Florence Nightingale was able to continue to work for the reform of public health care by becoming an invalid, unconsciously

---

*Florence Nightingale was born, perhaps not too surprisingly, in Florence. Her parents' choice of name for her was as unusual as their choice for her sister: it is simply because Florence became world-renowned that we regard her name as perfectly ordinary. Parthenope was the classical name for the Greek colony in what is now Naples. The Nightingale girls were perhaps fortunate that their parents did not move on to Sardinia at the crucial time.

protecting herself from the demands of society by illness, by frailty, by a withdrawal into ill health. Only in the sickroom could she find the time and space to fulfill her destiny. "Her invalidism," a modern historian has noted, "paradoxically enabled a life of almost uninterrupted exertion."[57]

Other women, without that sense of destiny, still knew that invalidism gave them permission to put themselves before others without the odium that this "selfish" behavior would have involved anywhere outside the sickroom. Mrs. Panton wrote that "a vast assistance to all invalids is the consciousness that, though they are helpless, yet they need not be fretted by constant companionship, nor by the feeling that they can as constantly be pounced upon . . . [They must have] the privacy, the sense of being alone, which is so precious to us all."[58]

Alice James was an invalid all her adult life. She possibly took her invalidism to extremes, but it may simply be that, as a highly intelligent woman who kept a diary in which she analyzed herself and her illness remorselessly, we know more about her mental state than about that of many other women in a similar situation. Born in 1848, Alice James grew up in Cambridge, Massachusetts,* and by her twentieth birthday she was well on her way to becoming a professional invalid. No letter mentioned her without also mentioning her health; she underwent cures, treatments, therapies. No organic problems were discovered, and her mother referred to "nervous turns" brought on by "exertion"; she considered these periods "genuine hysteria."[59]

After a period of normal life in her twenties, Alice relapsed as she approached her thirtieth birthday. Her father wrote, "Alice is half the time, indeed much more than half, on the verge of insanity and suicide."[60] It is important to note that it was in this time that two of her brothers had married, had children, begun their professional lives; her third brother, William, was teaching at Harvard, and he too had married; Henry had started on his career as a novelist, and had settled into

---

*Although this New England background makes the James family appear to be outside my remit, I am stretching the boundaries somewhat both because her years in England were her years of invalidism, and because of the unusually analytical nature of her writing.

a permanent comfortable bachelorhood. Alice, by contrast, had for a brief time joined Miss Anna Ticknor's Society to Encourage Studies at Home, an early type of correspondence course for those without formal education. She had, in the terms of the middle-class social world, failed: she was not married, and she therefore had no children; she had no overriding concerns, no charity work, no novel-writing, not even a busy social life, all of which would have appeared sufficiently ladylike while giving her a focus. Illness was a way of putting achievement definitively out of reach. This is not simply a modern take on the situation; her brother Henry wrote after her death that "tragic health was, in a manner, the only solution for her of the practical problem of life."[61]

When Alice was given a purpose, her health recovered: after her mother's death she cared for her father for more than a year, until his own death, without any of her usual relapses. As soon as he began to fail, she failed too. The day after his funeral she collapsed and needed nursing for a year afterward.

In the 1880s Alice left America for England, where she remained for the rest of her life, mostly with her companion Katherine Loring.* She remained an invalid in mind if not in body from now on. Improvements were hedged about with what her state "really" was: "I am gradually getting stronger & am able to do a great deal more, but as always happens as my physical strength increases my nervous distress & susceptibility grows with it, so that from an inside view it is somewhat an exchange of evils."[62] Everything in the household had to revolve around the invalid: the least lack of care or attention was punished by relapse. When a window was left open by an inch on a landing outside her sickroom, in "consequence I was laid up the next day with rheuma-

---

*Increasingly as time went on Alice James and Katherine Loring lived in a Boston marriage, a recognized form of companionship in America in the nineteenth century, whereby two women settled down together in a long-term emotional and financial partnership that, before Freud sexualized all aspects of life, was considered beneficial to unmarried women. What Boston marriages implied sexually probably varied from couple to couple. I would suggest that a strong romantic and weak-to-nonexistent sexual bond was probably the case between Alice James and Katherine Loring, if for no other reason than Alice's permanent invalidism.

tism in my head, unable to move or breathe for twelve hrs."[63] As Alice herself said in mockery, "How well one has to be, to be ill!"[64]

The difference between Alice and many other invalids was her outspoken desire for death, if only to prove that her illnesses had been physical all along: "Doctors tell you that you will die, or *recover!* But you *don't* recover. I have been at these alternations since I was nineteen and I am neither dead nor recovered."[65] When, in May 1891, she was finally diagnosed with an organic disease—breast cancer—she was jubilant: "To him who waits, all things come! . . . Ever since I have been ill, I have longed and longed for some palpable disease." Finally, after a lifetime, she had found something to distinguish her. It was, she told William, "the most supremely interesting moment in life." As a person beyond hope of recovery one becomes, she noted, "suddenly picturesque to oneself, and one's wavering little individuality stands out with cameo effect."[66]

Her wavering little individuality could be boosted only by her looming death. Not all invalids felt like that, but, as Alice was aware, not all families were like the Jameses. She noted, two weeks after the initial diagnosis, "Within the last year [Henry] has published the 'Tragic Muse,' brought out 'The American' & written a play . . . combined with William's ['Principles of] Psychology.[']. Not a bad show for one family! Especially if I get myself dead, the hardest job of all."* When she had finally achieved her difficult task, Henry acknowledged her desire: "She lies as the very perfection of the image of what she had longed for years, & at the last with pathetic intensity, to be." William responded, "What a blessed thing to be able to say, *that* task is over!"[67]

If purely in the nakedness of its longing, Alice James's attitude to death was, shall we say, unusual. The more conventional Victorians' attitude to death was, however, still very different from ours. For one thing, death occurred more regularly across the entire life span—infant and child mortality was higher, life expectancy was lower. It was also

---

*One is reminded of a very different mindset, but an equally transgressive impulse, in Sylvia Plath's "Lady Lazarus": "Dying / Is an art, like everything else. / I do it exceptionally well."

something that happened to most people at home: it was not the great unspoken that it was to become in the twentieth century.* The late-Georgian and early-Victorian Evangelical movement had ensured that death and dying were part of daily life. *The Rule and Exercises of Holy Dying*, a seventeenth-century treatise on the examination of the soul as preparation for eternal life, was, according to George Eliot, the main reference book in many Victorian homes.[69] Through the century, until the late 1870s, correct deathbed behavior was set in the pattern laid down by the Evangelicals. A good death was, for them, one in which the dying person had time to tie up all loose ends in his or her earthly life, in both spiritual and secular terms: repentance was made, prayers were said, all business was finished. Around the deathbed were the immediate family, praying for the soul of the departing one to be taken into heaven, saying their final farewells. These deathbed scenes were the staples of nineteenth-century fiction.†

Those who were left behind were expected to accept death in a spirit of submission to God. The deeply devout Philip Gosse had no trouble with this. Before she was diagnosed with cancer, Emily had written in her diary, "May this be a year of much blessing—a year of jubilee!" When Philip saw the diary after her agonizing, labored death, his response was in line with religious teaching: "I believe my beloved's

---

*It is outside the time frame of this book, but it is worth mentioning historian Pat Jalland's theory that it was the mass slaughter of World War I, together with the tidying away of the dying into hospitals, that combined to make death the great taboo, as sex had been earlier.[68]

†Florence Dombey, in *Dombey and Son*, may hold the record: she watched at the deathbeds of her mother, her brother, and her stepmother, although Mrs. Gaskell's *North and South* actually leads in deaths, if not deathbeds—three by natural causes, one work-related death, a suicide, and a railway accident. But Margaret Hale, the protagonist, was present at only one deathbed, her mother's. In Mrs. Gaskell's *Mary Barton*, Mrs. and Mr. Wilson are both present at the deaths of three people. With this kind of death toll it was justifiable of Dickens to write (about still another of Mrs. Gaskell's works) that "if it had ended happily it would have been a great success. As it is it . . . will link itself painfully, with the girl who fell down at the well, and the child who tumbled down the stairs. I wish to Heaven, her people would keep a little firmer on their legs!"[70]

prayer was fully answered, and that this *was* the best year of her life; but through much tribulation, through great agony of body, was her spirit made ripe for the glory . . . she was called to glorify Him whom she loved, by a patient endurance of his will, in bearing the most torturing pain."[71] Others had more trouble. Mrs. Warren's fictitious narrator, who had lost two of her children within eight months, reflected: "There was a very large amount of rebellion in my heart at the loss of Dot. 'Thy will be done,' though uttered a hundred times by my mouth, was never once said in my heart; but when Edith was stricken down rebellion vanished, and a humbleness arose, as in deprecation; but it required years of teaching to feel that what He had done must have been in love, not in anger."[72]

By the 1880s, ideas had changed radically. Dr. William Munk, the author of *Euthanasia, or Medical Treatment in Aid of an Easy Death*, was adamant that the dying should not, until the very last minute, know that their cases were hopeless: "To the dying there is no greater solace and cordial than hope—it is the most soothing and cheering of our feelings."* On the other hand, it should not be left too long either: "When the intimation that death is at hand has been postponed to the last possible moment, it comes upon the sufferer so late, that there may not be time for him to get over the shock of the first impression . . . An earlier intimation to the dying person of the great change he is about to undergo is in all respects desirable, and if the communication be made tenderly and with prudence, nothing but good is likely to result from it."[73] Beatrice Webb's mother was kept in ignorance of her impending death in 1882. She wanted to make bequests regarding her jewelry, but her daughters felt it was more important to keep her spirits up, and they told her she would be fine. In order to maintain this fiction, not all her daughters could be sent for to be present at her deathbed.[74]

---

*I cannot emphasize too strongly that the usage of "euthanasia" in his work was in its primary meaning of "gentle or easy death": Dr. Munk's book was concerned with how to control pain and ease the fears of the dying. The idea of mercy killing would have horrified him.

If, however, there was any hope of recovery at all, only positive comments about the patients' illness were to be made in their presence; it was feared that otherwise depression might prevent them from making the necessary effort. However, friends should be notified, so that all worldly affairs would be taken care of. And in the end even the patient must be warned, as "surely it is lamentable to think that any human being should leave the world unprepared to meet his Creator and Judge." Then "all that the dying person . . . requires, is to be left alone, and allowed to die in peace . . . The physician will not torment his patient with unavailing attempts to stimulate the dissolving system, from the idle vanity of prolonging the flutter of the pulse for a few more vibrations: if he cannot alleviate his situation, he will protect his patient against every suffering which has not been attached to it by nature."[75] "Alone" was a relative term. By midcentury it was expected that the doctor, the nurse, a minister of religion, and probably the immediate family would be present, although as time went on sometimes this last was no longer guaranteed. In *East Lynne* (1861), Isabel Vane confronts Alexander Carlyle after her father's death, from which she has been barred: "It is cruel so to treat me . . . Pent up here . . . When your father was dying, were you kept away from him?" Carlyle is shocked: "My dear young lady—a hardy, callous man may go where you may not."[76]

Jeannette Marshall's family did not have the same concerns. Reggie, Jeannette's brother, developed typhoid at age thirteen, in 1873. In his final hours, she wrote,

> he was asking for me! I went up & going quite close to the bed & putting my face well in the light as P[apa] told me I managed to say "here I am, darling, don't you know me?" & P[apa] said "here is Jeannette." Reggie opened his eyes very wide, raising the eyebrows, as if he was trying to see me, but there was *no* expression in them. I kissed him, his face & lips were cold & clammy, & then went to lie down on the sofa in the room next door . . . we were all crying, Mr C[astañeda, Dr. Marshall's assistant] & nurse too . . . at 7.30 M[ama] came down, & lifting up her hands, screamed out

quite hysterically "He's gone!" I comforted her as well as I cd. & made her take some wine. Nurse and Cook attended to the poor angel (that no doubt is what he is now!) . . . Poor P[apa] feels it *so* dreadfully! We were all 3 now sent to bed.[77]

Mrs. Marshall, who rarely went to church, could not find that Christian resignation which was preached as a response to death. Even the devout Mrs. Gaskell, although more outwardly accepting, remembered three years after her son's death how "I used to sit up in the room so often in the evenings reading by the fire, and watching my darling *darling* Willie, who now sleeps sounder still in the dull, dreary chapel-yard at Warrington. That wound will never heal on earth, although hardly any one knows how it changed me." Two years later she still thought of it as a "never-ending sorrow . . . which hallows this house."[78] Some took the death of children—at least, of other people's children—more easily. Marion Sambourne wrote of her sister Tabby coming to visit the day after Tabby's baby had died: "Tabby came to tea and dinner—seems to feel her baby's loss v. much. Very happy quiet day."[79] Certainly many women half-feared, half-expected to lose a child. Emily Gosse wrote in her journal, soon after Edmund turned five, "Should we be called on to weep over the early grave of the dear one whom now we are endeavouring to train for heaven, may we be able to remember that we never ceased to pray for and watch over him."[80]

How the dead were remembered varied as much as the responses to their death. Laura Forster wrote of one old man who had died of consumption: he had told her, "Do not be unhappy about me, but never forget me and talk about me always." On the other hand, Louise Creighton, whose brother Edward died at the age of ten, wrote much later: "I have been told since that after the funeral my father said to the assembled family that he must not be spoken of. I have no idea if this was the wish of both my father & mother because of the greatness of their sorrow. I never remember his being mentioned to me by either of them at any time in later years. My mother had a little round water-color portrait of him which hung inside her wardrobe. I used to see it when she opened her wardrobe, but she never showed it to me." One of Louise's own sons died in the First World War, and similarly she did not mention him in her memoir, begun five years after the Armistice.[81]

Long before memory had time to fade, arrangements for the funeral and formal mourning had to be set in motion. After Reggie Marshall's death his body remained in his parents' room, where he had been cared for throughout his illness. Plaster casts—probably death masks, although possibly a cast of a hand or arm—were taken, and so were photographs of him in his coffin. This was not uncommon: photographs of Lord Frederick Cavendish, murdered in 1882 in the Phoenix Park in Dublin by an Irish secret society of Fenian extremists, were taken of his body lying on a bed covered with flowers. Some of Reggie Marshall's hair was cut off for his parents and his siblings and, before his body was sealed in the inner coffin, they each rolled a piece of their own hair in foil, on which they "pricked . . . 'The hair of his Father, Mother, Sisters & Brother'" to place in the coffin with him. With the labeled hair was added the notice of his death which had appeared in *The Times*, inscribed "The Little Soldier." It was put in his left hand, and on his right was a mourning ring that Mrs. Marshall had inherited from her father when he died. The coffin was closed, and the family read poetry—a startlingly secular occupation for such a moment, even in this not very religious family—while the coffin was brought downstairs to the dining room, where it remained "standing under the gas light, dimly lit, with the black velvet pall bordered with broad white cambric over it." Six days after Reggie's death, just before the funeral, the family congregated for a final time around the coffin. "We put all our hands together on the lid & P[apa] said 'May he forgive us anything unkind we have ever done or said to him'; then we said 'Goodbye.'"[82]

It was usual for the body to remain at the family's house until the funeral: the body of Linley Sambourne's mother was brought from the house where she had died to rest in the Sambournes' morning room.[83] The blinds were drawn throughout the house as soon as a death took place, and were not raised again until after the funeral was over. This, and the return of close mourners to the house after the meal, were the only elements of the funeral that touched the house itself. The service was carried out at the cemetery, but during the period of funeral arrangements, the rigid etiquette of death carried mourners through. Arnold Bennett understood this need for busy formality. In *The Old Wives' Tale* "The funeral grew into an obsession, for multitudinous things had to be performed and done sumptuously and in strict accordance with precedent. There were the family mourning [clothes], the funeral repast, the choice of the text on the memorial card,* the composition of the legend on the coffin, the legal arrangements, the letters to relations, the selection of guests, and the questions of bell-ringing, hearse, plumes, number of horses, and grave-digging. Nobody had leisure for the indulgence of grief."[84]

As soon as a date and time were set for the funeral, a member of the family wrote to all those they hoped would attend. It was also possible to buy printed forms, which were black-edged. They read: "The favour of your company is requested on——next, the——of——, to attend the funeral of the late——. The mourners will assemble at—— late residence, at——, at——o'clock precisely, to proceed to——."[85] Whether women attended or not was open to debate. Many manuals said absolutely not, as women could not contain their emotions and would be overcome. Other books accepted that women did go; still others thought it was only upper- and lower-class women who did so (and yet Queen Victoria was not present at her beloved Albert's funeral). Jeannette Marshall and her mother did not attend Reggie's funeral, but Ada went with her father and brother, while Jeannette and her mother sat at home with a female relative for company.

Earlier in the century funerals had been elaborate affairs. The accompanying trappings were based on the aristocratic funerals of the past, although this was not generally realized by the participants. The attendants—employees of the undertaker—were the feathermen, who each carried a tray of waving black plumes; men holding staffs, or wands; and mutes, also with staffs, each of which had a "love ribbon" tied to it, in black normally, or in white for a young girl. In addition, at children's funerals the coffin and accoutrements were all white, the attendants wore white rather than black, and the horses had white plumes

---

*See p. 376.

The funeral of Lord Palmerston, 1865, from an engraving in the *Illustrated London News*. The coffin, covered with a pall with Palmerston's escutcheon, is carried into Westminster Abbey preceded by a featherman with a tray of plumes on his head and a mute carrying a staff with a weeper tied to it. Between the featherman and the mute (center) it is just possible to see a man's hat with a weeper tied around it. This is the funeral Arthur Munby thought a "*poor* and a mean business," with the coffin's pall so simple it was "tawdry."

and harnesses. The mourners too were given white gloves and scarves instead of the normal black.[86] The coffin or the pall was sometimes carried by the child's friends: "It is a pretty and affecting sight to see the pall over the coffin of a young lady borne by six of her female friends."[87] In the 1820s a funeral for a middle-class spinster included ten horsemen, four mutes, twenty-two pages, a featherman, and two feather pages. Ladies who attended funerals wore scarves and hoods; men wore black cloaks, which often were hired from the undertakers, and black streamers from their hats. Over the next decade men's hats became taller and taller, and the mute's hat had a "weeper," a band like a scarf, hanging nearly to his waist. Then midcentury these things began gradually to disappear, or to be cut down. In *David Copperfield*

(1849–50) David says defiantly, "I did not attend the funeral in character . . . I mean I was not dressed up in a black cloak and a streamer, to frighten the birds"—although had he been going to a social equal's funeral, rather than that of Barkis, the husband of his old nurse, one wonders if he might have been cloaked.[88]

From this height of complex formality, funerals could only become simpler, and a gradual move toward less ostentation crystallized in 1875 with the Burial, Funeral and Mourning Reform Association to encourage moderation and reduced expenditure. While the theory was welcomed, many thought that inexpensive funerals showed a lack of reverence generally, and a lack of respect for the dead in particular. When Lord Palmerston died in 1865 Arthur Munby was shocked and disgusted by his funeral: "Saw cortège in Pall Mall & at Abbey West door. A most *poor* and mean business: nothing noble or solemn or religious in the aspect of it or of those who thronged to see it . . . Note, that no clergy met the coffin at the Abbey gate: men took it on their shoulders; a tawdry pall was thrown over; they disappeared, without a prayer or a note of music, into the cold crowded nave."[89]

Even when simplicity had been the expressed wish of the deceased, people were dubious. "Simplicity" was understood to mean that no crepe scarves for the men or gloves for any of the mourners were provided, which many thought made the family seem mean. Jeannette Marshall, like Arthur Munby, was concerned with how things looked. When her grandmother died in 1876, "the funeral was *without* mourning coaches, scarves or hatbands . . . every one going in their own carriage. In order that people shd. not think it was meanness that prompted them doing so, they had four horses to the hearse, and a very handsome polished oak coffin. It is so horrible, the idea of saving every penny of what one's relations have left." Their coachman felt the same. On his own initiative he put a mourning band, which had almost entirely replaced the more elaborate weeper, on his hat, and wore black buttons and gloves.[90]

When he wrote his will in 1869, some years after Palmerston's death, Dickens asked for an unostentatious funeral, although he clearly distrusted his family's ability (or desire) to follow his instructions for a simple ceremony. He was vehement to the point of aggression: "I emphatically direct that I be buried in an inexpensive, unostentatious and strictly private manner . . . that those who attend my funeral wear no scarf, cloak, black bow, long hatband,* or other such revolting absurdity."[91] This request caused great difficulties, as it was expected by all that Dickens would be buried in Westminster Abbey. A compromise was finally reached: he was interred in the Abbey, but in a private ceremony. Marion Sambourne's father, a businessman, died nearly twenty years after Dickens wrote his will, in 1884, and he still felt that he needed to put in his will "that my executors shall conduct my funeral in the quietest and most inexpensive manner possible."[92]

But change was occurring, if slowly. By the early 1870s, the simplest funeral listed by *Cassell's Household Guide* cost £3 5s. For this one got a carriage, a horse, a smooth elm coffin (lined), the use of a pall, "mourner's fittings" (that is, the gloves, scarves, mourning bands, and so on that were supplied to the mourners by the undertaker), a coachman wearing a hatband, pallbearers, and an attendant with a hatband. Further up the scale a funeral costing £53, which many of the prosperous middle classes expected to pay, included a hearse and four horses, two mourning coaches with four horses, twenty-three plumes of "rich" ostrich feathers, and velvet coverings for the carriages and horses, with a plume of best feathers. The coffin had an inner elm shell, with a tufted mattress, lined and ruffled with fine cambric, and a pillow; an embroidered cambric shroud; a stout outside lead coffin with an inscription plate; an oak case 1½ inches thick, covered with black or crimson velvet; set nails; an engraved brass inscription plate; and four pairs of brass handles and grips, with matching lid ornaments. It was covered by a silk velvet pall (which was taken back by the undertaker at the end of the service), and the procession was formed by two mutes (with gowns, silk hatbands, and gloves), fourteen men as pages, feathermen, and coachmen (with truncheons and wands, silk hatbands, use of mourners' fittings), and an attendant with a silk hatband.[93] The mourners' accoutrements were carefully graded in quality. At a surgeon's funeral

*By this date, even the word "weeper" was disappearing.

Mourning dress for the fashionable, 1890. The dress on the left is covered with crepe for first, or full, mourning. The crepe is reduced to edging in second mourning (center), and on the right "ordinary" mourning means any fashionable dress in black silk or wool (note the return of the hat after 18 months of widows' caps). By the end of the century mourning was vastly less cumbersome than fifty years earlier.

the hatbands of the family were of crepe, those of his colleagues and friends were of silk, and his students had "half-crape."[94]*

It was a combination of snobbery and hard cash that changed the situation. As more and more of the upper classes requested (or were given) simple funerals, those in the middle classes felt they could follow suit, saving money and still being seen to do the right thing. By the end of the century, as Charles Booth noted in his monumental *Life and Labour of the People of London*, "as a rule, the poor pay proportionately rather

*For an explanation of the types of mourning fabric, see p. 380–81.

For those who could afford it, mourning clothes were bought new with each
bereavement. For them, "Mourning Warehouses" were created to ensure that
every style was readily available when sudden death occurred. Peter Robinson
had a regular department store as well, so its mourning warehouse was known
colloquially as Black Peter Robinson to distinguish it.

more for show than do the rich. Plumed hearses are no longer used,
except, it is said, by costermongers and chimney sweeps."[95]

After the funeral it was rare that mourners returned to the house
with the family. At the end of the service they were given memorial
cards, which had the deceased's name, age, and date of death, when and
where he or she was buried (including the location of the grave in the
cemetery), and a verse of scripture (although by 1887 "A Member of
the Aristocracy" wrote that these cards were now "quite out of date").
Family and friends who had been unable to attend the funeral were
sent a memorial card, should they want to visit the grave.[96]

Mourning accoutrements, formally, were used from the day of the
funeral, although in practice it was accepted that it took some time to
buy or make the required items. The letters telling of the death were

properly written by a family member on black-edged paper, sent in a black-edged envelope, the thickness of the black borders being calibrated to the position of the deceased, his or her relationship to the writer, and the time that had elapsed since the death. If the death was sudden and the recipient of the news was frail or elderly, sometimes the sender wrote the initial news on ordinary paper, so as not to cause too big a shock. Lady Stanley wrote to her daughter-in-law, over the death of a distant connection, "I *ought* to be in mourning for George Way, but I think I shall only mourn in *black wax* [that is, using black sealing wax but not black-edged paper], which you shall see *next* time so as not to *alarm* you now."[97]

Social life and its routines were moderated for the mourning period, although not at will. The family in mourning was expected to give up all social life in the short term. Friends and relations called on them within two weeks of the funeral (any later was a calculated slight), but the calls were formal ones, with cards left, as in the case of illness: the family was not expected to receive the callers. In the twelve months after a husband's death, his widow did not go out at all, and accepted visits only from relations and very close friends. However, as with aspects of dress, a modified form of social life could be carried out as long as it was not referred to directly. After the death of Lucy Robarts's father in *Framley Parsonage* (1861), Lucy is invited to call on Lady Lufton, a social activity expressly forbidden. Lady Lufton makes it possible by adding: "You will meet nobody, you know. So you need not regard it as going out. Fanny here will tell you that stepping over to Framley Court is no more going out, than when you go from one room to another."[98] When the widow was ready to enter society again, she left cards to indicate this. Widowers, because of their work outside the house, were expected to go back into society quickly—within a month or so. However, for the first weeks the entire family remained secluded. In *The Daisy Chain*, the mother of the family died in a carriage accident before her youngest child was baptized. Only the younger children were to go to the service: the church was "too far off, and the way lay too much through the town for it to be thought proper for the others to go."[99] The younger children, being below the age of society, had more leeway.

When Mark Pattison, the widely disliked Rector of Lincoln College, died in 1884, his widow wrote "shortly" after his death to invite her friend Mrs. Gell for dinner, "on mourning note-paper with a border half an inch thick!"[100] The solecism was twofold: she was returning to social life too early, and she was using the deepest mourning paper to do it. The time to begin social life again would have been once she had reverted to narrow borders. Lady Jebb, a committed socialite, understood these rules entirely:

> Black is very tiresome and unbecoming, and when for a change I put on my grey cloth of last year, [my husband] could not express sufficient delight at the change. But I entirely refused to accept an invitation to a fancy ball. "How can we go to a ball in fancy dress," I asked him, "when we are using the deepest of black-edged paper and cards?" I refused to accept unless he bought narrower edges, convincing even him that to answer a ball invitation on that paper savoured of the ridiculous. He wanted very much to go to the ball, about which I don't care a farthing, so I gained my point as to the paper.[101]

These were minor points, although not unimportant ones. The real concern was the clothing. One's dress was a way of placing oneself in society, particularly for more distant family connections and for friends, defining minutely the precise level one held. It was also a way of showing community solidarity: a black dress or armband worn for the death of a friend was a gesture of inclusion, as well as a form of mannerly condolence; for a statesman or a member of the royal family it was an indication of tribal connection. For two decades after the death of Prince Albert, in 1861, the intricate details of mourning clothes preoccupied much of the middle class. Men from any level of society usually contented themselves with a black hatband and armband in crepe—the vestigial remains of the earlier weepers—although variants were possible. Crosbie, in *The Last Chronicle of Barset* (1866–67), was understood to be in mourning for his unloved wife, "though there was nothing but his shirt-studs by which to tell it."[102]

Women at the lower end of the scale had to attempt on small incomes to obey rules laid down by the more prosperous. If a new black dress was possible, one was bought or made. Many handed mourning clothes on after their own period of mourning was ended. Otherwise, dyeing the daily dress already in wear was a less expensive solution. Dyers were kept in business almost entirely through dyeing clothes black for mourning, and their selling point was speed. One advertised, "We dye blacks every day, and special mourning orders can be executed in twenty-four hours when necessary."[103] For many others, simply making do had to serve. Mrs. Gaskell wrote to Marianne on the death of the Duke of Wellington in 1852: "I wish you & I could [both] get into my blk silk at once. However I must make my grey look mourning."[104]

For women who could afford it, however, the permutations were endless. Women in mourning, like household decoration, were the outward manifestation of the family's status.[105] Mourning clothes were now expected to be a fashionable dress in a narrow range of fabrics, and were wherever possible bought new after each death. A comic take on this serious subject appeared early on, in 1844:

> LADY: I wish, sir, to look at some mourning.
>
> SHOPMAN: Certainly; by all means . . . How deep would you wish to go, Ma'am? Do you wish to be very poignant? . . . We have the very latest novelties from the Continent. Here is one, Ma'am, just imported—a widow's silk—watered, you perceive, to match the sentiment. It is called "Inconsolable," as is very much in vogue in Paris for matrimonial bereavements. And we have several new fabrics introduced this season to meet the demand for fashionable tribulation.
>
> LADY: And all in the French style?
>
> SHOPMAN: Certainly—of course, Ma'am. They excel in the funebrè. Here, for instance, is an article for the deeply afflicted. A black crape—makes up very sombre and interesting. Would you allow me, Ma'am, to cut off a dress?* Or if you would prefer a velvet, Ma'am—

*Note that the meaning here is "a length of fabric to make a dress."

LADY: Is it proper, sir, to mourn in velvet?

SHOPMAN: O quite!—certainly. Just coming in. Now here is a
very rich one—real Genoa—and a splendid black. We call it
"The Luxury of Woe" . . . Only 18/– a yard, and a superb quality—in short, fit for the handsomest style of domestic calamity.

LADY: And as to the change of dress, sir; I suppose you have a
great variety of half-mourning?

SHOPMAN: Oh! Infinite—the largest stock in town. Full, and
half, and quarter, and half-quarter, shaded off, if I may say so,
like an India-ink drawing, from a grief *prononcé* to the slightest
nuance of regret.[106]

The tone was comic, but the reality it was reflecting was not so very different. An advertisement at the end of the century described a "Half-
Mourning Costume of a woollen velvet; violet ground striped with thick
lines of grey, white and black, sleeves of violet looking-glass velvet; the
consoling influence of such a costume could not fail to be great."[107]

Jay's Mourning Warehouse, or, more formally, Jay's London General
Mourning Warehouse, was one of the earliest shops to cater entirely to
this niche market. It opened in Regent Street, the most fashionable
London shopping street, in 1841, and was soon followed by Pugh's
Mourning Warehouse and by Peter Robinson's Court and General
Mourning House (which became known as Black Peter Robinson, to
distinguish it from its non-mourning branch). Black Peter Robinson
advertised that it kept a carriage ready at all times to send to the
bereaved at home, to show them the new fashionable mourning wear
and measure them for whatever they chose. The carriage was fitted
with full mourning accoutrements, so that nothing should be unseemly
in front of a house of grief: the coachman was in black, with crepe hatbands and armbands, and the two fitters also wore black.[108] The necessity of producing mourning clothes quickly was a major factor in the
increased availability of ready-to-wear dresses; the dissemination of
fashion, as we saw in Chapter 8, was reflected in mourning wear as well.

Black dresses alone were not enough for those with the luxury of
choice in mourning wear: the fabric had to be bombazine or crepe.

Bombazine was a wool, silk-and-wool, or cotton-and-wool twill fabric; crepe was a plainly woven silk fabric that was crimped with hot irons during the manufacture to produce a dull, nonreflective surface. (Occasionally one sees paramatta listed as a mourning fabric. This was a merino-and-silk or merino-and-cotton type of bombazine.) Crepe was a difficult fabric and did not wear well: it looked rusty as it aged, and had to be carefully revived by being steamed, sprinkled with alcohol, rolled in newspaper, and left to dry.[109] Silk or any other fabric with a shine or gloss was considered vulgar for the first period of mourning. In *Cranford* little Miss Mattie, who never spoke ill of anyone, could not have been more shocked by the wealthy and flamboyant Mrs. Fitz-Adam, who wore a silk dress too soon after her husband's death: "Bombazine would have shown a deeper sense of her loss."[110] The gradations of all forms of mourning were very delicate, and were frequently mocked: Mrs. Glegg, in George Eliot's *The Mill on the Floss*, planned in advance that if her husband failed to leave her a decent legacy on his death, she "would . . . cry no more than if he had been a second husband."[111]

As with the rules of society in general, the rules of mourning dress were detailed, complex, and constantly changing. An indication of the fluid nature of the rules is the number of magazine articles setting out the formal periods and dress for mourning. The population at large did not know, for example, that "mothers [mourning] for the mother-in-law or father-in-law of their married children should wear black for six weeks or so without crape. Second wives [mourning] for the parents of the first wife, should wear complimentary mourning for about three weeks."[112] (For a summary of mourning periods and suitable dress, see pp. 386–89.) In general, at the height of elaborate mourning, bereaved women were expected to dress entirely in black, apart from the indoor cap, which was white. Black bonnets were worn outside, and black umbrellas were carried, to "protect" women from the inappropriate good cheer of passing strangers, who would not otherwise have known of their bereavement. Even underwear had black ribbons. A widow, who bore the brunt of ceremonial mourning, was expected to wear a dress entirely covered with crepe for a year and a day, in "deep" or "first" mourning. Diamonds or pearls set in black enamel could be

Punch cartoons rarely dealt with death and almost never with mourning:
the subject was too serious. By 1890, as elaborate mourning was beginning to
disappear, it risked a small joke, but only at the expense of a criminal.
Emily (who has called to take Lizzie to the Great Murder Trial):
"What deep black, dearest!"
Lizzie: "Yes, I thought it would be only decent, as the poor Wretch
is sure to be found guilty."
Emily: "Ah! Where I was Dining last night, it was even betting which way
the Verdict would go, so I only put on *Half* Mourning!"

worn, and it was considered especially tasteful to set the initials of the
deceased in pearls in lockets, or to wear a cameo or portrait of the
deceased.[113] Jewelry made of the deceased's hair was also popular. Collars and cuffs were white, as were weepers, although these last were
dying out by the 1850s. The Marshall women, like many others, followed the rules overtly, while subverting them for practical reasons
when necessary. After Mrs. Marshall's mother died in 1876, they all got
"best" mourning dresses in crepe. But in wet weather, and when traveling, crepe became badly damaged very quickly. So the crepe was
saved for ceremonial wear, and at home the girls wore retrimmed

dresses in dark, dull fabrics, the thinking being "of course I shd. not be *visible* in it, but it will save my other."[114]

Although it was said, sweepingly, that the rules applied to everyone, in fact "everyone" meant only the middle and upper classes. Hannah Cullwick, on being informed of her Aunt Ellen's death, wrote: "I shall put some crape on my black straw bonnet & frock & Sarah has given me an old dress of Mrs Foster's I can wear. I wrote to my sister Ellen & told her about it. Clean'd the knives. Made the fires up & got dinner ready. Laid the kitchen cloth. Clean'd away after & clean'd the hearth & tables. Wash'd up in the scullery & had tea. Clean'd myself & did my bonnet up wi [*sic*] the crape. Got supper ready & laid the kitchen cloth. Clean'd away after. Rubb'd Mrs Smiths foot again & then to bed."[116]

Hannah, like most of the working classes, could make only a token gesture toward mourning. Those who could afford it marked their separation from those beneath them even more clearly by second mourning, which technically began a year after the death, although good taste obliged widows to wait a little longer before divesting their dresses of some of their crepe (which was all that second mourning meant), in order not to appear to have recovered too quickly. Second mourning lasted between six and nine months, gradually growing shorter as the century progressed. After second mourning, "ordinary" mourning began, and the widow could wear a black or a black-and-white dress in any fabric, which might even have ribbons on it, and jet jewelry. At the end of two years from the death, half-mourning began: at Black Peter Robinson, one bought half-mourning clothes in the Mitigated Affliction Department.[117] Should the widow so choose, lilac, purple, gray, white, and black-and-gray (black and white together was for deeper mourning) could all be worn for half-mourning. These elaborate changes of costume were encouraged by the shops that specialized in mourning wear. Jay's Mourning Warehouse advertised: "Ladies are particularly invited to a trial of the new Corbeau silks and Velvets introduced at this house ... more durable ... the colour very superior, unaffected by the strongest acids and even sea water."[118] The ladies in mourning were not doing chemistry experiments with the acids; rather, the mention of acids had to do with a fabric's washability (see p. 162). Bathing was considered a medicinal therapy, not a recreation, and so ladies could go bathing after a certain period without its seeming frivolous.

After a long period in black, returning to colored clothes meant, for those who could afford to follow the fashions, an entirely new wardrobe, as the old dresses were as much as three years behind the times. Jeannette Marshall was thinking of this when her grandmother was in her final illness: "The fact is that we are afraid to buy anything coloured, as we fear we shall have to go into mourning before long. It seems dreadful to think of these things beforehand, but at the same time it is no use buying a lot of dresses wh. one can't wear."[119] Lady Stanley worried less about the sentiment and more about the clothes: "We have just heard of the death of Mrs. Givson—I thought she would die soon when I got a coloured poplin from Ireland the other day."[120]

This was not a problem for those who could not afford to be fashionable, and it was also not a problem for the many women who, after the prescribed mourning period, decided to remain in their weeds— Queen Victoria was a notable example.* Others, especially as the century progressed, objected to mourning clothes altogether. In *The Old Wives' Tale*, Constance refuses to wear mourning for her husband in the Potteries in the late 1880s: "Her mother and she, on the death of her father [in 1864], had talked of the various disadvantages of weeds; her mother had worn them unwillingly, and only because a public opinion not sufficiently advanced had intimidated her."[121] In *Middlemarch* (1871–72), a lady's maid says to her widowed mistress, "If anybody was to marry me flattering himself I should wear these hijeous weepers two years for him, he'd be deceived by his own vanity, that's all."[122] Although Jeannette Marshall had refused to be "visible" out of deep mourning in the 1870s, by the mid-1880s she had changed with the times: she trimmed a mourning hat with gray gauze and crimson feathers, because "really one can't travel quite like a crow, abroad."[123]

---

*"Weed" (singular) initially meant an item of clothing, but by the end of the sixteenth century it had taken on its current meaning of black mourning dress, always in the plural.

Once women emerged from seclusion they had to reassess their position in the world. For widowers, life continued much as normal. After 1850, 14 percent of men aged 55–64 were widowed, compared with 30 percent of women.[124] The men, both numerically and from their stronger financial and social position, had a much better chance of remarrying. Widows frequently lost their income, and even more frequently their status, both of which had been given to them by their marriage. Unless a woman was particularly well-born or rich, without a husband she was adrift. Often her home went too: after the death of Linley Sambourne's father, his mother lived in turn for several months a year with each of her children, dependent on them for her upkeep.[125]

Although a woman who remarried was considered fortunate, there was also a faint distaste for her action: she was being unfaithful to the memory of her dead husband, which was almost as bad as physical infidelity. (A widower who remarried was providing a replacement mother for his children; this was seen as entirely normal.) George Eliot was in a particularly anomalous position. She had lived with G. H. Lewes, who could not divorce his wife, for a quarter of a century, and was shunned by "decent" women for the irregularity of her liaison. Two years after his death she married a friend of his, John Cross, to the consternation of her circle (partly because Cross was substantially younger than she). When she had lived in an immoral relationship, she was condemned; when she finally regularized her situation, she was condemned again. Even the most conventional women were not immune from censure. Lord Tennyson's sister Emily had been engaged to Arthur Hallam. Eight years after his premature death she became engaged once more. Mrs. Brookfield wrote: "Only *conceive* Emily Tennyson (I really can hardly even now believe it) Emily Tennyson is actually going to be married—and to whom after such a man as Arthur Hallam. To a boy in the Navy, *supposed* to be a Midshipman . . . Can you conceive anyone who he had loved, putting up with another? I feel so distressed about this, really it quite *hurts* me, I had such a romantic admiration for her, looked at her with such pity, and now my feeling about her is bouleversé."[126] And Lily Dale, in *The Small House at Allington*, says, "I should be disgraced in my own eyes if I admitted the love of another man" after being jilted. Despite her ex-fiancé's inconstancy, "It is to me almost as though I had married him."[127]

The alternative, however, was to be seen as one of the sad, spiteful, silly women caricatured in *Punch* and by contemporary novelists: without lives of their own, without an adequate income, getting older, getting poorer, and constantly expecting (fearing?) that they were being trifled with. For too many women, widowhood brought a descent down the social scale, out of the homes which they had been brought up to understand were their reasons for existence, and which were extensions of themselves and their place in the world.

MOURNING CLOTHES FOR WOMEN[115]*

	First mourning	Second mourning	Ordinary mourning	Half-mourning
Wife for husband	1 year, 1 day: bombazine covered with crepe; widow's cap, lawn cuffs, collars	6 months: less crepe	6 months: no crepe; silk or wool replaces bombazine; in last 3 months jet jewelry, ribbons can be added	6 months: colors: gray, lavender, mauve, black-and-gray
Daughter for parent	6 months: black with black or white crepe (for young girls). No linen cuffs and collars, no jewelry for first 2 months	4 months: less crepe	—	2 months as above

*Most mourning wear was worn by women. For close family members men after midcentury wore a hatband, and a black suit, for half the period of mourning prescribed for women. Widowers were the only exception, and a hatband and a black suit was expected for three months.

	First mourning	Second mourning	Ordinary mourning	Half-mourning
Mother for child	6 months: black with crepe. No linen cuffs and collars, no jewelry for first 2 months	4 months: less crepe	—	2 months as above
Mother for infant	3 months, often with no crepe	—	—	—
Wife for husband's parents	18 months in black bombazine with crepe	—	3 months in black	3 months as above
Parent for son- or daughter-in-law	6 months: black with crepe. No linen cuffs and collars, no jewelry for first 2 months	4 months: less crepe	—	2 months as above
Parent for son- or daughter-in-law's parent	—	—	1 month black	—
2nd wife for parent of a 1st wife	—	—	3 months black	—
Daughters for step-mother	12 months, as for mother if still at home; 6 if not living at home	—	—	—

	First mourning	Second mourning	Ordinary mourning	Half-mourning
Sister for sibling	4 to 6 months: if 6 months, 3 months in crepe; if 4 months, 2 months in crepe	—	If 6 months, 3 without crepe; if 4 months, 2 months in black	If 6 months, 1 month as above; if 4, no half-mourning
For sister- or brother-in-law	4 to 6 months: if 6 months, 3 months in crepe; if 4 months, 2 months in crepe	—	If 6 months, 3 without crepe; if 4 months, 2 months without crepe	If 6 months, 1 month as above; if 4 months, no half-mourning
2nd wife for brother or sister of a 1st wife	—	—	6 weeks black: not obligatory	—
Grand-daughter for grandparent	6 to 9 months: 3 months in crepe	—	3 months in black	If 9 months, 3 months as above
Niece for aunt or uncle	—	—	6 weeks to 3 months: if 3 months, 2 months in black; if 6 weeks, black for entire period	If 3 months, 1 month as above
Niece for uncle or aunt by marriage	—	—	6 weeks in black silk	—

	First mourning	Second mourning	Ordinary mourning	Half-mourning
Niece for great-uncle or great-aunt	—	—	5 weeks to 2 months: if 5 weeks, black for entire period; if 2 months, black for 1 month	If 2 months, 1 month as above
Aunt for nephew or niece	—	—	6 weeks to 3 months: if 3 months, 2 months in black; if 6 weeks, black for entire period	If 3 months, 1 month as above
For a 1st cousin	—	—	1 month to 6 weeks: if 1 month, black for the entire period; if 6 weeks, black for 3 weeks	If 6 weeks: 3 weeks as above
For 2nd cousin	—	—	3 weeks black, but rarely worn	—
For husbands' relations	As blood relations			
For "connections"	—	—	1 to 3 weeks, depending on level of intimacy	—

THE STREET

Sherlock Holmes, in "A Case of Identity," said to Watson that if they "could fly out that window hand in hand, hover over this great city, gently remove the roofs, and peep in at the queer things which are going on," it might be possible only then to encompass all of human nature.[1] This desire for an aerial view was not uncommon: the new urban spaces were so big, so complex, so unending—sprawling out into what had just recently been countryside—that it appeared the only way to understand the city. London was the biggest city, and it was often used as a paradigm for all the new urban spaces. From the ground, it was difficult to gain a perspective. In *Little Dorrit*, Dickens spoke for the general population, who had "nothing to see but streets, streets, streets. Nothing to breathe but streets, streets, streets . . . Miles of close wells and pits of houses, where the inhabitants gasped for air, stretched far away towards every point of the compass."[2]

Nathaniel Hawthorne, by contrast, found that his "first impression of London was of stately and spacious streets . . . There is little or no show or pretension . . . it has a plain, business air; an air of homely, actual life, of a metropolis of tradesmen."[3] Throughout the century, metropolitan councils had worked to ameliorate the character of the streets by a variety of local and municipal acts, which ensured that drainage was improved, roads were widened to accommodate increased carriage traffic, and minimum safety standards were achieved by paving and cleaning, with further safety then secured by better lighting and policing.

These streets were thronged, in a way that we have now forgotten. Women may have remained inside their houses far more than we do, but they were not isolated. G. A. Sala reported on the endless variety in the changing shifts of people: the clerks streaming to and from work, the water carts spraying the dust, crossing sweepers keeping the worst of the mud and dung away from the pedestrians, the potboys and shop staff taking the shutters down from the shop fronts.[4] And then there was the street life itself: not people going from place to place, but people whose place was the streets. These broke down into two groups: the vendors and the entertainers.[5]

The vendors in turn divided into three groups: the buyers, the sellers, and the menders. With women and servants at home all day, selling door to door was economically sound, whether it was the small watercress girls who took fresh cresses to the homes of the middle classes in time for breakfast or just before tea, or the butchers' boys calling for orders after breakfast and returning with the meat on trays carried high on their shoulders a few hours later. The butchers and their assistants were a cheerful sight in light blue smocks and dark blue aprons, and they harmonized their deliveries to these by skewering the customers' names and addresses to their orders on labels written out in bright blue ink. The baker delivered daily too, and liquid refreshment came from milkmen and -women, who wore white countrymen's smocks and carried two covered pails hung across a yoke. Sometimes a milkman drove a cow through the suburbs, drawing milk at the door, right into the customers' jug, to prove that no adulteration was taking place—although this did not prevent the less scrupulous dairymen from ensuring that their cows drank huge quantities of water before they set out. Until the 1880s there was a cow in St. James's Park, to supply milk on demand for nurses and children out for their daily walks. Stronger drink was delivered by potmen, carrying wooden

8 a.m. in St. James's Park, 1859: a dairyman has his cows tethered to supply
women and children with milk during their morning walk. One family is
already ensconced. On the right a regiment marches past a hot-potato stand,
and (center) a milliner's assistant delivers her wares.

frames divided lengthwise in two, holding metal jugs of porter and
stout. They arrived on weekdays at the supper hours at their regular
houses, but anyone could look out the window and stop them, as Dick
Swiveller did in *The Old Curiosity Shop*: "He commanded [the pot-
boy] to set down his tray and to serve him with a pint of mild porter."[6]

In the summer there were also cherry girls, strawberry girls, lavender girls, and flower merchants with a barrow or tray, calling "All a-
growin' and all a-blowin'!" and girls with "Ornaments for your
fire-stoves"; in the autumn came sellers of sawdust-stuffed draft exclud-
ers, invariably red; in the winter roasted-chestnut and baked-potato
men appeared; and all year round there was the muffin man with a bell
and his wares on a tray on his head, who "liked wet days best, 'cause
there's werry respectable ladies what don't keep a servant, and they

buys to save themselves going out."⁷ Teas were also improved by catching the cockles-and-mussels man, who did his best business in the late afternoon. The onion man in Islington in Edmund Gosse's youth was

> a tall bony Jersey Protestant with a raucous voice, who strode up our street several times a week, carrying a yoke across his shoulders, from the ends of which hung ropes of onions. He used to shout, at abrupt intervals, in a tone which might wake the dead:
>
> > Here's your rope . . .
> > To hang the Pope . . .
> > An a penn'orth of cheese to choke him.
>
> The cheese appeared to be legendary; he sold only onions.⁸

Less salubrious, but still useful, visitors were the catsmeat man, selling horsemeat from a barrow or basket, "and the man selling flypapers who always wore a battered old top-hat round which was a fly-paper spotted with trapped flies, calling 'Catch 'em alive-oh.' "⁹ Boys shoveled up dung from the horses in the street and sold it door to door as garden manure.

Some sellers had more permanent pitches: there were stalls from which costermongers sold fruit and vegetables, sweet stalls, stewed-eel stalls. Stalls that sold sheep's trotters or oysters usually stood outside pubs; apple or orange women sold from trays or baskets by theaters; shoeblacks, who were yet to be organized into the Shoeblack Brigade, under central control and with a uniform, had their own regular spots.

Those buying rather than selling provided households with a simple way of disposing economically of objects no longer wanted. The old-clothes men were predominantly Jewish, and as well as clothes they also bought clocks, hats, dripping—almost anything, in fact. They carried "a Dutch clock under their arm, bell ringing as they went along, calling 'Old clo'!' " and wearing, on top of their own top hats, any hats they had purchased that day. There were also men who bought hare and rabbit skins from the cooks, carrying them on the ends of poles as they made their rounds. There were "grubby old men with bulging disreputable sacks, wheezing out 'Any rags, bottles, or bones?' and equally grubby men not so old shouting, 'Old iron! Old iron! Any old iron?'"[10]

Then there were all the people who mended and repaired. They came calling every day, together with a further group of people who provided services of various kinds. Dustmen—garbagemen—wore hats with leather flaps covering their necks to protect them from the dust that flew as they emptied the dustbins into their cart. They rang a bell as they arrived, to give householders time to call their children in from the streets and close their windows and doors. There were also "gypsies . . . calling 'Chairs to mend? Any chairs to mend?' It was interesting to stand and watch fine flaunting gypsy women with plumed hats and richly coloured shawls sitting on the front-door steps of one of the houses while they deftly plaited the cane seats of broken chairs." The chair-menders often combined several services: while chairs were being mended they sold brooms, brushes, and other odds and ends, and the women told fortunes. The knife-grinder wheeled his barrow in front of him, loaded with a treadle and grindstone; and there were tinkers shouting "Any pots, pans, or kettles to mend?" while the tinker's wife and children followed behind, with their own barrow loaded with a furnace and tools.[11]

The lamplighter—usually an elderly man—carried a ladder and a handlamp. The crosspiece that still survives on some street lights was there to hold his ladder. He set it beside each lamp, climbed up, turned the cock, and held his handlamp to the mantle. He then repeated his journey in the morning to shut off each cock again. Chimney sweeps (by now mostly adults) carried their rods and brushes on their shoulders and announced themselves simply, shouting "Sweep!" On May 1 the Jack-in-the-Green took to the streets for the sweeps' annual holiday. This was a sweep with a wicker frame over him, like a beehive supported by his shoulders, and a dome over his head which was covered with greenery and flowers. His wife and children escorted him, playing mouth organs and tambourines; the girls wore their best white stockings, and they all danced: "How Jack reels and staggers in the midst of his green portable armour towards the close of the day! . . .

Merrily does the 'Sweepess' or 'Jackess' of the green jingle her bright brass ladle before the doors [for a tip]."[12]

This was only a small part of a very large street-entertainment world. By midcentury stilt-dancers were already disappearing, as were dancing dogs, but there were plenty of impromptu acts: little girls danced the hornpipe for spare change, acrobats spread small carpets and tumbled, or did feats of strength, balancers balanced swords, or ladders, on their chins, with small boys to climb the ladders (all these were usually outside pubs), ballad singers, with ballads hung over a clotheshorse, had a regular weekly route, singing the songs and then selling the words for a halfpenny. Raree shows were still to be seen: these were boxes supported on a stick, in which were pictures—sometimes rude, but more often engravings of public monuments or famous people—which could be viewed for a halfpenny. During the Crimean War (1853–56) and the Indian Mutiny (1857) topical images helped this form of entertainment survive a little longer. A Happy Family hand-barrow had a mouse that walked a tightrope and a bird that fired a toy cannon, while another bird was "killed," put in a coffin, and towed away. The bird-murderer was ceremoniously hanged from a gibbet that was operated by a bird-hangman.

By the end of the 1880s barrel organs and hurdy-gurdies, usually played by Italians accompanied by a monkey wearing a small scarlet coat or cloak and performing tumbling tricks, were both driven out by piano-organs, which made a bigger noise. Dancing bears were rare by the end of the century, but they appeared from time to time.* Compton Mackenzie, in Kensington at the end of the century, remembered a German band, "four or five middle-aged men with peaked caps blowing brass instruments [who] visited . . . once a week regularly," and "the

---

*In the 1850s and 1860s barbershops selling hair unguent advertised: "Bears' grease personally prepared," "Try our special Bears' grease," "Bears' grease fresh this week," or, more rarely, "We killed a bear this week." Occasionally a sad-looking bear was chained in the area to prove the product's freshness, but Alfred Bennett, who remembered seeing them in his childhood, suspected even then that it was a bear that was moved from shop to shop, for display, or a performing bear borrowed for the day.[13]

gentleman in a top-hat with bells round it who played simultaneously a drum, a pair of cymbals, a penny whistle, a concertina, and a triangle."[14]

There were several kinds of puppet show that traveled the suburban streets. There were dancing sailor puppets, girl puppets performing a ballet, or a skeleton dancing: his bones separated and left the puppet stage, dancing all the time, until only a dancing skull was left; then one by one the dancing bones returned and reassembled themselves. The greatest treat for children, however, was the traveling Punch and Judy show, announced by a man in a white top hat who played a mouth organ and a drum. Midcentury the story was very different from the one we know, being both more brutal and more moral. As Compton Mackenzie remembered it, Punch, having been out drinking,

came home and quarrelled with his wife; from words they got to blows, and there used to be a tremendous fight between them, and sorry we are to say the drunken old rascal swore dreadfully. At the last he struck Judy a tremendous blow with his truncheon, and she fell down, senseless, as if dead. Then the conscience of the hump-backed villain smote him, and he wept and wailed over her, until at last the doctor came, felt her pulse, and pronounced her dead. Punch was inconsolable for her loss, pronounced the doctor a quack, and then they went at it. Oh what a fight that was between Punch and the Doctor! . . . Punch was next tried, and knocked the judge off the bench for finding him guilty of murder, and sentenced to be hanged. Then the gallows was brought out, and you made sure that the old villain's career of crime was ended; but not a bit of it . . . He seemed willing enough to be hanged, but did not know how to place his neck in the halter; sometimes he put his arms through the noose, then half his body, but never by any chance did he allow the cord to touch his neck. At length he succeeded in persuading Jack Ketch to shew him the right way: the hangman did so, placed his own neck in the noose, received a crack on the head with the staff and a kick behind, and there he hung and swung to the delight of every beholder.[15]

Edmund Gosse was only allowed to watch from his window, as many middle-class children were, to prevent their mixing with the street children, lower-class children who played on the streets unchecked. Even from that distance,

> I was much affected by the internal troubles of the Punch family; I thought that with a little more tact on the part of Mrs Punch and some restraint held over a temper, naturally violent, by Mr Punch, a great deal of this sad misunderstanding might have been prevented.
>
> The momentous close, when a figure of shapeless horror appears on the stage, and quells the hitherto undaunted Mr Punch, was to me the bouquet of the entire performance. When Mr Punch, losing his nerve, points to this shape and says in an awestruck, squeaking whisper, "Who's that? Is it the butcher?" and the stern answer comes, "No, Mr Punch!" And then, "Is it the baker?" "No, Mr Punch!" "Who is it then?" . . . and then the full, loud reply, booming like a judgement-bell, "It is the Devil come to take you down to Hell," and the form of Punch, with kicking legs, sunken in epilepsy on the floor,—all this was solemn and exquisite to me beyond words.[16]

Children adored street entertainment, but there was a perpetual stream of complaints from householders unhappy at being sometimes held to ransom by street bands, who would not leave until they had been tipped—or who returned if they had been tipped too well. Charles Babbage, the mathematician and progenitor of the Difference Engine, ancestor of the computer, claimed to have been driven nearly mad by what he called "instruments of torture permitted by the Government to be in daily and nightly use in the streets of London." He wrote a pamphlet, *A Chapter on Street Nuisances*, in which he laid out his grievances, and separately he listed the 165 interruptions he had endured over ninety days from street musicians (including 37 disruptive monkeys, a thrown stone, and 23 further incidents, sadly only noted as "other").[17]* He was not alone. Augustus Mayhew was summonsed by the local magistrates court, charged with the assault of a peddler woman. His defense was that she had come to his door three times in one day, selling her flower stands, and had refused to take no for an answer. He added that "as many as 38 persons in one day" had come to the door, and he produced a list of them that included "Rags and bones," "Crockery," "Sixpence a peck, peas," "Fine young rabbits," "Roots all a-blowing, all a growing," "Crochet mats, slippers, writing-paper."† The magistrates, who perhaps also worked at home, found him not guilty and cautioned the peddler, despite the fact that Mayhew acknowledged having physically removed her from his doorstep.[18]

There were not only hawkers and entertainers on the streets. Industrialization had brought with it consumerism: trade was burgeoning, and women, as the guardians of the home and its decoration, were out and about, ensuring that no new fashion escaped them. The shops that opened in this period were not just successful: many of them were the foundations of great fortunes, and a good percentage have survived into the twenty-first century.** In the early part of the nineteenth century, before Victoria came to the throne, several shops had transformed

---

*This response appears out of proportion to the offense. Perhaps street bands, playing in public music that penetrated the private sphere, were disturbing for their mixing of the two spheres? Or perhaps the noise was simply worse than we can today imagine, like spending one's life in an elevator perpetually playing Mantovani.

†Note that Mayhew identified the peddlers by their cries alone.

**Shops that survived into the second half of the twentieth century include Bon Marché (founded 1818, as Peck's of Liverpool), Pullars of Perth (1826), Peter Robinson (1833), Marshall & Snelgrove (1837 as Marshall & Wilson, becoming Marshall & Snelgrove in 1848), Maples (1842), Gorringe's (1858), Derry & Toms (1862), Handley's of Southsea (1867), Army & Navy Co-operative (1871), Ponting's (1873), Robinson & Cleaver of Belfast (1894), Bourne & Hollingsworth (1894), and Penberthy's (1883, for which I feel a particular affinity, as my grandfather owned it midcentury). Those that continue today include Benjamin Harvey (1813, now Harvey Nichols), Kendal's of Manchester (1821, as The Bazaar, then becoming Kendal Milne), Jolly's of Bath (1830), Lilly & Skinner (1832), Dickins, Son & Stevens (1835, now Dickins & Jones), Bainbridge of Newcastle (1838), The Scotch House (1839), Harrods (1849), Aquascutum (1851, as Bax & Co., later Emary & Co.), Thomas

By 8 a.m. the streets are already crowded (1859). Shop assistants remove the
shutters that have protected their windows. The shoeblack boy is not yet part
of the Shoeblack Brigade that would be formed later in the century, which had
a uniform, and a central organization. Note the crosspiece on the streetlamp,
to hold the lamplighter's ladder (p. 394).

the whole idea of retail outlets. The Soho Bazaar (opened in 1816) sold
a wide range of goods under one roof—a precursor of the department
store—and also provided essential services such as a servants' registry
office. Shoolbreds (1817) and Maples (1842) made Tottenham Court
Road the destination for furniture for the middle classes—although it
became a byword for the cheap and shoddy for precisely this reason.

It has been suggested for the better part of a century that women on
the streets alone, together, or unaccompanied by men were either prostitutes or in danger of being mistaken for prostitutes. In government

---

Burberry (1856), Whiteley's (1863), John Lewis (1864), Bentalls (1867), Barkers
(1870), Peter Jones (1871), Liberty's (1875), The Irish Linen Co. (1875), D. H. Evans
(1879), Fenwick's (1882), Jaeger (1883), and Calman Links (1897).[19]

reports and newspaper articles the city was portrayed as dangerous, threatening, not somewhere that women could safely be, although many correspondents wrote in to *The Times* following these reports, commenting that if women were sensible, they could walk out in public with no trouble—and no escort.[20] Reading women's own writings of how they spent their time, and analyzing fiction, suggests that many decent women were habitually out in the streets without its being particularly remarkable. It is true that the Marshall girls were careful, when they left their Savile Row home, to walk away from the St. James's area, which was club- and theater-land, therefore male, and therefore territory where unaccompanied women did not venture. But they did walk, they did go to the park, just the two sisters together. And by the 1870s and 1880s, these previously no-go areas had been invaded and subdued: Bond Street, the Strand, the City had all been colonized by shops and therefore by women shoppers. The West End was a magnet for women, and even those who lived in suburbs that had a good high street and a number of large local department stores would still go "up" to town regularly. One resident of Crouch End, a suburb in north London, wrote that "I delight, as every fashionable woman does, in taking a journey once every season to the West End, and thoroughly doing the sights."[21] This meant shopping, window-shopping, visiting friends who lived in the West End, and perhaps going to a matinee or a museum, as well as having a meal—usually lunch or tea—at one of the new tea shops: an ABC, or a Lyons Corner House. (These ladies' tea shops were welcomed with enthusiasm not simply because they were safe environments for unaccompanied women when pubs, grill rooms, and many restaurants were not, but because they had lavatories for their female customers. Previously, women could go out only for as long as they didn't have to "go.") Marion Sambourne routinely went by herself to Westbourne Grove or the West End by Underground to go shopping, and to Oxford Street or Knightsbridge by omnibus, although Harrods, a grocery shop, was not her favorite destination—a "dirty place though cheap."[22]

Frances Mary Buss was the founder in 1850 of North London Collegiate School, one of the earliest girls' schools to focus on academic attainment. In the late 1840s she helped at her mother's small school in Camden, and from there she walked on her own to Queen's College to attend classes, and walked back in the evenings.[23] Charlotte Brontë's heroine in *Villette*, Lucy Snowe, was less used to being abroad in a large city; she thought that "to walk alone in London seemed enough of an adventure." When she went to the coffee room of a hotel she was perturbed, but found that a woman alone caused no stir:

> It cannot be denied that on entering this room I trembled some-
> what; felt uncertain, solitary, wretched; wished to Heaven I knew
> whether I was doing right or wrong; felt convinced it was the last,
> but could not help myself . . . There were many other people
> breakfasting at other tables in the room; I should have felt rather
> more happy if amongst them all I could have seen any women;
> however, there was not one—all present were men. But nobody
> seemed to think I was doing anything strange; one or two gentle-
> men glanced at me occasionally, but none stared obtrusively.[24]

In the 1860s Dickens showed Bella Wilfer ranging across town without an escort, walking from Oxford Street to Holloway, over three miles as the crow flies, without anyone's thinking it odd. She also walked from Holloway to the City to look for her father one evening, and she was noticeable then only because there were so few women in the financial district.[25]

Beatrix Potter fit much more closely our general perception of the sheltered Victorian miss. Her family went one night to the theater, but "when we got to Buckingham Palace Road her Majesty was having a Drawing-room . . . We stuck for about half an hour, and after all had to go back round by Westminster . . . Extraordinary to state, it was the first time in my life that I had been past the Horse Guards, Admiralty, and Whitehall, or seen the Strand and the Monument."[26] She was eighteen, and had lived in Kensington her whole life—only about as far from those sights as Bella had walked in one afternoon. True, Bella Wilfer was a fictional construct, but Molly Hughes, at exactly the same period, played outside by herself and went shopping alone for her mother when still a child. Money and social caste were not the only factors: Beatrix Potter came from a background not dissimilar to that of the Marshall sisters, who happily walked through the West End.

Apart from the possibility of danger, walking through the streets was a tiring and dirty business. Gwen Raverat knew the work involved: "It was difficult to walk freely in the heavy tweed 'walking skirts,' which kept on catching between the knees. Round the bottom of these skirts I had, with my own hands, sewn two and a half yards of 'brush braid,' to collect the worst of the mud; for they inevitably swept the roads, however carefully I might hold them up behind . . . After-wards the crusted mud had to be brushed off, which might take an hour or more to do."[27] In Gissing's *New Grub Street*, Marian, the daughter of an impecunious literary hack, goes out after dinner to visit friends who live only a twenty-minute walk away, but she takes the omnibus there and back.[28] An hour of brushing after every walk, and constricting clothing, made this a sensible option.

The spreading transport system came to women's aid: the Under-ground, omnibuses, railways, and trams all were useful, relatively inex-pensive means of transport, and no one was surprised to see women traveling alone. Segregation was the order of the day in transport, as it was elsewhere. It was not, for the most part, a male/female separation; instead, it was one based on class and money. Trains had three classes of travel, and in addition there were cheap "workmen's trains," to bring the manual laborers into central London, and other reduced-fare trains, scheduled earlier in the day than the general mass of commuters wanted to travel.* Many train companies had offered cheaper fares from the 1860s, and in 1883 the Cheap Trains Act made the workmen's

---

*Time, another of the great preoccupations of the age, was transformed by the development of the railways. Until the railway arrived at a town or village, each functioned on its own "local" time. As the trains began to spread into the coun-tryside running on strict schedules, variations were no longer tolerable. Synchro-nization was at first a laborious business. Initially a watch was set daily at the Admiralty and sent by the Irish Mail to Holyhead and then to Dublin, to take "London time" across the country. After 1842 it was settled that all stations would, via the telegraph, synchronize their clocks with Greenwich time, or "rail-way time" as it came to be known.[29]

By 9 a.m. the omnibuses are discharging clerks in the City of London (1859).
Many of these sit on the top deck on the "knife-board" seats, reached only by
a ladder. The routes are marked along the sides of the omnibuses, with the
start and finish points appearing at the back. The rest of the space is given up
to advertisements. A hansom cab goes past (left) with the passenger below and
the driver perched above, the reins passed over the top of the carriage.

trains compulsory. This enabled many of the less prosperous to follow
the middle classes out to the suburbs. The Underground was somewhat less segregated: it had two classes of travel. Omnibuses had only
one, but they began their service at eight o'clock, after the laborers
were already expected to be at work, and so they were middle class by
default. The fares were also more expensive than third class on the
trains, which kept them select.[30] If that did not, then the driver and
conductor often maintained what they considered to be a suitable standard. Hannah Cullwick wrote in her diary: "The first 'bus conductor
refused to take me in with the ladies, because I look'd shabby I suppose, which vex'd me for I was in a hurry. So I waited for the next &
he let me get inside." Sometimes, if only poorly dressed people were

waiting, the driver would just slow down, not stop, and the would-be passengers either had to jump while the bus was in motion or had to wait for a better-tempered driver. After the Underground opened in 1863, the working classes as a whole preferred it, for obvious reasons.[31]

In 1829 George Shillibeer had begun to run omnibuses between Paddington and the Bank, via Islington. By 1853 there were 3,000 buses in London alone, carrying an estimated million people a day.[32]* Each route had its own name and color: "Paragons, Paddingtons, Favourites, Nelsons, Royal Blues" were represented by "red, green, blue, drab, cinnamon colour."[34] The driver wore a white top hat, the conductor a black one. The conductor

> stood on a step to the left of the door, barely large enough for his feet, and supported himself by grasping a strap fixed high on the back of the bus and descending over his shoulder. From this proud eminence he hailed likely passengers, ogled the girls, and chaffed the drivers of following buses or other vehicles. His was supposed to be a pungent wit. One of his duties in the crinoline age was to lean down from his perch and prevent with his hand the oval that hoops or whalebone had to assume when squeezing through the narrow doorway from rising to an indelicate height, as they were somewhat prone to do. "It's as well I'm married," [a conductor] once remarked to an outside passenger; "my place ain't fit for a single bloke."[35]

"Outsides"—passengers who rode on the top of the bus—had to climb to the roof by an iron ladder, with only a strap to hold on to (later replaced by a rail). They sat on the "knife-board," a central bench running lengthwise and divided in two by a partition, so that the passengers sat back to back with their feet against the roof's edge. Women were expected not to ride on top: even if they could have managed the

---

*It is easy to see why the internal-combustion engine was initially regarded as a pollution reliever. Each omnibus used ten horses a day, and each horse daily ate twenty-one pounds of oats and hay.[33]

ladder, the lack of a skirting-board along the sides meant that people on the pavements could have seen up their skirts. In 1864 the ladder was replaced by stairs, and this was soon followed by a raised skirting-board along the roof. In the 1880s the knife-board was replaced altogether by "garden seats," the two-abreast seating that remains in use on most public transport, although it took some time for the prejudice regarding the propriety of women riding on top to dissipate. Sara Duncan told her stuffy London cousin that she had traveled "on an omnibus":

> "*In* an omnibus I suppose you mean. You couldn't very well be *on* it, unless you went on the top!" And Mrs. Portheris smiled rather derisively.
>
> "I did; I went on the top," I returned calmly. "And it was lovely."
>
> Mrs. Portheris very nearly lost her self-control in her effort to grasp this enormity. Her cap bristled again, and the muscles round her mouth twitched quite perceptibly.
>
> "Careering all over London on the top of an omnibus! . . . The top of an omnibus is not a proper place for you . . . you *must not* go there! Don't on any account do it again! It is a thing people never do!"[36]

There were also two or four box seats by the driver, which were usually reserved for regular male customers, who tipped the driver to keep them. Initially there were no tickets: the conductor charged as much as he thought he could get away with, and passed on to his employers as little as he thought he could get away with, sharing the rest with the driver. Molly Hughes remembered that in the 1870s "we stopped anywhere, for plenty of passengers rather than rapid progress was the main idea. I reckon that the journey from Islington to the West End took a good deal over an hour," to cover approximately two miles.[37] When tickets were first introduced, the conductors went on strike; after they had lost their battle, they did not always bother to stop when asked, as Hannah Cullwick knew well, because carrying more passengers no longer meant that they made more.

Inside, "the bus was a box lined with blue velvet, made to carry five each side . . . No air got in, except when the door was opened, for the little windows admitted only some so-called light. Straw on the floor, designed to keep our feet warm, was apt to get very wet and dirty."[38] G. A. Sala was firm that the inside was fit only for women:

> Men, don't ride inside . . . Inside an omnibus you are subjected to innumerable vexations and annoyances. Sticks or parasols are poked in your chest and in the back of your neck, as a polite reminder that somebody wants to get out, and that you must seize the conductor by the skirt of his coat, or pinch him in the calf of the leg, as an equally polite request for him to stop; you are half suffocated by the steam of damp umbrellas; your toes are crushed to atoms as the passengers alight or ascend; you are very probably the next neighbour to persons suffering under vexatious ailments, such as asthma, simple cold in the head, or St. Vitus's dance; it is ten to one but that you suffer under the plague of babies; and, five days out of seven, you will have a pickpocket, male or female, for a fellow-passenger. The rumbling, the jumbling, the jolting, and the concussions—the lurking ague in the straw when it is wet, and the peculiar omnibus fleas that lurk in it when it is dry, make the interior of one of these vehicles a place of terror and discomfort.[39]

The men who did travel inside were regarded by women passengers as a design feature that went with the bus. Sara Duncan noted the convenience of the "gentleman in the corner": "His arm, or his stick, or his umbrella, is always at the service of any lady who wants the bell rung. It seems to be a duty that goes with the corner seat, cheerfully accepted by every man that sits there."[40] Sala might have queried the adverb "cheerfully," but the rest seems accurate. Etiquette books were firm that no man needed to give up his seat for a woman, but conductors continued to ask "if any gentleman would go outside to oblige a lady," so they were probably shamed into it.[41]

The Underground opened in 1863, with the Metropolitan Railway line, which ran from Paddington to the City. As the "Tube" spread toward Notting Hill and then farther out, its speed and cheapness made it popular with commuters, even though the coke-burning engines filled the tunnels with smoke. Compton Mackenzie remembered that one decided whether to use the Underground or not depending on the destination: the Metropolitan Railway at Baker Street "was much fuller of fumes than the Temple, though not so full of them as Portland Road, or worst of all Gower Street."[42] Increasing the unease, the Underground was a target for Fenians, who set off an explosion between Charing Cross and Westminster in the 1870s, two more in the 1880s, and another in the 1890s.[43] Despite all these drawbacks, the Tube remained one of the easiest ways to travel longer distances across London. In 1875, in Trollope's *The Way We Live Now*, even Hetta Carbury, an upper-class girl, "trusted herself all alone to the mysteries of the Marylebone underground railway, and emerged with accuracy at King's Cross."[44]

The railways were considered perfectly safe for unaccompanied women, and even children; as a small child, Molly Hughes was sent from London to Cornwall on her own, with only a warning not to talk to strangers. However, not all the comforts supplied by the railway station were equally available. Some stations took segregation to an extreme, with separate entrances, staircases, waiting rooms, and booking halls for different classes of passenger. But for those who could afford them, trains had as many comforts as possible: they had gas lighting, and for an extra payment passengers could hire foot-warmers, filled with acetate of soda, which melted at 200°F and in the process of recrystallizing threw off heat for about twenty hours.[45] The restaurant or buffet in the station was a male preserve, just as most restaurants in cities were. When Molly married in 1897, nearly two decades after her first trip, her brothers accompanied her and her new husband to the station to see them off. There, as it was "not the thing" for her to appear in the buffet, she was parked in the train alone "with some light literature while the six boys went off to have a stirrup cup."[46]

Trains were the most comfortable method of traveling, and also the fastest: by midcentury it was estimated that one could get from

The inside of a railway carriage (*left*) with gas lighting. Note the window retains the shape of the old stagecoach windows, on which the train carriages were originally modeled. The man with the newspaper, wrapped carefully in a traveling rug, has a footwarmer at his feet. (*Right*) One of the many street vendors has his pitch on the platform, where he does a brisk trade in pies.

London Bridge Station to Brighton (about fifty miles) in less time than it took to get by road from London Bridge Station to Paddington (about five miles).* Traffic was, even by today's standards, appalling in most major cities. There were no traffic lights, no one-way streets; carriages took up more space than cars, and were subject to the vagaries of the horses pulling them. The main shopping hours were 11:00 to 12:30 and 2:00 to 4:00 in the winter (later in the summer). Sala called Regent Street the "Great Trunk Road in Vanity Fair," not simply because it was the main "trade route," but also for the number of people who flowed down it daily.[47] The afternoon shoppers and afternoon callers, as well as those out for a drive, all mixed together and created chaos. The Marshalls lived in Savile Row, and at the most congested

*Today the British have become resigned to the opposite: the fifty-mile trip is scheduled to take anything up to seventy minutes by train—far longer than it took the Victorians.

times it took them three-quarters of an hour to drive less than a quarter of a mile to the Piccadilly entrance of the Royal Academy in their carriage, or an hour to go less than half a mile up Bond Street.[48] In 1866 one Bond Street shop advertised that "ready access will always be found in Conduit Street when Bond Street is blocked," even though more than a decade earlier it had already been noted that "in the spring-tide of fashion, of a glorious summer's day . . . you could not cross Conduit-street under a lapse of a quarter of an hour, and carriages seemed to have come to an interminable lock."[49]

Toll roads and tollbars marked the separation of rural and urban. In the 1860s there were still 178 tollbars that prevented vehicles from entering London without payment. It cost from 2d. to 4d. to pass, while pedestrians crossed free, walking between posts set close together in the footpath to block carts. The only wheeled objects given free passage were prams and wheelbarrows.[50] There were still a few oddly rural pockets in most cities, despite the seething modernity. In the 1860s the French historian Hippolyte Taine noted sheep grazing outside Westminster Abbey; Samuel Butler in *The Way of All Flesh*, set at a roughly contemporaneous period, had Ernest Pontifex walk past Green Park, beside Piccadilly, one of the main thoroughfares of the modern city. There he saw "three sheep with very small lambs only a day or two old, which had been penned off for shelter and protection from the others that ranged in the park."[51]

Next to these rural idylls, the traffic thundered past. Accidents were common. Jeannette Marshall was in her father's carriage coming home from a concert at the Albert Hall when it knocked down an old lady. The woman recovered, but Jeannette described many more accidents, including some where the carriages were reduced to "matchsticks."[52] The number of carriage accidents increased dramatically in bad weather: snow or ice meant that the horses had to have nails driven into their shoes to keep a grip on the roads, and even then only the main roads were passable—they were cleared by men with shovels, and carts to remove the snow, while small side roads were left to wait for a thaw.

Women often stayed inside entirely during bad weather. Nominally waterproof fabric was first created in 1817, and a more effective rubberized material was developed in 1844, but it did not breathe and made the wearer sweat heavily; in addition, the smell of the rubberizing process lingered—it was said that a waterproof coat could be smelled across the street. It was not until 1851 that a "showerproof" wool fabric was developed that could be worn with relative comfort. Bax & Co. showed its "Aquascutum" cloth at the Great Exhibition of 1851, and the army soon ordered it for soldiers destined for the Crimea. Ladies at first were not supplied with outfits made from similar fabric, but instead had "Ladies Ventilating Waterproof Travelling Cloaks," which may have been rubberized, that is, nonporous. Burberry patented a "weatherproof" cloth called gabardine in 1870, and gradually rainwear became equally common for both sexes. By midcentury umbrellas were generally conveniently to hand, in London, at any rate. The London Umbrella Company rented out umbrellas from its depots throughout the city, charging a 4s. deposit and a fee of 4d. for three hours' use, or 9d. for up to twenty-four hours, with another 6d. for each additional twenty-four-hour period. The umbrella could be returned to any of the company's depots, most of which were at railway stations.[53] However, the sheer area of clothing to be protected made umbrellas of less use to women than to men, and until the arrival of waterproofs, it remained problematic for women to venture out in the wet. Their clothing, which already weighed nearly 40 pounds, became saturated, and it was difficult to walk. No waterproofing and heavy woollen dresses with flannel and wool petticoats, in streets where the rain created lakes of mud from the dirt and dung, which fouled even the most carefully held dress, ensured that avoiding the rain was not something that only prosperous middle-class women did. Many of the patrons of the National Gallery complained that its free admission policy meant that working-class women as well as the middle classes took refuge in the museum whenever it began to rain.

And yet rain was the least troublesome of the elements in this new industrial age. When the narrator of *Bleak House*, Esther Summerson, first arrived in London, she asked her guide "whether there was a great fire anywhere? For the streets were so full of dense brown smoke that scarcely anything was to be seen. 'O dear no, miss,' he said. 'This is a

London particular.' " The streets of London had become nothing more than "an oblong cistern to hold the fog."[54] London had been called "the big smoke" or simply "the smoke" from the eighteenth century for good reason. The Industrial Revolution had brought with it a pall that hung over all the major cities, made up of coal smoke, dirt, and dust pouring out of millions of chimneys, together with the mist that prevented the former elements from being burned off by the sun.

Even when there was no actual fog London was often hazy, except very early in the morning, or on warm summer Sundays, when factories were shut and only kitchen fires were in use. The smoke haze was bluish, dirty gray or brown, and had a pungent smell. By the 1880s, people used terms such as "day darkness" or "high fog" to describe a day when there was often no fog at ground level but the sun was blocked by atmospheric haze. Cities with similar coal-fire and industrial usage had a similar perpetual pall: Liverpool, Birmingham, Manchester, and Glasgow rarely had a clear sky, and "Middlesborough and Cleveland also succeed in almost excluding daylight from the district."[55] Edinburgh,* Brighton, Dundee, and Dublin had less trouble because they used less coal, having less industry and smaller populations.

Fogless days, however, were becoming rarer in most of the industrialized areas of the country. In addition to the dirt produced by industry, the climate was changing, bringing with it more fogs, which were thicker and of a different color than previously. Using meteorological records, one modern historian has estimated that between 1871 and 1875 there were 51 days a year in London that were foggy; between 1876 and 1880 it was 58 days a year; between 1881 and 1885 it was 62 days; and between 1886 and 1890 it was 74 days a year—a 50 percent increase in two decades.[57] Nathaniel Hawthorne gave a description of what a foggy day meant:

> This morning, when it was time to get up, there was but a glimmering of daylight; and we had candles on the breakfast-table, at

---

*Edinburgh's nickname of "Auld Reekie" had something to do with the smell of smoke, but more to do with sewage.[56]

nearly ten o'clock. All abroad, there was a dense, dim fog, brooding through the atmosphere, insomuch that we could hardly see across the street. At eleven o'clock, I went out into the midst of this fog-bank, which, for the moment, seemed a little more interfused with daylight; for there seem to be continual changes in the density of this dim medium, which varies so much that now you can but just see your hand before you, and, a moment afterwards, you can see the cabs dashing out of the duskiness, a score of yards off . . .

I went home by way of Holborn; and the fog was denser than ever—very black, indeed, more like a distillation of mud than anything else; the ghost of mud, the spiritualized medium of departed mud . . . On reaching home, I found the fog diffused through the parlour, though how it could have got in is a mystery. Since nightfall, however, the atmosphere is clear again.[58]

That was a lightish fog, for Hawthorne could see people passing by. The heavier fogs were "palpable fogs, that you could . . . bottle up for future inspection," said Sala.[59] They were, in another observer's description,

something like being imbedded in a dilution of yellow peas-pudding, just thick enough to get through it without being wholly choked or completely suffocated . . . every time you open your mouth you partake of it, and all day long you are compelled to burn lights and, in addition to the fog, inhale the fumes from gas, candle or lamp, which have no more chance of escape than you have, so burn on dim, yellow, and sulkily* . . . [Once outside] You step gingerly along, feeling your way beside the walls, windows, and doors, whenever you can, until at last you tumble headlong into some cellar . . . or perhaps it is an underground coal-

---

*This was not poetic license: the reduced oxygen in the foggy atmosphere meant that lights burned less brightly.

shed . . . you escape once more into the street; and, as you cannot
see a yard before you, break your shins over a milkman's can . . .
Even one well accustomed to the ins and outs of our far-stretch-
ing city is strangely deceived in distance, and the size objects
assume, as they loom in dim and gigantic dimensions through the
heavy fog. The gas-lamps appear as if placed three storeys high,
unless you stand close beneath them, for what light they emit is
nearly all thrown upward . . . Once take a wrong turning, and you
may consider yourself very fortunate if you ever discover the
right road again within three hours . . . You seem to go as much
backward as forward; and some old Cockneys do aver that the
surest way of reaching Temple-bar from Charing-cross would be
to . . . walk away manfully without once turning your head, and
that, by the end of three hours, you would be pretty sure of reaching the point aimed at, should you not be run over.[60]

A foggy winter day meant using torches to light the way—or staying at
home altogether. The woman on the right is attempting to avoid breathing
fume-laden air: deaths from respiratory problems went up by as much as
400 percent during a heavy fog.

Losing one's way from one moment to the next seems a picturesque exaggeration, but many writers insist on it: Gissing's Everard Barfoot arrived in Chelsea in dense fog, and "literally he groped along, feeling the fronts of the houses . . . After abandoning hope several times, and all but asphyxiated, he found by inquiry of a man with whom he collided that he was actually within a few doors of his destination. Another effort, and he rang a joyous peal at the bell. A mistake. It was the wrong house."[61] It was not only in fiction that these fogs prevented people from moving about. In Marion Sambourne's diary there are frequent notes such as "Fearful fog!!! third day. Lin started for Punch dinner but had to return," or, more simply, "Could not go out."[62]

Fogs were not just a nuisance: they were dangerous to health. In one week of prolonged fog in the winter of 1880 there were 2,200 deaths in London, of which 757 were attributed to respiratory problems—607 more deaths than in the same week the year before. In the following week there were another 3,376 deaths, of which 1,557 were respiratory—1,657 more deaths than that week in the previous year. The death rate in that single fortnight increased from 27.1 per 1,000 of the population in 1879 to 48.1 per 1,000 in the following year. (There was no epidemic illness sweeping the country at that date: in country towns not suffering from fog the death rate was 26.3 per 1,000 for the same fortnight.) Farmers suffered just as badly. In 1873, at a cattle show in Islington, hundreds of cattle died of suffocation, and more had to be put down for humanitarian reasons.[63] In that same fog sixteen people working near the river drowned, and another two in the Regent's Canal.[64]

Workers lost hundreds of hours: anyone doing close work, or work involving color (for example, dressmakers making mourning clothes, using black thread on black fabric), went for days at a time when they either had to work by expensive gas lighting throughout the day or, unable to afford that, could do nothing at all. One artist grumbled, "All through the next 4 months I doubt if there will be 15 hours a week of light fit to paint by."[65] Throughout the century there were repeated attempts to solve the problem. In 1843 a committee for "the Means and Expediency of Preventing the Nuisance of Smoke from Fires and Furnaces" met. In 1853 a bill was finally pushed through Parliament—the Smoke Nuisance Abatement (Metropolitan) Act—and there were further attempts to improve matters in later sanitary and public-health acts.[66] Nothing made a substantial difference, however, until meteorological conditions changed again at about the turn of the century: fogs began to lessen long before the Clean Air Act of 1956 eliminated them altogether. It is not known what caused these climate changes.

Yet what would our image of the Victorian world be without fogs? What would Sherlock Holmes be without fog swirling outside his window as he sits holed up in Baker Street? Would Robert Louis Stevenson have been able to achieve the same atmosphere in *The Strange Case of Dr Jekyll and Mr Hyde* without a setting where "a great chocolate-coloured pall lowered over heaven . . . here it would be dark like the back-end of the evening; and there would be a glow of a rich, lurid brown, like the light of some strange conflagration; and here, for a moment, the fog would be quite broken up, and a haggard shaft of daylight would glance in between the swirling wreaths . . . this mournful re-invasion of darkness, seemed . . . like a district of some city in a nightmare"?[67]

Many would not have argued with the nightmarish qualities of the city, but, as a surreal coda, we will finish with a description of the sunsets that appeared in 1883. The volcano on the island of Krakatoa in Indonesia, half the world away, had exploded in August 1883, and 70,000 cubic yards of dust were released into the atmosphere. In December the poet Gerard Manley Hopkins recorded one of a resulting series of remarkable apparitions over Britain:

A bright glow had been round the sun all day and became more remarkable towards sunset. It then had a silvery or steely look, with soft radiating streamers and little colour; its shape was mainly elliptical . . . There was a pale golden colour, brightening and fading by turns for ten minutes as the sun went down. After the sunset the horizon was . . . lined a long way by a glowing tawny light, not very pure in colour and distinctly textured in hummocks, bodies like shoals of dolphins, or in what are called gadroons, or as the Japanese conventionally represent waves . . .

The glowing vapour above this was as yet colourless; then this took a beautiful olive or celadon green . . . delicately fluted; the green belt was broader than the orange, and pressed down on and contracted it. Above the green in turn appeared a red glow, broader and burlier in make; it was softly brindled, and in the ribs or bars the colour was rosier, in the channels where the blue of the sky shone through it was a mallow colour. Above this was a vague lilac . . .[68]

Given the Victorian home, the olive, celadon, and lilac skies must have harmonized beautifully. These skies were as varied, and as wildly untamed, as many aspects of the house.

It is too easy for us to think of the Victorian era—or any part of the past—as "romantic." For some it was an endless succession of cold, dirt, and dark, of black bombazine and narrow stairs. For others, though, it was fuchsine and peacock blue, as well as celadon skies.

To emphasize either viewpoint at the expense of the other is to give only a partial picture. We may be able to do no more than peer through the windows of the past—but at least we can choose to do so through windows that have the curtains open and the rooms inside brightly lit.

NOTES

INTRODUCTION: HOUSE AND HOME

1   H. G. Wells, *Tono-Bungay* ([1909]; London, n.p., 1933), p. 138.

2   Henry James, *The Portrait of a Lady* ([1881]; rev. ed., New York: Charles Scribner's Sons, 1908), vol. 1, pp. 287–88.

3   Anthony S. Wohl, *The Victorian Family: Structure and Stresses* (London: Croom Helm, 1978), p. 9.

4   Alison Adburgham, *A Punch History of Manners and Modes, 1841–1940* (London: Hutchinson, 1961), p. 143.

5   There is not the space here to deal with this important development in any detail. However, Leonore Davidoff and Catherine Hall's superb *Family Fortunes: Men and Women of the English Middle Classes, 1780–1850* (London: Hutchinson, 1987) is a compelling study.

6   Catherine Hall, "The Sweet Delights of Home," in *From the Fires of Revolution to the Great War*, ed. Michelle Perrot, trans. Arthur Goldhammer, vol. 4 of *A History of Private Life*, ed. Philippe Ariès and Georges Duby (Cambridge, Mass.: The Belknap Press of Harvard University Press, 1990), p. 69.

7   Charles Dickens, *Great Expectations* ([1860–61]; Garden City, N.Y.: Nelson Doubleday, n.d.), p. 195.

8   [White, William Hale, pseudonym of] Mark Rutherford, *The Autobiography of Mark Rutherford, Dissenting Minister*, "edited by his friend Reuben Shapcott" (London: Trübner, 1881), pp. 250–51.

9   Cited by John Tosh, "New Man? The Bourgeois Cult of Home," in Gordon Marsden, ed., *Victorian Values: Personalities and Perspectives in Nineteenth-Century Society*, 2d ed. (London: Longman, 1998), pp. 78–87.

10   George and Weedon Grossmith, *The Diary of a Nobody* ([1892]; London, Folio Society, 1979), p. 13.

11 Cited in Elizabeth Wilson, *The Sphinx in the City: Urban Life, the Control of Disorder, and Women* (Berkeley: University of California Press, 1992), p. 52.

12 George Augustus Sala, *Gaslight and Daylight, with Some London Scenes They Shine Upon* (London: Chapman & Hall, 1859), p. 218.

13 Cited in Hall, "Sweet Delights of Home," p. 82.

14 Thorstein Veblen, *The Theory of the Leisure Class* ([1899]; Amherst, N.Y.: Prometheus Books, 1998), p. 112.

15 John Forster, *Life of Charles Dickens* (London: Chapman & Hall, 1874), vol. 3, pp. 473–74.

16 Cited in John R. Reed, *Victorian Conventions* (Athens, Ohio: Ohio University Press, 1975), pp. 226–27.

17 Charles Dickens, *The Mystery of Edwin Drood*, ed. Arthur J. Cox ([1870]; Harmondsworth: Penguin Books, 1985), p. 263.

18 Marianne Farningham, *Home Life* (London: James Clarke, 1889), pp. 10ff.

19 Sarah Stickney Ellis, *The Wives of England. Their Relative Duties, Domestic Influence, & Social Obligations* (London: Fisher, Son & Co., [1843]), p. 17.

20 George Gissing, *The Odd Women* ([1893]; London: Sidgwick & Jackson, 1915), p. 260.

21 Marion Jane Bradley, [c. 1854], Diary, British Library, Add MSS 3766 A–B.

22 George Gissing, *New Grub Street* ([1891]; Harmondsworth: Penguin Books, 1968), p. 156.

23 In particular John Tosh and Lieve Spaas have begun to map out this field; see the bibliography for their very useful works.

24 John Ruskin, "Of Queens' Gardens," in *Sesame and Lilies: Two Lectures* (London: Smith, Elder & Co., 1865), p. 149.

25 Sarah Stickney Ellis, *The Women of England: Their Social Duties and Domestic Habits*, 2d ed. (London: Fisher, Son & Co., [1839]), p. 26.

26 Gissing, *The Odd Women*, p. 313.

27 Arnold Bennett, *The Old Wives' Tale* ([1908]; Harmondsworth: Penguin Books, 1983), pp. 248–49.

28 Charles Dickens, *Bleak House*, ed. Norman Page ([1852–53]; Harmondsworth: Penguin Books, 1985), pp. 237–38.

29 Ibid., p. 249.

30 *Chambers Journal*, vol. 14, 1860, p. 307, cited in Sheila Sullivan, "Spectacular Failures: Thomas Hopley, Wilkie Collins, and the Reconstruction of Victorian Masculinity," in Martin Hewitt, ed., *An Age of Equipoise? Reassessing Mid-Victorian Britain* (Aldershot: Ashgate, 2000), pp. 84–108.

31 [Thomas Wright], *Some Habits and Customs of the Working Classes*, "by a Journeyman Engineer" (London: Tinsley Brothers, 1867), pp. 189–90.

32 Mrs. Henry Wood, *East Lynne*, ed. Andrew Maunder ([1861]; Peterborough, Ont.: Broadview Literary Texts, 2000), pp. 464–65.

33 [R. Kemp Philp], *The Practical Housewife, forming a complete Encyclopaedia of Domestic Economy*, by the editors of the "Family Friend" (London: Ward and Lock, 1855), p. 2.

34 Dickens, *Bleak House*, p. 908.

35 Christopher Dresser, *Studies in Design* (London: Cassell, Petter and Galpin, [1879]), p. 9.

36 Mrs. [Jane Ellen] Panton, *Homes of Taste: Economical Hints* (London: Sampson Low, Marston, Searle, & Rivington, 1890), p. 12.

37 J. A. Banks, "The Contagion of Numbers," in H. J. Dyos and Michael Wolff, eds., *The Victorian City: Images and Realities* (London: Routledge & Kegan Paul, 1973), pp. 105–22.

38 Hippolyte Taine, *Notes on England*, trans. W. F. Rae, 3d ed. (London: Strahan, 1872), p. 18.

39 Report of George Graham, the Registrar General, on the Census of 1851, pp. xxxv–xxxvi; Parliamentary Papers, 1852/3, vol. 85.

40 Sharon Marcus, *Apartment Stories: City and Home in Nineteenth-Century Paris and London* (Berkeley: University of California Press, 1999), p. 91.

41 Dickens, *Great Expectations*, p. 193–94.

42 See, for example, F. M. L. Thompson, *The Rise of Respectable Society: A Social History of Victorian Britain, 1830–1900* (Cambridge, Mass.: Harvard University Press, 1988), pp. 168–69.

43 Michael Anderson, "The Social Implications of Demographic Change," in F. M. L. Thompson, ed., *The Cambridge Social History of Britain, 1750–1950* (Cambridge: Cambridge University Press, 1990), vol. 2: *People and Their Environment*, pp. 1–70.

44 Cited in Leonore Davidoff, *The Best Circles: Society, Etiquette and the Season* (London: Croom Helm, 1973), p. 85.

45 *The Times*, 21 May 1923, p. 11; Mrs. Panton, *From Kitchen to Garret: Hints for Young Householders*, 4th ed. (London: Ward & Downey, 1888), pp. 30-31.

46 William Morris, *Collected Letters of William Morris*, ed. Norman Kelvin (Princeton, N.J.: Princeton University Press, 1984), 10 June 1890, vol. 3, p. 164.

47 Walter Scott, *Guy Mannering*, cited in Inga Bryden and Janet Floyd, eds., *Domestic Space: Reading the Nineteenth Century Interior* (Manchester: Manchester University Press, 1999), p. 13; Anthony Trollope, *The Last Chronicle of Barset* ([1866–67]; Oxford: Oxford World's Classics, 2001), p. 606.

48 Arthur Conan Doyle, *The Sign of the Four* ([1889]; New York: Quality Paperback Book Club, 1994), p. 18.

49 Anthony Trollope, *Framley Parsonage*, eds. David Skilton and Peter Miles ([1861]; Harmondsworth: Penguin Books, 1986), p. 73.

50 Cited in Donald Olsen, *The Growth of Victorian London* (London: Batsford, 1976), p. 188.

51 Zuzanna Shonfield, *The Precariously Privileged: A Professional Family in Victorian London* (Oxford: Oxford University Press, 1987), p. 9.

52 Peter Brimblecombe, *The Big Smoke: A History of Air Pollution in London since Medieval Times* (London: Methuen, 1987), p. 64.

53 Mrs. Panton, *From Kitchen to Garret*, p. 2.

54 Cited in Olsen, *Growth of Victorian London*, pp. 213 (Besant), 263, 23 (*The Builder*).

55 Anthony Trollope, *The Small House at Allington* ([1864]; Harmondsworth: Penguin Books, 1991), p. 436.

56 H. J. Dyos and D. A. Reeder, "Slums and Suburbs," in Dyos and Wolff, eds., *Victorian City*, pp. 359–86; Olsen, *Growth of Victorian London*, p. 241.

57 Derek Hudson, *Munby: Man of Two Worlds. The Life and Diaries of Arthur J. Munby, 1828–1910* (London: John Murray, 1972), 25 April 1860, p. 57.

58 Anthony Trollope, *Castle Richmond* (1860), cited by Julian Thompson in his edition of Trollope's *The Small House at Allington*, p. 687n.

59 George Augustus Sala, *Twice Round the Clock; or, the Hours of the Day and Night in London* (London: Houlston and Wright, 1859), pp. 50–52.

60 Robert Kerr, *The Gentleman's House; or, How to Plan English Residences, from the Parsonage to the Palace* (London: John Murray, 1864), p. 74.

61 Ibid., pp. 74–75.

62 Percival Gordon Smith and Keith Downes Young, "Architecture," in Shirley Forster Murphy, *Our Homes, and How to Make them Healthy* (London: Cassell, 1883), p. 39.

63 Beatrix Potter, *The Journal of Beatrix Potter, from 1881 to 1897*, transcribed from her code writing by Leslie Linder (London: Frederick Warne, 1966), 6 March 1883, p. 32.

64 Henry C. Burdett, "The Dwellings of the Middle Classes," in Transactions of the Sanitary Institute of Great Britain, 1883/4, pp. 237–41.

65 Alice James, *The Diary of Alice James*, ed. Leon Edel (Harmondsworth: Penguin Books,

1982), 17 June 1891, p. 215.

66 Stefan Muthesius, in his seminal *The English Terraced House* (London: Yale University Press, 1982), p. 7, noted in particular Newmarket Road, Norwich. I am indebted to his work for many of the ideas in this section.

67 Ibid., pp. 35, 32.

68 Sara Jeannette Duncan, *An American Girl in London* (London, Chatto & Windus, 1891), p. 33.

69 H. G. Wells, *Kipps: The Story of a Simple Soul*, ed. Peter Vansittart ([1905]; London: Everyman, J. M. Dent, 1993), p. 254.

70 Nathaniel Hawthorne, *The English Notebooks: 1853–1856* and *1856–1860*, ed. Thomas Woodson and Bill Ellis (Columbus, Ohio: Ohio State University Press, 1997), 10 September 1857, vol. 22, pp. 371–72.

CHAPTER 1. THE BEDROOM

1 This is a paraphrase by Donald Olsen, in *Growth of Victorian London*, p. 160.

2 Alice James, *Diary*, 17 June 1891, p. 213-14.

3 Shirley Nicholson, *A Victorian Household*, rev. ed. (Stroud: Sutton Publishing, 1994), pp. 65–67.

4 Mrs. [Mary] Haweis, *The Art of Housekeeping: A Bridal Garland* (London: Sampson Low, Marston, Searle, & Rivington, 1889), p. 55.

5 Anthony Trollope, *He Knew He Was Right*, ed. John Sutherland ([1869]; Oxford: Oxford World's Classics, 1998), p. 67.

6 Mrs. Panton, *From Kitchen to Garret*, p. 103.

7 Bennett, *The Old Wives' Tale*, p. 81.

8 Robert Edis, *Decoration & Furniture of Town Houses* (London: C. Kegan Paul, 1881), pp. 148ff.

9 Mrs. Haweis, *Art of Housekeeping*, p. 29.

10 Mrs. [Florence] Caddy, *Household Organisation* (London: Chapman & Hall, 1877), p. 163.

11 List from Nicholson, *A Victorian Household*, p. 25.

12 Mrs. Panton, *From Kitchen to Garret*, p. 116.

13 List from Nicholson, *A Victorian Household*, p. 25.

14 [Anon.], *Cassell's Household Guide: Being A Complete Encyclopaedia of Domestic and Social Economy . . .* (London: Cassell, Petter, and Galpin, 1869–71), vol. 1., pp. 183–84.

15 Mrs. Panton, *From Kitchen to Garret*, p. 112.

16 Ibid., p. 103.

17 Robert Brudnell Carter, "Lighting," in Murphy, *Our Homes*, p. 476.

18 Mrs. Panton, *From Kitchen to Garret*, p. 116; Murphy, *Our Homes*, p. 125.

19 Smith and Young, "Architecture," in Murphy, *Our Homes*, p. 86.

20 Carter, "Lighting," in Ibid., p. 398.

21 Mrs. Panton, *From Kitchen to Garret*, p. 119.

22 Robert James Mann, M.D., *Domestic Economy and Household Science . . .* (London: Edward Stanford, 1878), pp. 314–15.

23 Mrs. Haweis, *Art of Housekeeping*, p. 54.

24 *Cassell's Household Guide*, vol. 3, p. 29.

25 Caroline Davidson, *A Woman's Work Is Never Done* (London: Chatto & Windus, 1982), p. 130.

26 Mrs. Haweis, *Art of Housekeeping*, p. 40.

27 Cited in Irene and Alan Taylor, *The Assassin's Cloak: An Anthology of the World's Greatest*

Diarists (Edinburgh: Canongate Books, 2000), 14 March 1883, p. 144.

28 Jane Welsh Carlyle to Thomas Carlyle, *Letters and Memorials of Jane Welsh Carlyle*, ed. J. A. Froude (London: Longmans, Green, 1883), 18 August 1843, vol.1, pp. 241–42.

29 Ibid., 13 September 1852, vol. 2, p. 191.

30 Cited in Thea Holme, *The Carlyles at Home* (London: Oxford University Press, 1965), p. 121.

31 Phillis Browne, "House-Cleaning," in Murphy, *Our Homes*, p. 875.

32 My thanks to Lesley Hall and the contributors to the Victoria Mailbase for this information.

33 Ann Fraser Tytler, *Common Sense for Housemaids* (London, Hatchards, 1869), p. 13.

34 Mrs. Panton, *From Kitchen to Garret*, p. 108.

35 The figures in this paragraph and the footnote come from Charles Ansell, *On the Rate of Mortality at Early Periods of Life, the Age of Marriage, the Number of Children to a Marriage* . . . (London: National Life Assurance Society, Charles & Edwin Layton, 1874).

36 *A Few Suggestions to Mothers on the Management of Their Children* (London: J. & A. Churchill, 1884), p. vi, cited in Deborah Gorham, *The Victorian Girl and the Feminine Ideal* (London: Croom Helm, 1982), p. 81. I am indebted to Gorham's book for the idea framed in this paragraph.

37 Cited in Erna Olafson Hellerstein, Leslie Parker Hume, and Karen M. Offen, eds., *Victorian Women: A Documentary Account of Women's Lives in Nineteenth-Century England, France and the United States* (Brighton: Harvester Press, 1981), p. 227.

38 Patricia Branca, *Silent Sisterhood: Middle Class Women in the Victorian Home* (London: Croom Helm, 1975), pp. 82–84; Mrs. Panton, *From Kitchen to Garret*, p. 180.

39 Rudyard Kipling, "The Three Decker," in *Rudyard Kipling's Verse: Inclusive Edition, 1885–1932* (New York, Doubleday, Doran, 1938), p. 382.

40 Mrs. Panton, *From Kitchen to Garret*, p. 180.

41 Ursula Bloom, *Victorian Vinaigrette* (London: Hutchinson, 1956), p. 13. I am not entirely convinced by this book: she was born c. 1900, and so what she wrote had all been told to her by her mother and grandmother; her anecdotes reflect a preoccupation with twentieth-century pre-conceptions. I will therefore use examples from her work only when corroborating detail is available from more than one other source.

42 Cited in Antony and Peter Miall, *The Victorian Nursery Book* (London: J. M. Dent & Sons, 1980), pp. 17–19.

43 Queen Victoria, *Dearest Child: Letters Between Queen Victoria and the Princess Royal, 1858–61*, ed. Roger Fulford (London: Evans Bros., 1964), pp. 77–78.

44 Maud Berkeley, *Maud: The Diaries of Maud Berkeley*, adapted by Flora Fraser (London: Secker & Warburg, 1985), February 1898, p. 185.

45 Phyllis Cunnington and Catherine Lucas, *Costume for Births, Marriages and Deaths* (London: Adam & Charles Black, 1972), p. 17.

46 I am grateful to Jim Endersby for the information on Prince Albert.

47 Phyllis Rose, *Parallel Lives: Five Victorian Marriages* (London: Chatto and Windus, 1984), p. 149.

48 John Hawkins Miller, "'Temple and Sewer': Childbirth, Prudery and Victoria Regina," in Wohl, ed., *Victorian Family*, pp. 22–43.

49 Branca, *Silent Sisterhood*, pp. 78–80.

50 Ibid., pp. 85–87.

51 Dr. Charles Meigs, *Obstetrics: The Science and the Art* (Philadelphia, 1849), p. 318, cited by Miller, "Temple and Sewer," in Wohl, *Victorian Family*, p. 25. Although Dr. Meigs was American, the situation in Britain was not substantially different.

52 Charles Darwin, *The Correspondence of Charles Darwin, 1809–1882*, eds. Frederick

Burkhardt and Sydney Smith, 13+ vols. (Cambridge: Cambridge University Press, 1985–). Charles Darwin to Joseph Hooker, 3 February 1850, vol. 4, p. 311, 27 June 1854, vol. 5, p. 197, 1 August 1857, vol. 6, p. 438; Joseph Hooker to Charles Darwin, 29 June 1854, vol. 5, p. 199. My thanks to Jim Endersby for drawing this correspondence to my attention.

53 Mrs. Panton, *From Kitchen to Garret*, p. 180.

54 Edmund Gosse, *Father and Son*, ed. Peter Abbs ([1907]; Harmondsworth: Penguin Books, 1983), p. 39.

55 *Cassell's Household Guide*, vol. 1, p. 10.

56 Louise Creighton, *Memoir of a Victorian Woman: Reflections of Louise Creighton, 1850–1936*, ed. James Thayne Covert (Bloomington: Indiana University Press, 1994), p. 60.

57 Bloom, *Victorian Vinaigrette*, p. 14.

58 Patricia Jalland, *Death in the Victorian Family* (Oxford: Oxford University Press, 1996), pp. 46–47.

59 Branca, *Silent Sisterhood*, pp. 86–88.

60 Lorna Duffin, "The Conspicuous Consumptive: Woman as an Invalid," in Sara Delamont and Lorna Duffin, eds., *The Nineteenth-Century Woman: Her Cultural and Physical World* (London: Croom Helm, 1978), p. 35.

61 Branca, *Silent Sisterhood*, p. 86–88.

62 Mrs. Eliza Warren, *How I Managed My Children from Infancy to Marriage* (London: Houlston and Wright, 1865), p. 8.

63 Mrs. Panton, *From Kitchen to Garret*, pp. 180–91.

64 Mrs. [Isabella] Beeton, *Mrs Beeton's Book of Household Management*, ed. Nicola Humble ([1861]; Oxford: Oxford University Press, 2000), p. 488.

65 Ibid.

66 Ibid.

67 Mrs. Panton, *From Kitchen to Garret*, p. 163.

68 Patricia Branca, in *Silent Sisterhood*, thinks that the large number of articles advocating breastfeeding that appeared in journals aimed at a middle-class readership means that not many women were actually doing it. I am less certain: there are large numbers of articles in journals today advocating the same thing, aimed at the same middle-class readership, and yet this is the current trend in that socioeconomic group.

69 Mrs. Beeton, *Household Management*, p. 494.

70 Dr. Pye Chavasse, *Advice to a Mother on the Management of Her Offspring* (London: John Churchill, 1861), p. 30.

71 Mrs. Beeton, *Household Management*, p. 494.

72 Ibid., p. 498ff.

73 Chavasse, *Advice to a Mother*, pp. 14–16.

74 Mrs. Warren, *How I Managed My Children*, p. 9.

75 Houlston's Industrial Library, *The Nursery Maid: Her Duties, and How to Perform Them* (No. 27; London: Houlston and Sons, 1877), p. 15.

76 M. Vivian Hughes, *A London Home in the Nineties* (London: Oxford University Press, 1937), p. 208.

77 Dr. Bakewell, *Infant Mortality and Its Causes*, cited in Branca, *Silent Sisterhood*, pp. 100–104.

78 Chavasse, *Advice to a Mother*, p. 82–84.

79 Mrs. Frederick Pedley, *Infant Nursing and the Management of Young Children* (London: George Routledge and Sons, 1866), p. 42.

80 Chavasse, *Advice to a Mother*, p. 8; Mrs. Panton, *From Kitchen to Garret*, p. 185.

81 Mrs. Haweis, *Art of Housekeeping*, p. 50; Shonfield, *Precariously Privileged*, p. 72.

82 Cited in Cunnington and Lucas, *Costume for Births, Marriages and Deaths*, p. 38.

83 Chavasse, *Advice to a Mother*, p. 8.

84 Mrs. Pedley, *Infant Nursing*, p. 29; Rev. J. P. Faunthorpe, *Household Science: Readings in Necessary Knowledge for Girls and Young Women*, 5th ed. (London: Edward Stanford, 1889), p. 246.

85 Mrs. Panton, *From Kitchen to Garret*, p. 185.

86 William Squire, "The Nursery," in Murphy, *Our Homes*, p. 849.

CHAPTER 2. THE NURSERY

1 Davidoff and Hall, *Family Fortunes*, p. 375.

2 Kerr, *The Gentleman's House*, p. 144.

3 Squire, "The Nursery," in Murphy, *Our Homes*, pp. 860–62.

4 Ibid., p. 844.

5 Mrs. Panton, *From Kitchen to Garret*, pp. 164–74.

6 Hughes, *London Home in the Nineties*, p. 211.

7 Caroline Louisa Timings, *Letter from the Past: Memories of a Victorian Childhood* (privately published, 1954), p. 16.

8 Mrs. Panton, *From Kitchen to Garret*, pp. 164, 182, 124.

9 Caroline Clive, *From the Diary and Family Papers of Mrs Archer Clive, 1801–1873*, ed. Mary Clive (London: Bodley Head, 1949), 29 April 1842, 21 February 1842, p. 147.

10 Creighton, *Memoir*, pp. 57–58.

11 Bloom, *Victorian Vinaigrette*, p. 29.

12 Augustus Hare, *The Story of My Life* (London: George Allen, 1896–1900), vol. 1, p. 51.

13 Georgiana Burne-Jones, *Memorials of Edward Coley Burne-Jones* (London: Macmillan, 1904), vol. 1, pp. 230–31.

14 Samuel Butler, *The Way of All Flesh*, ed. James Cochrane ([1903, written 1873–80]; Harmondsworth: Penguin Books, 1986), p. 53.

15 Rev. T. V. Moore, "The Family as Government," in *The British Mothers' Journal*, May 1856, p. 99; cited in Branca, *Silent Sisterhood*, p. 109.

16 Frances Power Cobbe, *Duties of Women: A Course of Lectures* (London and Edinburgh: Williams & Norgate, 1881), p. 80.

17 Laura Forster, E. M. Forster Papers, King's College, Cambridge, Recollections, xxii/4, p. 74.

18 *Cassell's Household Guide*, vol. 1, p. 11.

19 Mrs. Warren, *How I Managed My Children*, pp. 33, 38; Marion Jane Bradley, Diary, British Library, Egerton 3766A, 3 November 1853.

20 Ibid., 30 April 1853.

21 Creighton, *Memoir*, pp. 11, 72.

22 Esther le Hardy, *The Home Nurse and Manual for the Sick-Room* (London: John Churchill, 1863), p. 174.

23 Adrian Forty, *Objects of Desire: Design and Society, 1750–1980* (London: Thames and Hudson, 1986), p. 68.

24 Creighton, *Memoir*, pp. 40, 4, 58.

25 Mrs. Warren, *How I Managed My Children*, pp. 41–42.

26 Mrs. Panton, *From Kitchen to Garret*, p. 115.

27 Gissing, *New Grub Street*, p. 157.

28 Wood, *East Lynne*, pp. 464–65.

29 Mrs. [Elizabeth] Gaskell, *Ruth*, ed. Alan Shelston ([1853]; Oxford: Oxford University Press, 1985), p. 266.

30 Marion Jane Bradley, Diary, British Library, Egerton 3766A, [?c.1891].

31 Timings, *Letter from the Past*, p. 17.

32 Mrs. [Elizabeth] Gaskell, *Private Voices: The Diaries of Elizabeth Gaskell and Sophia Holland*, ed. J. A. V. Chapple and Anita Wilson (Keele: Keele University Press, 1996), 10 March 1835, p. 52.

33 Ibid., p. 50.

34 Mrs. Gaskell to Anne Robson, *The Letters of Mrs Gaskell*, ed. J. A. V. Chapple and Arthur Pollard (Manchester: Manchester University Press, 1997), [1 September 1851], p. 159.

35 Jalland, *Death in the Victorian Family*, p. 5.

36 Thompson, *Rise of Respectable Society*, p. 115.

37 Gorham, *The Victorian Girl*, p. 15.

38 Mrs. Eliza Warren, *How I Managed My House on Two Hundred Pounds a Year* (London: Houlston and Wright, 1864), p. 15; Mrs. Beeton, *Household Management*, p. 487.

39 Dr. Pye Chavasse, *Advice to a Mother*, pp. 172–86.

40 Mrs. Gaskell, *Private Voices*, 8 April 1838, pp. 68–69.

41 Mrs. Pedley, *Infant Nursing*, pp. 52ff.

42 Mrs. Beeton, *Household Management*, pp. 501–5.

43 Mrs. Gaskell, *Private Voices*, 5 November 1836, p. 57.

44 Mrs. Beeton, *Household Management*, pp. 505–6.

45 Sally Mitchell, *Daily Life in Victorian England* (Westport, Conn.: Greenwood Press, 1996), p. 203.

46 Mrs. Pedley, *Infant Nursing*, p. 70.

47 Murphy, "Sickness in the House," in *Our Homes*, p. 901.

48 Creighton, *Memoir*, p. 87.

49 Hardy, *The Home Nurse*, p. 155–56.

50 Mrs. Beeton, *Household Management*, pp. 332–33.

51 Ibid., pp. 263, 265.

52 Mrs. Pedley, *Infant Nursing*, pp. 99ff.

53 Gwen Raverat, *Period Piece: A Cambridge Childhood* ([1952]; London: Faber and Faber, 1987), p. 53.

54 Creighton, *Memoir*, p. 1.

55 Compton Mackenzie, *My Life and Times: Octave One, 1883–1891* (London: Chatto & Windus, 1963), pp. 170–71.

56 Ibid., pp. 154–56.

57 Mrs. Gaskell to Anne Robson, *Letters*, 1 September 1851, p. 160.

58 Mrs. Gaskell, *Private Voices*, 5 November 1836, 14 October 1838, pp. 61, 69.

59 Marion Jane Bradley, Diary, British Library, Egerton 3766A, [October] 1854.

60 Mrs. Warren, *How I Managed My Children*, pp. 39–40.

61 Marion Jane Bradley, Diary, British Library, Egerton 3766A, 28 January 1853, March 1854, May 1854.

62 M. Vivian Hughes, *A London Girl of the Eighties* (London: Oxford University Press, 1936), pp. 47–50, 70.

63 Raverat, *Period Piece*, p. 62.

64 Charlotte M. Yonge, *The Daisy Chain, or, Aspirations: A Family Chronicle* ([1856]; London: Macmillan, 1886), p. 64.

65 Elizabeth Barrett Browning, *Aurora Leigh* (London: Chapman & Hall, 1857), I.403–14.

66 Eleanor Farjeon, *A Nursery in the Nineties* (London: Victor Gollancz, 1935), p. 381.

67 Creighton, *Memoir*, p. 15.

68 Cited on Lee Jackson's splendid web resource, www.victorianlondon.org/publications /improving.htm.

69 Christina Rieger, "'Sweet Order and Arrangement': Victorian Women Edit John Ruskin," *Journal of Victorian Culture*, vol. 6.2, Autumn 2001, pp. 231–49.

70 Creighton, *Memoir*, p. 28.

71 Anthony Trollope, *The Way We Live Now*, ed. Frank Kermode ([1875]; Harmondsworth: Penguin Books, 1994), p. 601.

72 Raverat, *Period Piece*, pp. 96–97.

73 Emily Faithfull, cited in E. Royston Pike, *Human Documents of the Victorian Golden Age, 1850–1875* (London: George Allen & Unwin, 1967), p. 200.

74 Ruskin, "Of Queens' Gardens," in *Sesame and Lilies*, pp. 135–37, 138–39, 148–49.

75 Gissing, *New Grub Street*, p. 70.

76 Gorham, *The Victorian Girl*, pp. 158, 161.

77 Hughes, *London Girl of the Eighties*, pp. 110, 210.

78 Florence Nightingale, "Cassandra," in Ray Strachey, *The Cause: A Short History of the Women's Movement in Great Britain* (London: Virago, 1978), pp. 406, 408.

79 Berkeley, *Maud*, February 1888, p. 21.

80 Sarah Stickney Ellis, *The Daughters of England: Their Position in Society, Character and Responsibilities* (London: Fisher, Son & Co., [1845]), pp. 90, 93.

81 Yonge, *The Daisy Chain*, pp. 177, 181–82, 413.

82 Cited in Hellerstein, Hume, and Offen, eds., *Victorian Women*, p. 69.

83 Cited in ibid., pp. 90, 94.

84 Shonfield, *Precariously Privileged*, pp. 65–68, 76–77.

85 Mrs. Pullan, *Maternal Counsels to a Daughter* (London: Darton, 1855), p. 81.

86 Mrs. Gaskell, *Private Voices*, p. 67.

87 Gissing, *The Odd Women*, p. 264.

88 Mrs. Panton, *From Kitchen to Garret*, p. 196.

89 *Our Mothers and Daughters* magazine, 182, again cited in Gorham, *The Victorian Girl*.

90 Hughes, *London Girl of the Eighties*, pp. 4, 1.

91 Anthony Trollope, *The Way We Live Now*, pp. 18-19.

92 Farjeon, *Nursery in the Nineties*, pp. 250–51.

93 Hughes, *London Girl of the Eighties*, pp. 3, 56.

94 Laura Forster, xxii/11–12, Reminiscences; xxii/4, pp. 160, E. M. Forster Papers, King's College, Cambridge.

95 Ibid., p. 187

96 Creighton, *Memoir*, p. 22.

97 Cited in Gorham, *The Victorian Girl*, p. 156.

98 Pamela Horn, *The Victorian Town Child* (Stroud: Sutton Publishing, 1997), p. 43.

99 Cited in Gorham, *The Victorian Girl*, p. 176.

100 Wichelo, Lily [Alice Clara Forster], Journal, E. M. Forster Papers, King's College, Cambridge, 30 July 1872.

CHAPTER 3. THE KITCHEN

1 Smith and Young, "Architecture," in Murphy, *Our Homes*, p. 147.

2 Charles Dickens, *The Old Curiosity Shop* ([1841]; Harmondsworth: Penguin Books, 1985), pp. 350–51.

3 Bennett, *The Old Wives' Tale*, pp. 68–69.

4   Arthur Munby, Diary, Trinity College Collection, vol. 7, October 1860, p. 79; cited in Leonore Davidoff and and Ruth Hawthorn, *A Day in the Life of a Victorian Domestic Servant* (London: George Allen & Unwin, 1976), p. 11.

5   Asa Briggs, *Victorian Things* (Harmondsworth: Penguin Books, 1990), p. 24.

6   Mrs. Panton, *Homes of Taste*, pp. 134–36, 138–39.

7   Dickens, *Great Expectations*, p. 196.

8   *The English Housekeeper, or, Manual of Domestic Management . . .*, 3d ed. (London, A. Cobbett, 1842), p. 76.

9   Mrs. Beeton, *Household Management*, p. 41.

10   E.g., Murphy, *Our Homes*, p. 72; Mrs. Panton, *From Kitchen to Garret*, pp. 12–13.

11   E.g., *The English Housekeeper*, p. 76.

12   Dr. John Simon, *City Medical Reports*, no. 2, 1850.

13   Arthur Conan Doyle, *A Study in Scarlet* ([1887]; New York: Quality Paperback Book Club, 1994), pp. 29–30.

14   Smith and Young, "Architecture," in Murphy, *Our Homes*, p. 129.

15   See Mrs. Quilp's "bower" in *The Old Curiosity Shop*, p. 74; Mrs. [Mary] Haweis, *The Art of Decoration* (London: Chatto & Windus, 1881), p. 45; Mrs. Panton, *From Kitchen to Garret*, p. 147.

16   Mrs. Panton, *From Kitchen to Garret*, pp. 53ff.

17   Holme, *Carlyles at Home*, pp. 147–50.

18   Kerr, *The Gentleman's House*, p. 113.

19   Douglas Galton, "Warming and Ventilation," in Murphy, *Our Homes*, p. 614.

20   C. J. Richardson, *The Englishman's House from a Cottage to a Mansion*, 2d ed. (London: John Camden Hotten, [1871]), pp. 404–5.

21   Muthesius, *The English Terraced House*, p. 49.

22   Mrs. Caddy, *Household Organization*, p. 49.

23   Cited in Briggs, *Victorian Things*, pp. 105–6.

24   Murphy, "Sickness in the House," in *Our Homes*, p. 897; Ross Murray, *The Modern Householder: A Manual of Domestic Economy in All Its Branches* (London: Frederick Warne, 1872), p. 664.

25   Cited in Nicholson, *A Victorian Household*, pp. 82–83.

26   Bennett, *The Old Wives' Tale*, p. 133.

27   Mrs. Panton, *From Kitchen to Garret*, pp. 40–41.

28   Creighton, *Memoir*, p. 11.

29   Murray, *The Modern Householder*, pp. 35–36.

30   Mrs. Haweis, *Art of Housekeeping*, pp. 36–37.

31   Ibid., p. 43.

32   Ibid., p. 40.

33   *Cassell's Household Guide*, vol. 3, pp. 17–19.

34   Potter, *Journal*, [summer 1886], p. 193.

35   George Godwin, *London Shadows: A Glance at the Homes of Thousands* (London: G. Routledge, 1854), p. 10.

36   Cited in Forty, *Objects of Desire*, pp. 108–9.

37   Grace Foakes, *My Part of the River*, cited in Janet Murray, *Strong-Minded Women and Other Lost Voices from Nineteenth-Century England* (Harmondsworth: Penguin Books, 1984), p. 179; my thanks to Hilary Mantel for information on Derbyshire customs, and Paul Bailey for London doorsteps, in the twentieth century.

38   Mrs. Haweis, *Art of Housekeeping*, p. 25.

39   Thomas Carlyle, *Reminiscences*, ed. J. A. Froude (New York: Charles Scribner's Sons, 1881), p. 346.

40 Gissing, *The Odd Women*, p. 260.

41 Charles Dickens, *Our Mutual Friend*, ed. Adrian Poole ([1864–65]; Harmondsworth: Penguin Books, 1997), pp. 281–82.

42 Mrs. Beeton, *Household Management*, p. 7.

43 Browne, "House-Cleaning," in Murphy, *Our Homes*, pp. 869–70.

44 Mrs. Haweis, *Art of Housekeeping*, p. 86–87.

45 Cited by Rieger, " 'Sweet Order and Arrangement,' " pp. 231–49.

46 *Paddington Times*, 1872, cited in Erika Diane Rappaport, *Shopping for Pleasure: Women in the Making of London's West End* (Princeton, N.J.: Princeton University Press, 2000), p. 40.

47 Houlston's Industrial Library, *The Lady's Maid: Her Duties, and How to Perform Them* (No. 22; London: Houlston and Sons, 1877), p. 23.

48 Nicholson, *A Victorian Household*, pp. 21–22.

49 Mrs. Panton, *From Kitchen to Garret*, pp. 12, 29.

50 *The English Housekeeper*, pp. 24–26.

51 Mrs. Haweis, *Art of Housekeeping*, pp. 101–6.

52 "Cre-fydd," *Cre-Fydd's Family Fare: The Young Housewife's Daily Assistant . . .* (London: Simpkin, Marshall, 1864), p. 316.

53 Murray, *The Modern Householder*, p. 37.

54 Mrs. Haweis, *Art of Housekeeping*, p. 95.

55 Raverat, *Period Piece*, p. 50.

56 Hannah Cullwick, *The Diaries of Hannah Cullwick, Victorian Maidservant*, ed. Liz Stanley (London: Virago, 1984), 22 March 1871, p. 158.

57 Elizabeth Grant, *The Highland Lady in Ireland: Journals, 1840–50*, ed. Patricia Pelly and Andrew Tod (Edinburgh: Canongate, 1991), 14 January 1840, p. 6.

58 Wilkie Collins, *Poor Miss Finch*, pp. 11, 65–66.

59 Mrs. [Elizabeth] Gaskell, *Cranford*, ed. Peter Keating ([1851–53]; Harmondsworth: Penguin Books, 1986), pp. 118, 185.

60 Mrs. Haweis, *Art of Housekeeping*, pp. 38–39.

61 Dickens, *Bleak House*, pp. 98–99.

62 Henry Mayhew, *Shops and Companies of London*, p. 17.

63 [Dr. Andrew Wynter], "The London Commissariat," in *The Quarterly Review*, vol. 95, no. 190, 1854, cited in Pike, *Human Documents*, pp. 58–59; Henry Mayhew et al., *London Characters and the Humorous Side of London Life*, 2d ed. (London: Stanley Rivers, 1881), p. 445.

64 [Wynter], "London Commissariat," cited in Pike, *Human Documents*.

65 Jane Brookfield, *Mrs Brookfield and Her Circle*, ed. Charles and Frances Brookfield (London, Sir Isaac Pitman and Sons, 1905), vol. 1, p. 214.

66 Quoted by Nicholson, *A Victorian Household*, p. 73.

67 The various methods of keeping food fresh in this paragraph and the one above come from: Mrs. Beeton, *Household Management*, pp. 236, 323, 324 (the source of the advice for keeping butter); Murray, *The Modern Householder*, p. 147; Faunthorpe, *Household Science*, p. 93–95; and [R. Kemp Philp], *The Lady's Every-Day Book: A Practical Guide in the Elegant Arts and Daily Difficulties of Domestic Life* (London, E. W. Allen, [c. 1873]), p. 174.

68 H. Seymour Tremenheere, Report addressed to H.M. Principal Secretary of state for the Home Department, relative to the Grievances complained of by the Journeymen Bakers, 1862; *Parliamentary Papers*, 1862, vol. 47.

69 [Wynter], "London Commissariat," in Pike, *Human Documents*.

70 Shirley Hibberd, *Water-Cresses without Sewage. Home Culture of the Water-Cress . . . For the Supply of the Household in all Seasons with Cresses of the Finest Quality, at a merely Nominal Cost of Money and Labour* (London: E. W. Allen, 1878).

71 Doyle, *A Study in Scarlet*, p. 37.

72 S. Stevens Hellyer, *The Plumber and Sanitary Houses: A Practical Treatise on the Principles of Internal Plumbing Work . . .* (London, T. B. Batsford, 1877), p. v.

73 Mrs. Haweis, *Art of Housekeeping*, p. 24.

74 Anne Hardy, "Parish Pump to Private Pipes: London's Water Supply in the Nineteenth Century," in W. F. Bynum and Roy Porter, eds., *Living and Dying in London* (Wellcome Medical History Supplement no. 11; London: Wellcome Institute, 1991), p. 79.

75 F. S. B. F. de Chaumont, Rogers Field, and J. Wallace Peggs, "Water," in Murphy, *Our Homes*, pp. 763–65.

76 Hardy, "Parish Pump to Private Pipes," in Bynum and Porter, eds., *Living and Dying in London*, p. 88.

CHAPTER 4. THE SCULLERY

1 Cited in Theresa M. McBride, *The Domestic Revolution: The Modernisation of Household Service in England and France, 1820–1920* (London: Croom Helm, 1976), p. 10.

2 Henry and Augustus Mayhew, *The Greatest Plague of Life* (London: David Bogue, 1847), p. 20.

3 Michael Anderson, ed., *British Population History from the Black Death to the Present Day* (Cambridge: Cambridge University Press, 1996), p. 5.

4 McBride, *Domestic Revolution*, p. 14.

5 Patricia Branca, "Image and Reality: The Myth of the Idle Victorian Woman," in Mary Hartman and Lois Banner, eds., *Clio's Consciousness Raised: New Perspectives on the History of Women* (New York: Harper Torchbooks, 1974), pp. 179–91.

6 Helen Corke, *In Our Infancy: An Autobiography. Part I: 1882–1912* (Cambridge: Cambridge University Press, 1975), p. 9.

7 Ford Madox Brown, *The Diary of Ford Madox Brown*, ed. Virginia Surtees (London, Yale University Press, 1981), p. xi.

8 Robert Edis, "Internal Decoration," in Murphy, *Our Homes*, p. 312.

9 Friedrich Engels, *The Condition of the Working-Class in England in 1844*, cited in *The Portable Victorian Reader*, ed. Gordon S. Haight (New York: Penguin Books, 1976), pp. 60–67.

10 Dickens, *Bleak House*, p. 181.

11 McBride, *Domestic Revolution*, pp. 74–75.

12 Holme, *Carlyles at Home*, p. 14.

13 Mary S. Hartman, *Victorian Murderesses* (London: Robson Books, 1977), p. 107.

14 Mrs. Haweis, *Art of Housekeeping*, p. 68.

15 Jane Welsh Carlyle to John A. Carlyle, 28 April 1850, in Thomas and Jane Welsh Carlyle, *The Collected Letters of Thomas and Jane Welsh Carlyle*, ed. Clyde de L. Ryals, Kenneth J. Fielding, et al. (Durham, N.C.: Duke University Press, 1970–), vol. 25, p. 74.

16 T. Henry Baylis, *The Rights, Duties and Relations of Domestic Servants, Their Masters and Mistresses . . .* (London: Sampson, Low, Son and Co., 1857; and 5th ed., 1896), p. 33.

17 Geraldine Jewsbury, *Selections from the Letters of Geraldine Endsor Jewsbury to Jane Welsh Carlyle*, ed. Mrs Alexander Ireland (London: Longmans, Green, 1892), [postmarked 20 April 1844], pp. 122–24.

18 Laura Forster, E. M. Forster Papers, King's College, Cambridge, xxii/11, pp. 184–85.

19 Houlston's Industrial Library, *The Nursery Maid*, pp. 73–74.

20 Hannah Cullwick, "Account of her own life during the last 6 years of her 30 years' servitude for hire," *Diaries*, p. 64.

21 Jessie Boucherett, "Legislative Restrictions on Woman's Labour," in *Englishwoman's Review*, 1873, cited in Pike, *Human Documents*, pp. 162–63.

22 George E. Arkell, in Charles Booth, *Life and Labour of the People of London*, 2d ser., vol. 3, "Industry" (London: Macmillan, 1892–97), pp. 68–70; Sala, *Twice Round the Clock*, pp. 55–56; Hannah Cullwick, *Diaries*, 25 December 1872, p. 261.

23 Davidoff and Hawthorn, *A Day in the Life*, p. 78.

24 Boucherett, "Legislative Restrictions," cited in Pike, *Human Documents*, pp. 162–63.

25 Henry Mayhew, "Letters to the Morning Chronicle," cited in *The Westminster Review*, vol. 53, 1850, p. 496.

26 E.g., McBride, *Domestic Revolution*, p. 99.

27 This is suggested by Nicola Humble, in her introduction and notes to Mrs. Beeton, *Household Management*, pp. xxi, 1001.

28 M. Taylor, cited in Davidoff, *The Best Circles*, p. 92.

29 Mrs. Beeton, *Household Management*, p. 446.

30 Galton, "Warming and Ventilation," in Murphy, *Our Homes*, p. 497.

31 [Philp], *The Lady's Every-Day Book*, p. 13.

32 Briggs, *Victorian Things*, p. 335.

33 *Cassell's Household Guide*, vol. 1, pp. 147–48.

34 Mrs. Beeton, *Household Management*, p. 452. Mrs. Eliza Warren, *Cookery for Maids of All Work* (London: Groombridge & Sons, 1856), pp. x–xiii.

35 "Cre-fydd," *Cre-Fydd's Family Fare*, p. 316.

36 Mrs. Gaskell to Marianne Gaskell, *Letters*, 2 March 1852, 25 September 1852, [?October 1852], p. 181.

37 Henry and Augustus Mayhew, *The Greatest Plague*, pp. 64–65.

38 Cullwick, *Diaries*, 14, 28, 31 July 1860, pp. 106–8.

39 Ibid., pp. 118–19.

40 Barry Reay, *Watching Hannah: Sexuality, Horror and Bodily De-formation in Victorian England* (London: Reaktion, 2002), p. 27.

41 Mrs. Panton, *From Kitchen to Garret*, pp. 151ff.

42 Mrs. Eliot James, *Our Servants, Their Duties to Us and Ours to Them* (London: Ward, Lock, 1883), pp. 170–74.

43 Hudson, *Munby: Man of Two Worlds*, p. 326.

44 Bloom, *Victorian Vinaigrette*, p. 15.

45 Henry and Augustus Mayhew, *The Greatest Plague*, p. 85.

46 Butler, *The Way of All Flesh*, p. 389.

47 Alison Adburgham, *Shops and Shopping, 1800-1914* (rev. ed.; London, George Allen and Unwin, 1981), pp. 194–95.

48 McBride, *Domestic Revolution*, p. 25.

49 Cullwick, *Diaries*, 17 December 1871, p. 183.

50 Wood, *East Lynne*, p. 204.

51 Jane Welsh Carlyle to Helen Welsh, *Collected Letters*, vol. 27, [?6 May 1852], p. 106.

52 Geraldine Jewsbury to Jane Welsh Carlyle, *Letters to Jane Carlyle*, 3 August 1852, pp. 441–42.

53 Mary Elizabeth Braddon, *Aurora Floyd* ([1863]; Oxford: Oxford World's Classics, 1996), pp. 177–78.

54 Cullwick, *Diaries*, 25 December 1871, p. 183.

55 Anne Brontë, *The Tenant of Wildfell Hall* ([1848]; Harmondsworth: Penguin, 1985), p. 36.

56 Dickens, *Great Expectations*, p. 184.

57 Mrs. Haweis, *Art of Housekeeping*, pp. 38–39.

58   Charles Dickens, *David Copperfield*, pp. 650–51.

59   Geraldine Jewsbury, *Letters to Jane Carlyle*, [postmarked 28 December 1849], p. 327.

60   Mrs. Eliza Warren, *Comfort for Small Incomes* (London: At the Office of "The Ladies' Treasury," 1866), pp. 18–20.

61   Mrs. Haweis, *Art of Housekeeping*, p. 114.

62   Ibid., p. 111.

63   R. Hall Bakewell, *Practical Hints on the Management of the Sick-Room* (London: John Snow, 1857), p. 45.

64   Adburgham, *Shops and Shopping*, p. 154.

65   Tytler, *Common Sense for Housemaids*, p. 13.

66   Cullwick, *Diaries*, 6 February 1872, p. 195.

67   Murray, *The Modern Householder*, p. 411; *Cassell's Household Guide*, vol. 1, pp. 38–39.

68   Rosalind Pritchard, ed., *London and Londoners, 1898* (London: Scientific Press, 1898), pp. 294–97.

69   Quoted in its entirety by Henry Mayhew in *The Shops and Companies of London* (London: Strand, 1865), p. 199.

70   For the information on Lever, see Forty, *Objects of Desire*, pp. 76–78; on Pears, see Lori Anne Loeb, *Consuming Angels: Advertising and Victorian Women* (New York: Oxford University Press, 1994), p. viii.

71   Gissing, *New Grub Street*, p. 279.

72   Iona and Peter Opie, *The Oxford Dictionary of Nursery Rhymes* (Oxford: Oxford University Press, 1952), p. 3, cited by Leonore Davidoff, "The Rationalisation of Housework," in Sheila Allen and Diana Leonard Barker, eds., *Dependence and Exploitation in Work and Marriage* (London: Longmans, 1976), p. 144.

73   Alfred Rosling Bennett, *London and Londoners in the Eighteen-Fifties and Sixties* (London: T. Fisher Unwin, 1924), pp. 28–29.

74   D. H. Lawrence, *The Rainbow* (London: Methuen, 1915), p. 53.

75   The laundry process described in the previous seven paragraphs has been compiled from a number of primary and secondary sources, including: Mrs. Beeton, *Household Management*, pp. 457–60; Faunthorpe, *Household Science*, pp. 330–39; Murray, *The Modern Householder*, pp. 413–15; *Cassell's Household Guide*, vol. 1, pp. 38–40; Mrs. Haweis, *Art of Housekeeping*, pp. 111–14; Davidson, *A Woman's Work is Never Done*, pp. 159–60; Patricia E. Malcolmson, *English Laundresses: A Social History, 1850–1930* (Urbana: University of Illinois Press, 1986), pp. 26–33; and Christina Walkley and Vanda Foster, *Crinolines and Crimping Irons: Victorian Clothes: How They Were Cleaned and Cared For* (London, Peter Owen, 1978), pp. 31–33, 50–52.

76   Hannah Cullwick, *Diaries*, 26 May 1871, p. 167.

77   Foakes, *My Part of the River*, cited in Murray, ed., *Strong-Minded Women*, pp. 177–78.

78   Elizabeth Wilson, *The Sphinx in the City*, p. 42.

79   Walkley and Foster, *Crinolines and Crimping Irons*, pp. 64, 32.

80   Ibid., p. 64–66; Dickens, *The Old Curiosity Shop*, p. 133.

81   Faunthorpe, *Household Science*, p. 335; Ernest H. Shepard, *Drawn from Memory* (London: Methuen, 1957), p. 28.

CHAPTER 5. THE DRAWING ROOM

1   Ellis, *Wives of England*, p. 219.

2   Mrs. Panton, *Homes of Taste*, p. 21.

3   Gissing, *New Grub Street*, p. 94.

4   *Building News*, vol. 32, no. 484, cited in Peter Gay, *Schnitzler's Century: The Making of Middle-Class Culture, 1815–1914* (New York: W. W. Norton, 2002), p. 271.

5   "MBH," *Home Truths for Home Peace, or, "Muddle" Defeated* (London: Effingham Wilson, 1851), p. 56.

6   Raverat, *Period Piece*, p. 177; Dickens, *Our Mutual Friend*.

7   J. H. Walsh, *A Manual of Domestic Economy* (London: G. Routledge, 1857). I am indebted to J. A. Banks for his analysis of these figures in *Prosperity and Parenthood: A Study of Family Planning among the Victorian Middle Classes* ([1954]; London: Gregg Revivals, 1993), pp. 49-50.

8   Berkeley, *Maud*, July 1894, p. 150.

9   John Gloag, *Victorian Comfort: A Social History of Design from 1830–1900* (London: Adam and Charles Black, 1961), p. 60.

10   Raverat, *Period Piece*, pp. 180–81.

11   Dickens, *Bleak House*, p. 296.

12   Mrs. Panton, *From Kitchen to Garret*, cited in Briggs, *Victorian Things*, p. 244.

13   Raverat, *Period Piece*, p. 126.

14   Rhoda and Agnes Garrett, *Suggestions for House Decoration in Painting, Woodwork, and Furniture* (London: Macmillan, 1876), p. 25.

15   See Owen Knowles, "Veneering and the Age of Veneer: A Source and Background for *Our Mutual Friend*," *The Dickensian*, vol. 81, no. 2, Summer 1985, pp. 88–96; Edis, "Internal Decoration," in Murphy, *Our Homes*, pp. 313, 319, 356.

16   Mrs. Panton, *From Kitchen to Garret*, p. 48.

17   George and Weedon Grossmith, *Diary of a Nobody*, p. 57.

18   [Philp], *Lady's Every-Day Book*, p. 6.

19   *Cassell's Household Guide*, vol. 1, pp. 18–19.

20   Mrs. Panton, *From Kitchen to Garret*, p. 86.

21   Charlotte Brontë, *Jane Eyre* ([1847]; [London]: Everyman Library, 1991), pp. 131–32.

22   Arnold Bennett, *Anna of the Five Towns* ([1902]; Harmondsworth: Penguin Books, 2001), p. 39.

23   Duncan, *An American Girl in London*, p. 53.

24   Wells, *Tono-Bungay*, p. 36.

25   George and Weedon Grossmith, *Diary of a Nobody*, p. 14; the Rev. H. R. Haweis, cited in Briggs, *Victorian Things*, p. 248.

26   Mrs. Panton, *From Kitchen to Garret*, p. 86.

27   Mrs. Panton, *Homes of Taste*, pp. 76–77.

28   Wilkie Collins, *Basil* ([1852]; London: Chatto & Windus, 1890), p. 61.

29   Ibid., pp. 31–32.

30   [Frances Mary Sibthorpe], *Home Is Home: A Domestic Tale* (London: William Pickering, 1851), p. 5.

31   Dickens, *Our Mutual Friend*, pp. 118, 128.

32   Cited in Susan Casteras, *Images of Victorian Womanhood in English Art* (Cranbury, N.J., and London: Associated University Presses, 1987), p. 140.

33   Edis, *Decoration & Furniture of Town Houses*, pp. 17–20.

34   Creighton, *Memoir*, pp. 34–35.

35   John Fleming and Hugh Honour, *The Penguin Dictionary of Decorative Arts*, 2d ed. (Harmondsworth: Viking, 1989), "Lincrusta."

36   Mackenzie, *My Life and Times*, Octavo I, p. 232.

37   Cited in Gloag, *Victorian Comfort*, p. 72.

38 Alfred Rosling Bennett, *London and Londoners*, pp. 145–47.

39 Mrs. Panton, *From Kitchen to Garret*, p. 78ff.

40 Raverat, *Period Piece*, p. 194.

41 Dickens, *Our Mutual Friend*, p. 135.

42 Trollope, *Last Chronicle of Barset*, p. 246.

43 Mrs. Haweis, *Art of Decoration*, pp. 353–54.

44 Mrs. Haweis cited in Thad Logan, *The Victorian Parlour* (Cambridge: Cambridge University Press, 2001), pp. 7–8; Mrs. Caddy cited in Briggs, *Victorian Things*, pp. 243–44; Mrs. [Lucy] Orrinsmith, *The Drawing Room, Its Decoration and Furniture* (London: Macmillan, 1877), pp. 5, 132–33.

45 Gerald Viewing, *Exchange and Mart: Selected Issues, 1868–1948*, intro. by John Mendes (Newton Abbot: David and Charles, 1970), p. 1.

46 Nicholson, *A Victorian Household*, pp. 59, 53.

47 Mrs. Panton, *From Kitchen to Garret*, p. 198.

48 Raverat, *Period Piece*, p. 102.

49 Creighton, *Memoir*, p. 8.

50 Percy Cruikshank, *Sunday Scenes in London and Its Suburbs* (London, published by the artist, 1854), pp. 29–38.

51 M. Vivian Hughes, *A London Child of the Seventies* (London: Oxford University Press, 1934), pp. 80–91; Mrs. Gaskell to Catherine Winkworth, *Letters*, 29 November 1848, pp. 63–64.

52 John Ruskin, *Praeterita: Outlines of Scenes and Thoughts Perhaps Worthy of Memory in My Past Life*, 3 vols. (Orpington and London: George Allen, 1899), vol. 2, p. 162. My thanks to Bob Davenport for bringing this passage to my attention.

53 Edmund Gosse, *Father and Son*, pp. 194–95.

54 Taine, *Notes on England*, p. 9.

55 Laura Forster, Reminiscences (1911), xxii/12, in E. M. Forster Papers, King's College, Cambridge.

56 Trollope, *Last Chronicle of Barset*, p. 788.

57 Cited in Corke, *In Our Infancy*, p. 12.

58 John Ruskin, *Praeterita*, vol. 1, p. 97. Again I am indebted to Bob Davenport for this quotation.

59 Laura Forster, Reminiscences, xxii/11, p. 72, in E. M. Forster Papers, King's College, Cambridge.

60 The soldiers and horse belonged to Ernest Shepard, *Drawn from Memory*, pp. 30–31; Raverat, *Period Piece*, p. 66; the Sambourne children, Nicholson, *A Victorian Household*, pp. 39–40, 43.

61 Mrs. Panton, *From Kitchen to Garret*, p. 85.

62 Michael Darby, *Stevengraphs* (St. Peter Port, Guernsey: A. Sprake & M. Darby, 1968).

63 Logan, *The Victorian Parlour*, p. 110.

64 Cited in Murphy, *Our Homes*, pp. 325–26.

65 Ibid., pp. 123–24.

66 Ibid., p. 367.

67 *The Times*, 21 October 1862, cited in Ralph Colp, Jr., *To Be an Invalid: The Illness of Charles Darwin* (Chicago: University of Chicago Press, 1977), p. 165; Mrs. Ada S. Ballin, *Personal Hygiene* (London: F. J. Rebman, 1894), p. 122.

68 Carter, "Lighting," in Murphy, *Our Homes*, p. 390. He was very fond of this subject, and returns to it again on pp. 397–98.

69 *Cassell's Household Guide*, vol. 1, pp. 92–93; vol. 2, pp. 204–6, 247–51; vol. 3, p. 118; vol. 4, p. 184, and passim; *The Young Ladies' Treasure Book. A complete cyclopaedia of practical instruction . . . for all indoor and outdoor occupations* (London, Ward, Lock & Co., [1884]), p. 47.

70 Mrs. Panton, *From Kitchen to Garret*, pp. 91ff.

71 Bennett, *The Old Wives' Tale*, pp. 64–65.

72 Shonfield, *Precariously Privileged*, pp. 86–87.

73 Mrs. Beeton, *Household Management*, pp. 443–44.

74 Mrs. Panton, *From Kitchen to Garret*, p. 68.

75 For the pasteboard watch case, see Yonge, *The Daisy Chain*, p. 370; the White Rabbit is in Lewis Carroll, *Alice's Adventures in Wonderland and What She Found There* ([1865]; New York: Heritage Reprints, 1941).

76 Cited in Lawrence Wright, *Home Fires Burning: The History of Domestic Heating and Cooking* (London: Routledge & Kegan Paul, 1964), p. 145.

77 All these are in *Cassell's Household Guide*, vol. 3, p. 13, but throughout the four volumes are many more fancywork suggestions.

78 Berkeley, *Maud*, December 1888, p. 42.

79 This insight comes from Leonore Davidoff, "The Rationalisation of Housework," in Sheila Allen and Diana Leonard Barker, eds., *Dependence and Exploitation*, pp. 121–51.

80 Berkeley, *Maud*, December 1888, December 1890, p. 101.

81 *Cassell's Household Guide*, vol. 1, pp. 129–30.

82 [Dinah Mulock Craik], *A Woman's Thoughts about Women* (London: Hurst and Blackett, 1858), pp. 5–8.

83 Bloom, *Victorian Vinaigrette*, p. 17.

84 Charles Dickens, *Dombey and Son*, ed. Peter Fairclough ([1848]; Harmondsworth: Penguin Books, 1985), p. 57.

85 E. F. Benson, *As We Were, A Victorian Peepshow* (London: Longmans, Green, 1930), cited in Logan, *The Victorian Parlour*, p. 10.

86 Jane Welsh Carlyle to Helen Welsh, *Collected Letters*, [?12/3/53], vol. 28, pp. 70–71.

87 Cited on www.victorianlondon.org/houses/ferns.htm.

88 A modern book on Victorian fern collecting is David Elliston Allen's *The Victorian Fern Craze: A History of Pteridomania* (London: Hutchinson, 1969). I have also used for this paragraph Shirley Hibberd, *Rustic Adornments for Homes of Taste* (London: Groombridge and Sons, 1857), from which the quotations are taken (pp. 60 and iii–iv); his *The Fern Garden: How to Make, Keep, and Enjoy It* (London: Groombridge and Sons, 1869); and [Harriet Martineau], *Life in the Sick-Room* (London: Edward Moxon, 1844).

89 Shirley Hibberd, *The Book of the Aquarium* (London: Groombridge and Sons, 1860), p. 2.

90 My thanks to Jim Endersby for drawing this inference.

91 Ann Thwaite, *Glimpses of the Wonderful: The Life of Philip Henry Gosse, 1810–1888* (London: Faber & Faber, 2002), p. 171.

92 *Cassell's Household Guide*, vol. 1, p. 17.

93 Ibid.; Henry D. Butler, *The Family Aquarium or Aqua-Vivarium* (New York: Dick and Fitzgerald, 1858), pp. 30–31; Hibberd, *Book of the Aquarium*, pp. 28–30.

94 Viewing, *Exchange and Mart*, p. 1.

95 [Philp], *Lady's Every-Day Book*, p. 17; Advertisement in "Espoir," *How to Live on a Hundred a Year, Make a Good Appearance, and Save Money* (London: Ward, Lock, and Tyler, [1874]), endpaper.

96 Carter, "Lighting," in Murphy, *Our Homes*, p. 418.

97 Most of the history of the development of the gas industry in this paragraph, and the two paragraphs on theaters and the Argand lamp, are taken from Wolfgang Schivelbusch's extraordinary work, *Disenchanted Night: The Industrialisation of Light in the Nineteenth Century*, trans. Angela Davies (Oxford: Berg, 1988), except where otherwise indicated. The information in this paragraph is to be found on pp. 25, 31–32; on theaters, pp. 45–46; the Argand lamp on pp. 10–13,

167–68. It is Schivelbusch (or his translator) who uses the word "Germany" for this decade before the unification of the German states; I have followed his example. The population comparison can therefore only be approximate: if the areas of Prussia not included in the German Confederation are taken into account, the figure rises to just over 52 million. (Thomas Nipperdey, *Germany: From Napoleon to Bismarck, 1800–1866*, trans. Daniel Nolan [Dublin: Gill and Macmillan, 1996], pp. 86–87.)

98 Charles Manby Smith, *The Little World of London* (1857), cited in Andrew H. Miller, *Novels Behind Glass: Commodity Culture and Victorian Narrative* (Cambridge: Cambridge University Press, 1995), p. 4.

99 The information on Swan lamps (in both the text and the footnote) is from Maureen Dillon, "'Like a Glow-worm who had lost its Glow': The Invention of the Incandescent Electric Lamp and the Development of Artificial Silk and Electric Jewellery," *Costume*, vol. 35, 2001, pp. 76–81.

100 Pritchard, *London and Londoners*, p. 22.

101 G. A. Sala, *Gaslight and Daylight*, p. 159.

102 Schivelbusch, *Disenchanted Night*, pp. 87ff.

103 Carter, "Lighting," in Murphy, *Our Homes*, pp. 426, 452.

104 Bennett, *The Old Wives' Tale*, p. 130; Murphy, *Our Homes*, p. 595.

105 Mrs. Panton, *From Kitchen to Garret*, pp. 53ff.

106 Carter, "Lighting," in Murphy, *Our Homes*, p. 436.

107 Adburgham, *Shops and Shopping*, p. 96.

108 George and Weedon Grossmith, *Diary of a Nobody*, p. 128.

109 Muthesius, *The English Terraced House*, p. 51; Mann, *Domestic Economy and Household Science*, p. 343.

110 Sarah Milan, "Refracting the Gaselier: Understanding Victorian Responses to Domestic Gas Lighting," in Bryden and Floyd, eds., *Domestic Space*, pp. 84–102.

111 Anthony Trollope, *Barchester Towers*, ed. Robin Gilmour ([1857]; Harmondsworth: Penguin Books, 1994), p. 78.

112 Carter, "Lighting," in Murphy, *Our Homes*, pp. 435, 420–21, 427, 443.

113 Murray, *The Modern Householder*, p. 39; Smith and Young, "Architecture," in Murphy, *Our Homes*, p. 75.

114 Mrs. Haweis, *Art of Housekeeping*, pp. 98–101.

115 Murray, *The Modern Householder*, p. 39.

116 [Philp], *Lady's Every-Day Book*, pp. 86–87.

117 Carter, "Lighting," in Murphy, *Our Homes*, pp. 442, 467.

118 Cited in Kate Flint, *The Victorians and the Visual Imagination* (Cambridge: Cambridge University Press, 2000), p. 239.

119 Schivelbush, *Disenchanted Night*, p. 40.

120 Mrs. Orrinsmith, *The Drawing-Room*, p. 64, cited in Schivelbush, *Disenchanted Night*, p. 185.

121 Cited in Milan, "Refracting the Gaselier," in op. cit., pp. 84–102.

122 Charlotte Brontë, *Jane Eyre*, pp. 200–201.

123 Mrs. Warren, *How I Managed My Children*, p. 55.

124 Mrs. Haweis, *Art of Housekeeping*, p. 34; Mrs. Panton, *From Kitchen to Garret*, p. 21; "MBH," *Home Truths for Home Peace*, p. 67.

125 [Dinah Mulock Craik], *Olive* ([1850]; London: Macmillan, 1893), p. 37; Gissing, *The Odd Women*, pp. 106–7.

126 Mrs. Warren, *A Young Wife's Perplexities* (London: Houlston and Sons, 1886), p. 35.

127 Mrs. Gaskell to Anne Robson, *Letters*, 23 December 1841, p. 45.

CHAPTER 6. THE PARLOR

1   Amy Levy, *Reuben Sachs* ([1888]; London: Persephone Books, 2001), p. 19.

2   Samuel Butler, *The Way of All Flesh*, p. 74.

3   Anderson, "Social Implications of Demographic Change," in Thompson, ed., *Cambridge Social History of Britain*, vol. 2, pp. 1–70.

4   William Rathbone Greg, "Why Are Women Redundant" (1862), cited in Murray, *Strong-Minded Women*, p. 51.

5   Mary Taylor, "The First Duty of Women," in *The Victorian Magazine*, June 1870, cited in ibid.

6   Cited in Casteras, *Images of Victorian Womanhood*, p. 77.

7   Bennett, *The Old Wives' Tale*, pp. 80–81.

8   [Craik], *A Woman's Thoughts about Women*, pp. 14–15, 19.

9   Yonge, *The Daisy Chain*, p. 657.

10 Shonfield, *Precariously Privileged*, pp. vi–vii.

11 Potter, *Journals*, 6 November 1895, pp. 398–99.

12 Ibid., 7 September 1895, pp. 149–50.

13 Berkeley, *Maud*, September 1891, p. 118.

14 Robert Browning, "Pippa Passes," Introduction, 11. 163–64, *Poetical Works, 1833–1864*, ed. Ian Jack (Oxford: Oxford University Press, 1970), p. 319.

15 Laura Forster, Reminiscences (1909), xxii/11, pp. 24–26, 110–11, in E. M. Forster Papers, King's College, Cambridge.

16 Gissing, *The Odd Women*, p. 228.

17 Ellis, *Daughters of England*, p. 392.

18 [Anon.], *Etiquette of Love* (Halifax: William Milner, 1849), pp. 28–31; "Shreds and Patches: Flirts and Flirtation," in *The Englishwoman*, June 1835, p. 456. Both cited in Casteras, *Images of Victorian Womanhood*, pp. 85–86.

19 Cited in Murray, *Strong-Minded Women*, pp. 109–10.

20 Trollope, *Small House at Allington*, p. 59.

21 Levy, *Reuben Sachs*, p. 127.

22 Mrs. Gaskell, *Ruth*, p. 216.

23 Dickens, *Bleak House*, p. 593.

24 Cited in Reed, *Victorian Conventions*, pp. 109–10.

25 Gissing, *The Odd Women*, pp. 156–57.

26 Shonfield, *Precariously Privileged*, pp. 21–24, for both the story and its interpretation.

27 Ibid., pp. 53–60.

28 The routine outlined in this paragraph and the next two, and the quotations (except as indicated otherwise), come from [Anon.], *Etiquette of Courtship and Matrimony* (London: Routledge, Warne, and Routledge, [c.1865]), pp. 8–9. Many other books give a formula so similar that a comparison appears unnecessary.

29 Creighton, *Memoir*, p. 39.

30 Yonge, *The Daisy Chain*, pp. 391–92.

31 Dickens, *Bleak House*, p. 175.

32 Mrs. Panton, *From Kitchen to Garret*, pp. 3, 19.

33 S. W. Partridge, *Upward and Onward: A Thought Book for the Threshold of Active Life* (1851), cited in Briggs, *Victorian Things*, p. 215.

34 Shonfield, *Precariously Privileged*, p. 195.

35 Rose, *Parallel Lives*, p. 52.

36 Sarah Thomas, *The Secret Diary of Sarah Thomas, 1860–1865*, ed. June Lewis (Moreton-in-the-Marsh: Windrush Press, 1994), 30 October 1860, p. 56.

37 Mrs. Gaskell to Anne Robson, *Letters*, 1 Sepember 1851, p. 160.

38 Samuel Butler, *The Way of All Flesh*, p. 79.

39 Wood, *East Lynne*, p. 372.

40 Gissing, *New Grub Street*, pp. 37, 80, 229, 262.

41 I am grateful to Malcolm Shifrin, Eileen Curran, Terry Meyers, and Miriam Elizabeth Burstein of the Victoria Mailbase, and the research desk of the Fawcett Library, for both positive and negative sightings of this elusive character.

42 [Ann Richelieu Lamb], *Can Women Regenerate Society?* (London: John W. Parker, 1844), p. 123.

43 *Punch*, 1859, cited on www.victorianlondon.org/women/wives.htm.

44 Murray, *Strong-Minded Women*, p. 118; Erna Reiss, *Rights and Duties of Englishwomen: A Study in Law and Public Opinion* (Manchester: Sherratt & Hughes, 1934), passim.

45 Susan Casteras, *Images of Victorian Womanhood*, pp. 101–2, notes the number of pictures, suggesting that they represent middle-class practice. It seems to me that the aspirational nature of many books and magazines may have created a false impression, and in actuality this very expensive ritual was confined to the very top end of the middle classes and upward.

46 Trollope, *Small House at Allington*, p. 493.

47 Cited in Adburgham, *Shops and Shopping*, pp. 130–33.

48 Thomas, *Secret Diary*, 18 August 1862, p. 140.

49 Creighton, *Memoir*, p. 44.

50 [Anon.], *The Etiquette of Courtship and Marriage* (London: Frederick Warne, [1866]), p. 57–58.

51 Ann Monsarrat, *And the Bride Wore . . . The Story of the White Wedding* (London: Gentry Books, 1973), p. 143.

52 Cunnington and Lucas, *Costume for Births, Marriages and Deaths*, pp. 280–81.

53 William Thackeray, *Vanity Fair*, ed. J. I. M. Stewart ([1847–48], Harmondsworth: Penguin Books, 1985), pp. 259–60.

54 Rev. Benjamin John Armstrong, *Armstrong's Norfolk Diary*, ed. Herbert B. J. Armstrong (London: Hodder and Stoughton, 1963), 7 February 1854, p. 46.

55 Apart from the quotations separately noted, these three paragraphs are compiled from information in: *Etiquette of Courtship and Marriage*; Cunnington and Lucas, *Costume for Births, Marriages and Deaths*; Monsarrat, *And the Bride Wore . . .*; Avril Lansdell, *Wedding Fashions, 1860–1980* (Princes Risborough: Shire Publications, 1983).

56 Cunnington and Lucas, *Costume for Births, Marriages and Deaths*, p. 116.

57 Ann Buck, "The Trap Re-baited: Mourning Dress 1860–90," in *High Victorian: Proceedings of the Second Annual Conference of the Costume Society* (London: Victoria and Albert Publications, 1968), p. 34.

58 Cunnington and Lucas, *Costume for Births, Marriages and Deaths*, p. 109, including the citation from the *Minister's Gazette of Fashion*.

59 Creighton, *Memoir*, p. 20.

60 Henry and Augustus Mayhew, *The Greatest Plague of Life*, pp. 22–23.

61 Monsarrat, *And the Bride Wore . . .*, pp. 129, 131.

62 *Etiquette of Courtship and Marriage*, pp. 43–45, 66–68; "A Member of the Aristocracy," *Manners and Rules of Good Society* (London: Frederick Warne, 1887), pp. 123–38; [W. T. Marchant], *Betrothals and Bridals: With a Chat About Wedding Cakes and Wedding Customs* (London: W. Hill & Son, 1879), p. 105.

63 Murray, *The Modern Householder*, p. 343.

64 Casteras, *Images of Victorian Womanhood*, pp. 101–2.

65 "A Member of the Aristocracy," *Manners and Rules of Good Society*, p. 138.

66 Henry and Augustus Mayhew, *The Greatest Plague*, p. 24.

67 *Etiquette of Courtship and Marriage*, pp. 84–87.

68 David I. Kertzer, "Living with Kin," in David I. Kertzer and Marzio Barbagli, *The History of the European Family* (London: Yale University Press, 2002), vol. 2, pp. 40–72.

69 Rose, *Parallel Lives*, p. 149.

70 Berkeley, *Maud*, March 1889, p. 51.

71 Dickens, *Our Mutual Friend*, pp. 666.

72 *Cassell's Household Guide*, vol. 1, p. 312.

73 Creighton, *Memoir*, p. 48.

74 Cited in Nicholson, *A Victorian Household*, pp. 65–67, 68, 129.

75 Creighton, *Memoir*, pp. 6, 28.

76 Raverat, *Period Piece*, p. 77.

77 Ibid., p. 148.

78 Mrs. Beeton, *Household Management*, pp. 15–16.

79 Nicola Humble, in her introduction to Mrs. Beeton, *Household Management*, pp. xxvi–xxvii.

80 Mrs. Gaskell to Catherine Winkworth, *Letters*, 11 November 1848, p. 62.

81 Charlotte Brontë, *Jane Eyre*, p. 202.

82 Holme, *Carlyles at Home*, pp. 18–19.

83 Jane Welsh Carlyle to Thomas Carlyle, *Collected Letters*, 10 August 1850, vol. 25, p. 143.

84 Jane Welsh Carlyle to Jeannie Welsh, ibid., 5 March 1851, vol. 26, p. 41.

85 These tasks were performed by, among others, Sarah Thomas, *Secret Diary*, and Jane Carlyle, *Collected Letters*.

86 Cited in Monica F. Cohen, *Professional Domesticity in the Victorian Novel: Women, Work and Home* (Cambridge: Cambridge University Press, 1998), p. 4.

87 Gissing, *The Odd Women*, pp. 214–15.

88 Ibid., p. 201.

89 Rose, *Parallel Lives*, p. 42.

90 Cited in Mary Lutyens, *The Ruskins and the Grays* (London: John Murray, 1972), pp. 126–27.

91 Jane Welsh Carlyle to Charlotte Sterling, *Collected Letters*, ?January 1851, vol. 26, p. 28.

92 Charles Dickens to Catherine Dickens, *Mrs and Mrs Charles Dickens: His Letters to Her*, ed. Walter Dexter (London: Constable, 1935), 8 November 1844, p. 109.

93 Laura Forster, Reminiscences, xxii/11, p. 76, E. M. Forster Papers, King's College, Cambridge.

94 Gissing, *New Grub Street*, p. 261.

95 Gissing, *The Odd Women*, p. 313.

96 Elizabeth Barrett Browning, *Aurora Leigh*, I.304–5.

97 Charlotte Brontë, *Jane Eyre*, p. 254; the pictures are all included in Casteras, *Images of Victorian Womanhood*, passim.

98 Coventry Patmore, *The Angel in the House* (London and Cambridge: Macmillan, 1863), Part I, Book II ("The Espousals"), Canto 8 ("The Koh-I-Noor"), Preludes I, part 1: "In Love," p. 250.

99 [Lamb], *Can Women Regenerate Society?* (1844), cited in Murray, *Strong-Minded Women*, pp. 28–31.

100 Charles Dickens, *The Personal History of David Copperfield* ([1849–50]; Garden City, N.Y.: Nelson Doubleday, n.d.), p. 721; *Our Mutual Friend*, p. 663.

101 [Craik], *Olive*, p. 9.

102 Cited in J. Howard Whitehouse, *Vindication of Ruskin* (London: George Allen and Unwin, 1950), p. 14.

103 Ibid., p. 16.

104 Cited in Lorna Duffin, "The Conspicuous Consumptive: Woman as an Invalid," in Delamont and Duffin, eds., *Nineteenth-Century Woman*, pp. 35–36.

105 Mary S. Hartman, *Victorian Murderesses*, pp. 109, 94–95.

106 Ann Blainey, *Fanny and Adelaide* (Chicago: Ivan R. Dee, 2001), p. 167.

107 Cited in Adrian Desmond and James Moore, *Darwin* (London, Michael Joseph, 1991), p. 257. All the spelling and punctuation is thus, including "Mary" for "Marry."

CHAPTER 7. THE DINING ROOM

1   These examples were quoted by Charles Eastlake, and cited in Asa Briggs, *Victorian Things*, p. 227.

2   Edis, *Decoration & Furniture of Town Houses*, pp. 17–20.

3   Rhoda and Agnes Garrett, *Suggestions for House Decoration*, pp. 25–34.

4   *Cassell's Household Guide*, vol. 1, p. 126.

5   Mrs. Caddy, *Household Organization*, pp. 104–17.

6   Edis, *Decoration & Furniture of Town Houses*, p. 122.

7   Briggs, *Victorian Things*, p. 22.

8   Mrs. Loftie, *The Dining Room* (London: Macmillan, 1878), pp. 12–14.

9   Cited in Gloag, *Victorian Comfort*, p. 42.

10   Timings, *Letter from the Past*, pp. 42–43.

11   Shepard, *Drawn from Memory*, p. 38.

12   Mrs. Panton, *From Kitchen to Garret*, pp. 8, 58–60.

13   Mrs. Panton, *Homes of Taste*, pp. 44, 55; Mrs. Loftie, *The Dining Room*, p. 71.

14   Creighton, *Memoir*, p. 34.

15   Mrs. Panton, *From Kitchen to Garret*, p. 64.

16   Briggs, *Victorian Things*, pp. 331, 335, 346; Geraldine Jewsbury, *Letters to Jane Welsh Carlyle*, [?1849], pp. 302–3; Mrs. Gaskell, *Cranford*, p. 83; Alfred Rosling Bennett, *London and Londoners*, p. 38; Pritchard, *London and Londoners*, p. 4; *The Times*, 8 May 1851, cited on www.victorianlondon.org/communications/frequency.

17   Mrs. Gaskell, *Ruth*, p. 231; Mrs. Gaskell to Marianne Gaskell, *Letters*, [late March 1859?], p. 545.

18   Farjeon, *Nursery in the Nineties*, p. 438.

19   *The English Housekeeper*, pp. 104–5; Wright, *Home Fires Burning*, pp. 122–31.

20   Dickens, *David Copperfield*, p. 336.

21   *Cassell's Household Guide*, vol. 1, pp. 38–39, gives details of the family on £140; Mrs. Haweis, *Art of Housekeeping*, pp. 101–6, on the £300–£500 family.

22   Economic Club of London, *Family Budgets* (London: P. S. King & Son, 1896), pp. 25–28; Mrs. Panton, *From Kitchen to Garret*, p. 26.

23   [Philp], *Lady's Every-Day Book*, pp. 11–12; Holme, *Carlyles at Home*, p. 6; Raverat, *Period Piece*, p. 54.

24   Mrs. Beeton, *Household Management*, p. 316.

25   Mrs. James, *Our Servants*, pp. 133–35.

26   Mrs. Beeton, *Household Management*, p. 390.

27   Mrs. Warren, *How I Managed My Children*, p. 34; Chavasse, *Advice to a Mother*, p. 94.

28   "Cre-fydd," *Cre-Fydd's Family Fare*, pp. xviii–xx.

29 Hannah Cullwick, *Diaries*, 22 January 1863, p. 117.

30 This was noted by Nicola Humble, editor of the World's Classics edition of *Household Management*, p. 611.

31 *Cassell's Household Guide*, vol. 1, p. 4; Mrs. Beeton, *Household Management*, pp. 205, 207, 213, 217, 273, are only some examples.

32 Potter, *Journals*, 5 March 1884, p. 70.

33 George and Weedon Grossmith, *Diary of a Nobody*, p. 77, and passim.

34 "Cre-fydd," *Cre-Fydd's Family Fare*, pp. xviii–xx. The text has been slightly edited for clarity.

35 Rose, *Parallel Lives*, p. 63; Mrs. Gaskell to Catherine Winkworth, *Letters*, 2 November 1848, p. 61; Dickens, *David Copperfield*, p. 562.

36 Henry and Augustus Mayhew, *Living for Appearances* (London: James Blackwood, 1855), p. 1.

37 Hannah Cullwick, *Diaries*, 18 July 1871, p. 171; George and Weedon Grossmith, *Diary of a Nobody*, pp. 53, 27.

38 Thomas Carlyle to Delia Bacon, *Collected Letters*, 8 June 1853, vol. 28, pp. 165–66.

39 Mrs. James, *Our Servants*, pp. 139–42.

40 Thomas, *Secret Diary*, 14 December 1860, p. 62.

41 [Philp], *Lady's Every-Day Book*, p. 12; Mrs. Beeton, *Household Management*, p. 248.

42 Ellis, *Daughters of Engand*, pp. 40, 46, 47.

43 Tytler, *Common Sense for Housemaids*, pp. 35ff.

44 Dickens, *David Copperfield*, p. 281; Mrs. Gaskell, *Private Voices*, 28 December 1838, p. 58; Hare, *Story of My Life*, vol. 2, p. 329.

45 Dickens, *Bleak House*, p. 87; Gissing, *The Odd Women*, p. 199.

46 Murray, *The Modern Householder*, p. 320.

47 [Philp], *Lady's Every-Day Book*, p. 41.

48 Yonge, *The Daisy Chain*, p. 213.

49 An excellent description of dinner *à la française* appears in Laura Forster, xxii/4-c, E. M. Forster Papers, King's College, Cambridge; more elaborate instructions can be found in [Philp], *The Practical Housewife*, p. 76; Mrs. James, *Our Servants*, pp. 143–49; and Tytler, *Common Sense for Housemaids*, pp. 35ff.

50 Mrs. Gaskell to Marianne and Meta Gaskell, *Letters*, December [?1847], p. 51.

51 Murray, *The Modern Householder*, p. 320.

52 Anon., *My Receipt Book: A Treasury of More than Six Hundred Receipts of Cooking and Preserving, by A Lady* (London: Groombridge and Sons, 1867), recipe 400.

53 Lady Jeune, *Lesser Questions* (London: Remington, 1894), p. 62.

54 Trollope, *Last Chronicle of Barset*, p. 403; Mrs. Beeton, *Household Management*, p. 401.

55 Laura Forster, xxii/4-c, E. M. Forster Papers, King's College, Cambridge.

56 Jane Brookfield, *Mrs Brookfield and Her Circle*, ed. Charles and Frances Brookfield (London: Sir Isaac Pitman and Sons, 1905), vol.1, p. 290.

57 [Philp], *Lady's Every-Day Book*, pp. 120–21.

58 *Cassell's Household Guide*, vol. 3, pp. 262–63.

59 Trollope, *Last Chronicle of Barset*, p. 245.

60 *Cassell's Household Guide*, vol. 1, p. 114.

61 Edward Ricket, *The Gentleman's Table Guide and Table Companion . . .* (London: Frederick Warne, 1873), pp. 28, 5.

62 Lewis Carroll, *Through the Looking-Glass, and What Alice Found There* ([1871]; New York: Heritage Press, 1941), p. 183.

63 Anthony Trollope, *Miss Mackenzie* (London: Chapman and Hall, 1865), vol. 1, p. 155.

64 *The English Housekeeper*, p. 119; Mrs. Beeton, *Household Management*, p. 119.

65 Mrs. Panton, *From Kitchen to Garret*, p. 26.

66 Mrs. Beeton, *Household Management*, pp. 327, 562, 900, 155; *The English Housekeeper*, pp. 249, 85; Faunthorpe, *Household Science*, p. 171.

67 *Cassell's Household Guide*, vol. 1, p. 111 and passim.

68 "Cre-fydd," *Cre-Fydd's Family Fare*, pp. 314–15.

69 *The English Housekeeper*, p. 229.

70 For the information on Harvey's Sauce I am grateful to Larry Bailis, President, Ketchup-World.

71 Brookfield, *Mrs Brookfield and Her Circle*, p. 367.

72 Nicola Humble, in Mrs. Beeton, *Household Management*, pp. 598–99n.

73 Anon., *My Receipt Book*, recipe 401.

74 Mrs. Beeton, *Household Management*, pp. 163, 167, 182, 194, 203, 238, 205.

75 Timings, *Letter from the Past*, p. 37.

76 Cited in Stephen van Dulken, *Inventing the Nineteenth Century: The Great Age of Victorian Inventions* (London: British Library, 2001), p. 48.

77 Sardines, George Boyce, *The Diaries of George Price Boyce*, ed. Virginia Surtees (Norwich: Real World, 1980), pp. 4 and 69n; meat and beans, Doreen Yarwood, *The British Kitchen: Housewifery since Roman Times* (London, B. T. Batsford, 1981), p. 116; soup, Loeb, *Consuming Angels*, p. 43; gravy balls, "Espoir," *How to Live on a Hundred a Year*, pp. 13ff.; and egg powder, *Cassell's Household Guide*, vol. 1, p. 27.

78 Laura Forster, xxii/11, pp. 185-6, E. M. Forster Papers, King's College, Cambridge.

79 Mrs. Beeton, *Household Management*, pp. 130–31, 133, 337, 119.

80 Bruce Haley, *The Healthy Body and Victorian Culture* (Cambridge, Mass.: Harvard University Press, 1978), p. 12.

81 Mrs. Beeton, *Household Management*, p. 103.

82 The information in these two paragraphs, except where otherwise noted, comes from the "Report of the Select Committee appointed to inquire into the Adulterations of Food, Drinks, and Drugs," 1st Report, pp. 1–3, *Parliamentary Papers*, 1854/5, vol. 8; and John Burnett, *Plenty and Want: A Social History of Diet in England from 1815 to the Present Day* (London: Thomas Nelson and Sons, 1966), pp. 190–96.

83 [Philp], *The Practical Housewife*, p. 180.

84 Burnett, *Plenty and Want*, pp. 195–96.

85 Sala, *Twice Round the Clock*, pp. 45–46.

86 Mrs. Beeton, *Household Management*, p. 168.

87 Mrs. Panton, *From Kitchen to Garret*, p. 34.

88 Mrs. Beeton, *Household Management*, p. 316.

89 Ibid., p. 367.

90 Charles Dickens, *Our Mutual Friend*, p. 134.

91 Laura Forster, xxii/4-c, E. M. Forster Papers, King's College, Cambridge.

92 Trollope, *Last Chronicle of Barset*, p. 242.

93 Raverat, *Period Piece*, p. 78.

94 "A Member of the Aristocracy," *Manners and Rules of Good Society*, n. 94.

95 Mrs. Beeton, *Household Management*, p. 327.

96 I am grateful to contributors to the Victoria Mailbase for their information on this subject.

97 Cited in Nicholson, *A Victorian Household*, pp. 71, 125.

98 My thanks to the Victoria Mailbase for this information.

99 Brookfield, *Mrs Brookfield and Her Circle*, pp. 209, 174.

100 Raverat, *Period Piece*, p. 78.

101 These suggestions appear in Ricket, *Gentleman's Table Guide*, p. 145.

102 The procedure for dinner parties is taken from: *Cassell's Household Guide*, vol. 3, p. 243; Mrs. [C. E.] Humphry, *Manners for Men* (London: Ward, Lock, 1898), pp. 56–82; Mrs. James, *Our Servants*, pp. 150ff.; "A Member of the Aristocracy," *Manners and Rules of Good Society*, pp. 41–46, 95–112; Murray, *The Modern Householder*, pp. 37–38; and Mrs. Panton, *From Kitchen to Garret*, pp. 30–31.

103 Gissing, *New Grub Street*, p. 274.

104 James Baldwin Brown, *The Gregarious Follies of Fashion* (London: James Clarke, 1876), p. 7.

105 Mrs. Beeton, *Household Management*, p. 24.

CHAPTER 8. THE MORNING ROOM

1   Thomas Carlyle, *Sartor Resartus* ([1833–34]; London: Chapman and Hall, 1896), p. 27.

2   "The Art of Dress," *Quarterly Review* (1847), vol. 79, pp. 375–76, cited in Casteras, *Images of Victorian Womanhood*, p. 69.

3   Raverat, *Period Piece*, p. 256.

4   The rules in this paragraph are all from Murray, *The Modern Householder*, pp. 372–74.

5   Mrs. Gaskell, *Cranford*, p. 40.

6   Brookfield, *Mrs Brookfield and Her Circle*, p. 118.

7   Shonfield, *Precariously Privileged*, p. 117.

8   Faunthorpe, *Readings in Necessary Knowledge*, p. 210.

9   Hughes, *London Girl of the Eighties*, p. 3.

10   Trollope, *Framley Parsonage*, p. 102.

11   Adburgham, *Shops and Shopping*, p. 114; K. Theodore Hoppen, *The Mid-Victorian Generation, 1846–1886* (Oxford: Clarendon Press, 1998), pp. 348–49.

12   Mrs. Beeton, *Household Management*, p. 5.

13   Mrs. Gaskell to Marianne Gaskell, *Letters*, [?May 1851], pp. 153–54.

14   Mrs. Panton, *From Kitchen to Garret*, p. 229.

15   Shonfield, *Precariously Privileged*, pp. 38–39.

16   Cited in Adburgham, *Shops and Shopping*, p. 143.

17   Shonfield, *Precariously Privileged*, p. 63.

18   C. Willet Cunnington, *The Perfect Lady* (London: Max Parrish, 1948), p. 43.

19   *Cassell's Household Guide*, vol. 3, p. 27; Murray, *The Modern Householder*, p. 371.

20   Shonfield, *Precariously Privileged*, p. 63.

21   Pamela Horn, *Pleasures and Pastimes in Victorian Britain* (Stroud: Sutton, 1999), p. 45; Nicholson, *A Victorian Household*, pp. 83–85.

22   Hughes, *London Home in the Nineties*, p. 162.

23   This is from Pritchard, *London and Londoners*, pp. 298–304, but many other books contain similar details.

24   Trollope, *He Knew He Was Right*, p. 64.

25   "Espoir," *How to Live on a Hundred a Year*, pp. 44ff.

26   Mrs. Gaskell, *Ruth*, pp. 129, 131.

27   Trollope, *Small House at Allington*, p. 28.

28   Adburgham, *Shops and Shopping*, pp. 123–25.

29   Raverat, *Period Piece*, pp. 258–59.

30   Sarah Levitt, *Victorians Unbuttoned: Registered Designs for Clothing, Their Makers and Wearers, 1839–1900* (London: George Allen & Unwin, 1986), pp. 74–75.

31   Adburgham, *Shops and Shopping*, p. 135.

32 Nicholson, *A Victorian Household*, pp. 86, 83–84.

33 Holme, *Carlyles at Home*, p. 100.

34 Faunthorpe, *Readings in Necessary Knowledge*, p. 211.

35 Hughes, *London Girl of the Eighties*, p. 13.

36 Laura Forster, Reminiscences, xxii/12, p. 23, E. M. Forster Papers, King's College, Cambridge.

37 Mrs. Gaskell to Marianne Gaskell, *Letters*, [?May 1851], pp. 155.

38 Cited in Levitt, *Victorians Unbuttoned*, p. 103.

39 Bloom, *Victorian Vinaigrette*, p. 33.

40 C. S. Lewis, *Surprised by Joy* (1955), cited in Christina Walkley, *Dressed to Impress: 1840–1914* (London: B. T. Batsford, 1989), p. 15.

41 Eleanor Acland, *Good-bye for the Present: The Story of Two Childhoods* (London: Hodder & Stoughton, 1935), pp. 140–41.

42 Raverat, *Period Piece*, p. 262.

43 Mrs. C. S. Peel, *Life's Enchanted Cup: An Autobiography, 1872–1933* (London: John Lane/The Bodley Head, 1933), p. 47; Mrs. Oliphant cited in Horn, *Pleasures and Pastimes*, p. 45.

44 John S. Haller, Jr., and Robin M. Haller, *The Physician and Sexuality in Victorian America* (Urbana: University of Illinois Press, 1974), p. 31; Horn, *Pleasures and Pastimes*, p. 51.

45 Farjeon, *Nursery in the Nineties*, p. 339.

46 Laura Marx Larargue to Jenny Marx, *The Daughters of Karl Marx: Family Correspondence, 1866–98* (London: André Deutsch, 1982), 20 March 1870, pp. 66–67.

47 Acland, *Good-bye for the Present*, p. 143.

48 Raverat, *Period Piece*, p. 264.

49 Baroness Staffe, *The Lady's Dressing-Room*, trans. Lady Colin Campbell (London: Cassell, 1892), p. 236.

50 Huysmans cited in Valerie Steele, *The Corset: A Cultural History* (London: Yale University Press, 2001), p. 115.

51 Haller and Haller, *The Physician and Sexuality*, p. 98.

52 From an unnamed fashion magazine, dated "1870s," cited in Cunnington, *The Perfect Lady*, p. 42.

53 Levitt, *Victorians Unbuttoned*, pp. 26–33.

54 Shonfield, *Precariously Privileged*, p. 71.

55 The debate on the nature of this correspondence has continued for some time. Many take it for granted that the correspondence was genuine—see Lawrence Stone, *The Family, Sex and Marriage in England, 1500–1800* (London: Weidenfeld and Nicolson, 1997); Helene E. Roberts, "The Exquisite Slave: The Role of Clothes in the Making of the Victorian Woman," *Signs: Journal of Women in Culture and Society*, 2, 1977)—while others see the letters as very obvious sexual fantasies—David Kunzle, "Dress Reform: A Response to Helene E. Roberts' 'The Exquisite Slave: The Role of Clothes in the Making of the Victorian Woman,'" *Signs: Journal of Women in Culture and Society*, 3, 1977; Steele, *The Corset*.

56 Steele, *The Corset*, p. 92.

57 Ibid., p. 100.

58 Cited in Horn, *Victorian Town Child*, pp. 25–26.

59 Kate Dickens cited in Rose, *Parallel Lives*, p. 168–69.

60 Yonge, *The Daisy Chain*, p. 620.

61 Alice James, *The Death and Letters of Alice James: Selected Correspondence*, ed. Ruth Bernard Yeazell (Berkeley: University of California Press, 1981), 21 February 1890, p. 13.

62 Cited in Catherine Robson, *Men in Wonderland: The Lost Girlhood of the Victorian Gentleman* (Princeton, N.J.: Princeton University Press, 2001), pp. 56, 52–53.

63 John Angell James, *Female Piety: or The Young Woman's Friend and Guide through Life to Immortality* (London: Hamilton, Adams, 1852), p. 160.

64 [Philp], *Lady's Every-Day Book*, p. 34.

65 Marion Jane Bradley, Diary, 18 October 1854, British Library, Egerton 3766A.

66 Hudson, *Munby: Man of Two Worlds*, pp. 18–19.

67 Hughes, *London Girl of the Eighties*, pp. 190–91.

68 Nicholson, *A Victorian Household*, p. 63.

69 Trollope, *Small House at Allington*, p. 205.

70 Duncan, *American Girl in London*, pp. 1–2.

71 Gissing, *The Odd Women*, pp. 185–86.

72 From an etiquette manual of the 1860s, cited in Davidoff, *The Best Circles*, p. 41.

73 "A Member of the Aristocracy," *Manners and Rules of Good Society*, pp. 6ff.

74 Mrs. Gaskell to Eliza Fox, *Letters*, 26 April 1850, p. 113.

75 Shonfield, *Precariously Privileged*, pp. 38–39.

76 George and Weedon Grossmith, *Diary of a Nobody*, pp. 64–65.

77 Nicholson, *A Victorian Household*, p. 54.

78 Ibid.

79 Mrs. Gaskell, *Cranford*, p. 41.

80 The information on the etiquette of calling in this and the previous four paragraphs, except where noted, comes from: Mrs. Beeton, *Household Management*, pp. 18–20, 28–29; "A Member of the Aristocracy," *Manners and Rules of Good Society*, pp. 16–28, 29–40; Murray, *The Modern Householder*, pp. 345–46.

81 Mrs. Gaskell to her sister-in-law Elizabeth Gaskell, *Letters*, c. 16 December 1833, p. 4.

82 Creighton, *Memoir*, p. 53.

83 Shonfield, *Precariously Privileged*, pp. 46–47.

84 Berkeley, *Maud*, January 1888, p. 18.

85 Dickens, *Our Mutual Friend*, p. 104.

86 Nightingale, "Cassandra," in Strachey, *The Cause*, pp. 400–401.

87 Davidoff, *The Best Circles*, p. 57.

88 Shonfield, *Precariously Privileged*, pp. 68–69.

89 Nicholson, *A Victorian Household*, p. 80.

90 Raverat, *Period Piece*, pp. 128–29.

91 Mrs. Beeton, *Household Management*, p. 13.

92 Raverat, *Period Piece*, p. 75.

93 Analyzed in Casteras, *Images of Victorian Womanhood*, p. 75.

94 Mrs. Beeton, *Household Management*, pp. 77–79.

95 Sarah Thomas, *Secret Diary*, 4 July 1860, p. 36.

96 Shonfield, *Precariously Privileged*, pp. 68–69.

97 Cited in Hall, "Sweet Delights of Home," p. 77.

98 Dickens, *Our Mutual Friend*, p. 210.

CHAPTER 9. THE BATHROOM AND THE LAVATORY

1 Olsen, *Growth of Victorian London*, p. 161.

2 Mrs. Haweis, *Art of Housekeeping*, pp. 28–29, gives the cost of installing hot water, but her conclusion as to its value concerns the lessees only.

3 Mrs. Panton, *From Kitchen to Garret*, p. 129.

4 Hoppen, *Mid-Victorian Generation*, pp. 337–38; Mrs. Haweis, *Art of Housekeeping*, p. 29.

5   Raverat, *Period Piece*, p. 183.

6   Mrs. Panton, *Homes of Taste*, pp. 129–31.

7   *Cassell's Household Guide*, vol. 1, pp. 45–46.

8   [Philp], *Lady's Every-Day Book*, pp. 28–30.

9   Raverat, *Period Piece*, p. 57.

10 Nicholson, *A Victorian Household*, p. 87.

11 Berkeley, *Maud*, April 1892, p. 126.

12 Raverat, *Period Piece*, p. 183.

13 Stephen Halliday, *The Great Stink of London: Sir Joseph Bazalgette and the Cleansing of the Victorian Capital* (Stroud: Sutton, 1999), p. 43.

14 First Report of the Commissioners of the Exhibition of 1851, *Parliamentary Papers*, 1852, vol. 26, Appendix 30.

15 Erika Diane Rappaport, *Shopping for Pleasure*, pp. 83–85.

16 The information in this and the previous two paragraphs was taken from: Munroe Blair, *Ceramic Water Closets* (Princes Risborough: Shire Publications, 2000), pp. 12, 13–19, 27–34; Halliday, *Great Stink of London*, p. 42; Hoppen, *Mid-Victorian Generation*, pp. 337–38; Murphy, *Our Homes*, pp. 140–41; and Roy Palmer, *The Water Closet, A New History* (Newton Abbot: David & Charles, 1973), pp. 33–45.

17 Browne, "House-Cleaning," in Murphy, *Our Homes*, p. 885.

18 Cullwick, *Journal*, 3 March 1872, p. 214.

19 All from Palmer, *The Water Closet*, pp. 80–87.

20 Diana Holman Hunt, *My Grandmothers and I* ([1960], London: Hamish Hamilton, 1987), pp. 32–33. This scene took place during World War I, but the life her grandmother lived was still firmly rooted in the Victorian age, and it seems useful to quote this passage none the less.

21 Jenni Calder, *The Victorian Home* (London: B. T. Batsford, 1977), pp. 18–19.

22 Smith and Young, "Architecture," in Murphy, *Our Homes*, pp. 66, 63–64.

23 Ibid., pp. 73, 90; Kerr, *The Gentleman's House*, p. 168.

24 Smith and Young, "Architecture," in Murphy, *Our Homes*, p. 66.

25 Hellyer, *The Plumber*, p. v.

26 Nicholson, *A Victorian Household*, p. 87.

27 Haley, *Healthy Body*, p. 8; Murphy, *Our Homes*, p. 503.

28 These two paragraphs are heavily indebted to Haley, *Healthy Body*, pp. 6–7.

29 Cited in Halliday, *Great Stink of London*, pp. 133–34.

30 Cited in Wilson, *Sphinx in the City*, p. 26.

31 The list appears in Flint, *The Victorians and the Visual Imagination*, p. 157.

32 Halliday, *Great Stink of London*, p. ix.

33 Raverat, *Period Piece*, p. 34.

34 Cited in Halliday, *Great Stink of London*, p. 46.

35 Hudson, *Munby: Man of Two Worlds*, p. 40.

36 Halliday, *Great Stink of London*, p. ix.

37 Benjamin Richardson, "Introduction," in Murphy, *Our Homes*, pp. 12–13.

38 Halliday, *Great Stink of London*, p. 124; Martine Segalen, "Material Conditions of Family Life," in Kertzer and Barbagli, *History of the European Family*, vol. 2, pp. 3–39.

CHAPTER 10. THE SICKROOM

1   Smith and Young, "Architecture," in Murphy, *Our Homes*, p. 86.

2   Anthony Todd Thomson, *The Domestic Management of the Sick-Room* (London: Longman,

Orme, Brown, Green, & Longman's, 1841), pp. 124ff.

3 Dickens, *The Old Curiosity Shop*, p. 136.

4 Mrs. Beeton, *Household Management*, p. 467.

5 Ibid., p. 362.

6 Dickens, *David Copperfield*, p. 555.

7 Florence Nightingale, *Notes on Nursing: What It Is and What It Is Not* (London: Harrison, [1860]), p. 6.

8 Trollope, *Small House at Allington*, p. 424.

9 Potter, *Journals*, 11 October 1895, p. 398.

10 Laura Forster, Journal, 15 May 1864, xxii/4, p. 2, E. M. Forster Papers, King's College, Cambridge.

11 Ibid., xxii/12, p. 22.

12 Miriam Bailin, in *The Sickroom in Victorian Fiction: The Art of Being Ill* (Cambridge: Cambridge University Press, 1994), p. 29, discusses these authors and others.

13 Eugene Bouchut, *Practical Treatise on the Diseases of Children and Infants at the Breast*, pp. 12–13, cited in Hellerstein, Hume, and Offen, eds., *Victorian Women*, p. 228.

14 Mrs. Gaskell, *Ruth*, p. 389.

15 Bakewell, *Practical Hints on the Management of the Sick-Room*, pp. 5–6, 7, 15, 37–38, 43.

16 *Cassell's Household Guide*, vol. 3, p. 122–23.

17 Cited in Jalland, *Death in the Victorian Family*, p. 112.

18 Haley, *Healthy Body*, p. 5.

19 Alice James, *Death and Letters*, 3–7 January [?1886], pp. 108–9.

20 My thanks to Melanie Wilson and the Victoria Mailbase for this information.

21 Thomas, *Secret Diary*, 12 December 1860, p. 61.

22 Alfred Rosling Bennett, *London and Londoners*, p. 33.

23 Corke, *In Our Infancy*, p. 22.

24 Jewsbury, *Letters to Jane Carlyle*, [postmarked 27 September 1849], p. 298.

25 The information on the Gosse family comes from Edmund Gosse, *Father and Son*, pp. 37, 47, 71, 72, 75, 137; Philip Henry Gosse, *A Memorial of the Last Days on Earth of Emily Gosse* (London: James Nisbet, 1857); and Ann Thwaite, *Glimpses of the Wonderful*. The material that follows is taken entirely from these volumes unless otherwise stated.

26 Jalland, *Death in the Victorian Family*, p. 10.

27 Sherwin B. Nuland, "A Very Wide and Deep Dissection," review of Barron H. Lerner, *The Breast Cancer Wars*, in *New York Review of Books*, 20 September 2001.

28 Ann Thwaite, *Edmund Gosse: A Literary Landscape, 1849–1928* (London: Secker and Warburg, 1984), p. 29.

29 Cited in Thwaite, *Glimpses of the Wonderful*, p. 195.

30 Alice James, *Diary*, 3 September 1891, p. 218.

31 This photograph is reprinted in Alice James, *Death and Letters*, between pages 22 and 23.

32 Thomson, *Domestic Management of the Sick-Room*, pp. 105–11.

33 Ibid., pp. 315–20; Mrs. Buck, *Simple Recipes for Sickroom Cookery* (London: Simpkin, Marshall, 1885), p. 16.

34 Anthony Trollope, *Doctor Thorne* ([1858]; London: J. M. Dent & Sons, 1908), pp. 456–57.

35 Thomson, *Domestic Management of the Sick-Room*, p. 118.

36 Thomson, *Domestic Management of the Sick-Room*, pp. 112–18; Mrs. Beeton, *Household Management*, p. 467.

37 Timings, *Letter from the Past*, p. 28.

38 Murray, *The Modern Householder*, p. 689.

39 Arnold Bennett, *The Old Wives' Tale*, pp. 402–3, 405.

40 Deborah Gorham, *The Victorian Girl*, p. 15, notes the gender-specific infant-mortality figures; I am indebted to her work for this, and for her suggestions of enclosure in the house, and enclosure in clothing.

41 Thomson, *Domestic Management of the Sick-Room*, pp. 27–28.

42 Mrs. Gaskell, *Ruth*, pp. 246–47.

43 John Burnett, *Organ Diseases of Women* (London: Homoeopathic Publishing, 1896), pp. v–vi.

44 I. Baker Brown, *On the Curability of Certain Forms of Insanity* (London: Robert Hardwicke, 1866), pp. 14–15.

45 Mrs. Panton, *Within Four Walls: A Handbook for Invalids* (London: "The Gentlewoman" Offices, 1893), p. 24.

46 Cited in Bailin, *Sickroom in Victorian Fiction*, p. 1.

47 Nicholson, *A Victorian Household*, pp. 36–37, 47.

48 Jewsbury, *Letters to Jane Carlyle*, [postmarked 25 June 1845], p. 164; Mrs. Panton, *From Kitchen to Garret*, p. 112.

49 Jane Welsh Carlyle to Thomas Carlyle, *Collected Letters*, 29 December 1853, vol. 28, p. 365.

50 These are all cited by Bruce Haley in his fascinating *Healthy Body*, pp. 12–13. Any cursory reading of the *Collected Letters* will yield half a dozen more examples in any half a dozen pages.

51 These and many more are cited by Miriam Bailin, in her *Sickroom in Victorian Fiction*, pp. 6, 7, 23, 25–26, to which I am indebted.

52 Hudson, *Munby, Man of Two Worlds*, p. 17.

53 Raverat, *Period Piece*, pp. 121–22.

54 Colp, *To Be an Invalid*, p. 32.

55 The theory of arsenic poisoning, as I have reproduced it here, is taken from John H. Winslow, *Darwin's Victorian Malady: Evidence for Its Medically Induced Origin* (Philadelphia: American Philosophical Society, 1971), pp. 26–28, 79–84, and passim.

56 Nightingale, "Cassandra," in Strachey, *The Cause*, pp. 402, 396.

57 Bailin, *Sickroom in Victorian Fiction*, pp. 32–36.

58 Mrs. Panton, *Within Four Walls*, p. 27.

59 Letters from Mrs. James in Alice James, *Death and Letters*, [1868], pp. 10–12. All the information on Alice James's illness and death comes from her diary and letters, to be found in *The Diary of Alice James*, ed. Leon Edel, and *The Death and Letters of Alice James*, ed. Ruth Bernard Yeazell, and the excellent introduction and notes therein, which are cited separately below.

60 *Death and Letters*, [summer 1878], p. 15.

61 Cited by Leon Edel in his introduction, *Diary*, p. 6.

62 Alice James to Catharine Walsh, *Death and Letters*, 21/24 November [?1885], p. 104.

63 Ibid., 11/15 November 1886, p. 110.

64 *Diary*, 18 July 1890, p. 129.

65 Ibid., 27 August 1890, p. 142.

66 Alice James to William James, *Death and Letters*, 30 July 1891, pp. 41–42; *Diary*, 3 May 1891, pp. 206–8.

67 Alice James's diary cited in *Death and Letters*, p. 2; William and Henry James's letters cited in ibid., pp. 44–45.

68 See Jalland, *Death in the Victorian Family*.

69 Cited in ibid., p. 18. I am indebted to Jalland's book for my discussion of the Evangelical response to death in this paragraph.

70 Dickens to W. H. Wills, 12 December 1850; *Correspondence: The Letters of Charles Dickens*, The Pilgrim Edition, ed. Madeline House, Graham Storey, and Kathleen Tillotson; vol. 6,

1850–52, ed. Graham Storey, Kathleen Tillotson, and Nina Burgis (Oxford: Clarendon Press, 1988), p. 231. I am grateful to Kathryn Smith for this reference, to Mary Haynes Kuhlman for the reference to *North and South*, and to Marguerite Finnigan for the reference to *Mary Barton*.

71 Philip Gosse, *Memorial*, p. 2.

72 Mrs. Warren, *How I Managed My Children*, pp. 50–51.

73 Dr. William Munk, *Euthanasia, or Medical Treatment in Aid of an Easy Death* (London: Longmans, Green, 1887), pp. 22, 26–67.

74 The information comes from Jalland, *Death in the Victorian Family*, p. 51–52.

75 Ibid., pp. 28, 87–88.

76 Wood, *East Lynne*, p. 130.

77 Shonfield, *Precariously Privileged*, pp. 26–28.

78 Mrs. Gaskell to ?Anne Shaen, [?24 April 1848]; Mrs. Gaskell to Eliza Fox, 26 April 1850, *Letters*, pp. 57, 111; Creighton, *Memoirs*, p. 2.

79 Nicholson, *A Victorian Household*, p. 99.

80 Quoted in Edmund Gosse, *Father and Son*, p. 68.

81 Laura Forster, xxii/11, p. 179, E. M. Forster Papers, King's College, Cambridge; Creighton, *Memoirs*, p. 2.

82 The description of Reggie Marshall's death, and all citations, come from Shonfield, *Precariously Privileged*, pp. 28–30.

83 Nicholson, *A Victorian Household*, p. 131.

84 Arnold Bennett, *The Old Wives' Tale*, pp. 114–15.

85 *Cassell's Household Guide*, vol. 3, p. 292.

86 Lou Taylor, *Mourning Dress: A Costume and Social History* (London, George Allen and Unwin, 1983), pp. 169–70.

87 *Enquire Within Upon Everything*, in *The "Enquire Within" and "Reason Why" Series* (London: Houlston & Wright, 1865), pp. 247–48.

88 Dickens, *David Copperfield*, p. 419. I am indebted to Cunnington and Lucas, *Costume for Births, Marriages and Deaths,* p. 196, for the information in this paragraph, except where otherwise noted.

89 Hudson, *Munby: Man of Two Worlds*, pp. 211–12.

90 Shonfield, *Precariously Privileged*, p. 82.

91 Peter Ackroyd, *Dickens* (London: Vintage, 1999), p. xiii.

92 Nicholson, *A Victorian Household*, p. 48.

93 Both inventories from *Cassell's Household Guide*, vol. 3, p. 292.

94 Cunnington and Lucas, *Costume for Births, Marriages and Deaths*, p. 149.

95 Charles Booth, *Life and Labour of the People of London*, 1st ser., vol. 1, "Industry," pp. 205–9.

96 *Cassell's Household Guide*, vol. 1, pp. 344–46; "A Member of the Aristocracy," *Manners and Rules of Good Society*, pp. 227–28.

97 Cited in Adburgham, *Shops and Shopping*, p. 62.

98 Trollope, *Framley Parsonage*, p. 145.

99 Yonge, *The Daisy Chain*, p. 39.

100 The Hon. Mrs. Gell, *Under Three Reigns, 1860–1920* (London: Kegan Paul, Trench, Trubner, 1927), p. 103.

101 Cited in Adburgham, *Shops and Shopping*, p. 63.

102 Trollope, *Last Chronicle of Barset*, p. 241.

103 Cited in Adburgham, *Shops and Shopping*, p. 57.

104 Mrs. Gaskell to Marianne Gaskell, *Letters*, [15 November 1852], p. 209.

105 Lou Taylor, *Mourning Dress*, pp. 134, 136.

106 Henry Mayhew, ed., *The Shops and Companies of London . . .* (London, 1865), pp. 219–20.

107 Cited in Cunnington and Lucas, *Costume for Births, Marriages and Deaths*, p. 249.

108 Ibid., pp. 65, 241.

109 Walkley, *Crinolines and Crimping Irons*, p. 36.

110 Mrs. Gaskell, *Cranford*, p. 108.

111 George Eliot, *The Mill on the Floss*, ed. Gordon S. Haight ([1860]; Oxford: Oxford University Press, 1998), p. 126.

112 *Sylvia's Home Journal*, 1881, cited in Adburgham, *Shops and Shopping*, p. 64.

113 Cunnington and Lucas, *Costume for Births, Marriages and Deaths*, pp. 252–53.

114 Zuzanna Shonfield, *Precariously Privileged*, p. 85.

115 Source: "A Member of the Aristocracy," *Manners and Rules of Good Society*, pp. 222–28.

116 Cullwick, *Diaries*, 24 February 1863, pp. 117–18.

117 Cunnington and Lucas, *Costume for Births, Marriages and Deaths*, p. 249.

118 Ibid., p. 247.

119 Shonfield, *Precariously Privileged*, p. 82.

120 Cited in Adburgham, *Shops and Shopping*, pp. 62–63.

121 Arnold Bennett, *The Old Wives' Tale*, p. 275.

122 George Eliot, *Middlemarch*, ed. W. J. Harvey ([1871-72]; Harmondsworth: Penguin Books, 1985), p. 846.

123 Shonfield, *Precariously Privileged*, p. 85.

124 Jalland, *Death in the Victorian Family*, p. 230.

125 Nicholson, *A Victorian Family*, p. 47.

126 Both examples cited in Rose, *Parallel Lives*, pp. 228–29, 301–2.

127 Trollope, *Small House at Allington*, p. 596.

Chapter 11. The Street

1   Arthur Conan Doyle, "A Case of Identity," in *The Adventures of Sherlock Holmes* ([1892]; New York: Quality Paperback Book Club, 1994), p. 56.

2   Dickens, *Little Dorrit*, pp. 67–68, cited in Wilson, *Sphinx in the City*, p. 26.

3   Nathaniel Hawthorne, *The English Notebooks*, 7 September 1855, vol. 21, pp. 306–7.

4   Sala, *Twice Round the Clock*, pp. 51–69.

5   The following paragraphs on street life, to p. 397, have been compiled from: Alfred Rosling Bennett, *London and Londoners*, pp. 39–58, 60–62, 69–70; Arnold Bennett, *The Old Wives' Tale*, pp. 56–57; Edmund Gosse, *Father and Son*, pp. 85–87; Mackenzie, *Life and Times*, Octave I, pp. 208–10; Thomas Miller, *Picturesque Sketches of London, Past and Present* (London: Office of the National Illustrated Library, 1852), pp. 255–61; Shepard, *Drawn from Memory*, pp. 16–22.

6   Dickens, *The Old Curiosity Shop*, p. 331.

7   From Mayhew's *London Labour and the London Poor*, cited in Mrs. Beeton, *Household Management*, p. 608, editor's note.

8   Edmund Gosse, *Father and Son*, pp. 85–86.

9   Alfred Rosling Bennett, *London and Londoners*, p. 39; Mackenzie, *Life and Times*, Octave I, pp. 208–10.

10 Mackenzie, *Life and Times*, Octave I, pp. 208–10.

11 Ibid.

12 Miller, *Picturesque Sketches of London*, p. 261.

13 Alfred Rosling Bennett, *London and Londoners*, pp. 100–101.

14   Mackenzie, *Life and Times*, Octave I, pp. 208–10.

15   Ibid., pp. 255–56.

16   Edmund Gosse, *Father and Son*, pp. 86–87.

17   Charles Babbage, *A Chapter on Street Nuisances* (London: John Murray, 1864), pp. 4–5; Michael T. Bass, M.P., *Street Music of the Metropolis* (London: John Murray, 1864), pp. 20–22.

18   *The Times*, 9 July 1872, p. 11d.

19   Adburgham, *Shops and Shopping*, pp. 284–87.

20   See, for example, *The Times*, 9 January 1862, p. 10; Eliza Lynn Linton's essay in *Temple Bar*, April 1862, p. 132.

21   Cited in Rappaport, *Shopping for Pleasure*, p. 4.

22   Nicholson, *A Victorian Household*, p. 85.

23   Gorham, *The Victorian Girl*, p. 151.

24   Charlotte Brontë, *Villette*, ed. Mark Lilly ([1853]; Harmondsworth: Penguin Books, 1985), p. 121.

25   Dickens, *Our Mutual Friend*, pp. 589, 649.

26   Potter, *Journals*, 18 March 1885, p. 136.

27   Raverat, *Period Piece*, p. 260.

28   Gissing, *New Grub Street*, p. 208.

29   Michael Freeman, *Railways and the Victorian Imagination* (London: Yale University Press, 1999), p. 46.

30   Olsen, *Growth of Victorian London*, pp, 318–22.

31   Cullwick, *Diaries*, 30 July 1860, and editor's note on the behavior of bus drivers, pp. 110, 113.

32   Adburgham, *Shops and Shopping*, pp. 79, 145.

33   Briggs, *Victorian Things*, p. 415.

34   Alfred Rosling Bennett, *London and Londoners*, p. 84; [R. S. Surtees], *Mr Sponge's Sporting Tour* ([1853]; London: Folio Society, [1981]), p. 5.

35   Alfred Rosling Bennett, *London and Londoners*, pp. 81–82.

36   Duncan, *An American Girl in London*, pp. 42–43.

37   Hughes, *London Child of the Seventies*, p. 39.

38   Ibid., pp. 38–39.

39   Sala, *Twice Round the Clock*, pp. 219–20.

40   Duncan, *An American Girl in London*, pp. 133–34.

41   Mrs. Humphry, *Manners for Men*, p. 41.

42   Mackenzie, *Life and Times*, Octave I, p. 178.

43   Flint, *The Victorians and the Visual Imagination*, p. 162.

44   Trollope, *The Way We Live Now*, p. 696.

45   Galton, "Warming and Ventilation," in Murphy, *Our Homes*, p. 568.

46   Hughes, *London Home in the Nineties*, p. 179.

47   Sala, *Twice Round the Clock*, p. 157.

48   Shonfield, *Precariously Privileged*, p. 47.

49   Advertisement cited in Adburgham, *Shops and Shopping*, p. 101; [Surtees], *Mr Sponge's Sporting Tour*, p. 188.

50   Alfred Rosling Bennett, *London and Londoners*, p. 90.

51   Taine, *Notes on England*, p. 18; Butler, *The Way of All Flesh*, p. 362.

52   Shonfield, *Precariously Privileged*, p. 47.

53   I am grateful to Alison Adburgham, *Shops and Shopping*, pp. 80–90, for all the foregoing fashion information in this paragraph.

54   Dickens, *Bleak House*, pp. 76, 83.

55   The Hon. R. Russell, F.M.S., *London Fogs* (London: Edward Stanford, 1880), p. 608.

56 Brimblecombe, *The Big Smoke*, p. 113.

57 Ibid., p. 111.

58 Hawthorne, *The English Notebooks,* 8 December 1857, vol. 22, pp. 443–44.

59 Sala, *Gaslight and Daylight*, p. 64.

60 Miller, *Picturesque Sketches of London*, pp. 243–47.

61 Gissing, *The Odd Women*, p. 235.

62 Cited in Nicholson, *A Victorian Household*, p. 83.

63 Russell, *London Fogs*, pp. 26, 22–23.

64 Brimblecombe, *The Big Smoke*, pp. 122–23.

65 Cited in Caroline Dakers, *The Holland Park Circle: Artists and Victorian Society* (London: Yale University Press, 1999), p. 238.

66 Brimblecombe, *The Big Smoke*, p. 101.

67 Robert Louis Stevenson, *The Strange Case of Dr Jekyll and Mr Hyde* (London: Longmans, Green, 1896), pp. 41–42.

68 Gerard Manley Hopkins, in *Nature*, no. 29, 3 January 1884, pp. 222–23, cited in Flint, *The Victorians and the Visual Imagination*, pp. 57–58.

SELECT
BIBLIOGRAPHY

PRIMARY SOURCES

Acland, Eleanor. *Good-bye for the Present: The Story of Two Childhoods, Milly, 1878–88, and Ellen, 1913–24*. London: Hodder & Stoughton, 1935.

[Anon.]. *Cassell's Household Guide: Being A Complete Encyclopaedia of domestic and Social Economy, and Forming A Guide to Every Department of Practical Life*. London: Cassell, Petter, and Galpin, 1869–71.

[Anon.]. *Corner Cupboard, a Family Repository*. London: Houlston & Stoneman, 1858.

[Anon.]. *The English Housekeeper, or, Manual of Domestic Management: containing advice on the conduct of household affairs, and Practical Instructions concerning the store-room, the pantry, the larder, the kitchen, the cellar, the dairy . . . The whole being intended for the use of young ladies who undertake the superintendence of their own housekeeping*, 3d ed. London: A. Cobbett, 1842.

[Anon.]. *The "Enquire Within" and "Reason Why" Series*. London: Houlston & Wright, 1865.

[Anon.]. *The Etiquette of Courtship and Marriage*. London: Frederick Warne, [1866].

[Anon.]. *Etiquette of Courtship and Matrimony: with a complete guide to the forms of a wedding*. London: Routledge, Warne, and Routledge, [c. 1865].

[Anon.]. *Etiquette of Love*. Halifax: William Milner, 1849.

[Anon.]. *The Habits of Good Society: A Handbook of Etiquette for Ladies and Gentlemen*. London: J. Hogg & Sons, 1859.

[Anon.]. *Modern Household Cookery: A New Work for Private Families. By "A Lady."* London: T. Nelson, 1860.

[Anon.]. *My Receipt Book: A Treasury of More than Six Hundred Receipts of Cooking and Preserving, by A Lady*. London: Groombridge and Sons, 1867.

[Anon.]. *Steam Power from House Dust for Electric Lighting and Other Purposes*. London: Refuse Disposal Co., 1892.

[Anon.]. *The What-Not, or Ladies' Handy-Book*. London: Kent, 1861.

Ansell, Charles. *On the Rate of Mortality at Early Periods of Life, the Age of Marriage, the Number of Children to a Marriage, the Length of a Generation, and other statistics of families, in the upper and professional classes*. London: National Life Assurance Society, Charles & Edwin Layton, 1874.

Armstrong, Rev. Benjamin John. *Armstrong's Norfolk Diary*. Ed. Herbert B. J. Armstrong. London: Hodder and Stoughton, 1963.

Babbage, Charles. *A Chapter on Street Nuisances*. London: John Murray, 1864.

Bakewell, R. Hall. *Practical Hints on the Management of the Sick-Room*. London: John Snow, 1857.

Ballin, Mrs. Ada S. *Personal Hygiene*. London: F. J. Rebman, 1894.

Barker, Lady. *The Bedroom and Boudoir*. London: Macmillan, 1878.

Bass, Michael T., M.P. *Street Music of the Metropolis*. London: John Murray, 1864.

Baylis, T. Henry. *The Rights, Duties and Relations of Domestic Servants, Their Masters and Mistresses, with a short account of servants' institutions and their advantages*. London: Sampson, Low, Son and Co., 1857; 5th ed., 1896.

Beeton, Mrs. [Isabella]. *Mrs Beeton's Book of Household Management* [1861]. Ed. Nicola Humble. Oxford: Oxford University Press, 2000.

[Beeton, Samuel]. *Beeton's Complete Etiquette for Gentlemen: A Guide to the Table, the Toilette and the Ball-Room, with Hints on Courtship, Music and Manners*. London: Ward, Lock, and Tyler, [1876].

Bennett, Alfred Rosling. *London and Londoners in the Eighteen-Fifties and Sixties*. London: T. Fisher Unwin, 1924.

Bennett, Arnold. *The Old Wives' Tale*. [1908]. Harmondsworth: Penguin Books, 1983.

———. *Anna of the Five Towns*. [1902]. Harmondsworth: Penguin Books, 2001.

Berkeley, Maud. *Maud: The Diaries of Maud Berkeley*. Adapted by Flora Fraser. London: Secker & Warburg, 1985.

Bloom, Ursula. *Victorian Vinaigrette*. London: Hutchinson, 1956.

[Bodichon, Barbara]. "A Brief Summary in Plain Language of the Most Important Laws Concerning Women; Together with a Few Observations Thereon." London: John Chapman, 1854.

Booth, Charles. *Life and Labour of the People of London*, 1st ser., vol. 1, "Industry." London: Macmillan, 1892–97.

Bradley, Marion Jane. [c. 1854]. Diary. British Library, Add MSS 3766 A–B.

Braddon, Mary Elizabeth. *Aurora Floyd*. [1863]. Oxford: Oxford World's Classics, 1996.

Brontë, Anne. *The Tenant of Wildfell Hall*. [1848]. Ed. G. D. Hargreaves. Harmondsworth: Penguin Books, 1985.

Brontë, Charlotte. *Jane Eyre*. [1847]. [London]: Everyman Library, 1991.

———. *Villette*. [1853]. Ed. Mark Lilly. Harmondsworth: Penguin Books, 1985.

Brookfield, Jane. *Mrs Brookfield and Her Circle*. Ed. Charles and Frances Brookfield. 2 vols. London: Sir Isaac Pitman and Sons, 1905.

Brown, Ford Madox. *The Diary of Ford Madox Brown*. Ed. Virginia Surtees. London: Yale University Press, 1981.

Brown, I. Baker. *On the Curability of Certain Forms of Insanity*. London: Robert Hardwicke, 1866.

Brown, James Baldwin. *The Cholera: How to Rob It of Its Terror: or, The Mercies of Judgment*. London: A. M. Piggott, 1853.

———. *The Gregarious Follies of Fashion. An Address to the Younger Generation*. London: James Clarke, 1876.

Browning, Elizabeth Barrett. *Aurora Leigh*. London: Chapman & Hall, 1857.

Browning, Robert. *Poetical Works, 1833–1864*. Ed. Ian Jack. Oxford: Oxford University Press, 1970.

Buck, Mrs. *Simple Recipes for Sickroom Cookery*. London: Simpkin, Marshall, 1885.

Buckton, Catherine M. *Our Dwellings, Healthy and Unhealthy*. London: Longmans, Green, 1885.

Burne-Jones, [Georgiana] Lady. *Memorials of Edward Coley Burne-Jones*. London: Macmillan, 1904.

Butler, Henry D. *The Family Aquarium or Aqua-Vivarium. A "New Pleasure" for the Domestic Circle: being a Familiar and complete Instructor upon the subject of the Construction, Fitting-Up, Stocking and Maintenance of the Fluvial and Marine Aquaria, or River and Ocean Gardens*. New York: Dick and Fitzgerald, 1858.

Butler, Samuel. *The Way of All Flesh*. [1903; written 1873–80]. Ed. James Cochrane; introduction by Richard Hoggart. Harmondsworth: Penguin Books, 1986.

Caddy, Mrs. [Florence]. *Household Organisation*. London: Chapman and Hall, 1877.

Cantlie, James. *Degeneration Amongst Londoners*. London: Field & Tuer, 1885.

Carlyle, Jane. *Letters and Memorials of Jane Welsh Carlyle*. Ed. J. A. Froude. (London: Longmans, Green, 1883.

Carlyle, Thomas. *Reminiscences*. Ed. J. A. Froude. New York: Charles Scribner's Sons, 1881.

Carlyle, Thomas, and Jane Welsh Carlyle. *The Collected Letters of Thomas and Jane Welsh Carlyle*. 28+ vols. Ed. Clyde de L. Ryals, Kenneth J. Fielding, et al. Durham, N.C.: Duke University Press, 1970– .

Carroll, Lewis. *Alice's Adventures in Wonderland, and What She Found There.* [1865]. New York: Heritage Reprints, 1941.

———. *Through the Looking-Glass, and What Alice Found There.* [1871]. New York: Heritage Press, 1941.

Charles, Richard. *The Cabinet-Maker: A Journal of Designs* (Nos. 1-8, 1868, London).

Chavasse, Dr. Pye Henry. *Advice to a Mother on the Management of Her Offspring.* London: John Churchill, 1861.

[Clarke, W. S.]. *The Suburban Homes of London: A Residential Guide.* London: Chatto & Windus, 1881.

Clive, Caroline. *From the Diary and Family Papers of Mrs Archer Clive, 1801–1873.* Ed. Mary Clive. London: Bodley Head, 1949.

Cobbe, Frances Power. *Duties of Women: A Course of Lectures.* London and Edinburgh: Williams & Norgate, 1881.

Collins, Wilkie. *Basil.* [1852]. London: Chatto & Windus, 1890.

———. *Poor Miss Finch.* [1872]. London: Chatto & Windus, 1891.

Compton Burnett, J. *Organ Diseases of Women, Notably Enlargements and Displacements of the Uterus, and Sterility, Considered as Curable by Medicines.* London: Homoeopathic Publishing, 1896.

Corke, Helen. *In Our Infancy: An Autobiography. Part I: 1882-1912.* Cambridge: Cambridge University Press, 1975.

[Craik, Dinah Mulock]. *A Woman's Thoughts about Women.* London: Hurst and Blackett, 1858.

[———]. *Olive: A Novel.* [1850]. London: Macmillan, 1893.

"Cre-fydd." *Cre-Fydd's Family Fare: The Young Housewife's Daily Assistant, on all matters relating to cookery and housekeeping.* London: Simpkin, Marshall, 1864.

Creighton, Louise. *Memoir of a Victorian Woman: Reflections of Louise Creighton, 1850-1936.* Ed. James Thayne Covert. Bloomington: Indiana University Press, 1994.

———. *A Victorian Family as Seen through the Letters of Louise Creighton to Her Mother, 1872–1880.* Ed. James Thayne Covert. Lewiston, N.Y.: Edwin Mellen, 1998.

Cruikshank, Percy. *Sunday Scenes in London and Its Suburbs.* London, published by the artist, 1854.

Cullwick, Hannah. *The Diaries of Hannah Cullwick, Victorian Maidservant.* Ed. Liz Stanley. London: Virago, 1984.

Davey, Richard. *A History of Mourning.* London: Jay's, 1889.

Dickens, Charles. *Bleak House.* [1852–53]. Ed. Norman Page. Harmondsworth: Penguin Books, 1985.

———. *The Christmas Books.* Vol. 1, *A Christmas Carol* [1843] *and The Chimes* [1844]. Ed. Michael Slater. Harmondsworth: Penguin Books, 1985.

———. *Dombey and Son.* [1848]. Ed. Peter Fairclough. Harmondsworth: Penguin Books, 1985.

———. *Great Expectations.* [1860–61]. Garden City, N.Y.: Nelson Doubleday, n.d.

———. *Little Dorrit.* [1857]. Ed. John Holloway. Harmondsworth: Penguin Books, 1985.

———. *The Mystery of Edwin Drood.* [1870]. Ed. Arthur J. Cox. Harmondsworth: Penguin Books, 1985.

———. *The Old Curiosity Shop.* [1841]. Ed. Angus Easson. Harmondsworth: Penguin Books, 1985.

———. *Our Mutual Friend.* [1864–65]. Ed. Adrian Poole. Harmondsworth: Penguin Books, 1997.

———. *The Personal History of David Copperfield.* [1849–50]. Garden City, N.Y.: Nelson Doubleday, n.d.

———. *Correspondence: The Letters of Charles Dickens.* The Pilgrim Edition. Ed. Madeline House, Graham Storey, and Kathleen Tillotson. Oxford: Clarendon Press, 1965– .

———. *Mr and Mrs Charles Dickens. His Letters to Her.* Ed. Walter Dexter, with a foreword by their daughter Kate Perugini. London: Constable, 1935.

Doyle, Arthur Conan. *The Adventures of Sherlock Holmes.* [1892]. New York: Quality Paperback Book Club, 1994.

———. *The Sign of the Four.* [1889]. New York: Quality Paperback Book Club, 1994.

———. *A Study in Scarlet.* [1887]. New York: Quality Paperback Book Club, 1994.

Dresser, Christopher, *Principles of Decorative Design.* London: Cassell, Petter & Galpin, 1873.

———. *Studies in Design.* London: Cassell, Petter & Galpin, [1879].

Duncan, Sara Jeannette. *An American Girl in London.* London: Chatto & Windus, 1891.

Eastlake, C. L. *Hints on Household Taste.* London: Longman & Co., 1868.

Economic Club of London. *Family Budgets; Being the Income and Expenses of Twenty-Eight British Households, 1891–94.* London: P. S. King & Son, 1896.

Edis, Robert W. *Decoration & Furniture of Town Houses.* London: C. Kegan Paul, 1881.

Eliot, George. *Middlemarch.* [1871–72]. Ed. W. J. Harvey. Harmondsworth: Penguin Books, 1985.

———. *The Mill on the Floss.* [1860]. Ed. Gordon S. Haight. Oxford: Oxford University Press, 1998.

Ellis, Sarah Stickney. *The Daughters of England: Their Position in Society, Character and Responsibilities.* London: Fisher, Son & Co., [1845].

———. *The Mothers of England: Their Influence & Responsibility.* London: Fisher, Son & Co., 1843.

————. *The Wives of England: Their Relative Duties, Domestic Influence, & Social Obligations.* London: Fisher, Son & Co., [1843].

————. *The Women of England: Their Social Duties and Domestic Habits.* 2d ed. London: Fisher, Son & Co., [1839].

"Espoir," *How to Live on a Hundred a Year, Make a Good Appearance, and Save Money.* London: Ward, Lock, and Tyler, [1874].

Facey, James William, Jr. *Elementary Decoration: A Guide to the Simpler Forms of Everyday Art, as Applied to the Interior and Exterior Decoration of Dwelling-Houses.* London: Crosby Lockwood, 1882.

Farjeon, Eleanor. *A Nursery in the Nineties.* London: Victor Gollancz, 1935.

Farningham, Marianne. *Home Life.* London: James Clarke, 1889.

Faunthorpe, Rev. J. P., ed. *Household Science: Readings in Necessary Knowledge for Girls and Young Women.* 5th ed. London: Edward Stanford, 1889. [NB: Although it does not say so, this book is an expanded version of R. J. Mann's *Domestic Economy,* q.v., with some interesting variations.]

Forster, John. *Life of Charles Dickens.* London: Chapman & Hall, 1874.

Forster, Laura. xxii/14-c: Country dinners, 1857–70; xxii/11–12, Recollections; xxii/4; Journal, 1864–65, 1870, ?1872, xxi/1-a. E. M. Forster Papers, King's College, Cambridge.

Freeling, Arthur. *The Young Bride's Book; Being Hints for Regulating the Conduct of Married Women, with a Few Medical Axioms.* London: Henry Washbourne, 1839.

Garrett, Rhoda and Agnes. *Suggestions for House Decoration in Painting, Woodwork, and Furniture.* London: Macmillan, 1876.

Gaskell, Mrs. [Elizabeth]. *Cranford.* [1851–53]. Ed. Peter Keating. Harmondsworth: Penguin Books, 1986.

————. *Ruth.* [1853]. Ed. Alan Shelston. Oxford: Oxford University Press, 1985.

————. *Further Letters of Mrs Gaskell.* Ed. John Chapple and Alan Shelston. Manchester: Manchester University Press, 2000.

————. *The Letters of Mrs Gaskell.* Ed. J. A. V. Chapple and Arthur Pollard. Manchester: Manchester University Press, 1997.

————. *Private Voices: The Diaries of Elizabeth Gaskell and Sophia Holland.* Ed. J. A. V. Chapple and Anita Wilson. Keele: Keele University Press, 1996.

Gell, The Hon. Mrs. *Under Three Reigns, 1860–1920.* London: Kegan Paul, Trench, Trübner, 1927.

Gissing, George. *New Grub Street.* [1891]. Harmondsworth: Penguin Books, 1968.

————. *The Odd Women.* [1893]. London: Sidgwick & Jackson, 1915.

Godwin, George. *London Shadows: A Glance at the Homes of Thousands.* London: G. Routledge, 1854.

Gosse, Edmund. *Father and Son.* [1907]. Ed. Peter Abbs. Harmondsworth: Penguin Books, 1983.

Gosse, Philip Henry. *A Memorial of the Last Days on Earth of Emily Gosse*. London: James Nisbet, 1857.

Grant, Elizabeth. *The Highland Lady in Ireland: Journals, 1840–50*. Ed. Patricia Pelly and Andrew Tod. Edinburgh: Canongate, 1991.

Grossmith, George and Weedon. *The Diary of a Nobody*. [1892]. London: Folio Society, 1979.

Hardy, Esther le. *The Home Nurse and Manual for the Sick-Room*. London: John Churchill, 1863.

Hare, Augustus. *The Story of My Life*. 6 vols. London: George Allen, 1896–1900.

Haweis, Mrs. [Mary]. *The Art of Beauty*. 2d ed. London: Chatto & Windus, 1883.

———. *The Art of Decoration*. London: Chatto & Windus, 1881.

———. *The Art of Dress*. London: Chatto & Windus, 1879.

———. *The Art of Housekeeping: A Bridal Garland*. London: Sampson Low, Marston, Searle, & Rivington, 1889.

Hawthorne, Nathaniel. *The English Notebooks: 1853–1856* and *1856–1860* (vols. 21 and 22). Ed. Thomas Woodson and Bill Ellis. Columbus, Ohio: Ohio State University Press, 1997.

Hayek, F. A. *John Stuart Mill and Harriet Taylor: Their Correspondence and Subsequent Marriage*. London: Routledge & Kegan Paul, 1951.

Hellyer, S. Stevens. *The Plumber and Sanitary Houses: A Practical Treatise on the Principles of Internal Plumbing Work, or the Best means for effectually excluding Noxious Gases from our Houses*. London: T. B. Batsford, 1877.

Hibberd, Shirley. *The Book of the Aquarium; or, Practical Instructions on the formation, stocking, and management in all seasons, of collections of marine and river animals and plants*. London: Groombridge and Sons, 1860.

———. *The Fern Garden: How to Make, Keep, and Enjoy It; or, Fern Culture Made Easy*. London: Groombridge and Sons, 1869.

———. *Rustic Adornments for Homes of Taste, and Recreations for Town Folk, in the Study and Imitation of Nature*. London: Groombridge and Sons, 1857.

———. *Water-Cresses without Sewage. Home Culture of the Water-Cress: A Practical Guide to the Cultivation of the Water-cress in pans, troughs, beds, and forcing frames, For the Supply of the Household in all Seasons with Cresses of the Finest Quality, at a merely Nominal Cost of Money and Labour*. London: E. W. Allen, 1878.

———. *Water for Nothing: Every House Its Own Water Supply*. London, Effingham Wilson, 1879.

Holman Hunt, Diana. *My Grandmothers and I*. [1960]. London: Hamish Hamilton, 1987.

Houlston's Industrial Library. *The Lady's Maid: Her Duties, and How to Perform Them*. No. 22. London: Houlston and Sons, 1877.

———. *The Nursery Maid: Her Duties, and How to Perform Them*. No. 27. London: Houlston and Sons, 1877.

Hudson, Derek. *Munby: Man of Two Worlds. The Life and Diaries of Arthur J. Munby, 1828–1910*. London: John Murray, 1972.

Hughes, M. Vivian. *A London Girl of the Eighties*. London: Oxford University Press, 1936.

———. *A London Home in the Nineties*. London: Oxford University Press, 1937.

———. *A London Child of the Seventies*. London: Oxford University Press, 1934.

Humphry, Mrs. [C. E.]. *Manners for Men*. London: Ward, Lock, 1898.

James, Alice. *The Diary of Alice James*. Ed. Leon Edel. Harmondsworth: Penguin Books, 1982.

———. *The Death and Letters of Alice James: Selected Correspondence*. Ed. Ruth Bernard Yeazell. Berkeley: University of California Press, 1981.

James, Henry. *The Portrait of a Lady*. [1881]. New York: Charles Scribner's Sons, 1908.

James, Mrs. Eliot. *Our Servants, Their Duties to Us and Ours to Them*. London: Ward, Lock, 1883.

James, John Angell. *Female Piety: or the Young Woman's Friend and Guide through Life to Immortality*. London: Hamilton Adams, 1852.

Jeaffreson, John Cody. *Brides and Bridals*. London: Hurst and Blackett, 1872.

Jeune, Lady. *Lesser Questions*. London: Remington, 1894.

Jewsbury, Geraldine. *Selections from the Letters of Geraldine Endsor Jewsbury to Jane Welsh Carlyle*. Ed. Mrs Alexander Ireland. London: Longmans, Green, 1892.

Kerr, Robert. *The Gentleman's House; or, How to Plan English Residences, from the Parsonage to the Palace*. London: John Murray, 1864.

[Lamb, Ann Richelieu]. *Can Women Regenerate Society?* London: John W. Parker, 1844.

Levy, Amy. *Reuben Sachs*. [1888]. London: Persephone Books, 2001.

———. *Miss Meredith*. London: Hodder and Stoughton, 1889.

[Linton, Eliza Lynn]. *The Girl of the Period*. [1868]. London: J. G. Berger, 1883.

Linton, Eliza Lynn. *Ourselves: A Series of Essays on Women*. London: G. Routledge & Sons, 1870.

Loftie, Mrs. *The Dining Room*. London: Macmillan, 1878.

"MBH." *Home Truths for Home Peace, or, "Muddle" Defeated, A Practical Inquiry into What Chiefly Mars or Makes the Comfort of Domestic Life*. London: Effingham Wilson, 1851.

Mackenzie, Compton. *My Life and Times, Octave One, 1883–1891; Octave Two, 1891–1900*. London: Chatto & Windus, 1963.

Mann, Robert James, M.D. *Domestic Economy and Household Science for home education; and for school mistresses and pupil teachers*. London: Edward Stanford, 1878.

[Marchant, W. T.] *Betrothals and Bridals: With a Chat About Wedding Cakes and Wedding Customs*. London: W. Hill & Son, 1879.

[Martineau, Harriet]. *Life in the Sick-Room: Essays by an Invalid*. London: Edward Moxon, 1844.

Marx, daughters. *The Daughters of Karl Marx: Family Correspondence, 1866–98*. Commentary and notes by Olga Meier, trans. and adapted by Faith Evans, intro. by Sheila Rowbotham. London: André Deutsch, 1982.

Mayhew, Henry, ed. *The Shops and Companies of London and the Trades and Manufactories of Great Britain*. London, 1865.

Mayhew, Henry, et al. *London Characters and the Humorous Side of London Life* [1874]. 2d ed. London: Stanley Rivers, 1881.

Mayhew, Henry and Augustus. *The Greatest Plague of Life; or, the Adventures of a Lady in Search of a Good Servant. By one who has been "almost worried to death."* London: David Bogue, 1847.

———. *Living for Appearances*. London: James Blackwood, 1855.

"A Member of the Aristocracy." *Manners and Rules of Good Society, or, Solecisms to Be Avoided*. London: Frederick Warne, 1887.

Miller, Thomas. *Picturesque Sketches of London, Past and Present*. London: Office of the National Illustrated Library, 1852.

Morris, William. *Collected Letters of William Morris*. Ed. Norman Kelvin. Princeton, N.J.: Princeton University Press, 1984.

Munby, Arthur J. *Faithful Servants: Being Epitaphs and Obituaries Recording Their Names and Services*. London: Reeves and Turner, 1891.

Munk, Dr. William. *Euthanasia: or, Medical Treatment in Aid of an Easy Death*. London: Longmans, Green, 1887.

Murphy, Shirley Forster. *Our Homes, and How to Make Them Healthy*. London: Cassell, 1883.

Murray, Ross. *The Modern Householder: A Manual of Domestic Economy in All Its Branches*. London: Frederick Warne, 1872.

Muthesius, Hermann. *The English House*. Ed. and intro. by Dennis Sharp, trans. Janet Seligman. Oxford: Blackwell Scientific, 1979; reprint of 1904 edition.

Neale, The Late Rev. J. M. *The Invalid's Hymn-book: Being a Selection of Hymns Appropriate to the Sick-Room, Original or Translated*. London: J. T. Hayes, 1866.

Nightingale, Florence. "Cassandra." In Ray Strachey, *The Cause: A Short History of the Women's Movement in Great Britain*. London: Virago, 1978.

"One of the Sisterhood." *A Defence for the Girl of the Period*. London: Robert Hardwicke, 1868.

Orrinsmith, Mrs. [Lucy]. *The Drawing Room, Its Decoration and Furniture*. London: Macmillan, 1877.

Panton, Mrs. [Jane Ellen]. *From Kitchen to Garret: Hints for Young Householders*. 4th ed. London: Ward & Downey, 1888.

———. *Homes of Taste: Economical Hints*. London: Sampson Low, Marston, Searle, & Rivington, 1890.

———. *Nooks and Corners.* London: Ward & Downey, 1889.

———. *Suburban Residences, and How to Circumvent Them.* London: Ward & Downey, 1896.

———. *Within Four Walls: A Handbook for Invalids.* London: "The Gentlewoman" Offices, 1893.

Parkyn, Ernest Albert. *The Law of Master and Servant, with a chapter on apprenticeship.* London: Butterworth, 1897.

Patmore, Coventry. *The Angel in the House.* London and Cambridge: Macmillan, 1860 (Book I) and 1863 (Book II).

Pedley, Mrs. Frederick. *Infant Nursing and the Management of Young Children.* London: George Routledge and Sons, 1866.

Peel, Mrs. C. S. *Life's Enchanted Cup: An Autobiography, 1872–1933.* London: John Lane/The Bodley Head, 1933.

[Philp, R. Kemp]. *The Lady's Every-Day Book: A Practical Guide in the Elegant Arts and Daily Difficulties of Domestic Life. By the author of "Enquire Within," "Best of Everything," Etc.* London: E. W. Allen, [c. 1873].

———. *The Practical Housewife, forming a complete Encyclopaedia of Domestic Economy. By the editors of the "Family Friend."* London: Ward and Lock, 1855.

Potter, Beatrix. *The Journal of Beatrix Potter, from 1881 to 1897.* Transcribed from her code writing by Leslie Linder. London: Frederick Warne, 1966.

Pritchard, Rosalind, ed. *London and Londoners, 1898: What to see; what to know; what to do; where to shop; and practical hints.* London: Scientific Press, 1898.

Pullan, Mrs. *Maternal Counsels to a Daughter.* London: Darton, 1855.

Raverat, Gwen. *Period Piece: A Cambridge Childhood.* [1952]. London: Faber & Faber, 1987.

Richardson, C. J. *The Englishman's House from a Cottage to a Mansion.* 2d ed. London: John Camden Hotten, [1871].

Ricket, Edward. *The Gentleman's Table Guide and Table Companion to the Art of Dining and Drinking, with Table Habits and Curious Dishes of the Various Nations, &c., &c., with practical recipes for wine cups, American drinks, punches, cordials, recherché bills of fare, with service of wines, &c.* London: Frederick Warne, 1873.

Ruskin, John. *Sesame and Lilies: Two Lectures by John Ruskin, LL.D.* 1. "Of Kings' Treasures"; 2. "Of Queens' Gardens." London: Smith, Elder & Co., 1865.

Russell, the Hon. R., F.M.S. *London Fogs.* London: Edward Stanford, 1880.

Rutter, J. O. N. *The Advantages of Gas in Private Houses.* London: Virtue Bros., 1865.

Sala, George Augustus. *Gaslight and Daylight, with Some London Scenes They Shine Upon.* London: Chapman & Hall, 1859.

———. *London Up to Date.* London: Adam and Charles Black, 1894.

————. *Twice Round the Clock; or, The Hours of the Day and Night in London.* London: Houlston and Wright, 1859.

[Sibthorpe, Frances Mary]. *Home Is Home: A Domestic Tale.* London: William Pickering, 1851.

Squire, Peter. *A Companion to the Medicine Chest; Giving the Properties and doses of the Most Useful Domestic Medicines, Also Directions for Sick-Room Cookery.* London: John Churchill and Sons, 1866.

Stables, Gordon. *The Girl's Own Book of Health and Beauty.* London: Jarrolds and Sons, 1892.

Staffe, Baroness. *The Lady's Dressing-Room.* Trans. Lady Colin Campbell. London: Cassell, 1892.

Stephen, Mrs. Leslie [Julia Prinsep]. *Notes from Sick Rooms.* London: Smith, Elder, & Co., 1883.

Stevenson, Robert Louis. *The Strange Case of Dr Jekyll and Mr Hyde.* London: Longmans, Green, 1896.

[Surtees, R. S.]. *Mr Sponge's Sporting Tour.* [1853]. London: Folio Society (facsimile of Bradbury and Evans first edition), [1981].

————. *Ask Mama, or The Richest Commoner in England.* London: Bradbury and Evans, 1858.

Taine, Hippolyte. *Notes on England.* Trans. W. F. Rae, 3d ed. London: Strahan, 1872.

Thackeray, William. *Vanity Fair.* [1847–48]. Ed. J. I. M. Stewart. Harmondsworth: Penguin Books, 1985.

Thomas, Sarah. *The Secret Diary of Sarah Thomas, 1860–1865.* Ed. June Lewis. Moreton-in-the-Marsh: Windrush Press, 1994.

Thomson, Anthony Todd. *The Domestic Management of the Sick-Room, necessary, in aid of medical treatment, for the cure of diseases.* London: Longman, Orme, Brown, Green, & Longman's, 1841.

Timings, Caroline Louisa. *Letter from the Past: Memories of a Victorian Childhood.* Privately published, 1954.

Trollope, Anthony. *Barchester Towers.* [1857]. Ed. Robin Gilmour. Harmondsworth: Penguin Books, 1994.

————. *Doctor Thorne.* [1858]. London: J. M. Dent & Sons, 1908.

————. *Framley Parsonage.* [1861] Ed. David Skilton and Peter Miles. Harmondsworth: Penguin Books, 1986.

————. *He Knew He Was Right.* [1869]. Ed. John Sutherland. Oxford: Oxford World's Classics, 1998.

————. *The Last Chronicle of Barset.* [1866–67]. Ed. Stephen Gill. Oxford: Oxford World's Classics, 2001.

————. *Miss Mackenzie.* London: Chapman and Hall, 1865.

————. *The Small House at Allington.* [1864]. Ed. Julian Thompson. Harmondsworth: Penguin Books, 1991.

————. *The Way We Live Now*. [1875]. Ed. Frank Kermode. Harmondsworth: Penguin Books, 1994.

Tytler, Ann Fraser. *Common Sense for Housemaids*. London: Hatchards, 1869.

Veblen, Thorstein. *The Theory of the Leisure Class*. [1899]. Amherst, N.Y.: Prometheus Books, 1998.

Walsh, J. H. *A Manual of Domestic Economy: Suited to Families Spending from £100 to £1000 a Year*. London: G. Routledge, 1857.

Ward and Lock. *Ward and Lock's Home Book: A Domestic Cyclopaedia*. London: Ward and Lock, 1866.

Warren, Mrs. Eliza. *How I Managed My House on Two Hundred Pounds a Year*. London: Houlston and Wright, 1864.

————. *Cookery for Maids of All Work*. London. Groombridge & Sons, 1856.

————. *Comfort for Small Incomes*. London: At the Office of "The Ladies' Treasury," 1866.

————. *How I Managed My Children from Infancy to Marriage*. London: Houlston and Wright, 1865.

————. *A Young Wife's Perplexities*. London: Houlston and Sons, 1886.

Wells, H. G. *Kipps: The Story of a Simple Soul*. [1905]. Ed. Peter Vansittart. London: Everyman, J. M. Dent, 1993.

————. *Tono-Bungay*. [1909]. London: n.p., 1933.

[White, William Hale, pseud. of] Mark Rutherford. *The Autobiography of Mark Rutherford, Dissenting Minister*, "edited by his friend Reuben Shapcott." London: Trübner, 1881.

Wichelo, Lily [Alice Clara Forster]. Journal. 1872. E. M. Forster Papers, King's College, Cambridge.

Wood, Mrs. Henry. *East Lynne*. [1861]. Ed. Andrew Maunder. Peterborough, Ont.: Broadview Literary Texts, 2000.

[Wright, Thomas]. "Some Habits and Customs of the Working Classes, by a Journeyman Engineer." London, 1867.

Young, William. *Town and Country Mansions and Suburban Homes*. London: Spon, 1879.

Yonge, Charlotte M. *The Daisy Chain, or, Aspirations: A Family Chronicle*. [1856]. London: Macmillan, 1886.

SECONDARY SOURCES

Ackroyd, Peter. *Dickens*. London: Vintage, 1999.

Adburgham, Alison. *A Punch History of Manners and Modes, 1841–1940*. London: Hutchinson, 1961.

————. *Shops and Shopping, 1800–1914: Where, and in What Manner, the Well-*

Dressed Englishwoman Bought Her Clothes. Rev. ed. London: George Allen and Unwin, 1981.

Allen, David Elliston. *The Victorian Fern Craze: A History of Pteridomania*. London: Hutchinson, 1969.

Allen, Rick, ed. *The Moving Pageant: A Literary Sourcebook on London Street-Life, 1700–1914*. London: Routledge, 1998.

Allen, Sheila, and Diana Leonard Barker, eds. *Dependence and Exploitation in Work and Marriage*. London: Longmans, 1976.

Altick, Richard D. *Victorian People and Ideas*. London: J. M. Dent & Sons, 1974.

Ames, K. L. *Death in the Dining Room and Other Tales of Victorian Culture*. Philadelphia: Temple University Press, 1992.

Anderson, Gregory. *Victorian Clerks*. Manchester: Manchester University Press, 1976.

Anderson, Michael. "The Social Implications of Demographic Change." In F. M. L. Thompson, ed., *The Cambridge Social History of Britain, 1750–1950*. Cambridge: Cambridge University Press, 1990.

Anderson, Michael, ed. *British Population History from the Black Death to the Present Day*. Cambridge: Cambridge University Press, 1996.

Ashton, Rosemary. *Thomas and Jane Carlyle: Portrait of a Marriage*. London: Chatto & Windus, 2002.

Ayres, Brenda. *Dissenting Women in Dickens' Novels: The Subversion of Domestic Ideology*. Westport, Conn.: Greenwood Press, 1998.

Bailin, Miriam. *The Sickroom in Victorian Fiction: The Art of Being Ill*. Cambridge: Cambridge University Press, 1994.

Banham, Joanna, Sally Macdonald, and Julia Porter. *Victorian Interior Design*. London: Cassell, 1991.

Banks, J. A. *Prosperity and Parenthood: A Study of Family Planning among the Victorian Middle Classes*. [1954]. London: Gregg Revivals, 1993.

Banks, J. A., and Olive Banks. *Feminism and Family Planning in Victorian England*. Liverpool: Liverpool University Press, 1964.

Barrett, H., and J. Phillips. *Suburban Style: The British Home, 1840–1960*. London: Macdonald, 1987.

Beetham, Margaret. *A Magazine of Her Own? Domesticity and Desire in the Woman's Magazine, 1800–1914*. London: Routledge, 1996.

Beetham, Margaret, and Kay Boardman, eds. *Victorian Women's Magazines: An Anthology*. Manchester: Manchester University Press, 2001.

Behlmer, George K. *Friends of the Family: The English Home and Its Guardians, 1850–1940*. Stanford, Calif.: Stanford University Press, 1998.

Blair, Munroe. *Ceramic Water Closets*. Princes Risborough: Shire Publications, 2000.

Branca, Patricia. *Silent Sisterhood: Middle Class Women in the Victorian Home*. London: Croom Helm, 1975.

Breward, Christopher. *The Hidden Consumer: Masculinities, Fashion and City Life, 1860–1914*. Manchester: Manchester University Press, 1999.

Briggs, Asa. *Victorian Things*. Harmondsworth: Penguin Books, 1990.

Brimblecombe, Peter. *The Big Smoke: A History of Air Pollution in London since Medieval Times*. London: Methuen, 1987.

Bryden, Inga, and Janet Floyd, eds. *Domestic Space: Reading the Nineteenth Century Interior*. Manchester: Manchester University Press, 1999.

Burn, W. L. *The Age of Equipoise: A Study of the Mid-Victorian Generation*. London: George Allen & Unwin, 1964.

Burnett, John. *A History of the Cost of Living*. Harmondsworth: Penguin Books, 1969.

———. *Plenty and Want: A Social History of Diet in England from 1815 to the Present Day*. London: Thomas Nelson and Sons, 1966.

Burton, Elizabeth. *The Early Victorians at Home, 1837–1861*. London: Longman, 1972.

Bynum, W. F., and Roy Porter, eds. *Living and Dying in London*. Wellcome Medical History Supplement no. 11. London: Wellcome Institute, 1991.

Calder, Jenni. *The Victorian Home*. London: B. T. Batsford, 1977.

———. *Women and Marriage in Victorian Fiction*. London: Thames and Hudson, 1976.

Carey, John. *The Intellectuals and the Masses. Pride and Prejudice among the Literary Intelligentsia*. London: Faber and Faber, 1992.

Cartwright, Frederick F. *A Social History of Medicine*. London: Longman, 1977.

Casteras, Susan. *Images of Victorian Womanhood in English Art*. Cranbury, N.J., and London: Associated University Presses, 1987.

Caton, Donald. *What a Blessing She Had Chloroform: The Medical and Social Response to the Pain of Childbirth from 1800 to the Present*. New Haven: Yale University Press, 1999.

Chapman, Tony, and Jenny Hockey, eds. *Ideal Homes? Social Change and Domestic Life*. London: Routledge, 1999.

Chase, Karen, and Michael Levenson. *The Spectacle of Intimacy: A Public Life for the Victorian Family*. Princeton, N.J.: Princeton University Press, 2000.

Choi, Tina Young. "Writing the Victorian City: Discourses of Risk, Connection, and Inevitability." *Victorian Studies*, vol. 43, no. 4, Summer 2001, pp. 561–89.

Cohen, Monica F. *Professional Domesticity in the Victorian Novel: Women, Work and Home*. Cambridge: Cambridge University Press, 1998.

Colley, Ann C. *Nostalgia and Recollection in Victorian Culture*. Basingstoke: Macmillan, 1998.

Colp, Ralph, Jr. *To Be an Invalid: The Illness of Charles Darwin*. Chicago: University of Chicago Press, 1977.

[Costume Society, The]. *High Victorian: Proceedings of the Second Annual Con-*

ference of the Costume Society. London: Victoria and Albert Publications, 1968.

Crossick, Geoffrey, ed. *The Lower Middle Class in Britain, 1870–1914.* London: Croom Helm, 1977.

Cunnington, C. Willet. *The Perfect Lady.* London: Max Parrish, 1948.

Cunnington, C. Willet, and Phillis Cunnington. *The History of Underclothes.* London: Michael Joseph, 1951.

Cunnington, Phillis, and Catherine Lucas. *Costume for Births, Marriages and Deaths.* London: Adam & Charles Black, 1972.

Dakers, Caroline. *The Holland Park Circle: Artists and Victorian Society.* London: Yale University Press, 1999.

Davidoff, Leonore. "'Adam Spoke First and Named the Orders of the World': Masculine and Feminine Domains in History and Sociology." In H. Corr and L. Jamieson, eds., *The Politics of Everyday Life: Continuity and Change in Work, Labour and the Family.* London: Macmillan, 1990.

———. *The Best Circles. Society, Etiquette and the Season.* London: Croom Helm, 1973.

———. *Worlds Between: Historical Perspectives on Gender and Class.* Cambridge: Polity Press, 1995.

Davidoff, Leonore, Megan Doolittle, Janet Fink, and Katherine Holden. *The Family Story: Blood, Contract, and Intimacy, 1830-1960.* London: Longman, 1999.

Davidoff, Leonore, and Catherine Hall. *Family Fortunes: Men and Women of the English Middle Classes, 1780–1850.* London: Hutchinson, 1987.

Davidoff, Leonore, and Ruth Hawthorn. *A Day in the Life of a Victorian Domestic Servant.* London: George Allen & Unwin, 1976.

Davidson, Caroline. *A Woman's Work Is Never Done: A History of Housework in the British Isles, 1650–1950.* London: Chatto & Windus, 1982.

Delamont, Sara, and Lorna Duffin, eds. *The Nineteenth-Century Woman: Her Cultural and Physical World.* London: Croom Helm, 1978.

Delgado, Alan. *Victorian Entertainment.* Newton Abbot: David & Charles, 1971.

Desmond, Adrian, and James Moore. *Darwin.* London: Michael Joseph, 1991.

Dickerson, Vanessa D. *Keeping the Victorian House: A Collection of Essays.* New York: Garland Publishing, 1995.

Dillon, Maureen. "'Like a Glow-worm who had lost its Glow', The Invention of the Incandescent Electric Lamp and the Development of Artificial Silk and Electric Jewellery." *Costume,* vol. 35, 2001, pp. 76–81.

Duff, David. *Punch on Children: A Panorama, 1845–1865.* London: Frederick Muller, 1975.

Dutton, Ralph. *The Victorian Home: Some Aspects of Nineteenth-Century Taste and Manners.* London: B. T. Batsford, 1954.

Dyhouse, Carol. *Girls Growing Up in Late Victorian and Edwardian England.* London: Routledge & Kegan Paul, 1981.

———. *Feminism and the Family in England, 1880–1939.* Oxford: Blackwell, 1989.

Dyos, H. J. *Victorian Suburb: A Study of the Growth of Camberwell.* Leicester: Leicester University Press, 1961.

Dyos, H. J., and Michael Wolff, eds. *The Victorian City: Images and Realities.* London: Routledge & Kegan Paul, 1973.

Ehrenreich, Barbara, and Deirdre English. *For Her Own Good: 150 Years of the Experts' Advice to Women.* London: Pluto Press, 1979.

Flint, Kate. *The Victorians and the Visual Imagination.* Cambridge: Cambridge University Press, 2000.

Forty, Adrian. *Objects of Desire: Design and Society, 1750–1980.* London: Thames and Hudson, 1986.

Foucault, Michel. "Of Other Spaces: Utopias and Heterotopias," In N. Leach, ed., *Rethinking Architecture: A Reader in Cultural Theory.* London: Routledge, 1997.

Freeman, Michael. *Railways and the Victorian Imagination.* London: Yale University Press, 1999.

Freeman, Sarah. *Mutton and Oysters: Food, Cooking and Eating in Victorian Times.* London: Gollancz, 1989.

Gay, Peter. *The Bourgeois Experience from Victoria to Freud.* Vol. 1, *Education of the Senses.* New York: Oxford University Press, 1984. Vol. 2, *The Tender Passion.* London: Oxford University Press, 1986. Vol. 3, *Cultivation of Hatred.* New York: W. W. Norton, 1993. Vol. 4, *The Naked Heart.* London: Fontana, 1998. Vol. 5, *Pleasure Wars.* London: HarperCollins, 1998.

———. *Schnitzler's Century: The Making of Middle-Class Culture, 1815–1914.* New York: W. W. Norton, 2002.

Gere, Charlotte. *Nineteenth Century Decoration: The Art of the Interior.* London: Weidenfeld & Nicolson, 1989.

Gilbert, Sandra, and Susan Gubar. *The Madwoman in the Attic: A Study of Women and the Literary Imagination in the Nineteenth Century.* New Haven: Yale University Press, 1979.

Ginsburg, Madeleine. *Victorian Dress in Photographs.* London: Batsford, 1982.

Gloag, John. *Victorian Comfort: A Social History of Design from 1830–1900.* London: Adam & Charles Black, 1961.

———. *Victorian Taste: Some Social Aspects of Architectural and Industrial Design from 1820–1900.* London: Adam & Charles Black, 1962.

Gorham, Deborah. *The Victorian Girl and the Feminine Ideal.* London: Croom Helm, 1982.

Grier, K. *Culture and Comfort: Parlor-Making and Middle-Class Identity.* Washington, D.C.: Smithsonian Institute Press, 1988.

Guy, Josephine M., ed. *The Victorian Age: An Anthology of Sources and Documents*. London: Routledge, 1998.

Haley, Bruce. *The Healthy Body and Victorian Culture*. Cambridge, Mass.: Harvard University Press, 1978.

Hall, Catherine. "The Sweet Delights of Home." In *From the Fires of Revolution to the Great War*, ed. Michelle Perrot, trans. Arthur Goldhammer, vol. 4 of *A History of Private Life*, ed. Philippe Ariès and Georges Duby. Cambridge, Mass.: Belknap Press of Harvard University Press, 1990.

Haller, John S., Jr., and Robin M. Haller. *The Physician and Sexuality in Victorian America*. Urbana: University of Illinois Press, 1974.

Halliday, Stephen. *The Great Stink of London: Sir Joseph Bazalgette and the Cleansing of the Victorian Capital*. Stroud: Sutton, 1999.

Hardy, Anne. *The Epidemic Streets: Infectious Disease and the Rise of Preventative Medicine, 1856–1900*. Oxford: Clarendon Press, 1993.

Hartman, Mary S. *Victorian Murderesses: A True History of Thirteen Respectable French and English Women Accused of Unspeakable Crimes*. London: Robson Books, 1977.

Hartman, Mary, and Lois Banner, eds., *Clio's Consciousness Raised: New Perspectives on the History of Women*. New York: Harper Torchbooks, 1974.

Heidegger, Martin. "Building, Dwelling, Thinking." In N. Leach, ed., *Rethinking Architecture: A Reader in Cultural Theory*. London: Routledge, 1997.

Hellerstein, Erna Olafson, Leslie Parker Hume, and Karen M. Offen, eds. *Victorian Women: A Documentary Account of Women's Lives in Nineteenth-Century England, France and the United States*. Brighton: Harvester Press, 1981.

Helly, D. O., and S. Reverby, eds. *Gendered Domains: Rethinking Public and Private in Women's History*. Ithaca, N.Y.: Cornell University Press, 1992.

Hewitt, Martin, ed. *An Age of Equipoise? Reassessing Mid-Victorian Britain*. Aldershot: Ashgate, 2000.

Holme, Thea. *The Carlyles at Home*. London: Oxford University Press, 1965.

Hoppen, K. Theodore. *The Mid-Victorian Generation, 1846–1886*. Oxford: Clarendon Press, 1998.

Horn, Pamela. *The Victorian Town Child*. Stroud: Sutton, 1997.

———. *The Rise and Fall of the Victorian Servant*. Dublin: Gill and Macmillan, 1975.

———. *Pleasures and Pastimes in Victorian Britain*. Stroud: Sutton, 1999.

Houghton, Walter E. *The Victorian Frame of Mind, 1830–1870*. New Haven: Yale University Press, 1957.

Huggett, Frank E. *Life Below Stairs: Domestic Servants in England from Victorian Times*. London: Book Club Associates, 1977.

Hunter, Michael. *The Victorian Villas of Hackney*. London: Hackney Society, 1981.

Jalland, Patricia. *Death in the Victorian Family*. Oxford: Oxford University Press, 1996.

Jervis, Simon, and Leonée Ormond. *Linley Sambourne House*. London: Victorian Society, 1987.

Johnson, James H., and Colin G. Pooley. *The Structure of Nineteenth Century Cities*. London: Croom Helm, 1982.

Jordanova, Ludmilla. *Sexual Visions: Images of Gender in Science and Medicine between the Eighteenth and Twentieth Centuries*. Hemel Hempstead: Wheatsheaf, 1989.

Kelly, Ann. "Ponds in the Parlour: The Victorian Aquarium." *Things*, summer 1995, pp. 55–68.

Kertzer, David I., and Marzio Barbagli. *The History of the European Family*. Vol. 2, *Family Life in the Long Nineteenth Century, 1789–1913*. London: Yale University Press, 2002.

Knoepflmacher, U. C. *Ventures into Childland: Victorians, Fairy Tales, and Femininity*. Chicago, University of Chicago Press, 1998.

Knoepflmacher, U. C., and G. B. Tennyson, eds. *Nature and the Victorian Imagination*. Berkeley: University of California Press, 1977.

Knowles, Owen. "Veneering and the Age of Veneer: A Source and Background for *Our Mutual Friend*." *The Dickensian*, vol. 81, no. 2, Summer 1985, pp. 88–96.

Lansdell, Avril. *Wedding Fashions, 1860–1980*. Princes Risborough: Shire Publications, 1983.

Langland, Elizabeth. *Nobody's Angels: Middle-Class Women and Domestic Ideology in Victorian Culture*. Ithaca, N.Y.: Cornell University Press, 1995.

Lasdun, Susan. *Victorians at Home*. London: Weidenfeld & Nicolson, 1981.

Lawton, Richard, ed. *The Census and Social Structure: An Interpretative Guide to Nineteenth Century Censuses for England and Wales*. London: Frank Cass, 1978.

Leach, N., ed. *Rethinking Architecture: A Reader in Cultural Theory*. London: Routledge, 1997.

Levitt, Sarah. *Victorians Unbuttoned: Registered Designs for Clothing, Their Makers and Wearers, 1839–1900*. London: George Allen & Unwin, 1986.

Lewis, Jane, ed. *Labour and Love: Women's Experience of Home and Family, 1850–1940*. Oxford: Basil Blackwell, 1986.

Little, Jo, Linda Peake, and Pat Richardson, eds. *Women in Cities: Gender and the Urban Environment*. London: Macmillan Education, 1988.

Lockwood, David. *The Blackcoated Worker: A Study in Class Consciousness*. London: George Allen & Unwin, 1958.

Loeb, Lori Anne. *Consuming Angels: Advertising and Victorian Women*. New York: Oxford University Press, 1994.

Logan, Thad. *The Victorian Parlour*. Cambridge: Cambridge University Press, 2001.

Lutyens, Mary. *The Ruskins and the Grays*. London: John Murray, 1972.

Malcolmson, Patricia E. *English Laundresses: A Social History, 1850–1930.* Urbana: University of Illinois Press, 1986.

Marcus, Sharon. *Apartment Stories: City and Home in Nineteenth-Century Paris and London.* Berkeley: University of California Press, 1999.

Marsden, Gordon, ed. *Victorian Values: Personalities and Perspectives in Nineteenth-Century Society.* 2d ed. London: Longman, 1998.

Marshall, John, and Ian Willox. *The Victorian House.* London: Sidgwick & Jackson, 1986.

McBride, Theresa M. *The Domestic Revolution: The Modernisation of Household Service in England and France, 1820-1920.* London: Croom Helm, 1976.

McCracken, G. *Culture and Consumption: New Approaches to the Symbolic Character of Consumer Goods and Activities.* Bloomington: Indiana University Press, 1988.

Miall, Antony and Peter. *The Victorian Nursery Book.* London: J. M. Dent & Sons, 1980.

Miller, Andrew H. *Novels Behind Glass: Commodity Culture and Victorian Narrative.* Cambridge: Cambridge University Press, 1995.

Mills, Dennis, and Kevin Schürer, eds. *Local Communities in the Victorian Census Enumerators' Books.* Oxford: Leopard's Head Press, 1996.

Mitchell, Sally. *Daily Life in Victorian England.* Westport, Conn.: Greenwood Press, 1996.

Monsarrat, Ann. *And the Bride Wore . . . The Story of the White Wedding.* London: Gentry Books, 1973.

Mumford, Lewis. *The City in History: Its Origins, Its Transformations, and Its Prospects.* Harmondsworth: Penguin Books, 1966.

Murray, Janet. *Strong-Minded Women and Other Lost Voices from Nineteenth-Century England.* Harmondsworth: Penguin Books, 1984.

Muthesius, Stefan. *The English Terraced House.* London: Yale University Press, 1982.

Nead, Lynda. *Myths of Sexuality, Representations of Women in Victorian Britain.* Oxford: Basil Blackwell, 1988.

———. *Victorian Babylon: People, Streets and Images in Nineteenth-Century London.* London: Yale University Press, 2000.

Nelson, Claudia. *Boys Will be Girls: The Feminine Ethic and British Children's Fiction, 1857–1917.* London and New Brunswick, N.J.: Rutgers University Press, 1991.

Nelson, Claudia, and Ann Sumner Holmes, eds. *Maternal Instincts: Visions of Motherhood and Sexuality in Britain, 1875–1925.* Basingstoke: Macmillan, 1997.

Nicholson, Shirley. *A Victorian Household.* Rev. ed. Stroud: Sutton, 1994.

Nord, Deborah Epstein. *Walking the Victorian Streets: Women, Representation and the City.* Ithaca, N.Y.: Cornell University Press, 1995.

Norris, Herbert, and Oswald Curtis. *Costumes and Fashion.* Vol. 6, *The Nineteenth Century.* London: J. M. Dent & Sons, 1933.

Olsen, Donald. *The City as a Work of Art: London, Paris, Vienna.* New Haven: Yale University Press, 1986.

———. *The Growth of Victorian London.* London: Batsford, 1976.

Oppenheim, Janet. *Shattered Nerves: Doctors, Patients and Depression in Victorian England.* New York: Oxford University Press, 1991.

Palmer, Arnold. *Movable Feasts: A Reconaissance of the Origins and Consequences of Fluctuations in Meal-Times . . .* New York: Oxford University Press, 1952.

Palmer, Roy. *The Water Closet: A New History.* Newton Abbot: David & Charles, 1973.

Peterson, Audrey C. "Brain Fever in Nineteenth Century Literature: Fact and Fiction." *Victorian Studies,* vol. 19, 1975/6, pp. 437–65.

Picker, John M. "The Soundproof Study: Victorian Professionals, Work Space, and Urban Noise." *Victorian Studies,* vol. 42, 1998/9, pp. 427–53.

Pike, E. Royston. *Human Documents of the Age of the Forsytes.* London: George Allen & Unwin, 1969.

———. *Human Documents of the Victorian Golden Age, 1850–1875.* London: George Allen & Unwin, 1967.

Pinchbeck, Ivy. *Women Workers and the Industrial Revolution, 1750–1850.* London: Frank Cass, 1967.

Pinchbeck, Ivy, and Margaret Hewitt. *Children in English Society.* London: London: Routledge & Kegan Paul, vol. 2, 1973.

Porter, Roy. *Bodies Politic: Disease, Death and Doctors in Britain, 1650–1900.* London: Reaktion, 2001.

Rappaport, Erika Diane. *Shopping for Pleasure: Women in the Making of London's West End.* Princeton, N.J.: Princeton University Press, 2000.

Ravetz, Alison. "The Victorian Coal Kitchen and its Reformers." *Victorian Studies,* vol. 11, 1968, pp. 435–60.

Reader, W. J. *Professional Men: The Rise of the Professional Classes in Nineteenth-Century England.* London: Weidenfeld and Nicolson, 1966.

Reay, Barry. *Watching Hannah: Sexuality, Horror and Bodily De-formation in Victorian England.* London: Reaktion, 2002.

Reed, John R. *Victorian Conventions.* Athens, Ohio: Ohio University Press, 1975.

Rees, Barbara. *The Victorian Lady.* New York: Gordon & Cremonesi, 1977.

Reiss, Erna. *Rights and Duties of Englishwomen: A Study in Law and Public Opinion.* Manchester: Sherratt & Hughes, 1934.

Rieger, Christina. " 'Sweet Order and Arrangement': Victorian Women Edit John Ruskin." *Journal of Victorian Culture,* vol. 6.2, Autumn 2001, pp. 231–49.

Roberts, Helene E. "The Exquisite Slave: The Role of Clothes in the Making of the Victorian Woman." *Signs: Journal of Women in Culture and Society,* 2, Spring 1977, pp. 554–69.

Robson, Catherine. *Men in Wonderland: The Lost Girlhood of the Victorian Gentleman*. Princeton, N.J.: Princeton University Press, 2001.

Rose, Phyllis. *Parallel Lives: Five Victorian Marriages*. London: Chatto & Windus, 1984.

Rubinstein, David, ed. *Victorian Homes*. Newton Abbot: David & Charles, 1974.

Rybczynski, Witold. *Looking Around: A Journey through Architecture*. London: Scribner, 2002.

Schivelbusch, Wolfgang. *Disenchanted Night: The Industrialisation of Light in the Nineteenth Century*. Trans. Angela Davies. Oxford: Berg, 1988.

———. *The Railway Journey: The Industrialisation of Time and Space in the Nineteenth Century*. 2d ed. Leamington Spa: Berg, 1986.

Schlör, Joachim. *Nights in the Big City: Paris, Berlin, London, 1840-1930*. Trans. Pierre Gottfried Imhof and Dafydd Rees Roberts. London: Reaktion, 1998.

Shepard, Ernest H. *Drawn from Memory*. London: Methuen, 1957.

Shonfield, Zuzanna. *The Precariously Privileged: A Professional Family in Victorian London*. Oxford: Oxford University Press, 1987.

Showalter, Elaine. *The Female Malady: Women, Madness and English Culture*. London: Virago, 1987.

———. *A Literature of Their Own*. Princeton, N.J.: Princeton University Press, 1977.

Sigsworth, Eric M., ed. *In Search of Victorian Values: Aspects of Nineteenth-Century Thought and Society*. Manchester: Manchester University Press, 1988.

Simpson, David, ed. *Subject to History: Ideology, Class and Gender*. Ithaca, N.Y.: Cornell University Press, 1991.

Small, Hugh. *Florence Nightingale: Avenging Angel*. New York: St. Martin's Press, 1998.

Spaas, Lieve, ed. *Paternity and Fatherhood: Myths and Realities*. Basingstoke: Macmillan, 1998.

Spalding, Frances. *Gwen Raverat: Friends, Family, and Affections*. London: Harvill Press, 2001.

Steele, Valerie. *The Corset: A Cultural History*. London: Yale University Press, 2001.

Storey, Gladys. *Dickens and Daughter*. London: Frederick Muller, 1939.

Taylor, Irene and Alan. *The Assassin's Cloak: An Anthology of the World's Greatest Diarists*. Edinburgh: Canongate Books, 2000.

Taylor, Lou. *Mourning Dress: A Costume and Social History*. London: George Allen and Unwin, 1983.

Thompson, F. M. L. *The Rise of Respectable Society: A Social History of Victorian Britain, 1830–1900*. Cambridge, Mass.: Harvard University Press, 1988.

———. *Hampstead: Building a Borough, 1650–1964*. London: Routledge and Kegan Paul, 1974.

———. ed. *The Cambridge Social History of Britain, 1750–1950*. Cambridge: Cambridge University Press, 1990.

Tosh, John. *A Man's Place: Masculinity and the Middle-Class Home in Victorian England*. London: Yale University Press, 1999.

Tosh, John, and Michael Roper, eds. *Manful Assertions: Masculinities in Britain Since 1800*. London: Routledge, 1991.

Thwaite, Ann. *Edmund Gosse: A Literary Landscape, 1849–1928*. London: Secker & Warburg, 1984.

———. *Glimpses of the Wonderful: The Life of Philip Henry Gosse, 1810–1888*. London: Faber & Faber, 2002.

Van Dulken, Stephen. *Inventing the Nineteenth Century: The Great Age of Victorian Inventions*. London: British Library, 2001.

Vicinus, Martha, ed. *Suffer and Be Still: Women in the Victorian Age*. London: Methuen, 1980.

———. *A Widening Sphere: Changing Roles of Victorian Women*. Bloomington: Indiana University Press, 1977.

Vickery, Amanda. "Golden Age to Separate Spheres? A Review of the Categories and Chronology of English Women's History." *Historical Journal*, 36 (1993), pp. 383–414.

Viewing, Gerald. *Exchange and Mart: Selected Issues, 1868–1948*. Intro. by John Mendes. Newton Abbot: David and Charles, 1970.

Vries, Leonard de. *Victorian Advertisements*. Text by James Laver. London: John Murray, 1968.

Walkley, Christina. *Dressed to Impress: 1840–1914*. London: B. T. Batsford, 1989.

———. *The Ghost in the Looking Glass: The Victorian Seamstress*. London: Peter Owen, 1981.

Walkley, Christina, and Vanda Foster. *Crinolines and Crimping Irons: Victorian Clothes: How They Were Cleaned and Cared For*. London: Peter Owen, 1978.

Waugh, Norah. *Corsets and Crinolines*. London: B. T. Batsford, 1954.

Welsh, Alexander. *The City of Dickens*. Oxford: Clarendon Press, 1971.

White, Cynthia L. *Women's Magazines, 1693–1968*. London: Michael Joseph, 1970.

Whitehouse, J. Howard. *Vindication of Ruskin*. London: George Allen and Unwin, 1950.

Wilson, Elizabeth. *The Sphinx in the City: Urban Life, the Control of Disorder, and Women*. Berkeley: University of California Press, 1992.

Winslow, John H. *Darwin's Victorian Malady: Evidence for Its Medically Induced Origin*. Philadelphia: American Philosophical Society, 1971.

Winer, James. *London's Teeming Streets, 1830–1914*. London: Routledge, 1999.

Wohl, Anthony S., ed. *The Victorian Family: Structure and Stresses*. London: Croom Helm, 1978.

Wolff, Janet. *Feminine Sentences: Essays on Women and Culture*. Oxford: Polity Press, 1990.

Woodward, John, and David Richards, eds. *Health Care and Popular Medicine in Nineteenth Century England: Essays in the Social History of Medicine.* London: Croom Helm, 1977.

Wright, Lawrence. *Home Fires Burning: The History of Domestic Heating and Cooking.* London: Routledge & Kegan Paul, 1964.

Yarwood, Doreen. *The British Kitchen: Housewifery since Roman Times.* London: B. T. Batsford, 1981.

PICTURE CREDITS

The author and publisher make grateful acknowledgment for permission to reproduce the following:

COLOR PLATES

Carlyle Outside 6 Cheyne Row, 1859, ink and wash, by H. and W. Greaves (National Trust Photographic Library/Michael Boys).

The Governess, no date, watercolor, by Alice Squire (Geffrye Museum, London Bridgeman Art Library).

Mrs. Carlyle's bedroom at Carlyle's house (National Trust Photographic Library/Michael Boys).

Childhood, 1855, oil on canvas, by James Collinson (National Gallery of Canada, Ottawa).

Waiting to Go Out, no date, oil on canvas, by James Hayllar (Roy Miles Esq./Bridgeman Art Library).

The Introduction, no date, oil on canvas, by Emily Crawford (Fine Art Photographic Library Ltd./Fine Art of Oakham).

The kitchen at Carlyle's house (National Trust Photographic Library/Michael Boys).

Hannah Cullwick, photographed by Arthur Munby c. 1860 (by kind permission of the Master and Fellows of Trinity College; Cambridge).

The First Place, 1860, oil on canvas, by A. Erwood (Private Collection/Bridgeman Art Library).

Housemaid polishing silver, no date (Hulton Archive/Getty Images).

Advertisement for the "Thorough Washing Machine," no date (V & A Picture Library).

Trade card for Wilson Cookers, c. 1900 (Mary Evans Picture Library).

A Game of Cards, no date, oil on canvas, by Nancy A. Sabine Pasley (Geffrye Museum, London/Bridgeman Art Library).

The library, or drawing room, at Carlyle's house (National Trust Photographic Library/Michael Boys).

"Mixie and I invariably lose our shuttlecock in the gas," illustration by Maud Berkeley from *The Diaries of Maud Berkeley*, adapted by Flora Fraser, 1985 (illustration © Lorraine Wood).

Past and Present (1), 1858, oil on canvas, by Augustus Leopold Egg (Tate Gallery, London).

The Only Daughter, no date, oil on canvas, by James Hayllar (Christies Images).

Signing the Marriage Register, no date, oil on canvas by James Charles (Bradford City Art Gallery/Bridgeman Art Library).

Our Dining Room at York, 1838, by Mary Ellen Best (Private Collection/Bridgeman Art Library).

A dining room with electric light, from *The Electric Light in Our Homes* by Robert Hammond, 1883 (Mary Evans Picture Library).

Woman's Mission: Companion to Manhood, 1863, oil on canvas, by George Elgar Hicks (Tate Gallery, London).

At the Bazaar (The Empty Purse), 1857, oil on canvas, by James Collinson (Tate Gallery, London).

Strange Faces, 1862, watercolor, by Frederick Walker (Yale Center for British Art/Bridgeman Art Library).

The dressing room at Carlyle's house (National Trust Photographic Library/Michael Boys).

"Improved wash-down closet" by Doulton & Co. (V & A Picture Library).

"Domestic Sanitary Regulations," *Punch* cartoon c. 1851 (National Trust Photographic Library/John Hammond).

Late-nineteenth-century nursery bathroom at Lanhydrock House, Cornwall (National Trust Photographic Library/Andreas von Einsiedel).

Old Schoolfellows, 1854, oil on canvas, by Alfred Rankley (Private Collection/Bridgeman Art Library).

Doubtful Hope, 1875, oil on canvas, by Frank Holl (The Forbes Collection, New York).

A Funeral Bearer, c. 1830–40, oil on canvas, by the Reverend Septimus Buss (Museum of London).

A Young Widow, 1877, watercolor and gouache, by Edward Killingworth Johnson (V & A Picture Library).

Omnibus Life in London, 1859, oil on canvas, by William Maw Egley (Tate Gallery, London).

Detail from *St. Pancras Hotel and Station from Pentonville Road*, no date, oil on canvas, by John O'Connor (Museum of London/Bridgeman Art Library).

Street hawker selling baked potatoes, 1892, platinum print, by Edgar Scamell (V & A Picture Library).

Schoolgirls, 1880, oil on canvas, by George Clausen (Yale Center for British Art/Bridgeman Art Library).

INTEGRATED ILLUSTRATIONS

page 19 "Spend the afternoon in the drawing-room," line drawing from *Drawn from Memory* by E. H. Shepard, 1957 (©1957 E. H. Shepard, reproduced by permission of Curtis Brown Ltd., London).

page 77 "Trailing round the Park," line drawing from *Drawn from Memory* by E.H. Shepard, 1957 (©1957 E. H. Shepard, reproduced by permission of Curtis Brown Ltd., London).

page 103 Cook and housemaid in the kitchen, from *The Sunday at Home*, 1872 (Mary Evans Picture Library).

page 166 "Airing my nightshirt over the gas," line drawing from *Drawn from Memory* by E. H. Shepard, 1957 (©1957 E. H. Shepard, reproduced by permission of Curtis Brown Ltd., London).

page 227 A late-Victorian drawing room (Hulton Archive/Getty Images).

page 327 "My first attempt to use the new invention for the hot water was *not* a success." Illustration by Maud Berkeley, from *The Diaries of Maud Berkeley*, adapted by Flora Fraser, 1985 (illustration ©Lorraine Wood).

page 414 "Using torches to light the way in a foggy London street by night" by William Small, from *The Graphic*, November 9, 1872 (Mary Evans Picture Library)

INDEX

Page numbers in *italics* refer to illustrations.

A NOTE ABOUT
THE AUTHOR

JUDITH FLANDERS'S first book, *A Circle of Sisters: Alice Kipling, Georgiana Burne-Jones, Agnes Poynter and Louisa Baldwin*, was short-listed for the Guardian First Book Award in 2001. She is a frequent contributor to print publications including the *Times Literary Supplement*, the *Telegraph*, the *Spectator*, the *Guardian*, and the *Evening Standard*.